This book was presented to
the Library by

Daisaku Ikeda

President

Soka Gakkai International

A CENTENNIAL BOOK

One hundred books
published between 1990 and
1995 bear this special imprint of
the University of California Press.
We have chosen each Centennial Book
as an example of the Press's finest
publishing and bookmaking
traditions as we celebrate the
beginning of our second
century.

UNIVERSITY OF CALIFORNIA PRESS
Founded in 1893

THE PAPERS OF MARTIN LUTHER KING, JR.

Sponsored by

The Martin Luther King, Jr.,
Center for Nonviolent Social Change, Inc.,

in association with

Stanford University and Emory University

The King family, January 1939. Back row, left to right: Alberta Williams King,
Martin Luther King, Sr., and Jennie Celeste Parks Williams. Front row,
left to right: Alfred Daniel King, Christine King, and Martin Luther King, Jr.
Permission granted by Christine King Farris. Photo courtesy of the
State Historical Society of Wisconsin.

THE PAPERS OF MARTIN LUTHER KING, JR.

VOLUME I:

Called to Serve
January 1929–June 1951

Senior Editor

Clayborne Carson

Volume Editors

Ralph E. Luker
Penny A. Russell

Advisory Editor

Louis R. Harlan

UNIVERSITY OF CALIFORNIA PRESS

Berkeley   Los Angeles   London

University of California Press
Berkeley and Los Angeles, California

University of California Press, Ltd.
London, England

Library of Congress Cataloging in Publication Data
King, Martin Luther, Jr., 1929–1968.
   [Papers]
   The papers of Martin Luther King, Jr. / senior editor, Clayborne
Carson : volume editors, Ralph E. Luker, Penny A. Russell : advisory
editor, Louis R. Harlan.
     p. cm.
   Includes bibliographical references and index.
   Contents: v. 1. Called to serve. January 1929–June 1951.
   ISBN 0-520-07950-7 (cloth : alk. paper)
   1. Afro-Americans—Civil rights. 2. Civil rights movements—
United States—History—20th century. 3. King, Martin Luther, Jr.,
1929–1968—Archives. 4. United States—Race relations. I. Carson,
Clayborne, 1944– . II. Luker, Ralph. III. Russell, Penny A.
IV. Title.
E185.97.K5A2   1992
323′.092—dc20
                                    91-42336
                                       CIP

Printed in the United States of America
9 8 7 6 5 4 3 2 1

The paper used in this publication meets the minimum require-
ments of American National Standard for Information Sciences—
Permanence of Paper for Printed Library Materials, ANSI
Z39.48–1984.∞

*My call to the ministry . . .
came about in the summer of 1944 when I felt an inescapable
urge to serve society. In short, I felt a sense of responsibility
which I could not escape.*

MARTIN LUTHER KING, JR.
February 1948

Publication of this volume was made possible by the financial
and material support of the following major contributors:

National Endowment for the Humanities
National Historical Publications and Records Commission
James Irvine Foundation
Ford Foundation
Rockefeller Foundation
Stanford University
Emory University
IBM Corporation
Intel Corporation
The Stanford University Associates of the
Martin Luther King, Jr., Papers Project

The publishers acknowledge gratefully the many
individuals and foundations that have contributed to the
publication of the Papers of Martin Luther King, Jr.

Our special thanks to Marilyn Solomon, chair, and Maxine
Griggs, co-chair, the Friends of the Martin Luther King,
Jr., Papers Project; and to Franklin Murphy, Joan
Palevsky, and Mary Jane Hewitt for their support.

Leadership Grants
The Times Mirror Foundation
The Ahmanson Foundation
AT&T Foundation

Sponsors
Mr. and Mrs. Clarence Avant
BankAmerica Foundation
Earl and June Cheit
Fleishhacker Foundation
Koret Foundation
August and Susan Frugé
Joseph and Deborah Goldyne
Mr. and Mrs. Richard Heggie
Sally Lilienthal
Max Palevsky
Joan Palevsky

TABLE OF CONTENTS

THE PAPERS

I : CHILDHOOD

II : MOREHOUSE YEARS

III : CROZER YEARS

ACKNOWLEDGMENTS

Like the social movements that made possible King's historic achievements, the Martin Luther King, Jr., Papers Project has relied on the cooperation and good will of many people and institutions. As director of the King Papers Project, I have had the pleasure of participating in a collective effort with people who still believe in King's dream. Realizing the enormity of the task of assembling, annotating, and publishing King's most significant papers, my primary task has been to enlist the support of talented people and to secure the resources they require. Preparation of the initial two volumes of King's papers has brought together an exceptional group of researchers who have received vital assistance from enlightened and generous financial supporters, document donors, and advisors. As in all collective endeavors, the King Project has experienced conflicts and setbacks, but commitment has ultimately triumphed. The following acknowledgments constitute a kind of narrative of a small-scale social movement.

Institutional Support

After becoming director of the King Project in 1985, I came to appreciate the uniqueness of its initiator and sponsor, the Martin Luther King, Jr., Center for Nonviolent Social Change, Inc. The Project is an outgrowth of the King Center's long-term effort to preserve King's legacy by assembling the nation's largest archive focused on the modern African-American freedom struggle. King Center officials played a crucial role in initiating and facilitating the Project's activities.

In particular, the Project reflects the vision of the person who selected me as director. As the King Center's founding president and chief executive officer and as executrix of the King estate Mrs. Coretta Scott King has been an essential starting point for the Project's effort to assemble and publish this comprehensive edition of her late husband's writings and public statements. She made available to the project valuable documents that had remained in her personal possession. Meeting with me and other editors on numerous occasions, Mrs. King spent many hours discussing Project matters. Even on those few occasions when we disagreed over some issues, she was always gracious and open to my views. She also inspired student researchers and staff members during her visits to the Project's offices at Stanford University and Emory University.

Mrs. King also enhanced the Project by selecting an editorial Advisory Board that includes a remarkable group of distinguished scholars and former associates of Dr. King. I quickly discovered that many members of the Board not only contributed to the Project's prestige but also to its work. Chaired by Mrs. King, the Board has met three times to discuss the Project's progress, and individual members often talked with me informally on other occasions. In addition to Mrs. King and Mrs. Christine King Farris, members include Louis R. Harlan, who generously agreed to serve as the advisory editor for the initial two volumes. His singular knowledge of documentary editing, the result of his highly regarded edition of Booker T. Washington's papers, enabled us to learn from his experience and avoid many mistakes. Dr. Harlan consulted with us on numerous occasions and his critical advice has greatly improved this edition. John Hope Franklin contributed the kind of wise advice regarding scholarly and non-scholarly matters that can only result from a long and distinguished career. I have fond memories of our long discussions at his home about difficult and sensitive issues relating to these volumes. Vincent Harding's friendship and understanding similarly enabled the Project to confront the issues that have emerged during the past six years. David Garrow made an extraordinary contribution to our work by sharing his research finds and by carefully reading early manuscript drafts. We also consulted on several occasions with Robert A. Hill, editor of Marcus Garvey's papers, and learned valuable lessons from him about the use of computers in the preparation of a documentary edition. On many occasions, other Advisory Board members, including Lerone Bennett, Jr., Ira Berlin, Robert L. Green, Darlene Clark Hine, Bernard Lafayette, John Maguire, Otis Moss, Joseph Roberts, Jr., Harry H. Wachtel, Preston N. Williams, Harris Wofford, and Andrew Young, have unselfishly provided advice, encouragement, and research leads.

King Center vice president and treasurer Christine King Farris was also a valued participant in Advisory Board meetings and worked closely with me and other staff members. As the King Center's financial administrator, she devoted many hours to the Project's needs. In addition, she allowed us to photocopy her personal collection of documents about her brother's early life and family background. I am especially grateful for her permission to publish many photographs from her collection. The Farris collection and Mrs. Farris's many suggestions for research have been particularly useful in preparing the initial volumes of this documentary edition.

Many other King Center officials have contributed their time to the project. These include the King Center's interim chief operating officer, Dr. Cleveland Dennard, whose wise words of advice were particularly helpful during the fall of 1990. His predecessor, William H. (Chip) Wheeler, also devoted many hours to the Project's work. Other King Center personnel who have assisted the Project included Delores Harmon, Mrs. King's assistant; Barbara Harrison, Mrs. Farris's assistant; Isaac Clark in the business office; Lloyd Davis of the King holiday commission; and Diane Ware of the King Library and Archives.

After Mrs. King selected me as director of the Project, I successfully sought support from Stanford University in order to establish a King Project office on my campus. Provost James Rosse's consistent support was crucial as the Stanford office grew from a few researchers gathered around my history department desk to a substantial research center housed in a wing of offices in Cypress Hall. He remained steadfast in his support even during periods when I was doubtful about the Project's future, and during the recent period of financial retrenchment at Stanford. President Donald Kennedy also became a valued supporter for the project after meeting with Mrs. King in 1985 to formalize the institutional ties. Michael Jackson, then assistant to the president, used his position effectively and tactfully to further the interests of the Project. He listened patiently as I explained needs and complained about problems, and then translated my wishes into proposals that could be acted upon by Stanford administrators. Many other Stanford officials assisted the Project in various ways, including the vice-provost and dean of Graduate Studies, Elizabeth Traugott, whose support and guidance has been most helpful.

Other Stanford officials who have worked closely with the Project include history department administrator Nan Bentley; Associate Dean Cecilia Burciaga; Pat Cook in the Human Resources department; Phyllis Perreault, vice president for Planning and Management; Susan Perry, former chief librarian at Meyer Library; and history department chairs Peter Stansky, Paul Robinson, James Sheehan, and David M. Kennedy. Iris Brest provided useful legal advice. Eileen Walsh and Kathleen O'Toole of the Stanford News Service helped us cope with numerous press inquiries during the fall of 1990. Other Stanford administrators who have helped the Project include Andrew Lisac and Andrea Parra of the Office of Graduate Studies, Alicia Restrepo in the department of facilities management, and Loraine Sinclair, history department graduate secretary.

The development of the Project's state-of-the-art document and bibliographic databases benefited greatly from the advice and assistance of various computer professionals at Stanford, particularly Malcolm Brown, Sandy Laws, Jeff Mapes, Randy Melen, Becky Morton, Tony Navarette, Lynn Sinclair, and Jeffrey Rensch. Robert Street provided funds to help set up the Project's computer database. The financial assistance of David Weber and the technical expertise of LaVonne Gallow of the Research Libraries Group allowed us to install a vital national computer database. On numerous occasions, the Project received help from staff members of the Stanford University Libraries, including Kathy Fehrn, Jim Knox, Sonia Moss, and Michael Ryan.

I am also thankful for the advice and support of members of our Stanford Faculty Advisory Committee. Since the early days of the King Project, I have depended upon the wise and supportive counsel of William Gould of the Law School. Professors Barton Bernstein of the history department, Sandra Drake of the English department, and David Tyack of the School of Education remain strong and knowledgeable advisors and advocates of the project. Their critical readings of manuscripts were particularly useful.

In 1987 the University of California Press became another vital element in the King Project's institutional foundation. Mrs. King and I agreed that the Press was the best of the large number of publishers who bid for the right to publish the King Papers. I have never regretted that decision. The Press has aided our work in numerous ways that extend beyond the normal obligations of a publisher. We admire their patience and appreciate their solid backing of the Project. Director James Clark and assistant director Lynne Withey have been involved in all of the many discussions regarding complex contractual and editorial issues. Jeanne Sugiyama's editorial advice has been offered with sensitive regard for our sometimes fragile egos. We have been fortunate to have worked with other members of the Press's talented staff, including Ann Canright, Chet Grycz, Jane-Ellen Long, Mary Renaud, and Steve Renick.

Establishment of the Emory University office of the King Papers resulted from discussions initiated by Coretta Scott King with president James T. Laney. Provost Billy E. Frye, former associate provost Sheila Bennett, and Marcy Alexander of the provost's office played key roles in the office's creation. Dean George Jones of the Graduate School is in large measure responsible for its continued support and Thomas Stitt of the Graduate School office provided valuable administrative assistance. The support of the Emory Faculty Advisory Committee, including Delores Aldridge, Dan Carter, Robert Franklin, Richard Joseph, Robin Kelley, Richard Long, and Thee Smith, has also been crucial.

Financial Supporters

The King Project has been fortunate to have received long-term financial support from several institutions. The Project's first grant came from the National Historical Publications and Records Commission (NHPRC), an agency that still funds the Project. Roger Bruns gave special attention to the Project's needs during his term as NHPRC director, making clear to me that his concern extended beyond his professional responsibilities. Similarly, the former NHPRC acting director, Mary Giunta, has also been a constant source of support, encouragement, and advice during the entire life of the Project. Roger's and Mary's wise counsel was particularly vital during the Project's difficult first year. We are also grateful for the research assistance of the NHPRC's Sara Dunlap Jackson.

The National Endowment for the Humanities has been a vitally important source of funding since 1986. Our initial program officer, David Nichols, and his replacement, Douglas M. Arnold, have devoted considerable attention to the Project. Margot Backas and Kathy Fuller have also offered supportive, unobtrusive advice.

A grant from the Irvine Foundation enabled the Stanford office to involve gifted and dedicated student interns from Stanford and other universities in the King Project's research. Irvine Foundation President Dennis Collins has understood the special value of the Project as a training ground for students of color interested in pursuing scholarly careers as a result of their work in the Project.

Private donors are another valuable source of funding for the Project. Among the contributors during the first five years of the Project were Diane and James Geocaris, Penny Brooke Jameson, and James and Janice Rosse. Other individuals have assisted the King Project's fund-raising efforts. A group of Stanford alumni and alumnae formed the Associates of the Martin Luther King, Jr., Papers Project in order to assist the Project in many ways, including the raising of funds. Ira D. Hall, Jr., chaired this informal group, which includes Michon Fulgham, Diane F. Geocaris, Ronald E. Goldsberry, L. Tyrone Holt, Lydia Kennard, and Beverly P. Ryder. Henry Organ, then of Stanford's Office of Development, gave helpful fund-raising advice during the early days of the project and has remained a consistent supporter. Evelyn Kelsey and Carolyn Barnes of Stanford's Office of Development worked for several years on the project's behalf. Other supporters include Ron McPherson, Ben Bowser, Ellious Dunson, and Betty Dunson of the Martin Luther King, Jr., Association of Santa Clara Valley.

Staff Members

During her tenure as director of the King Library and Archives, D. Louise Cook played a crucial role in initiating the King Project. During 1984, Ms. Cook wrote the Project's initial funding proposals, outlining its objectives and overall plan. From 1985 until the fall of 1987, when she left to take a position at the Carter Library, Ms. Cook served as the Project's managing editor, drafting grant applications and administering the Project's activities at the King Center. She also contributed her unparalleled knowledge of the King Archive's vast collection of civil rights materials, a collection that she helped build.

The contributions of volume editors Ralph Luker and Penny Russell permeate this entire volume. Ralph played a particularly important role in preparing the section of the introductory essay concerning A. D. Williams and Martin Luther King, Sr. His own research and that of students working with him have greatly increased our understanding of the religious roots of King, Jr. Moreover, he and his staff at Emory University conducted extensive research in the Atlanta area and wrote initial drafts of many of the document annotations and headnotes.

Penny Russell focused her attention on the document section of the first two volumes, guiding the transcription of documents and the writing of headnotes and footnotes. As the initial staff member in 1985, she acquired an unsurpassed understanding of the entire universe of documents acquired by the King Project. She was the axle around which the project revolved. She benefited from the help of Peter Holloran, who joined the project in 1985 as a Stanford sophomore and became so essential that we hired him after his graduation. Since Penny left the Project in June 1990, he has, as contributing editor, ably guided the first two volumes through the publication process.

Associate editor Stewart Burns made numerous contributions to the Project's work on the first two volumes, although Volume III has been the primary focus of his work.

The Stanford office could not have survived without the dedication and talent of the many individuals who have worked in it. Even before the office had a budget capable of paying for her services, Rachel Bagby volunteered to help. She served capably as the King Project's associate director for four years, handling personnel and financial matters. Her varied skills, which extend from lawyering to medicinal singing to financial management, proved essential as the Project grew.

Susan Carson volunteered to assist the King Project when it became obvious that we needed help in organizing the vast number of documents. Becoming the Project's librarian and archivist in 1988, she designed our computerized database and has trained and supervised the student researchers who have entered thousands of records. From 1989 to 1991, she was assisted on a full-time basis by Megan Maxwell, another of the multi-talented former Stanford students who have stayed with the project after graduation as paid staff members.

Margaret Jacobs was the Project's first office worker at a time when staff responsibilities were delimited vaguely. She was followed by Madeline Larsen and Karl B. Knapper, both of whom helped to establish bureaucratic order where little had existed before. Norma Pugh, an executive on loan from IBM Corporation, assisted in the Project's financial administration during the 1990–91 academic year. Others who have served ably include research coordinators Joy Asfeld, David Howard-Pitney, Faye McNair-Knox, and Joyce McNair.

In addition to the editors listed on the title pages, several scholars contributed to the Project during their abbreviated terms. From 1988 to 1990, Dr. A. B. Assensoh served the King Project in several capacities, first as assistant editor assigned to the Stanford office and then as both associate editor and director of research at the King Center. Dr. Lillian Ashcraft-Eason served as the project's assistant editor at the King Center from 1986 to 1987, and Dr. Charles T. Banner-Haley served in the same capacity from 1988 to 1989.

Student Researchers: Stanford Office

The Project depends on the skills and resources of the many undergraduate and graduate students whose hard work and enthusiasm are vital to our ongoing research. Working under the direction of the editors and other staff members, students have made important contributions to the King Project's work. Stanford graduate students who have been active in the King Project include: Vincent Gilliam, Konrad Hamilton, Leslie Harris, Tom Jackson, Lorna Meyer, Karen Parker, James Tracy, and Katherine Weinert.

Undergraduates included Doug Abrams, Dan Aladjem, Arian Ardie, Chip Bartlett, Holly Bartling, Meltin Bell, Diane Bisgeier, Hal Black, Lesley Bonnet, Sheila Cain, Rudy Carrasco, Antoinette Carter, Darlene Carter, Noam Christopher, Greg Crossfield, Alexandra d'Arbeloff, Andrew Efron, Demetrius Eudell, Lyn Fairchild, Jeff Follett, Carolyn Frazier, Jennifer Freudenberg, Kathryne Gambrell, Claudine Gay, Jay Gilbert, Alan Glenn, Jamie Green, Christina Halvorson, Jeff Harkavy, Andrea Harper, Venessa Herlon, Elizabeth Hunter, Canetta Ivy, Louis Jackson, Mark L. Jeter, Bradley Joondeph, Anthony Katz, David Kazanjian, Amanda Kemp, Katherine Kohner, Michelle Latvala, Janet Lewis, Sheryl Loving, Janet Mercer, Sharon Metzger, Tanya Murphy, Alex Niles, Stephen Ostrander, Andrew Patzman, Brian Perrone, Julie Plaut, Tonya Rhodes, Michelle Robinson, Nathaniel Sheidley, Jason Snipes, Jon Sterns, Cheryl Taylor, David Troutt, Christopher Walcott, Lorna Weissinger, and Andrew Wilcox.

The Project has also benefited from the participation of a number of students from other universities and colleges who worked at our Stanford offices under a program funded by the Irvine Foundation. These graduate and undergraduate students include Yvette M. Alex (Ohio State University), Alicia L. Alexander (Howard University), Britt Anderson (University of Pennsylvania), Elizabeth Baez (Williams College), David M. Carson (Howard University), Margo Crawford (Swarthmore College), Allison Dorsey (University of California, Irvine), Loree D. L. Jones (Spelman College), Tony Miles (University of California, Los Angeles), Michele Mitchell (Northwestern University), Mikal Muharrar (Yale University), Pamela Nadasen (Columbia University), Dean

Robinson (Yale University), Jaymes Terry (University of Oregon), and Michael Warren (Yale University).

Student Researchers: King Center and Emory Offices

The work of the editors in Atlanta also depended on the valued assistance of students from Emory, other Atlanta-area students, and King Center interns. Emory graduate students Gilbert Bond, Jonathan Byrd, and Edward Munn were particularly vital members of the Project's staff. Dorothy Carr and Vanita Maynard served as research assistants at the Project's King Center office. Among the other students who contributed were Douglass P. Aucoin, Jessie Audette, David Berry, Josephine Bradley, Bruce A. Calhoun, Margaret Calhoun, Mary K. Clements, Michele Combs, Kenneth J. Cribbs, Masharn Doans, Alisa Anne Duffey, Linda Friedrich, Carmen Gillespie, Jeffrey Goodis, David Harmon, Phyllis Lea Heaton, Danny Horne, Luther Ivory, Jacqueline Jones, Richard Lee, Michael McMullen, Glenda Minter, Barry J. Morris, David E. Neuwirth, Rob Page, Shuva Paul, Christopher Pinc, Leonard Scriven, Andrea Simpson, Bruce Stephenson, Scott Switalla, Franklin Thomas, Audia Wells, Debra Jean Williams, Kim A. Williams, and Brian Woods.

Other Acquisition and Research Assistance

The institutions and individuals that provided documents relating to King deserve the greatest thanks, for without their care and assistance a documentary edition of King's papers would not be possible. The King collection at the King Center is the core of our collection. The King collection at Boston University, which is the largest holding of pre-1962 materials, has been critically important to the initial volumes of the King Papers. We are grateful for the generous assistance of Howard Gotlieb, director of Special Collections, and the members of his staff, particularly Margaret Goostray, assistant director of Special Collections.

To supplement the documents obtained from the King Center and from Boston University, we contacted scores of archives, resulting in the identification of more than one hundred and fifty manuscript collections with King-related material. Archives that assisted us in locating documents for our initial volumes include the Afro-American History and Cultural Museum, Philadelphia; American Baptist Historical Society; Atlanta Public Schools; Atlanta Historical Society; Atlanta-Fulton County Public Library; Woodruff Library, Atlanta University Center; Birmingham Public Library; School of Theology, Boston University; Archives and Manuscripts, Catholic University of America; Colgate-Rochester Divinity School; Special Collections, Emory University; Special Collections, Fisk University; Fulton County (Georgia) Probate Court; William Russell Pullen Library, Georgia State University; Georgia Department of Archives and History; Georgia Department of Human Resources; Greene County (Georgia) Historical Society; Andover-Harvard Theological Library, Harvard Divinity School; Henry County (Georgia) Probate Court; Moorland-Spingarn Research Center, Howard University; Manuscripts Division, Library of Congress; Special Collections, Mercer University; Morehouse College Archives; Albin O. Kuhn Library and Gallery, University of Maryland, Baltimore County; U.S. National Archives and Records Service; Rare Books and Manuscripts, New York Public Library; Schomburg Center for Research in Black Culture, New York Public Library; Morris Library, Southern Illinois University; the State Historical Society of Wisconsin; and the Swarthmore College Peace Collection. The many librarians and archivists at these institutions have been of invaluable assistance to the Project. Their efforts on our behalf were boundless and their expertise indispensable in our search for documents. The tireless effort and dedication of several individuals require special mention. Esme Bhan and Karen L. Jefferson of the Moorland-Spingarn Research Center and Linda Matthews of Emory's Special Collections helped the Project in countless ways.

Dr. King's acquaintances and colleagues are among the most important sources of documents. We attempted to contact many of those who had known King during his early life, including his colleagues at Morehouse College, Crozer Theological Seminary, and Boston University. Although many had not yet donated their valuable papers to an archive, they graciously allowed us to make photocopies of documents in their possession. Among those individuals who donated documents or photocopies of documents pertaining to the initial two volumes are Thelma B. Archer, Lillian Barbour, J. T. Blasingame, Percy A. Carter, Timothy Y. H. Chow, Everett L. Dargan, Griffith Davis, John David Erb, Hardy Franklin, Jr., Julian O. Grayson, W. T. Handy, Lydia Pelzer Kirkland, Nathaniel Leach, Samuel P. Long, Jr., Elaine Pace-Holmes, Mark A. Rouch, S. Paul Schilling, Kenneth L. Smith, Francis E. Stewart, Willard Williams, Marcus G. Wood, and Ira Zepp, Jr. George D. Kelsey and W. Thomas McGann not only provided photocopies of documents, but also granted permission to publish their writings in this volume. The following individuals and institutions also permitted us to publish their documents: Gladys Bean, Mrs. Brailsford R. Brazeal, Theodore Enslin, Hazel Yates Gray, Phoebe Burney Hart, Karen Jefferson of the Moorland-Spingarn Research Center, Isabella M. Tobin, Joan Blanton Tucker, and David F. Wright of the University of Edinburgh. Mrs. Woodie Brown, Reverend M. L. King, Sr.'s sister, graciously talked with us about her family.

The Project has also gained access to several collections of papers belonging to institutions that played a major part in Dr. King's life. The papers of Dexter Avenue King Memorial Baptist Church and Ebenezer Baptist Church have been made available to us, providing important documents from King's life as pastor of the two churches. Reverend Murray Branch of Dexter Avenue King Memorial Baptist Church and David Fiskum of Ebenezer Baptist Church facilitated the Project's examination of the papers. Nathaniel Leach of Second Baptist Church in Detroit and Dean Lawrence E. Carter of the Martin Luther King, Jr., Memorial Chapel at Morehouse College also provided important documents and assistance.

Many other people have contributed their time and energy to participate in the Project. Some are community people who have wanted to share in our work, others are scholars who have provided information and discussion of our findings, and others have special skills that enabled us to expand the horizons of our work. Among the many who deserve mention are Margo Davis, Tina DiFiliciantonio, William Geoghegan, Kathryn Kershner, Linda Jolivet, Gregory Palmer, Joan Peters, Barbara Plum, Cherel Sampson, William Tucker, Jane Wagner, and Ed Williams.

Several scholars without official ties to the Project also provided vital assistance. These include Taylor Branch, James Cone of Union Theological Seminary, and George Fredrickson and Paul Robinson of Stanford. Candace Falk and the staff of the Emma Goldman Papers Project have given much appreciated advice and support. There are doubtless other individuals and organizations who participated in and contributed to the success of the King Papers Project. Failure to mention them simply reflects the limits of my memory rather than of my gratitude.

CLAYBORNE CARSON
12 SEPTEMBER 1991

INTRODUCTION

In the quiet recesses of my heart, I am fundamentally a clergyman, a Baptist preacher. This is my being and my heritage for I am also the son of a Baptist preacher, the grandson of a Baptist preacher and the great-grandson of a Baptist preacher.

> Martin Luther King, Jr.,
> August 1965

Martin Luther King, Jr., was born in Atlanta about noon on Tuesday, 15 January 1929. The difficult delivery occurred in the second-floor master bedroom of the Auburn Avenue home his parents shared with his maternal grandparents. From the moment of his birth, King's extended family connected him to African-American religious traditions. His grandparents A. D. Williams and Jennie Celeste Williams had transformed nearby Ebenezer Baptist Church from a struggling congregation in the 1890s into one of black Atlanta's most prominent institutions. Martin Luther King, Sr., would succeed his father-in-law as Ebenezer's pastor, and Alberta Williams King would follow her mother as a powerful presence in Ebenezer's affairs. Immersed in religion at home and in church, King, Jr., acquired skills and contacts that would serve him well once he accepted his calling as a minister. He saw his father and grandfather as appealing role models who combined pastoring with social activism. Although King's theological curiosity and public ministry would take him far from his Auburn Avenue origins, his basic identity remained rooted in Baptist church traditions that were intertwined with his family's history.

King, Jr.'s family ties to the Baptist church extended back to the slave era. His great-grandfather Willis Williams, "an old slavery time preacher" and an "exhorter," entered the Baptist church during the period of religious and moral fervor that swept the nation in the decades before the Civil War.[1] In 1846, when Willis joined Shiloh Baptist Church in the Penfield district of Greene County, Georgia (seventy miles east of Atlanta), its congregation num-

---

1. G. S. Ellington, "A Short Sketch of the Life and Work of Rev. A. D. Williams, D.D.," in *Programme of the Thirtieth Anniversary of the Pastorate of Rev. A. D. Williams of Ebenezer Baptist Church,* 16 March 1924, CKFC.

bered fifty white and twenty-eight black members.[2] His owner, a wealthy planter named William N. Williams, joined later.[3]

Although subordinate to whites in church governance, blacks actively participated in church affairs and served on church committees. In August 1848, members of such a committee investigated charges of theft against Willis. After listening to the committee's report the church expelled him, but two months later the church minutes reported that "Willis, servant to Bro. W. N. Williams, came forward and made himself confession of his guilt and said that the Lord had forgiven him for his error. He was therefore unanimously received into fellowship with us."[4]

Extant records provide no documentation of Willis's ministry, but he probably helped recruit some of the slaves who joined the church during a major revival in 1855. Between April and December of that year, nearly a hundred blacks, more than one-tenth of the slaves in the Penfield district, joined the congregation. Among them was a fifteen-year-old named Lucrecia (or Creecy) Daniel. Shiloh's minutes report that she "related an experience and was received" into church membership in April 1855.[5] She and Willis were married in the late 1850s or early 1860s, and she bore him five children—including

---

2. Records of Shiloh Baptist Church indicate that after several others joined the church on 1 November 1846, "Willis, servant boy of William N. Williams, came forward and was also received" by the pastor. One of the oldest Baptist congregations in the state, Shiloh was founded in 1795. Both enslaved and free African-Americans were admitted as full members, but only free black members were mentioned with last names in the church minutes. See Arthur F. Raper, *Preface to Peasantry: A Tale of Two Black Belt Counties* (Chapel Hill: University of North Carolina Press, 1936), p. 356; James Porter, "Shiloh Baptist Church minutes," 1 November 1846, SBCM-G-Ar: Drawer 34, box 36; and Bruce A. Calhoun, "The Family Background of Martin Luther King, Jr.: 1810–1893," King Project seminar paper, 1987, Martin Luther King, Jr., Center for Nonviolent Social Change.

3. William Williams, one of the county's wealthiest slave owners, became a pillar of the church, serving as its clerk and as its delegate to meetings of the Georgia Baptist Association. His and his wife's combined holdings placed them in the top 15 percent of Greene County's landowners and in the top 20 percent of the county's slave owners. There is no documentation regarding Williams's treatment of Willis and his other slaves, but in 1859 Williams became patrol commissioner, supervising slave catchers in the Greene County militia district. See Thaddeus Brockett Rice and Carolyn White Williams, *History of Greene County, Georgia, 1786–1886* (Macon, Ga.: J. W. Burke Company, 1961), p. 628; Census entries for William Williams, 1850 and 1870, Greene Co., Ga.; Greene Co., Ga., "Tax Digest Record for William Williams," 1854 and 1859, G-Ar; Greene Co., Ga., "Slave Digest Record for William Williams," 1850, G-Ar; Arthur F. Raper, *Tenants of the Almighty* (New York: Macmillan, 1943), pp. 366, 372; "Shiloh Baptist Church minutes," 3 January 1852 and passim, SBCM-G-Ar: Drawer 34, box 36.

4. R. B. Edmonds, "Shiloh Baptist Church minutes," 15 October 1848, SBCM-G-Ar: Drawer 34, box 36. See also minutes for 16 July 1848 and 20 August 1848.

5. William Sanders, "Shiloh Baptist Church minutes," 15 April 1855, SBCM-G-Ar: Drawer 34, box 36. The identification of "Creecy, servant to Mrs. N. E. Daniel," as the wife of Willis can be inferred from the documentary evidence. The census of 1870 locates sixty-year-old Willis Williams living with thirty-year-old Creecy, thirteen-year-old Benjamin, and twelve-year-old Randal Williams on the plantation of his seventy-two-year-old former owner, William Williams (Census entry for Willis Williams, 22 June 1870, Greene Co., Ga.). Family tradition holds that Willis Williams's wife was "Lucrecia" or "Creecy" (Ellington, "Short Sketch"; and unsigned sketch, "Adam Daniel Williams," in *History of the American Negro and His Institutions: Georgia Edition*, ed. A. B. Caldwell [Atlanta: A. B. Caldwell, 1917], p. 210).

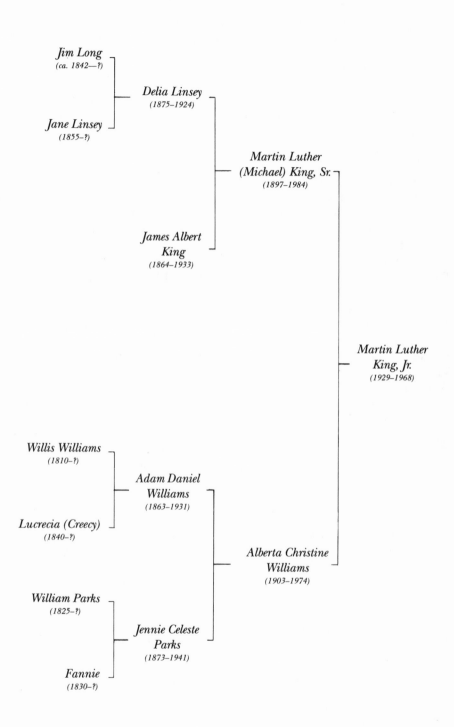

Jim Long
(ca. 1842—?)

Jane Linsey
(1855–?)

Delia Linsey
(1875–1924)

James Albert
King
(1864–1933)

Martin Luther
(Michael) King, Sr.
(1897–1984)

Martin Luther
King, Jr.
(1929–1968)

Willis Williams
(1810–?)

Lucrecia (Creecy)
(1840–?)

Adam Daniel
Williams
(1863–1931)

Alberta Christine
Williams
(1903–1974)

William Parks
(1825–?)

Fannie
(1830–?)

Jennie Celeste
Parks
(1873–1941)

Adam Daniel (A. D.), who celebrated 2 January 1863, the day after the effective date of the Emancipation Proclamation, as his birthday.[6]

The family left Shiloh Baptist Church when it, like other southern congregations, divided along racial lines at the end of the Civil War. At war's end, Shiloh's 144 black members outnumbered the 77 white members, but in the following years all the black members left. Willis Williams and his family may have joined other black members of Shiloh in organizing a large black-controlled Baptist church in Penfield.[7]

A. D.'s desire to follow his father's calling was evident even as a child, when "it was his greatest pleasure to preach the funeral of snakes, cats, dogs, horses or any thing that died. The children of the community would call him to preach the funeral and they would have a big shout."[8] Although he was unable to attend school because of the demands of sharecropping, the seven-year-old A. D. reportedly "attracted the people for miles around with his ability to count."[9]

A. D. Williams probably spent his childhood on the Williams plantation. After the death of his father in 1874, A. D. and his family moved from the Williams plantation to nearby Scull Shoals, a rural community on the Oconee River.[10] Several years later, in the early 1880s, A. D. and his family joined Bethabara Baptist Church in northern Greene County. With the help of his pastor, the Reverend Parker Poullain, A. D. worked through a blueback speller and the first, second, and third readers. Williams underwent a conversion experience that confirmed his religious commitment. Poullain baptized A. D. in August 1884, and tutored him in preparation for a preaching career. Finally, in April 1888, Williams earned his license to preach.[11]

The number of black Baptist churches, many of which were affiliated with Georgia's Missionary Baptist Convention, increased rapidly during the 1870s and 1880s, but general economic conditions in Greene County's Oconee

6. Adam Daniel's and his twin sister Eve's actual birthdate was probably earlier in the 1860s. The census of 1870 lists Adam Daniel Williams as nine years old, suggesting that he was born in 1861; his twin sister, Eve, is listed as seven. The census of 1880 lists both him and Eve as eighteen, implying a birthdate of 1862 (Census entry for Willis Williams, 22 June 1870, Greene Co., Ga.; census entry for A. D. Williams, 1880, Greene Co., Ga.). For A. D. Williams's claim of 2 January 1863 as his birthdate, see "Rev. A. D. Williams," *Atlanta Independent*, 4 April 1904; Ellington, "Short Sketch"; and "Adam Daniel Williams," in Caldwell, ed., *History of the American Negro*, p. 212.

7. The fragmentary church records show no sign of the Williams family at Shiloh Baptist after Emancipation. See Bartow Davis Ragsdale, *Story of Georgia Baptists* (Atlanta: Foote and Davies, 1938), 3:65, 3:312; Raper, *Preface to Peasantry*, p. 356; and Clarence M. Wagner, *Profiles of Black Georgia Baptists* (Atlanta: Bennett Bros., 1980), p. 65.

8. Ellington, "Short Sketch." See also "Adam Daniel Williams," in Caldwell, ed., *History of the American Negro*, p. 212.

9. Ellington, "Short Sketch." Ellington noted that A. D. Williams had only three weeks of schooling during his youth.

10. See Ellington, "Short Sketch"; Census entry for A. D. Williams, 15 June 1880, Greene Co., Ga.; and Calhoun, "Family Background."

11. Ellington, "Short Sketch"; and "Adam Daniel Williams," in Caldwell, ed., *History of the American Negro*, p. 212. Williams also later studied with the Reverend Henry M. Smith of Crawford, clerk of the Jeruel Baptist Association which was composed of rural black congregations.

In 1870, Martin Luther King, Jr.'s maternal great-grandfather was recorded in the federal census of Greene County, Georgia. The entry listed his family members, including the twins, Adam and Eve.

River Valley declined during the latter decade. Surrounding farmlands were much less profitable than in the past, and many blacks migrated from the area.[12] During the late 1880s and early 1890s, A. D. Williams tried to make a living as an itinerant preacher, while supplementing his income with other work.[13] An injury in a sawmill accident left him with only the nub of a thumb on his right hand. Seeking better opportunities elsewhere, A. D. Williams joined the black exodus from Greene County. In January 1893 he left for Atlanta.[14]

Arriving in Atlanta "with one dime and a five dollar gold piece" during the unusually cold winter of 1893, Williams used the gold piece to secure treatment for a sore throat.[15] At the end of the summer after working in a machine shop, he accepted invitations to preach at Springfield Baptist Church in Atlanta and a Baptist church in nearby Kennesaw, Georgia.[16] Finally, on 14 March 1894, Williams was called to the pastorate of Atlanta's Ebenezer Baptist Church. One of many small Baptist congregations in the city, Ebenezer had recently lost its founding pastor, the Reverend John Andrew Parker, who had organized the church eight years earlier.[17] Williams took over a church with thirteen members and "no church house at all"—a challenging situation in which he quickly demonstrated his leadership abilities, adding some sixty-five members to the church his first year. His attempt in 1896 to leave for another pastorate was "frustrated by the providence of God"; yet at Ebenezer he was "an overwhelming success." Ebenezer, his biographer recounted, "continued to grow in strength and popularity and so did he."[18]

Williams supplemented his income by serving as minister of other congre-

---

12. Powell Mills, a major employer, closed in 1884 and was destroyed in a devastating flood three years later. For more information on Greene County economic conditions, see E. Merton Coulter, "Scull Shoals: An Extinct Georgia Manufacturing and Farming Community," *Georgia Historical Quarterly* 48 (March 1964): 51–63; Raper, *Tenants of the Almighty*, pp. 111–112, 365; and Rice and Williams, *History of Greene County*, pp. 380–381.

13. "Adam Daniel Williams," in Caldwell, ed., *History of the American Negro*, p. 212; and Ellington, "Short Sketch." Although A. D. Williams's name does not appear on the extant rolls of ministers in the Jeruel Baptist Association minutes during these years, a transcriptionist's error may be at fault. The rolls list an "O. W. Williams" of Crawford, Georgia, in 1891, and an "E. D. Williams" in 1892. See *Minutes of Jeruel Baptist Association, Convened with Thankful Baptist Church, Days Station, Oglethorpe County, Georgia, September 24th, 25th, 26th, and 27th, 1891* (Augusta: Georgia Baptist Book Print, 1891); and *Minutes of Jeruel Baptist Association, Convened with Spring Creek Baptist Church, The Fork, Greene County, Georgia, September 21st, 22nd, 23rd, and 24th, 1892* (Augusta: Georgia Baptist Book Print, 1892).

14. [C. Shaw?], "Rev. John Parker," [1950?], EBCR; Christine King Farris, interview by Ralph E. Luker, 6 February 1989, MLKJrP-GAMK; and Ellington, "Short Sketch."

15. Ellington, "Short Sketch."

16. Ellington, "Short Sketch"; and "Adam Daniel Williams," in Caldwell, ed., *History of the American Negro*, p. 212.

17. Reverend Parker had studied at Atlanta Baptist Seminary and earned his living as a drayman. See [C. Shaw?], "Rev. John Parker"; and E. R. Carter, *The Black Side: A Partial History of the Business, Religious, and Educational Side of the Negro in Atlanta, Ga.* (Atlanta: N.p., 1894), pp. 243–250.

18. Ellington, "Short Sketch." Three biographical sketches of A. D. Williams published in his lifetime gave three different figures for Ebenezer's membership at the time Williams began his ministry: a newspaper's sketch reported seventeen members, Caldwell estimated seven members,

gations in the Atlanta area before deciding to focus his energies on building Ebenezer.[19] Recognizing that his long-term success as an urban minister required that he overcome academic shortcomings, Williams also enrolled at Atlanta Baptist College, taking both the elementary English and the ministers' courses of study. In May 1898 Williams received his certificate from the ministerial program.[20]

During the 1890s Williams also met his future wife, Jennie Celeste Parks. Born in Atlanta in April 1873, Jennie Parks was one of thirteen children. Her father, William Parks, supported his family through work as a carpenter. At age fifteen, Jennie Parks began taking classes at Spelman Seminary, becoming, according to one account, "one of Spelman's lovely girls"; her graces included "culture, unfeigned modesty, and [a] devotion to home life."[21] Parks left Spelman in 1892, however, without graduating. Married to A. D. Williams on 29 October 1899, she was a deeply pious woman who always kept a Bible nearby and was "a model wife for a minister." On 13 September 1903, she gave birth at home to their only surviving child, Alberta Christine Williams, the mother of Martin Luther King, Jr.[22] During the early years of the century, the family lived in several houses in the Auburn Avenue area, which was then home to both whites and blacks.[23]

Like many other contemporary black ministers from similar backgrounds, Williams built his congregation by means of forceful preaching that addressed the everyday concerns of poor and working-class residents. Despite his deficiencies "from a technical educational point of view," a biographer insisted

and Ellington counted thirteen members in 1893; see "Rev. A. D. Williams," *Atlanta Independent,* 12 April 1904; and "Adam Daniel Williams," in Caldwell, ed., *History of the American Negro,* p. 213.

19. "Adam Daniel Williams," in Caldwell, ed., *History of the American Negro,* p. 213; and Ellington, "Short Sketch."

20. Ellington, "Short Sketch." Organized as the Augusta Baptist Institute by the black Baptist churches of Augusta in 1867, the school sought to prepare newly emancipated black men for teaching and preaching. In 1879 the Institute was relocated to Atlanta and renamed the Atlanta Baptist Seminary. Its name was later changed to Atlanta Baptist College and then to Morehouse College, in honor of Dr. Henry Morehouse, a white executive of the American Baptist Home Mission Society. Morehouse College operated under the sponsorship of the Society. See A. W. Pegues, *Our Baptist Ministers and Schools* (Springfield, Mass.: Willey, 1892), pp. 587–591, 609–617; Carter, *Black Side,* pp. 28–35, 52–55; *Catalogue of the Atlanta Baptist Seminary, 1895–1896* (Atlanta: Atlanta Seminary Press, 1896); *Catalogue of the Atlanta Baptist Seminary, 1897–1898* (Atlanta: Atlanta Seminary Press, 1898); *Georgia Baptist,* 2 June 1898; Edward A. Jones, *A Candle in the Dark: A History of Morehouse College* (Valley Forge, Pa.: Judson Press, 1967), pp. 17–47, 53–67; and Addie Louise Joyner Butler, *The Distinctive Black College: Talladega, Tuskegee, and Morehouse* (Metuchen, N.J.: Scarecrow Press, 1977), pp. 102–103.

21. Ellington, "Short Sketch." In 1881 the Atlanta Baptist Female Seminary was founded in the basement of Friendship Baptist Church; subsequently it was renamed Spelman Seminary, in honor of the mother-in-law of John D. Rockefeller, a financial supporter.

22. Ellington, "Short Sketch"; Census entry for A. D. Williams and Jennie Celeste Parks Williams, 18 June 1900, Fulton County, Ga.; and Marriage license for A. D. Williams and Jennie Celeste Parks, 29 October 1899, Fulton County, Ga. See Loree Dionne Lynne Jones, "A Study of Spelman Seminary, Jennie Celeste Parks Williams, and Alberta Christine Williams King," King Project seminar paper, 1987, Martin Luther King, Jr., Center for Nonviolent Social Change.

23. Census entries for A. D. Williams and Jennie Celeste Parks Williams, 18 June 1900 and 28 April 1910, Fulton County, Ga.; and Atlanta City Directories, 1897–1905, 1907.

Page from the 1910 federal census with entries for A. D. Williams and his family.

that Williams's "experience and profound thought and his intensive pra
ways in expounding the gospel, places him easily with the leading preac
of his day and generation."[24] In 1900 the Ebenezer congregation purcha
a building at Bell and Gilmore streets that formerly housed the white Fi.
Baptist Church, and there they remained for thirteen years. Thanks to W
liams's efforts, the congregation experienced steady growth, attracting ninety
one new members in 1903 for a total membership of four hundred at year's
end. Nevertheless, Ebenezer was still overshadowed by the much larger Big
Bethel AME and Wheat Street Baptist churches on Auburn Avenue.[25]

In addition to building his own congregation, Williams participated in the
establishment of new regional and national Baptist institutions. In September
1895, he joined two thousand other delegates and visitors at Friendship Baptist Church to organize the National Baptist Convention, the largest black
organization in the United States. By 1904 Williams was president of the Atlanta Baptist Ministers Union, chairman of both the executive board and the
finance committee of the General State Baptist Convention, and a member of
the Convention's educational board and its Baptist Young Peoples Union and
Sunday School board.[26]

Black-white relations in Atlanta were undergoing major changes during the
early years of the twentieth century. Booker T. Washington's historic address
delivered at Atlanta's Cotton States and International Exposition of 1895 had
signaled the beginning of a period of rapid economic growth and intensified
racial restrictions. Black migrants sought to participate in the city's economic
growth, and by 1900 black Atlantans constituted nearly 40 percent of the city's
population. In 1900, some black residents departed from Washington's ac-
commodationist strategy by launching an unsuccessful streetcar boycott to
protest new regulations requiring segregation on all public transportation. In
the same year, the Georgia Democratic Party adopted rules that barred the
participation of blacks in the party's primary.[27]

24. Ellington, "Short Sketch."

25. Indenture between Oscar Davis and the Trustees of Ebenezer Baptist Church, 26 May
1899, Fulton County, Ga., G-Ar; Indenture between Mrs. D. C. Shaw and the Trustees of Ebenezer Baptist Church, 20 June 1900, Fulton County, Ga., G-Ar; Indenture between the Fifth
Baptist Church and the Trustees of Ebenezer Baptist Church, 12 December 1900, Fulton County,
Ga., G-Ar; and "Rev. A. D. Williams," *Atlanta Independent*, 2 April 1904.

26. For more information on the origin of the National Baptist Convention and Williams's
involvement in denominational activities, see James Melvin Washington, *Frustrated Fellowship: The
Black Baptist Quest for Social Power* (Macon, Ga.: Mercer University Press, 1986), pp. 159–185;
Porter, "Black Atlanta," pp. 71, 209–212; *Georgia Baptist*, 2 June, 21 July, and 27 October 1898;
and *Atlanta Independent*, 12 April and 17 June 1904. The Atlanta Baptist Ministers Union, in
which A. D. Williams and Martin Luther King, Sr., were prominent for six decades, was an organization of black Baptist ministers in the city. The General State Baptist Convention was one
of two black Baptist conventions in Georgia from 1893 to 1915. In 1893, a dispute over leadership
of the Missionary Baptist Convention of Georgia led to the establishment of the General State
Baptist Convention. In 1915, the two conventions were reunited as the General Missionary Baptist Convention of Georgia. See Wagner, *Profiles of Black Georgia Baptists*, pp. 79–81.

27. For more information on these events, see *Georgia Baptist*, 17 May 1900; Walter White, *A
Man Called White* (New York: Viking Press, 1948), pp. 20–21; Clarence A. Bacote, "The Negro

Williams, along with other black religious leaders, was a pioneering advocate of a distinctive African-American version of the social gospel, endorsing a strategy that combined elements of Washington's emphasis on black business development and W. E. B. Du Bois's call for civil rights activism. In mid-February 1906, A. D. Williams joined five hundred black Georgians in organizing the Georgia Equal Rights League to protest the white primary system. They elected William Jefferson White as president and AME Bishop Henry McNeal Turner and CME Bishop R. S. Williams as vice presidents. White urged the delegates to recognize the importance of both black economic development and civil protest. Turner, one of the most prominent black religious leaders of the period, was an outspoken advocate of racial pride and a caustic critic of prevailing racial policies. "To the Negro . . . the American flag is a dirty and contemptible rag," he cried. "Hell is an improvement upon the United States when the Negro is involved."[28] The convention's address to the public protested lynching, peonage, the convict lease system, inequitable treatment in the courts, inferior segregated public transportation, unequal distribution of funds for public education, and exclusion of black men from the electorate, juries, and the state militia. A. D. Williams and Turner signed the address along with sixteen other leaders including Atlanta University professor W. E. B. Du Bois; Atlanta Baptist College president-elect John Hope; J. Max Barber, editor of *The Voice of the Negro*; and Peter James Bryant, pastor of Wheat Street Baptist Church.[29]

Soon after this gathering, in September 1906, African-American advancement efforts received a serious setback when Atlanta experienced a major race riot. Newspaper reports and rumors of black assaults on white women had already inflamed the fears of whites. When white gangs assaulted iso-

---

in Atlanta Politics," *Phylon* 16 (1955): 333–350; Bacote, "Negro Proscriptions, Protests, and Proposed Solutions in Georgia, 1880–1908," *Journal of Southern History* 25 (November 1959): 474; August Meier and Elliott Rudwick, "The Boycott Movement Against Jim Crow Streetcars in the South, 1900–1906," *Journal of American History* 55 (March 1969): 756–775; Jean Martin, "Mule to MARTA," *Atlanta Historical Bulletin* 20 (Winter 1976): 14–26; and John Dittmer, *Black Georgia in the Progressive Era* (Urbana: University of Illinois Press, 1977), pp. 16–17, 94–97.

28. Edwin S. Redkey, ed., *Respect Black: The Writings and Speeches of Henry McNeal Turner* (New York: Arno, 1971), pp. 196–197.

29. Augusta's William Jefferson White issued the call for a convention of black Georgians to consider a wide range of grievances in December 1905. Founder of the Augusta Institute, trustee of Atlanta Baptist College, founder and editor of the *Georgia Baptist*, and pastor of Augusta's Harmony Baptist Church, White was the venerated patriarch of Georgia's black Baptists. See "A Call For a Conference," *Voice of the Negro* 3 (February 1906): 90; "The Macon Convention" and "The Leaders of the Convention," *Voice of the Negro* 3 (March 1906): 163–166; "Address of the First Annual Meeting of the Georgia Equal Rights Convention," *Voice of the Negro* 3 (March 1906): 175–177; "A Few Corrections," *Voice of the Negro* 3 (April 1906): 291; Redkey, ed., *Respect Black: The Writings and Speeches of Henry McNeal Turner*, pp. 196–199; Dittmer, *Black Georgia*, pp. 173–174; *Atlanta Independent*, 9 December 1905, 20 January 1906, 27 January 1906, and 24 February 1906; W. J. Simmons, "Rev. W. J. White: Editor of the *Georgia Baptist*," in *Men of Mark: Eminent, Progressive, and Rising* (Cleveland: George M. Rewell, 1887), pp. 791–792; and "Rev. William Jefferson White, D.D.," in Pegues, *Our Baptist Ministers and Schools*, pp. 526–539.

lated African Americans, they met little opposition from police. Larger mobs of whites, numbering in the thousands, then attacked and looted black businesses near Auburn Avenue. Rioters derailed trolley cars and beat to death blacks who happened to be on the streets. Commerce in the city almost ceased for three days as many Atlantans remained in their homes. After five days of violence, the city resumed a sullen peace. Official accounts listed one white and twenty-six black deaths and more than 150 blacks seriously wounded. The riot destroyed the illusion that Atlanta was a New South paradigm of racial harmony and reinforced the trend toward increased residential segregation in the Auburn Avenue neighborhood, which now became a center of African-American economic and social life in Atlanta.[30]

Williams and other black Atlanta residents faced new racial barriers in the years after the riot, but Auburn Avenue businesses thrived during the following two decades as the black community turned inward, supporting its own institutions. Although Williams continued to oppose racial discrimination, he benefited from the new realities of white flight from and black movement into the Auburn Avenue area. Several years after the riot, Williams purchased the two-story Queen Anne–style building on Auburn Avenue in which King, Jr., would be born.[31] An Odd Fellow, Williams also served on the order's Industrial Commission, which planned to develop Odd Fellow City, an African-American community near Elberton, Georgia. He joined Bishop Turner in a controversial business venture, the Silver Queen Mining Company, which sold stock in a silver mine in Mexico. Benjamin Davis, editor of the black newspaper the *Atlanta Independent,* criticized the venture as "a fake, pure and simple" and offered space in the newspaper to Turner and Williams "to explain their connection with this fraudulent scheme" to the "many thousands of poor Negroes that are being defrauded throughout the state."[32] Turner responded that stock was sold "to colored people only" because the corporation was a "colored organization" and "a stepping stone to teach our people how to do business, and put some money in their pockets." He said he had visited the mine with two reputable mining engineers. "The reports from these two gentlemen were good," he concluded, "and there is no fake about the Company, but a straight, fair, square proposition."[33] Although Turner's re-

---

30. For more information on the Atlanta race riot, see Charles Crowe, "Racial Violence and Social Reform—Origins of the Atlanta Riot of 1906," *Journal of Negro History* 53 (July 1968): 234–256; Charles Crowe, "Racial Massacre in Atlanta, September 22, 1906," *Journal of Negro History* 54 (April 1969): 150–169; Dittmer, *Black Georgia,* pp. 123–131; and Clarence A. Bacote, "Some Aspects of Negro Life in Georgia, 1880–1908," *Journal of Negro History* 43 (July 1958): 186.

31. For more information on the house, which was constructed in 1895, see U.S. Department of the Interior, "Historic Structure Report: The Martin Luther King Birth Home" (Denver: National Park Service, n.d.).

32. "Is It a Fraud?" *Atlanta Independent,* 25 September 1909.

33. "Judge for Yourself," *Atlanta Independent,* 2 October 1909. See also Dittmer, *Black Georgia,* pp. 13–14; Porter, "Black Atlanta," pp. 126–158; and Silver Queen Mining Company, Stock certificate for A. D. Williams, 28 January 1908, CKFC. On Davis and Turner, see Mungo Melanchthon Ponton, *The Life and Times of Bishop Henry M. Turner* (Atlanta: A. B. Caldwell, 1917);

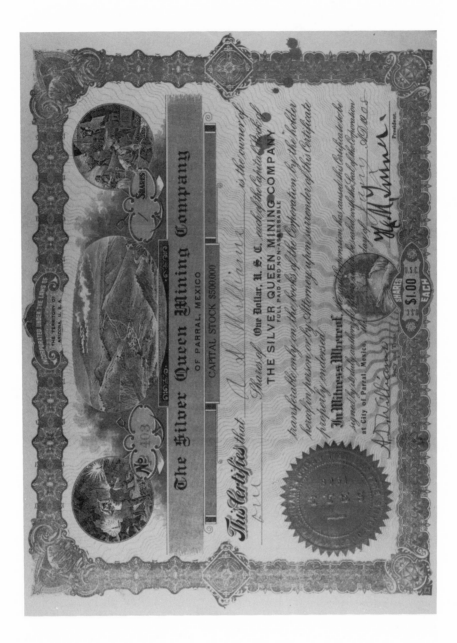

sponse did not satisfy Davis, the reputations of the two preacher-entrepreneurs suffered no permanent damage because of the controversy.

Williams continued to involve himself in business ventures that capitalized on and enhanced his success as Ebenezer's pastor. By the beginning of 1913 the growing congregation had 750 members and was planning further expansion. In January the church purchased a lot on the corner of Auburn Avenue and Jackson Street. Six months later it announced plans to raise $25,000 for a new church building, which would include an auditorium and gallery seating 1,250 people. "Few Churches in the city have made strides more rapidly," conceded the *Independent*, "nor have contributed more to the moral and intellectual growth of the city. Dr. Williams is an earnest, conscientious and well-informed minister whose influence in the city is acknowledged and appreciated."[34] In March 1914 Ebenezer celebrated the beginning of Williams's third decade as its pastor by breaking ground for the new building. While the basement was under construction, the congregation worshipped in a hall above a storefront on Edgewood Avenue. That spring many of the older children of the church, including ten-year-old Alberta Williams, were converted in a ten-day revival, baptized in a borrowed pool at Wheat Street Baptist Church, and formally admitted to church membership. When the basement was capped with a roof in the late spring of 1914, "there was a great march" as worshippers entered the basement to hold services for the first time. Ebenezer's building was finally completed in 1922.[35]

As he consolidated his institutional base at Ebenezer, A. D. Williams continued to expand his regional influence. In the fall of 1913 he was elected moderator of the Atlanta Missionary Baptist Association.[36] He played a role in power struggles among Baptist leaders, including a dispute within the National Baptist Convention over ownership of the National Baptist Publishing House.[37] He also served as treasurer of Atlanta's YMCA campaign and of the

---

J. Minton Batten, "Henry M. Turner: Negro Bishop Extraordinary," *Church History*, 7 (September 1938): 231–246; E. Merton Coulter, "Henry M. Turner: Georgia Preacher-Politician During the Reconstruction Era," *Georgia Historical Quarterly* 48 (December 1964): 371–410; John Dittmer, "The Education of Henry McNeal Turner," in *Black Leaders of the Nineteenth Century*, ed. Leon Litwack and August Meier (Urbana: University of Illinois Press, 1988), pp. 253–272; "Benjamin Jefferson Davis," in *Who's Who in Colored America: A Biographical Dictionary of Notable Living Persons of Negro Descent in America*, ed. Joseph J. Boris (New York: Who's Who in Colored America Corp., 1927), 1:52–53; and Benjamin J. Davis, Jr., *Communist Councilman from Harlem: Autobiographical Notes Written in a Federal Penitentiary* (New York: International Publishers, 1969), pp. 21–39, 145–160.

34. "Ebenezer Baptist Church," *Atlanta Independent*, 12 July 1913.

35. *Atlanta Independent*, 14 March 1914. See also J. H. Edwards, "Ebenezer History," March 1976, EBCR; and Fulton County, Ga., Bond for Title between A. J. Delbridge and A. D. Williams, 10 January 1913.

36. A. D. Williams was moderator of the Atlanta Missionary Baptist Association from 1913 until 1920. Martin Luther King, Sr., was later moderator of the association for more than twenty years. See Atlanta Missionary Baptist Association, "Minutes of the Fifty-second Annual Session of the Atlanta Missionary Baptist Association, Inc.," Atlanta, 13 October 1955.

37. In 1915, the National Baptist Convention was incorporated in order to claim ownership of the National Baptist Publishing House in Nashville, Tennessee. Insisting that the publishing

Georgia State Baptist Convention, where he had fiduciary responsibility for a new youth reformatory established by the convention in Macon, Georgia. In 1914 Williams became chairman of the finance committee of the Morehouse College Alumni Association; that same year, the college honored him with a Doctor of Divinity degree.[38]

Early in 1917, A. D. Williams became involved in an effort, initiated by Atlanta University graduate Walter White, to organize a local branch of the National Association for the Advancement of Colored People (NAACP).[39] After the branch was chartered, he and other NAACP members, along with members of the Neighborhood Union, a black women's group, launched a prolonged campaign to improve conditions in black schools. The catalyst was the plan by the Board of Education to close seventh-grade classes in its black schools in order to pay for a new junior high school for white students. A committee, which included branch president Harry H. Pace, Lugenia Burns Hope of the Neighborhood Union, and her husband, Morehouse president John Hope, presented a petition protesting the plan to the all-white school board. A. D. Williams represented the black Baptist ministerial alliance at the meeting with the board. "You, with fifty schools, most of them ample, efficient

---

house was his property, its director Richard H. Boyd led his followers out of the National Baptist Convention, Inc., to form the National Baptist Convention, Unincorporated. In November 1916, hoping to explain his position, Boyd appeared at a meeting of the General Missionary Baptist Convention of Georgia, where Benjamin Davis sought to introduce him. A. D. Williams and Peter James Bryant of Wheat Street Baptist Church seized the rostrum and declared that they would not allow Boyd to speak. See *Atlanta Independent*, 22 May 1915, 25 November 1916, and 15 September 1917; Wagner, *Profiles of Black Georgia Baptists*, pp. 79–81, 134; Lewis Garnett Jordan, *Negro Baptist History, U.S.A.* (Nashville, Tenn: Sunday School Publishing Board, [1930]), pp. 126–142, 247–255; Owen D. Pelt and Ralph Lee Smith, *The Story of the National Baptists* (New York: Vantage Press, 1960), pp. 97–109; and Joseph Harrison Jackson, *A Story of Christian Activism: The History of the National Baptist Convention, U.S.A., Inc.* (Nashville, Tenn.: Townsend Press, 1980), pp. 93–126.

38. For more details on Williams's activities during the period, see *Atlanta Independent*, 25 August 1911, 10 September 1911, 31 May 1913, 15 November 1913, 21 February 1914, 22 May 1915, and 14 August 1915; Morehouse College, *Annual Catalogue, 1917–1918*, p. 95; Dittmer, *Black Georgia*, p. 179; and Jones, *A Candle in the Dark*, pp. 91–92.

39. At the end of 1916, following several unsuccessful efforts, Walter White began to organize a local branch of the NAACP. At an organizing conference held in February 1917, Harry H. Pace, an executive of Standard Life Insurance Company, was elected president and Walter White, Standard Life's cashier, was elected secretary. NAACP national field secretary James Weldon Johnson addressed the conference in a crowded assembly room of Atlanta Life Insurance Company. Although police officers were stationed around the room, he noted, the crowd was not intimidated. "The organization conference which was held at Atlanta was unique," Johnson recalled years later; "it was the only one in which no woman was invited to take part. There were present fifty or so of the leading colored men of the city; lawyers, doctors, college professors, public school teachers, editors, bankers, insurance officials, and businessmen" (James Weldon Johnson, *Along This Way: The Autobiography of James Weldon Johnson* [New York: Viking Press, 1933], pp. 315–316). For further information on the creation of the Atlanta NAACP branch, see *Atlanta Independent*, 10 February 1917 and 24 February 1917; Minutes of the Board of Directors Meeting, 9 April 1917, NAACPP-DLC: Part I, Reel 1; Reports from the Annual Meetings of the NAACP, 7 January 1918, NAACPP-DLC: Part I, Reel 4; and White, *A Man Called White*, pp. 28–31.

and comfortable, for the education of your children," said the petitioners, "can square neither your conscience with your God nor your conduct with your oaths, and behold Negro children in fourteen unsanitary, dilapidated, unventilated school rooms, with double sessions in half of the grades, no industrial facilities, no preparation for high schools and no high schools for the blacks." In the end, the school board acceded to the petitioners' plea to reinstate the seventh grade for blacks.[40]

The issue of black schools spurred membership in the new NAACP branch, which climbed to four hundred by the end of March. Yet subsequent petitions to the school board—for better school buildings, a commercial and industrial junior high, a high school for black students, and the elimination of double sessions in all public schools—met with no success. Thereafter, wartime mobilization and rebuilding after a devastating fire in May 1917 caused popular commitment to the NAACP to wane.[41] By June 1918, membership had declined to forty-nine due to Walter White's departure for the NAACP's New York office and the resignation of the branch president. The enervated branch appealed to Atlanta's Baptist and Methodist ministerial associations for support. In response, A. D. Williams agreed to serve as branch president and was formally elected on 9 July.[42]

Williams—described in one account as "a forceful and impressive speaker, a good organizer and leader, a man of vision and brilliant imagination, which he sometimes finds it necessary to curb"—experienced initial success as an NAACP leader.[43] A month after his election, he announced an ambitious drive to attract five thousand new members. The *Atlanta Independent* illustrated its confidence in Williams's ability to revive the organization with a front page cartoon depicting a black gladiator, whose shield was the NAACP, slaying the hydra-headed monster of the grandfather clause, lynching, peonage, and segregation. The branch did grow: to 1,400 members within five months. During his tenure, the newly invigorated NAACP spearheaded a major effort to register black voters in anticipation of a local referendum on school taxes and bond issues for public works that would allocate a dispropor-

40. *Atlanta Independent*, 24 February 1917. A Neighborhood Union investigation of black schools in 1913 found students studying in unsanitary, poorly equipped, crowded classrooms. The group protested these conditions to the school board, which took only token remedial action. See *Atlanta Independent*, 18 October 1913; and Jacqueline Anne Rouse, *Lugenia Burns Hope: Black Southern Reformer* (Athens: University of Georgia Press, 1989), pp. 74–79. For more information on the schools campaign see Edgar A. Toppin, "Walter White and the Atlanta NAACP's Fight for Equal Schools, 1916–1917," *History of Education Quarterly* 7 (Spring 1967): 8–10.

41. On 21 May, a fire fueled by a strong wind burned through the heart of Atlanta, gutting nearly two thousand buildings, including many churches. The "Great Conflagration" left ten thousand people homeless, most of them black. See *Atlanta Independent*, 26 May 1917; Garrett, *Atlanta and Its Environs* 2:700–706, 730; John Robert Smith, "The Day of Atlanta's Big Fire," *Atlanta Historical Journal* 24 (Fall 1980): 58–66; and Alan Patureau, "Atlanta's Other Great Fire," *Atlanta Journal and Constitution*, 17 May 1987.

42. Toppin, "Walter White and the Atlanta NAACP," pp. 12–15; Adam Daniel Williams, "Speech to the Tenth Annual Convention of the NAACP," 26 June 1919, NAACPP-DLC: Part I, Reel 8; and White, *A Man Called White*, pp. 32–37.

43. "Adam Daniel Williams," in Caldwell, ed., *History of the American Negro*, p. 214.

tionate share of the funds raised to white institutions. The 2,500 black Atlantans who paid the poll tax and overcame other obstacles to become registered voters were able to defeat the education measures in the nonpartisan referendum.[44] When local authorities put the issues to a vote again in April 1919, Atlanta's NAACP submitted a petition to the mayor and the Board of Education outlining the inadequate conditions in black schools and stating the group's terms for supporting the bond issues and tax increase. Again black Atlantans, not convinced by official promises, helped to defeat the measures.[45]

In June 1919, A. D. Williams led an Atlanta delegation to the NAACP national convention in Cleveland. In a speech there, Williams told how black voters had rejected the referenda in Atlanta and attributed the rapid increase in black voter registration to the work of women. "We got our women organized and put the women in different districts and we had meetings weekly," Williams explained. "There is one gentleman [who] said we couldn't get members by having meetings; we got a number that way. . . . Night after night people came forward and paid their dollar. That was done largely because the women were allowed to make speeches. They made such speeches you would be surprised." Williams ended by extending an invitation from the governor of Georgia, the mayor of Atlanta, and the Atlanta Chamber of Commerce to hold the organization's 1920 convention in that city, still notorious as the site of the 1906 riot. "Somebody says it is not time to go down to Atlanta now, but it is, you are due there," Williams asserted.[46] After some hesitation, the NAACP voted to make Atlanta the site of its first national convention in the South.[47]

By May 1920, however, when the NAACP convened at Auburn Avenue's Big Bethel AME Church, Williams had been forced to step down as branch president. The preceding year some NAACP members had moved to boycott the white press in favor of black newspapers such as the *Atlanta Independent*. Williams opposed the move. In retaliation, the editor of the *Independent*, Benjamin Davis, lashed out, attacking Williams in scurrilous cartoons and editorials and charging him with "suppression of speech, arbitrary ruling, despotism in the chair," and other misuses of authority.[48] Nevertheless, Williams

---

44. *Atlanta Independent*, 18 January, 8 March, and 15 March 1919; "The Atlanta Negro Vote," *Crisis* 18 (June 1919): 90–91; "Address Delivered by Miss Cora Finley at the Tenth Anniversary Conference of the NAACP," 25 June 1919, NAACPP-DLC: Part I, Reel 8; "The Atlanta Branch," *Crisis* 18 (July 1919): 141; Cora Finley, "Registered Fighters," *Crisis* 18 (August 1919): 181; White, *A Man Called White*, p. 37; Garrett, *Atlanta and Its Environs*, 2:756; Toppin, "Walter White and the Atlanta NAACP," p. 15; and Dittmer, *Black Georgia*, pp. 147–148.

45. The memorial pointed out the inadequate number and condition of black schools, pay inequity for black teachers, and limited library services, public services, and health and recreational facilities in the black community (*Atlanta Independent*, 8 March and 15 March 1919). Although black leaders claimed responsibility for defeating the measures, it was alleged in the white press (*Atlanta Georgian*, 24 April 1919) that the loss was due to manipulation of the black vote by the Georgia Railway & Power Company.

46. A. D. Williams, "Speech to the Tenth National Convention," 26 June 1919, NAACPP-DLC: Part I, Reel 8; and *Crisis* 19 (August 1919): 193. For the activities of black women in the Atlanta election campaigns see Rouse, *Lugenia Burns Hope*, pp. 74–79.

47. *Crisis* 20 (March 1920): 249; and "The Atlanta Conference," *Crisis* 20 (April 1920): 322.

48. *Atlanta Independent*, 3 May 1919.

served on the local host committee for the NAACP conference, an event that enhanced the city's reputation for racial tolerance. "Atlanta treated us royally," NAACP leader Mary White Ovington recalled, "and there were white men . . . who attended our sessions every evening. The press gave us unusually fine publicity, featuring on its front page our demands for unsegregated traveling accommodations and for the vote."[49]

Williams remained active in racial advancement efforts, achieving another victory in the school bond election of March 1921. With the addition of women to the electorate, black voter registration more than doubled in two years. This rise in representation, combined with the results of the 1919 balloting, convinced white leaders to make firm commitments to the black community. The bond issues now passed overwhelmingly in a record turnout. Several million dollars were earmarked to build eighteen new schools, including four black elementary schools and Atlanta's first public secondary school for black students. Martin Luther King, Jr., would receive most of his public education in two of the new schools, David T. Howard Elementary School and Booker T. Washington High School.[50]

In the fall of 1922, the *Atlanta Independent* endorsed Williams for the newly vacant post of president of the General Missionary Baptist Convention of Georgia. "Dr. Williams may not be the most learned philosopher among our preachers, the best scholar or the deepest theologian, but he is easily the best businessman, and that is what the state Baptist convention needs at its head," editor Benjamin Davis argued.[51] That November, however, Williams lost the election.[52] Even so, by then his institutional ties reached broadly and deeply throughout Atlanta's black community. Williams was on the executive board of the General Missionary Baptist Convention of Georgia, chaired its Mission Board, and served as a trustee of its Central City College in Macon. He had also served the Baptist community as president of the Atlanta Baptist Ministers Union and moderator of the Atlanta Missionary Baptist Association for seven years, as Georgia's representative on the Foreign Mission Board of the National Baptist Convention for a dozen years, and as floor leader of Georgia's delegation for six years.[53] In the last of these roles, he had attended the tumultuous National Baptist Convention held in St. Louis in December 1922, where he participated in the unsuccessful effort to

---

49. *Atlanta Independent,* 26 June 1919, 2 August 1919, 23 August 1919, 16 May 1920, and 5 June 1920; Mary White Ovington, "Reminiscences," *Baltimore Afro-American,* 7 January 1933; and Johnson, *Along This Way,* pp. 356–357.

50. For more information on the 1921 bond campaign and the schools funded by the bonds, see *Atlanta Constitution,* 1, 6, and 9 March 1921; *Atlanta Independent,* 27 September 1923; Henry Reid Hunter, *The Development of the Public Secondary Schools of Atlanta, Georgia: 1845–1937* (Atlanta: Atlanta Public Schools, 1974), pp. 51–56; Garrett, *Atlanta and Its Environs,* 2:795–796; and Toppin, "Walter White and the Atlanta NAACP," p. 16.

51. *Atlanta Independent,* 28 September 1922.

52. The victor was Professor James M. Nabrit of Morehouse College. See *Atlanta Independent,* 30 November 1922.

53. *Atlanta Independent,* 14 and 28 February 1924; *Programme of the Thirtieth Anniversary of the Pastorate of Rev. A. D. Williams of Ebenezer Baptist Church,* 16 March 1924, CKFC.

elect Peter James Bryant of Atlanta's Wheat Street Baptist Church to succeed the convention's first president, Elias Camp Morris. In the end, the Reverend Lacey Kirk Williams of Chicago's Olivet Baptist Church won the election, after a two-month campaign marked by "bitter feelings" and "the ugliest things ever said by one preacher about another."[54]

A. D. Williams regained some of his earlier prominence as a civil rights leader in February 1924, when he was reelected as president of the moribund Atlanta NAACP branch. Despite earlier criticisms, the *Atlanta Independent* reported Williams's return in hopeful terms: "It was the ballot that gave Atlanta Negroes modern . . . schoolhouses and facilities; and it was the inspiration that the race received from the local branch under the leadership of Dr. A. D. Williams that put the fight in their bones."[55] Williams's program for the revitalization of the branch called for drives to increase membership to two thousand and to register ten thousand black voters; he also advocated passage of bond issues for more and better schools, boycotts of office buildings where black people were barred from elevators, and improved park and recreational facilities for the black community. Williams and other NAACP leaders aggressively promoted branch membership and voter registration and eventually won additional funding for Atlanta's beleaguered black public schools.[56]

In the meantime, Williams was unable to prevent a decline in Ebenezer's membership from nine hundred in 1918 to three hundred by 1924.[57] As he entered the seventh decade of his life and his fourth decade as pastor of Ebenezer, he faced strong competition from younger ministers. Some members, too, may have left to join the northern migration. Although Williams himself had thought of moving during the years after World War I, by the mid-1920s he realized that his future, for better or worse, was at Ebenezer. By then he had met Michael King, the man who would become his son-in-law and reinvigorate his pastorate.

❧

Like A. D. Williams a quarter of a century earlier, King had come to Atlanta from rural Georgia with little money or education but with a fierce desire to succeed. In 1920, when he first met Alberta Williams, the Reverend Williams's daughter, King was twenty-three and studying elementary English at a preparatory school. She was sixteen and attending Spelman Seminary's four-year high school program. Even before meeting her, he had heard about her "gracious manners, captivating smile and scholarly manner" and knew that she

---

54. Jordan, *Negro Baptist History*, pp. 142–143; Jackson, *A Story of Christian Activism*, pp. 125–128; and *Atlanta Independent*, 28 September 1922.

55. *Atlanta Independent*, 7 February 1924.

56. *Atlanta Independent*, 19 April, 29 November, 6 December, 13 December, 20 December 1923; 7 February, 6 March, 20 March 1924; 25 February, 25 March 1926; 11 August 1927; and 13 September 1928.

57. *Atlanta Independent*, 28 February 1924.

had "organized a fine choir in her father's church." He told incredulous friends of his plan to marry the daughter of one of Atlanta's most prominent ministers although he had not yet met her. Driven by his desire to be taken seriously as a suitor and a minister, King struggled to rectify his educational deficiencies by attending night classes until he was able to afford day school. "I had no natural talent for study," he admitted, "and my learning came after long, long hours of going over and over and over the work until I was falling asleep saying my lessons to myself." The school principal drilled King in English syntax. He also encouraged his pupil to register to vote. When King sought to do so, however, he discovered the maze of obstacles placed in the way of black people, including the poll tax, literacy test, and even elevators to the "colored registration office" that did not work. He made several attempts before becoming a registered voter.[58]

King's determination was rooted in his childhood experiences with poverty and racism. His grandfather Jim Long had been used by his owner to breed slaves, conceiving children with several women. Census records show that after the Civil War, Long maintained at least two families in Henry County, where he also registered to vote during Reconstruction.[59] Long's relationship with Jane Linsey produced a daughter, Delia, who married James Albert King, King, Jr.'s grandfather.[60] Little is known about James King's early life and heritage, except that he was probably of Irish-African ancestry and was born outside the South.[61] Following their marriage in Stockbridge on 20 August 1895, twenty-year-old Delia Linsey and thirty-one-year-old James King became sharecroppers, moving from place to place in Henry and Clayton counties. After 1900 they settled in Stockbridge, an area of unexceptional farmland later romanticized in Margaret Mitchell's *Gone With the Wind*. Unlike

---

58. Martin Luther King, Sr., with Clayton Riley, *Daddy King: An Autobiography* (New York: William Morrow, 1980), pp. 15, 62, 64–66.

59. Born about 1842 in Virginia or Georgia, Long and his two brothers registered in 1867, despite intimidating activity by the Ku Klux Klan, which was organized in Henry County the previous year. See Henry County, Ga., Voter Qualification Form for James Long, 11 August 1867, G-Ar; and Ranier, *Henry County, Georgia*, pp. 283–284.

60. Census records for 1870 show that Jim Long settled after the war in Henry County, where he lived with his wife, Francis, and five children. In 1880, Jim and Francis Long lived with their ten children in Henry County's Stockbridge district. The records suggest that Jim Long maintained another family, which included twenty-seven-year-old Jane Linsey and their five children. See Census entries for James Long and family, 1870 and 29 June 1880, Henry County, Ga.; Census entry for Jane Linsey and family, 28 June 1880, Henry County, Ga.; and Woodie King Brown, interview by Ralph E. Luker, 21 April 1989, MLKJrP-GAMK.

61. Information regarding James Albert King's lineage is contradictory. The 1900 census reported that he was born in Ohio and that his father was born in Pennsylvania and his mother in Ohio. In 1910, though, the census listed his father's place of birth as Ireland, while the 1920 census reported his place of birth as Georgia, an unlikely location given the absence of records placing King or his father in Georgia before the 1890s. See Census entry for James Albert King and family, 23 June 1900, Clayton County, Ga.; and Census entries for James Albert King and family, 11 May 1910 and 14 January 1920, Henry County, Ga. Jim King's death certificate, filed by Martin Luther King, Sr., stated that Jim King and his parents were born in Georgia; see Georgia Department of Public Health, Bureau of Vital Statistics, Certificate of Death for James King, 17 November 1933, GAHR.

Page from the 1910 federal census with entries for James King and his family.

Willis Williams's Greene County, Henry County never had many large plantations. It was a section of hard-scrabble farms, where black and white people alike scratched a living from hard red clay. Like many families, the Kings were poor; the county tax lists record little personal property for James King.[62]

The large King family included nine children (plus one who died in infancy). Michael (or M. L.), the second child and first son, was born on 19 December 1897.[63] During his childhood, King later recalled, "my mother had babies, worked the fields, and often went during the winter to wash and iron in the homes of whites around town." His father's life followed the unchanging seasonal labors of a sharecropper: spring sowing of cotton in fields fertilized with foul-smelling guano; summer weeding; fall picking and chopping; and winter turning of the resistant soil. The rewards were paltry, made even more so by the inability of powerless blacks to prevent cheating by whites. On one occasion, Michael King remembered accompanying his father to "settle up" with the white landlord. When he pointed out that his father was due more money, the landlord threatened him. A fight was narrowly averted, but the King family was forced off the property and had to seek aid from a white landowner who employed Delia King and Woodie, Michael's older sister, as laundresses. The family then moved into a little frame building on his property.[64]

For Delia King and her children, the rituals of the black church offered relief from this life of hardship. Although the family occasionally attended a local Methodist as well as the Baptist church, they established enduring ties with Floyd Chapel Baptist Church in Stockbridge. Its Sunday services, Wednesday prayer meetings, baptisms, weddings, funerals, and special Christmas and Easter services offered welcome diversions. "Church was a way to ease the harsh tone of farm life, a way to keep from descending into bitterness," Michael King wrote. "Papa was not religious, and although I don't think he was very enthusiastic about my attending so many church affairs, he never interfered with Mama's taking me." Unable to find solace in religion, James King became increasingly cynical in the face of the economic and racial hardships of his life. His family became targets of his angry outbursts, fueled by alcoholism.[65]

The King children attended school from three to five months a year at the

---

62. Marriage license for James Albert King and Delia Linsey, 20 August 1895, Henry County, Ga., HCPC; Tax Digest Records for James Albert King, 1897–1898, 1901–1907, 1910–1913, 1916–1918, Henry County, Ga., G-Ar; and Tax Digest Records for James Albert King, 1900, Clayton County, Ga., G-Ar. See also Alisa Duffey and Phyllis Heaton, "The King Family: 1880–1920," King Project seminar paper, 1987, Martin Luther King, Jr., Center for Nonviolent Social Change.

63. Although King would later date his birth in 1899, the census records for 1900 and 1910 support an earlier birthdate. See Census entry for James Albert King, 23 June 1900, Clayton County, Ga.; and Census entry for James Albert King, 28 April 1910, Henry County, Ga. Although M. L. King was christened Michael L., he later changed his name to Martin Luther; see note 98.

64. King, Sr., with Riley, *Daddy King*, pp. 25, 40–44.

65. Ibid., pp. 26–27.

STATE OF GEORGIA,

COUNTY OF Henry

of _____ 1867, _____ day

PERSONALLY APPEARED before me this

COUNTY,

who states that he resides in the 11 Election Precinct of Henry

GEORGIA, and who makes oath as follows:

"I, Jam Long _____ do solemnly swear in the presence of Almighty God, that I am a citizen of the State of Georgia; that I have resided in said State for _____ months next preceeding this day, and now reside in the County of Henry _____ in said State; that I am 21 years old; that I have not been disfranchised for participation in any rebellion or civil war against the United States, nor for felony committed against the laws of any State or the United States; that I have never been a member of any State Legislature, nor held any executive or judicial office in any State, and afterwards engaged in insurrection or rebellion against the United States, or given aid or comfort to the enemies thereof; that I have never taken an oath as a member of Congress of the United States, or as an officer of the United States, or as a member of any State Legislature, or as an executive or judicial officer of any State, to support the Constitution of the United States, and afterwards engaged in insurrection or rebellion against the United States, or given aid and comfort to the enemies thereof; that I will faithfully support the Constitution and obey the laws of the United States, and will, to the best of my ability, encourage others so to do. So help me, God."

The said Jas Long _____ further swears that he has not been previously registered under the provisions of "An Act supplementary to 'an act to provide for the more efficient government of the rebel States'—passed March 2, 1867—and to facilitate restoration," under this or any other name, in this or any other Election District; and further, that he was born in Virginia _____ and naturalized by _____ on the _____ day of _____, 18 _____ in the _____

SWORN TO AND SUBSCRIBED before me _____

Register of the 3½ Registration District.

After emancipation, King's paternal great-grandfather James Long signed this oath of allegiance to the federal government in order to register to vote in Henry County, Georgia. Photo courtesy of the Georgia Department of Archives and History.

Stockbridge Colored School. Michael King's teacher, the wife of his pastor, taught 234 children in all the grades. "We had no books, no materials to write with, and no blackboard for her to use in instructing us," King wrote. "But I loved going, particularly when we began learning numbers, which always had a fascination for me."[66]

According to his memoirs, King experienced a number of brutal incidents as he grew up in a troubled family in the rural South.[67] On one occasion, when he was fetching milk for his mother, he was stopped by a sawmill owner who demanded that King get a bucket of water for the sawmill workmen. The youngster politely declined, whereupon the white man beat him and kicked over his milk. King ran home and explained what had happened. His enraged mother then returned with her son to the mill to confront the owner; when he acknowledged that he had hit the boy, she knocked him down and pummeled him. Jim King, upon hearing of the incident, took his rifle to the mill and threatened to kill the man. That evening, white men mounted on horses visited the King house in search of the father. Having heard that they were after him, however, King had already fled. He lived for months in the woods, but by the time tempers had cooled enough for him to return to his family, he was drinking heavily, and Delia was in poor health. One evening Jim King came home drunk and began to assault his wife. Michael came to his mother's defense and subdued his father. The next day, he promised not to challenge his father's authority; Jim, in turn, pledged never to hit his wife again.[68]

Within the walls of Floyd Chapel Baptist Church, meanwhile, Michael grew to respect the few black preachers who were willing to speak out against racial injustice, despite the risk of violent white retaliation. He also admired ministers, such as his own pastor, the Reverend W. H. Lowe, who could recite Scripture largely from memory, preach in rich cadence, and lead traditional Baptist congregational a capella singing. "The human voice was the rural church's organ and piano," King recalled.[69] By age ten Michael King had developed his own talent for singing, and during his teenage years he was a member of an a capella gospel group that toured local churches. He gradually

---

66. Ibid., p. 37. See also *Henry County Weekly*, 14 July 1905; and Henry County School Census, Stockbridge Colored School, 1903, 1908, and 1913, G-Ar.

67. King reported witnessing the lynching of a black man by white mill workers. Although lynchings were common enough in the rural Georgia of his youth, there was no report in the *Henry County Weekly* or the *Henry County News* of a lynching or a murder in the Stockbridge area that fits King's description. See Duffey and Heaton, "King Family," pp. 4, 16–18; and King, Sr., with Riley, *Daddy King*, pp. 30–31.

68. King, Sr., with Riley, *Daddy King*, pp. 39–45; and L. D. Reddick, *Crusader Without Violence* (New York: Harper & Brother, 1959), pp. 44–45. These versions of the story vary in detail, but the *Daddy King* version corresponds best with Jim King's disappearance from the Henry County tax records in 1911 and 1912; see Tax Digest Records, 1911 and 1912, Henry County, Ga., G-Ar; and Duffey and Heaton, "King Family," pp. 14–15.

69. King, Sr., with Riley, *Daddy King*, p. 27. King remembered his childhood minister explaining the meaning of hymns to the congregation and urging them "to sing with the spirit and understanding" (King, Sr., "What Part Should Singing Play In Our Church Worship?" *Georgia Baptist*, 1 March 1936).

developed an interest in preaching, initially practicing eulogies on the family's chickens, which he then dispatched. By the end of 1917 he had decided to become a minister, choosing the Baptist church because its nonhierarchical structure seemed to offer more opportunities for a person, such as himself, with little formal education. (Like many other rural preachers, King was barely literate; his religious training was limited to instruction from his pastor and his experience as a church member. School records indicate that by age fifteen, he had learned to read but could not write.)[70] After the minister and deacons of his church licensed him to preach, a small rural church between Jonesboro and Atlanta invited King to become its pastor. Overcoming the resistance of church officers who felt he was too young, King was able to convince his examiners that he should be ordained. By that time, he had already developed a conception of his role as a pastor concerned about the everyday lives of his congregation.[71]

In the spring of 1918 King left Stockbridge to make his home in Atlanta, an attractive place for an ambitious young country preacher. He joined his older sister, Woodie, who had left Stockbridge for the city a year or so earlier. King roomed with a family near Auburn Avenue. He worked first in a vulcanizing shop that made tires. When he failed to get a raise, he quit to load cotton bales and then drove a truck for a firm that sold barbers' chairs.[72]

By the summer of 1919 Woodie King had moved from her first residence with a cousin and was boarding at the Williams home. Michael King seized the opportunity to introduce himself to Alberta Williams. He began to see her regularly before asking her to "consider entering a courtship" with him. The courtship persisted even when Alberta Williams, at her father's insistence, departed to attend Hampton Normal and Industrial Institute in Virginia.[73] Her parents welcomed King into the family circle eventually treating him as a son and encouraging the young minister to overcome his educational deficiencies as the elder Williams had done three decades earlier.

❦

In March 1924, shortly after A. D. Williams celebrated his thirtieth anniversary as pastor of Ebenezer Baptist Church, Alberta returned to Atlanta after completing a two-year teaching program at Hampton. Her engagement to Michael King was announced at Ebenezer's Sunday services. Because the school board did not allow married women in classrooms, Alberta Williams taught only briefly in Rockdale County and at Atlanta's W. H. Crogman Elementary School before her marriage.[74] Meanwhile King served as pastor of several churches in nearby College Park, while studying at Bryant Preparatory School. Shortly after the engagement, his mother died, prompting his

---

70. Henry County School Census, 1913, G-Ar.
71. King, Sr., with Riley, *Daddy King*, p. 45.
72. King, Sr., with Riley, *Daddy King*, pp. 59–60; and *Atlanta City Directory*, 1919.
73. King, Sr., with Riley, *Daddy King*, pp. 68–72.
74. Ellington, "Short Sketch"; Jones, "Spelman Seminary," p. 12; and King, Sr., with Riley, *Daddy King*, p. 72.

father to request his return to help on the farm. Instead of complying, he followed the urging of Alberta Williams and her father to finish at Bryant and to seek admission to Morehouse College.[75] Despite being twice refused admission owing to poor test scores, King, backed by influential alumnus A. D. Williams, appealed his case to President John Hope and Dean Samuel Howard Archer. He was finally admitted as a beginning student at the Morehouse School of Religion in the fall of 1926.[76]

Like Williams, King studied in Morehouse's three-year minister's degree program, headed by Dr. Charles Hubert. Although he found the work difficult, he received encouragement from Hubert, who offered helpful criticisms of sermons King prepared. He recalled failing an introductory course in English twice and only receiving a passing grade on his third attempt in summer school. To study for a biology course, he relied on the help of classmate Melvin H. Watson (the son of a longtime clerk of Ebenezer Baptist Church). His closest friend was Sandy Ray of Texas, a fellow seminarian. "We shared an awe of city life, of cars, of the mysteries of college scholarship, and, most of all, of our callings to the ministry," King recalled.[77]

On Thanksgiving Day 1926, the Reverend Michael Luther King and Alberta Christine Williams were married at Ebenezer. Atlanta's most prominent black Baptist ministers—Bryant of Wheat Street, E. R. Carter of Friendship, and James M. Nabrit of Mt. Olive—performed the ceremony. When the newlyweds moved into an upstairs bedroom of the Williams's house on Auburn Avenue, many people assumed that King would succeed his father-in-law at Ebenezer. Williams encouraged him to consider the possibility, but King initially resisted. He was already serving two congregations at College Park and East Point, and he was still learning the ministry. If he was to be Williams's successor, he wanted to merit the position, not inherit it.[78]

---

75. Delia King died in 1924, and her youngest daughter, Ruby, suffered a ruptured appendix shortly thereafter and died. Still reeling from these losses, Jim King was ordered to leave his sharehold. With his remaining children, he moved to College Park near Atlanta, where he earned a living as a porter and day laborer. He remained there until his death on 17 November 1933. See Georgia State Board of Health, Bureau of Vital Statistics, Certificate of Death for Delia Lindsay King, 27 May 1924, GAHR; King, Sr., with Riley, *Daddy King*, pp. 73–75, 88; Rainer, *Henry County, Georgia*, p. 331; *Atlanta City Directory*, 1928; Georgia Department of Public Health, Bureau of Vital Statistics, Certificate of Death for James Albert King, 17 November 1933, GAHR; and *Atlanta Daily World*, 19 November 1933.

76. At the time, the Morehouse faculty included Brailsford R. Brazeal in economics; Walter R. Chivers, E. Franklin Frazier, and Garry W. Moore in sociology; Claude B. Dansby in mathematics; William Kemper Harreld in music; Edward A. Jones in French; Samuel M. Nabrit in biology; Benjamin E. Mays in philosophy and psychology; and Nathaniel P. Tillman in English. See Morehouse College, *The Torch '23; Morehouse Alumnus* 1 (November 1928); Butler, *Distinctive Black College*, pp. 111–112; Jones, *A Candle in the Dark*, pp. 108–109, 284–285; Benjamin E. Mays, *Born to Rebel: An Autobiography* (Athens: University of Georgia Press, 1987), pp. 66–98; and King, Sr., with Riley, *Daddy King*, pp. 75–77.

77. King, Sr., with Riley, *Daddy King*, pp. 77–79, 87; *Morehouse College Catalogue, 1928–1929* (Atlanta: Morehouse College, 1928), p. 106; and *Morehouse College Catalogue, 1929–1930* (Atlanta: Morehouse College, 1929), p. 110.

78. Adam Daniel Williams and Jennie Celeste Parks Williams, Wedding Invitation for Marriage of Alberta Christine Williams and Michael Luther King, 25 November 1926, EBCR; and King, Sr., with Riley, *Daddy King*, pp. 80–82.

According to King's recollections, A. D. Williams inspired him in many ways. Both men preached a social-gospel Christianity that combined a belief in personal salvation with the need to apply the teachings of Jesus to the daily problems of their black congregations. Both also avoided an overreliance on emotional oratory, which sometimes was meant to disguise lack of content. King later noted his high regard for Williams's sermons. "[He] could preach with force and power. Some of the things I started off to do as a preacher he corrected . . . He turned me around and put me on the right road."[79]

The family of M. L. and Alberta Williams King grew rapidly. On 11 September 1927, the first child was born to the Kings and named Willie Christine for her grandfather and for her mother. M. L. King, Jr., the first son and grandson in the extended family, was born next on 15 January 1929. A second son—named Alfred Daniel Williams, after his grandfather—arrived on 30 July 1930, a month after King, Sr., received his bachelor's degree in theology.[80]

The black community into which King, Jr., was born had changed substantially during his grandfather's forty years in Atlanta. The city's population had grown from 65,500 people in 1890 to 270,500 in 1930, while the percentage of blacks in the city had declined from 43 to 33 percent. Because of legal and social restrictions, Atlanta's blacks were now heavily concentrated in the "Sweet Auburn" district and in southwest Atlanta near Morehouse, Spelman, and Atlanta University.[81] In 1928, just as Benjamin Davis's *Independent* was foundering, W. A. Scott launched the *Atlanta World*. The new paper flourished, becoming the *Atlanta Daily World* in 1932, the first black-owned daily newspaper in the country. At the same time, older black leaders such as A. D. Williams were gradually being replaced by a new generation of ministers that included King, Sr., who was, by then, president of the Atlanta Sunday School and Baptist Young Peoples Union convention and moderator of the Atlanta Missionary Baptist Association.

A. D. Williams died on 21 March 1931. The massed choirs of Ebenezer,

---

79. Martin Luther King, Sr., interview by E. A. Jones, [1972?], MLKJrP-GAMK. See also King, Sr., with Riley, *Daddy King*, p. 82.

80. King, Sr., with Riley, *Daddy King*, pp. 83, 87–88; and Georgia Department of Public Health, Bureau of Vital Statistics, Certificate of Birth for Martin Luther King, Jr., 15 January 1929 [revised 12 April 1934 and 23 July 1957], GAHR.

81. In 1929, Morehouse, Spelman, and Atlanta University joined in forming the Atlanta University Center. Morehouse and Spelman specialized in educating undergraduate men and women respectively, and Atlanta University concentrated on graduate and professional education. Later, Clark University, Morris Brown College, the Interdenominational Theological Center, and Morehouse Medical School affiliated with the Atlanta University Center institutions, creating the largest center of African-American higher education in the United States. See Porter, "Black Atlanta," p. 294; Henderson and Walker, "Sweet Auburn," p. 17; Garrett, *Atlanta and Its Environs* 2:842; Myron W. Adams, *A History of Atlanta University* (Atlanta: Atlanta University Press, 1930), pp. 115–118; Clarence A. Bacote, *The Story of Atlanta University: A Century of Service, 1865–1965* (Atlanta: Atlanta University Press, 1969), pp. 256–315; Jones, *A Candle in the Dark*, pp. 113–132; and George A. Sewell and Cornelius V. Troup, *Morris Brown College: The First Hundred Years, 1881–1981* (Atlanta: Morris Brown College, 1981), pp. 135–143.

Dr. C.H. Johnson

CERTIFICATE OF BIRTH
GEORGIA DEPARTMENT OF PUBLIC HEALTH
Bureau of Vital Statistics

59431

1. PLACE OF BIRTH

Registered No. 5576

County Fulton   Militia District (Number and Name) 1061   State of Georgia

City or Town Atlanta   Ward   NON-RESIDENT (Yes or No)

Street and Number (No.)   (Street) 501 Auburn Ave.,
(If birth occurred in hospital or institution, give its name instead of street and number)

2. FULL NAME OF CHILD Michael King, Martin Luther, Jr.
(If not yet named, leave space blank)

3. SEX male   6. LEGITIMATE? (Are parents married?) yes   7. BORN Alive Jan. 15th, 1929   (Month, Day, Year) 19   at   M
(Alive or Dead)   (Hour)

4 and 5. If plural birth indicate with check (√) whether twin, triplet or quadruplet, also give order of birth. TWIN No. (1 or 2)   TRIPLET No. (1, 2 or 3)   QUADRUPLET No. (1, 2, 3 or 4)

	FATHER		MOTHER
8. FULL NAME	M. L. King	14. FULL MAIDEN NAME	Alberta Williams,
9. RESIDENCE (P. O. Address)	501 Auburn Ave.	15. RESIDENCE (P. O. Address)	501 Auburn Ave.,
10. COLOR or RACE	negro	16. COLOR or RACE	negro
11. AGE at last birthday	29 (years)	17. AGE at last birthday	26 (years)
12. BIRTHPLACE (P. O. Address)	Stockbridge, Ga.	18. BIRTHPLACE (P. O. Address)	Atlanta, Ga.
13a. Trade, profession or particular kind of work done, as spinner sawyer, bookkeeper, etc.	Minister	19a. Trade, profession or particular kind of work done as housekeeper, typist, nurse, clerk, etc.	Housewife
13b. Industry or business in which work is done, as cotton mill, sawmill, bank, etc.		19b. Industry or business in which work is done, as own home, lawyer's office, cotton mill, etc.	

DECEASED

20. Number of children born alive to this mother, not counting this birth 1   21. Number of children of this mother living, not counting this birth 1   21a. Number of stillbirths of this mother, not counting this birth 0

(b) Was a one per cent. solution of silver nitrate used in this baby's eyes as provided by law? (yes or no) yes

22. CERTIFICATE OF ATTENDING PHYSICIAN OR MIDWIFE
I HEREBY CERTIFY, That I attended the birth of the above mentioned child who was born as stated in item (7)

MIDWIFE   PHYSICIAN

(Signed)   Midwife   (Signed) Chas H Johnson M.D.

(Address)   (Address) 250 Auburn Ave

Date   19   Date 4/17/34   19
(Given name of child added from a supplemental report)

FILED: Date 4/17/34   19   Date   7-23-57

(Signed) L. Thornton   (Signed)   J M Long
(Local Registrar)   (Registrar)

Martin Luther King, Jr.'s birth certificate.
Original in the Georgia Department of Human Resources.

Liberty, Traveler's Rest, and Wheat Street Baptist churches sang at his funeral, "a huge and emotional ceremony," as King, Sr., recalled.[82] The sixteen eulogies included offerings by Benjamin Davis; W. A. Fountain and J. S. Flipper, bishops of the AME church; John Hope, president of Atlanta University and Morehouse; Florence M. Read, president of Spelman; Dr. Will Alexander of the Commission on Inter-racial Cooperation; and Dr. James M. Nabrit of the General Missionary Baptist Convention of Georgia. Letters, resolutions, and telegrams of condolence and tribute came from across the country. The *Georgia Baptist*'s obituary was effusive: "'A. D.' was a sign post among his neighbors, and a mighty oak in the Baptist forest of the nation," it said. "Born in the country and with limited literary preparation, his wealth of native ability, tact and application made him a man among men and a force to be reckoned with in local, state, and national economic and ecclesiastical councils. He was a preacher of unusual power, an appealing experimentalist, a persuasive evangelist, and a convincing doctrinarian."[83]

As a child, King, Jr., was constantly reminded of the depth of his family's roots in Ebenezer Church and Atlanta's black community. Although his father's increasingly impressive accomplishments would in time overshadow those of his grandfather, Williams's influence at Ebenezer remained strong even after his death. King, Sr., did not leave Traveler's Rest to succeed his father-in-law until the fall of 1931, by which time he had sufficiently overcome his feeling of unpreparedness in assuming the post. It took several years, however, before he gained the full trust and support of Ebenezer's deacons— years in which he provided remarkably effective leadership and restored the church to financial security.[84]

Beyond his grandfather's legacy, the forces shaping King, Jr.'s emerging personality were the stable influences of family, church, and community. King remembered his childhood as one of harmony. In an autobiographical statement written in early adulthood, King, Jr., depicted a happy childhood spent "in a very congenial home situation," with parents who "always lived together very intimately." He could "hardly remember a time that they ever argued (My father happens to be the kind who just [won't] argue), or had any great fall out."[85]

---

82. King, Sr., with Riley, *Daddy King*, p. 90.

83. "Rev. Adam Daniel Williams" and "Noted Atlanta Divine Dies," *Georgia Baptist*, 10 April 1931. See also Lizzie Hunnicut, "In Memoriam," *Georgia Baptist*, 25 August 1931; and Ebenezer Baptist Church, Program for Rev. Adam Daniel Williams's Funeral Service, 24 March 1931, CKFC.

84. King, Sr., with Riley, *Daddy King*, pp. 91–95.

85. King, Jr., "An Autobiography of Religious Development," p. 360 in this volume. Adult recollections of childhood are often unreliable as historical evidence, but the available accounts of King's childhood display an underlying consistency while differing over details. For more information on King, Jr.'s childhood, see King, Sr., with Riley, *Daddy King*; and King, Jr., *Stride Toward Freedom* (New York: Harper & Brothers, 1958). For other sources that rely on first-hand knowledge of King's childhood, see Reddick, *Crusader Without Violence*; and Lerone Bennett, Jr., *What Manner of Man* (Chicago: Johnson Publishing Co., 1964, sixth revised edition, 1986).

Hidden from view were his parents' negotiations regarding their differing notions on discipline. His father believed strict discipline was sometimes necessary to prepare his offspring for the often cruel society they would enter. "To prepare a child for a world where death and violence are always near drains a lot of energy from the soul," King, Sr., later explained. "Inside you, there is always a fist balled up to protect them. And a constant sense of the hard line between maintaining self-respect and getting along with the enemy all around you."[86]

As a father, King, Sr., found it difficult to control his temper and to soften the sharper edges of personality that had enabled him to survive the hardships of his early life. "My impatience made it very hard for me to sit down with the boys and quietly explain to them the way I wanted things done."[87] L. D. Reddick, an acquaintance of the King family, described the household as "father-centered," a place where King, Sr.'s word, "considerate and benevolent as he tried to make it, was final."[88] The elder King's own recollections, however, suggest that his paternal desires were neither unbending nor always obeyed. Although he believed that the "switch was usually quicker and more persuasive" in disciplining his boys (Christine was "exceptionally well-behaved"), he increasingly deferred to his wife's less stern but effective approaches to child rearing, recognizing that her gentleness and empathy did not result in permissiveness—"they couldn't get up early enough in the morning to fool her." King, Sr., later acknowledged that his wife "insisted . . . as the children grew older, that any form of discipline used on them by either of us had to be agreed upon by both parents." His own difficult relationship with his embittered, violence-prone father prepared him to accept the possibility that only his wife could "investigate and soothe" his oldest son's "sensitivities." "We talked a lot about the future of the kids, and she was able to understand that even when I got very upset with them, it was only because I wanted them to be strong and able and happy."[89] King, Jr., would later describe "Mother Dear" as being "behind the scene setting forth those motherly cares, the lack of which leaves a missing link in life."[90]

Protected and loved by concerned, confident, and accommodating parents, the King children also benefited from the presence in their household of Jennie Celeste Williams. As "First Lady" of Ebenezer, Williams was involved in most aspects of church governance, heading the Missionary Society for many years. She represented the church in local Baptist organizations and in the Woman's Convention, an auxiliary to the National Baptist Convention. Known as "Mama" to her grandchildren, she was especially protective of her first grandson and "could never bear to see him cry." Referring to her as "saintly," King, Jr., acknowledged her considerable impact on his childhood. "She was very dear to each of us, but especially to me," he later wrote. "I sometimes

---

86. King, Sr., with Riley, *Daddy King,* p. 94.
87. King, Sr., with Riley, *Daddy King,* p. 130.
88. Reddick, *Crusader Without Violence,* p. 51.
89. King, Sr., with Riley, *Daddy King,* pp. 130, 131.
90. King, Jr., "Autobiography of Religious Development," p. 360 in this volume.

think that I was [her] favorite grandchild. I can remember very vividly how she spent many evenings telling us interesting stories."[91]

Beyond the family home, the King children spent most of their time at Ebenezer church. As King, Jr., later explained, "the church has always been a second home for me." Nearly all his initial friendships developed there. "My best friends were in Sunday School, and it was the Sunday School that helped me to build the capacity for getting along with people."[92] Even King, Jr.'s earliest letters to his parents, written between the ages of eleven and fifteen, convey an intimate knowledge of Baptist church life, including such details as congregational governance, ward meetings, church finances, and social events.

In addition to observing his father's leadership role, King, Jr.'s church activities also brought him into close association with his mother, who was Ebenezer's organist and choir director. As in other African-American Baptist churches, the music and singing at Ebenezer played a major role in attracting and holding members. King, Sr., believed that "religious ideas and ideals have been shaped as much by gospel songs as by gospel sermons."[93] Alberta King's musical talent caused her to be in demand at various Baptist gatherings in Georgia and even at meetings of the National Baptist Convention. In 1937, a year before graduating from Morris Brown College, Alberta King initiated a series of annual musicales featuring the church's choirs. Ebenezer's choirs also performed at the 1939 Atlanta premiere of *Gone with the Wind.* By the early 1940s the annual concerts were attracting overflowing crowds. From the age of four, King, Jr., often performed with his mother at Ebenezer and at other churches and religious gatherings, singing such songs as "I Want to Be More and More Like Jesus" with his mother providing accompaniment.[94] His father recalled his son's appreciation for church "ceremonies and ritual, the passionate love of Baptist music."[95]

The King children observed their father's increasingly evident achievements as a minister. Faced with mortgage foreclosure on Ebenezer in the years after A. D. Williams's death, King, Sr., reinvigorated the church through successful membership and fundraising drives, and was able to pay off the note within four years. The family's living standard also improved. Indeed, King, Sr., later stated, "the deacons took great pride in knowing that young Reverend King was the best-paid Negro minister in the city."[96] In 1934, his finances were such that he could attend the World Baptist Alliance in Berlin. Traveling by ocean liner to France, King and ten other ministers journeyed by train from Paris to Rome, then by boat to Tunisia, Libya, and Egypt. The tour was highlighted by visits to historic sites in Palestine and the Holy Land.

----

91. Reddick, *Crusader Without Violence*, p. 51; King, Jr., "Autobiography of Religious Development," p. 359 in this volume.

92. King, Jr., "Autobiography of Religious Development," p. 361 in this volume.

93. King, Sr., "What Part Should Singing Play In Our Church Worship?"

94. Ebenezer Baptist Church Anniversary Program, 9–16 March 1936, EBCR; Wagner, *Profiles of Black Georgia Baptists*, p. 94; Reddick, *Crusader Without Violence*, p. 56.

95. King, Sr., with Riley, *Daddy King*, p. 127.

96. King, Sr., with Riley, *Daddy King*, p. 94.

"In Jerusalem, when I saw with my own eyes the places where Jesus had lived and taught, a life spent in the ministry seemed to me even more compelling," King recalled. Upon arrival in Berlin—where they noted many ominous signs of the rise of Adolf Hitler—the group joined thousands of Baptist clergymen from around the world. King's return to Atlanta in August 1934 was front-page news in the *Atlanta Daily World*.[97] The increasing prominence and relative affluence of Ebenezer's pastor was also reflected by the now-final transformation of his name: from Michael King to Michael Luther King to Martin Luther King (although close friends and relatives continued to refer to him and his son as Mike or M. L.).[98]

Despite the senior King's relative wealth, the family did not join the migration to the more prestigious neighborhoods that were being settled by middle-class blacks. King's anti-elitist attitudes were cultivated by his parents who discouraged him from developing feelings of class superiority. The King children often heard the story of A. D. Williams's stern rebuke of a parishioner who had corrected his grammar: "I done give a hundred dollars but the gentleman who corrected me *has* given nothing."[99] King, Jr., worked at a variety of jobs—delivering the *Atlanta Journal* from age eight and holding manual labor positions as a teenager. He connected the "anti capitalistic feelings" he had developed by late adolescence with his childhood observations of "the numerous people standing in bread lines" during the Depression.[100]

At about age six, King, Jr., had an experience that profoundly affected his attitudes toward white people. When a white playmate he had known for three years entered Atlanta's segregated school system, his friend's father told his son that he could no longer play with King. "I never will forget what a great shock this was to me," King, Jr., later recalled. He remembered discuss-

---

97. Ibid., p. 97; and "Royally Welcomed on Return," *Atlanta Daily World,* 28 August 1934.

98. Documents from this period indicate that King, Sr.'s name change was achieved gradually rather than through a single legal process, which was not required under Georgia law. By the time he moved to Atlanta and enrolled in Morehouse College, he identified himself as M. L. King, or formally as Michael Luther King, which appeared on his wedding invitation in 1926. He stated in his autobiography that his mother and father had different preferences regarding his name: his mother preferring Michael, after the archangel, his father insisting that he have the names of Jim King's brothers, Martin and Luther. See King, Sr., with Riley, *Daddy King,* p. 26. The coincidence of the name change and King, Sr.'s visit to Germany may also suggest an attempt to identify with the founder of Protestantism. After returning from Europe in 1934, he rarely referred to himself as Michael Luther King and typically used either Martin Luther King or M. L. King. As for King, Jr., his birth certificate was filed on 12 April 1934, before the European tour, under the name Michael King, but was altered on 23 July 1957 to list King as Martin Luther, Jr. Atlanta public school transcripts for King, Jr., obtained by the King Papers Project, initially listed him as M. L. King, although this record was altered, probably during the 1930s, to identify him as Martin Luther King, the name that is also on his elementary school "Test Scores and Ratings" (Dulcie Shrider, Records Manager, Atlanta Public Schools to King Papers Project, 9 June 1987).

99. Reddick, *Crusader Without Violence,* p. 84. This story is told slightly differently by King, Sr.: "I have give a hundred dollars while the man with the good speech have give nothin'!" (King, Sr., with Riley, *Daddy King,* p. 90).

100. King, Jr., "Autobiography of Religious Development," p. 359 in this volume.

ing the matter with his parents over dinner and realizing for the first time "the existence of a race problem." King's parents told him of the "tragedies" of racism and recounted "some of the insults they themselves had confronted on account of it. I was greatly shocked, and from that moment on I was determined to hate every white person." Although his parents told him that he "should not hate the white man, but that it was my duty as a Christian to love him," he was not satisfied. "The question arose in my mind, how could I love a race of people who hated me and who had been responsible for breaking me up with one of my best childhood friends?"[101]

King, Jr.'s schooling officially began in January 1935. A year earlier he had tried to join his sister in the first grade of Yonge Street Elementary School; the attempt to enter school early was apparently foiled, however, when a teacher overheard him talking about his fifth birthday party. After a half-year as a first grader, though, he was promoted to the second grade anyway. In the fall of 1936, he entered the third grade at David T. Howard Elementary School, where he remained through the sixth grade.[102] He then entered the Laboratory High School of Atlanta University, an experimental, progressive private school that appealed to black residents seeking alternatives to Atlanta's crowded public schools. He completed two years there—earning generally good grades except for a failing grade in social studies—before the school was closed.[103]

---

101. Ibid., pp. 362–363 in this volume. A different account, mentioning two white playmates, appears in *Stride Toward Freedom* (pp. 18–19): "My mother took me on her lap and began by telling me about slavery and how it had ended with the Civil War. She tried to explain the divided system of the South—the segregated schools, restaurants, theaters, housing; the white and colored signs on drinking fountains, waiting rooms, lavatories—as a social condition rather than a natural order. Then she said the words that almost every Negro hears before he can yet understand the injustice that makes them necessary: 'You are as good as anyone.'" King's father also recounted this incident—mentioning "two young sons of a local grocery-store owner": Alberta "sat and talked with him for hours. He was a curious youngster who really did wonder constantly about this peculiar world he saw all around him. 'Don't you be impressed by any of this prejudice you see,' she told him. 'And never think, son, that there is anything that makes a person *better* than you are, especially the color of his skin'" (King, Sr., with Riley, *Daddy King*, p. 130). See also King, Jr., BBC interview by John Freeman on "Face to Face," 29 October 1961, MLKJrP-GAMK.

102. His sister later recalled that he was "not too studious" during his elementary school days, although she remembered that he enjoyed competing in spelling bees. King's elementary school grades were generally satisfactory; a fifth grade intelligence test rated him slightly below the mean for youngsters his age. See Reddick, *Crusader Without Violence*, p. 54; Jerry Tallmer, "Martin Luther King, Jr., His Life and Times," *New York Post*, 8 April 1968; "Christine King Farris," *USA Weekend*, 17–19 January 1986; Christine King Farris, "The Young Martin," *Ebony* 41 (January 1986): 56–58; and "Martin Luther King, Jr.'s Grade School Records, 1934–1940," APS-GAP.

103. Reddick, *Crusader Without Violence*, p. 54. King's report cards from the Laboratory High School are: Beulah Bolen, Report Card in Science for King, January 1942; B. A. Jones, Report Card in 8th Grade Social Studies for King, 23 January 1942; E. R. Thomas, Report Card in 8th Grade Shop for King, 23 January 1942; E. R. Thomas, Report Card in P.E. for King, 23 January 1942; Roland G. Anderson, Report Card in 8th Grade Math for King, 26 January 1942; Mary J. Dean, Report Card in 8th Grade Art for King, 26 January 1942; and Report Card in 8th or 9th Grade English for King, September 1941–June 1942; all in CKFC.

During King's childhood and teenage years, he became increasingly aware of his father's vocal opposition to segregation. The elder King not only engaged in individual acts of dissent, such as riding the "whites only" City Hall elevator to reach the voter registrar's office, but also was a leader of organizations such as the Atlanta Civic and Political League and the NAACP. In 1939, he proposed, to the opposition of more cautious clergy and lay leaders, a massive voter registration drive to be initiated by a march to City Hall. At an Ebenezer rally of more than a thousand activists, King referred to his own past and urged black people toward greater militancy. "I ain't gonna plow no more mules," he shouted. "I'll never step off the road again to let white folks pass. I am going to move forward toward freedom, and I'm hoping everybody here today is going right along with me!"[104] A year later King, Sr., braved racist threats when he became chair of the Committee on the Equalization of Teachers' Salaries, organized to protest discriminatory policies that paid higher salaries to white teachers than to blacks with equivalent qualifications and experience. With NAACP legal help, the movement resulted in significant gains.

Although too young to understand fully his father's activism, King, Jr., later wrote that he and his siblings wondered how their father avoided being physically attacked during the "tension-packed atmosphere" of their childhood years. Dinner discussions in the King household often touched on political matters as King, Sr., expressed his views about "the ridiculous nature of segregation in the South." Fearing that they might endure humiliating treatment, King forbade his children to attend segregated theaters. King, Jr., later remembered witnessing his father standing up to a policeman who stopped the elder King for a traffic violation and referred to him as a "boy." According to King, Jr., his indignant father responded by pointing to his son and asserting, "This is a boy. I'm a man, and until you call me one, I will not listen to you." The shocked policeman "wrote the ticket up nervously, and left the scene as quickly as possible."[105]

On another occasion during the voting rights campaign, King, Jr., again witnessed his father's determination not to accept racial discrimination. His father requested a pair of shoes at a downtown store. When the white clerk told the two that they must go to the back of the store for service, King, Sr., refused and left the store. Years later, King, Jr., recalled the incident: "I still remember walking down the street beside him as he muttered, 'I don't care how long I have to live with this system, I will never accept it.'"[106]

King, Sr.'s activism shaped his son's understanding of the ministry and presaged King, Jr.'s own career. Along with other "progressive" black Baptist preachers, the elder King stressed the need for an educated, politically-active ministry. In 1942 he spearheaded an effort in the National Baptist Conven-

---

104. King, Sr., with Riley, *Daddy King*, pp. 100, 104–107, 124–125. King incorrectly dated the march to 1935 rather than 1939; see *Atlanta Daily World*, 8 November 1939.

105. King, Jr., *Stride Toward Freedom*, p. 20.

106. King, Jr., *Stride Toward Freedom*, p. 19. See also the description of this incident in King, Sr., *Daddy King*, pp. 108–109.

tion to pressure President Franklin Roosevelt to eliminate racial discrimination on trains. In an earlier speech expressing his views on "the true mission of the Church," King, Sr., told his fellow clergymen that the church must

> touch every phase of the community life. Quite often we say the church has no place in politics, forgetting the words of the Lord, "The spirit of the Lord is upon me, because he hath anointed me to preach the Gospel to the poor; he hath sent me to heal the broken-hearted, to preach deliverance to the captives, and the recovering of sight to the blind, to set at liberty them that are bruised." . . .
>
> In this we find we are to do something about the broken-hearted, poor, unemployed, the captive, the blind, and the bruised. How can people be happy without jobs, food, shelter and clothes? . . .
>
> God hasten the time when every minister will become a registered voter and a part of every movement for the betterment of our people. Again and again has it been said we cannot lead where we do not go, and we cannot teach what we do not know.
>
> As ministers a great responsibility rests upon us as leaders. We cannot expect our people to register and become citizens until we as leaders set the standard.[107]

King, Jr.'s recollections suggest that he entered his teenage years with enormous admiration for his father's social commitment and with a sense of religion as a constant source of support. Upon the traumatic occasion of his grandmother's death on 18 May 1941, he accepted his parents' spiritual guidance. King learned about the fatal heart attack of Jennie Celeste Williams while attending a parade without his parents' permission. Grieved by the death of his beloved "Mama" and remorseful about his transgression, King initially reacted by impulsively jumping from a second-floor window of his home. Neither King nor his father later mentioned a suicide attempt in their autobiographical statements, but the elder King's account confirms the distress and guilt his son felt: "He cried off and on for several days afterward, and was unable to sleep at night." King, Sr., explained that death "was a part of life that was difficult to get used to" and that God had "His own plan and His own way, and we cannot change or interfere with the time He chooses to call any of us back to Him."[108] King, Jr., later described his grandmother's death as a major formative experience of his youth: "It was after this incident for the first time that I talked at any length on the doctrine of immortality. My parents attempted to explain it to me and I was assured that somehow my grandmother still lived."[109]

Despite his acceptance of many of his parents' religious beliefs, King was uncomfortable with the fervent emotionalism he sometimes observed in the church. In an autobiographical sketch King wrote while a graduate student at Crozer Theological Seminary, he remembered the lack of "dynamic conviction" that had accompanied his decision to join the church, made when a guest

---

107. King, Sr., Moderator's Annual Address, Atlanta Missionary Baptist Association, 17 October 1940, CKFC.

108. King, Sr., with Riley, *Daddy King*, p. 109.

109. King, Jr., "Autobiography of Religious Development," p. 362 in this volume.

evangelist led a revival at Ebenezer. He admitted that he "had never given this matter a thought" and joined only when his sister took the step: "after seeing her join I decided that I would not let her get ahead of me, so I was the next." That King so vividly recalled this childhood event, which culminated in his baptism, may explain his later discomfort with emotional "conversion" experiences. "Conversion for me was never an abrupt something," he explained after recounting his baptism. "I have never experienced the so called 'crisis moment.'" In his sketch, King described his conversion as the "unconscious" and "gradual intaking of the noble ideals set forth in my family and my environment," but he also reported that he entered his teenage years with lingering questions about those Baptist beliefs that he considered "fundamentalist." King noted that none of his Sunday school teachers had "ever doubted the infallibility of the Scriptures. Most of them were unlettered and had never heard of Biblical criticism." He accepted such teachings only until he was twelve: "this uncritical attitude could not last long, for it was contrary to the very nature of my being. I had always been the questioning and precocious type. At the age of 13 I shocked my Sunday School class by denying the bodily resurrection of Jesus. From the age of thirteen on doubts began to spring forth unrelentingly." [110]

King's religious doubts occurred just as many aspects of his life were changing. Following the death of his grandmother, the family moved from the house on Auburn to a larger yellow brick house three blocks away at 193 Boulevard, thus fulfilling a childhood ambition of King, Sr., to own such a home. Enjoying the benefits of his family's affluence, King, Jr., became active in the social life of middle-class Atlanta. He could not remain isolated, however, from southern racism. After delivering the *Atlanta Journal* for five years, he was denied the job of manager of a deposit station. As one account put it, "such a top post, even in Negro neighborhoods was reserved for white men. It involved handling money and coming into the downtown office where the cashiers and clerks were mostly young white women." [111]

Another change in King's life resulted from the closure of the Atlanta Laboratory School in 1942. Skipping the ninth grade, the thirteen-year-old started tenth grade at the public Booker T. Washington High. During his second year at the school he won a preliminary public speaking contest, which allowed him to participate in a state oratorical contest sponsored by the black Elks in Dublin, Georgia. On the way home from the competition, King and other black students were cursed by the bus driver when they refused to give up their seats to white passengers. They reluctantly complied with his directive only when their speech teacher warned them against becoming involved in a potentially dangerous incident. More than two decades later, King recalled his feelings as he stood during that ride to Atlanta: "It was the angriest I have ever been in my life." [112]

---

110. Ibid., p. 361 in this volume.
111. Reddick, *Crusader Without Violence*, p. 56.
112. King, Jr., "Interview," *Playboy*, January 1965, p. 66. On the oratorical contest, which was part of a national competition, see *Atlanta Daily World*, 16 and 22 April 1944.

King's speech from the contest, "The Negro and the Constitution," was published in the 1944 high school annual. The text reflected King's early political views. "We cannot have an enlightened democracy with one great group living in ignorance," he insisted. Neither could the nation be healthy with "one tenth of the people ill-nourished, sick, harboring germs of disease," or "orderly and sound with one group so ground down and thwarted that it is almost forced into unsocial attitudes and crime." King warned: "We cannot be truly Christian people so long as we flaunt the central teachings of Jesus: brotherly love and the Golden Rule. We cannot come to full prosperity with one great group so ill-delayed that it cannot buy goods. So as we gird ourselves to defend democracy from foreign attack, let us see to it that increasingly at home we give fair play and free opportunity for all people." [113]

Following completion of the eleventh grade at Washington High, King had an opportunity to begin college education a year early. Because enrollment at Morehouse College, the alma mater of both King, Sr., and A. D. Williams, had declined because of the wartime draft, president Benjamin E. Mays allowed promising high school juniors to fill out the entering class of 1944. Although King's grades at Washington were not strong, he demonstrated his capacity for college work in a special admissions test. Before beginning at Morehouse, however, King left for his first extended stay away from home, joining about one hundred other students working on a tobacco farm near Simsbury, Connecticut. Established during World War I by John Hope and supervised since the 1930s by Morehouse mathematics professor Claude B. Dansby, the summer work program allowed students to earn and save money to pay college expenses.

The letters King wrote home from Connecticut reveal a fifteen-year-old who was both a child responding to his parents' wishes and a teenager relishing this departure from the world of his childhood. Most startling for King was his first exposure to racial attitudes outside the segregated South. Writing to his father, he commented on things he "never [anticipated] to see." Upon traveling north from Washington, D.C., he observed "no discrimination at all." Whites were "very nice. We go to any place we want to and sit any where we want to." A letter to his mother referred to his attendance at a church service in Simsbury: "Negroes and whites go [to] the same church." After a weekend trip into Hartford, he told his mother about the lack of discrimination in public places. Having eaten at one of Hartford's "finest" restaurants, he commented, "I never [thought] that a person of my race could eat anywhere." [114] These experiences in the North increased King's already strong resentment of racial segregation. [115]

While in Connecticut King participated in various religious activities, in-

---

113. King, Jr., "The Negro and the Constitution," p. 110 in this volume.

114. King, Jr., to King, Sr., 15 June 1944; King, Jr., to Alberta Williams King, 11 June 1944; and King, Jr., to Alberta Williams King, 18 June 1944; pp. 111–116 in this volume.

115. King, Jr., later remembered his first time sitting behind a curtain in a dining car: "I never will forget the deep sense of resentment. . . . Although I was only thirteen years old, this experience disturbed me greatly" (draft of *Stride Toward Freedom*, MLKP-MBU; Box 94A, folder 17B).

cluding singing in a boy's choir that appeared on a local radio program and leading student religious meetings on Sunday evenings. Despite the doubts of his high school years, King's religious commitment became stronger as he demonstrated his preaching abilities. He informed his mother: "As head of the religious Dept. I have to take charge of the Sunday service I have to speak from any text I want to."[116] Four years later he referred to the summer of 1944 as a crucial period in his religious evolution, a time when he "felt an inescapable urge to serve society . . . a sense of responsibility which I could not escape."[117]

In September 1944, King returned to Atlanta to begin his studies at Morehouse College. While the buildings on the small campus had not changed much since the days when his father had been a student, the goals and standing of the college had. Since Mays had become president in 1940, Morehouse had begun to reverse the decline that began during John Hope's final years. Under this new leadership, the college regained its earlier vitality. Not only did Mays—the first Morehouse president with an earned doctoral degree—instill a belief in its students that "Morehouse men" were distinctive in their talent and commitment to racial uplift, but he also worked hard to improve the quality of the faculty, increasing salaries and encouraging professors to pursue doctorates.[118]

Mays was also an innovative, politically-engaged scholar. His first book, *The Negro's God,* published in 1938, was a pioneering study of African-American Christianity, and reflected Mays's enthusiasm for prophetic, social-gospel religious teachings. A trip to India increased his appreciation of the philosophy of Mohandas K. Gandhi, who had given the Indian masses "a new conception of courage." Mays asserted that "when an oppressed race ceases to be afraid, it is free."[119] He often criticized American Christian institutions for not challenging segregation.[120] Believing that black colleges should be "experiment stations in democratic living," Mays challenged Morehouse students to struggle against segregation rather than accommodate themselves to it.[121] Noting the difficulty many students encountered in developing "a critical but secure

116. King, Jr., to Alberta Williams King, 18 June 1944, p. 116 in this volume.

117. King, Jr., Application for Admission to Crozer Theological Seminary, p. 144 in this volume.

118. Mays, *Born to Rebel,* pp. 170–178; and Jones, *A Candle in the Dark,* p. 152.

119. Mays, "The Color Line Around the World," *Journal of Negro Education* 6 (April 1937): 141.

120. Mays's militancy is evident in the articles he wrote during this period. See his "Color Line Around the World," pp. 134–143; "The American Negro and the Christian Religion," *Journal of Negro Education* 8 (July 1939): 530–538; "Veterans: It Need Not Happen Again," *Phylon* 6, no. 3 (1945): 205–211; "Democratizing and Christianizing America in This Generation," *Journal of Negro Education* 14 (Fall 1945): 527–534; "Segregation in Higher Education," *Phylon* 10, no. 4 (1949): 401–406. Mays later wrote that while president "I never ceased to raise my voice and pen against the injustices of a society that segregated and discriminated against people because God made them black" (*Born to Rebel,* p. 188). In 1950 he edited a collection of Walter Rauschenbusch's writings entitled *A Gospel for the Social Awakening.*

121. Mays, "The Role of the Negro Liberal Arts College in Postwar Reconstruction," *Journal of Negro Education* 9 (July 1942): 402.

religious position" to replace the orthodox religious views of their precollege years, he argued that black colleges should seek to inform students about the importance of the church in African-American life. Students needed "contact with people who demonstrate in their person the fact that religion counts," Mays argued, adding that "a religion which ignores social problems will in time be doomed." Religion must "give direction to life—a direction that is neither communistic nor fascistic—not even the direction of a capitalistic individualism."[122]

Mays inspired a generation of Morehouse students who gathered for his Tuesday morning lectures in which he stressed intellectual excellence, religious piety, and commitment to racial advancement. He later recalled King as an eager listener, often responding to his lectures by debating certain points. These contacts led to a "real friendship which was strengthened by visits to his home and by fairly frequent chats."[123] King later described Mays as "one of the great influences in my life."[124]

King's enthusiasm for Mays's teachings developed only gradually. There is little evidence that King exhibited a serious interest in his studies during most of his stay at Morehouse. Younger than most of the other 204 students in his class and uncertain about his career plans, King initially paid more attention to his social life than to his classwork. Although he lived with his parents and did not join a fraternity, King was socially active. Not only was he president of the sociology club and a member of the debating team, student council, glee club, and minister's union, but he also joined the Morehouse chapter of the NAACP, and played on the Butler Street YMCA basketball team.[125]

Among King's first acquaintances at the college was another Morehouse freshman, Walter R. McCall, a preministerial student five years older than King who would soon become his best friend. McCall recalled that King was an "ordinary student" during this period: "I don't think [King] took his studies *very* seriously, but seriously enough to get by." King "loved the lighter side of life," even when it meant disobeying his father's injunctions against sinful behavior. "Many times [his father] opposed our dancing and things like that," McCall remembered, "but he would slip off anyway and go. Many times he and I as well as his sister and some more girls would congregate at his house while his Daddy was at church and we'd put on a party."[126]

Documentary evidence regarding King's studies at Morehouse is scanty, making his intellectual development there difficult to trace. Later accounts

---

122. Mays, "The Religious Life and Needs of Negro Students," *Journal of Negro Education* 9 (July 1940): 337, 341, 342.

123. Mays, *Born to Rebel*, p. 265.

124. King, Jr., *Stride Toward Freedom*, p. 145. Mays's influence on King is also discussed by Robert E. Johnson, William G. Pickens, and Charles V. Willie in Renee D. Turner, "Remembering the Young King," *Ebony* 43 (January 1988): 42–46; and Oliver "Sack" Jones in an interview by Herbert Holmes, 8 April 1970, MLK/OH-GAMK.

125. King, Jr., Application for Admission to Crozer Theological Seminary, p. 144 in this volume; YMCA, Certificate of Participation in Annual Basketball League, 1947–1948, ATL-AAHM.

126. Walter R. McCall, interview by Herbert Holmes, 31 March 1970, MLK/OH-GAMK.

Year & Course, grouped by semester	Instructor	Grade	Credit Hours
1944-1945			
Introductory Biology	Mary L. Reddick	C	3
Composition and Reading		C	6
History of Civilization	Thomas J. Curry	C	3
Freshman Mathematics	Claude Dansby	B	3
Church History	Lloyd O. Lewis	C	3
Freshman Hygiene	Marshall B. Arnold	P	1
Freshman Orientation	Brailsford R. Brazeal	P	
Physical Education	Marshall B. Arnold	P	
Introductory Biology	Mary L. Reddick	C	3
Composition and Reading		C	6
History of Civilization		C	3
Freshman Mathematics	Claude Dansby	B	3
Church History	Lloyd O. Lewis	C	3
Freshman Hygiene	Marshall B. Arnold	P	1
Freshman Orientation	Brailsford R. Brazeal	P	
Physical Education	Marshall B. Arnold	P	
1945-1946			
Elementary French	Evelyn Wynona Moore?	C	4
Introduction to General Literature	Gladstone Lewis Chandler	C	3
General Psychology	Joseph L. Whiting	C	3
Matter and Energy	Burwell Towns Harvey	B	3
Introduction to Sociology	Walter R. Chivers	B	3
Physical Education	Marshall B. Arnold	P	
Elementary French	Evelyn Wynona Moore?	B	4
Introduction to General Literature	Gladstone Lewis Chandler	C	3
Educational Psychology	Joseph L. Whiting	C	3
Matter and Energy	Burwell Towns Harvey	B	3
Introductory Sociology	Walter R. Chivers	B	3
Physical Education	Marshall B. Arnold	P	

Year & Course, grouped by semester	Instructor	Grade	Credit Hours
[continued]			
1946-1947			
Shakespeare	Nathaniel P. Tillman	B	3
American Literature		C	3
Intermediate French	Evelyn Wynona Moore?	C	3
Bible	George D. Kelsey	B	3
Contemporary Social Trends in America	Walter R. Chivers	B	3
Social Psychology	Walter R. Chivers	B	3
Shakespeare	Nathaniel P. Tillman	B	3
American Literature		B	3
Intermediate French	Evelyn Wynona Moore?	D	3
Bible	George D. Kelsey	A	3
Social Anthropology	Walter R. Chivers	B	3
Seminar in Sociology	Walter R. Chivers	P	
1947-1948			
Introduction to Philosophy	Samuel Williams	C	3
Classics in English		B	3
Social Institutions	Walter R. Chivers	B	3
Social Legislation	Madrid B. Turner	B	3
Statistics	Walter R. Chivers	Inc.	
Introduction to Philosophy	Samuel Williams	B	3
Principles and Methods of Statistics	Walter R. Chivers	C	3
English Fundamentals		P	
Seminar in Sociology		P	
Intercultural Relations	Walter R. Chivers	B	3
Language and Thinking	Nathaniel P. Tillman	C	3
[*Urban Sociology?*]	Madrid B. Turner?	B	3

suggest, however, that he benefited from Morehouse's liberal arts curriculum and from the personal attention of the school's faculty. During his first year, for example, he received the valuable help of Professor Gladstone Lewis Chandler in preparing for the John L. Webb oratorical competition, in which he won second prize in 1946 and 1948.[127]

During King's second year, he took his first course with sociologist Walter Richard Chivers, an outspoken critic of segregation, who became King's advisor when he chose sociology as his major. Chivers wrote several articles during the 1940s about racial discrimination and the role of black leaders in the struggle against oppression. He praised social reformers, such as Harlem's militant minister, Adam Clayton Powell, but offered caustic criticism of cautious "talented tenth Negro leaders." Although his discussions of working-class issues were clearly influenced by Marx, Chivers did not openly advocate socialism, and he rejected communism as akin to totalitarian fascism.[128] His emphasis on the economic roots of racism certainly contributed to King's increasingly anticapitalist sentiments. As classmate Lerone Bennett, Jr., later recalled, King saw Chivers's notion "that money was the root not only of evil but also of race" confirmed when he took a summer job and observed that blacks were paid less than whites performing the same tasks.[129]

King's growing awareness of social and political issues is evident in the few writings that survive from his undergraduate years. In a letter to the editor of the *Atlanta Constitution* written the summer before his junior year, for example, he reacted to a series of racially-motivated murders in Georgia. King summarized black goals: "We want and are entitled to the basic rights and opportunities of American citizens: The right to earn a living at work for which we are fitted by training and ability; equal opportunities in education, health, recreation, and similar public services; the right to vote; equality before the law; some of the same courtesy and good manners that we ourselves bring to all human relations."[130] Invited during his junior year to write an article for the February 1947 Founders' Day issue of the school paper, the *Maroon Tiger,* King used the opportunity to warn students about their "mis-

---

127. "King later described [Chandler] as 'one of the most articulate, knowledgeable and brilliant professors' at Morehouse, 'one of those rare unique individuals who was so dedicated to his work that he forgot himself into immortality'" (King to Mrs. G. Lewis Chandler, 28 September 1965, quoted in Stephen B. Oates, *Let the Trumpet Sound* [New York: Harper & Row, 1982], p. 17).

128. See the following works by Walter R. Chivers: "Current Trends and Events of National Importance in Negro Education," *Journal of Negro Education* 12 (Winter 1943): 104–111; "Negro Business and the National Crisis," *Opportunity* (April 1942): 113–115; "Modern Educational Leadership of Negroes," *Southern Frontier* 3 (October 1942); and "Negro Church Leadership," *Southern Frontier* 3 (December 1942) and 4 (January 1943).

129. Bennett, *What Manner of Man,* p. 28. King drew a somewhat different conclusion when he described his summer work experiences, years later in *Stride Toward Freedom:* "During my late teens I worked two summers, against my father's wishes—he never wanted my brother and me to work around white people because of the oppressive conditions—in a plant that hired both Negroes and whites. Here I saw economic injustice firsthand, and realized that the poor white was exploited just as much as the Negro" (King, *Stride Toward Freedom,* p. 90).

130. King, Jr., "Kick Up Dust," Letter to the Editor, *Atlanta Constitution,* 6 August 1946, p. 121 in this volume.

conception of the purpose of education. Most of the 'brethren' think that education should equip them with the proper instruments of exploitation so that they can forever trample over the masses. Still others think that education should furnish them with noble ends rather than means to an end." To save men from "the morass of propaganda" was "one of the chief aims of education," according to King. "The function of education, therefore, is to teach one to think intensively and to think critically."[131] Another essay, written at the end of his junior year, addressed the topic "Economic Basis for Cultural Conflict" and appeared in a departmental journal Chivers helped produce.[132]

During his junior year, King's evolving sociopolitical views merged with the new understanding of Christian theology he gained from religion professor George D. Kelsey, a theologian widely known and respected for his annual Institute for the Training and Improvement of Baptist Ministers. While King, Sr., described Kelsey as a teacher who "saw the pulpit as a place both for drama, in the old-fashioned, country Baptist sense, and for the articulation of philosophies that address the problems of society," the younger King was attracted to his professor's tough-minded approach to theological issues. Kelsey (who gave King his only A at Morehouse) stressed the implications of the Christian gospel for social and racial reform while also insisting that the Kingdom of God could "never be realized fully within history" because the sinful nature of man "distorts and imposes confusion even on his highest ideas."[133] Kelsey's writings of the 1940s evinced a personal struggle to reconcile the Protestant notion of individual salvation with the realization that religious individualism often encourages pessimism about progressive social reform.[134] He also provided some of the intellectual resources King needed to resolve the conflict between the religious traditions of his youth and the secular ideas he had learned in college. As King later commented, that conflict continued until he took Kelsey's course and realized "that behind the legends

---

131. King, Jr., "The Purpose of Education," pp. 123–124 in this volume. See also the recollections of Charles V. Willie, in Renee D. Turner, "Remembering the Young King," *Ebony* 43 (January 1988): 46. King's essay was undoubtedly influenced by Mays's ideas. Mays had presented an argument similar to King's in a 1942 article: "One of the fundamental defects in the world today is the fact that man's intellect has been developed to a point beyond his integrity and beyond his ability to be good. . . . The trouble with the world lies primarily in the area of ethics and morals. It will not be sufficient for the Negro liberal arts colleges, nor any colleges, to produce clever graduates, men fluent in speech and able to argue their way through; but rather honest men who can be trusted both in public and private life—men who are sensitive to the wrongs, sufferings, and injustices of society and who are willing to accept responsibility for correcting the ills" (Mays, "The Role of the Negro Liberal Arts College in Postwar Reconstruction," pp. 407–408).

132. This article, which has not been located by the King Papers Project, is mentioned in "M'house Students Publish Annual Sociology Digest," *Maroon Tiger*, May–June 1948.

133. King, Sr., with Riley, *Daddy King*, p. 141; and Kelsey, "Protestantism and Democratic Intergroup Living," *Phylon* 7 (1947): 77–82.

134. See Kelsey, "Social Thought of Contemporary Southern Baptists" (Ph.D. diss., Yale University, 1946); and Kelsey, "Negro Churches in the United States," in *Twentieth Century Encyclopedia of Religious Knowledge*, ed. Lefferts A. Loetscher (Grand Rapids, Mich.: Baker Book House, 1955), 2:789–791.

and myths of the Book were many profound truths which one could not escape."[135]

The influence of Chivers and Kelsey was evident in an essay entitled "Ritual" that King probably wrote during his senior year. Reflecting his self-conscious straddling of the line between his social science training and his religious vocation, King acknowledged that, although as a pretheological student he would be expected "to defend certain aspects of sacred ritual, therefore becoming unscientific," his aim was "to be as unbiased and scientific as possible."[136]

While King's enthusiasm for Kelsey's critical approach to biblical studies set him apart from his father's scriptural literalism, it also enabled him to think more seriously about an idea he had previously rejected: entering the ministry. King, Sr., had always wanted both sons to become ministers and eventually, perhaps, to serve as pastors for Ebenezer, but he also recognized the wisdom of his wife's entreaties that their children be allowed to make their own career choices. He later expressed the hope that his sons could make use of his connections among Baptists—"family ties, school and fraternal relationships, the so-called hometown connections that kept phones ringing and letters moving in consideration of help requested and granted, favors offered and accepted. The world is too tough for anyone to think of challenging it alone."[137] Yet A. D. and M. L. were unwilling to conform to paternal expectations: A. D. dropped out of Morehouse before deciding on a ministerial career, and King, Jr., spent his first three years at Morehouse planning to become a lawyer, or perhaps a physician, but certainly not a minister like his father.

King, Jr.'s reluctance to become a minister stemmed largely from his rejection of religious practices that appealed to emotions rather than to the intellect. His persistent questioning of literal interpretations of biblical texts evolved during his Morehouse years into criticism of traditional Baptist teachings. He later wrote that his college days were "very exciting ones," especially the first two years when "the shackles of fundamentalism were removed from my body."[138] Although his break with orthodoxy may have strengthened his

---

135. King, Jr., "Autobiography of Religious Development," p. 362 in this volume. Kelsey (who remembered the class as occurring during King's sophomore year) recalled that King "stood out in class not simply academically, but in the sense that he absorbed Jesus' teachings with his whole being. I made it my business to present lectures on the most strenuous teachings of Jesus. It was precisely at this time that Martin's eyes lit up most and his face was graced with a smile" (quoted in Turner, "Remembering the Young King," p. 44). For Kelsey's restrained letter supporting King's seminary application, see Kelsey to Charles E. Batten, 12 March 1948, p. 155 in this volume.

136. King, Jr., "Ritual," p. 128 in this volume. "Ritual" is the only extant essay from King's Morehouse education.

137. King, Sr., with Riley, Daddy King, p. 128.

138. King, Jr., "Autobiography of Religious Development," p. 363 in this volume. Despite King, Jr.'s definition of his father's theology as "fundamentalist," the term is a misleading description of King, Sr.'s conservatism on matters of biblical interpretation. In a 1956 interview, King, Jr., noted that he was disturbed that "most Negro ministers were unlettered, not trained in

determination not to become a minister, it also opened him to liberalism as a potentially acceptable religious orientation. King wrote later that the circumstances of his call to the ministry were unusual, for even though he had experienced a sense of calling, he continued to waver about his career choice during his first three years at Morehouse. He recalled wondering "whether [the church] could serve as a vehicle to modern thinking. I wondered whether religion, with its emotionalism in Negro churches, could be intellectually respectable as well as emotionally satisfying." [139]

King was probably leaning toward a career as a minister by the end of his junior year, but making a final decision was nevertheless difficult. On the one hand, he could not ignore his father's hopes and his friends' expectations. His fellow students who heard him speak at campus events admired his oratorical skills; as one classmate recalled, "he knew almost intuitively how to move an audience." [140] On the other hand, he continued to deprecate the emotionalism he associated with Baptist preaching. While remaining skeptical of his father's doctrinal conservatism, King saw his father as a model. He would later explain that King, Sr.'s influence "had a great deal to do with my going in the ministry. He set forth a noble example that I didn't [mind] following." [141] Perhaps even more influential than his father, Mays and Kelsey were also crucial role models. "Both were ministers, both deeply religious, and yet both were learned men, aware of all the trends of modern thinking," King, Jr., later explained. "I could see in their lives the ideal of what I wanted a minister to be." [142] His decision was, in short, a summation of King's earlier experiences and influences.

> It came neither by some miraculous vision nor by some blinding light experience on the road of life. Moreover, it was a response to an inner urge that gradually came upon me. This urge expressed itself in a desire to serve God and humanity, and the feeling that my talent and my commitment could best be expressed through the ministry. [143]

King told close friends at Morehouse of his intention to become a minister, but he probably continued to debate the idea during the summer. Returning

---

seminaries, and that gave me pause. I revolted, too, against the emotionalism of much Negro religion, the shouting and stamping. I didn't understand it, and it embarrassed me" (William Peters, "'Our Weapon Is Love,'" *Redbook* 107 [August 1956]: 42).

139. King, Jr., quoted in "Attack on the Conscience," *Time*, 18 February 1957, p. 18. A Morehouse classmate, William G. Pickens, recalled that King's image of the black Baptist preacher was negative: "He saw them as anti-intellectual and prone to establish or maintain emotionalism as the chief sign of salvation" (quoted in Turner, "Remembering the Young King," p. 46).

140. Samuel DuBois Cook, quoted in Turner, "Remembering the Young King," p. 42.

141. King, Jr., "Autobiography of Religious Development," p. 363 in this volume.

142. Peters, "'Our Weapon Is Love,'" p. 42.

143. King's 7 August 1959 statement written in response to a request by Joan Thatcher, Publicity Director of the Board of Education and Publication of the American Baptist Convention, Division of Christian Higher Education, 30 July 1959, MLKP-MBU, quoted in Mervyn Alonzo Warren, "A Rhetorical Study of the Preaching of Doctor Martin Luther King, Jr., Pastor and Pulpit Orator" (Ph.D. diss., Michigan State University, 1966), pp. 35–36.

with other students to the Connecticut tobacco farm where he had worked in
1944, King once again led weekly religious gatherings. While there, he tele-
phoned his mother to tell her of his decision. Upon his return to Atlanta at
summer's end, he discussed his plans with other family members before finally telling his father. "I finally decided to accept the challenge to enter the
ministry," King recalled. "I came to see that God had placed a responsibility
upon my shoulders and the more I tried to escape it the more frustrated I
would become."[144] That autumn, King, Jr., delivered a trial sermon at Ebenezer, attracting a large and appreciative audience. "M. L. had found himself," King, Sr., recalled. "I could only thank God, pretty regularly, for letting
me stay around long enough to be there."[145] Immediately after the sermon,
the Ebenezer congregation licensed him to preach, and he joined the church
as associate pastor to his father. During his final year at Morehouse, he
preached occasionally at Ebenezer before being ordained as a minister in February 1948.

After King decided to become a minister and to pursue graduate studies at
a seminary, he became more serious and focused during his final year at Morehouse. In addition to Kelsey and Mays, Samuel W. Williams provided King
with another example of an academically trained, socially committed minister.
A leader of the People's Progressive Party in Georgia, Williams supported the
presidential campaign of Henry A. Wallace.[146] King took an introductory philosophy course from Williams, who also preached at local churches. During
his senior year, King's commitment to social change was strengthened when
he joined the Intercollegiate Council, an interracial student group that met
monthly at Emory University to discuss various issues. Despite opposition
from his father, King actively participated in these meetings. The encounters
with white students helped King overcome the antiwhite feelings he had felt
since childhood.[147]

---

144. Ibid.
145. King, Sr., with Riley, *Daddy King*, p. 141.
146. In a mock presidential election during the spring of 1948, a "Wallace for President"
committee (led by Morehouse student Floyd B. McKissick) succeeded in winning the support of
a majority of Morehouse students. Williams's hopes for the radical political party were dashed in
the November general election, however, when less than 1 percent of Georgia's voters favored
Wallace. Nine months later, Williams resigned from the leadership of the Progressive Party over
differences in "basic philosophy." Soon thereafter he published two articles, one outlining his
understanding of the party's failure to appeal to large numbers of Georgia voters, black or white,
the other presenting a Christian critique of Communism: "The People's Progressive Party of
Georgia," *Phylon* 10 (September 1947): 226–230; and "Communism: A Christian Critique," *Journal of Religious Thought* 6 (Autumn/Winter 1949): 120–135. See also "Wallace Committee," *Maroon Tiger*, March–April 1948; "Student Poll Favors Wallace; Supports A. Philip Randolph,"
Maroon Tiger, May–June 1948; *Congressional Quarterly's Guide to U.S. Elections* (Washington, D.C.:
Congressional Quarterly, Inc., 1985), p. 357; and Progressive Party Correspondence, 1949,
SWWC-GAU.
147. King, Jr., "Autobiography of Religious Development," pp. 362–363 in this volume.
King was later quoted as saying, "I was ready to resent all the white race. As I got to see more
of white people, my resentment was softened, and a spirit of cooperation took its place. But I
never felt like a spectator in the racial problem. I wanted to be involved in the very heart of it"

As he approached the end of his undergraduate years, King applied to several northern, theologically liberal seminaries, including Crozer Theological Seminary. His father, who already admired his son's qualities as a preacher ("His voice, his delivery, the structure and design of his sermons all set him apart from anyone I'd ever heard in my life"), was disappointed that King, Jr., would not become co-pastor at Ebenezer, but reluctantly agreed to support his son's education. King, Sr., feared his son might not return to the segregated South, but he also recognized that King, Jr., would be able to "broaden his knowledge tremendously" at a northern seminary.[148] He secured letters from his father and several family friends, but the comments of those who knew King well were restrained in their assessments of his intellectual ability, often focusing on King's family background and social skills. Morehouse religion professor Lucius M. Tobin, who had not taught King, could report only that he came from "a fine family" and was "a little above average in scholarship." Mays similarly recommended King, along with another student, but conceded that King was "not brilliant," only a person capable of "B work" or, "with good competition," perhaps "even better." George D. Kelsey described King's Morehouse record as "short of what may be called 'good'" but contended that King was an underachiever who had come "to realize the value of scholarship late in his college career." Brailsford R. Brazeal similarly saw evidence of academic growth and sought to explain King's average grades by referring to his "comparatively weak high school background." Even King, Sr.'s positive letter was vague, referring to the fact that King was only fifteen when he entered college and was "above his age in thought."[149]

When he began his seminary studies in the fall of 1948, nineteen-year-old King was younger than most of his Crozer classmates. He probably realized that he would have to become more diligent in his studies if he were to succeed at the small Baptist institution in Chester, Pennsylvania, a small town southwest of Philadelphia. As one of eleven black students (six of them in King's class) in a student body numbering more than ninety, King was self-consciously aware that he represented his race and was determined to do well in his studies. King's only extant letter from his Crozer years, written to his mother during his first term, mentions the social distractions of a Temple student he had once dated and another "fine chick" in Philadelphia, but King also insists that he never went "anywhere much but in these books" and did not think about girls because he was "[too] busy studying."[150] King, evidently wishing to break with the relaxed attitude he had had toward his Morehouse studies, quickly immersed himself in Crozer's intellectual environment. He

------

("Attack on the Conscience," *Time,* 18 February 1957, p. 18). See also Brailsford Brazeal, interview by Judy Barton, 16 February 1972, MLK/OH-GAMK; and King, Sr., with Riley, *Daddy King,* pp. 141–142.

148. King, Sr., with Riley, *Daddy King,* p. 144.

149. Lucius M. Tobin to Charles E. Batten, 25 February 1948; Benjamin Elijah Mays to Batten, 28 February 1948; George D. Kelsey to Batten, 12 March 1948; King, Sr., to Batten, 5 March 1948; and Phoebe Burney to Batten, 9 March 1948; pp. 151–155 in this volume.

150. King, Jr., to Alberta Williams King, October 1948, p. 161 in this volume.

later recalled struggling to avoid confirming racial stereotypes: "If I were a minute late to class, I was almost morbidly conscious of it and sure that everyone noticed it. Rather than be thought of as always laughing, I'm afraid I was grimly serious for a time. I had a tendency to overdress, to keep my room spotless, my shoes perfectly shined and my clothes immaculately pressed."[151]

The Crozer environment encouraged King's increasing intellectual seriousness. Nearly all students lived in private dormitory rooms on campus, situated on a bucolic hillside. Students found that most of their daily needs were satisfied by the seminary's facilities, which included a library, dining rooms, tennis courts, and other amenities. The letter King received from Crozer's dean before the start of the term emphasized the school's academic quality—it was a fully accredited theological seminary with an "excellent faculty of consecrated Christian teachers"—and its informality, made possible by extensive personal contacts between students and full-time faculty, all of whom lived on campus.[152] His transition was eased when former Morehouse classmate Walter McCall joined him at Crozer after the first term. In addition, King often had dinner at the nearby home of the Reverend J. Pius Barbour, a King family acquaintance who had left Morehouse to become Crozer's first black graduate and who was then pastor of Chester's Calvary Baptist Church. "He is full of fun, and he has one of the best minds of anybody I have ever met," King informed his mother.[153]

King immersed himself in his studies and in the European-American theological readings assigned by his Crozer professors. He enrolled in six courses during his first term at Crozer, the most important of which was James Bennett Pritchard's Introduction to the Old Testament—a demanding required course that constituted eight of King's thirteen credit hours for the term. Pritchard was a noted biblical scholar who had earned his doctorate at the University of Pennsylvania and had taught at Crozer since 1942. King quickly demonstrated his willingness to accept Pritchard's biblical interpretations based on historical and archaeological research. In one of his first papers for Pritchard, King eagerly expressed his independence from religious fundamentalism. "No logical thinker can doubt the fact that . . . archaeological findings are now [indispensable] to all concrete study of Hebrew-Christian religion," King commented in discussing the application of the "scientific method" to Old Testament study. Yet, King concluded, while such findings might reveal that biblical stories have mythological roots, they did not necessarily undermine the essential truths of the Old Testament, which remained "one of the most logical vehicles of mankind's deepest devotional thoughts and aspirations, couched in language which still retains its original vigour and its moral intensity."[154]

King's preference for politically engaged religion was also evident in an-

---

151. Quoted in Peters, "'Our Weapon Is Love,'" p. 72.
152. Charles E. Batten to King, Jr., 29 October 1947, p. 126 in this volume.
153. King, Jr., to Alberta Williams King, October 1948, p. 161 in this volume.
154. King, Jr., "Light on the Old Testament from the Ancient Near East," pp. 163, 180 in this volume.

Year & Course, grouped by trimester	Instructor	Grade	Credit Hours
1948-1949			
Introduction to the Old Testament	James B. Pritchard	B −	8
Preaching Ministry of the Church	Robert E. Keighton	B +	2
Orientation for Juniors	Edwin Ewart Aubrey	C −	2
Public Speaking	Robert E. Keighton	P	1/3
Choir	Ruth B. Grooters	P	1/3
Church Music (Elem. Harmony & Sight Singing)	Ruth B. Grooters	C +	1/3
History and Literature of the New Testament	Morton Scott Enslin	B	8
Great Theologians	George W. Davis	A −	2
Preparation of the Sermon	Robert E. Keighton	A	2
Public Speaking	Robert E. Keighton	C +	1/3
The Gospels	Morton Scott Enslin	B +	4
Christian Mysticism	George W. Davis	B +	4
Practice Preaching	Robert E. Keighton	A −	4
Public Speaking	Robert E. Keighton	C	1/3
1949-1950			
Public Worship	Robert E. Keighton	B +	4
Greek Religion	Morton Scott Enslin	B	4
Christian Theology for Today	George W. Davis	B +	4
The Development of Christian Ideas	George W. Davis	A	4
Christian Theology for Today	George W. Davis	A	4
Preaching Problems	Robert E. Keighton	B +	2
Conduct of Church Services	Robert E. Keighton	B	2
Pastoral Counseling	Seward Hiltner	Audit	
Outline History of Christianity	Raymond J. Bean?	B +	8
The History of Living Religions	George W. Davis	B +	4
1950-1951			
American Christianity—Colonial Period	Raymond J. Bean	A	4
Religious Development of Personality	George W. Davis	A	4
The Minister's Use of the Radio	Robert E. Keighton	A	2
Problems of Esthetics (taken at University of Pennsylvania)			4
Philosophy of Religion	George W. Davis	A	4
Theological Integration	Sankey L. Blanton	A	4
Kant (taken at University of Pennsylvania)			4
Advanced Philosophy of Religion	George W. Davis	A	4
Christian Social Philosophy II	Kenneth L. Smith	A	4
Christianity and Society	Kenneth L. Smith	A −	4

other paper discussing scholarship on Jeremiah. King argued that despite his failure to affect the social order of his time, Jeremiah's insistence on a personal relationship with God was ultimately a valuable contribution to Christianity. The prophet, King insisted, demonstrated that Christians should never "become sponsors and supporters of the status quo. How often has religion gone down, chained to a status quo it allied itself with." In refuting the cynical notion that religion was "simply the reflection of the State's opinion of itself foisted upon the divine," Jeremiah taught that religion could be a vehicle of social progress: "Religion, in a sense, through men like Jeremiah, provides for its own advancement, and carries within it the promise of progress and renewed power."[155]

King gained further exposure to historical biblical scholarship during his second term, in Morton Scott Enslin's History and Literature of the New Testament. A sometimes intimidating, Harvard-trained expert in the history of early Christianity, Enslin had taught at Crozer since 1924 and edited the *Crozer Quarterly* since 1941. Like Pritchard, Enslin was known to give few high grades, and he returned King's papers with numerous critical comments and corrections written in almost illegible, miniature script. King's papers for Enslin, in which he acknowledged Christianity's indebtedness to earlier religious traditions, were, like those for Pritchard, competent but unimaginative and derivative. In them he continued to affirm the value of biblical scholarship while also insisting that such scholarship did not undermine essential Christian values.

King began to forge his own theological perspective during the fall term of his second year, when he enrolled in George Washington Davis's two-term course, Christian Theology for Today. Davis, who attended Colgate-Rochester Divinity School and received a doctorate from Yale before joining Crozer's faculty in 1938, was a northern Baptist influenced by the social gospel of Walter Rauschenbusch. He emphasized the social implications of Christianity, reinforcing the social reform motivations that had led to King's decision to become a minister. Although King had already been exposed to the social-gospel teachings of Mays and Kelsey, Davis expanded King's understanding of the philosophical underpinnings of modern Christian liberalism, particularly the notion that God's reality was revealed through the historical unfolding of his moral law. Davis's impact on his twenty-year-old student was immediate. King's essays for Davis displayed a greater degree of intellectual engagement than had the historical essays written for Pritchard and Enslin. So theologically compatible were King and Davis that King took a total of seven courses from him. Under Davis's tutelage, King began to see theology as a storehouse of ideas that could reinforce the religious beliefs derived from his formative experiences.

Although King's essays for Davis were more reflective than those he had written during his first year, they were still flawed by unacknowledged textual

---

155. King, Jr., "The Significant Contributions of Jeremiah to Religious Thought," pp. 194–195 in this volume.

appropriations from theologians King consulted. His bibliography or notes nearly always identified his sources, but the lack of adequate citations and quotation marks obscured the extent to which King relied upon the work of others. The available documentary evidence does not provide a definite answer to the question whether King deliberately violated the standards that applied to him as a student, yet his academic papers do contain passages that meet a strict definition of plagiarism—that is, *any* unacknowledged appropriation of words or ideas. At the same time, his essays also contain views consistent with those King expressed in other papers and exams written at the time; thus, even though King's writings were often derivative, they remain reliable expressions of his theological opinions.[156]

King, in his papers for Davis, reaffirmed his acceptance of critical biblical scholarship while leaving room in his perspective for some traditional Christian beliefs that could not be reconciled with scholarly findings. He agreed with the liberal view of the Bible as "a portrayal of the experiences of men written in particular historical situations" and as a progressive revelation of the divine, rather than as the literal word of God.[157] Although he saw Jesus as human, he affirmed "an element in his life which transcends the human," a divine quality that was "not something thrust upon Jesus from above, but . . . a definite achievement through the process of moral struggle and self-abnegation."[158] He rejected literal interpretations of Christian beliefs that contradicted "the laws of modern science," insisting instead that such beliefs—the divinity of Jesus, the virgin birth, the second coming, and the bodily resurrection—should be understood metaphorically. The true meaning of the kingdom of God, in short, involved the creation of "a society in which all men and women will be controlled by the eternal love of God."[159] Christians who probed "into the deeper meaning of these doctrines" would find, he stated, "that they are based on a profound foundation."[160] Contrasting liberalism with fundamentalism, King portrayed fundamentalists as "willing to preserve certain ancient ideas even though they are contrary to science."[161]

In another paper, King declared that biblical scholars did not destroy religious belief; instead they served "to prepare the ground for constructive

---

156. For a fuller discussion of the plagiarism issue, see the Martin Luther King, Jr., Papers Project, "The Student Papers of Martin Luther King, Jr.: A Summary Statement on Research," *Journal of American History* 78 (June 1991): 23–31; and Clayborne Carson et al., "Martin Luther King, Jr., as Scholar: A Reexamination of His Theological Writings," ibid., pp. 93–105.

157. King, Jr., "How to Use the Bible in Modern Theological Construction," p. 253 in this volume.

158. King, Jr., "The Humanity and Divinity of Jesus," pp. 260 and 262 in this volume.

159. King, Jr., "The Christian Pertinence of Eschatological Hope," pp. 272–273 in this volume.

160. King, Jr., "What Experiences of Christians Living in the Early Christian Century Led to the Christian Doctrines of the Divine Sonship of Jesus, the Virgin Birth, and the Bodily Resurrection," p. 226 in this volume.

161. King, Jr., "The Sources of Fundamentalism and Liberalism Considered Historically and Psychologically," p. 242 in this volume.

building." The Bible is subject to historical analysis, King explained: "This advance has revealed to us that God reveals himself progressively through human history, and that the final significance of the Scripture lies in the outcome of the process."[162]

Several of King's papers for Davis reflect his effort to refine his theological perspective by either identifying himself with or setting himself apart from particular theologians or theological schools. In an essay entitled "The Place of Reason and Experience in Finding God," for example, King rejected both agnosticism, which eliminates "mystery from the universe," and fundamentalism, which claims certainty about the nature of divinity; rather, he reiterated, "genuine Christian faith" accepts "that the search for God is a process not an achievement." This stance led King to discard, as "one of the perils of our time," the views of Karl Barth and other "crisis" or neo-orthodox theologians who argued that man, corrupted by original sin, could never come to know God through reason. Instead King identified himself with the views of Boston University personalist theologian, Edgar S. Brightman, who saw human awareness of God's presence as the very essence of religious experience.

Brightman's personalism appealed to King because it recognized the importance of nonintellectual sources of theological knowledge, including one's own experiences. Echoing Brightman and other personalists, he confidently insisted that religious experience was important in finding God. "No theology is needed to tell us that love is the law of life and to disobey it means to suffer the consequences," King wrote. "It is religious experience which shows us that much of the misery and weakness of men's lives is due to [the] personal fault of the individual." Moreover, King argued, all people, not just the intellectual elite, were capable of searching for God through experience.[163] While granting the utility of reason in the search for knowledge of the divine, King concluded by appropriating a Brightman formulation: "We must grant freely, however, that final intellectual certainty about God is impossible. . . . We can never gain complete knowledge or proof of the real. . . . But we cannot give up the search because of this limitation. Certainly if God is the real that we are seeking, we can always learn more about him. Thus, reason, when sincerely and honestly used, is one of [the] supreme roads that leads man into the presence of God."[164]

While King remained hostile to fundamentalist Christianity, he increasingly acknowledged the limitations of liberal theology and even of the theological enterprise itself. Still accepting a broad framework of theological understanding based on biblical criticism and the social gospel, he increasingly referred to his personal experiences to explain his gradual move toward greater ortho-

---

162. King, Jr., "How to Use the Bible in Modern Theological Construction," pp. 253–254 in this volume.

163. King, Jr., "The Place of Reason and Experience in Finding God," p. 234 in this volume.

164. Ibid. Cf. Edgar S. Brightman, *The Finding of God* (New York: Abingdon Press, 1931), pp. 69, 72.

doxy. In an essay for Davis entitled "How Modern Christians Should Think of Man," he argued that liberals too "easily cast aside the term sin, failing to realize that many of our present ills result from the sins of men." King admitted that his conception of man was

> going through a state of transition. At one time I find myself leaning toward a mild neo-orthodox view of man, and at other times I find myself leaning toward a liberal view of man. The former leaning may root back to certain experiences that I had in the south with a vicious race problem. Some of the experiences that I encountered there made it very difficult for me to believe in the essential goodness of man. On the other hand part of my liberal leaning has its source in another branch of the same root. [In] noticing the gradual improvements of this same race problem I came to see some noble possibilities in human nature. Also my liberal leaning may root back to the great imprint that many liberal theologians have left upon me and to my ever present desire to be optimistic about human nature.

He had, he acknowledged, become "a victim of eclecticism," seeking to "synthesize the best in liberal theology with the best in neo-orthodox theology." Discarding "one-sided generalizations about man," he concluded that "we shall be closest to the authentic Christian interpretation of man if we avoid both of these extremes." [165]

As King became more critical of liberal theology, he also focused on the theological issue that he considered most crucial: the nature of divinity. Never having experienced God's presence directly through an abrupt experience of conversion, he sought ideas that would provide a conception of God consistent with his own experiences. Although King indicated in the middle of his second year "that the most valid conception of God is that of theism," which he defined as the notion that God was "a personal spirit immanent in nature and in the value structure of the universe," he would continue to struggle with this difficult issue long afterward. [166] King's acceptance of personalist theology resulted from his desire to view religious experience, rather than philosophical rigor, as a necessary foundation for religious rectitude. In another paper for Davis, King concluded that the "ultimate solution" to the vexing problem of the sources of evil in a God-created universe was "not intellectual but spiritual. After we have climbed to the top of the speculative ladder we must leap out into the darkness of faith." [167]

King's increasing tendency to acknowledge the validity of some neo-orthodox criticisms of Christian liberalism may have been related to events in his personal life that contradicted Crozer's ethos of interracial harmony. Most accounts of King's experiences at Crozer suggest that he actively sought out social contacts with white students and faculty members. His immersion in the social and intellectual life of a predominantly white, northern seminary may

---

165. King, Jr., "How Modern Christians Should Think of Man," pp. 274–275 in this volume.
166. King, Jr., "Examination Answers, Christian Theology for Today," p. 290 in this volume.
167. King, Jr., "Religion's Answer to the Problem of Evil," p. 432 in this volume.

have had psychological costs, however, for King learned that he could not insulate himself from the realities of antiblack prejudice. On one occasion a white southern student pulled a gun on King, in the mistaken belief that King had victimized him as a prank.[168] During the summer after his second year at Crozer, King was involved in another incident of harassment that reminded him of his vulnerability to racial discrimination when he ventured off campus. Not only were he and three friends refused service at a tavern, but the owner became abusive and picked up a gun, which he took outside and fired into the air. (He later claimed that, fearing a robbery, he wanted to alert his watchdog.) Almanina Barbour, daughter of J. Pius Barbour, urged the outraged King to sue the establishment. Although the Camden branch of the NAACP agreed to handle the case as a violation of New Jersey's 1945 legislation prohibiting racial discrimination in public facilities, the matter was dropped when several witnesses refused to testify.[169]

In addition to these reminders that he had not left racism behind in the South, King confronted the realization that he would have to tailor his academic training to fit his needs as a pastor of a black congregation. The unenthusiastic evaluation he received as a participant in Crozer's fieldwork program suggests King's difficulty in reconciling what he was learning at seminary with the ingrained religious beliefs he had brought from black Atlanta. Designed to aid students in their development as clergymen, fieldwork in King's case involved training at black churches in the area. Although King had refined his preaching while at Crozer, listeners' accounts suggest that his practice sermons were designed to engage the mind, not the emotions.[170] King was an experienced preacher, of course, having assisted his father at Ebenezer during the previous three summers; the final evaluation written by the Reverend William E. Gardner suggests, however, that King may have become somewhat estranged from his Ebenezer roots. While Gardner saw King as superior in judgment, decisiveness, neatness, poise, and self-confidence, he also noted an "attitude of aloofness, disdain & possible snobbishness which prevent his coming to close grips with the rank and file of ordinary people," as well as "a smugness that refuses to adapt itself to the demands of ministering effectively to the average Negro congregation."[171]

Despite this evaluation, King's buoyancy and self-assurance were evident in the most extended biographical statement he would write during his college career. While enrolled in Davis's course The Religious Development of Personality in late 1950, King insisted in a paper, "An Autobiography of Religious Development," that his basic religious and social views were decisively

---

168. Reddick, *Crusader Without Violence*, p. 82.

169. See W. Thomas McGann, Statement on Behalf of Ernest Nichols, *State v. Ernest Nichols*, pp. 327–328 in this volume.

170. Taylor Branch, *Parting the Waters: America in the King Years, 1954–63* (New York: Simon and Schuster, 1988), pp. 75–77.

171. Gardner was the pastor of First Baptist Church in Corona, New York. See William E. Gardner, Crozer Theological Seminary Field Work Department: Rating Sheet for Martin Luther King, Jr., pp. 380–381 in this volume.

shaped, not by his academic training, but by his formative experiences. His father's "noble" example, he said, and the influences of his childhood had led him to enter the ministry. Despite periods of doubt and a continuing antipathy toward religious emotionalism, King considered his early years and his intense, daily involvement in church life as the bedrock of his religious faith: "At present I still feel the [effects] of the noble moral and ethical ideas that I grew up under. They have been real and precious to me, and even in moments of theological doubt I could never turn away from them. Even though I have never had an abrupt conversion experience, religion has been real to me and closely knitted to life. In fact the two cannot be separated; religion for me is life."[172]

As King became absorbed in the concerns of philosophical or systematic theology, he did not abandon his interest in Christian ethics and the social role of the Christian church. During King's last months at Crozer, he took two courses with Kenneth L. Smith, a strong advocate of social-gospel thought. The courses—Christianity and Society, and Christian Social Philosophy— served as a forum for discussion of modern social issues, including the problems associated with capitalism and the appropriateness of Marxian solutions to those problems.[173] Unsigned student papers from this class suggest that students examined a wide range of issues—church-state relations, the American economy, and Cold War foreign policy, for example—and challenged their own and one another's political beliefs. One unsigned paper entitled "War and Pacifism," often attributed to King, probably accurately expressed King's changing position on the issue during this period. "Though I cannot accept an absolute pacifist position," the author began, "I am as anxious as any to see wars end and have no desire to take part in one." Challenging the views of American pacifist leader A. J. Muste, who had spoken at Crozer during November of King's second year, the paper argued that absolute pacifism would lead to anarchy.[174] Not only did such a position allow "no grounds for

---

172. King, Jr., "Autobiography of Religious Development," p. 363 in this volume. The dependability of the paper is limited by the fact that King self-consciously fits his life experiences into the framework of then-popular theories of personality and attitudinal development during childhood. In his notes for the course, for example, King defines an attitude as a "habitual manner of reaction with strong emotional components." King was encouraged to see his childhood experiences as of primary importance to his religious development: "The social reaction in the home is of primary importance in a child's religious dev. This is because out of experience grows concepts and only through finding mutual love between parents can the child conceive of a God of love . . . Rel. finds the beginning of its ethical quality in the early soc. situation which involves distinctions of right and wrong" (King, "Class Notes, Religious Development of Personality," 12 September 1950–22 November 1950, MLKP-MBU: Box 106, folder 22).

173. According to his account in *Stride Toward Freedom*, King had read Marx during his spare time in 1949. He concluded that Marx had "pointed to weaknesses of traditional capitalism, contributed to the growth of a definite self-consciousness in the masses, and challenged the social conscience of the Christian churches" (*Stride Toward Freedom*, p. 95).

174. King reported in his autobiography that after hearing Muste speak, he felt that "while war could never be a positive or absolute good, it could serve as a negative good in the sense of preventing the spread and growth of an evil force" (*Stride Toward Freedom*, p. 95). According to another report of Muste's talk, he received "a fairly good reception, marred by the chilly attitude

maintaining even a police force, since there is no real difference in kind between war and police action," but it also isolated "war from other ethical problems and [ignored] the fact that war is actually a symptom of deeper trouble." The conclusion was probably consistent with King's beliefs at the time:

> Since man is so often sinful there must be some coercion to keep one man from injuring his fellows. This is just as true between nations as it is between individuals. If one nation oppresses another a Christian nation must, in order to express love of neighbor, help protect the oppressed. This does not relieve us of our obligation to the enemy nation. We are obligated to treat them in such a way as to reclaim them to a useful place in the world community after they have been prevented from oppressing another. We must not seek revenge.[175]

Although this paper reflects the neo-orthodox ideas of Reinhold Niebuhr, Smith recalled that King remained a fervent advocate of the social-gospel Christianity he had derived from both his childhood experiences and his study of Walter Rauschenbusch.[176] Smith later recounted his arguments with King "about the relative merits of the social ethics of Rauschenbusch and Reinhold Niebuhr," with King arguing against Niebuhr.[177] King's later account of his Crozer years, in *Stride Toward Freedom*, probably overstates the extent of his intellectual engagement with the ideas of Niebuhr, for this is not confirmed by the documentary record. While King, like many other liberal theological students of the early 1950s, was undoubtedly influenced by Niebuhr's ideas, few of his papers mention Niebuhr's writings. Rather, King's increasing awareness of the neo-orthodox critique of liberalism derived from a variety of sources in addition to Niebuhr.

Aware of the intellectual deficiencies of social-gospel Christianity, King

---

of the acting president, and the worst outburst of invective . . . from a vet who apparently had a tough time during the war and is having a difficult time living with himself" (Charles Walker to Bayard Rustin, 14 November 1949, FORP-PSC-P).

175. "War and Pacifism," p. 435 in this volume. Although the evidence for King's authorship of this document is inconclusive, there is no convincing information identifying one of the other unsigned papers as the one submitted by King. One of the three papers that may have been authored by King linked democracy to the rise of Protestant Christianity. The Reformation, the author maintained, "was not primarily theological but social." It was part of a social movement, in which "the sacredness of man and his rights were the cardinal doctrines," attempting to overcome the "weight of centuries of oppression." In the New World, the ideals of religious dissenters "were imposed on their political action and we have the foundation of an essentially Christian nation." Having been linked in their origins, democracy and Protestant Christianity were interdependent. "So long as the Christian ideals hold true for individual men, so long will democracy grow and flourish. When Christianity dies, democracy too will fade away and die for it will have lost the wellspring of its life" ("Christianity and Democracy," 20 February 1951–4 May 1951, MLKP-MBU: Box 112, folder 17).

176. King asserted that his initial reading of Rauschenbusch's *Christianity and the Social Crisis* "left an indelible imprint on my thinking by giving me a theological basis for the social concern which had already grown up in me as a result of my early experiences" (King, Jr., *Stride Toward Freedom*, p. 91). See also Kenneth L. Smith, "Reflections of a Former Teacher," *Bulletin of Crozer Theological Seminary*, April 1965, p. 3.

177. Smith, "Reflections of a Former Teacher," p. 3. Smith also speculated that King's direct-action approach to civil rights indicated an eventual acceptance of Niebuhr's brand of realism.

sought a theological framework that combined scholarly rigor with an emphasis on personal experience of God's immanence. Such a theology would allow him to reconcile his emotional roots in the nurturing, sustaining environment of Ebenezer with the sense of intellectual rectitude he had sought in graduate study. King's search led him to the personalism of Boston University's Edgar S. Brightman. As early as his second year at Crozer, he had made favorable comments about Brightman's writings, and during the second term of his last year he again encountered Brightman in Davis's course on the philosophy of religion. Assessing Brightman's book *A Philosophy of Religion,* he conceded that Brightman's personalism left him "quite confused as to which definition [of God] was the most adequate." In general, however, he was persuaded by Brightman's inclusive notion of "essential" beliefs that underlay particular religious practices and concepts of God. Rejecting atheism as "philosophically unsound and practically disadvantageous," King affirmed religion "that gives meaning to life" and provides "the greatest incentive for the good life." He expressed his enthusiasm for a philosophical perspective that offers a rationale for the emotionally rich religious life he had known as a child: "How I long now for that religious experience which Dr. Brightman so cogently speaks of throughout his book," King concluded. "It seems to be an experience, the lack of which life becomes dull and meaningless." The third-year seminarian reflected on his struggle to achieve a sense of religious contentment: "I do remember moments that I have been awe awakened; there have been times that I have been carried out of myself by something greater than myself and to that something I gave myself. Has this great something been God? Maybe after all I have been religious for a number of years, and am now only becoming aware of it."[178]

By the time of his graduation, King's intellectual confidence was reinforced by the experience of having successfully competed with white students during his Crozer years. He was elected student body president, became the class valedictorian, and was the recipient of the Pearl Plafker award for scholarship. He was also accepted for doctoral study at Boston University's School of Theology, where he would be able to work directly with the personalist theologians he had come to admire. He had convinced his teachers that he was destined for further success as a minister and leader, perhaps even as a scholar. Davis's confidential assessment of King's abilities was that he would "make an excellent minister or teacher. He has the mind for the latter." Enslin considered him a "very able man. All is grist that comes to his mill. Hard working, fertile minded, rarely misses anything which he can subsequently use." He added a prediction: "He will probably become a big strong man among his people." Crozer dean Charles Batten saw King as "undoubtedly one of the best men in our entire student body," one of Crozer's "most bril-

---

178. King, Jr., "A Conception and Impression of Religion Drawn from Dr. Brightman's Book Entitled *A Philosophy of Religion,*" pp. 411 and 415–416 in this volume.

liant students," a person with "a keen mind which is both analytical and constructively creative."[179]

Although King's understanding of the modern literature of systematic theology was still in flux at the end of his stay at Crozer, he had refined his basic
ideas about the nature of God. His essays reflected a gradual movement from
an acceptance of liberal theological scholarship toward an increasing skepticism about rational inquiry as a means of achieving religious understanding.
He had found new value in his early religious experiences. King's seminary
years had also been characterized by an ambiguous relationship to the values
of the academy. Rather than developing proficiency as an original scholar,
King had become skilled at appropriating ideas and texts that defined his
evolving religious identity. As a student, he had been dutiful, inquisitive, well
read, and able to win the approval of his professors, but his theological beliefs
were subtly derivative, based on a priori assumptions about the nature of divinity and increasingly suited to his anticipated needs as a preacher rather
than a scholar. King's discovery of personalist theology had both strengthened
his ties with African-American Baptist traditions and encouraged him to pursue further theological study at Boston University.

The religious ideas King brought to the seminary were modified but not
drastically altered as his intellectual sophistication grew. Indeed, although he
sought scholarly understanding of religion, his writings at Crozer consisted of
an eclectic body of ideas that was rendered coherent not by his academic training but by his inherited values. He saw God as immanent in the world, accessible through reason and personal experience, yet also transcendent, a being
not limited by human conceptions of reality. Although King would further
refine his beliefs about the nature of God, at Crozer he had reached theological conclusions that would remain central to his worldview.

---

179. Crozer Theological Seminary Placement Committee: Confidential Evaluations of Martin
Luther King, Jr., by George W. Davis, Morton Scott Enslin, and Charles E. Batten, 15 November
1950, 21 November 1950, and 23 February 1951, respectively, pp. 334, 354, and 406–407 in this
volume; and Charles E. Batten, "Martin L. King," 1951, pp. 390–391 in this volume.

The Reverend Adam Daniel
(A. D.) Williams in 1904.
He was Martin Luther King, Jr.'s
maternal grandfather. Photo
from the *Atlanta Independent*,
2 April 1904.

Shiloh Baptist Church near Penfield in Greene County,
Georgia. Photo courtesy of the Greene County Historical Society.

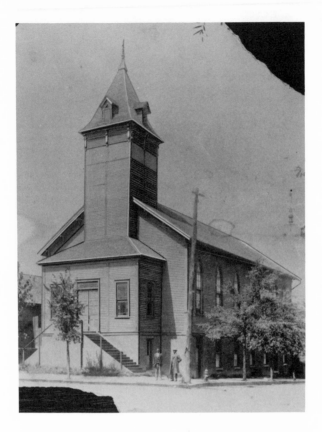

Between 1900 and 1913, A. D. Williams's growing Ebenezer congregation worshipped in this building at the corner of Gilmer and Bell streets in Atlanta. Photo and permission courtesy of Christine King Farris.

APTIST CHURCH, AND (INSERT) REV. A. D. WILLIAMS, THE PASTOR

Ebenezer Baptist Church was built on the corner of Jackson Street and Auburn Avenue in Atlanta between 1914 and 1922. A. D. Williams is pictured in the upper right corner. Photo and permission courtesy of Christine King Farris.

Jennie Celeste Parks Williams (ca. 1920). She was Martin Luther King, Jr.'s maternal grandmother. Photo and permission courtesy of Christine King Farris.

Below: Detail from a group portrait of some of the delegates who attended the Tenth Anniversary Conference of the NAACP held during 21–28 June 1919. A. D. Williams is standing in the fourth row (from the bottom), third from the right. From the Lloyd O. Lewis Papers, Special Collections, the University Library, University of Illinois at Chicago.

Above: Michael King, Martin Luther King, Jr.'s father, was the pastor of Atlanta's Union Baptist Church (ca. 1920).

Right: James Albert King in 1924. He was Martin Luther King, Jr.'s paternal grandfather. Photo and permission courtesy of Christine King Farris.

Alberta Williams King on her graduation in 1938 from Atlanta's Morris Brown College. Photo and permission courtesy of Christine King Farris.

Martin Luther King, Sr., on his graduation from Atlanta's Morehouse College in 1930. Photo and permission courtesy of Christine King Farris.

Above: Martin Luther King, Jr., with his sister Christine in 1930. Photo and permission courtesy of Christine King Farris.

Opposite page: Martin Luther King, Jr., at a birthday party in Atlanta in June 1935 (front row, fourth from the left). Photo courtesy of the Schomburg Center for Research in Black Culture, The New York Public Library (Astor, Lenox and Tilden Foundations).

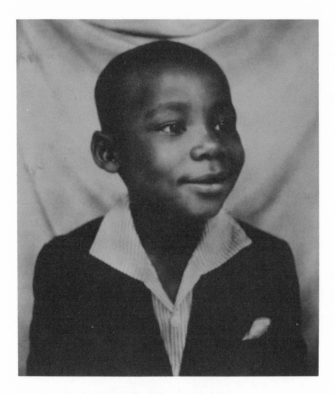

Martin Luther King, Jr.,
at the age of six. Photo
and permission courtesy
of Christine King Farris.

Alberta Williams King ca. 1940. Photo and permission courtesy of Christine King Farris.

Alberta Williams King directed the Ebenezer Baptist Church choir at the premiere of the movie, Gone with the Wind in Atlanta. Martin Luther King, Jr., sang in the choir. Photo and permission courtesy of Life.

Martin Luther King, Sr., and Alberta Williams King in Utah en route to California to attend the National Baptist Convention in September 1949. Photo and permission courtesy of Christine King Farris.

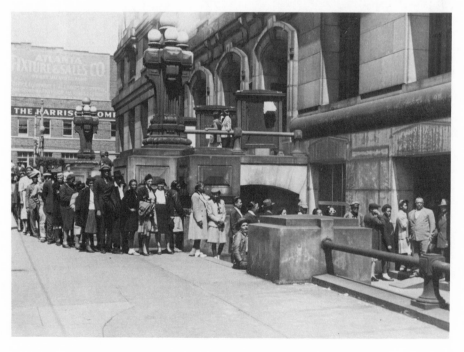

Atlanta citizens wait in line to register to vote in August 1946.
Photo courtesy of the Library of Congress, NAACP Papers.

The King family on the Morehouse College campus. Joel King, one of Martin Luther King, Jr.'s uncles, is at the far right of the picture. Photo and permission courtesy of Christine King Farris.

Martin Luther King, Jr., with his sister Christine, sometime during his years at Morehouse College. Permission courtesy of Christine King Faris. Photo courtesy of the State Historical Society of Wisconsin.

Below: Martin Luther King, Jr., attending a lecture at Morehouse College. Photo courtesy of Moorland-Spingarn Center, Howard University.

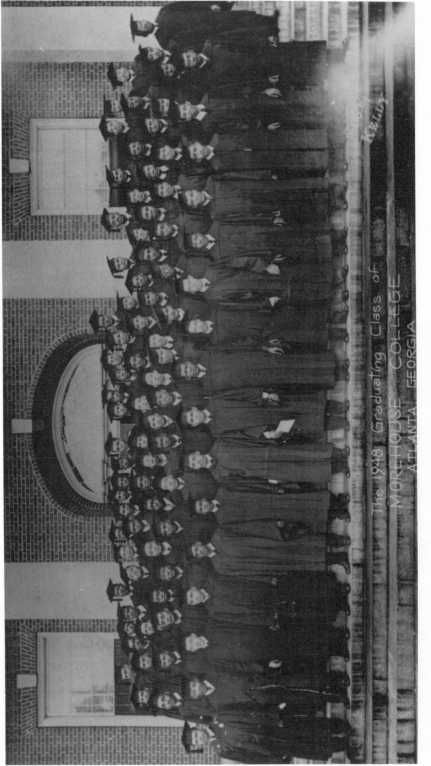

The Morehouse College graduating class of 1948. Martin Luther King, Jr., is in the front row, second from the left. Photo courtesy of Morehouse College.

Martin Luther King, Jr., and his sister Christine
at the joint baccalaureate service for Morehouse and Spelman
Colleges. Photo and permission courtesy of Christine King Farris.

Martin Luther King, Jr., and his uncle Joel King watch Martin Luther King, Sr., deliver a sermon at a Baptist church in Philadelphia in 1949. Photo and permission courtesy of Christine King Farris.

The King family and Walter R. McCall at the Crozer
Theological Seminary commencement service in May
1951. Photo and permission courtesy of
Christine King Farris.

Martin Luther King, Jr., with his mother, ca. 1951. Permission courtesy of
Christine King Farris. Photo courtesy of the State Historical
Society of Wisconsin.

1810	Willis Williams—one of King, Jr.'s maternal great-grandfathers—is born in Georgia.
February 1825	William Parks—one of King, Jr.'s maternal great-grandfathers—is born in Georgia.
January 1830	Fannie—one of King, Jr.'s maternal great-grandmothers—is born in Georgia. She later married William Parks.
1840	Lucrecia (Creecy)—one of King, Jr.'s maternal great-grandmothers—is born in Georgia. She later married Willis Williams.
1842 or 1844	Jim Long—one of King, Jr.'s paternal great-grandfathers—is born in Virginia.
1855	Jane Linsey—one of King, Jr.'s paternal great-grandmothers—is born in Henry County, Georgia.
2 January 1863	Adam Daniel (A. D.) Williams—the son of Lucrecia and Willis Williams—is born near the town of Penfield in Greene County, Georgia.
December 1864	James Albert King—King, Jr.'s paternal grandfather—is born in Ohio.
April 1873	Jennie Celeste Parks—the daughter of Fannie and William Parks—is born in Atlanta, Georgia.
1874	Willis Williams dies.
July 1875	Delia Linsey—the daughter of Jane Linsey and Jim Long—is born in Henry County, Georgia.
March 1894	A. D. Williams becomes pastor of Atlanta's Ebenezer Baptist Church.
20 August 1895	James Albert King marries Delia Linsey in Stockbridge, Georgia.

Chronology	19 December 1897	Michael King—son of Delia and James Albert King—is born in Stockbridge, Georgia. He is later known as Martin Luther King.
	29 October 1899	A. D. Williams marries Jennie Celeste Parks in Fulton County, Georgia.
	13 September 1903	Alberta Christine Williams—daughter of Jennie Celeste and A. D. Williams—is born in Atlanta.
	25 November 1926	Michael Luther King marries Alberta Christine Williams at Ebenezer Baptist Church.
	1927	
	27 April	Coretta Scott is born in Heiberger, Alabama. Her parents are Obie and Bernice Scott.
	11 September	Willie Christine King—King, Jr.'s sister—is born in Atlanta.
	15 January 1929	Michael King [later known as Martin Luther King, Jr.] is born at 501 Auburn Avenue in Atlanta.
	1930	
	June	King, Sr., receives bachelor of arts degree in theology from Morehouse College.
	30 July	Alfred Daniel Williams King—King, Jr.'s brother, A. D.—is born in Atlanta.
	1931	
	21 March	A. D. Williams dies of a heart attack.
	October	King, Sr., is chosen to succeed his father-in-law, A. D. Williams, as pastor of Ebenezer Baptist Church in Atlanta.
	1932	
	January	King, Jr., enters nursery school.
	April	King, Sr., is officially installed as pastor of Ebenezer.
	3 September	King, Sr., attends the National Baptist Convention in Cleveland, Ohio.

5 July	King, Sr., attends the first interdenominational institute for black clergymen at Atlanta University.
Fall	King, Jr., enters the first grade at Yonge Street Elementary School with his six-year-old sister, Christine.
18 November	James Albert King dies.

1934

January	King, Jr., reveals to his first-grade teacher that he is only five years old and is expelled from school.
20 January	Atlanta's black Baptists join local white Baptists in inviting the Baptist World Alliance to meet in the city but insist that they will tolerate no segregation at the conference.
March	Atlanta's black public school teachers demand the same pay scale as that of the city's white public school teachers.
	King, Sr., is elected first vice president of the Atlanta Baptist Ministers Union.
12 April	King, Jr.'s birth certificate is filed, under the name Michael King.
14 July–10 August	King, Sr., tours the Middle East and Europe with ten other Baptist ministers from the United States. They attend the Baptist World Alliance in Berlin.
4 September	King, Sr., attends the National Baptist Convention in Oklahoma.
24 October	The Atlanta Baptist Ministers Union holds mock elections to instruct potential black voters on voting procedures.
14 November	King, Jr., accompanied by his mother, Alberta Williams King, sings at a meeting of the General Missionary Baptist Convention of Georgia at Mount Vernon Baptist Church in Newnan, Georgia.

1935

28 January	King, Jr., reenters the first grade at Yonge Street Elementary School and after half a year advances to the second grade.

77

30 January	King, Sr., stages a protest against the segregation of elevators at the Fulton County Courthouse.
27 March	King, Sr., becomes president of the Atlanta Baptist Ministers Union.
11 April	King, Sr., preaches at a service commemorating the fifty-third anniversary of the Reverend E. R. Carter's ministry at Friendship Baptist Church in Atlanta.
11 May	King, Sr., and other leaders of the Atlanta Baptist Ministers Union call for black voter registration.
9 June	King, Sr., is elected president of the Atlanta District Baptist Young Peoples Union and Sunday School Convention.
2 July	King, Sr., becomes acting moderator of the Atlanta Missionary Baptist Association.
August–September	King, Sr., and the Atlanta branch of the NAACP lead a voter registration drive in anticipation of a local school bond referendum.
3 September	King, Sr., attends the National Baptist Convention in New York.
11 September	King, Jr., enters the second grade at Yonge Street Elementary School.
17 October	King, Sr., is elected moderator of the Atlanta Missionary Baptist Association.
1936	
7 January	King, Sr., is reelected president of the Atlanta Baptist Ministers Union.
26 February	King, Sr., is chosen to lead the NAACP membership drive in Atlanta.
6 March	King, Sr., joins other speakers in addressing a mass meeting of the NAACP at Wheat Street Baptist Church.
9 April	King, Sr., addresses the annual Lenten service at the Butler Street YMCA, speaking on "The Compelling Vision of the Kingdom of God."
3 May	King, Jr., is baptized after Ebenezer's two-week annual revival, led by guest evangelist Rev. H. H. Coleman of Macedonia Baptist Church in Detroit.

1 June	King, Sr., steps down as president of the Atlanta District Baptist Young Peoples Union and Sunday School Convention.
21–26 July	King, Sr., attends the General Missionary Baptist Convention of Georgia at Tabernacle Baptist Church in Augusta.
8 September	King, Jr., enters the third grade at Atlanta's David T. Howard Colored Elementary School.
11 September	King, Sr., has an automobile accident en route to the National Baptist Convention in Jacksonville, Florida. His mother-in-law, Jennie Celeste Parks Williams, suffers minor injuries.
4 November	Howard Thurman, dean of the chapel at Howard University, addresses Morehouse students on Mahatma Gandhi's campaign against British imperialism in India.

1937

	King, Jr., begins delivering the *Atlanta Journal*.
March	King, Sr., completes term as president of the Atlanta Baptist Ministers Union.
September	Alberta Williams King initiates a series of annual musicals by Ebenezer's choirs.
4 September	King, Sr., and Alberta Williams King attend the National Baptist Convention in Los Angeles, California.
10 September	King, Jr., enters the fourth grade at Howard Elementary School.
10 November	Robed Ku Klux Klansmen parade on Auburn Avenue in Atlanta.
19 November	King, Sr., is defeated by the Reverend L. A. Pinkston of Augusta in a bid for the presidency of the General Missionary Baptist Convention of Georgia. Six months earlier, Pinkston was the visiting evangelist at Ebenezer's spring revival.

1938

2 February	King, Sr., speaks at Atlanta's annual Lincoln-Douglas Day celebration.
2 March	King, Sr., is elected to the executive committee of the Atlanta Civic and Political League and pledges to seek the support of black ministers for the League's voter registration drive.

20 March	The Reverend Melvin Watson delivers the anniversary sermon, which culminates the weeklong celebration of Ebenezer's fifty-first anniversary.
3 May	King, Sr., speaks at a meeting of the Atlanta Civic and Political League.
June	Alberta Williams King graduates from Morris Brown College with a bachelor of arts degree.
7 June	King, Sr., again urges black ministers to cooperate with voter registration efforts at a meeting of the Atlanta Civic and Political League at Ebenezer.
4 September	The Atlanta Civic and Political League issues a report criticizing the inadequate facilities of the city's black schools.
10 September	King, Jr., enters the fifth grade at Howard Elementary School.
October	The Atlanta Civic and Political League and the Atlanta Missionary Baptist Association lead black opposition to the passage of a school bond issue that provides inadequate funds for black schools. The bond issue is defeated in November.
5 December	King, Sr., is reappointed to the executive committee of the Atlanta branch of the NAACP.

1939

1 April	King, Sr., is the featured speaker for father's night at Howard Elementary School.
7 April	King, Sr., is elected president of the Atlanta Ministers Council, an interdenominational organization of ministers dedicated to fighting "the Negroes' battles along civic, political, and educational lines."
June	King, Sr., makes an extended tour of the western states following the National Baptist Sunday School and Young Peoples Union Congress in Tulsa, Oklahoma.
July	King, Sr., attends the General Missionary Baptist Convention of Georgia in Savannah.
22–28 July	King, Sr., chairs the committee on local arrangements as Atlanta hosts the quadrennial meeting of the Baptist World Alliance.

11 September	King, Jr., enters the sixth grade at Howard Elementary School. Chronology
10 October	King, Sr., is reelected moderator of the Atlanta Missionary Baptist Association.
8 November	King, Sr., as head of the Atlanta Baptist Ministers Union, leads several hundred black Atlantans on a voter registration march to City Hall.
14 November	Ebenezer hosts the annual meeting of the General Missionary Baptist Convention of Georgia.
6 December	King, Sr., presides at a meeting of the Atlanta Ministers Council.
15 December	King, Jr., and members of Ebenezer's choir sing at the Junior League gala ball celebrating the premiere of *Gone with the Wind* at Loew's Grand Theater in Atlanta.
1940	
January	King, Sr., conducts a two-week revival at Shiloh Baptist Church in Columbus, Ohio.
March	The Atlanta Baptist Ministers Union requests Rich's department store to provide restroom and lunchroom accommodations for its black customers.
5 April	King, Sr., delivers a sermon at the installation of his brother, Joel King, as pastor of Mt. Zion Baptist Church in Griffin, Georgia.
6 June	King, Jr., graduates from Howard Elementary School.
10 July	King, Sr., is reelected president of the Atlanta Ministers Council.
23 July	King, Sr., attends the General Missionary Baptist Sunday School and Baptist Training Union Convention of Georgia in Columbus.
1 August	Benjamin Mays is appointed president of Morehouse College.
7–8 August	The Atlanta branch of the NAACP and the Atlanta Baptist Ministers Union oppose a proposed city bond issue because it sets aside insufficient funds for black schools.
September	King, Jr., enters the seventh grade at Atlanta University Laboratory School.

2–5 September	King, Sr., attends the National Baptist Convention in Birmingham, Alabama.
15–17 October	King, Sr., is reelected moderator of the Atlanta Missionary Baptist Association, and on 17 October addresses the group on "the true mission of the Church."
1 November	Benjamin Mays speaks at a service to dedicate Ebenezer's new organ.
9 November	King, Sr., preaches at a meeting of the General Missionary Baptist Convention of Georgia.
25–29 November	Morehouse and Ebenezer host the annual training school of the Atlanta District Sunday School and Baptist Training Union Convention.
	At the end of 1940, Ebenezer Baptist Church reports 2,400 members, the largest membership in its history.

1941

16 February	King, Sr., speaks on "Goals Toward Which We Should Strive Today as a Minority Group" at Atlanta's annual Lincoln-Douglas Day celebration.
16 March	Charles D. Hubert, the dean of the Morehouse School of Religion, preaches the anniversary sermon at Ebenezer.
18 May	Jennie Celeste Parks Williams, King, Jr.'s grandmother, dies of a heart attack while serving as the women's day speaker at Mount Olive Baptist Church.
Summer	The King family moves from 501 Auburn Avenue to 193 Boulevard.
17–22 June	King, Sr., is the chairman of the Georgia delegation at the National Baptist Convention in Texas.
13–15 October	King, Sr., presides at a meeting of the Atlanta Baptist Ministers Association.
	Ebenezer Baptist Church reports three hundred people joined the church during 1941.

1942

	At thirteen, King, Jr., becomes the youngest assistant manager of a newspaper delivery station for the *Atlanta Journal*.

January	After half a year in the eighth grade at Atlanta University Laboratory School, King, Jr., enrolls in the ninth grade.
9–15 March	Charles H. Haynes, a member of the faculty at Talladega College in Alabama, preaches at Ebenezer's fifty-fifth anniversary celebration.
September	King, Jr., enters the tenth grade at Booker T. Washington High School.
12 September	King, Sr., helps draft a resolution adopted by the National Baptist Convention calling on President Roosevelt to appoint a citizens committee to ensure that black and white train passengers are treated equally.
13–15 October	King, Sr., presides at a meeting of the Atlanta Missionary Baptist Association at the Butler Street YMCA.

1943

11 January	The Atlanta Civic and Political League holds a mass meeting at Ebenezer to discuss the condition of public schools and other issues.
8 February	The Atlanta branch of the NAACP initiates a membership drive.
2 March	King, Sr., and other officers of the Atlanta Civic and Political League are reelected during a meeting at the Prince Hall Masons Building in Atlanta.
17 March	Morehouse College president Benjamin Mays addresses the Atlanta Baptist Ministers Union.
16 May	King, Sr., delivers the baccalaureate sermon at Union Baptist Institute in Athens.
26 May	King, Sr., speaks at the anniversary service of Mt. Pleasant Baptist Church in Atlanta.
14 June	King, Sr., chairs a meeting of the Atlanta Citizens' Committee on the Equalization of Teachers' Salaries.
15 August	King, Sr., conducts a revival at First Baptist Church in Carrollton, Georgia.
September	King, Jr., enters the eleventh grade at Booker T. Washington High School.
22 September	The Atlanta Baptist Ministers Union condemns the use of forced black labor in cotton fields near Athens, Georgia.

12–14 October	The Atlanta Missionary Baptist Association re-elects King, Sr., as moderator.
19 December	John W. Webb, national leader of the black Masons, speaks at Ebenezer.

1944

20 February	King, Sr., addresses an NAACP membership rally.
13 April	King, Jr., wins the right to represent Booker T. Washington High School in the state competition of the Elks' oratorical contest.
17 April	King, Jr., travels to Dublin, Georgia, to deliver his oration "The Negro and the Constitution." Although he does not win the contest, his speech is later printed in the Booker T. Washington High School yearbook, *The Cornellian.*
Summer	King, Jr., participates in a summer work program for Morehouse students, picking tobacco on a farm in Simsbury, Connecticut. At the end of the summer, King, Jr., is admitted to Morehouse College as an early admissions student.
20 September	King begins his freshman year at Morehouse, taking Freshman Mathematics, Church History, Composition and Reading, History of Civilization, and Introduction to Biology.

1945

10 January	King, Sr., is elected vice president of the Atlanta Civic and Political League.
15 February	King, Sr., leads a protest against segregated elevators at the Fulton County Courthouse.
June	King, Sr., receives an honorary doctor of divinity degree from Morris Brown College.
5–9 September	King, Jr., accompanies King, Sr., as he leads the Atlanta delegation to the National Baptist Convention in Detroit.
19 September	King, Jr., begins his sophomore year at Morehouse, taking Elementary French, Introduction to General Literature, Introduction to Sociology, Matter and Energy, General Psychology, and Educational Psychology.
16–19 October	King, Sr., is reelected moderator of the Atlanta Missionary Baptist Association.

12 November	King, Sr., is elected president of the Atlanta Morehouse Club. Chronology
16–17 November	The Georgia NAACP convention meets at Ebenezer.
1946	
	As a sophomore at Morehouse, King, Jr., wins second prize in the John L. Webb Oratorical Contest.
19 January	Mary McLeod Bethune speaks at Ebenezer.
March	King, Sr., leads a revival at Metropolitan Baptist Church in Pittsburgh.
Spring	Walter R. Chivers, Morehouse sociology professor, inaugurates an annual institute on family living.
2 April	The U.S. Supreme Court, in the case of *Primus King v. State of Georgia,* declares the "white primary" to be unconstitutional, thus removing a significant legal barrier to black voting in the state.
10 May	NAACP official Ella Baker speaks at a mass meeting of the All Citizens Registration Committee at Wheat Street Baptist Church in Atlanta.
Summer	King, Jr., quits his job as a laborer at the Atlanta Railway Express Company when a white foreman calls him "nigger."
6 August	The *Atlanta Constitution* publishes King, Jr.'s letter to the editor stating that blacks "are entitled to the basic rights and opportunities of American citizens."
4–8 September	The National Baptist Convention meets in Atlanta.
25 September	King, Jr., begins his junior year at Morehouse; his courses include Shakespeare, the Bible, American Literature, Intermediate French, Contemporary Social Trends, Social Anthropology, and a seminar in Sociology.
15–19 October	King, Sr., presides at the annual meeting of the Atlanta Missionary Baptist Association.
5 November	Eugene Talmadge is elected governor of Georgia. Black Georgia Baptists plan to protest his inauguration, on 9 January 1947, with a day of prayer.

21 December   Eugene Talmadge dies before taking office as
                                       governor.

1947

January/February   King, Jr.'s article, "The Purpose of Education," is
                                       published in the Morehouse student paper, the
                                       Maroon Tiger.

12 March   King, Jr., is elected chair of the membership com-
                                       mittee of the Atlanta NAACP Youth Council in a
                                       meeting on the Morehouse College campus.

14 March   King, Jr., opens an Ebenezer anniversary service
                                       with a song.

24 April   King, Sr., is elected a trustee of Morehouse
                                       College.

Summer   King, Jr., works on a tobacco farm in Simsbury,
                                       Connecticut.

24 September   King, Jr., begins his senior year at Morehouse
                                       College, enrolling in Social Psychology, Classics in
                                       English, Social Institutions, Social Legislation, Ur-
                                       ban Sociology, Intercultural Relations, Introduc-
                                       tion to Philosophy, Principles and Methods of Sta-
                                       tistics, and a seminar in Sociology.

Fall   King, Jr., preaches a trial sermon at Ebenezer.

27 October   King, Jr., requests an application for admission to
                                       Crozer Theological Seminary in Chester,
                                       Pennsylvania.

1948

                                       King, Jr., wins second prize in the John L. Webb
                                       Oratorical Contest.

20 February   King, Jr., offers the prayer at graveside memorial
                                       services for former Morehouse College presidents
                                       John Hope and Samuel H. Archer.

25 February   King, Jr., is ordained and appointed associate pas-
                                       tor at Ebenezer.

22 March   King, Sr., preaches at Morehouse College Chapel.

April   King, Jr., accepts Crozer's offer of admission.

25 April   King, Jr., preaches "Life is What You Make It" in
                                       the morning and "The Meaning of Christian Liv-
                                       ing" in the evening at Liberty Baptist Church in
Atlanta.

8 June	King, Jr., receives his bachelor of arts degree in sociology from Morehouse and Christine King receives her bachelor of arts degree in economics from Spelman College. Chronology
Summer	King, Jr., serves as associate pastor of Ebenezer.
11 July	King, Jr., is guest speaker at a meeting of the Negro Cultural League at Ebenezer.
1 August	King, Jr., delivers sermon at Ebenezer's evening service on "External Versus Internal Religion."
8 August	Walter R. McCall delivers sermon on "The Destruction of Pride" at Ebenezer's morning service, and King, Jr., preaches "The Tests of Goodness" in the evening.
22 August	King, Jr., preaches at Ebenezer's morning service on "God's Kingdom First."
	King, Jr., performs the wedding ceremony of Samuel P. Long and Ruth Bussey at Thankful Baptist Church in Decatur, Georgia.
5 September	King, Jr., preaches at Ebenezer.
11–12 September	King, Jr., spends the weekend in New York City with his sister, Christine, a first-year graduate student at Columbia University.
14 September–24 November	During the first term of his first year at Crozer Theological Seminary, King takes Public Speaking, Preaching Ministry of the Church, Introduction to the Old Testament, Orientation for Juniors, Choir, and Church Music.
30 November–16 February 1949	King, Jr., takes Great Theologians, the History and Literature of the New Testament, Preparation of the Sermon, and Public Speaking.

1949

20 February	King, Jr., delivers the annual youth day sermon at Ebenezer.
22 February–6 May	King, Jr., is enrolled in Christian Mysticism, Practice Preaching, and Public Speaking.
Summer	King, Jr., serves as assistant pastor of Ebenezer.
12 June	King, Jr., preaches in the morning at Atlanta's Mt. Pleasant Baptist Church and in the evening at Ebenezer.

3 July	King, Jr., delivers a sermon on "The Voice of Hope" at Ebenezer.
5–8 July	King, Sr., lectures on "The Pastor as Administrator and Organizer" at the annual ministers' conference held at Morehouse.
31 July	King, Jr., preaches "The Two Challenging Questions" at Ebenezer.
14 August	King, Jr., is the youth day speaker at Zion Hill Baptist Church in Atlanta.
4 September	King, Jr., preaches "The Great Paradox" in the morning and "The Significance of the Cross" in the evening at Ebenezer.
7 September	William B. Hartsfield is elected mayor of Atlanta by a coalition of black and affluent white voters that will dominate the city's politics for the next four decades.
13 September–23 November	During the first term of his second year at Crozer, King, Jr., enrolls in Public Worship, Greek Religion, and Christian Theology for Today. Later that year he is named chairman of the student body's devotional committee.
26 September–10 June 1950	King, Jr., audits a course on the Philosophy of History at the University of Pennsylvania.
November	King, Jr., hears A. J. Muste defend pacifism in a lecture at Crozer.
29 November–15 February 1950	King, Jr., is enrolled in Preaching Problems, Pastoral Counseling, Conduct of Church Services, the Development of Christian Ideas I, and Christian Theology for Today.
11 December	The Reverend William H. Gray, Jr., of Philadelphia preaches for men's day at Ebenezer.
23 December–2 January 1950	According to his later published account, King, Jr., spends Christmas vacation reading Karl Marx, and he "carefully scrutinizes" *Das Kapital* and *The Communist Manifesto*.
1950	
19 February	King, Jr., preaches "Walking with the Lord" at Ebenezer's morning service.
21 February–5 May	King, Jr., takes courses on the History of Living Religions and the History of Christianity.

23 February	The Atlanta branch of the NAACP votes to support a lawsuit filed by King, Sr., as head of a citizens' committee seeking to win equal pay for black teachers. Chronology
Spring	King, Jr., hears Mordecai Johnson, president of Howard University, preach at Philadelphia's Fellowship House on Mohandas K. Gandhi's *satyagraha* as a method of social change.
May	King, Jr., is elected president of the student body at Crozer.
12 June	King, Jr., Walter R. McCall, Pearl E. Smith, and Doris Wilson are refused service by Ernest Nichols at Mary's Cafe in Maple Shade, New Jersey. Nichols fires a gun into the air when they persist in their request for service. He is arrested and charged, but later, when witnesses fail to testify, the case is dropped.
16 June	King, Jr., is arrested for speeding in Claymont, Delaware, on his way to Atlanta.
17 June	A. D. King and Naomi Barber are married at Ebenezer.
18 June	King, Jr., preaches "The Lord God Omnipotent Reigneth" at Ebenezer.
Summer	King, Jr., serves as assistant pastor of Ebenezer.
30 July	King, Jr., is youth day speaker at Liberty Baptist Church.
12 September– 22 November	King, Jr., enters his senior year at Crozer, taking courses on American Christianity—Colonial Period, Minister's Use of the Radio, and Religious Development of Personality. He serves as student pastor at the First Baptist Church in Queens, New York.
20 September– 3 February 1951	King, Jr., audits courses on the Problems of Esthetics and Kant at the University of Pennsylvania.
28 November– 15 February 1951	King, Jr., enrolls in Philosophy of Religion and Theological Integration at Crozer.
10 December	The Reverend J. H. Jackson of Chicago is men's day speaker at Ebenezer.
15 December	King, Jr., is accepted as a student in the Post-Graduate School of the Faculty of Divinity at Edinburgh University, Scotland.

1951

11 January	King, Jr., is admitted to Boston University's School of Theology.
3 February	King, Jr., takes the Graduate Record Examination.
18 February	King, Jr., preaches "Nothing in Particular" at Ebenezer.
20 February–4 May	King, Jr., is enrolled in Advanced Philosophy of Religion, Christian Social Philosophy, and Christianity and Society.
6–8 May	King, Jr., graduates from Crozer with a bachelor of divinity degree, delivering the valedictory address at commencement. He receives both the Pearl Plafker Memorial Award as the graduating student who, "in the judgment of the faculty, has been the outstanding member of his class during his course in the seminary," and the J. Lewis Crozer Fellowship, which provides $1,200 toward graduate school.
12 May	King, Jr., preaches "The World Crisis & A Mother's Responsibility" at Ebenezer.
Summer	King, Jr., serves as pastor in charge at Ebenezer.
29 June	King, Sr., offers the benediction at the evening session of the NAACP's annual conference in Atlanta.

The purpose of the Martin Luther King, Jr., Papers Project is to produce an authoritative, multivolume edition of King's works. The chronologically arranged volumes provide complete, accurate, and annotated transcriptions of King's most important publications, sermons, speeches, correspondence, unpublished manuscripts, and other papers. We examined thousands of King-related documents and recordings and selected those that were biographically or historically significant to King's life, thought, and leadership. Because only a small proportion of all the available documents could be published, we developed certain principles and priorities to guide our selection process.

King's writings were assigned highest priority for inclusion. Because of their impact on the public, all of King's published writings were included. Although many of these writings are already accessible, few have been annotated and some exist only in obscure periodicals. King's public statements—his sermons, speeches, interviews, and recorded comments—were given the next highest priority for selection. King's unpublished manuscripts, such as his student papers, were included when they provided information about the development of his ideas. Letters to and from King reveal much about his life and thought. Preference was given to correspondence that influenced King or revealed his impact on others. Routine correspondence and office-generated replies to unsolicited letters were excluded.

Documents produced by others were selected in cases of clear biographical or historical significance to King. This category included confidential academic evaluations, published and unpublished interviews, transcripts or reports of meetings in which King participated, documents from legal proceedings involving King, and FBI transcripts of King's conversations. Correspondence not directly involving King and time-specific printed matter concerning King's activities (such as church programs or political leaflets) were transcribed only if they had special historical value.

To further assist scholars and others seeking information on King-related primary documents, each volume includes a "Calendar of Documents" that describes items not chosen for publication. In addition, the King Papers Project's descriptions of King-related document collections are available in the electronic database of the Research Libraries Information Network (RLIN). This edition of King's papers is part of a broader, long-term effort to facilitate access, through various print and electronic media, to all the research material that the Project has located and assembled.

Editorial Apparatus

Annotations enhance readers' understanding of documents. Headnotes preceding documents explain the context of their creation and briefly summarize their contents. Editorial footnotes, as well as headnotes, may also identify in- 91 dividuals, organizations, and other references in the document. Significant comments written in the margins are annotated as well. In the first two volumes, these comments consist mainly of the remarks of King's professors, although not every correction of grammar or spelling is noted. Editorial footnotes are placed at the bottom of the page. For those papers which King annotated, his footnotes are treated as sidenotes and placed as close to the individual callouts as possible. To enable readers to better understand King's citation practices, we provided footnotes that give full references for and quotations from sources containing passages similar or identical to King's. We did not attempt to decide whether his use of sources was appropriate. On occasion editorial footnotes also describe variations contained in different versions of documents.

Each document is introduced in almost all cases by a title, date, and place of origin. Existing titles are used when available and are designated by quotation marks. Punctuation, capitalization, and spelling irregularities or errors in titles are silently corrected. Names are standardized. For untitled materials, descriptive titles are assigned (Application for Admission to Crozer Theological Seminary). In King's correspondence, the title contains the author or the recipient, leaving King's participation implied (To Crozer Theological Seminary). The date and place of origin appear after the title. When the date was not specified in the document, we assigned it, presented it in italics, and enclosed it in brackets. We provided a range date when a specific date was not available. (A more detailed explanation of how titles, dates, and other cataloging information were assigned appears at the end of the volume in the "Calendar of Documents.")

The source note following each document provides information on the characteristics of the original document and its provenance. Codes are used to describe the document's format, type, version, and signature (see below, "List of Abbreviations"). "TLS" for example identifies the letter as a typed letter with a signature. The location of the original document is described next, using standard abbreviations based on the Library of Congress's codes for libraries and archives.

Transcription Practices

Our transcriptions reproduce the source document or recording as accurately as possible, adhering to the exact wording and punctuation of the original. Errors in spelling, punctuation, and grammar are neither corrected nor indicated by *sic*. Such errors and stylistic irregularities may offer important insights into the author's state of mind and the conditions under which a document was composed. Other features that cannot be adequately reproduced, such as signatures and handwritten marginal comments, are noted and described in the text or in footnotes. All editorial explanations are italicized and enclosed by square brackets. In a few cases, the document is presented as a facsimile.

Transcripts of recordings can never reproduce all the qualities of an oral presentation, but we sought to replicate to the extent possible King's sermons and speeches as they were delivered. When King forcefully stressed certain

"The Influence of the
Mystery Religions on Christianity" ——————— Title

[29 November 1949–15 February 1950] —— Range date
[Chester, Pa.] —— Place of origin

King wrote this paper for the course Development of Christian Ideas, taught by Davis. The essay examines how Christianity developed as a distinct religion with a set of central tenets and how it was influenced by those pagan religions it assimilated. King repeats material from an earlier paper, "A Study of Mithraism," but he extends the discussion here to the influence of other mystery religions. Davis ——— Headnote

position. They covered an enormous range, and manifested a great diversity in character and outlook, "from Orphism to Gnosticism, from the orgies of the Cabira to the fervours of the Hermetic contemplative."*[2] However it is to be noticed that these Mysteries possessed many fundamental likenesses; (1) All held that the initiate shared in symbolic (sacramental) fashion the experiences of the god. (2) All had secret rites for the initiated. (3) All offered mystical cleansing from sin. (4) All promised a happy future life for the faithful.† ——— Document

It is not at all surprising in view of the wide and growing influence of these religions that when the

King's footnotes ———————

* Angus, The Mystery Religions and Christianity, p. vii.

† Enslin, Christian Beginnings, pp. 187, 188.

Document description ———————

AHDf. MLKP-MBU: Box 113, folder 23.

Editors' footnotes

2. S. Angus, The Mystery-Religions and Christianity (London: John Murray, 1925), p. vii: "These Mysteries covered an enormous range, and manifested a great diversity in character and outlook, from Orphism to Gnosticism, from the orgies of the Cabiri to the fervours of the Hermetic contemplative."

words, they are italicized in an effort to convey his emphasis. As is the case with other orators and preachers in the African-American tradition, King's audience played an integral role in his orations, encouraging him with enthusiastic exclamations. Despite the difficulties presented by the spontaneous and simultaneous nature of the audience's response, these interjections are italicized, enclosed in parentheses, and placed within King's text.

1. Capitalization, boldface, symbols, subscripts, superscripts, abbreviations, strikeouts, and deletions are replicated regardless of inconsistency or usage.

2. The line breaks, pagination, and vertical and horizontal spacing of the original are not replicated. A blank line signals a break in the text other than a straightforward paragraph break. The transcription regularizes spacing and indentation of paragraphs, outlines, and lists, as well as the spacing of words, initials, and ellipses.

3. The underlining of book titles, court cases, or other words and phrases in typescripts is reproduced. Since underlining practices were often inconsistent (sometimes breaking between words, sometimes not), we regularized the various types to continuous underscoring.

4. Silent editorial corrections were made only in cases of malformed letters, single-letter corrections of words in typescript, and the superimposition of two characters.

5. The author's use of hyphens is replicated, but end-of-line hyphens are silently deleted unless the usage is ambiguous. Dashes between numbers are rendered as en-dashes. Em-dashes, which are rendered in several styles in the original manuscripts, are regularized.

6. Insertions in the text by the author (usually handwritten) are indicated by curly braces ({ }) and placed as precisely as possible.

7. Many of King's academic essays contain footnotes which are numbered in various styles. King's footnotes are reproduced as sidenotes. We replaced the various footnote numbering systems King used with a sequence of symbols. The order of the symbols used is asterisk (*), dagger (†), double dagger (‡), section mark (§), parallels (‖), number sign (#). If more than six sidenotes appear on a page, the symbols are doubled as needed.

8. Small capital letters are used to simulate telegrams and printed forms. King's handwritten or typed answers on the latter are set in boldface.

9. Spelling, punctuation, and paragraphing are provided for transcriptions of audio recordings. Certain sharply stressed phrases are italicized to indicate emphasis, though this is done sparingly. Audience responses are enclosed in parentheses and italicized; multiple responses are separated by commas within the parentheses. The first occurrence of the audience's response is noted as follows: (*Audience: Lord help him*). Since individual words occasionally cannot be distinguished, some responses are described: (*Laughter*).

10. Conjectural renderings of text are set in italic type and placed within brackets; speculative conjectures are accompanied by a question mark: [*rousers?*].

11. In cases of illegible text, the extent of the illegibility is indicated: [*2 words*
    illegible].
12. Illegible crossed-out words are indicated with the phrase [*strikeout illeg-ible*]. If the strikeout is by someone other than the author, it is not rep-licated, but it is described in a footnote.
13. If the remainder of a document is lost or unintelligible, the condition is described: [*remainder missing*].
14. In a very few cases, long documents are excerpted. Editorial omissions within a transcription are designated by bracketed ellipses ([. . .]) and described in the annotation.
15. Signatures are reproduced in the following manner: [*signed*] name. For example,

> Sincerely,
> [*signed*] Phoebe Burney
> Mrs. John W. Burney

If the signature and typewritten complimentary closing are identical, the signature is described using the convention: [*signed as below*].
16. Examination questions, when available from archival sources, are pro-vided in italics and brackets before the answers.
17. Printed letterheads are not reproduced, but any significant information contained in them is explained in the headnote or in a footnote. The internal address, salutation, and complimentary closing of a letter are reproduced left-aligned, regardless of the original format.

Collections and Repositories

ATL-AAHM	Alton T. Lemon Papers, Afro-American History and Cultural Museum, Philadelphia, Penn.
APS-GAP	Atlanta Public Schools Records Collection, Atlanta Public Schools, Professional Library, Atlanta, Ga.
BEMP-DHU	Benjamin E. Mays Papers, Moorland-Spingarn Research Center, Howard University, Washington, D.C.
CA-GAM	College Archives, Morehouse College, Atlanta, Ga.
CKFC	Christine King Farris Collection (in private hands)
CSKC	Coretta Scott King Collection (in private hands)
CRO-NRCR	Crozer Theological Seminary Records, Colgate-Rochester Divinity School, Rochester, N.Y.
DABCC	Dexter Avenue King Memorial Baptist Church Collection (in private hands)
DCF-GAM	Dean of the Chapel's Files, Morehouse College, Atlanta, Ga.
DNA	United States National Archives and Records Service, National Archives Library, Washington, D.C.
EBCR	Ebenezer Baptist Church, Miscellaneous Records (in private hands)
EPH	Elaine Pace-Holmes Papers (in private hands)
FCPCR-GAFC	Fulton County Probate Court Records, Fulton County Court House, Atlanta, Ga.
FORP-PSC-P	Fellowship of Reconciliation Papers, Swarthmore College Peace Collection, Swarthmore, Pa.
GAHR	Georgia Department of Human Resources, Vital Records Service, Atlanta, Ga.
G-Ar	Georgia Department of Archives and History, Atlanta, Ga.
GD	Griffith Davis Papers (in private hands)
GMM	Mercer University, Macon, Ga.
HCPC	Henry County Probate Court, McDonough, Ga.
HSl-GAU	Henry P. Slaughter Collection, Woodruff Library, Atlanta University Center, Atlanta, Ga.
JK	Joe Kirkland Papers (in private hands)
JOG	Julian O. Grayson Papers (in private hands)
MLK/OH-GAMK	Martin Luther King, Jr., Oral History Collection, King Library and Archives, Atlanta, Ga.
MLKP-MBU	Martin Luther King, Jr., Papers, 1954–1968, Boston University, Boston, Mass.
MLKJrP-GAMK	Martin Luther King, Jr., Papers, 1950–1968, King Library and Archives, Atlanta, Ga.

Abbreviations	NAACPP-DLC	National Association for the Advancement of Colored People Papers, 1909–1965, Library of Congress, Washington, D.C.
	RKC-WHi	Richard Kaplan Collection, State Historical Society of Wisconsin, Madison, Wis.
	SBCM-G-Ar	Shiloh Baptist Church Minutes, Georgia Department of Archives and History, Atlanta, Ga.
	SCRBC-NN-Sc	Schomburg Center for Research in Black Culture Photograph Collection, Schomburg Center, New York Public Library, New York, N.Y.
	SLP	Samuel P. Long, Jr., Papers (in private hands)
	SPS	S. Paul Schilling Collection (in private hands)
	SWWC-GAU	Samuel W. Williams Collection, Woodruff Library, Atlanta University Center, Atlanta, Ga.
	TAP	Thelma B. Archer Papers (in private hands)
	WTMc	W. Thomas McGann Papers (in private hands)

Abbreviations Used in Source Notes

The following symbols are used to describe characteristics of the original documents:

Format
A	Autograph—author's hand
H	Handwritten—other than author's hand
P	Printed
T	Typed

Type
D	Document
Fm	Form
L	Letter or memo
Ph	Photo
W	Wire or telegram

Version
c	Copy (carbon)
d	Draft
f	Fragment

Signature
I	Initialed
S	Signed
Sr	Signed with representation of author

I

Childhood

To Martin Luther King, Sr.

[*13 June 1937*]
Atlanta, Ga.

*Nine-year-old Willie Christine King, eight-year-old Martin Luther King, Jr.,
and six-year-old Alfred Daniel Williams King send their father a Father's Day
greeting.*

REV M L KING SR
501 AUBURN AVE ATLA

DEAR DADDY WE LOVE YOU AND WE HOPE YOU ARE HAPPY ON FATHERS DAY AND
EVERY OTHER DAY FROM YOUR CHILDREN

WILLIE CHRISTINE M L JR A D KING.

PWSr. CKFC.

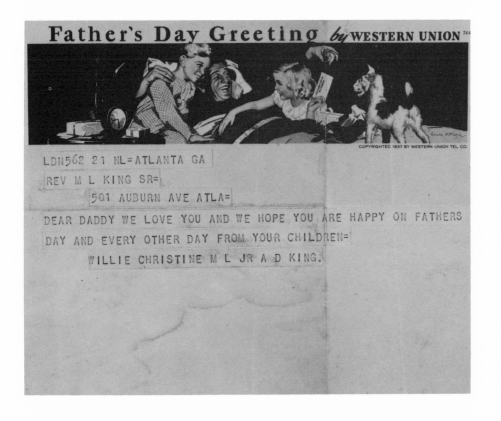

1 April 1939
Atlanta, Ga.

Eight years after the death of A. D. Williams, his influence remained strong in the family. His widow, his daughter, and his three grandchildren published this poem in his memory in the Georgia Baptist, *the official publication of the General Missionary Baptist Convention of Georgia.*

Eight years ago you left us,
And the wound has never healed
From the shock of your sudden going,

And the loss time has revealed
We are striving hard to meet you
In heaven some sweet day,
Where we may dwell together once more
As the ages roll away.

Mrs. J. C. Williams, wife,
Mrs. Alberta Williams King, daughter,
Christine King
M. L. King, Jr.,
A. D. Williams King,
   Grandchildren

PD. *Georgia Baptist,* 1 April 1939.

To Martin Luther King, Sr.

18 January 1940
Atlanta, Ga.

Three days after his eleventh birthday, King, Jr., uses a child's typewriter to write to his father, who was preaching at a two-week revival at Shiloh Baptist Church in Columbus, Ohio. "Mother Dear" is his mother, Alberta Williams King. "Mama" refers to his grandmother, Jennie Celeste Parks Williams. The ward was a residential subdivision of Ebenezer Baptist Church's congregation. "Uncle Jim and Aunt Essie" are King, Sr.'s younger brother, James Albert King, Jr., and his wife, Esther King. "Miss Rutland" is Miss Carrie Rutland, a member of Ebenezer Church and a neighbor of the King family on Auburn Avenue. "The Ray familly" refers to the family of the Reverend Sandy Ray, a friend of King, Sr., since their

I am getting along fine and hoppe you are the same we got your letter. We are praying that you might have a safe trip home. I am doing fine in my scool work. Mother dear bought me a hat for my birthday present from you. We have been having warm wether every day since Tuesday. We went to the ward Tuesday and we had a very nice metting. Uncle Jim and Aunt Essie said hello. I hope you are having a nice metting. And we are looking for coal wether tomorrow it was in the paper. At the scout metting Tuesday and we had fifteen boys and we are doing fine in scouting. Mama said hello and keep well and so did Miss Rutland give love to the Ray familly I am going to end

Your truly
Your son M. L. Jr

TL. CKFC.

To Martin Luther King, Sr.

24 January 1940
Atlanta, Ga.

William Gibson was a handyman and a hymn leader at Ebenezer Baptist Church. King, Jr., comments on one of Atlanta's rare snowstorms.

Dear Daddyy

Just a few lines to let you know that I am feeling fine and hope you are the same. We are having some snow and the last report we heard the snow was a {little} more than ten and a half inches and we are really having a fine time makeing snow men and throwing snow balls. And the policemen made everybody clean off their sidewalks and Christine and I cleaned off and it was a hard job. I received your letter and I am glad you liked my typeing. I am

---

1. Sandy F. Ray (1898–1979) graduated with Martin Luther King, Sr., from Morehouse College in 1930. He served Baptist churches in LaGrange, Georgia; Chicago, Illinois; Columbus, Ohio; and Macon, Georgia, before moving to Cornerstone Baptist Church in Brooklyn, New York, where he was pastor for forty years. Ray served as president of the New York State Baptist Convention and as an officer of the National Baptist Convention for many years. In 1953, he was one of six candidates for president of the National Baptist Convention. Ray remained a close family friend. In 1958, King, Jr., convalesced in Ray's Brooklyn parsonage after being stabbed while autographing copies of *Stride Toward Freedom*, and Ray offered the eulogy at the funeral of Alberta Williams King in 1974.

ATLANTA GA.,

JANUARY 24, 1940

DEAR DADDYY

JUST A FEW LINES TO LET YOU KNOW THAT I AM FEELING
FINE AND HOPE YOU ARE THE SAME. WE ARE HAVING SOME
SNOW AND THE LAST REPORT WE HEARD THE SNOW WAS A LITTLE
MORE THAN TEN AND A HALF INCHES AND WE ARE REALLY
HAVING A FINE TIME MAKEING SNOW MEN AND THROWING
SNOW BALLS. AND THE POLICEMEN MADE EVERYBODY CLEAN
OFF THEIR SIDEWALKS AND CHRISTINE AND I CLEANED OFF
AND IT WAS A HARD JOB. I RECEIVED YOUR LETTER AND I
AM GLAD YOU LIKED MY TYPEING. I AM KEEPING THE FIRE
BURNNING BUT MR. GIBSON HAD TO PUT SOME COAL IM THE
BASEMENT BECAUSE IT GAVE OUT. WE CAN NOT GO TO
UNTIL MONDAY BECAUSE IT IS TO BAD.

YOUR TRULY

Martin Luther King

keeping the fire burnning but Mr. Gibson had to put some coal im the basement because it gave out. We can not go to {[s]chool} until Monday because it
is to bad.

Your truly
[*signed*] Martin Luther King

TALS. CKFC.

To Alberta Williams King

20 June 1940
Atlanta, Ga.

*The following two letters are to King's parents, who were attending the Sunday
School and Baptist Young Peoples Union Congress of the National Baptist
Convention. In this letter, King mentions a movie on the life of Thomas Edison
and a ward meeting of the Ebenezer Baptist Church congregation. Having
recently completed the sixth grade at the David T. Howard School, King also asks
his mother about registering at Atlanta University's Laboratory High School,
which he will enter in the fall of 1940. Lillian Watkins was church secretary at
Ebenezer Baptist Church and often published articles about the congregation in the*
Atlanta Daily World. *Mrs. Mamie Williams was the King family's neighbor on
Auburn Avenue and a member of Ebenezer. "Mother Holly" refers to Mrs.
Margaret Holley, also an Ebenezer member. King's concluding sentence refers to
his own payment for the papers from his newspaper route.*

Dear Mother:

   I am felling fine and hope you are the same. I am praying that you and
daddy have successful trip back home. I know you are have a nice time and I
wish I was there to. At the ward Tuesday night, we raised $8.10. Give love
to the Ray family. Mana and Lillian said helo, they are doing fine. Give love to
daddy and tell him I will write him sone. Listen mother dear where I am going
to school write me and tell me because if I am going to Lab I will have to
register by Monday. Mother dear tell daddy that Mrs. Mamie Wms. next door
died last night. And mother Holly died this morning. We went to the shore
Tuesday, and Tom Edison and it was very intering. I have a nuf money to get
all of my paper this week.

from your son
[*signed*] Martin L. King Jr.

P. S.   When you are idle and nothing to do with your time sit down and write
me a few lines

ALS. CKFC.

Atlanta Ga
June 2o 1940

Dear Mother:

I am felling fine and hope you are the same. I am praying that you and daddy have successful trip back home. I know you are have a nice time and I wish I was there to. At the ward Thurs. night we raised $3.10. Give love to the Ray family. Mama and Lillian said hello they are doing fine. Give love to daddy and tell him I will write him soon. Listen mother dear when I am going to school write me and tell me because if I am going to Lab I will have to register by Monday. Mother dear tell daddy that Mrs. Mamie Wms. next door died last night. And mother Holly died this morning. We got to the show Tuesday. We saw Edison and it was very entertaining. I have near money to get all of my paper this week.

The first page of Martin Luther King, Jr.'s letter to his mother, 20 June 1940.

23 June 1940
Atlanta, Ga.

*King's letter to his father mentions activities at Ebenezer Baptist Church. In King,
Sr.'s absence, other Baptist ministers assisted with pastoral duties. The Reverend
John Henry Edwards, a member of Ebenezer since 1914, preached at the morning
and evening services. The Reverend C. S. Jackson, pastor of Atlanta's Israel and
Salem Baptist churches, and the Reverend J. D. Sims of Piney Grove Baptist
Church conducted Mother Holley's funeral on Sunday afternoon. The "June
drive" mentioned in the letter refers to a church fundraising campaign conducted
by Ebenezer members born in the month. "Aunt Florence and uncle Joel" are King,
Sr.'s brother, the Reverend Joel King, and his wife, Florence King. "Ida" is King,
Jr.'s great-aunt, Ida Worthem, the sister of Jennie Celeste Parks Williams. The
Reverend Roland Smith's request refers to the Baptist Young Peoples Union
convention of the General Missionary Baptist Convention of Georgia, which will
begin on 3 July. "Emnit" is King's boyhood friend Emmett Proctor, the grandson
of C. L. Harper, the first principal of Booker T. Washington High School.*

Dear Daddy:

How are you feeling, fine I hope. I am being a good boy while you are away.
We had good church services all day today. No one joined the church but
Rev. Edward brought too good sermon. Mother Holleys funral was today and
Rev Sims and Rev C. S. Jackson preached the funral. We are working hard to
makt the June drive tune out like you wont it. Give love to Aunt Florence and
uncle Joel. Mama Lillian and aunt Ida are doing fine. Rev. Smith wonts to
know how many, dalegates are coming to the convention from Ebernezer. Tell
mother dear helo and tell her I made 35¢ off of my paper this week and have
some more to colect. Today we raised $11.86 in Sunday today Emnit came
back today and his mother to.

Your Son
[*signed*] Martin Luther King Jr

ALS. CKFC.

Contest Winner

M. L. KING, Jr.
The elimination contest of the Washington high school, under the direction of the committee on Elks' orations, was held at the Service Men's Center Thursday morning at 10:30 o'clock.

From the *Atlanta Daily World*, 16 April 1944.

"The Negro and the Constitution"

[*May 1944*]
Atlanta, Ga.

On 13 April 1944, in his junior year at Atlanta's Booker T. Washington High School, King, Jr., won an oratorical contest sponsored by the black Elks. With the runner-up at Washington High, Hiram Kendall, he won the right to represent the school at the statewide contest held at First Baptist Church in Dublin, Georgia. Kendall was a runner-up at the state contest. The theme of both contests was "The Negro and the Constitution." According to later accounts, during the bus trip to the contest, King and his teacher, Sarah Grace Bradley, were told by the driver to surrender their seats to newly boarding white passengers. King resisted at first, but his teacher finally persuaded him to leave his seat. They stood for several hours during the bus ride to Atlanta.[1]

King's oration was published in May 1944 at the end of his junior, and final, year at Washington High in the school annual, The Cornellian. *More polished than other pieces that King wrote as a teenager, the essay probably benefited from adult editing and from King's awareness of similar orations. Citing the experiences of the black opera singer Marian Anderson as an example, the oration outlines the contradictions between the nation's biblical faith and constitutional values and the continuing problem of racial discrimination. But the conclusion is marked by a hopeful rhetorical flourish: "My heart throbs anew in the hope that inspired by the example of Lincoln, imbued with the spirit of Christ, [America] will cast down the last barrier to perfect freedom," said the young King. "And I with my brother of blackest hue possessing at last my rightful heritage and holding my head erect, may stand beside the Saxon—a Negro—and yet a man!"*

Negroes were first brought to America in 1620 when England legalized slavery both in England and the colonies and America; the institution grew and thrived for about 150 years upon the backs of these black men. The empire of King Cotton was built and the southland maintained a status of life and hospitality distinctly its own and not anywhere else.

On January 1, 1863 the proclamation emancipating the slaves which had been decreed by President Lincoln in September took effect—millions of Negroes faced a rising sun of a new day begun. Did they have habits of thrift or principles of honesty and integrity? Only a few! For their teachings and duties had been but two activities—love of Master, right or wrong, good or bad, and loyalty to work. What was to be the place for such men in the reconstruction of the south?

America gave its full pledge of freedom seventy-five years ago. Slavery has been a strange paradox in a nation founded on the principles that all men are

---

1. *Atlanta Daily World*, 16 April and 22 April 1944; Ted Poston, "Fighting Pastor: Martin Luther King," *New York Post*, 10 April 1957; Playboy interview with Martin Luther King, Jr., *Playboy*, January 1965.

created free and equal. Finally after tumult and war, the nation in 1865 took a new stand—freedom for all people. The new order was backed by amendments to the national constitution making it the fundamental law that thenceforth there should be no discrimination anywhere in the "land of the free" on account of race, color or previous condition of servitude.

Black America still wears chains. The finest Negro is at the mercy of the meanest white man. Even winners of our highest honors face the class color bar. Look at a few of the paradoxes that mark daily life in America. Marian Anderson was barred from singing in the Constitution Hall, ironically enough, by the professional daughters of the very men who founded this nation for liberty and equality. But this tale had a different ending. The nation rose in protest, and gave a stunning rebuke to the Daughters of the American Revolution and a tremendous ovation to the artist, Marian Anderson, who sang in Washington on Easter Sunday and fittingly, before the Lincoln Memorial. Ranking cabinet members and a justice of the supreme court were seated about her. Seventy-five thousand people stood patiently for hours to hear a great artist at a historic moment. She sang as never before with tears in her eyes. When the words of "America" and "Nobody Knows De Trouble I Seen" rang out over that great gathering, there was a hush on thee sea of uplifted faces, black and white, and a new baptism of liberty, equality and fraternity. That was a touching tribute, but Miss Anderson may not as yet spend the night in any good hotel in America. Recently she was again signally honored by being given the Bok reward as the most distinguished resident of Philadelphia. Yet she cannot be served in many of the public restaurants of her home city, eveen after it has declared her to be its best citizen.[2]

So, with their right hand they raise to high places the great who have dark skins, and with their left, they slap us down to keep us in "our places." "Yes, America you have stripped me of my garments, you have robbed me of my precious endowment."

We cannot have an enlightened democracy with one great group living in ignorance. We cannot have a healthy nation with one tenth of the people ill-nourished, sick, harboring germs of disease which recognize no color lines—obey no Jim Crow laws. We cannot have a nation orderly and sound with one group so ground down and thwarted that it is almost forced into unsocial attitudes and crime. We cannot be truly Christian people so long as we flaunt the central teachings of Jesus: brotherly love and the Golden Rule. We cannot come to full prosperity with one great group so ill-delayed that it cannot buy goods. So as we gird ourselves to defend democracy from foreign attack, let us see to it that increasingly at home we give fair play and free opportunity for all people.

---

2. Marian Anderson was barred from singing in Constitution Hall in 1939. She received the Bok Award on 18 March 1941. See her autobiography, *My Lord, What a Morning* (New York: Viking, 1956), pp. 184–192, 274–275.

Today thirteen million black sons and daughters of our forefathers con- tinue the fight for the translation of the 13th, 14th, and 15th amendments from writing on the printed page to an actuality. We believe with them that "if freedom is good for any it is good for all," that we may conquer southern armies by the sword, but it is another thing to conquer southern hate, that if the franchise is given to Negroes, they will be vigilant and defend even with their arms, the ark of federal liberty from treason and destruction by her enemies.

The spirit of Lincoln still lives; that spirit born of the teachings of the Nazarene, who promised mercy to the merciful, who lifted the lowly, strengthened the weak, ate with publicans, and made the captives free. In the light of this divine example, the doctrines of demagogues shiver in their chaff. Already closer understanding links Saxon and Freedman in mutual sympathy.

America experiences a new birth of freedom in her sons and daughters; she incarnates the spirit of her martyred chief. Their loyalty is repledged; their devotion renewed to the work He left unfinished. My heart throbs anew in the hope that inspired by the example of Lincoln, imbued with the spirit of Christ, they will cast down the last barrier to perfect freedom. And I with my brother of blackest hue possessing at last my rightful heritage and holding my head erect, may stand beside the Saxon—a Negro—and yet a man!

PD. EPH.

To Alberta Williams King

11 June 1944
Simsbury, Conn.

Although King had just completed his junior year in high school, he spent the summer of 1944 working with Morehouse College students on a Connecticut tobacco farm owned by Cullman Brothers, Inc.[1] This, the first of four letters he wrote that summer, comments on attending a nonsegregated church in Simsbury and leading Sunday services for the other students in the program. King later traced his call to the ministry to "the summer of 1944 when I felt an inescapable urge to serve society."[2] King asks his mother to see Clinton Nathaniel Cornell, principal of Booker T. Washington High School, about the results of the test he had taken to gain early admission to Morehouse.

---

1. At the top of the letter, King writes "Cullman Bro Inc.," as part of the return address.
2. See King, Application for Admission to Crozer Theological Seminary, February 1948, p. 144 in this volume.

Dear Mother:

I received your letter and was very glad to here from you. I am doing fine and still having a nice time. Tell everybody at home hello. We went to church Sunday in Simsbury and we were the only negro's there Negroes and whites go the the same church. Sunday morning we had church in the boad house and I lead it I an the religious leader I have to speak on some text every Sunday to 107 boys we really have good meetings.

Our work is very easy we have to get up a 6:00 every day and be in the bed a 10:00. I have a job in the Kicthin so I get better food than any of the boys and more I get as much as I want. Tell daddy hello and I am praying for the church and all. I will write again soon.

Your Son
[*signed*] M. L.

P. S.   Dont forget to see Mr Conell about the test as soon as possible

ALS. CKFC.

To Martin Luther King, Sr.

15 June 1944
Simsbury, Conn.

Writing to his father from the tobacco farm in Connecticut, King expresses his surprise at the lack of racial discrimination in the North. He mentions attending a white church in Simsbury and tells his father, "We go to any place we want to and sit any where we want to."

Dear father:

I am very sorry I am so long about writing but I having been working most of the time. We are really having a fine time here and the work is very easy. We have to get up every day at 6:00. We have very good food. And I am working kitchen so you see I get better food.

We have service here every Sunday about 8:00 and I am the religious leader we have a Boys choir here and we are going to sing on the air soon. Sunday I went to church in Simsbury it was a white church. I could not get to Hartford {to church} but I am going next week. On our way here we saw some things I had never antiscipated to see. After we passed Washington the was no discrimination at all the white people here are very nice. We go to any place we want to and sit any where we want to.

K Dear father:

I am very sorry I am so long about writing but I having been working most of the time. We are really having a fine time here and the work is very easy. We have to get up every day at 6:00. We have very good food. And I am working kitchen so you see I get better food.

We have service here every Sunday about 8:00 and I am the religious leader we have a Boys choir here and we are going to sing on the air soon. Sunday I went to church in Simsbury it was a white church. I could not get to Hartford no church but I am going next week. On our way here we saw some things I had never anticipated to see. After we passed Washington the was no discrimination at all the white people here are very nice. We go to any place we want to and sit any where we want to.

Tell everybody I said hello and I am still thinking of the church and reading my bible. And I am not doing any thing that I would not doing front of you.

Your Son
M. L. Jr.

Tell everybody I said hello and I am still thinking of the church and reading
my bible. And I am not doing any thing that I would not doing front of you.

Your Son
[*signed*] M. L. Jr.

ALS. CKFC.

To Alberta Williams King

18 June 1944
Simsbury, Conn.

After receiving a letter from his mother, King informs her of his activities in
Connecticut, which included leading student religious services. He refers to his
brother, A. D., and his sister, Christine. King asks that Christine inform him of
his Morehouse admission test results. Mrs. Phoebe Burney was dean of women
at Clark College and a member of Ebenezer.[1]

Dear Mother Dear:

I recieved your letter to-day and was very glad to hear from you.

Yesterday we didn's work so we went to Hardford we really had a nice time there. I never though that a person of my race could eat anywhere but we [*strikeout illegible*] ate in one of the finest resturant in Hardford. And we went to the largest shows there. It is really a large city. Tell A. D. I hope him luck in summer school. Be sure to tell Christine write me and tell me about the test while you are gone. On

On our way here we stoped in Spartinburgh S.C. and it is a pretty large place. And we also many large ships some as large as the Bethel Church and larger we also saw many airplanes. We went under the Hudson river and entered New York. It is the largest place I have ever seen in my life. We might go there the 4th of July or either Boston Mass they are both near here. The sun has begun to get pretty hot, But that is not the begaining they {say} it is

---

1. Phoebe Fraser Burney (1902–) attended Fisk University from 1918 to 1923. From 1930 to 1941, she was director of religious education for the southeastern region of the Congregational church. She received her B.A. from Clark College in 1935, her M.A. in religious education from Gammon Theological Seminary in 1938, and did additional study in education at Boston University in 1940. She was a secretary in the endowment office at Morehouse College from 1941 until 1943, when she became dean of women at Clark College, where she remained until 1958. She later served as dean of City College at Chattanooga, Tennessee, and dean of education at the University of Tennessee, Chattanooga.

going to be so hot here in July that you can hardly take it but I am going to take in some dayhow.

I am very I didn't tell you about the locks but I just forget it. I received and thank you very much. My job in the kitchen is very easy I just do the extra work I give out the lunches and serve what ever they have to drink. Please send me Mrs. Burney's address and other members.

As head of the religious Dept. I have to take charge of the Sunday service I have to speak from any text I want to. Be sure to send me my Drivers ticket.

Mother dear I want you to send me some fried chikens and rolls it will not be so much. And also send my brown shoes the others have worn out.

Mother I cant send but ten dollars home this week because they took out for railroad fare and boad it will be the same for the next two week. We are going to get a raise to five or six dollar in July.

Your Son
[*signed*] M. L.

ALS. CKFC.

To Alberta Williams King

5 August 1944
Simsbury, Conn.

King notes that his friend Emmett Proctor ("Weasel"), who had joined him for the summer's work in Connecticut, has left for Washington, D.C. He refers to a preview of the Eighth Annual Musical of the Ebenezer Baptist Church choir, which was directed by his mother. The young men on the Connecticut tobacco farm raised funds for Morehouse in anticipation of a visit from the president, Benjamin E. Mays, and his wife, Sadie Mays.

Dear Mother:

How are you all getting along. I am doing fine. I received your letter and was very glad to hear from home.

As you know Weasel left last week for Washington last week. I think season will close Sept the 9th. I read the program of the musical and {I know} it was very good.

I dont think I will put you to the troble of sending The fried because I am getting pretty food here now. But I will go over to see the lady when I go to Harford. I wont have much time because we are working all day every Sunday and going bach overtime everyday.

Dr. May's of Morehouse and his wife will be here tonight he will speak to us. We took up money here for Morehouse and we raised [*strikeout illegible*]
$135 we are going to present it to them tonight.

I am sending $25 home this week I had planed to send $30 every week but   30 Aug
we are losing plenty of money because of rain. Will write again soon   1944

[*signed*] M. L. Jr.

ALS. CKFC.

To Alberta Williams King

30 August 1944
Simsbury, Conn.

*Responding to a letter in which his mother informed him of his admission to
Morehouse, King explains that Claude B. Dansby, the mathematics professor who
accompanied the students to Connecticut, will consult with Dean Brailsford R.
Brazeal about the registration of those students who were delayed in getting back to
Atlanta from Connecticut. Years later King recalled his return to the segregated
South: "It was a bitter feeling going back to segregation. It was hard to
understand why I could ride wherever I pleased on the train from New York to
Washington, and then had to change to a Jim Crow car at the nation's capital in
order to continue the trip to Atlanta."* [1]

Dear Mother

I received your letter and was very glad to hear from you.

I was very glad to hear that I can enter Morehouse. I cannot get home until
the 15th Because I signed the to leave the 12th and if I leave before the 12th I
cannot get my railroad fare and they are also giving us a bonus for about
$25.00 if I leave before the 12th I cant get nither of them. I asked Mr. Dansby
about entering school late and he said he would see Dean and explain it to
him it is a lot of boys here that are entering late. Mr. Dansby is giving some of
the boys the Math test here and they wont have to take it when they get there
I think I will take it. I will leave here Sept 12 Tues after next and get home
the 15th because I am stoping in N. York for about a day.

[*signed*] M. L.

ALS. CKFC.

---

1. Ted Poston, "Fighting Pastor: Martin Luther King," *New York Post*, 10 April 1957. See also
Coretta Scott King, *My Life with Martin Luther King, Jr.* (New York: Holt, Rinehart and Winston,
1969), p. 85.

II

Morehouse Years

"Kick Up Dust,"
Letter to the Editor, *Atlanta Constitution*

6 August 1946
Atlanta, Ga.

During the summer after his sophomore year at Morehouse, King wrote this letter
to the editor of Atlanta's largest newspaper. Although King does not make clear his
reasons for writing, the letter was probably written in response to the racially
motivated murders of two black couples in Walton County, Georgia, and of Macio
Snipes, a black World War II veteran.[1] In the letter, King is critical of those who
attempt to "obscure the real question of rights and opportunities." Years later,
King, Sr., observed that he and his wife had "no intimation of [King, Jr.'s]
developing greatness . . . until as a teenager he wrote a letter to the editor of a
local paper which received widespread and favorable comment."[2]

Editor Constitution:

I often find when decent treatment for the Negro is urged, a certain class
of people hurry to raise the scarecrow of social mingling and intermarriage.
These questions have nothing to do with the case. And most people who kick
up this kind of dust know that it is simple dust to obscure the real question of
rights and opportunities. It is fair to remember that almost the total of race
mixture in America has come, not at Negro initiative, but by the acts of those
very white men who talk loudest of race purity. We aren't eager to marry white
girls, and we would like to have our own girls left alone by both white toughs
and white aristocrats.

We want and are entitled to the basic rights and opportunities of American
citizens: The right to earn a living at work for which we are fitted by training
and ability; equal opportunities in education, health, recreation, and similar
public services; the right to vote; equality before the law; some of the same
courtesy and good manners that we ourselves bring to all human relations.

M. L. KING, JR.
Morehouse College.

PD. *Atlanta Constitution*, 6 August 1946.

---

1. On 26 July 1946, the *Atlanta Constitution* reported the killing of Macio Snipes, the only black
person to vote in his district in Taylor County, Georgia. On the day after he voted, four white
men shot Snipes to death. On 27 July, the newspaper reported that twenty white men stopped
and shot two black couples who were driving near Monroe, Georgia. The *Constitution* expressed
"a heartfelt sense of shame and embarrassment" over these incidents, but repeated its opposition
to "legislation that would make instances of mob violence a matter for Federal authorities" (*Atlanta Constitution*, 26, 27, and 29 July 1946).

2. Quoted in Lucy P. Bolds, ed., *Martin Luther King, Jr.: Profile of Greatness, A Student Symposium*
(Atlanta: Religious Heritage of the Black World, 1973), p. viii.

"The Purpose of Education"

[*September 1946–January 1947?*]

[*Atlanta, Ga.*]

This essay, written sometime during King's junior year at Morehouse, may be an early draft of the article of the same name published in the Maroon Tiger. *He suggests that education should not only "teach man to think intensively" but also provide "worthy objectives upon which to concentrate."*

Last week we attempted to discuss the purpose of religion. This week our attention moves toward education. I will attempt to answer the question, what is the purpose of education?

To my mind, education has a two-fold function in society. On the one hand it should discipline the mind for sustained and persistent speculation. On the other hand it should integrate human life around central, forcusing ideals. It is a tragedy that the latter is often neglected in our educational system.

Education should equip us with the power to think effectively and objectively. To think is one of the hardest things in the world, and to think objectively is still harder. Yet this is the job of education. Education should cause us to rise beyond the horizon of legions of half truth, prejudices and propaganda. Education should enable us to "weigh and consider," to discern the true from the false, the relevant from the irrelevant, and the real from the unreal.[1] The first function of education, therefore, is to teach man to think intensively. But this is not the whole of education. If education stops here it can be the most dangerous force in society. Some of the greatest criminals in society have been men {who} possessed the power of concentration and reason, but they had no morals. Perhaps the most dangerous periods in civilization have been those periods when there was no moral foundation in society.

Education without morals is like a ship without a compass, merely wandering nowhere. It is not enough to have the power of concentration, but we must have worthy objectives upon which to concentrate. It is not enough to know truth, but we must love truth and sacrifice for it.

ADS. MLKP-MBU: Box 118, folder 6.

---

1. "Read not to contradict and confute; nor yet to believe and take for granted; nor to find talk and discourse; but to weigh and consider" (Francis Bacon, "Of Studies," in *The Works of Francis Bacon*, ed. James Spedding, R. L. Ellis, and D. D. Heath [New York: Hurd and Houghton, 1877], p. 252). King used the phrase "weigh and consider" in three papers written at Crozer Theological Seminary ("Light on the Old Testament from the Ancient Near East," 14 September–24 November 1948, p. 180 in this volume; "The Sources of Fundamentalism and Liberalism Considered Historically and Psychologically," 13 September–23 November 1949, p. 237; and Book review of *A Functional Approach to Religious Education* by Ernest J. Chave, 12 September–22 November 1950, p. 355).

January–February 1947
Atlanta, Ga.

Writing in the campus newspaper, the Maroon Tiger, *King argues that
education has both a utilitarian and a moral function.*[1] *Citing the example of
Georgia's former governor Eugene Talmadge, he asserts that reasoning ability is
not enough. He insists that character and moral development are necessary to give
the critical intellect humane purposes. King, Sr., later recalled that his son told
him, "Talmadge has a Phi Beta Kappa key, can you believe that? What did he use
all that precious knowledge for? To accomplish what?"*[2]

As I engage in the so-called "bull sessions" around and about the school, I
too often find that most college men have a misconception of the purpose of
education. Most of the "brethren" think that education should equip them
with the proper instruments of exploitation so that they can forever trample

---

1. In 1925, the *Maroon Tiger* succeeded the *Athenaeum* as the campus literary journal at Morehouse. In the first semester of the 1947–1948 academic year, it won a First Class Honor Rating
from the Associated Collegiate Press at the University of Minnesota. The faculty adviser to the
Maroon Tiger was King's English professor, Gladstone Lewis Chandler. King's "The Purpose of
Education" was published with a companion piece, "English Majors All?" by a fellow student,
William G. Pickens. Among the many prominent black academicians and journalists who served
an apprenticeship on the *Maroon Tiger* staff were Lerone Bennett, Jr., editor of *Ebony;* Brailsford
R. Brazeal, dean of Morehouse College; S. W. Garlington, city editor of New York's *Amsterdam
News;* Hugh Gloster, president of Morehouse College; Emory O. Jackson, editor of the *Birmingham World;* Robert E. Johnson, editor of *Jet;* King D. Reddick of the *New York Age;* Ira De A. Reid,
chair of the Sociology Department at Atlanta University; and C. A. Scott, editor and general
manager of the *Atlanta Daily World.* See *The Morehouse Alumnus,* July 1948, pp. 15–16; and Edward A. Jones, *A Candle in the Dark: A History of Morehouse College* (Valley Forge, Pa.: Judson Press,
1967), pp. 174, 260, 289–292.
2. Martin Luther King, Sr., with Clayton Riley, *Daddy King: An Autobiography* (New York: William Morrow, 1980), p. 143. In an unpublished autobiographical statement, King, Sr., remembered a meeting between Governor Eugene Talmadge and a committee of blacks concerning the
imposition of the death penalty on a young black man convicted of making improper remarks to
a white woman. King, Sr., reported that Talmadge "sent us away humiliated, frustrated, insulted,
and without hope of redress" ("The Autobiography of Daddy King as Told to Edward A. Jones"
[n.d.], p. 40; copy in CKFC). Six months before the publication of King's article, Georgia's race-
baiting former governor Eugene Talmadge had declared in the midst of his campaign for a new
term as governor that "the only issue in this race is White Supremacy." On 12 November, the
black General Missionary Baptist Convention of Georgia designated his inauguration date, 9
January 1947, as a day of prayer. Talmadge died three weeks before his inauguration. See William Anderson, *The Wild Man from Sugar Creek: The Political Career of Eugene Talmadge* (Baton
Rouge: Louisiana State University Press, 1975), pp. 226–237; Joseph L. Bernd, "White Supremacy and the Disfranchisement of Blacks in Georgia, 1946," *Georgia Historical Quarterly* 66
(Winter 1982): 492–501; Clarence M. Wagner, *Profiles of Black Georgia Baptists* (Atlanta: Bennett
Brothers, 1980), p. 104; and Benjamin E. Mays, *Born to Rebel: An Autobiography* (Athens: University of Georgia Press, 1987), pp. 221–223.

over the masses. Still others think that education should furnish them with noble ends rather than means to an end.

It seems to me that education has a two-fold function to perform in the life of man and in society: the one is utility and the other is culture. Education must enable a man to become more efficient, to achieve with increasing facility the ligitimate goals of his life.

Education must also train one for quick, resolute and effective thinking. To think incisively and to think for one's self is very difficult. We are prone to let our mental life become invaded by legions of half truths, prejudices, and propaganda. At this point, I often wonder whether or not education is fulfilling its purpose. A great majority of the so-called educated people do not think logically and scientifically. Even the press, the classroom, the platform, and the pulpit in many instances do not give us objective and unbiased truths. To save man from the morass of propaganda, in my opinion, is one of the chief aims of education. Education must enable one to sift and weigh evidence, to discern the true from the false, the real from the unreal, and the facts from the fiction.

The function of education, therefore, is to teach one to think intensively and to think critically. But education which stops with efficiency may prove the greatest menace to society. The most dangerous criminal may be the man gifted with reason, but with no morals.

The late Eugene Talmadge, in my opinion, possessed one of the better minds of Georgia, or even America. Moreover, he wore the Phi Beta Kappa key. By all measuring rods, Mr. Talmadge could think critically and intensively; yet he contends that I am an inferior being. Are those the types of men we call educated?

We must remember that intelligence is not enough. Intelligence plus character—that is the goal of true education. The complete education gives one not only power of concentration, but worthy objectives upon which to concentrate. The broad education will, therefore, transmit to one not only the accumulated knowledge of the race but also the accumulated experience of social living.

If we are not careful, our colleges will produce a group of close-minded, unscientific, illogical propagandists, consumed with immoral acts. Be careful, "brethren!" Be careful, teachers!

PD. *Maroon Tiger* (January–February 1947): 10. Copy in GD.

27 October 1947
Atlanta, Ga.

King writes to Crozer Theological Seminary in Chester, Pennsylvania, asking for
an application and a seminary catalog. J. Pius Barbour, a friend of his father and
a graduate of Crozer, probably encouraged him to apply to Crozer.[1] Crozer
president Edwin E. Aubrey had taught Morehouse president Benjamin Mays at the
University of Chicago and spoke at Morehouse's baccalaureate in 1945.

Crozer Theological Seminary
Chester, Pa.

Dear Sir:

After reading and hearing much about your seminary I have become intensely interested in it. I am now a senior at Morehouse College, and I hope
to enter some Theological school after graduating.

I would like very much to secure an application blank and also a catalog of
your school

Will you please send this material as soon as possible.

Yours truly,
[*signed as below*]
M. L. King, Jr.

K/w

TLS. CRO-NRCR.

---

1. J. Pius Barbour (1894–1974) received his B.A. degree from Morehouse College in 1917.
At Crozer Theological Seminary, Barbour earned a Bachelor of Divinity degree in 1936 and a
Master of Theology degree in 1937. Barbour served two churches in Texas before joining the
faculty of Tuskegee Institute from 1919 to 1921. From 1921 to 1931, he was the pastor of Day
Street Baptist Church in Montgomery, Alabama, and from 1931 to 1933 of Mt. Olive Baptist
Church in Fort Wayne, Indiana. In 1933, he became pastor of Calvary Baptist Church in Chester,
Pennsylvania. As editor of the *National Baptist Voice*, Barbour gained a national reputation as
one of the most prominent theological spokesmen of his generation for the National Baptist
Convention.

From Charles E. Batten

29 October 1947
Chester, Pa.

Responding to King's letter of inquiry, Charles E. Batten of Crozer Theological
Seminary, who served the small Baptist seminary as registrar and librarian,
introduces King to Crozer and invites his application.¹ Batten discusses features of
seminary life that would be significant for King, such as the "personal contact"
and "informality" the school encouraged among faculty and students.

My dear Mr. King:

I have your letter of October 27 inquiring about Crozer. Under separate cover I have sent you a copy of our latest catalogue together with a pamphlet entitled, "The Crozer Pattern." After you read this material, if you have any questions, please do not hesitate to write me.

I am enclosing herewith an application blank. If you are interested in coming to Crozer, I would suggest as early an application as possible. I think that it is good for men to decide as soon as possible where they wish to do their theological work. Then too, there is always the problem of accommodations.

I do not know how well acquainted you are with Crozer but I am sure you will be interested in knowing that Crozer is fully accredited by the American Association of Theological Schools. We have an excellent faculty of consecrated Christian teachers who are leaders in their respective subjects. All full-time faculty members reside on the campus hence there is much opportunity for personal contact between students and professors. Life on the campus is marked by an informality and a high sense of community responsibility as professors and students face their respective tasks in theological education.

In any graduate school the library is an important feature. Crozer has a complete and usable library with an open stack system.

There is a wide offering in courses. The curriculum is marked by its flexibility. Because the school is a small one, attention can be given to the individual needs of students. Through an agreement with the University of Pennsylvania, students at Crozer are admitted to courses in the Graduate Schools of the University in fields related to their seminary studies. Thus the resources of a large metropolitan university are available to Crozer students.

---

1. Charles Edward Batten (1910–1963) earned a B.S. degree from Temple University in 1935 and a B.D. from Crozer in 1938. Batten was registrar at Crozer from 1938 to 1948, librarian from 1943 to 1948, and dean from 1948 to 1953. He became minister of education at an Episcopal church in Winchester, Massachusetts, in 1954 and a professor of Christian education at the Episcopal Theological School in Cambridge in 1956.

I trust I shall hear from you. You may be sure of our interest in you and our willingness to cooperate in every possible way.

31 Jan 1948

With all good wishes, I am

Sincerely,
Charles E. Batten

CEB:w

TLc. CRO-NRCR.

"Ritual"

[*25 September 1946–31 January 1948?*]
[*Atlanta, Ga.?*]

Probably written for a sociology course with Walter R. Chivers during King's junior or senior year, this paper is one of the few extant academic papers from his Morehouse years.[1] *As a "pre-th[e]ological" student and major in sociology, he grapples with the problem of writing "scientifically" about religious matters. In this paper King considers both sacred and secular rituals, including those of the Ku Klux Klan and college fraternities. Chivers gave the paper an A — and commented: "This is a good analysis. Your thought is good. Learn to do two things: (1) Proof read and correct your ms. before submitting it; (2) How to document and check your references." In this and other academic essays, King's citations are presented as notes in the inner margin.*

   I. Introduction
  II. Definition
 III. Classification of Ritual
     A. Sacred
         (a) Life Cycle Ritual
             1. Baptism
             2. Birth
             3. Ritual Dances
             4. Marriage (sacred)
             5. Others

---

1. Walter R. Chivers (1896–1969) received an A.B. from Morehouse College in 1919. After graduating from the New York School of Social Work in 1924, he joined the Morehouse faculty as an instructor in sociology. In 1946 Chivers initiated an annual Institute on Successful Marriage and Family Living, sponsored by Morehouse. He remained associated with the college until his retirement in 1968.

         (b) Ritual For Group Welfare
             1. Mass
             2. Communion
             3. Feast Days
             4. Others

    B. Secular
         (a) Secret Societies
             1. Clubs
             2. Age Groups
             3. Fraternities
             4. Lodges
             5. Ku Klux Klan
             6. Others
         (b) Etiquette
             1. Standing
             2. Smiling
             3. Removal of hat
             4. Words of thanks

V. Changes of Rites
    A. Causes
             1. Cultural change
             2. Individualism

  {B.}

VI. Conclusion

    The present study represents an attempt to apply the scientific {method to an} analysis of ritual. Being a pre-thological student it would ordinarily be expected of me to defend certain aspects of sacred ritual, therefore becoming unscientific; but I will attempt to be as unbaised and scientific as possible.[2] For the most part the study has been confined to the forms and functions of ritual in contemporary America, though occasional references are made to titualism characteristic of other cultures, even as far back as Greek and Hebrew culture.[3]

    In order to keep the study within reasonable limits it has been necessary to confine the analysis to what appears to be the most important features. So very complex and all pervasive is the phenomenon of ritu-

---

2. Chivers wrote "good" in the margin.

3. Chivers corrected "titualism" to "ritualism" and added an "s" to the end of the sentence.

31 Jan
1948

alism that a complete picture would involve innumerable details of all single aspects involved in ritual. In this respect the present study conforms to accepted methodological standards in institutional research. This study will deal with both sacred and secular ritual. For the purpose of this discussion the terms "ritual" and "ceremonial" will be used synonymously. Let us now look into the meaning of ritual.

"Ritual," in the words of Ruth Benedick, "is a form of prescribed and elaborated behavior and occurs both as the spontaneous inventions of the individual especially of the compulsion neurotic, and as a culture trait."* From this definition we can easily see that ritual is found in all forms of prescribed behavior. In other words ritual is any repetitive symbolic act which is socially established. As used in this sense the term may indicate either those simple, person-to-person acts such as handshaking or tipping one's hat, or else those formal collective procedures such as a Catholic Mass, the inauguration of a president, the graduation of college students, or the initiation of a neophyte into a secret order.

In most discussions of ritual it is often discussed as aspect of religion and has been considered the origin of religion, but it is by no means a phenomenon peculiar to religion, as we saw in the definition above. I will agree that most of the ritualistic occasions are sacred and are often, therefore religious; but many secular occasions are similarly elaborated.[5] Durkheim, the French sociologist, contends that ritual is only to be associated with that which is sacred;[6] but this contention must certainly be challenged, for the most extreme ritualistic formalism has no religion connec-

* Ruth Benedick, "Ritual," Enclopedia Of Sociology[4]

---

4. Chivers underlined "Ritual" and "Enclopedia Of Sociology," and in each instance (text and footnote) circled the misspelled name, correcting it to "Benedict." He marked the Encyclopedia of Sociology and commented, "I don't know this reference." The citation is Ruth Benedict, "Ritual," in *Encyclopedia of the Social Sciences*, ed. Edwin R. A. Seligman and Alvin Johnson (New York: Macmillan, 1934), 13:396–397. The word "inventions" in the middle of the quotation should be "invention"; likewise, the correct phrase at the end of the quotation should be "cultural trait."

5. Benedict, "Ritual," p. 396: "It is ordinarily discussed as an aspect of religion and has even been considered the origin of religion, but it is by no means a phenomenon peculiar to religion. The occasions which are ritualistically elaborated are usually solemn and are often therefore religious; but many secular occasions are similarly elaborated."

6. Chivers asked, "How does he define sacred?"

tions,[7] as we shall see later in the study. I will agree that in many instances secular ritual grows out of sacred ritual, but certainly are they not to be used identical. Durkheim fails to see that ritual may surround any field of behavior. Let us look for the moment into the realm of sacred ritual.

We shall begin this discussion by giving a few of the ritualistic practices connected with individual or life cycle ritual. The first rite under discussion is that of baptism. As a sacrament of admission to the church, baptism always stood until the religious divisions of Post-Reformation days. It so stands for the vast majority of Christians at present. The origin of the rite is uncertain, but according to most of the theological data I have come across, it seems probable that it was a spiritualization of the old Levitical washing.[8] Diverse intrepretations of baptism have been given by theologians. To John the Baptist, it was a fitting symbol of the spiritual purification that followed the repentence of sin. With Paul, baptism was not merely the symbol of cleansing from sin, it involved a new relationship to Christ, and a participation in his death and resurrection. Baptism still stands as one of the basic symbolic acts connected with sacred ritual.

The ceremonies associated with the birth of a child is also a very important aspect of life cycle ritual. Leaving contemporary America for the moment, I have chosen for an example the Buka people in the Northwestern part of Bougainville in the Solomon Island.* Among these people the beginning of pregnancy is symbolically marked; the woman makes a belt of a special creeper and wears it in place of a loin cloth; furthermore, during pregnancy, she must abstain from eating certain foods. Toward the end of pregnancy a ritual is performed to make delivery easy. When the expectant mother feels the child birth beginning, the husband goes to fetch one of her female relatives and then goes to another but where he must spend his time in complete idleness for three days. During this period, he must carry no account, carry or lift no heavy objects. It is believed that if he did so, the child would be injured.

* Blackwood, Beatrice, Both sides of Buka Passage, 1935

---

7. Benedict, "Ritual," p. 396: "The contention of Durkheim . . . that religion arises from ritualism as such must be challenged, for the most extreme ritualistic formalism . . . "

8. Chivers asked for a reference.

His reintroduction to his normal rate of interaction begins on the fourth day, after he has seen his wife and child he is allowed to wander around the village once more. Actually these prohibitions are nothing more than ritualistic ceremonies. Of course, in a more complex society like our own, the ceremonies connected with child birth are much different, yet they are present.

The ritual dance is also a striking phenomena to study in relation to ritualism. I will use for an example the vodun dance as found in the Haitian Culture.* According to Herskoirts the vodun dance is the most public aspect of Haitian peasant ritual and also the most important social occasion.

* Herskoirts, Life In A Haitian Valley, New York, 1937.[9]

The vodun dance may be said to be nothing more than a symbolic way of becoming possessed of the gods. A release of psychic {tension} is undoubtedly afforded those who become possessed.[10] When a possession occurs, the songs for the deity who has "arrived" are taken up as the drums play the rhythm of the god. As the possession comes on, the devotee falls to the ground, rolling before the drums, or staggers blindly about the dancing-space. After a while he begins to dance.[11] Gradually his dancing becomes calmed until he is taken to a near-by house where he rests and if, as often happens, he has rolled in muddy ground during his possession, he washes and changes his clothes.[12] This, in short, is the theory behind the ritual dance.

The ritual connected with marriage is the simplest of all ceremonies with which we have to deal. There is always a general increase of interaction between

---

9. Chivers circled the name "Herskoirts" and underlined the title. The complete citation is Melville J. Herskovits, *Life in a Haitian Valley* (New York: Alfred A. Knopf, 1937).

10. Herskovits, *Life in a Haitian Valley*, p. 178: "A release of psychic tension is undoubtedly afforded those who become possessed."

11. Herskovits, *Life in a Haitian Valley*, p. 183: "When a possession occurs, the songs for the deity who has 'arrived' are taken up as the drums play the rhythm of the god. As his possession comes on, the devotee falls to the ground, rolling before the drums, or staggers blindly about the dancing-space, or otherwise follows the characteristic behavior attributed to his god. After a time he begins to dance."

12. Herskovits, *Life in a Haitian Valley*, p. 184: "Gradually his dancing becomes calmed, until he is taken either to the *maison de servitude* or to a near-by house, where he rests and if, as often happens, he has rolled on muddy ground during his possession, he washes and changes his clothes."

two groups, involving, as a rule, gift giving and feasting. It is interesting to know that most of the ceremonies connected with marriage were borrowed from Jewish and Pagan customs. The presentation of the man and woman by their parents and friends, the joining of their right hands, the giving and receiving of a ring, the veiling of the bride, and the crowning of the married couple with chaplets and flowers, were all in use in the fourth century A.D.[13] This ceremony remains one of the most sacred of all ritual in our culture.

Other life cycle riturl which will not be discussed in detail are puberty ceremonies, funeral ceremonies, circumcision etc. Each of these is built around definite ritualistic practices.

Now we past from the realm of life cycle ritual to the ritual for group welfare. It must be remembered that both are equally important in institutional research. The Catholic Mass, in my opinion is the most important phase of ritual for group welfare.[14] I will elaborate on the mass a little more than I have on previous aspects of ritual, because of the extreme formal and ritualistic practices found therein. I will approach the Mass from a somewhat social-psychological point of view. That is to say I will go into such matters as the character of social interaction within the church, the influence of the ritualistic experiences on attitudes and values, and particularly the effect of the ritual on youthful members.

The ritual centering around the mass with all of its formalism is the principal feature which sets off Catholicism from Protestatism.[15] In the ceremony of the mass there are three factors, the belief, the ritual, and the response of the worshiper. Of all of these, the symbolic trapping, the ritual, is the most important. Why is it that this mechanical factor tends to confirm people in their old faiths and hold them in the

---

13. Oscar Hardman, *A History of Christian Worship* (Nashville, Tenn.: Cokesbury Press, 1937), pp. 73–74: "The presentation of the man and woman by their parents and friends, the joining of their right hands, the giving and receiving of a ring, the veiling of the bride by the priest, and the crowning of the married couple with chaplets and flowers, were all in use at this time [from the fourth to the seventh centuries]."

14. Chivers underlined "most important phase" and asked, "Do you mean this?"

15. Luther Sheeleigh Cressman, "Ritual the Conserver," *American Journal of Sociology* 35 (January 1930): 569: "The ritual centering about the Mass and all its manifold implications is the principal feature which sets off Catholicism from Protestantism."

church?[16] According to Cressman[17] this is due to the general psychological principle that we respond to a repeated total situation or to a part of the original one as though it were the entire original situation. In other words a part may call forth a response given originally to the whole. The ritual which the child is taught for years to become accustomed to almost becomes second nature to him. This is why it is almost impossible to separate the Catholic trained person from the church; too many stimuli release the old reactions.[18]

The story is told of a Bishop of the church of England who was once called upon to advise one of the country's leading scientific men, a former devout worshipper in the Anglo-Catholic church. The Scientist came to the Bishop because he had lost his faith. The Bishop being wise knew that this was no case for argument. He understood both human nature and the power of the majestic ritual of his church. So the Bishop advised his friend to try an experiment; to continue to attend church, especially at the mass, as he had always done in the days before he lost his faith and see if he did not regain the faith which he had lost. A few weeks later the scientist was back in the Bishop's office. He had come back to assure the Bishop that the experiment was successful, that once more he had found himself secure in the faith of his fathers. The ritual had done its work.[19] Every priest

---

16. Cressman, "Ritual the Conserver," p. 569: "In the ceremony of the Mass there are three factors, the beliefs, the ritual, and the response of the worshipers. The ritual is but the trappings, the mere mechanics of worship. Why is this mechanical factor the decisive one that results in the development of modernism, yet tends to confirm people in their old faiths and bind them to the church?"

17. Chivers underlined "Cressman" and remarked, "Document."

18. Cressman, "Ritual the Conserver," pp. 569–570: "This is due to the general psychological principle that we respond to a repeated total situation or to a part of the original one as though it were the entire original situation. In other words, a part may call forth a response given originally to the whole. . . . The long years in which the child is taught to become accustomed to the ritual of his church until it becomes almost second nature with it makes well-nigh impossible the separation of the Catholic trained person from the church because too many stimuli release the old reactions."

19. Cressman, "Ritual the Conserver," p. 564: "Bishop Gore, of the Church of England, once found himself called upon to advise one of his country's leading scientific men, a former devout worshiper in the Anglo-Catholic church. The caller had come to the bishop because he had lost his faith. The good bishop was a wise and gentle person and knew that this was no cause for argument. He understood both human nature and the power of the majestic ritual of his church. So he advised his troubled friend to try an experiment; to continue to attend his church for worship, especially at the Mass, as he had always done in the days before he had lost his faith,

knows the power of ritual. The ritual has a certain emotional effect upon the worshipper that produces a certain mystic ecstasy or "emotional thrill." Once this ecstasy has been experienced the worshipper is safe so far as the church is concerned. So the statement that we often hear, "Give me a child for the first seven years of its life and I do not care who has it for the rest,"[20] is often true.

Protestantism, on the other hand is much different. There is no ritual like the mass, which serves to imbibe the old faith. The nearest thing psychologically, which Protestantism has to offer is the evangelistic revival.[21] This is, in my opinion, one reason why it is so easy to find Protestans withdrawing from his own denomination or from any church connections whatsoever.[22] In other words there is no psychological mechanism established in Protestantism which will serve to hold its members once the intellectual grounds for beliefs are shaken.[23] I do not argue the Protestantism has no basic ritual and no binding force, all religions do, but I do argue that the definite pattern of worship found in Catholicism has a greater psychological effect than that found in Protestantism. All of this goes on to justify Luther Cressman in saying, "ritual is the powerful conservation force binding the members of a religion which invokes its aid so firmly to their faith that the appeal to reason is of no avail."*[24]

* "Ritual the Conserver," American Journal of Sociology XXXV, 1929

and see if he did not regain the old sureness of conviction which he had lost. Some months later, the bishop found his old friend again in the study. He had come to thank the bishop and to assure him that the experiment had been successful, that once more he found himself secure in the faith of his fathers. . . . The ritual had done its work."

20. Cressman, "Ritual the Conserver," p. 568: "Its emotional effect upon the worshiper is the production of a certain mystic ecstasy, the 'religious thrill,' as it has been called. And once this ecstasy has been experienced the worshiper is safe as far as his church goes. The folk saying, often invidious, that the Catholic church says, 'Give me a child for the first seven years of its life and I do not care who has it for the rest' is a recognition of this fact."

21. Cressman, "Ritual the Conserver," p. 570: "The nearest thing, psychologically, which Protestantism has to offer is the evangelistic revival."

22. Cressman, "Ritual the Conserver," p. 565: "In a conflict between the church and the individual in the Catholic communion, the individual makes every effort to remain in the bosom of his church, whereas in Protestantism he too often withdraws from his own denomination or from any church connection whatsoever."

23. Cressman, "Ritual the Conserver," p. 570: "No psychological mechanism is established which will serve to hold its members to the church once the intellectual grounds for belief are shattered by the use of the scientific method or for any other reason."

24. The quotation should read: "[Ritual] is a powerful conservative force binding the members of a religion which invokes its aid so firmly to their faith that the appeal to reason is of no avail" (Cressman, "Ritual the Conserver," p. 572).

Another important aspect of ritual for public welfare is that of holy communion or the Eucharist. This is the central and most characteristic act of Christian worship—It remains the unshaken faith of the church that Christ himself instituted the Eucharist and the night in which he was betrayed, and that he expressly ordered its observance as a memorial of His sacrificial death and intended it to be a means of sacramental association with Himself as Victor over all the powers of evil.[25]

To miss communion in many churches is considered a major sin. For instance Catholicism put major emphasis on its observance. Why? Because Christ himself instituted it, supposively. It is interesting to know that the Catholics believe this communion is beyond a mere symbol. They believe that the substance is transformed into the very body and boood of Christ. The basis of the whole thing is built around the concept of eating the God.

In this analysis feast days are certainly characteristic of ritual for public welfare. All feasts are divided into two classes, feasts of precept and feasts of devotion. The feasts of precept are holydays on which the Faithful in most Catholic countries refrain from unnecessary servile labor and attend Mass. These include all the Sundays in the year, Christmas Day, the circumcism, the Epiphany, the Immaculate Conception and the Assumption of the Blessed Virgin, St. Joseph, St. Peter and St. Paul, and all Saints. The feasts of devotion, which form the second division, are purely ecclesiastical feasts, and are of three grades, double, semi-double, and simple.[26] Throughout Christendom, feast days have been considered very important.

---

25. Hardman, *History of Christian Worship*, pp. 28–29: "The central and most characteristic act of Christian worship is the Eucharist. Its dominical institution has been denied: but it remains the unshaken faith of the Church that our Lord Himself instituted the Eucharist on the night in which He was betrayed, and that He expressly ordered its observance as a memorial of His sacrificial death and intended it to be a means of sacramental association with Himself as Victor over all the powers of evil."

26. Hardman, *History of Christian Worship*, p. 233: "All feasts are divided into two classes, feasts of precept and feasts of devotion. The former are holy days on which the Faithful in most Catholic countries refrain from unnecessary servile labour and attend Mass. These include all the Sundays in the year, Christmas Day, the Circumcision, the Epiphany, the Ascension, Corpus Christi, the Immaculate Conception and the Assumption of the Blessed Virgin, St. Joseph, St. Peter and St. Paul, and All Saints. The feasts of devotion, which form the second division, are purely ecclesiastical feasts and are of three grades, double, semi-double, and simple."

We now leave the realm of sacred ritual entering into the broad realm of secular ritual, which, in my opinion, is just as important as sacred ritual. As was stated above, secular ritual, in many instances, becomes more elaborate than sacred ritual. Let us open the discussion with a consideration of secret societies. This discussion will cover such organizations as clubs, age groups, Fraternities, Lodges, Ku Klux Klan, Honor Societies, Philanthropic Societies and Insurance Societies.

By way of introduction of the subject it may be well to mention what appears to be almost a universal characteristic of secret societies, namely, the secrecy of the ritual themselves. As Simmel says, "that which is most striking about the treatment of the ritual in secret societies is not merely the precision with which it is observed, but first of all the anxiety with which it is guarded as a secret as though the unveiling of it were precisely as fatal as betrayal of the purposes and victims of the society, or even the existence of the society altogether."* Even those secret societies which never hid their motives or aims will take special precautions against disclosure of the secret ritual. One of the most exstream forms of disloyalty in any secret society, is to expose to non-members the ritualistic traits. It is one of the obligations of every member to honor this ritualistic secrecy throughout life. Let us look into some of these secre societies. But before doing so I must admit some difficulties I encountered. As we know a classification or interpretation of secret societies according to their secret ritual is a difficult task, because of the emphasis placed against their disclosure. So in no way should the purpose of this study be interpreted as an exposure of fraternal secrets. All of the printed rituals that are copyrighted may be found in the library of Congress. Where there was any doubt about their ~~authority~~ {authenticity} of the printed ritual, I contacted students on Morehouse's campus who are fraternity {members}, and friends in the city who are lodge members.[28]

* George Simmel, "The Sociology of Secrecy," American Journal of Sociology, XI 1946.[27]

27. King added the word "most" at the beginning of the quotation and substituted the phrase "purposes and victims" for the original "purposes and actions." Chivers circled the date and volume and wrote "no," indicating that the year was incorrect. The citation should read George Simmel, "The Sociology of Secrecy and Secret Societies," *American Journal of Sociology* 11, no. 4 (January 1906): 441–498.

28. As a student at Morehouse, King was not a member of a fraternity. He later joined Alpha Phi Alpha, a black social fraternity, in 1952 as a graduate student at Boston University.

Of all the secret orders those in support of the status quo in this country appear to be far in the numerical majority. Perhaps the most distinctive among all these societies is the Ku Klux Klan, committed to a philosophy of "one hundred per cent Americanism", white supremacy and nationalistic isolation. This organization is avowedly antagonistic to Catholic, Jewish, or Negro influences.[29] The most ritualistic trait found within the Ku Klux Klan is the "Fiery cross." This symbol is always featured conspicuously in Klan meetings. During the prosperous days of the Klan the burning cross was a familiar scene: often it would be placed on a hill or mountain top as signal to the countryside that "the Klan rides" or as a warning to unconventional persons in the vicinity. It is the symbol of Klan morality and Klan power. At mass initiation ceremonies, usually conducted in the open, the lighting is provided by an illuminated cross. The symbol of the Klan is a simple Latin cross with no embellishments or decoration.[30]

Greek letter fraternities are also very important in relation to secular ritual. Such fraternities are: Phi Beta Sigma, Alpha Phi Alpha, etc. The whole make-up of fraternal life is built around ritualism. The symbol of the fraternity, the fraternity colors, the initiation period and the oath of secrecy are nothing more than ritualistic practices. Let me give briefly a few of the ritualistic practices found in fraternities. First, most fraternities have as one of their recognition signs the fraternal handclasp. Like titles and pass words they are symbolic in character.[31] Second, we find that

29. Noel P. Gist, "Secret Societies: A Cultural Study of Fraternalism in the United States," *University of Missouri Studies* 15, no. 4 (1 October 1940): 25–26: "Of all the secret political orders those in support of the *status quo* in this country appear to be far in the numerical majority. . . . Perhaps the most distinctive among all these societies, . . . is the Ku Klux Klan, committed to a philosophy of 'one hundred per cent Americanism,' white supremacy, Protestantism, nationalistic isolation, and economic individualism. Avowedly antagonistic to Catholic, Jewish, Negro, or Communistic influences, . . ."

30. Gist, "Secret Societies," p. 116: "During the prosperous days of the Klan in the early 1920's the burning cross was a familiar scene: often it would be placed on a hill or mountain top as a signal to the countryside that 'the Klan rides' or as a warning or threat to unpatriotic or unconventional persons in the vicinity. It was the symbol of Klan morality and Klan power. At mass initiation ceremonies, usually conducted in the open, the lighting is provided by an illuminated cross. The symbol of the Klan is a simple Latin cross with no embellishments or decorations."

31. Gist, "Secret Societies," p. 126: "Most secret societies have as one of their recognition signs the fraternal handclasp. Some orders even have a special grip for each of the degrees. Like titles and passwords, they are symbolic in character."

most fraternities have a symbolic coloring. While the colors and their symbols vary considerably, there is one fairly common color combination—red, white, and blue—signifying, no doubt, the patriotic sentiments of the members.[32]

The well-nigh universal propensity of human beings to assist their fellow in time of distress finds expression in Philanthropic societies so common to the western world. These organizations combine social activities with the task of providing protection to member whose economic status is jeopardized by the circumstances of life. Here are the Knights of Pythias, the independent order of Odd Fellows, the improved order of Red Men, and other well-known societies.[33] Space will not permit me to go into details of the ritualistic practices of each of these, but it is to be understood that the basis of each of them is ritualistic.

Similar to the Philanthropic society is the fraternal insurance organization. While devoted to the principle of brotherhood, the mechanisms of mutual aid of such organizations are more formal and their devotion to ritual and ceremony usually less pronounced.[34]

Lodges also have a very important position in an analysis of secular ritual. Let us look into the Freemasonry centers its ritualistic drama on Biblical legends relating to King Solomon's Temple.[35] All of the "degrees" found in Masonry are nothing more than symbolic practices.

There are two things all lodges have in common. One is the oath of the lodge. Conscious of the power of ritual as a modifier of human behavior and especially as a solidifying influence in group life, lodges

---

32. Gist, "Secret Societies," p. 127: "While the colors and their symbols vary considerably, there is one fairly common color combination—red, white, and blue—signifying, no doubt, the patriotic sentiments of the members."

33. Gist, "Secret Societies," p. 24: "The well-nigh-universal propensity of human beings to assist their fellows in times of distress finds expression in the benevolent societies so common to the western world.... The organizations combine 'social' activities with the task of providing protection and succor to members whose economic status or even existence is jeopardized by the circumstances of life. Here are the Masonic order, the Knights of Pythias, the Independent Order of Odd Fellows, the Improved Order of Red Men, and other well-known societies."

34. Gist, "Secret Societies," p. 24: "Similar to the benevolent society is the fraternal insurance organization. While likewise devoted to the principle of brotherhood, the mechanisms of mutual aid of such organizations are more formal and their devotion to ritual and ceremony usually less pronounced."

35. In the original document page 11 ends with "Freemasonry centers" and page 12 begins with "its ritualistic drama." King (or King's typist) omitted several lines of the essay.

have employed these ritualistic devices to further the
cohesiveness of the group.[36] Second is the oath of secrecy. This is the most conspicuous aspect of ritualistic obligation. It is the formal promise to keep inviolate the secrets of the order. The candidate must not
write, print, or impart verbally any of the secrets relating to passwords, ritual, or other secret features.
These are the supreme taboos of secret fraternalism.
To make them more compulsive for religious-minded
persons the name of deity is usually associated with
the obligation, the candidate promising "in the presence of Almighty God" to conceal none of the ritualistic secrets.[37]

Another important phase of secular ritual is that of
Etiquette. Etiquette has been defined by one as the
body of forms of conventional decorum into which
one's behavior is cast." In the Western world etiquette
is inculcated at such an early age until it is often mistaken as an unborn drive. Thus, standing to show respect is thought by many to be instinctive until people
show respect by sitting. Most of the manifestations of
emotion such as smiling, are determined by convention, most of which can be traced to ritual. Although
I have classified etiquette under secular ritual, I think
I can be justified in saying that there are certain sacred traits found therein. Some sociologists argue
that etiquette centers around divinity. For instance,
etiquette often consists in practices arising from the
belief that the superior equals a god.[38] In short, all

36. Gist, "Secret Societies," p. 92: "Conscious of the potency of ritual as a modifier of human
behavior and especially as a solidifying influence in group life, fraternalists have employed certain ceremonial devices the obvious purpose of which is to further the cohesiveness of the group."

37. Chivers changed "conceal" to "reveal." Gist, "Secret Societies," p. 93: "The most conspicuous aspect of the ritualistic obligation, as noted above, is the formal promise to keep inviolate the
secrets of the order. . . . The candidate must not write, print, or impart verbally any of the secrets
relating to passwords, ritual, or other secret features. These are the supreme taboos of secret
fraternalism. To make them more compulsive for religious-minded persons the name of the deity
is usually associated with the obligation, the candidate promising 'in the presence of Almighty
God' to conceal the secrets."

38. A. M. Hocart, "Etiquette," in *Encyclopaedia of the Social Sciences* 5:615: "Etiquette is the
body of forms of conventional decorum into which one's behavior is cast. In the western world
etiquette is inculcated at such an early age that it becomes automatic and is therefore often mistaken for a reflex expression of emotions. Thus, standing to show respect is thought to be instinctive until peoples are found who show respect by sitting. Reflex manifestations of emotion, such
as smiling, are invariable. Variable expressions of the same feeling are determined by conventions, most of which can be traced to ritual. Since ritual centers around divinity, so does etiquette. . . . Etiquette often consists in practices arising from the belief that the superior equals
a god."

etiquette is social ritual, and when we give words of thanks, or remove our hats we are indulging in ritualistic practices.

The other aspects of secular ritual which will not be discussed in detail are: saluting the flag, singing school songs, and observing national holidays. Because these are not discussed they must not be considered unimportant; in institutional research they are very important.

Throughout this whole discussion, ritual has appeared to be something stable. Although ritual displays an extraordinary stability, its nature is of course not absolutely rigid; it grows, alters, and decays. Ritual change can be attributed to two things. First, the element of migration; secondly, the element of strong individualism. The whole course of ritual evolution is affected by the constant borrowings of races and creeds from on another, and the ever present tendency to develope new forms from old. Moreover, the individualism of strong men has had a very decided influence upon the simplification, or total or partial destruction of ritual. A good example of this can be found in Dr. Harry Emerson Fosdick who, in his church, puts little or no emphasis on the ritualistic aspects of religion.[39] The more educated individuals become the less formal and ritualistic they become.

The conclusion I have thus reached deductively from a consideration of the fundamental ideas of sacred and secular ritual is very interesting. First, the most striking thing about ritual, both in the secular and sacred realm, is the precision with which it is observed. In many instances it becomes the be-all and end-all of all social occasions. Moreover, {ritual is looked upon as an end within itself} rather than a means to an end. Too often do individuals think the complete task is finish when they attend Mass, take all sacraments, or, in short observe all rituals. But real

---

39. Harry Emerson Fosdick (1878–1969) was a liberal Baptist preacher who studied at Colgate University, Union Theological Seminary, and Columbia University. As pastor of First Presbyterian Church in New York City, he achieved national prominence in the 1920s by challenging fundamentalism. In 1925, Fosdick became pastor of Park Avenue Baptist Church, which became the nondenominational Riverside Church in 1930. As pastor of Riverside Church, professor of practical theology at Union Seminary, and a prolific author, Fosdick was one of Protestant liberalism's most influential voices for four decades. See his autobiography, *The Living of These Days* (New York: Harper, 1956), and Robert Moats Miller's biography, *Harry Emerson Fosdick: Preacher, Pastor, Prophet* (New York: Oxford University Press, 1985).

religion goes beyond a form of ritual; that is, it is not to end in recitation of prayers, offering of sacrifice and other outward ceremonies. Its aim is to please the deity, and if the deity is one who delights in charity and mercy and purity more than the singing of hymns, and the burning of candles, his worshippers will best please him, not by bowing before him, and by filling the church with costly gifts, but by being pure and charitable toward men.

On the other hand I noticed that ritual is a form of control. It must be remembered that all ritual is not propitiation.[40] As one says, "ceremonies are the bond that holds the multitude together, and if the bond be removed, those multitude falls into confusion." The recognition of a new-born child, the emancipation of slaves, the inheritance of property, marriage, adoption, initiation, installation of officers, ordination and treaty—these have this in common, that they bind somebody to do for others, for the family, or for the group at large, what hitherto has not been laid upon him.

Thirdly, I noticed that ritual is solomn. It serves, not only to be remembered, but to leave a moral impress. A coronation or a ring as giver in marriage, as a miniature drama intended to produce an effect upon the feeling of the person who receives it.

What can we conclude to be the overall concept of ritual? It serves to stimulate the imagination by certain picturesque, dramatic actions, and words which calls up the conception of something larger in power, life or numbers than the here and now—God, society, the dead, or the unborn.

Selected Bibliography

Books

Blackwood, Beatrice Both Sides of Buka Passage,
1935
Frazer Golden Bough, 2nd ed. II
Hardman, C. A History of Christian Worship
Nashville, Tenn. Cokesbury press 1937

---

40. Chivers commented, "Not mentioned previously."

Feb   Herskoirts, M. <u>Life In A Haitian Valley</u> New York,
1948   1937
          Lang, Andrew <u>Magic and Religion</u>, London New
              York: 1907

                              Articles

          Cressman "Ritual the Conserver" <u>American Journal
              of Sociology</u> XXXV, 1929
          Gist, N. P. "Secret Societies" <u>The University of
              Missouri Studies</u> XV 1940
          Seligman & Johnson "Ritual" <u>Encyclopedia Of Social
              Sciences</u> XIII[41]
          Simmel, George "The Sociology of Secrecy"
              <u>American Journal of Sociology</u>, XI 1946

          THDS. MLKP-MBU: Box 113, folder 19.

---

41. Chivers wrote question marks in the margin by the first three articles and "Incomplete" at the end of the bibliography.

Application for Admission
to Crozer Theological Seminary

[*February 1948*]
[*Atlanta, Ga.*]

*Shortly after his nineteenth birthday, King applied for admission to Crozer
Theological Seminary. His application indicates the date of his joining the church
(1 May 1936), the date of his early decision to enter the ministry (summer of
1944), and his various student activities at Morehouse College. As character
references King lists George D. Kelsey, Morehouse professor of religion; Lucius M.
Tobin, chaplain at Morehouse; Benjamin E. Mays, Morehouse president; John
Burney and Phoebe Burney, members of Ebenezer Baptist Church; and his father.*

TO THE FACULTY OF
CROZER THEOLOGICAL SEMINARY,
CHESTER, PA.

GENTLEMEN:

HAVING FILLED OUT TO THE BEST OF MY ABILITY THE QUESTIONNAIRE THAT
YOU FORWARDED ME AT MY OWN REQUEST, I HEREBY MAKE APPLICATION FOR

142

ADMISSION TO CROZER THEOLOGICAL SEMINARY FOR THE ACADEMIC YEAR BEGIN-   Feb
NING **Sept. 1948.**   1948

SIGNATURE   [*signed*] **M. L. King Jr.**
DATE OF APPLICATION

ACCOMPANYING THIS APPLICATION THERE SHOULD BE:
1. A SMALL UNMOUNTED PHOTOGRAPH.
2. TRANSCRIPT OF COMPLETE COLLEGE AND GRADUATE WORK.
3. A MEDICAL CERTIFICATE OF HEALTH.
4. A LICENSE TO PREACH FROM THE LOCAL HOME CHURCH, OR A RECOMMEN-
   DATION TO STUDY FOR THE MINISTRY FROM THE HOME CHURCH OR A COPY
   OF THE CERTIFICATE OF ORDINATION.

SOME OF THE QUESTIONS BELOW ARE OF A PECULIARLY PERSONAL NATURE, BUT
FRANK ANSWERS ARE SOLICITED SO THAT THE STUDENT MAY BE THE MORE INTEL-
LIGENTLY GUIDED. NATURALLY, ANSWERS TO SUCH QUESTIONS ARE REGARDED AS
STRICTLY CONFIDENTIAL.

I. PERSONAL AND FAMILY HISTORY OF THE APPLICANT:
NAME IN FULL   **Martin Luther King Jr**
PERMANENT ADDRESS   **193 Boulevard N. E.**
PRESENT ADDRESS   **Same**
PLACE OF BIRTH   **Atlanta, Ga.**   DATE   **1–15–29**   RACE   **Negro**
   NATIONALITY   **American**
FATHER'S NAME   **M. L. King Sr.**
   RACE   **Negro**   NATIONALITY   **American**
   EDUCATION   **Graduate of Morehouse**   OCCUPATION   **Minister**
   RELIGIOUS INTERESTS AND ACTIVITIES   **Pastor**
MOTHER'S MAIDEN NAME   **Alberta Williams**
   RACE   **Negro**   NATIONALITY   **American**
   EDUCATION   **Graduate of Spelman College**
   RELIGIOUS INTERESTS   **Minister of Music in Church**
ARE YOU MARRIED?   **No**   IF SO, GIVE WIFE'S MAIDEN NAME
   WIFE'S EDUCATION
   WIFE'S BUSINESS EXPERIENCE   **Teaching**
   GENERAL STATE OF HEALTH
   CHILDREN, IF ANY, NAMES   AGES

II. GENERAL PHYSICAL CONDITION OF THE APPLICANT:
HEIGHT **5'7"**   WEIGHT **150**
HAVE YOU EVER HAD A PROLONGED SICKNESS? **No**   GIVE DETAILS
HAS NERVOUS CONDITION EVER INTERFERED WITH YOUR BUSINESS OR WITH
STUDIES? **No**
IF SO GIVE DETAILS
HAVE YOU ANY PHYSICAL DISABILITIES THAT MIGHT INTERFERE WITH AN EFFEC-
TIVE MINISTRY? **No**
IF SO GIVE DETAILS
GIVE LATEST DATES OF INOCULATION FOR VARIOUS PREVENTABLE DISEASES

143

III. RELIGIOUS ACTIVITIES AND INTERESTS OF THE APPLICANT:
DATE WHEN YOU JOINED THE CHURCH   **May 1ˢᵗ 1936**
PLACE   **Atlanta, Ga.**   DENOMINATION   **Baptist**
MEMBERSHIP IN OTHER CHURCHES
PRESENT CHURCH MEMBERSHIP   **Ebenezer Baptist**
SPECIFY ACTIVITIES IN VARIOUS RELIGIOUS ORGANIZATIONS
OFFICES HELD IN SUCH ORGANIZATIONS
ARE YOU LICENSED OR ORDAINED?   **Yes, I am licensed**
GIVE YOUR PERSONAL REASONS FOR THE DECISION TO STUDY FOR THE GOSPEL
MINISTRY   **My call to the ministry was quite different from most explinations Ive heard. This dicision came about in the summer of 1944 when I felt an inescapable urge to serve society. In short, I felt a sense of responsibility which I could not escape.**

IV. EDUCATIONAL ATTAINMENTS OF THE APPLICANT:
HIGH SCHOOL ATTENDED   **Booker Washington High**
YEAR OF ENTRANCE   **1942**   DATE OF GRADUATION   **1944**
COLLEGE OR UNIVERSITY: YEAR OF ENTRANCE   **1944**   DEGREES   YEAR
THEOLOGICAL SEMINARIES: YEAR OF ENTRANCE
EXPLANATION OF FAILURES IN ANY COURSES IN ANY OF THE ABOVE
INDICATE COLLEGE HONORS
STUDIES MAJORED IN DURING COLLEGE OR UNIVERSITY WORK   **Sociology**
SPECIAL INTELLECTUAL INTERESTS
EXTRA-CURRICULAR ACTIVITIES IN COLLEGE IN WHICH YOU WERE INTERESTED
Member of Glee Club—Student council—minister's union—basketball and track teams—debating team—President of sociology club.

The transcript will be [*strikeout illegible*] **sent by the school.**

V. PRACTICAL EXPERIENCE OF THE APPLICANT:
WHAT BUSINESS EXPERIENCE HAVE YOU HAD?   **None**
WHAT TEACHING EXPERIENCE?   **None**
WHAT EXPERIENCE IN PREACHING OR IN OTHER TYPES OF RELIGIOUS LEADERSHIP   **I have served as assistant to my father for six months**
INDICATE THE TYPE OF RELIGIOUS WORK TO WHICH AT THE PRESENT TIME YOU ARE MOST ATTRACTED

VI. FINANCIAL CONSIDERATIONS:
DID YOU PERSONALLY FINANCE YOUR WAY THROUGH COLLEGE?   **No**
HAVE YOU ANY FINANCIAL OBLIGATION OTHER THAN THOSE OF THE CURRENT, PERSONAL TYPE? IF SO INDICATE   **No**
CAN YOU FINANCE YOURSELF IN WHOLE OR IN PART DURING YOUR SEMINARY STUDIES?   **In ~~part~~ {whole}**
IF NOT, CAN YOU ARRANGE FOR AID FROM PRIVATE SOURCES?
ESTIMATE THE POSSIBILITIES AND IF NECESSARY INDICATE YOUR FINANCIAL NEEDS AS NEARLY AS POSSIBLE

VII. AS PERSONAL CHARACTER REFERENCES, PLEASE FILL OUT THE NAME AND ADDRESS OF:

NAME   ADDRESS

1. A PROFESSOR OF YOUR COLLEGE   **Dr. George Kelsey—Morehouse College**   Feb
2. YOUR PASTOR, OR PASTORS   **Rev. L. M. Tobin—**   " " "   1948
3. SECRETARY OF YOUR STATE MISSION BOARD   **Pres. B. E. Mays** " " "
   {Dr. Benjamin Mays Morehouse College, Atlanta, Ga.}
4. **Dr. John Burney 434 Houston St. N.E. Atlanta, Ga.**
5. **Dean Phoeby Burney Clark College Atlanta, Ga.**
6. **Rev. M. L. King Sr. 193 Boulevard N.E. Atlanta, Ga.**[1]
7.

THE FACULTY OF CROZER THEOLOGICAL SEMINARY WILL MEET TO CONSIDER
APPLICANTS FOR ADMISSION AND FOR STUDENT-AID FOR THE FOLLOWING ACA-
DEMIC YEAR. APPLICATIONS WILL BE TAKEN UP IN THE ORDER IN WHICH THEY
ARE RECEIVED. WE DESIRE SEVEN REFERENCES WITH WHOM WE MAY CORRESPOND.
YOU WILL GIVE THE NAMES OF A PROFESSOR OF YOUR COLLEGE, YOUR PASTOR,
AND FIVE OTHERS. WE SUGGEST THE PRESIDENT OF YOUR COLLEGE, LAY LEADERS
IN YOUR CHURCH, OR OTHERS WHO KNOW OF YOU AND YOUR WORK WELL ENOUGH
TO GIVE A SATISFACTORY APPRAISAL OF YOUR CHARACTER AND ABILITY.

AFmS. CRO-NRCR.

---

1. All six names were marked with a check by an unknown person.

APPLICATION FOR ADMISSION

TO

Crozer Theological Seminary

To the Faculty of
Crozer Theological Seminary,
Chester, Pa.

Gentlemen:

Having filled out to the best of my ability the questionnaire that you forwarded me at my own request, I hereby make application for admission to Crozer Theological Seminary for the academic year beginning *Sept. 1948*

Signature *M. L. King Jr.*

Date of Application _____

Accompanying this application there should be:

1. A small unmounted photograph.
2. Transcript of complete college and graduate work.
3. A medical certificate of health.
4. A license to preach from the local home church, or a recommendation to study for the ministry from the home church or a copy of the certificate of ordination.

Some of the questions below are of a peculiarly personal nature, but frank answers are solicited so that the student may be the more intelligently guided. Naturally, answers to such questions are regarded as strictly confidential.

I. Personal and family history of the applicant:

Name in full *Martin Luther King Jr.*

Permanent address *193 Boulevard N.E.*

Present address *Same*

Place of birth *Atlanta, Ga.* Date *1-15-29* Race *Negro* Nationality *American*

Father's name *M. L. King Sr.* Race *Negro* Nationality *American*

Education *Graduate of Morehouse College* Occupation *Minister*

Religious interests and activities *Pastor*

Mother's maiden name *Alberta Williams* Race *Negro* Nationality *American*

Education *Graduate of Spelman College* Religious interests *Minister Of Music in Church*

Are you married? *No* If so, give wife's maiden name

Wife's education

Wife's Business experience _____ Teaching

General state of health

Children, if any, Names _____ Ages

II. General physical condition of the applicant:

Height *5' 7"* Weight *150*

Have you ever had a prolonged sickness? *No* Give details

Has nervous condition ever interfered with your business or with studies? *No*

If so give details

Have you any physical disabilities that might interfere with an effective ministry? *No*

If so give details

Give latest dates of inoculation for various preventable diseases

III. Religious activities and interests of the applicant:

Date when you joined the Church *May 1ˢᵗ 1936*

Place *Atlanta, Ga.* Denomination *Baptist*

Membership in other churches

Present church membership *Ebenezer Baptist*

Specify activities in various religious organizations

Offices held in such organizations

Are you licensed or ordained? *Yes, I am licensed*

Give your personal reasons for the decision to study for the Gospel Ministry *My call to the ministry was quite different from most applications I've heard. The decision came about in the summer of 1944 when I felt an inescapable urge to serve society. In short, I felt a sense of responsibility which I could not escape*

IV. Educational attainments of the applicant:

High School attended *Booker Washington High*

Year of entrance *1942* Date of graduation *1944*

College or University: year of entrance *1944* Degrees _____ Year _____

Theological Seminaries: year of entrance

Explanation of failures in any courses in any of the above

Indicate college honors

Studies majored in during college or university work *Sociology*

Special intellectual interests

Extra-curricular activities in college in which you were interested *Member of Glee Club – Student council – minister's union – Basketball and track team – debating team – President of sociology club.*

The transcript will be ~~not~~ sent by the school.

V. Practical experience of the applicant:

What business experience have you had? *None*

What teaching experience? *None*

What experience in preaching or in other types of religious leadership *I have served as assistant to my father for six months*

Indicate the type of religious work to which at the present time you are most attracted

VI. Financial Considerations:

Did you personally finance your way through college? *No*

Have you any financial obligation other than those of the current, personal type? If so indicate *No*

Can you finance yourself in whole or in part during your Seminary studies?

If not, can you arrange for aid from private sources?

Estimate the possibilities and if necessary indicate your financial needs as nearly as possible

VII. As personal character references, please fill out the name and address of:

Name   Address

1. A professor of your college *Dr. George Kelsey — Morehouse College*
2. Your pastor, or pastors *Rev. L. M. Tobit — " " "*
3. Secretary of your State Mission Board *Pres. B. E. Mays " " "*
4. *Dr. John Burney 434 Houston St. N. E. Atlanta, Ga.*
5. *Dean Phoebe Burney Clark College Atlanta, Ga.*
6. *Rev. M. L. King Jr. 193 Boulevard N.E. Atlanta, Ga.*
7. *Dr. Benjamin Mays, Morehouse College, Atlanta, Ga.*

The Faculty of Crozer Theological Seminary will meet to consider applicants for admission and for student-aid for the following academic year. Applications will be taken up in the order in which they are received. We desire seven references with whom we may correspond. You will give the names of a professor of your college, your pastor, and five others. We suggest the president of your college, lay leaders in your church, or others who know of you and your work well enough to give a satisfactory appraisal of your character and ability.

Certification of Minister's
License for Martin Luther King, Jr.

4 February 1948
Atlanta, Ga.

*Lillian Watkins, the secretary at Ebenezer Baptist Church, sent this brief letter to
Crozer Theological Seminary to verify King's status as a licensed minister as
requested in the application. Watkins states that King is to be ordained on 18
February 1948, but in his letter of 5 March recommending his son to Crozer,
King, Sr., notes that the ordination was on 25 February.*

To Whom it may Concer:

This is to certify that Martin Luther King, Jr., is a lincensed Minister, by
vote of Ebenezer Baptist Church, Atlanta Georgia.
He will be ordained Wednesday February 18th, 1948.

[*signed as below*]
Lillian D. Watkins

TLS. CRO-NRCR.

From Charles E. Batten

18 February 1948

My Dear Mr. King:

I was very happy to receive your application for admission to the Crozer
Theological Seminary together with the material enclosed with it. Your transcript has arrived. As soon as I hear from your references, I shall let you know
officially concerning your admission to Crozer. I trust everything will work
out satisfactorialy for you to be a student with us.
With all good wishes, I am

Sincerely,
Charles E. Batten

CEB:w

Mr. Martin L. King, Jr.
193 Boulevard N.E.
Atlanta, Georgia

TLc. CRO-NRCR.

25 February 1948
Atlanta, Ga.

Lucius M. Tobin, professor of religion at Morehouse and pastor of Providence Baptist Church in Atlanta, recommends King to Crozer Theological Seminary. Tobin was a close family friend who served on the committee for King's ordination at Ebenezer Baptist Church on the day that this letter was written.[1]

Mr. Charles E. Batten, Dean
Crozer Theological Seminary
Chester, Pa.

Sir.—

I am happy to recommend Martin L. King as a prospective student at Crozer. The applicant has not been in my class at Morehouse. I am informed that he is a little above the average in scholarship. In personality and ability he shows promise for the ministry. Mr King comes from a fine family. His father is one of the most progressive pastors in the city of Atlanta. Mr King has had some experience in working with him. I do not hesitate in saying that he should do well in the ministry, once he has had the type of training given at Crozer.

I tried to persuade him to enter Colgate-Rochester, my school. I am glad he has chosen Crozer for which I have the highest respect.

I am sure you will get his academic standing from the registrar's office of Morehouse College.

Sincerely yours
[*signed as below*]
L. M. Tobin

TLS. CRO-NRCR.

---

1. Lucius M. Tobin (1898–1984) was a native of Greenville, South Carolina, and valedictorian of his graduating class at Virginia Union University in 1923. He earned an M.A. in sociology at the University of Michigan in 1928 and a B.D. at Colgate-Rochester Divinity School in 1938. In 1944 he became pastor of Atlanta's Providence Baptist Church and a member of the philosophy and religion department at Morehouse College. He taught at Morehouse until 1954 and served as pastor at Providence until 1969.

Benjamin Elijah Mays to Charles E. Batten

28 February 1948
Atlanta, Ga.

*Benjamin E. Mays, president of Morehouse,[1] is restrained in his assessment of
King but nevertheless recommends King to Crozer, along with another student
whose name the depository has deleted from the document for reasons of privacy. In
his autobiography, Mays indicates a relationship with King closer than that
suggested in this letter, mentioning "a real friendship which was strengthened
by visits in his home and by fairly frequent chats on the campus and in my office.
Many times, during his four years at Morehouse, he would linger after my
Tuesday morning address to discuss some point I had made—usually with
approval, but sometimes questioning or disagreeing." Responding to King's later
description of him as a "spiritual mentor," Mays remarked that he had not been
aware of the extent of his influence on King as a student. After King completed his
doctorate, Mays offered him a faculty position at Morehouse College, and during
the 1960s he convinced King to teach part-time at his institution.[2]*

Mr. Charles E. Batten
Crozer Theological Seminary
Chester, Pennsylvania

Dear Mr. Batten:

I want to endorse the applications for both Martin L. King, Jr. and [*name deleted*]. I have no reservations in recommending these two men. Both of them
should graduate from Morehouse College in June. They are men of good integrity; they adjust well, and I believe, that they would do a good job at Crozer.

You will see from their records that they are not brilliant students, but they
both have good minds. I believe they have academic averages around B−,
certainly between C and B. I am of the opinion that they both can do substan-

---

1. Benjamin Elijah Mays (1894–1984) earned his A.B. in 1920 from Bates College and his
M.A. in 1925 and Ph.D. in 1935 from the University of Chicago. After teaching at Morehouse
College from 1921 to 1924, Mays served on the faculty of South Carolina State College. In 1934,
he became dean of the School of Religion at Howard University in Washington, D.C. In 1940,
Mays was appointed president of Morehouse, where he served for more than thirty years. He
was the author of *The Negro's God* (1938), *Seeking to Be Christian in Race Relations* (1946), *A Gospel
for the Social Awakening* (1950), *Born to Rebel* (1971), and *Lord, the People Have Driven Me On* (1981).

2. Benjamin E. Mays, *Born to Rebel* (New York: Scribner, 1971), pp. 265, 266. King, Sr., states
that Mays's "inspirational messages at Morehouse chapel services" influenced King, Jr.'s decision
to enter the ministry. See Martin Luther King, Sr., with Clayton Riley, *Daddy King: An Autobiography* (New York: William Morrow, 1980), p. 140.

tial B work and with good competition, they may do even better. I hope you will see your way clear to accept them.

Sincerely yours,
[*signed as below*]
Benjamin E. Mays
President

M/H

TLS. CRO-NRCR.

Martin Luther King, Sr., to Charles E. Batten

5 March 1948
Atlanta, Ga.

King, Sr.'s letter of recommendation to Crozer speaks highly of his son's abilities and achievements: entering college at the age of fifteen and being ordained and appointed associate pastor of Ebenezer Baptist Church at eighteen. He mentions Mays, professor of philosophy Samuel Williams, and professor of religion Lucius M. Tobin who knew King, Jr., as a student at Morehouse. The Reverend Leander Asbury Pinkston, an alumnus of Morehouse and pastor of Atlanta's Traveler's Rest Baptist Church, served as president of the General Missionary Baptist Convention of Georgia from 1937 to 1959.

Crozer Theological Seminary
Chester, Pa.

Dean Charles E. Batten,

In reply to your letter relative to Martin Luther King, Jr. He is completing his college work at Morehouse in June. He entered college at the age of 15, is a good student and very conscientious in his work.

In my opinion he is above his age in thought. In fact he has always been a very steady child, quite scholarly. From childhood he always wanted {to} possess scholarship.

He was licensed to preach June 1947, and was voted Associate Pastor in the Ebenezer Baptist Church. He was ordained February 25th 1948. Serving on the council were Dr. B. E. Mays, President Morehouse College, Reverends Samuel Williams, L. M. Tobin, Morehouse and Dr. L. A. Pinkston, Pres. State Baptist Convention of Georgia, and several of our local pastors. This is stated merely as a suggestive background of his christian ministry.

He possesses a very pleasing personality, makes and holds friends easily, among youth and adults. I am

very truly yours,
[*signed as below*]
M. L. King, Sr

K/w

TLS. CRO-NRCR.

Phoebe Burney to Charles E. Batten

9 March 1948
Atlanta, Ga.

Phoebe Burney, dean of women at Clark College, was a longtime friend of the King family and a member of Ebenezer Baptist Church. In 1955, King invited her to be the women's day speaker at Dexter Avenue Baptist Church.

Mr. Charles E. Batten, Dean
Crozer Theological Seminary
Chester, Pennsylvania

Dear Mr. Batten:

In reply to your inquiry concerning Martin Luther King, Jr., 193 Boulevard, N.E., Atlanta, Georgia, I am glad to be able to vouch for his mental ability, moral stamina and apparent sincerity in efforts expressive of the course, The Ministry, which he has chosen.

He is a hard worker, clear thinker, persistent searcher after the truth in any situation. I have seen him grow from home to school, college, community and finally to aid his father as Pastor's Assistant in Ebenezer Baptist Church, one of the largest fellowships in this city.

I feel he is deserving of consideration in his request for admission to Crozer Theological Seminary.

Sincerely yours,
[*signed*] Phoebe Burney
Mrs. John W. Burney
Dean of Women

/mdl

TLS. CRO-NRCR.

12 March 1948
Atlanta, Ga.

As professor of religion and director of the Morehouse School of Religion, George D. Kelsey recommends King for admission to Crozer.[1] King had earned his only A as an undergraduate in the second semester of Kelsey's Introduction to the Bible, which focused on the "strenuous" ethical teachings of Jesus. Although Kelsey concedes shortcomings in King's academic record, years later he remembered that King "stood out in class not simply academically, but in the sense that he absorbed Jesus' teachings with his whole being."[2] Keeping in touch by letter and telephone over the years, King would seek Kelsey's advice on chapters of Stride Toward Freedom.

Mr. Charles E. Batten, Dean
Crozer Theological Seminary
Chester, Pennsylvania

Dear Mr. Batten:

The academic record of Martin Luther King, Jr. in Morehouse College is short of what may be called "good;" but I recommend that you give his application serious consideration. King is one of those boys who came to realize the value of scholarship late in his college career. His ability exceeds his record at Morehouse, and I believe his present attitude will lift his achievement to the level of his ability.

He impresses me as being quite serious about the ministry and as having a call rather than a professional urge. His record as a citizen in Morehouse is good. He gets along well with people, is friendly and courteous.

Yours sincerely,
[*signed as below*]
George D. Kelsey, Director
SCHOOL OF RELIGION

TLS. CRO-NRCR.

---

1. George Dennis Sale Kelsey (1910–) received his A.B. from Morehouse College in 1934, his B.D. from Andover-Newton Theological School in 1937, and his Ph.D. in 1946 from Yale University. He taught religion and philosophy at Morehouse from 1938 to 1948 and served as a visiting professor at Gammon Theological Seminary. From 1945 to 1948, he was also director of the Morehouse School of Religion. After leaving Morehouse, Kelsey was employed by the National Council of Churches from 1948 to 1952 as associate director of the field department. In 1952 he joined the faculty at Drew University. Kelsey's books include *Racism and the Christian Understanding of Man* (1965).

2. Renee D. Turner, "Remembering the Young King," *Ebony* 43 (January 1988): 44.

Brailsford R. Brazeal to Charles E. Batten

23 March 1948
Atlanta, Ga.

*Brazeal, dean of men at Morehouse College, notes that King and another student
(whose name was deleted for reasons of privacy) have "developed considerably" as
undergraduates and that they will "mix well interracially."*[1]

Dean Charles E. Batten
Crozer Theological Seminary
Chester, Pennsylvania

Dear Dean Batten:

Your letter to President B. E. Mays about Mr. M. L. King and [*name deleted*]
who are seniors at Morehouse College has been referred to my office for consideration because Dr. Mays is out of the city.

I regret that I can not at the moment let you know just where Messrs. King
and [*name deleted*] rank in relationship to the other members of the senior class
because we are not able to compile the list until the end of the present semester. We have checked on the record of each one of the men involved. Mr.
King has a quality point average of 2.48 which is virtually midway between a
"C" and a "B" average. [*sentence deleted*] I might state that these two young
men have developed considerably since beginning their studies at Morehouse
College. They had to work hard in order to overcome a comparatively weak
high school background. I believe that Mr. King has succeeded in doing this
to a slightly greater degree than has [*name deleted*]. I believe that these young
men will be able to take care of themselves scholastically and otherwise if they
are given a chance to study at Crozer Theological Seminary, and I also believe
that they will mix well interracially.

---

1. Brailsford Reese Brazeal (1905–1981) received his B.A. from Morehouse College, graduating with honors in 1927. He earned an M.A. from Columbia University and became academic
dean and professor of economics at Morehouse in 1928. After he received his Ph.D. in economics
from Columbia in 1942, Brazeal revised his dissertation for publication as *The Brotherhood of
Sleeping Car Porters* (1946). King took one of Brazeal's courses at Morehouse, Freshman Lectures,
in his first year, 20 September 1944–4 June 1945. As a Morehouse student, he participated
in the Atlanta chapter of a Georgia interracial student group that Brazeal had helped organize in 1926 or 1927. See Brailsford Brazeal, interview by Judy Barton, 16 February 1972,
MLK/OH-GAMK.

I am glad to recommend these applicants for the serious and favorable consideration of the Committee on Admissions. If you desire additional information about these young men please let me know.

With every kind wish, I am

Yours sincerely,
[*signed as below*]
B. R. Brazeal

BRB/g

TLS. CRO-NRCR.

Charles E. Batten's Notes
on Martin Luther King, Jr.'s
Academic Record at Morehouse College

[*23 March 1948*]

Using information from Brazeal's letter of 23 March and King's transcripts,
Batten summarizes King's academic preparation.

King, Martin L.
Academic average 2.48 between C + B.
Coverage—Good.
   Lacks—Ethics, logic, history of philos.
     has intro. philos.
   History—only hist of civil.
     Church hist.
     But has several soc. sc. courses.

AD. CRO-NRCR.

III

Crozer Years

To Alberta Williams King

[*October 1948*]
[*Chester, Pa.*]

Soon after entering Crozer Theological Seminary, King wrote to his mother recounting experiences from his first months at school. He tells of his difficulty with assignments in Hebrew, probably referring to James Bennett Pritchard's survey course on the Old Testament, one of King's first classes at Crozer. King also reports on his relations with women friends and tells of dining often at the home of J. Pius Barbour, a family friend and pastor at Calvary Baptist Church in Chester, Pennsylvania.

Sunday Night
10:30

Dear Mother,

Your letter was received this morning. I often tell the boys around the campus I have the best mother in the world. You will never know how I appreciate the many kind thing you and daddy are doing for me. So far I have gotten the money (5 dollars) every week.

As to my wanting some clippings from the newspapers, I must answer yes. I wondered why I you hadn't sent many, especially the Atlanta world.

You stated that my letters aren't newsey enough. Well I dont have much news. I never go anywhere much but in these books. Some times the professor comes in class and tells us to read our [*strikeout illegible*] asignments in Hebrew, and that is really hard.

Do you know the girl I used to date at Spelman (Gloria Royster). She is in school at Temple and I have been to see her twice. Also I met a fine chick in Phila who has gone wild over the old boy. Since Barbor told the members of his church that my family was rich, the girls are running me down. Of course, I dont ever think about them I am to busy studying.

I eat dinner at Barbors home quite often. He is full of fun, and he has one of the best minds of anybody I have ever met.

I haven't had time to contact any of your friends up this way. Maybe I will get to it pretty soon.

I hope you will explain to the members why I haven't written any of them. I am going to write a letter to the entire church next week. It should be there by the ~~forth~~ {first} Sunday.

I hear from Christine every week.[1] I try to answer her as regularly as possible. I hope she will somehow get adjusted to that accounting.

---

1. King's sister, Christine, was in the first term of a master's program in education at Columbia University in New York.

Rev. Ray was here Friday at the state convention. He told me to come up anytime I get ready. He is looking for you and dad in November.

Well I guess I must go back to studying. Give everybody my Regards.

Your son
[*signed*] "M. L."

ALS. CKFC.

"Light on the Old Testament from the Ancient Near East"

[*14 September–24 November 1948*]
[*Chester, Pa.*]

Written during King's first semester at Crozer Theological Seminary for James Bennett Pritchard's class on the Old Testament, the topic and content of the essay reflect Pritchard's interests in biblical studies, which was the strength of the seminary's faculty. Pritchard exposed his students to ancient Near Eastern texts, his edition of which secured his professional reputation.[1] Pritchard later recalled: "I do have, of course, vivid memories of [King] in my class in Old Testament and of his interest in the Hebrew Prophets. On a more informal level were the numerous occasions when he came to our home on the campus to stay with our two young daughters when we would be out for the evening. They too came to know and to appreciate him."[2] Pritchard gave the paper a B and commented: "Good conclusion! You must watch spelling, be consistent in your use of caps, etc. You have organized your material in such a way that it is apparent that you have grasped the significance of extra biblical matter for OT study."

With the rise of the science of archaeology many valuable facts have emerged from behind the fog of obscurity into the light of understanding. For years the door of the ancient near east remained locked, and the average mind was content with it being locked; it was content in accepting legendary truth for historical truth. But beginning with the year of 1890 the pendulum of interpretation began swinging

---

1. James Bennett Pritchard (1909–) received an A.B. from Asbury College and a B.D. from Drew University. He earned his Ph.D. at the University of Pennsylvania. He taught biblical studies at Crozer Theological Seminary from 1942 to 1954, at the Church Divinity School of the Pacific from 1954 to 1962, and at the University of Pennsylvania from 1962 to 1978. His major works include *Ancient Near Eastern Texts Relating to the Old Testament* (1950); *The Ancient Near East in Pictures Relating to the Old Testament* (1954); and *Archaeology and the Old Testament* (1958).

2. James B. Pritchard to Coretta Scott King, 22 February 1987, MLKJrP-GAMK.

* According to Wright
and Filson scientific ar-
chaeology did not com-
mence until 1890. See
Wright and Filson. The
Westminster Atlas of the
Bible, (Philadelphia: Westminster Press, 1942),
p. 10.[3]

in another direction.* A group of competent scholars
came on the scene who were both curious and dis-
content. They were not willing to accept those things
which appeared to be mythological and legendary as
historical truths. They dared, in the face of a world
of fundamentalists, to apply the scientific method to
a study of the old testament.[4] IT was these men who
subpoenaed the old testament to appear before the
judgement seat of reason. They realized that if they
wanted to get an objective standard of reference they
would they would have to go beyond the pages of
the old testament into the path that lead to that
locked door.

Fortunately, through numerous excavations and
assiduous decipherings, that door has been opened.
Ever since that time we have been able to get a critical,
unbaised, and scientific light upon the old testament.
No logical thinker can doubt the fact that these archaeological findings are now indispensable to all
concrete study of Hebrew-Christian religion. These
findings have proved to us that there are many striking analogies between the ideas expressed in the Old
Testament and those found in surrounding cultures
of the near east. For an instance the cosmogonic and
theogonic views of the old testament are almost identical with those of Babylonian mythology. This is not
to say that the pentateuch writers sat down and copied these views verbatim. The differences of expression attest to that fact. But after being in contact
with these surrounding cultures and hearing certain
doctrines expressed, it was only natural for some of
these views to become a part of their sub-conscious
minds. When they sat down to write they were expressing consciously that which had dwelled in their
sub-conscious minds.[5]

The present study represents an attempt to apply

---

3. The introductory article in the *Westminster Atlas*, "The Rediscovery of the Biblical World,"
was written by William Foxwell Albright. Pritchard noted, "This is Albright, not Wright and
Filson!"

4. Throughout this paper Pritchard used proofreading marks to indicate that King should
have capitalized the words "old testament" and "near east."

5. King used similar wording in a paper for Morton S. Enslin the following year: "But after
being in contact with these surrounding religions and hearing certain doctrines expressed, it was
only natural for some of these views to become a part of their subconscious minds. When they
sat down to write they were expressing consciously that which had dwelled in their subconscious
minds" ("A Study of Mithraism," 13 September–23 November 1949, p. 212 in this volume).

the scientific method to an analysis of the old testament in the light of these archaeological findings. The plan of this study involves taking successively five socities and relating their powerful influence upon the Old Testament writers. These socities are Sumer, Babylonia, Egypt, Ras Shamra, and Arabia. This study will not deal with the social and economic structure of these socities as such, but more with their literary compositions.

Before we enter the general discussion one question needs to be answered. Why is knowledge of these societies important for old testament study, specifically Mesopotamia? First, Mesopotamia is the locale for the oldest culture and literature known to man. Its literature reached the height that Greek masterpieces reached. The literature of this culture "furnishes new, rich, and unexpected source material to the archaeologist and anthropologist, to the ethnologist and the student of folklore, to the students of the history of religion and of the history of literature."*

* S. N. Kramer, Sumerian Mythology, (Philadelphia: American Philosophical society), p. viii.

Second, the invention or developement of writing was carried out in Mesopotamia. It was this culture which developed the cuneiform system of writing which was later adopted by most of the surrounding cultures.

Third, the study of these cultures of the near east is necessary for a thorough understanding of the Bible. It was the religious and spiritual concepts of these peoples which had profound influence upon the Hebrews and Greeks. Moreover, by way of the Judaeo-Christian religion many of these spiritual and religious concepts have been able to creep into the modern civilized world.[6]

Sumer and the Bible

If you look at a map of Mesopotamia you will observe at the lower end the city of Babylon. South of the city of Babylon lies that great city Sumer,[7] from which its grasping fingers captured, in the fourth millennium before Christ, a cultural dominance which tainted the minds of the entire near east. The in-

---

6. S. N. Kramer, *Sumerian Mythology* (Philadelphia: American Philosophical Society, 1944), p. vii: "Moreover, by way of Judaism, Christianity, and Mohammedanism, not a few of these spiritual and religious concepts have permeated the modern civilized world."

7. Pritchard crossed out "city" and inserted "land."

habitants of this area were a non-Semitic, non Indo-European people. For the moment we will examine the spiritual and religious concepts of these people as revealed in their literature. First let us look into the myths of origins.

The most significant material for the Sumerian conception of the creation of the universe is to be found in the introductory passage of a poem which was entitled, "Gilgamesh, Enkidu, and the Nether World," by Dr. Kramer.* The introductory passage reads as follows:

* Ibid., p. 30

> After heaven had been moved away from
>   earth,
> After earth had been separated from heaven
> After the name of man had been fixed;
>
> After An had carried off heaven,
> After Enlil had carried off earth,
> After Ereshkigal had been carried off into kur
>   as its prise.
>
> After he had set sail, after he had not sail,[8]
> After the father for Kur had set sail
> After Enki for Kur had set sail;
>
> Against the king the small ones it (Kur)
>   hurled,
> Against Enki, the large ones it hurled,
> Its small ones, stones of the hand,
> Its large ones, stones of . . . reeds,
> The keel of the boat of Enki,
> In battle, like the attacking storm overwhelm;[9]
>
> Against Enki, the water at the rear of the boat,
> Like a lion strikes down.[10]

If we analyse this passage we will immediately see that many significant questions remain unanswered. Such question as, from whence did heaven and earth come and who separated heaven and earth? Fortunately, DR. Kramer found the answers to these questins in other texts. Thus the cosmogonic concepts of the Sumerians can be summed up as follows: In the beginning was the primeval sea (Nammu). It is probable that the Sumerians believed that the primeval

---

8. The original line reads: "After he had set sail, after he had set sail."

9. King omits two lines in this stanza without using ellipses: "Against the king, the water at the head of the boat, / Like a wolf devours."

10. Kramer, *Sumerian Mythology*, pp. 37–38.

sea was eternal. The primeval sea begot the cosmic mountain which united heaven (An) and earth (Ki). Heaven (An) and earth (Ki) united giving rise to the air-god Enlil. Enlil, the air-god then separated heaven (An) and earth (Ki).

Now comes the process of organizing the universe. Enlil and Ninlil his wife begot Nammu (the moon-god) who traveled across the sky giving light to the "pitch-dark sky." Also the stars and the planets were scattered out. Nammu and Ningal gave rise to Utu the sun-god. Enlil, the air-god, does all of the organizing of earth. He appoints several minor deities to take care of seeds, cattle, ect.

Finally we come to the creation of man which concludes our study of Sumerian cosmogony and theogony. In short, the creation of man was a result of the combined efforts of the goddess Nammu, the goddess Nimmah, and the god Enki. It is significant to note that these gods fashioned man from clay. Following this creation story there is a detailed description of the purpose of man being created given in the introduction to the myth "Cattle and Grain." Actually man was created to relieve the gods from certain work.

WE can readily see that the most obvious similarity between this version and the Biblical version of creation is that of the creation of man. Although they differ as to the purpose for which man was created, they both agree that man was fashioned from clay. Of course, there are many more similarities existing between these versions, but they will be discussed in more detail when we come to the Babylonian documents (which in turn are based upon Sumerian sources).

The Sumerian deluge story is another interesting myth emerging from Sumerian literature. This story first appears on the fragment of a Sumerian tablet found at Nippur, which is a site north of Shuruppak.*

The poem opens dealing with the creation of men and animals. It goes on to tell how some deity founded five cities: Eridu, Badtibira, Larak, Sippar, and Shuruppak. The poem continues with Ziusudra, the Sumerian Noah, being informed that man would be destroyed. At this time he is appointed to build a large boat in which he would be saved. In the next intelligible part of the poem we find the flood under way. The next time the text is clear we read how Ziusudra receives eternal life. AT this point it is interesting to note that Ziusudra was the tenth antediluvian

* H. V. Hilprecht. The Excavations in Assyria and Babylonia, (1903) pp. 289–568.

king. There may be some correspondence between this tradition of ten antediluvian {kings}, and the Hebrew record of ten patriarchs from Adam to Noah.*

* George A. Barton. Archaeology and the Bible, 7th ed. (1937) p. 320

This, in short, outlines the ancient Sumerian story of the flood. From this we can at least see that the Hebrews were not at all original in their deluge story. This deluge story, like the Sumerian creation story, will be discussed in more detail in the next phase of our study.

Babylonia and the Bible

If you will look at your map again, you will notice in the lower valley of Mesopotamia an area known as Babylonia. This area lies some fifty-five miles south of the present Baghdad. For the moment let us turn to the religious and spiritual concepts of this nation as presented in its literature.

First consider the Babylonian Epic of creation or Enuma Elish ("when above").†[11] When George Smith found among the ruins of King Ashurbanipal's great library at Nineveh an account of this story, he presented certain facts which revolutionized, in a sense, our conception of history. For years the average individual believed that the biblical creation story was an original document. Now there appears on the scene a document which proves conclusively that a creation story of similar content existed in Babylonian mythology, and even beyond that in Sumerian mythology. Let us look into its content.

† Alexander Heidel. The Babylonian Genesis, (1943)

First we must admit that "enuma elish" is not primarily a creation story. Only two of the seven tablets deal with creation. The story is actually a hymn in honor of the Babylonian god, Marduk. The priests, who were responsible for the epic, were trying to prove that Marduk, in defeating Tiamat, became the chief god of the pantheon. Therefore, Babylon was the supreme city since it was the city of Marduk. In other words the epic was more political than religious.‡ Of course, this study is concerned with the cosmogonic and theogonic views growing out of this epic. Therefore, no futher discussion of the object of this epic is necessary.

‡ Alexander Heidel. The Gilgemesh Epic and Old Testament Parallels, (Chicago: University of Chicago Press, 1946). p. 3
{Ibid., p. 3.}

The account opens with the birth of the chief gods,

---

11. Alexander Heidel, *The Babylonian Genesis* (Chicago: University of Chicago Press, 1942), p. 1.

Tiamat (goddess of sea water) and Apsu (god of fresh water). They became the mother and father of all the gods. During the course of time the under gods revolted {against} their parents. Apsu becomming very angry announced his intention of destroying them. The god Ea, becomes aware of the plan, and ends up slaying Apsu. About this time Marduk, the hero of the epic, is born. At the same time Tiamat seems to be gathering a host of under-gods whose bodies are filled with poison. Kingu, one of Tiamat's offspring, is exalted to rule over the entire force of under-gods. At this point the first tablet closes.

Tiamat was now ready to declare war on the gods who were responsible for Apsu's death. After learning of Tiamat's plans the gods became afraid but Marduk volunteered to be their champion. Along with his acceptance as their champion, Marduk requested that he be made the higest god in the pantheon if he killed Tiamat. In tablet three we find the gods in the midst of a banquet discussing the coming war. In tablet four Marduk is found preparing for the war. The epic tells us:

> He made a bow and decreed it as his weapon
> An arrow he caused to ride thereon and fixed
>   the bow cord;
> He lifted up the club and grasped it in his
>   right hand;
> The bow and the quiver he hung on his side.
> The lightning he set before him;
> With a blazing flame he filled his body,
> He made a net to enclose Tiamat within it.

Marduk is now fully prepared to enter war. When Marduk comes before Tiamat he says, "come on let us, me and thee, do battle!" The action opens:

> Tiamat and Marduk, the wisest of the gods
>   took there stands opposite each other.
> They pressed on to the battle, they
>   approached in combat.
> The lord spread out his net and enmeshed
>   her,
> The evil wind following after, he let loose in
>   her face.
> When Tiamat opened her mouth to devour
>   him,
> He drove in the evil wind so that she could not
>   close her lips.
> As the raging winds filled her belly,

Her belly was distended and she opened her
mouth.
He shot off an arrow, it tore her belly,
It cut through her inward parts, it pierced her
heart.
When he had subdued her, he destroyed her
life;
He cast down her carcass and stood upon it.

After finishing this task Marduk captured the other
gods of Tiamat and cast them into prison. Then he
returns to Tiamat,

The lord rested, to look at her body to see,
How he might divide the colossus and create
wondrous things therein.
He split her open like a mussel into two parts;
Half of her he set in place and formed the sky.
He fixed the bar and posted guards;
He commanded them not to let the water
escape.[12]

Now we find Marduk establishing the earth which he
called Esharra. Then he places the gods. Anu occu-
pies the skies, Enlil the air, and Ea the waters underneath the earth. This ends tablet four. The part of
tablet five which remains tells how Marduk set up the
stars and the moon.

In the next tablet comes the creation of man. Here
Marduk slays Kingu, the leader of the gods who
caused all of the strife. With the blood that flowed out
of his arteries the gods fashioned man. IN creating
man the gods were relieved from their work. The
epic closes with Marduk becoming the chief god of
the pantheon.

Obviously there are many interesting similarities between the creation story presented in enuma elish and
that presented in Genesis. The most striking similarities between these two accounts is the order of creation. These similarities may be listed as follows: 1. Both
accounts agree that a divine spirit created the cosmic
matter. 2. Both accounts assume that primeval chaos
consisted of a mass of waters. In both cases the mass of
water has the same name. The Hebrews called it thom
(deep); The Babylonians called it Tiamat (deep).*

* Barton, op. cit., p. 295

---

12. This quotation and the two preceding it are from Heidel, *Babylonian Genesis*, pp. 28–32.

3. In both accounts the fifth event of creation is the creation of dry land. 4. In both accounts the creation of the sun, moon, and stars is the sixth event. 5. In both accounts the creation of man was the seventh event. 6. In both cases the divine spirit (or divine spirits) rested on the day after man was created. From this we can see that the Genesis version and the Babylonian version of creation are well-nigh identical. The important difference lies in the fact that the former is monotheistic and the latter polytheistic.

At this point we may present the comparison between the Hebrew, the Babylonian, and the Sumerian stories dealing with the creation of man. According to the Bible man was made from clay. The purpose of his creation was to have dominion over all other animals. In the Babylonian story man was made of the the blood of one of the troublesome gods who was killed for that purpose. He was created primarily to serve the gods and free them from the need of working for their bread. The Sumerian version, which is older than either version, says that man was made from clay as in the biblical version. The purpose for which he was created was to free the gods from laboring for their sustenance, as in the Babylonian version. So much for enuma elish.

Another Babylonian myth which has given a new light upon the Old Testament is the Gilgamesh Epic. This epic is truely one of the great literary masterpieces of all times. It compares favorably with Homer's Odyssey and other great epics of world history. The part of the epic which interests us most in this study begins with the death of Enkidu, the great friend of Gilgamesh. Gilgamesh ie found lamenting:

> My friend whom I love has become
>   like clay, Enkidu whom I love has become like
>   clay.
> Shall I not sleep like him?
> Shall I rise through all eternity?

His sole interest now lies in finding a method to attain eternal life. He now thinks of Utnapishtim, the Babylonian Noah or the Sumerian Ziusudra, who had received immortal life. We find him undertaking this hazardous journey. As he continues his journey he is told by Ishtar,

> O Gilgamesh, whither runnest thou?
> The life thou seekest thou shalt not find.
> When the gods created mankind,

They alloted death to mankind,
But life they retained in their keeping.
Thou, O Gilgamesh, let thou belly be full;
Day and night be thou merry;
Make every day a day of rejoicing
Day and night do thou dance and play,
Let thou raiment be clean,
Thy head be washed, and thyself be bathed in water.
Cherish the little one holding thy hand,
And let the wife rejoice in thy bosom.
This is the lot of mankind!*

* Alexander Heidel. The Gilgamesh Epic and Old Testament Parallels, (Chicago: University of Chicago Press, 1946). p. 38 [13]

It is significant to note that this passage seems to have a close nexus with Ecclesiastes (9:7–9). The ideas of these two passages are well-nigh identical. Well anyway, Gilgamesh continues his long and arduous journey. At last he reaches Utnapishtim. The question of immortality arises, in which Gilgamesh asks Utnapishtim how he entered company with the gods and obtained everlasting life. Utanapishtim begins:

Shuruppak there is, a city which thou knowest,
Which on the bank of the Euphrates was
    founded.
That city was old and the gods in it
Were moved in their hearts to send the deluge,
    they the great gods.

The story continues telling how the gods reveal their plans to Utnapishtim through the wall of a reed hut. After taking these instructions he builds a huge ark which is 120 cubits or nearly 200 feet on each side. On the boat he loads all the silver and goal and embarkes with his family and relatives. The flood came. The climax of the deluge is pictured:

Six days and six nights
Ranged the wind, the deluge, the hurricane
    devastated the land,[14]
When the seventh day arrived, the hurricane,
    the deluge, the shock of battle was broken
Which had smitten like an army.
The sea became calm, the cyclone died away,
    the deluge ceased.

13. Alexander Heidel, *The Gilgamesh Epic and Old Testament Parallels* (Chicago: University of Chicago Press, 1946), p. 70, rather than p. 38.

14. King's source, S. H. Langdon, capitalized "Deluge" and wrote "raged" rather than "ranged" (*The Mythology of All Races,* vol. 5: *Semitic* [Boston: Marshall Jones Company, 1931]).

I looked upon the sea and the sound of voices ended.
And all mankind had turned to clay.
Like a roof the hedged park was levelled.
I opened a window and a light fell on my cheek.
I kneeled and sat down to weep,
Tears streaming on my cheeks.
I looked on the quarters of the billowing sea.
A region stood out at a distance of twelve double
    hour marches.
The boat touched upon Mount Nisir.
Mount Nisir held it fast and allowed it not to move.

On the seventh day Utnapishtim sent forth a dove
which returned because it could find no resting place.
Following this Utnapishtim is found offering a sacrifice to the gods. Finally Utnapishtim is pictured
kneeling before Enlil receiving these words:

Formerly Utnapishtim was a man
But now Utnapishtim and his wife shall be like
    the gods.
Utnapishtim shall dwell far away at the mouth
    of the rivers.*

* S. H. Langdon. Semitic
Mythology, (Boston: Mar-
shall Jones Press, 1941).
pp. 210–223.

The above account of the deluge so closely resembles the biblical account (Genesis 6:9 to 9:17)
that it hardly needs explination, but for the sake of
accuracy let me briefly list the similarities. 1. In both
accounts there is a desire within the divine powers to
destroy mankind. 2. In both accounts the secret is revealed to a hero. 3. In both accounts a vessel is built
and the family of the hero is taken in. 4. In both accounts all mankind is destroyed. 5. In both accounts
a bird is sent out immediately after the flood. 6. In
both accounts the ark rests on a mountain. 7. In both
accounts the hero makes sacrifices to the divine power
(or divine powers).

Looking at the flood story from an objective angle
we obviously see that the Hebrews have done nothing
but taken a polytheistic picture and placed it in a
monotheistic frame, thereby producing from Babylonian mythology an almost verbatim story.

We turn now to the code of Hammurabi which is
one of the most important monuments in the history
of the human race. Containing as it does the laws
which were enacted by a king of Babylonia in the
third millenium B.C., whose rule extended over the
whole of Mesopotamia from the mouths of the rivers
Tigris and Euphrated to the Mediterranean coast, we

must regard it with interest.[15] The code is significant for the present study because many of the laws of the Bible were taken directly from it.

The code incuuded nearly 300 paragraphs of legal provisions touching all phases of life. Let uu discuss briefly the important provisions of this code. We immediately see that false accusation is grounds for death (#3). Kidnaping and house-breaking were punishable by death (#6, 14, 21). In the case of stealing at a fire, the thief was to be thrown into the fire (#25). There were numerous laws dealing with the duties of soldiers and tax collectors (#26–41). Marriage was legal only when there was a legal contract, of course divorces were permissible (#128–143). In the case of adultery both man and woman would be killed (#129). A married woman was permitted to hold property (#150). If a man caused the death of another man's daughter his oun daughter was to be put to death. Also if a patient died on the operation table the doctor's hand could be cut off (#215–222). Many other things were covered in the code which will not be mentioned here.

Now let us notice some of the similarities between this code and the later Hebrew laws. With the above laws from Hammurabi's code can be compared the following Hebrew laws: A false witness was to be visited with the penalty which he purposed to bring upon his brother (Deut. 19:18, 19).[16] The stealing and selling of a man was a capital offense (Exodus 22:2). Breaking in a house meant death (Exodus 21:16).[17] In the case of adultery both the man and the other man's wife were put to death (Deuteronomy 22:22). This law is identical with that found in Hammurabi's code. Deuteronomy (19:21) states exactly the same priciple of retaliation as found in Hammurabi's code, "eye for eye" and tooth for tooth."*

* C. H. W. Johns. The Oldest code of Laws in the World, (Edinburgh: T. & T. Clark, 1903)[18]

---

15. C. H. W. Johns, *The Oldest Code of Laws in the World* (Edinburgh: T. & T. Clark, 1903), p. v: "The Code of Hammurabi is one of the most important monuments in the history of the human race. Containing as it does the laws which were enacted by a king of Babylonia in the third millennium B.C., whose rule extended over the whole of Mesopotamia from the mouths of the rivers Tigris and Euphrates to the Mediterranean coast, we must regard it with interest."

16. George A. Barton, *Archeology and the Bible*, 6th edition (Philadelphia: American Sunday-School Union, 1933), p. 379: "Hebrew law was similar; a false witness was to be visited with the penalty which he had purposed to bring upon his brother (Deut. 19: 18, 19)."

17. King reversed the citations from Exodus.

18. The references are from pp. 2–47.

The differences between these two systems of law exist because the Hebrews did not have highly organized courts as did the Babylonians. Moreover, the social communities were different. For an instance the institution of slavery was not as firmly established in Israel as it was in Babylonia. The Hebrews had to take these laws and fit them into the framwork of their social order. From this we are almost led to believe that if there had been no differences in the two social orders the two systems of law would have been identical. Of course, Barton would disagree with this opinion, arguring that these similarities did not come about because of a direct borrowing, but because of similar intellectual outlooks.*

* Barton, op. cit., p. 406

If we delve further into Babylonian literature we will find a myth entitled, <u>Adapa</u>, which is strickingly similar to the Biblical story of the fall of man. This story "seems intended to explain the mortality of man as opposed to the immortality of the gods."† The story opens explaining the qualities and functions of Adape, the son of Ea.[20] He was a semi-divine being and a priest of the temple of Ea at Eridu. It was his duty to provide the ritual bread and water for this temple. IN carring out this duty he did quite a bit of fishing. One day while fishing the south wind blew and overturned his boat. Becoming angry because of this event he broke the "wings of the south wind." At this point Anu calls Adape to account for this misdeed. Adape' father immediately warns him what is about to happen and tells him how to gain the pity of Tammuz and Gishzida. He also tells him not to eat the food nor take the drink that would be offered him for it would be the food and drink of death. Of course, Ea was wrong, rather the food and water offered to him were the food and water of life. Therefore, by rejecting it he was deprived of eternal life.

† Hasting, <u>Encyclopaedia of Religion and Ethics,</u> Vol. II (1910) p. 314.[19]

We immediately see that this myth coincides with (Genesis 2 and 3). Let us list the points of comparison: 1. The "food of life" in Adape belongs to the same category as the "tree of life" in Genesis. 2. Both Adapa and Adam had gained knowledge. In both the

---

19. Pritchard asked, "Who wrote the article?" King's reference is to the article "Babylonians and Assyrians" by H. Zimmern.

20. Pritchard corrected King's misspelling of "Adapa" here and in the remainder of the paper.

knowledge was a power which was an attribute of divinity. This knowledge caused Adape to break the wing of the south wind; it tempted Adam and Eve "to become like God, knowing good and evil" (Genesis 3:5). 3. Both were punished for what they did. Adapa was subjected to sickness, disease, and restlessness. Adam was subject to the monotony of toil and his wife, Eve, to the pangs of childbirth. 4. Both were clothed in a special type of clothing as a consequence of their deeds.* This, in short, concludes our study of Babylonia. Now we turn to another great culture of the ancient near east.

* Barton, op. cit. pp. 311–12.

Egypt and the
Old Testament

We now turn to ancient Egypt which was another great center of civilization that left its mark upon the Old Testament. We know that the Hebrews remained in Egypt about four hundred years. It is certainly obvious that they assimilated some of the Egyptian culture during their sojourn there. IN order to get to the roots of Egyptian culture we must dig into its literature. Thus, we will follow this course.

The first phase of Egyptian literature that we will consider here is the composing of proverbs. I think I can be safe in saying that the composing of proverbs were begun in Egypt. One of the first and, to many, the greatest proverb writers to appear on the Egyptian scene was Ptahhotep, who was a grand vizier under a Pharaoh of the fifth dynasty (ca. 2675 B.C. According it other calculations about 2870 B.C.). We find him saying to his son, "Be not arrogant because of thy knowledge and have no confidence in that thou art a learned man. Take counsel with the ignorant as with the wise; for the limits of art cannot be reached, and no artist fully possesseth his skill. A good discourse is more hidden than the precious green stone, and yet it is found with slave girl over the mile-stone." He warns his son that "covetousness is a malady, diseaseful, incurable." He makes it very clear that "he who hath heard becomes a hearer."† Throughout the teachings of Ptahhotep we see many proverbs which are strikingly similar to those found in the Biblical book of Proverbs. It was the greatness of Ptahhotep's proverbs that led Breasted to say, "these maxiams of Ptahhotep constitute the

† Adolf Erman. The Literature of the Ancient Egyptians (1927) pp. 54–65

earliest formulation of right conduct to be found in any literature."*

Another important figure who contributed greatly to Egyptian literature was Amenemope. Like Ptahhotep, he offered sound advice to his son on honesty, integrity, self control and kindness. It was essentially this profound advice that proved to be of lasting influence to the Hebrews. We find striking parallels of Amenemope in Jeremiah, Psalms, and Proverbs. Here is one parallel:

Amenemope	Proverbs (15:16f.)
Better is poverty in the hand of God,	Better is little, with the fear of Jehovah,
Than riches in the storehouse.	Than great treasure and trouble therewith.
Better are loaves when the heart is joyous,	Better is a dinner of herbs, where love is,
Than riches in unhappiness.	Than a stalled ox and hatred therewith.†

This is only one instance of many where there is a direct similarity between the wisdom of Amenemope and Biblical versions.

Before we close our study of Egypt and its relationship to Old Testament literature, we must consider Amenhotep IV (Akhnaton). This interesting character was a king of the eighteenth dynasty (ca 1570–1150 B.C.), who through many lofty ideals became "the first individual of history."‡ His greatest contribution to Egyptian culture was his new idea of God. He introduced solar monotheism at a time when his nation was steeped in the tradition of polytheism. Unfortunately, his monotheism died with him.

Either for the temple service or for personal devotions the king composed two hymns to Aton, which are quite relevant for our present study. The one-hundred-and-fourth Psalms of the Hebrews shows a notable similarity to this hymn both in thought and sequence.[23] Some very interesting phrases which ap-

* J. W. Breasted. The {Dawn} of Conscience, (New York: C. Scribner's sons, 1933). p. 129 [21]

† Breasted, op. cit., pp. 372–378.

‡ J. H. Breasted. A History of Egypt, (New York: C. Scribner's sons, 1905). p. 265. [22]

21. Pritchard noted that the correct initials were "J. H." The quotation from Breasted should read, "the Maxims of Ptahhotep furnish us with the earliest formulation of right conduct to be found in any literature."

22. The correct citation should be p. 356, not p. 265.

23. J. H. Breasted, *A History of Egypt* (New York: Scribner, 1905), p. 371: "The one hundred and fourth Psalm of the Hebrews shows a notable similarity to our hymn both in the thought and the sequence."

pear in Akhnaton and the Bible are: "The earth is in
darkness like death" (cf. Psalm 104:20); "all serpents
they sting" (cf. Psalm 104:21); "thou didst create the
earth according to thy heart" (cf. Psalm 104;24).
From these few examples we are {able} to see the tremendous amount of influence that this hymn had on
the Biblical writers. With these explinations we now
leave Egypt.

Ugarit and the
Old Testament

In 1929 some very important tablets were discovered at a site on the nothern coast of Syria known
as Ras Shamra. The discovery of these tablets was
one of the most important discoveries made in the
near east. They afford us valuable evidence as to
the nature of religion in Syria and Palestine several
centuries before the Israelite monarchy, and also constitute a new revelation for the study of the Old
Testament.[24]

This spot (Raṣ es Shamra) was known in its earlier
history as Ugarit. The town seems to have been in existence well before 2000 B.C., but it didn't rise to importance until the second millenium when the Phoe-
nicians took possession of it.[25]

The language spoken by the Ugaritic people was
Senetic.[26] It was very closely connected to Hebrew.
For this reason Hebrew and Ugaritic poetry are very
similar.

Although the religious ideas of the Bible are quite
different from those found in Ugarit, the former
being monotheistic and the latter being polytheistic,
there are many striking similarities between the two.
For an instance, more than one Ugarit tablet mentions the serpent Leviathan, and the monster is described in exactly the same terms in (Isaiah 27:1).
It is also significant to note that the same two adjec-

---

24. J. W. Jack, *The Ras Shamra Tablets and Their Bearing on the Old Testament* (Edinburgh: T. &
T. Clark, 1935), p. 6: "Their discovery is one of the most important made in the Near East. They
afford us valuable evidence as to the nature of religion in Syria and Palestine several centuries
before the Israelite monarchy, and constitute a new revelation for the study of the Old
Testament."

25. Jack, *Ras Shamra Tablets*, p. 3: "The town seems to have been in existence well before 2000
B.C., . . . but it rose to importance by the beginning of the second millennium when the Phoeni-
cians took possession of it."

26. Pritchard changed "Senetic" to "Semitic."

tives namely "swift" and "crooked" are applied to the Biblical version.* The servant of Aleyn is described as "HE who rides upon the clouds" (cf. Isaiah 19:1). The Biblical verse, "I know my redeemer liveth," can be compared to the Ugarit verse, "I know that Aleyn son of Baal liveth." In Ugarit appears the phrase, "from generation to generation" (cf. Ex. 17:16, Dt. 22:7, Ps. 10:6, Is. 13:20). The Ugaritic phrase, "the dew of heaven, the fat of earth" is found with little change in Genesis 27:28, 29. The Ugaritic phrase, "eat of the tables spread, drink of the jars wine," can be compared to Proverbs 9:5, "eat of my bread, and drink of the wine which I have mingled." At Ugarit wine was called "blood of vines;" in Genesis 49;11, it is called the "blood of grapes."† Other phrases which appear both in Ugaric and the Bible are: "The mount of God" (1 Kings 19:8); "the river of God" (Psalms 46:4); "house of ceder" (2 Sanual 7:2).

Many more similar phrases exist, but these are sufficient to show the intimate relationship between these Syrian tablets and the literature of the Old Testament.[28]

Arabia and the
Old Testament

We come now to the last phase of this study. This phase deals with another area of the ancient near east which had profound influence on the Bible namely, Arabia. A basic core of belief and institutional life came out of this desert. According to Montgomery, "the central nerve of Hebrew religion leads back to Arabia."‡[29] A peculiar touch and atmosphere of Biblical life came from the free moving nomadic life we call Arabia.

Throughout the Old Testament we are aware of an Arabian influence. "The legendary account of the garden of Eden presupposes the scenery of a desert oasis, with its rivers springing up miraculously from

* J. W. Jack. The Ras Shamra tablets and their bearing on the Old Testament, (Edinburgh: T. & T. Clark, 1935). p. 46.

† Cyrus Gordon. The loves and wars of Baal and Anat, (Princeton: Princeton University Press, 1943). p. 8.[27]

‡ James Montgomery. Arabia and the Bible, (Philadelphia: University of Penn. Press, 1934). p. 15.

---

27. The correct citation should be p. xiii.

28. Jack, *Ras Shamra Tablets*, p. 49: "We have said sufficient to show the intimate relationship between these Syrian tablets and the literature of the Old Testament."

29. James Montgomery (*Arabia and the Bible* [Philadelphia: University of Pennsylvania Press, 1934], p. 5) quoted Nielsen, who wrote that "the central nerve of the Hebrew religion leads back to Old-Arabia."

* Montgomery, op. cit.,
p. 3

nowhere and emptying into the desert sands."* In (Genesis 4) we have three classes that appear throughout Arabian history: Jabal, the father of flock keepers; Jubal, the father of minstrels and Tubalcain. Tamechs' taunt song (Genesis 4:23–24) is our earliest example of the Arabian satire.[30] The Israelite journey to the land of Egypt during the time of economic crisis is also typical of Arabian nomads. In the prophetic literature of the Bible the prophets often refer to the nomadic life of their people as a time of pure worship. In the words of Wright and Filson, "the close relation of God and people, as symbolized in the covenant, was Israel's nomadic heritage, and the most important factor saving her from idolatry. These basic elements of patriarchal religious life were idealized in la later Israel and always remained as a purifying agent, not only among such extreamists as the Nazirites and Rechabites, but among the great prophets as well."†

† Filson and Wright, op. cit. p. 5.

There are many characters in the Bible who are full of Arabian characteristics. For an instance Jephthal is more of an Arab than an Israelite. His sacrifice of his daughter is parallel to Arabian tradition. Deborah is a typical Arab in Judges 4 and 5.

From these parallels we obviously see that Arabia had profound influence on the Old Testament. This is not to say that we can explain away Israel's unique conception of God simple by reference to the Arabian Desert, but the contention is that the ideal background of Hebrew religion lay in the desert, not in the scenes of urban civilization, and to that background the prophets constantly appealed.[31]

Conclusion

What now is the conclusion of the whole matter. First, we must conclude that the Old Testament has its roots not only in the history of the Hebrew peo-

---

30. Montgomery, *Arabia and the Bible*, p. 5: "We have three classes that appear all through Arabian history: Jabal the father of such as dwell in tents and have flocks; his brother Jubal, the father of those who handle the harp and pipe; and Tubalcain . . . Lamech's taunt-song, vv. 23–24, is our earliest example of the Arabian Hij'a or battle-satire." Pritchard corrected King's "Tamechs'" to "Lamechs'."

31. Preface to Wright and Filson, *Westminster Atlas*, p. 5: "This does not mean, however, that we can explain away Israel's unique conception of God simply by reference to the Arabian desert or nomadic life. . . . The ideal background of her religion lay in the desert, not in the scenes of urban civilization, and to that background the prophets constantly appealed."

ple. Instead, one must consider the Old Testament in relation to all the ancient civilizations of the near east. Modern archaeology has proven to us that many of the ideas of the Old Testament have their roots in the ideas of surrounding cultures. Many would argue that these archaeological findings have proven to be very pernicious to modern religion. They argue that archaeologists have robbed the Old Testament of any claim to uniqueness. Of course, any logical thinker must believe the contrary. For from attempting to destroy the unefulness of the Old Testament, archaeologist are attempting to give a better understanding of the contents of the Bible. They realize that religion, as for as possible, must be scientifically tenable. It is my opinion that "Biblical criticism" and "Biblical archaeology" will serve to justify the position of the church in modern culture, especially in the face of modern youth who are taught to "weigh and consider."

Second, we must conclude that many of the things which we have accepted as true historical happenings are merely mythological. They are merely modified links connected to the wide chain of mythology. Again this conclusion will shock many. But why so? One needs only know that a myth serves the purpose of getting over an idea that is in the mind of the author. Therefore, it becomes just as valuable as the factual. Dr. Bevan succinctly stated it: "We have documents which record actual historical events with the names of persons who lived and acted more or less in the way described; then, as we follow back the story, we find ourselves in a past with which the real history is apparently continuous, but which is in truth only only a work of imagination, a mythical past set behind [*strikeout illegible*] the historical events and and concealing the real past out of which in actual fact the historical process came."* If we accept the Old Testament as being "true" we will find it full of errors, contradictions, and obvious impossibilities—as that the Pentateuch was written by Moses. But if we accept it as "truth" we will find it to be one of the most logical vehicles of mankind's deepest devotional thoughts and aspirations, couched in language which still retains its original vigour and its moral intensity.

* S. H. Hooke. In the Beginning, (Oxford: Clarendon Press, 1947). p. 149.

THDS. MLKP-MBU: Box 113, folder 19.

"The Significant Contributions
of Jeremiah to Religious Thought"

24 Nov
1948

[*14 September–24 November 1948*]
[*Chester, Pa.*]

*In this paper for Pritchard's course on the Old Testament, King examines
Jeremiah's contributions to religious thought, particularly his New Covenant, his
argument against "artificial worship," and his conception of personal religion.
King interprets Jeremiah's spirituality as a form of "public pietism," which
emphasizes the social responsibility of the prophet, his public exposure, and the
extreme isolation in which he experiences the transforming encounter with the
divine. King concludes by summarizing Jeremiah's message for contemporary
Christianity: "the worst disservice that we as individuals or churches can do is to
become sponsors and supporters of the status quo." Pritchard gave King a B + and
commented at the end: "You have made good use of the commentaries available to
you and have written with enthusiasm in a convincing manner!"*

The peculiar importance of Jeremiah, both as a
man and as an actor in an unique tragedy, is visible
throughout his writings. The personality of Jeremiah
is one of the most fascinating studies in Old Testament history. There is no other of the sacred authors
who has taken us with such intimacy into his life, both
public and private.[1] We not only get the kernal of his
discourses, but we are able to dwell with him in his
moments of disillusionment; we are aware of the "inner conflict between his desire for inconspicuous retirement and his devotion to truth and civil duty;"*
we hear him as he secretly talks with God. His life
and character are full of surprises which stimulate
thought on great moral and religious problems. From
this we must not conclude that the Book of Jeremiah
is infalliable. That book which bears his name is
not orderly arranged, that many dates are not exact,
are all obvious facts to the serious student.[2] But we
should marvel in the fact that so much authentic material about the life and times of this great character
has survived.

Jeremiah came to prophesy at a time which was
ripe for a mighty appeal to be made to the masses and

* R. C. Knox. Knowing
The Bible. (New York:
Macmillan Co., 1936).
p. 99.

---

1. Pritchard asked in the margin, "What is a 'sacred author'?"
2. Pritchard replaced "all" with "both."

to take advantage of the new spirit of the time that had taken hold of Judah. He saw that the wind of pride and evil had become the whirlwind of spiritual desolation. He saw Judah and the moral and spiritual degeneracy into which she had sunk. Isaiah and Micah had raised their voices and gave a tremendous impetus to the revival work of Hezekiah. Zephaniah had done likewise at the beginning of Josiah's reign, and a little before his time. The time had come for another voice to be raised, to sound the note of warning to Judah. It was this great prophet that appeared at the capital and the Temple, whose message sprang from a heart touched with the deepest tenderness. Such was the prophet Jeremiah—such potency, such persuasion, such pleading in pointing out to Judah the way of escape from impending doom.

The Life and Times
of Jeremiah

Jeremiah was born of priestly parentage, toward the middle of the seventh century, in the little town of Anathoth. He prophesied under Josiah and his sons from the year 626 to the fall of Jerusalem in B.C. 587 (1:2f). He was contemporary with four of the ~~minor~~ prophets, Zephaniah, Habakkuk, Ezekiel, Daniel.[3]

As stated above, Jeremiah possessed a dynamic personality. "The Book of Jeremiah," says A. B. Davidson, "does not so much teach religious truths as present a religious personality. Prophecy had already taught its truths; its last effort was to reveal itself in a life."* Jeremiah was above everything a hero of the inner life. His inner experiences can be traced throughout the Book. He was in perpetual pain because of the stubborness of his people (8:18, 21, 22; 15:18), and their tragedy caused his tears to flow day and night (9:1; 10:19). He loved his people with his whole heart (8:18–22; 14:20, 21). This deep love for his own people expressed itself at times in impatience with them, and a desire to escape from them (4:31; 8:21, 22; 9:12). Amid the bewildering changes of his time, Jeremiah was made to realize that he had been marked from his mother's womb for a great errand

* A. B. Davidson. "Jeremiah." In: Hastings, James. Dictionary of the Bible. Vol. II p. 576.[4]

---

3. Pritchard underlined "Daniel" and wrote a question mark in the margin.
4. Pritchard corrected King's footnote to read: "A. B. Davidson. 'Jeremiah,' in Hastings, <u>Dictionary of the Bible</u>, Vol. II, p. 576."

and yet this errand becomes his shame and torture (cf. 1:5 with 15:10; 20:14ff.). Because Jeremiah possessed this mild and peculiarly sensitive disposition, many came to call him "the weeping prophet." It would be a great mistake, however, to suppose that he was lacking in courage. A careful study of the facts will show that he was one of the bravest men in Judah.

What were the conditions of the world during the life of Jeremiah? Stated briefly, the most important events which occured within the life of Jeremiah were these: (1) An invasion by the Scythians (ca. 626 B.C.). (2) The discovery of the Book of the Law (Deuteronomy) in the Temple, and resulting reforms by King Josiah (ca. 621 B.C.). (3) The overthrow of the Assyrians by the Chaldeans (Babylonians), in 612 B.C. (4) Immediately after the fall of Assyria, the armies of Egypt invaded Judah, defeating King Josiah (ca. 608 B.C.). (5) The contest for world supremacy between the Babylonians and the Egyptians. In 605 B.C. the Egyptians were defeated at the battle of Carchemish. Then comes the reign of Nebuchadrezzar. (6) The first attack of Jererusalem in 598 B.C. The entire city falls in 587 B.C.[5]

Such were the conditions that characterized the times of Jeremiah. Only through gaining a thorough knowledge of these moving events will we be able to understand the prophecies of Jeremiah, for prophecies spring out of immediate occasions. The situations they deal with, the personal moods, attitudes and temptations they are meant to meet, are always contemporary.

In this paper there is an attempt to present Jeremiah's contributions to religious thought. In order to keep the study within reasonable limits it has been necessary to confine the analysis to what appears to be the most important points. In this respect I will present three contributions. (1) Prophecies against Unreal Worship. (2) The New Covenant. (3) Personal religion.

The New Covenant

An important element in the teaching of Jeremiah is the establishment of a New Covenant. This

---

5. This list follows that of Raymond C. Knox, *Knowing the Bible* (New York: Macmillan, 1937), pp. 97–98.

prophecy immediately impresses us by the wonderful spirituality of its tone, and by its evangelical character. Dr. Driver laconically states: "By his conception of the New Covenant, Jeremiah surpasses in spirituality and profundity of insight every other prophet of the Old Testament."*

Many recent writers have been reluctant to admit that this prophecy came from Jeremiah. They have raised many critical questions which demand attention. One great objection is brought out by Duhm.[6] He argues that the passage is in prose and a style characteristic of the late expanders of the Book. Of course an outstanding scholar like Skinner has given profound arguments to the contrary.† Even Pfeiffer does not accept the Duhn theory.‡ In this study time will not permit me to discuss the details of this argument either pro or con, but only to say that if the prophecy did not come directly from the mouth of Jeremiah it came through the memory of a reporter of the Prophet, Baruch or another. Therefore, we may still be justified in listing this prophecy as a major contribution of Jeremiah to religious thought.

Jeremiah realized that the covenant made at Mount Sinai had failed to accomplish its purpose. He saw that Israel had become apostate; "they obeyed not, nor inclined their ear, but walked every one in the stubbornness of their evil heart" (11:8; 31:32). This was due to a serious defect inherent in the Old Covenant. Instead of being a spiritual asset it was a snare and a delusion. Instead of leading men to their knees it filled them with foolish presumption, until he strikes out at the priest and scribe and law. (8:8). This rebellion against the Old Covenant came to its climax and crown, when in his later activities the prophet brought forth that noblest of all spiritual conceptions, the New Covenant. The shortcomings of the Old Covenant would be removed in the new. "I will put my law in their inner parts and in their heart will I write it; and I will be their God, and they shall be my people. And they shall teach no more every man his neighbor, and every man his brother,

* S. R. Driver, An Introduction to the Literature of the Old Testament, (New York: Charles Scribner's Sons, 1903). p. 275

† J. Skinner, Prophecy and Religion, (Cambridge: The University Press, 1922). pp. 320–327.

‡ Robert H. Pfeiffer, Introduction to the Old Testament, (New York: Harper and Brothers Publishers, 1948). p. 517.[7]

---

6. King refers to Bernhard Duhm, who wrote *Das Buch Jeremia* (Tübingen: J. C. B. Mohr, 1901).

7. Pfeiffer's arguments against Duhm appear on page 504 of his *Introduction to the Old Testament* (New York: Harper & Brothers, 1948). King's citation to page 517 refers to Pfeiffer's commentary, which assumes Jeremiah's authorship.

saying, know Jehovah; for they shall all know me, from the least of them unto the greatest of them, saith Jehovah: for I will forgive their iniquity and their sin will I remember no more." (31:31ff). In every {respect} the New Covenant will differ from the Old. The law written upon stone is to be replaced by the law written in the heart. As stated by Dr. Matthews, "this law written in the heart required no Torah, canonized by an emotionally conditioned populace and then easily subverted by legalism. Nor were manuals of worship, altars, and a Temple, that so often become ends in themselves, required to aid the spirit of man in communing with his Maker. Nor was residence in the Holy Land essential to the highest religious life. True religion was not rooted in the soil of Palestine, but in the hearts of men and women."* The law written in the heart will become an inseparable part of man's moral being. Principles would take the place of external ordinances. Such principles as truth, and justice, and purity, love to God and love to man, would be enshrined in the hearts of men. This, said Jeremiah, would lead to an ideal state, in which the sins of the people would be forgiven. The children of the New Covenant would be the sons of God, no longer subject to external laws of the state, but ruled by impulses to good, acting upon the heart as a principle which grows from within.

Such was the New Covenant which Jeremiah was the first to conceive. Let us briefly list the positive features of the religious relationship established by the New Covenant. (1) Inwardness: "I will put my law in their inner parts;" (2) Individualism: "all shall know Me;" (3) Forgiveness of sins: "their sins I will remember no more."† All of this states one central truth, the inwardness of true religion. It is this inwardness of true religion which causes men to do the will of God spontaneously from inward inclination rather than from commands of an external law. No one can deny the fact that this prophecy, although rather idealistic, is one of the profoundest anticipations in all the Old Testament. "Liberating religion from all externals, at the same time the New Covenant strengthened and democratized it by placing responsibilities squarely on the shoulder of the individual, and purified and deepened it by making it a matter of conscience. The New Covenant, the law written in the heart, was one of the great visions of religion."‡

* I. G. Matthews, The Religious Pilgrimage of Israel, (New York: Harper & Brothers Publishers, 1947). p. 164.

† Skinner, op. cit., p. 329.

‡ Matthews, op. cit. p. 165.

Unreal Worship—Temple
and Sacrifice

Another line which can be added to the column of Jeremiah's contributions to religious thought is his stand against artificial worship. This attact {was} started against the Temple. As we know the Deuteronomic reformation culminated in the centrelization of national worship in the Temple at Jerusalem. This Temple was the pivot of the nation's religion. It was a national institution, linked intimately with the fortunes of the race. In the course of years elaborate ceremonies were enacted, and the priests prescribed sacrifices, and the smoke of burnt-offerings rose high from the altar. The Temple was the apple of the people's eye. To criticise it was to set aflame the fires of both religion and patriotism. And this was the very thing that Jeremiah did.[8] He saw that the Temple had been relegated to a position of empty formalism which substituted a superficial reverence for the doing of Yahweh's will. He saw that sacrificial offerings were taking the place of sacrificial living. All of these conditions led Jeremiah to cry out against the evils of the Temple and sacrifice. All of this is found in the sermon which Jeremiah preached in the Temple (7). "The primary purpose of this address was to utter a strong polemic against the Temple and the worship there. Anything which Jeremiah may have added about the future fate of the people was subsidiary to this leading aim."* For the moment let us look into the assumptions growing out of this address.

In the first place, Jeremiah declares that public religion is an organized hypocrisy. In it religion was divorced from morality.[9] He saw that the Temple was worse than a false defense, for it was given to aiding

* Adam C. Welch, Jeremiah His Times and His Work, (London: Oxford University Press, 1928) p. 137

---

8. T. Crouther Gordon, *The Rebel Prophet: Studies in the Personality of Jeremiah* (New York: Harper & Brothers, 1932), p. 105: "[The Temple] was the centre and pivot of the nation's religion. . . . It was a national institution, linked intimately with the fortunes of the race, for since the day when Solomon consecrated it, kings had risen and fallen under its shadow. . . . In the course of centuries an elaborate liturgical ceremony came to be enacted there, and the priests prescribed sacrifices, and the smoke of burnt-offerings rose high from the altar. . . . The Temple was the apple of the people's eye. To touch it was to set aflame the fires of both religion and patriotism. And this was just the very thing that the prophet did."

9. John Skinner, *Prophecy and Religion* (Cambridge: Cambridge University Press, 1940), p. 175: "In the first place, Jeremiah declares that the public religion, the religion of which the Temple is the centre and symbol is an organized hypocrisy. In it religion was divorced from morality as completely as in the earlier days when worship was accompanied by flagrant immoralities."

the evils of the day.[10] It had become in Yahweh's eyes, a cave for robbers to shelter themselves in.[11] Men stole, murdered, played the fool, and broke their promises, only to run under the shadow of the Temple for protection.[12]

> Behold, ye trust in lying words that cannot
>   profit.
> Will ye steal, murder, and commit adultery
>   and sware falsely,
> And burn incense unto Baal, and walk after
>   other gods whom ye know not;
> And come and stand before me in my house,
>   which is called by my name, and say,
> We are delivered to do all these abominations
>   (7:8–10).

Here one can see the profound convictions of a striving prophet. He deals with a problem that is a danger of all religions. It states the important truth that ritual is never to be used as an end within itself, but only as a means to an end.[13] It would be unfair to say to say that the functionnaries of the Temple deliberately meant to inculcate evil or immorality, but they drifted into the belief that the Temple was more important than the distinction of good and evil, the sacrifices more vital than sin. It therefore took the fortitude and mind of Jeremiah to expose these pressing faults.

All of this would seem to throw the fault on the Deuteronomists, but not rightly so. The Deuteronomists had no intention to bring about this state of things. They set out to organize religion, and we must admit that it brought about considerable external success. The Deuteronomists, however, failed to see that religion is not something which can be organized, rather it is a spontaneous outflow from men's contact with a divine spirit. As soon as an external compulsion is attempted it leads inevitably to hypocrisy. This

---

10. Gordon, *Rebel Prophet*, p. 107: "The Temple was worse than a false defence, for as the prophet goes on to make plain, it was given to aiding and abetting the evils of the day."

11. Skinner, *Prophecy and Religion*, p. 175: "[The Temple] might have been the place where Yahwe's gracious presence was experienced if they had hallowed His name by lives lived in piety and righteousness; but used as they use it it has become even in Yahwe's eyes a cave for robbers to shelter themselves in."

12. Gordon, *Rebel Prophet*, pp. 107–108: "Men stole, murdered, played the fool, and broke their promises, only to run under the shadow of the Temple for protection."

13. King used similar language in "Ritual," 24 September 1947–31 January 1948, p. 140 in this volume: "ritual is looked upon as an end within itself rather than a means to an end."

is the marked difference between the reformers and Jeremiah. The former were content to see crowds observe the ritual, even if their lives did not make the mark. Jeremiah cared nothing about external ritual if it did not produce internal change.*

In the second place, Jeremiah announces that since the Temple has become the symbol of a false religion God is about to make an end to it. At this point Jeremiah again went contrary to tradition, for those on the traditional side claimed that with the Temple in their midst the Hebrews could stand inviolable against the world.[14] Even Isaiah had proclaimed in the previous century that God would not allow the Temple to be desecrated. The Deuteronomists believed the same. Against all of the spiritual orthodoxy Jeremiah argues to the contrary. The very first point of his speech is:

> "Trust ye not in lying words, saying, the Temple of the Lord, The Temple of the Lord, the Temple of the Lord, are these. (7:4).[15]

The Temple might have been the bulwark of the nation in past days, but times are changed, and the only thing that could save it now was to thoroughly improve both methods and practices, to see strick justice present, to prevent the exploitation of strangers, the orphan and the widow, and to avoid the murder of the innocent. Only on these conditions would they survive and retain their land (7:5, 6, 7).[16] With history on his side the prophet points to the remains of Shiloh, and pronouced the doom of the Temple to be as certain as the fate that had overtaken the old sanctuary.

> "But go ye now unto my place which was in Shiloh, where I set my name at the first, and see what I did to it for the wickedness of my people Israel. And now because you have done all these works, saith the Lord, and I spake unto you, rising up early and speaking,

* cf. Skinner, op. cit., pp. 175–76.

---

14. Pritchard corrected "the Hebrews" to "Israel."

15. Cf. Gordon, *Rebel Prophet*, p. 107.

16. Gordon, *Rebel Prophet*, p. 107: "The Temple may have been the bulwark of the nation in past days, but times are changed, and the only things that can save it now are to thoroughly improve both methods and practices, to see strict justice done as man to man, to prevent the exploitation of the stranger, the orphan and the widow, and to avoid the murder of the innocent. Only on this condition would the people survive and retain their land (vii. 5, 6)."

but ye heard not and I called you, but ye answered not; therefore will I do unto this house, which is called by my name wherein ye trust, and unto the place which I gave to you and to your fathers, as I have done to Shiloh. (7:12–14)

Personal Religion

Important as are his other contributions to the body of religious truth, Jeremiah's teaching on Personal Religion is of greatest permanent value. With Jeremiah religion is an immediate, personal relationship between Jehovah and the individual soul; it means obedience and devotion of the individual to his God. "I will give them a heart to know me, that I am Jehovah: and they shall be my people and I will be their God; and they shall return unto me with the whole heart" (24:7). Here Jeremiah passes beyond his predecessors in the direction of the teaching of Jesus. Through his inner struggles, Jeremiah was able to experience a more personal and more tempestuous relation with his God.

This idea of personal religion is expressed nowhere greater than in the life of Jeremiah. Despised and rejected by men he clung the more tenaciously to Jehovah and His will. He was sustained by that fellowship with Heaven which made his "inner resistance superior to every outward pressure." On the one hand we hear him cry,

> "I am become a laughing stock all the day, every one mocketh me. The word of Yahweh is made to me a reproach and a derision all the day." (20;7f).

Again he cries,

> "Woe is me, my mother, that thou hast borne me a man of strife and contention to the whole earth." (15;10).

On the other hand we hear Jeremiah saying that he is sustained by his life with God. "I am with thee saith Yahweh, to deliver thee." With this promise Jeremiah began his ministry, and he ~~has left us~~ has left us the record of how it became fulfilled. It is probable that Jeremiah himself wrote down from time to time the account of his intercourse with God; or else he dictated it to Baruch.

That Jeremiah stood alone is in a real sense correct. In many instances he could cry with Elijah, "I, even I only, am left, and they seek my life to take it away" (I

189

Kings 19;10).[17] The prophet had literally nothing left but God. To God therefore he went for companionship, relief, encouragement, assurance and all that was needed to go on. "Out of the Hebrew prophet, there is created in Jeremiah a new spiritual type—the Old Testament saint: the man who, when flesh and heart fail, finds in God the strength of his heart and his portion forever."* It remains for us to sketch briefly the outstanding features of this type of personal religion, as exhibited in Jeremiah.

* Skinner, op. cit., p. 223.

First, his religion is marked by its strong individualism. In the case of Jeremiah this is naturally accounted for by the peculiar circumstances of his life; it was through such experiences that Jeremiah had to move from the realm of national religion to that of personal religion.[18] Throughout the "Confessions"† we can see that Jeremiah felt himself absolutely cut off from religious fellowship with men. The bond between him and his nation was broken, therefore he threw his all on Yahweh.[19] When he couldn't understand certain problems facing society he went to Yahweh. Listen as he cries to Yahweh:

† The term has been applied to such passages as 11:18–23; 12:1–6; 15:10–21; 17:9–18; 18:18–23; 20:7–12;

> "Righteous art thou, O Yahweh, when I
>   contend with thee;
> Yet would I reason the cause with thee:
> Wherefore doth the way of the wicked
>   prosper?
> Wherefore are they at ease that deal very
>   treacherously?
> Thou art near in their mouth and for from
>   their heart." (12:1f)

Over against their treachery Jeremiah sets his own integrity.

> "But thou, O Yahweh, knowest me;
> thou seest me, and triest my heart towards
>   thee." (12:3)

---

17. Skinner, *Prophecy and Religion*, p. 219: "With greater truth than Elijah he could have said 'I, even I only, am left, and they seek my life to take it away' (I Kings xix. 10, 14)."

18. Skinner, *Prophecy and Religion*, p. 223: "It remains for us to sketch briefly the outstanding features of this type of piety, as exhibited in Jeremiah. Its first and most obvious characteristic is its strongly marked *individualism*. In the case of Jeremiah this is naturally accounted for by the peculiar circumstances of his life; and it may be that only an altogether exceptional experience like his could have found a path from the national and prophetic religion of ancient Israel to the personal religion of the later Jewish Church and Christianity."

19. Skinner, *Prophecy and Religion*, p. 223: "in writing the 'Confessions' he felt himself absolutely cut off from religious fellowship with men. The bond between him and his nation was broken."

In this we can see that tone of sincerity which sounds throughout Jeremiah's life. We can see the purity of one who always lives intimately with God. Finally we see Jeremiah as he reaches complete trust and harmony with his God; Yahweh is his "hope" (17:14) and his strong protector against his persecutors (17:11). Having completely overcome his despair, Jeremiah found his deepest joy in the world of Yahweh (15:16) and became, as Yahweh had said at the time of his call (1:18), a wall of brass capable of resisting all attack (15:20).

Second, out of Jeremiah's piety grows a trust in the unerring righteousness of God. It was this trust in the unerring righteousness of God that was the basis of his personal religion. He saw Yahweh as the Righteous Judge, the all-seeing Searcher of hearts, who gives to every man according to his deeds (17:10; 12:1; 12:3; 20:12). Jeremiah came to this conception of God because of the divine working within him. It was the eye of Yahweh that was forever searching the thoughts and intents of the heart.[20] Jeremiah's great moral sincerity grew out of his realization of the omniscience and righteousness of God.[21]

Third, Jeremiah is original in his exercise of prayer.[22] Jeremiah "is the father of true prayer, in which the wretched soul expresses both its subhuman misery and its superhuman confidence . . . The Psalms would not have been composed without Jeremiah."* How far the other prophets went in the realm of prayer we do not know. Some scholars hold that the prophetic revelation always came in answer to prayer. Of course, as Skinner reminds us, this is mainly a generalization from the case of Jeremiah which may or may not be legitimate.† We may conclude in this in-

* See Pfeiffer, Introduction to the Old Testament, (New York: Harper & Brothers Publishers, 1948). p. 514.[23]

† Skinner, op. cit., p. 254.

---

20. Skinner, *Prophecy and Religion*, p. 225: "The basis of Jeremiah's personal religion is his trust in the unerring righteousness of God. . . . Yahwe was to him the Righteous Judge, the all-seeing Searcher of hearts, who gives to every man according to his deeds (xvii. 9, xii. 3, xx. 12). This conception of God is a reflexion of the process by which he experienced the divine working within him. . . . to Jeremiah it is the eye of Yahwe searching the thoughts and intents of the heart, and bringing to light things hidden from himself."

21. Skinner, *Prophecy and Religion*, pp. 225–226: "Now this note of *moral sincerity*, springing from a vivid realisation of the omniscience and righteousness of God, is one that is repeatedly struck in the meditations and prayers of the Psalter."

22. Skinner, *Prophecy and Religion*, p. 227: "Jeremiah is original above all in the exercise of prayer."

23. Pritchard commented above King's footnote: "This is Wellhausen as quoted in Pfeiffer."

stance, as in many others, that Jeremiah's experience was unique.[24] He prays for healing.

> "Heal me, O Lord, and I shall be healed;
> Save me, and I shall be saved;
> For thou art my praise." (17:14).

Again he prays for help against his adversaries.

> "Let them be confounded that persecute me,
>   but let me not be confounded;
> Let them be dismayed, but let not me be
>   dismayed:
> Bring upon them the day of evil, and destroy
>   them with double destruction." (17:18).

But to Jeremiah prayer was more than petition. It was no escape from the harsh realities of life. It was an "intimate converse with God, in which his inner life is laid bare, with its perplexities and struggles and temptations."* It is such a prayer that contains the assurance of an answer. In one of the most touching passages of his "Confessions," Jeremiah becomes aware of the answer which solves all of his internal problems.

* Ibid., p. 214.

> "Therefore thus saith the Lord, if thou return, then will I bring thee again, and then shall stand before me: and if thou take forth the precious from the vile,
> Thou shalt be as my mouth; let them return unto thee; but return not thou unto them. And I will make thee unto this people a brasen wall: and they shall fight against thee, but they shall not prevail against thee, for I am with thee to save thee and to deliver thee out of the hand of the wicked, and I will redeem thee out of the hand of the terrible." (15:19, 20, 21).[25]

Jeremiah, throughout all his doubts and difficulties, was able to be carried forward by the secret as-

---

24. Skinner, *Prophecy and Religion*, p. 227: "How far the older prophets were men of prayer is a question which we have slight means of answering. The theory of Oehler, Riehm, Giesebrecht and others, that the prophetic revelation always came in answer to prayer, is mainly a generalisation from the case of Jeremiah, which may or may not be legitimate. We may suspect that in this respect, as in so many others, Jeremiah's experience was *sui generis*."

25. Skinner, *Prophecy and Religion*, p. 214: "Now such prayer contains in itself the assurance of its answer; and in one striking passage, which we must regard as the climax of the 'Confessions,' Jeremiah comes to clear consciousness of the answer which solves the problem of his personal relation to God." After this sentence Skinner quotes Jeremiah 15:19ff.

surance that this business was not his business but God's business, and this alone supported him under the most pressing perplexities and loneliness.[26] All of this leads us to conclude that Jeremiah was the First of the Mystics. He was the mystic of the mystics. In Jeremiah "is mysticism pure and simple, mysticism in its finest and clearest form. It is neither the religion which is taught, nor the religion which is caught. It is the mystic's inmost and intense communion with the Divine."* This helps us to understand why Jeremiah took certain stands in life. His communion with God, which was for him the biggest single fact in life, led him ~~to~~ inevitably to the undermining of ecclesiastical religion. The Temple he slashes with scone and ridicule (7:9).[27] In another passage he scones the magical properties of the Ark (3:16). He stings with sweeping criticism the priests who were suppose to be the mediators between God and man. At one time he even challenges the validity of the Scriptures (8:8).[28] But amid all of that Jeremiah proved that God can be found.

In all of this discussion of personal religion, we have only dealt with the life of Jeremiah and his relationship to God. But what about other individuals? One might well ask the question, did Jeremiah ever reach the point of believing that all individuals could have personal relations with God as he did? The answer is yes. He concluded this from his own experiences. He perceived that what religion was to him it must be to all men—the response of the heart to the voice of God.[29] It was this thought that was continu-

* T. C. Gordon, The Rebel Prophet, (New York: Harper & Brothers Publishers, 1932). p. 220.

---

26. Gordon, *Rebel Prophet,* p. 224: "And yet, throughout all his doubts and difficulties the prophet was carried forward by the secret assurance that this business was not his business but God's business, and this alone supported him under the most pressing perplexities and loneliness."

27. Pritchard underlined "scone" and wrote a question mark in the margin.

28. Gordon, *Rebel Prophet,* p. 219: "His direct communion with God, which was for him the biggest single fact in his life, led him to the inevitable corollary of minimising the utility of material aids, and in the most logical and understandable fashion he sets about the undermining of ecclesiastical religion. The Temple he slashes with his scorn and ridicule, . . . (vii. 9–10). In another passage, if it is not post-exilic, he scorns the magical properties of the Ark, and promises that men shall come to be so personally in communion with God that the Ark shall never cross their minds (iii. 16). The priests, who pose as the intermediaries between Jehovah and His people, Jeremiah stings with his sweeping criticisms. He even challenges the validity of the Scriptures, which even the most simple-minded were willing to revere (viii. 8)."

29. Skinner, *Prophecy and Religion,* p. 334: "Something of this Jeremiah had learned in his own life; and if he saw but dimly, he perceived that what religion was to him it must be to all men—the response of the heart to the voice of God within."

ally touching the balloon of nationality until finally it burst. This was a supreme contribution, for it shifted the center of gravity in Judaism from the nation to the individual.[30]

Conclusion

We must conclude that Jeremiah left certain ineffaceable contributions to religious thought which are still relevant to our contemporary culture. He stepped on the religious stage sounding the trumpet for a new idea of God, and the signal for another forward march of the soul.[31] He had seized on a great and revolutionary truth, and with that truth, like a pillar of cloud by day and of fire by night, went ahead of his times. In many instances the picture drawn by Jeremiah is an idealistic one, and an ideal which has not yet been realized—the New Covenant for example. But the ideal is there; it at least serves as a standard by which we may measure ourselves, a goal which we may all strive to attain.

Again Jeremiah is a shining example of the truth that religion should never sanction the status quo. This more than anything else should be inculcated into the minds of modern religionists, for the worst disservice that we as individuals or churches can do to Christianity is to become sponsors and supporters of the status quo. How often has religion gone down, chained to a status quo it allied itself with. Durkheim and other sociologists rejoice to find in each religion simply the reflection of the State's opinion of itself foisted upon the divine, and along this they agree that no advancement can be looked for in spiritual affairs.[32] Therefore, we must admit that men like Jeremiah are valuable to any religion. Religion, in a sense, through men like Jeremiah, provides for its

---

30. Pfeiffer, *Introduction to the Old Testament*, p. 515: "Just as the 'Confessions' are the part of Jeremiah's book which had the most profound literary influence, so they also disclose the chief contribution of the prophet to religious growth, namely, the shift of the center of gravity in Judaism from the nation to the individual, from external acts to an attitude of mind."

31. Gordon, *Rebel Prophet*, p. 93: "And yet, as each rebel stepped upon the religious stage, it was but the trumpet for a new idea of God, the signal for another forward march of the soul, for without the spiritual rebel the soul of man would sicken and die."

32. Pritchard wrote a question mark at the end of this sentence and asked at the bottom of the page, "fn?" Gordon, *Rebel Prophet*, p. 93: "Durkheim and his confreres rejoice to find in each religion simply the reflection of the State's opinion of itself, foisted upon the Divine, and along this line they agree that no advancement can be looked for in spiritual affairs."

own advancement, and carries within it the promise of progress and renewed power.[33] But what is societies reaction to such men? It has reacted, and always will re-act, in the only way open to it. It destroys such men. Jeremiah died a martyr.[34]

It is obvious that if we judge Jeremiah by the ordinary standards of the world, his work was a failure. He was lightly esteemed in life. He became the supreme example of what Deutero-Isaiah called the suffering servant. He was despised and rejected, a man of sorrows and acquainted with grief.[35] But in after years his unheeded prophecies became the favourite book of the scattered Hebrew race. Many of the Psalms, as we saw above, re-echo his words, and depict scenes such as only Jeremiah could have passed through. It is for these reasons that Jeremiah came to be regarded as the greatest of them all (Matt. 16:14; John 1:21).

THDS. MLKP-MBU: Box 115, folder 17.

---

33. Gordon, *Rebel Prophet*, p. 94: "Religion, in a sense, through the prophet, provides for its own advancement, and carries within it the promise of progress and renewed power."

34. Pritchard wrote an "X" after "martyr" and commented in the margin, "not literally."

35. This sentence is an allusion to Isaiah 53:3. "He is despised and rejected by men, / A Man of sorrows and acquainted with grief."

"The Ethics of Late Judaism as Evidenced in the Testaments of the Twelve Patriarchs"

[30 November 1948–16 February 1949]
[Chester, Pa.]

This paper was written for Morton Scott Enslin's course on the history and literature of the New Testament, which exposed King to biblical criticism.[1] In observing that "many of the works of this period [late Judaism] were infinitely more valuable than those that received canonicity," King challenges the wisdom of canonical decisions and argues that many of the great ethical principles normally associated with the New Testament actually had their origins in late Judaism. He

---

1. Morton Scott Enslin (1897–1983) graduated from Harvard with a doctorate in theology. In 1924 he became professor of New Testament studies at Crozer Theological Seminary. In 1941 he became editor of the *Crozer Quarterly*. His publications include *The Ethics of Paul* (1930); with Kirsop Lake, *Six Collations of New Testament Manuscripts* (1933); and *Christian Beginnings* (1938).

describes how early Christian values such as chastity, compassion, forgiveness, and temperance were foreshadowed in the Testaments of the Twelve Patriarchs, a late Judaic document. Enslin noted numerous grammatical, spelling, and writing errors but gave the essay an A −. Although he thought the bibliography "a bit slim," Enslin wrote that this was "a well-written and competent paper. It shows evidence of thought and study. I have enjoyed reading it." King received a B for the course.

For a number of centuries, it was generally held that the period between the Old and New Testaments was a period of silence, and that no spiritual development was achieved within it. It was believed that this period of silence was broken when the New Testament appeared on the stage of history. Now the pendulum of interpretation is swinging in another direction. Most competent scholars have cast such positions out of the window. They would all agree that in reality there was no period of silence. To be sure, it was a period of great spiritual progress, and in many instances greater than any preceding it in Old Testament times, even though the Old Testament was its logical prelude.[2] To my mind, many of the works of this period were infinitely more valuable than those that received canonicity.[3] The materials to justify such statements are found mainly in the Apocrypha and the Pseudepigrapha.[4] These works, although presented pseudonymously, are of lasting significance to the Biblical student.[5]

---

2. Enslin replaced the phrase "To be sure" with "On the contrary" and wrote a question mark in the margin.

3. Enslin underlined "infinitely more valuable" and asked, "Is this not a bit sweeping?"

4. The Apocrypha refers to books of the Septuagint, or Greek Old Testament, not included in the Hebrew Bible. Pseudepigrapha is a term that suggests the ascription of false names to authors of works. It usually refers to pseudonymous Jewish texts written in the centuries shortly before and shortly after the death of Jesus and not included among the canonical books of the Septuagint. The Apocrypha and Pseudepigrapha thus consist of certain extracanonical writings of Jews from the Hellenistic and Roman periods. Although these works were never officially canonized, they were very influential. Since the discovery of the Dead Sea Scrolls and a renewed appreciation of the diversity of thought during this period, the Apocrypha and Pseudepigrapha have been indispensable in scholarly reconstructions of the early history of Judaism and Christianity.

5. King used R. H. Charles's phrase "period of silence" in this paragraph and paraphrased the passage in Charles that reads: "These two centuries were in many respects centuries of greater spiritual progress than any two that had preceded them in Israel. The materials for such a proof are to be found in a minor degree in the Apocrypha . . . but mainly in the Pseudepigrapha . . . issued pseudonymously" (Introduction to Robert Henry Charles, *Religious Development Between the Old and New Testaments* [London: Williams & Norgate, 1914], p. 8).

In this paper, however, we are mainly interested in the ethics of this period (late Judaism) as evidenced in one of the pseudepigraphic works—The Testaments of the Twelve Patriarchs. This work was written in Hebrew in the latter years of John Hyrcanus (ca. 109–106 B.C.).[6] The author was a Chasid* who had a great deal of admiration for the high-priesthood of the great Maccabean family. In fact, the work was written on behalf of the Messianic claims of John Hyrcanus.[7] The book has many valuable contributions, but its overwhelming value lies in the ethical teaching found therein. It was these high ethical principles which left an ineffaceable impression on many of the New Testament writers, and also upon our Lord. The language and thought of the New Testament writers prove conclusively that they were directly acquainted with the Testaments of the Twelve Patriarchs. All of this goes ~~on~~ to prove the importance of the book. The ethical teaching of this great work serves as a bridge connecting the ethics of the Old and New Testaments.[8] Therefore, no logical thinker can doubt the fact that knowledge of this work is a sine qua non to all concrete study of Hebrew-Christian religion.

For the moment let us turn our attention to a critical analysis of this important work.[9] The critical analysis is limited to the question of authorship. Because of conflicting Jewish and Christian elements found in the book, questions of authorship have arisen. To account for these conflicting views, Grabe—in his "Spicileguim Patrum" (Oxford, 1714)—arrived at the conclusion through critical analysis, that the basis of the work is Jewish, though there are many Christological interpolations. This hypothesis was immediately com-

* A Chasid, according to Charles, was a Pharisee of the early type.

---

6. Enslin underlined "ca." and told King to "underscore Latin or other foreign letters words or terms." Robert Henry Charles, *The Testaments of the Twelve Patriarchs: Translated from the Editor's Greek Text and Edited, with Introduction, Notes, and Indices* (London: Adam & Charles Black, 1908), p. xv: "The Testaments of the Twelve Patriarchs were written in Hebrew in the latter years of John Hyrcanus."

7. Enslin underlined "Messianic" and commented in the margin, "I am dubious about this."

8. Charles, *Testaments of the Twelve Patriarchs*, p. xvii: "The main, overwhelming value of the book lies not . . . but in its ethical teaching, which has achieved a real immortality by influencing the thought and diction of the writers of the New Testament, and even those of our Lord. This ethical teaching . . . helps to bridge the chasm that divides the ethics of the Old and New Testaments."

9. Enslin underlined "critical analysis" and commented in the margin: "Is this the proper term? Your following paragraphs scarcely warrant so sweeping a term."

bated by Corrodi.[10] Other scholars such as Nitzsch and Ritschl assigned the work to a Christian author; the former to a Jewish Christian and the latter to a Gentile Christian. Each of these views were vigorously assailed by other critics.

In recent years the picture has changed quite a bit. Such scholars as Schnapp, Conybeare, Preuschen and Bousset, have notably confirmed Grabe's hypothesis.[11] Therefore, it is now generally accepted {that} the groundwork of the book is the work of a single author of the Pharisaic school.[12]

Before entering the general discussion, a brief summary of the content of the book needs to be given. The writings consist of the last words and exhortations of the twelve sons of Jacob to their Children. Each testament indicates the virtues inculcated or the vices condemned by each of these patriarchs in turn.

It is also observed that in each testament three elements can be distinguished. (1) The patriarch gives a brief history of his life, in which he emphasizes his particular virtue or vice. This history is generally a midrashic expansion of certain biblical statements, but in some cases it contains materials that are in direct conflict with them.[13] (2) The patriarch next proceeds to exhorts his descendants to emulate the virtues and to avoid the vices. (3) Finally, the patriarch deals with the prophetic visions of his descendant's future. Here he emphasizes the authority of Levi and Judah, and foretells the tragedy that they will face if they fall into sin and disown the supremacy of Levi and Judah.

The present study represents an attempt to provide in condensed form a survey of late Jewish ethics as

---

10. Charles, *Testaments of the Twelve Patriarchs*, p. xxxviii: "To account for these conflicting Jewish and Christian elements, Grabe (*Spicil. Patrum*, 1714, i 129–144, 335–374) suggested that the book was written by a Jew and subsequently interpolated by a Christian. This hypothesis, however, was for the time . . . successfully combated by Corrodi."

11. Charles, *Testaments of the Twelve Patriarchs*, p. xxxix: "Nitzsch . . . describes the author as a Jewish Christian of Alexandria who had imbibed many of the Essene doctrines that were then current. Ritschl . . . assigns the book to a Gentile Christian, appealing principally to T. Benj. xi. (a Christian interpolation). Ritschl's view was vigorously assailed. . . . Recent research has notably confirmed Grabe's hypothesis."

12. Charles, *Testaments of the Twelve Patriarchs*, p. liv: "I have with some hesitation come to the conclusion that the groundwork is the work of a single writer of the Pharisaic school."

13. Enslin circled the first "b" in "biblical" and wrote: "See p. 1. Be consistent." On the first page Enslin had noted King's use of "Biblical," with a marginal note referring him to this spot.

evidenced in the Testaments of the Twelve Patriarchs. The plan of the study involves taking successively each of the twelve patriarchs, and presenting, what I consider, his outstanding ethical teaching. This method is employed with an attempt to give a comprehensive study of the book. Many of the patriarchs deal with more than one ethical principle, but in this {study} only one will be considered from each. The value of this study may be found in the textual quotations taken directly from the Testaments of the Twelve Patriarchs, supporting and illustrating the ethical priciple of each patriarch. Throughout the paper comparisons will be made of both Old and New Testament passages which are similar to passages found in this work.

Reuben: Unchastity.[14]

Purity has been considered the characteristic feature of the Jewish home and family life throughout the ages. Not only the home, but the body and soul must be pure. Impure thoughts are considered both immoral and unethical. Judaism is all out in forbidding sensual abandonment, the breaking down of family ties, and every impure act or thought in the relation between the sexes. This demand for chastity reaches a high peak in the Testaments of the Twelve Patriarchs. We find Reuben warn-ing his children against looking on a woman with lustful eyes (cf. Matt. 5:28). "Pay no heed to the face of a woman, nor associate with another man's wife, nor meddle with the affairs of womankind."* He continues, "and command the women likewise not to associate with men, that they also may be pure in mind. For constant meetings, even though the ungodly deed be not wrought, are to them an irremediable disease and to us a destruction of Beliar and an eternal reproach."†

It is interesting to notice that the impure thought, according to Reuben, is as destructive as the impure act. Even the desire for licentiousness is destructive, to say nothing of licentious conduct. This is a noble ethical principle which was re-echoed in the teaching of our Lord some years later.‡

How is one protected against lustful thoughts in the hour of temptation? It is only by the singleness of

* T. Reuben 3:10.

† T. Reuben 6:2, 3; cf. T. Jud. 14:2, 3; 15:2; T. Dan 5:5.

‡ See Matt. 5:28.

14. Enslin circled the period and wrote: "Omit period in a title head. (So hereinafter.)"

heart in the fear of God. It was these noble principles that preserved for the New Testament one of the highest conceptions of moral purity the world has ever known.

Simeon: Envy.

Of all sins, envy is one of the most insidious. This fact was expressed long ago in the ethics of late Judaism. Simeon, one of the twelve patriarchs, warns his children against the spirit of deceit and envy. "For envy," he warns, "ruleth over the whole mind of a man, and suffereth him neither to eat nor to drink, nor to do any good thing. But it even suggesteth (to him) to destroy him that he envieth, and so long as he that is envied flourisheth, he that envieth fadest away."* Here we see that envy brings about a dual destruction. It destroys both him that is envied and him that envies.

This is one of the most remarkable statements on the subject of envy in all ancient literature. The author is aware of the fact that envy poisons the atmosphere of old time friendship, warps the judgment, embitters the heart, and substitutes unkind criticism for sympathetic understanding and cynicism for courage.

How does one get rid of this destructive element, envy? It is only through loving your brother with a good heart that the spirit of envy will be withdrawn from you. This is the solution which Simeon gives. In other words, love is the logical substitute for envy.

It is significant to observe that Simeon conceives of envy as destroying the total personality. It is not a bath that dampens certain portions of the personality, but a flood that drowns the entire inner self. Therefore, the person who envies,, according to Simeon, can never achieve peace of mind, for his personality is forever distorted.

Levi: Retribution.

The question of retribution is an important ethical tenet in any religion. Of course, it might be argued that the question of retribution is a theological concept rather than an ethical principle. To my mind, it may be both, therefore I will treat it from the point of view of the latter. This ethical teaching is found in the testament of Levi. It is this principle that leads to the highest ethical consciousness in the end: "the reward of a good deed is a good deed, and the punishment of sin is sin."

Throughout the testament of Levi this ethical principle is discussed. He says to his children, "perform righteousness on earth that ye may find treasures in heaven;* sow good works in your souls that ye may reap them in life. But if you sow evil things ye shall reap every trouble and affliction."† Here we see that the author believed in the lasting honesty of the universe. He was aware of the fact that things dont happen haphazardly in this universe, but on the contrary they have causes; after every cause there is a concomitant effect.[16] Moreover, it was his conviction that there is order in the moral realm of the universe just as there is order in the natural realm.

This is truly a great ethical contribution. Even the apostle Paul discovered it in later years (it is probable that he was acquainted with these very passages) and declared, "whatsoever a man sowoth, that shall he also reap."‡ This is a principle that we in the modern world cannot minimize, for more than anything else, faith in God presupposes that this is an honest universe.

Judah: Temperance

In the testament of Judah, many ethical principles are discussed, such as courage, avarice, fornication and temperance.[17] But I think greater emphasis is placed on the question of temperance. Therefore, my discussion will be limited to temperance.

It is amazing to read what sane advice this old writer gives in regards to the question of temperance and abstinence. He laconically states, "if ye drink wine with gladness, be ye modest with fear of God. For if in your gladness the fear of God departeth, then drunkenness ariseth and shamelessness stealeth in. But if you would live soberly do not touch wine at all, lest ye sin in words of outrage . . . and perish before your time."§ He continues by telling his children that

* cf. Luke 12:21.[15]

† T. Levi 13:5, 6.

‡ Gal. 6:7.

§ T. Jud. 16:2–3.

---

15. Enslin marked the "c" of "cf." to be capitalized and instructed King, "Begin all notes with capital letter."

16. Enslin changed "dont" to "do not" and commented, "Avoid these contractions in formal writing."

17. Enslin inserted a comma before "and" and commented, "The omission of the comma before 'and' in 'a, b and c' is illogical although frequently written today."

drunkenness turns ones mind from truth and brings about lustful thoughts.*

This demand for temperance is not to be interpreted as an attempt to bring about asceticism. To argue that late Judaism (or even early Judaism) insisted upon asceticism is a false assumption. It rather desired that one should keep all in equipoise, granting every mental and physical faculty as much as it can bear, without overburdening another at its expense. Through such teaching one was to cultivate a conscious will to self-discipline, one was to learn moderation and how to rise above mere desire and prove stronger than things material.

This is a great contribution. This sound, sane and, cool-headed tendency, which condemns anything excessive, unbounded, extravagant and unnatural, makes itself felt today. It should serve as a profound challenge to the modern reader.[18]

Issachar: Simplicity.

The testament of Issachar reveals a very important ethical principle of late Judaism. This ethical teaching is that of simplicity. Issachar is presented as a single-hearted husbandman who works for the joy of working (3:1, 3, 5). He is free from malice, envy and greed (3:3); shuns lust (4:4); offers freely to God and his father (3:6), and to the poor (3:8). He accordingly admonishes his children to walk in simplicity, and to refrain from envy and all lustful thoughts, prying into no secrets, but loving God and man.

We are not to think of this simplicity which Issachar speaks of as simplicity of mind; but it is simplicity of heart. It is the type of simplicity that causes a man to know but one woman; it causes one to avoid the drinking of wine and the telling of falsehood; it causes one to love God with all his might, and every man even as his children.

At first sight this ethical principle, like that of temperance, would appear to asceticism.[19] But, in reality, it wasn't. To be sure, asceticism, as stated above, was never a characteristic of early or late Judaism,—notwithstanding the fact that ascetic groups occasion-

---

18. Enslin wrote in the margin, "Cf the [*evan.?*] preachers' insistence on this 'golden mean' in Greek thought."

19. Enslin underlined and questioned the phrase "appear to asceticism."

ally appeared on the scene—for Judaism was always a religion that was apart of everyday life.[20] It seems to me that this demand for simplicity was a desire for high ethical character rather than a total divorcement from life. In other words, man (according to Issachar) was to forever choose, through living the simple life, the higher values.

Zebulun: Compassion.

The testament of Zebulun presents a profound example of the demand for compassion in the ethics of late Judaism. Zebulun in the Testaments of the Twelve Patriarchs, unlike the rabbinical conception, is presented as a fisherman who supplies his household with fish and gives of his store to the stranger, the sick, the aged and the needy that he may be blessed by God for his compassion.* He goes on to tell his children that it was his deep compassion for Joseph which restrained Simeon and Gad from bloodshed. When the other brothers took the twenty pieces of silver for which they sold Joseph and used it to buy sandals, Zebulun refused to share in the money. He, therefore, admonishes his children to show mercy to every man, to walk with neither grudge nor malice, but to love one another. It is his firm conviction that if man showeth compassion on his fellow beings, so will God show compassion on him. It is interesting to notice that compassion was not to end with human beings, but beast also were to receive compassion.†

This is from all angles a noble principle, for it presupposes that all wealth belongs to God. Even man himself is the possession of God. Here we find no distinction between the rich and the poor, for all men are the children of God. According to this view, a gentle sympathetic attitude, a friendly word of courage and of cheer is the summum bonum of life. It forbids one to confine his care to his own welfare and to be indifferent to the misfortune of others. This is truly a great ethical principle.

Dan: Anger.

Anger has always been an injurious emotion. It is dangerous because it places one in a state where

* T. Zeb. ch. 6.

† T. Zeb. 5:1.

---

20. Enslin marked the insertion of a space between "a" and "part."

thinking ceases and passion takes its course. This was realized long ago by the {the author of the} Testaments of the {Twelve} Patriarchs. Dan is found telling his children a moving story of how anger overtook him. While under the influence of Belial,[21] he relates to his children, he had been filled with anger against Joseph, and had planned to kill him that he might supplant him in the heart of his father.* Dan accordingly warns his children against anger, because "anger is blindness and does not suffer one to see the face of any man with truth." Anger heeds neither parent, nor brother, nor prophet, nor righteous man, nor friend.† Anger first of all gives provocation by word, then it leads to action. Therefore, he exhorts his children to refrain from anger either at spoken words or at misfortune.‡

* T. Dan ch. 1.

† T. Dan 2:3.

‡ T. Dan 4:2, 3.

These are noble statements on the question of anger. It again reveals to us that the author had great insight into the deeper problems of human life.[22]

Naphtali:
Natural Goodness

In the testament of Naphtali, we are immediately attracted by his theory of natural goodness. He does not hesitate in saying that God made everything good. He seems to think that in the very nature of man is a spark of goodness. It is every mans job to develope this spark into a flame. Out of this theory grows his whole ethical contribution. So he says to his children, "be ye, therefore, not eager to corrupt your doings through covetousness or with vain words to beguile your souls, because if ye keep silence in purity of heart, ye shall understand how to hold fast the will of God, and to cast away the will of Beliar."§

§ T. Naphtali 3:1, 2.

Gad: Forgiveness.

One of the most important ethical principles found in late Judaism was that of forgiveness. In order to understand its importance, as Charles reminds us, we must contrast the Old Testament's concept of forgiveness with that of the New Testament. Without analyzing the content of the Old and New Testaments scru-

---

21. Enslin circled the final "l" and commented, "You spelled it Beliar on an early page."

22. Enslin asked, "Do these constant little compliments add anything? They seem almost pasted on and a bit amateurish."

tinizingly, one would easily conclude that the two types of forgiveness are the same.[23] But careful analyzation will prove to the contrary. In the New Testament, it is understood throughout that one can only receive the divine forgiveness on the condition that he forgives his neighbour.[24] A few passages will illustrate this point.

"Forgive us our debts as we also have forgiven our debtors . . . For if ye forgive men their trespasses, your heavenly father will also forgive you. But if ye forgive not men their trespasses, neither will your Father forgive your trespasses."*

"Whensoever ye stand praying, forgive, if ye have aught against any one, that your Father also which is in heaven may forgive you your trespasses."†

"Let all bitterness, and wrath, and anger, and clamour, and railing be put away from you, with all malice: and be ye kind to another, even as God also in Christ forgave you."‡

In the Old Testament, we get an altogether different point of view. One could receive divine pardon in the Old Testament, and yet have the most bitter feelings toward his neighbour.[26] Let us look at a few examples.

"The Lord is on my side among them that help me: Therefore shall I see my desire upon them that hate me."§

"Behold God is mine helper: the Lord is with them that uphold my soul. He shall reward evil unto mine enemies: cut them off in thy truth."‖

"Do thou, O Lord, have mercy upon me, and raise me up, that I may requite them."#

From these passages we can see that our Lord was justified in his statement, "ye have heard that it was said, thou shall love thy neighbour, and hate thine enemy."** Thus we may conclude that in most instances the two types of forgiveness are different.††

Now after seeing the differences of these two great

* Matt. 6:12, 14, 15.

† Mark 11:25, 26.[25]

‡ Eph. 4:31, 32.

§ Ps. cxviii. 7.

‖ Ps. 54:4–5.

Ps. 41:10.

** Matt. 5:43.
†† Charles, Testaments of the Twelve Patriarchs, p. xcii.

---

23. Enslin deleted "analyzing" and "scrutinizingly" and inserted the phrase "a careful analysis of" in place of "analyzing." He also substituted "might" for "would."

24. Charles, *Testaments of the Twelve Patriarchs*, p. xcii: "In the New Testament from the first page to the last it is either explicitly stated or implicitly understood that a man can only receive the divine forgiveness on condition that he forgives his neighbour."

25. Only Mark 11:25 is actually used in the text.

26. Charles, *Testaments of the Twelve Patriarchs*, p. xcii: "But the penitent in the Old Testament could accept and enjoy the divine pardon, and yet cherish the most bitter feelings towards his own personal enemy."

moral issues found in the Old and New Testaments, we are able to see the significant contribution found in the Testaments of the Twelve Patriarchs. We find Gad warning his children against hatred. "Love ye one another from the heart; and if a man sin against thee, speak peaceable to him, and in thy soul hold not guile.* And if he confess and repent, forgive him.† [27] Here we obviously see that our Lord in all probability had some acquaintance with the Testament of the Twelve Patriarchs.[28] The parallels in thought and language attest to that fact.[29]

* cf. Lev. 19:17; Matt. 18:15.

† cf. Luke 17:3.

It is significant to notice that the meaning of forgiveness as expressed in the Testaments of the Twelve Patriarchs is the same as that found in the New Testament. It means "the restoring the offender to communion with us, which he had forfeited through his offence."‡ The author is aware of the fact that forgiveness does not take away the fact of sin. But one thing it does; it reestablishes the old personal relationships that have been broken by sin, and makes them deeper and sweeter, it may even be by awakened love and responsive gratitude. That great thing forgiveness does—and to have been alienated and then reconciled through forgiveness is about the most searching experience that the human heart ever goes through.

‡ Charles, op. cit., p. xciv.

How is this process of forgiveness carried out? First, if a man sins against you, you must treat him with love and kindness. If he admits his wrong, you are to forgive him. If he fails to admit his offence, you must not lose your temper with him, lest he becomes poison[30] by your temper, and you become guilty of a double sin. In such a case, the offender, even though he denies his guilt, when he is reproved will feel a sense of shame, or he will not.[31] If he feels this sense

---

27. Enslin circled the quotation mark preceding "Love" and asked, "Where is the end of that quotation?"

28. Charles, *Testaments of the Twelve Patriarchs,* pp. xciii–xciv: "Now that we have grasped the conflicting attitudes of the Old and New Testaments on this great moral and religious question, we are able to appreciate the value of the contribution which the Testaments make in this direction. This contribution is found in T. Gad vi. 3–7. . . . So perfect are the parallels in thought and diction between these verses and Luke xvii. 3, Matt. xviii. 15, 35, that we must assume our Lord's acquaintance with them."

29. Enslin underlined "attest to that fact" and wrote, "suggest that possibility (?)."

30. Enslin questioned the meaning of this phrase.

31. Enslin underlined the final phrase of the sentence and commented that it was "a bit awkward."

of guilt he will repent. If he will not repent for his wrongdoing, he must be left to God.*

* T. Gad 6:3–7.

I have given more space to this ethical principle than I have given to any other previously, because of its tremendous influence on the Christian tradition. It reveals to us that the teachings of [*strikeout illegible*] late Judaism on the question of forgiveness is a connecting link between the conceptions found in the Old and New Testaments. The modern reader is amazed to see how the author of the Testaments of the Twelve Patriarchs had such a wonderful insight into the kernal of this question. No one can fully destroy its relevance today. We can see with greater appreciation the words of the prayer given to all men, "forgive us our trespasses, as we forgive them that trespass against us."

Asher: The Two Characters of Vice and Virtue.

The demand for ethical living presupposes that there is freedom of will, the free choice to will the good and do it or to hate the evil and avoid it. The teachers of late Judaism clearly recognized the significance of moral freedom. Asher says to his children: "Two ways hath God given to the sons of men, and two inclinations, and two kinds of action, and two modes (of action), and two issues. Therefore all things are by twos, one over against the other. For there are two ways, of good and evil, and with these are the two inclinations in our breasts discriminating them. Therefore if the soul take pleasure in the good (inclination), all its actions are in righteousness; and if it sin it straightway repenteth. For, having its thoughts set upon righteousness; and casting away wickedness, it strightway overthroweth the evil, and uprooteth the sin."† The importance of this passage can hardly be exaggerated, for it deals with a high ethical principle. Although the idea had been expressed before,‡ it is carried to its deeper meaning in this book. The author of the Testaments of the Twelve Patriarchs will not accept a doctrine of hereditary sin, neither will he accept the doctrine of inevitable fate. He will only accept the view that the universe is essentially honest.

† T. Asher 1:3–7.

‡ See Jer. 21:8.[32]

32. This citation is from Charles, *Testaments of the Twelve Patriarchs*, p. 161.

This is a lofty contribution which serves as a dynamic influence to later Judaism and Christian thought. Even the Sadducees and the Pharisees, the parties who, according to Josephus were of conflicting views, came in agreement on the question of freedom of will.[33]

Joseph: Brotherly Love.

The testament of Joseph deals with two important ethical principles. In the first part (ch. 1–10) he deals with the problem of chastity. In the second part (ch. 10–17) he appears as the model of brotherly love.[34] The former is written in poetical style; the latter, which is chronologically earlier, is written in simple prose, so that it is quite evident that the work {is of} two different authors.[35]

Since the question of chastity was discussed above, I will limit this discussion to the question of brotherly love. Joseph is found dwelling on the fact that, lest he should put his brothers to shame, he never revealed his birthplace and his family either to the merchants, who had bought him as a slave, or to Potiphar, whose wife had fallen in love with him at first sight, or to any of the enuchs of Pharaoh who stripped and beat him. "Therefore," said he to his children, "love one another, and with long-suffering hide each other's faults, for God delighteth in the unity of brethren."* He even goes futher by saying, "if any one seeketh to do evil unto you, do well unto him, and ye shall be redeemed of the Lord from all evil."†[37]

* T. Joseph 17:3.[36]

† T. Joseph 18:2.

Benjamin

The Testament of Benjamin deals with an ethical principle (purity of heart) which has already been discussed in the Testament of Reuben, therefore it would be needless repetition to reiterate this principle here.

---

33. Enslin underlined "came in agreement on the question of freedom of will" and asked: "What evidence have you for this statement?"

34. Enslin circled the "10" in both sets of parentheses and placed a question mark in the margin.

35. King is summarizing the discussion on the division of the Testament of Joseph found in Charles, *Testaments of the Twelve Patriarchs*, p. 172.

36. Enslin corrected the citation to "17:2 and 3."

37. Enslin marked "if" to be capitalized, added ellipses after "unto him," and commented, "Indicate any omissions or other deviation from quoted material."

So we may leave Benjamin by saying that he saw purity of heart as the highest virtue.

16 Feb
1949

Conclusion

We must conclude that the ethics of late Judaism reached a very high peak. So high and lofty were these ideals, that even today we cannot completely escape them.[38] We might have to modify these ideals to fit the conditions of the twentieth century, but we can never cast them out altogether. Although the form of the situations have changed, the substance of truth is the same.

In many instances, the pictures drawn by the author of this great work were idealistic, and ideals which all Jews did not attain any more than we attain all of our ideals. But the ideals were there; they at least served as standards by which he could measure himself, or goals which he could strive to attain. It was these ideals which later influenced the two great characters who will remain dear to us as long as the cords of memory shall lengthen—Jesus and Paul.

BIBLIOGRAPHY

Charles, R. H., <u>Testaments Of The Twelve Patriarchs</u>, London: Adam And Charles Black, 1908.
Charles, R. H., <u>Religious Development Between The Old And The New Testaments</u>, New York: Henry Holt and Co., n.d.

THDS. MLKP-MBU: Box 113, folder 19.

---

38. Enslin underlined "escape" and inquired, "Is this the word you want?"

William H. Gray, Jr., to Martin Luther King, Sr.

8 October 1949
Philadelphia, Pa.

Gray, the pastor of Bright Hope Baptist Church in Philadelphia, tells King, Sr., of his recent meeting at Crozer with King, Jr.[1] The relationship between the Gray and King families would continue for many years.

Reverend M. L. King, Sr.
Pastor
Ebenezer Baptist Church
Auburn Avenue at Jackson Street Northeast
Atlanta, Georgia

Dear Reverend King:

I am most appreciative of your letter of September twenty-eighth which your son was kind enough to forward to me from Crozer, and I assure you that I would consider it quite an honor to speak for your Men's Day Program on Sunday morning, December 11.

I would appreciate it, however, if you would be kind enough to allow me until October 20 to write you a final word of acceptance, since I would like to clear up some previous speaking commitments which I have made, and which might preclude my serving you on the date in question. One informal commitment which has been pending is with Reverend Maynard Jackson there in Atlanta, and I am hoping to hear from him soon. I hope that there will be no conflict to prevent my serving you.

I was very pleased to have met your son at Crozer recently. He seems to be quite a fine young gentleman, and I am sure that you and Mrs. King must be proud of the record he is making for himself and his family. {This is about you—Come over to see me when you are in Phila. and have an opportunity to visit. [*word illegible*]}[2]

Asking your prayers in my behalf, and with kindest personal regards, I remain

Sincerely yours,
Wm. H. Gray, Jr.

WHG/czs

cc: Reverend M. L. King, Jr.

TALc. MLKP-MBU: Box 117, folder 50.

---

1. William Herbert Gray, Jr. (1911–1972), received his B.S. from Bluefield State College in 1933 and his M.S. and Ph.D. from the University of Pennsylvania in 1934 and 1942, respectively. He was president of Florida Normal and Industrial College at St. Augustine from 1941 to 1944 and of Florida Agricultural and Mechanical University at Tallahassee from 1944 to 1949. In 1949, he succeeded his father as pastor of Bright Hope Baptist Church in Philadelphia.

2. Gray inserted this invitation to King, Jr., and sent him a copy of the letter.

"A Study of Mithraism"

[*13 September–23 November 1949*]
[*Chester, Pa.*]

*During the first semester of his second year at Crozer, King wrote this paper for
Enslin's course on Greek religion. Mithraism, a sect of Zoroastrianism characterized
by the worship of Mithra as the defender of the truth, was a monotheistic mystery
religion prevalent in the Roman empire before the acceptance of Christianity in the
fourth century. Followers of Mithra became less common after the Roman emperors
banned their cults, and Christianity gained the popularity that once belonged to
Mithraism. Enslin gave the essay an A and wrote: "This is an exceedingly good
paper. You have given a very complete picture of the essential details and you have
presented this in a balanced and restrained way. And furthermore you know how to
write. You should go a long way if you continue to pay the price."*

The Greco-Roman world in which the early church
developed was one of diverse religions. The conditions of that era made it possible for these religions to
sweep like a tidal wave over the ancient world. The
people of that age were eager and zealous in their
search for religious experience. The existence of this
atmosphere was vitally important in the development
and eventual triumph of Christianity.

These many religions were not alike in every respect; to draw this conclusion would lead to a gratuitous and erroneous supposition. But it is to be noticed
that they possessed many fundamental likenesses;
(1) All held that the initiate shared in symbolic (sacramental) fashion the experiences of the god. (2) All
had secret rites for the initiated. (3) All offered mystical cleansing from sin. (4) All promised a happy future life for the faithful.*

* Enslin, Christian Be-
ginnings, pp. 187, 188.

It is not at all surprising in view of the wide and
growing influence of these religions that when the
disciples in Antioch and elsewhere preached a crucified and risen Jesus they should be regarded as the
heralds of another mystery religion, and that Jesus
himself should be taken for the divine Lord of the
cult through whose death and resurrection salvation
was to be had.

It is at this point that we are able to see why knowledge of these cults is important for any serious New
Testament study. It is well-nigh impossible to grasp
Christianity through and through without knowledge
of these cults. That there were striking similarities between the developing church and these religions can-

not be denied. Even Christian apologist had to admit that fact. For an instance, in the mystery-religions identification between the devotee and the Lord of the cult was supposed to be brought about by various rites of initiation; the taurobolium, or bath of blood; the eating of flesh of the sacrifical beast and the like. Now there was something of this in Paul too, for he thought of the believer as buried with Christ in baptism and as feeding upon him in the eucharist. This is only one of many examples that I could give to prove the similarity between the developing Christian Church and the Mystery Religions.

This is not to say that a Saint Paul or a Saint John sat down and copied these views verbatim. But after being in contact with these surrounding religions and hearing certain doctrines expressed, it was only natural for some of these views to become a part of their subconscious minds. When they sat down to write they were expressing consciously that which had dwelled in their subconscious minds.[1] It is also significant to know that Roman tolerance had favoured this great syncretism of religious ideas. Borrowing was not only natural but inevitable.

One of the most interesting of these ancient cults was Mithraism, which bore so many points of resemblance to Christianity that it is a challenge to the modern student to investigate these likenesses and learn more about them. Mithraism is perhaps the greatest example of paganism's last effort to reconcile itself to the great spiritual movement which was gaining such sturdy influence with its purer conception of God.* Ernest Renan, the French philosopher and Orientalist, expressed the opinion that Mithraism would have been the religion of the modern world if anything had occured to halt or destroy the growth of Christianity in the early centuries of its existence. All this goes to show how important Mithraism was in ancient times.

The present study represents an attempt to provide

* Dill, Roman Society From Nero to Marcus Aurelius, p. 585.

---

1. King used similar phrasing in a paper written the previous year: "This is not to say that the pentateuch writers sat down and copied these views verbatim. The differences of expression attest to that fact. But after being in contact with these surrounding cultures and hearing certain doctrines expressed, it was only natural for some of these views to become a part of their subconscious minds. When they sat down to write they were expressing consciously that which had dwelled in their sub-conscious minds" ("Light on the Old Testament from the Ancient Near East," 14 September–24 November 1948, p. 163 in this volume).

a survey of the general character of the Mithraic re- ligion. The main source of reference for this study was the magnificent work of Cumont. In order to give a comprehensive picture of this mystery cult, I will discuss four points:

(1) The origin and dissemination of Mithraism
(2) The doctrines of Mithraism
(3) The liturgy of Mithraism
(4) The influence of Mithraism on Christianity

The Origin and Dissemination of Mithraism

The history of Mithraism lies deep in the roots of the past. Documents which belong to the fourteenth century before Christ have been found in the Hittite capital of Boghaz Keui, in which the names of Mithra, Vanuna, Indra, and the Heavenly Twins are recorded.[2] It is also known that they were written long before the separation of the Indian and Iranian races. But to give the exact origin of this cult and to determine exactly where Mithra came from would be merely conjecture.

Many have held the opinion that Mithra came originally from the high plateuas of the Hindukush;[3] and the differences in his nature, when he is found later in India and Iran, were due to environmental influences in the two distinctly different areas. In the Vedas he was associated with Varuna and was invoked together with him as a light god. The Iranians, however, placed Mithra in the position of Archangel. Although Ahura Mazda was the supreme god, he created Mithra equal to himself and made him chief among the yazatas. Evidence of his exalted position lies in the fact that the longest yasht, eight times longer than that in honour of Ahura Mazda, is dedicated to Mithra.* He possessed many attributes, the most important being his office of defender of truth and all good things. In the Avesta,† Mithra is represented as the genius of celestial light. He emerges

* Dhalla, History of Zoroastrianism, p. 183.

† This is the sacred book of the religion of Iran.

---

2. W. R. Halliday, *The Pagan Background of Early Christianity* (London: University Press of Liverpool, n.d.), p. 283: "Documents which belong to the fourteenth century before Christ have been found in the Hittite capital of Boghaz Keui, in which the names of Mitra, Varuna, Indra, and the Heavenly Twins, the Nasatyas, are recorded."

3. Enslin marked "Hindukush" and wrote that it was "more commonly written as two words."

from the rocky summits of eastern mountains at dawn, and goes through heaven with a team of four white horses; when the night falls he still illumines the surface of the earth "ever walking ever watchful." He is not sun or moon or any star, but a spirit of light, ever wakeful, watching with a hundred eyes. He hears all and sees all: none can deceive him.*[4] Mithra was the god of wide pastures and the giver of gifts. He was worthy of sacrifice and worship and desired the respect and prayer of the faithful, on whom he bestowed bounteous gifts. On the other hand, he was a warrior of violent and bitter nature; the forces of evil were his enemies, and he joined with Sraosha (Obedience) and Rashnu (Justice) in opposing them.

The fame of Mithra spread as the Persian empire expanded, and he became particularly strong in Asia Minor. Many of the Persian Kings grew very fond of Mithra and sponsored worship of him. It was during this time that the worship of Mithra developed into an independent religion. It is interesting to know that as Mithraism was spreading through the Persian empire, it was constantly borrowing ideas from other cultures. When it came in contact with Semitic star worship, it assimilated much of it as well as some of the mythology of ancient Babylon. Also the cult incorporated many local practices and ideas from Asia Minor. Finally it was influenced to a certain extent by Hellenistic culture. After having consolidated its theology and drawing into its ranksxmany converts in Asia Minor and Persia, Mithraism had almost reached its climax. It was, however, the latest religion of its kind to become popular in the Roman empire.†

The greatest agency of propagation of Mithraism was the army. Under the Roman policy of conscription troops from conquered lands were sent to serve in other parts of the empire. Among the forces which were drawn up in that fashion were soldiers from such places as Cappadocia, Commagene, Pontus and Armenia, where Mithraism was extremely popular.

* Cumont, Mysteries of Mithra, pp. 2, 3.

† Mithraism was not popular in the Roman empire until ca. A.D. 100.

---

4. Franz Cumont, *The Mysteries of Mithra* (Chicago: Open Court, 1910), pp. 2–3: "In the Avesta, Mithra is the genius of the celestial light. He appears before sunrise on the rocky summits of the mountains; during the day he traverses the wide firmament in his chariot drawn by four white horses, and when night falls he still illumines with flickering glow the surface of the earth, 'ever waking, ever watchful.' He is neither sun, nor moon, nor stars, but with 'his hundred ears and his hundred eyes' watches constantly the world. Mithra hears all, sees all, knows all: none can deceive him."

When these men were sent out to foreign outpost to serve in the Roman army they did not forget their religious customs. Converts were quickly gained within the army. Evidences of the diffusion of Mithraism by the army has been found in Scotland, Africa, Spain, Germany, and almost every locality where Roman troops were sent.

A second means of spreading Mithraism in the empire was through slaves who were sent to Italy from Asia Minor. Many of these slaves became public servants in the great bureaus of the government. It was these slaves who were missionaries for Mirtha in Italy and who practiced his mysteries in the very heart of the Roman world.

There was a third group which spread the Mithraic religion. This group consisted of Syrian merchants who established trading posts throughout the empire. Cumont is of the opinion that most of these Syrians belonged to the upper classes and were not the true worshippers of Mithra. He argues that it was the slaves and servants of these merchants who were followers of Mithra; and they introduced the religion to the inhabitants of maritime towns where their masters engaged in trading.*

* Cumont, op. cit., p. 63.

The great expansion of Mithraism in the ancient world can be traced to these three sources in almost every case. The slaves were forever looking for a better day, and they beleived that through worshipping Mithra that day would eventually come. As for the soldiers they found Mithraism very appealing because it offered them the protection of a deity who they believed would help them to be victorious in combat. After seeing these facts it is very easy to understand why these worshippers were so zealous in spreading their religion. It was a part of their total make-up. To argue that many were drawn into this cult through curiosity alone is certainly an unwarranted assumption. To be sure, the iniatory rites (as we will see later in the paper) were so strenuous that only the sincere and earnest converts would have wished to take part in them.

After the cult became popular throughout the Roman Empire, it received many converts from the upper classes. It had been spread by slaves and freedmen for the most part, but it did {not} remain a religion of the lower classes alone. As stated above, even the emperors gave it their approval.

Whether the religion of Mithra gained great influence in Greece is still under discussion by many scholars. There seems to be many conflicting statements about this question.[5] Cumont writes, "It may be said, in a general way, that Mithra remained forever excluded from the Hellenic world. The ancient authors of Greece speak of him only as a foreign god worshipped by the kings of Persia."[*] Dhalla says that Mithra "is the only Iranian divinity who won popularity for himself in Greece."[†] George Foot Moore says of Mithraism that "it never took root in the lands of Hellenistic culture."[‡] The majority of opinions seem to support the fact that Mithraism was excluded from Hellenized countries. It is probable that the name of Mithra was well-known in these lands, but the inhabitants declined to worship him.

The worship of Mithra, which had had its very first introduction into the western part of the empire only a short time before the birth of Christ and had not begun to expand until the end of the first century, became widespread and popular in a remarkably short time. It was during the same period, of course, that christianity was beginning to develop and reach out into new territories. The question immediately arises, why did the two religions not conflict?

One reason that the two religions did not conflict in the early years of their growth in the Roman Empire is that their activities for a while took place in different geographical areas. Another reason why these religions did not clash with each other was because each thought the other was too insignificant for serious competition. It is apparent, therefore, that geographically and socially these religions did not clash for a while.

The Doctrines
Of Mithraism

Unfortunately, there is practically no literary evidence for the inner history of Mithraism. A few scattered facts may be gathered from the remains of Christian polemics, a great deal of information about the overall character of the ideas to which they gave expression may be gotten from the writings of Neo-

[*] Cumont, op. cit., p. 9.[6]

[†] Dhalla, History of Zoroastrianism, p. 303.

[‡] Moore, History of Religions, Vol. 1, p. 600.

---

5. Enslin underlined "many" and wrote in the margin: "It is pretty generally recognized that it never 'took' in Greece. Dhalla's view is not widely held."

6. The quotation is actually from page 33.

Platonists and a close examination of mystical papyri.[7] 23 Nov 1949
Fortunately, these numerous monuments have been synthesized in the scholarly work of Cumont. From this work we are able to get with a degree of certainty the mythological and eschatological teaching of this cult. For the moment let us look into these teachings.

First we turn to the cosmogonic views of Mithraism. It is interesting to know how Mithraic preachers sought to explain the origin of the world. They explained it in terms of a series of successive generations. The first principle begot a primordial couple, the Heaven and the Earth; and the Earth, who was impregnated by her brother, gave birth to the vast Ocean. This group formed the supreme triad of the Mithraic Panthean.[8]

At times these cosmic divinities were personified in quite different names from their original ones. The Heaven was called Ormazd or Jupiter, the Earth was identified with Spenta-Armaiti or Juno, and the Ocean was called Apam-Napat or Neptune.[9]

As was stated above, Jupiter (Heaven) and Juno (Earth) were the sovereign couple. They gave birth not only to Neptune (Ocean) who became their peer, but to many other immortals. Shahrivar or Mars, Valcun or Atar, Bacchus or Haoma, Silvanus or Drvaspa, Diana or Luna are but a few of the long line of immortals. These innumerable multitude of divinities composed the celestial court.* This in short sums up the cosmogonic views of the Mithraic religion.

The doctrine of the immortality of the soul was another view which was very prominent in Mithraism.

* Cumont, op. cit., pp. 111, 112.

---

7. Halliday, *Pagan Background*, pp. 289–290: "It is profoundly to be regretted that we possess practically no literary evidence for the inner history of Mithraism, nor indeed of any of the pagan mystery religions of this period. A few random facts may be elicited from the *obiter dicta* of Christian polemic, a good deal of information about the general character of the ideas to which they gave expression may be gleaned from the difficult study of Gnosticism in its pagan and Christian forms, from the writings of the Neo-Platonists, and from the careful examination of magical papyri."

8. Cumont, *Mysteries of Mithra*, p. 109: "The first principle, according to an ancient belief found in India as well as in Greece, begot a primordial couple, the Heaven and the Earth; and the latter, impregnated by her brother, gave birth to the vast Ocean which was equal in power to its parents, and which appears to have formed with them the supreme triad of the Mithraic Pantheon."

9. Cumont, *Mysteries of Mithra*, p. 111: "The Heavens were naught less than Ormazd or Jupiter, the Earth was identified with Spenta-Armalti or Juno, and the Ocean was similarly called Apam-Napat or Neptune."

217

Mithraism insisted that the soul was immortal and its temporary sojourn in a body was a period of trial. The worshipper's action determined the posthumous fate of his soul. Of course, he was not alone in his attempt to attain purity and truth; Mithra stood by his side as a divine helper.[10]

The background of Mithraic eschatology was provided by that theory of the relation of the soul to the universe. It was believed that the soul descended at birth {from} the eternal home of light through the gate of Cancer, passing down through the seven planetary spheres to earth. As the soul passed through each stage it accumulated more and more impurity. It was possible for the initiate, while in his trial period on earth, to gain purity through the practice of courage and truth.[11]

After death there was judgment of the soul. Mithra, the protector of the truth, presided over the judgment court. If the soul had lived an impure life, it was dragged down to the infernal depths, where it received a thousand tortures. If, on the contrary, its good qualities outweighed the bad, it rises through the gate of caprocorn, passing in reverse order through the planetary sphere. At each stage the impurities which the soul picked up in its downward flow gradually diminished. The end of this great rise was supreme happiness and eternal bliss.

The doctrine of resurrection of the flesh was also a basic belief in the Mithraic circle. It was believed that the long struggle between the principles of good and evil would one day end. At this time a great bull would reappear on earth; and Mithra would redescend and reawaken men to life. All would come forth from the tombs with the same appearance they had on earth. All mankind would unite into a great

---

10. Halliday, *Pagan Background*, p. 294: "In Mithraism the soul was regarded as immortal, and its temporary sojourn in an earthly body was a period of trial. Upon the degrees of purity and truth which was attained by the worshipper, and upon the part played by him in fighting upon the side of Good, depended the posthumous fate of his soul. In this mortal life Mithras stands by the side of the initiate as a divine helper."

11. Halliday, *Pagan Background*, pp. 294–295: "The background of Mithraic eschatology was provided by that theory of the relation of the soul to the universe. . . . The soul was thought to have descended at birth from the eternal home of light through the gate of Cancer, passing down through the seven planetary spheres to earth. At each stage it became more heavily weighted by accumulated impurity. During its time of trial upon earth came the opportunity to acquire purity through moral struggle, that is to say, by the conquest of passions and appetites and the practice of courage, endurance, fortitude, and truth."

union, at which time the god of truth would separate the good from the bad. Then the great bull would be sacrificed. The fat of this bull would be mingled with the consecrated wine, and would be offered to the just. From this they would receive immortality. After this great event, Jupiter-Ormazd would cause a great fire to fall from heaven which would destroy all the wicked. The Spirit of Darkness would be completely destroyed. The universe would then enjoy eternal happiness and peace.

There was another doctrine which remained fundamental to Mithraism throughout its history. It was the doctrine of dualism. This doctrine was taken from Zoroastrianism. This doctrine accounted for the problem of evil by supposing that the world was a battleground between the Good Principle, Ahura Mazda, and the Evil Principle, Ahriman. The powers of good were identified with Light or Day, and the powers of evil were identified with Darkness or Night. These two powers were in a state of perpetual war. It was Mithra, the spirit of light and truth who became naturally a celestial warrior on the side of Ahura Mazda.* [12]

* Halliday, The Pagan Background of Early Christianity, pp. 285, 286.

It was many of these doctrines that became very influential in later years to the Christian religion. They molded the thinking of the ancient world.

Mithraic Liturgy

According to a text of St. Jerome, there were seven degrees of initiation which the Mithraic convert passed through. At each stage he assumed a different name: (1) Raven, (2) Occult, (3) Soldier, (4) Lion, (5) Persian, (6) Runner of the sun, (7) and Father. It is probable that there were slight variations of names of the grades from East to West. Each grade had its appropriate mask and costume.

The taking of the first three degrees did not authorize the status of full participation in the Mysteries. These initiates were called the Servants. Only

---

12. Halliday, *Pagan Background*, pp. 283–284: "The great Iranian prophet accounted for the problem of evil by supposing that the world was a battleground between the Good Principle, Ahura Mazda, and the Evil Principle, Ahriman. The powers of Good were identified with Light or Day in conflict with the powers of Evil, Darkness or Night, and Mithras, the spirit of light and truth, became naturally a celestial warrior on the side of Ahura Mazda."

the Mystic who had received the Leontics could become a "Participant". At the top of this structure were the Fathers, who probably presided over the sacred ceremonies and had command over the lower classes.[13]

It was possible to enter the lowest grades at infancy. Whether or not the initiate had to remain in each grade for a fixed length of time is not known. Cumont is of the opinion that the Fathers decided when the initiate was sufficiently prepared to move to the higher grade.*

One of the prominent features in the ceremony of initiation was the sacrament (sacramentum) or military oath of loyalty to the service of the god and to the fellow members of the brotherhood. In this oath the initiate promised to depart from certain sins and follow a life of moral behavior. Moreover, he promised not to reveal to the uninitiated the rites and knowledge he was about to learn.

Although our knowledge of the liturgy of Mithraism is inevitably fragmentary, we know that there was a form of baptism designed to wash away the sins of the initiate. This rite was probably carried out by sprinkling holy water, or in an actual immersion. At another stage in the development the initiated was sealed with a brand in his forehead. It appears that this mark was burned with a red-hot iron. This ineffaceable imprint was always a reminder to the initiate of what he had vowed. In the grade of soldier, the initiate was offered a crown which he caused to fall on his shoulder, saying that Mithra was his only crown. In the grade of Lion, the initiate's tongue and hands were purified with honey.[14]

Another important Mithraic ceremony was the celebration of a communion service which was in memory

* Cumont, op. cit., p. 156.

---

13. Cumont, *Mysteries of Mithra*, p. 155: "The taking of the first three degrees did not authorize participation in the Mysteries. These initiates, comparable to the Christian catechumens, were the Servants . . . Only the mystics that had received the Leontics became Participants . . . At the summit of the hierarchy were placed the Fathers, who appear to have presided over the sacred ceremonies (*pater sacrorum*) and to have commanded the other classes of the faithful."

14. Halliday, *Pagan Background*, p. 304: "Our knowledge of the initiatory rites of Mithraism is inevitably fragmentary. We know that in this, as in many contemporary cults, a form of baptism represented the mystical washing away of sin. The initiated in certain grades were sealed upon the forehead with the mark of their calling, probably with a brand. At the initiation into the grade of Soldier, the neophyte was offered a crown which he renounced with the words 'Mithras is my crown.' The tongue and the hands of a Lion were purified with honey."

of the last meal which Helios and Mithra partook together upon earth.[15] Here the celebrant took consecrated bread and mingled it with the juice of Haoma.
It is quite obvious that only the initiate who had attained the degree of Lions could take this communion.

The worship services were carried on in chapels
or Mithraea. These chapels were technically called
"caves" spelaea. They were probably called "caves"
because they were either constructed in natural caves
or in subterranean buildings. In most of the Mithraea
there was a portico which led into a second sacristry,
where the ritual dresses were probably kept. Beyond
the sacristry lay the shrine. It was here that most of
the ritual was performed. On each side were benches
where the new converts were probably seated. At the
end of the building there was an apse, in which stood
the relief of Mithra slaying the bull. It is probable that
this was veiled with curtains. The walls of the building
were very fascinating; they were covered with paintings and mosaics of mystical designs.[16]

The worship period was conducted by the priest,
who bore the title of sacerdos. The priest was considered the intermediary between God and man. It was
his duty to administer the sacraments. He also presided at the formal dedications. He probably had to
see that a perpetual fire burned upon the altars. He
addressed a prayer to the sun three times a day, at
dawn, at noon, and at dusk. This, in short, gives the
overall function of the priest.

It was a characteristic of Mithraism to be organized
in small and apparently independent communities.
In this community the individual had a right to hold
property. For the management of the affairs of the
community, officers were selected. The officers were

---

15. Halliday, *Pagan Background*, p. 304: "One of the principal Mithraic ceremonies was the
celebration of a communion service in memory, it was thought, of the last meal of which Helios
and Mithra partook together upon earth."

16. Halliday, *Pagan Background*, pp. 298–299: "The chapels or Mithraea in which the worship
of the cult was carried on, were technically called 'caves,' *spelaea*, and were constructed either in
a natural cave or, for obvious reasons, more often in a subterranean building which was made to
resemble a cave. . . . In the most usual type of Mithraeum a portico led off the road into a vesti-
bule, this led into a second sacristy, where probably the ritual dresses, etc., were kept; beyond
this again lay the shrine. . . . At the end of the building opposite to the entrance was an apse, in
which stood the relief of Mithra slaying the bull. It would appear that this was normally veiled
with curtains, . . . The walls of the building were covered with paintings and mosaics of mystical
design."

masters (magistri) or president, the curators (cura-
tores), the attorneys (defensores), and the patrons
(patroni).

Mithraism possessed a characteristic that was unique
and which for a time may have been an asset but in
the end was probably a weakness. It was a cult for
men only. In some cases young boys were taken into
the lower orders, but under no circumstances were
women admitted. Women were compelled to seek
salvation in some other cult, for Mithraism excluded
them entirely. "It has been surmised that the frequent juxtaposition of Mithraea (places of worship)
and temples of the Magna Mater was due to the fact
that the wives and daughters of the Mithraists were
addicted to the worship of the latter."* In the exclusion of women Mithraism missed "that ardent re-
ligiosity and fervent proselytism of devout women
which had so large a share in pushing the fortunes
of Isis and Cybele or in propagating the tenets of
Christianity."†

* Moore, op. cit., p. 600.

† Halliday, op. cit., p. 310.

The Influence of
Mithraism on Christianity

When Mithraism is compared with Christianity,
there are surprisingly many points of similarity. Of all
the mystery cults Mithraism was the greatest competi-
tor of Christianity. The cause for struggle between
these two religions was that they had so many traditions, practices and ideas that were similar and in
some cases identical.

Many of the similarities between these two religions
have already been alluded to, but there are many others of greater or lesser significance. The belief in immortality, a mediator between god and man, the observance of certain sacramental rites, the rebirth of
converts, and (in most cases) the support of high ethical ideas were common to Mithraism as well as to
Christianity. In fact, the comparison became so evident that many believed the Christian movement itself became a mystery cult. "Jesus was the divine
Lord. He too had found the road to heaven by his
suffering and resurrection. He too had God for his
father. He had left behind the secret whereby men
could achieve the goal with him."‡

‡ Enslin, op. cit., p. 190.

There were many other points of similarity between these two groups. Let us look at a few of them:

(1) Both regarded Sunday as a holy day.[17] (2) December 25 came to be considered as the anniversary of the birth of Mithra and Christ also. (3) Baptism and a communion meal were important parts of the ritual of both groups. (4) The rebirth of converts was a fundamental idea in the two cults. (5) The struggle with evil and the eventual triumph of good were essential ideas in both religions. (6) In both religions only initiates who passed through certain preliminary phases of introduction were admitted to the mysteries which brought salvation to converts. There were many more similarities between Christianity and Mithraism—most of them purely superficial. These which have been mentioned are largely only surface likenesses because the reasoning behind them is quite different, but the general effect is almost startling.

The sacraments of baptism and the eucharist have been mentioned as rites which were practiced both by christians and pagans. It is improbable, however, that either of these {were} introduced into Christian practices by association with the mystery cults. The baptismal ceremony in both cases (christian and mystery) was supposed to have the effect of identifying the initiate with his saviour. But although baptism did not originate with the Christians, still it was not copied from the pagans. It seems instead to have been carried over from Jewish background and modified by the new ideas and beliefs of the Christians. The eucharist, likewise though similar in some respects to the communion meal of Mithraism, was not a rite borrowed from them. There are several explanations regarding the beginning of the observance of the Lord's Supper. Some held that the sacrament was instituted by Jesus himself. Others saw it as an outgrowth from Jewish precedents. Still others felt that, after the death of Jesus, the disciples saw in their common meal an opportunity to hold a kind of memorial service for him.

On the whole, early Christians were not greatly concerned about the likenesses between the Mithraic cult and their own. They felt at first that these competitors were not worthy of consideration, and few references to them are found in Christian literature.

---

17. Enslin asked in the margin, "How early did Christians make this the [*first?*] day?"

When Mithraism became widespread and powerful, it attracted so much attention that certain Christian apologists felt the need to present an explanation for the similarities in their respective characteristics. The only one they could offer was quite naive, but it was in keeping with the trends of thought in that age. They maintained that it was the work of the devil who helped to confuse men by creating a pagan imitation of the true religion.[18]

The greatest influence of Mithraism on Christianity lies in a different direction from that of doctrine and ritual. It lies in the fact that Mithraism paved the way for the presentation of Christianity to the world of that time. It prepared the people mentally and emotionally to understand the type of religion which Christianity represented. It was itself in varying degrees, an imperfect example of the Galilean cult which was to replace it. It encouraged the movement away from the state religions and the philosophical systems and toward the desire for personal salvation and promise of immortality. Christianity was truly indebted to Mithraism for this contribution, for it had done this part of the groundwork and thus opened the way for Christian missionary work.

Conclusion

That Christianity did copy and borrow from Mithraism cannot be denied, but it was generally a natural and unconscious process rather than a deliberate plan of action. It was subject to the same influences from the environment as were the other cults, and it sometimes produced the same reaction. The people were conditioned by the contact with the older religions and the background and general trend of the time.

Many of the views, while passing out of Paganism into Christianity were given a more profound and spiritual meaning by Christians, yet we must be indebted to the source. To discuss Christianity without mentioning other religions would be like discussing the greatness of the Atlantic Ocean without the slightest mention of the many tributaries that keep it flowing.

---

18. The previous two paragraphs also appear in another essay by King, "Influence of the Mystery Religions on Christianity," 29 November 1949–15 February 1950, pp. 309–310 in this volume.

{2} Cumont, Franz, <u>The Mysteries of Mithra</u>, The
      Open Court Publishing Co., Chicago, 1910.

      Dhalla, M. N., <u>History of Zoroastrianism</u>, Ox-
      ford University Press N. Y., 1938 pp. 183–
      192.

{4}} Dill, Samuel, <u>Roman Society From Nero To
      Marcus Aurelius</u>, Macmillan and Co., 1905,
      pp. 585–626.

{5}} Enslin, Morton S., <u>Christian Beginnings</u>, Har-
      per and Brothers Publishers N. Y. and Lon-
      don, 1938, pp. 186–200.

{(8)} Halliday, W. R., <u>The Pagan Background of
      Early Christianity</u>, The University Press of
      Liverpool, London, N.D., pp. 281–311.

{(10)} Moore, George F., <u>History of Religions</u>, Vol. 1,
      Charles Scribner's Sons, N.Y., 1913, pp. 357–
      405, 592–602.

THDS. MLKP-MBU: Box 113, folder 19.

"What Experiences of Christians
Living in the Early Christian Century
Led to the Christian Doctrines
of the Divine Sonship of Jesus,
the Virgin Birth, and the Bodily Resurrection"

[13 September–23 November 1949]
[Chester, Pa.]

*During King's second year at Crozer Theological Seminary, he took a two-term
required course in systematic theology, Christian Theology for Today, with George
W. Davis.*[1] *For the first assignment of the first term, Davis asked his students to use
George Hedley's* The Symbol of the Faith, *an examination of the Apostles'
Creed. In this essay, King follows the book's structure and argument closely. When*

---

1. George Washington Davis (1902–1960) earned his B.A. at the University of Pittsburgh in
1924, his B.D. (1928) and Th.M. (1929) at Rochester Theological Seminary, and his Ph.D. under
the direction of Douglas Clyde Macintosh at Yale University (1932). Davis was the pastor of
churches in Calais, Maine, and Columbus, Ohio, before becoming professor of Christian theology
at Crozer Theological Seminary in 1938, where he taught for the remainder of his career.

*he discusses the "probable" influence of Greek mythology on Christian thought,
Davis prods, "Is there any doubt about it?" On balance, King shows himself
willing to abandon scriptural literalism, remaining confident that this would not
undermine the "profound foundation" of the Christian doctrines. Davis
commented, "Well done," and gave the paper an A−.*

In order to understand the meaning and the significance of any doctrine or any creed it is necessary to study the experiences of the individuals that produced them. Doctrines and creeds do not spring forth uncaused like Athene sprang from the head of Zeus, but they grow out of the historical settings and the psychological moods of the individuals that set them forth. All ideas, however profound or however naive, are produced by conditions and experiences that grow from the producers' environment.

In this paper we shall discuss the experiences of early Christians which lead to three rather orthodox doctrines—the divine sonship of Jesus, the virgin birth, and the bodily resurrection. Each of these doctrines is enshrined in what is known as "the Apostles' Creed." It is this creed that has stood as a "Symbol of Faith" for many Christians over the years. Even to this day it is recited in many churches. But in the minds of many sincere Christians this creed has planted a seed of confusion which has grown to an oak of doubt. They see this creed as incompatible with all scientific knowledge, and so they have proceeded to reject its content.

But if we delve into the deeper meaning of these doctrines, and somehow strip them of their literal interpretation, we will find that they are based on a profound foundation. Although we may be able to argue with all degrees of logic that these doctrines are historically and philolophically untenable, yet we can never undermind the foundation on which they are based. As Dr. Hedley has so cogently stated, "What ultimately the creed signifies is not words, but spirit."*

* George Hedley, The Symbol of the Faith, p. 7.

The first doctrine of our discussion which deals with the divine sonship of Jesus went through a great process of developement. It seems quite evident that the early followers of Jesus in Palestine were well aware of his genuine humanity. Even the synoptic gospels picture Jesus as a victim of human experiences. Such human experiences as growth, learning, prayer, and defeat are not at all uncommon in the life of Jesus.[2] How then did this doctrine of divine sonship come into being?

We may find a partial clue to the actual rise of this doctrine in the spreading of Christianity into the Greco-Roman world. I need not elaborate on the fact that the Greeks were very philosophical minded people. Through philosophical thinking the Greeks came to the point of subordinating, distrusting, and even minimizing anything physical. Anything that possessed flesh was always underminded in Greek thought. And so in order to receive inspiration from Jesus the Greeks had to apotheosize him. We must remember that the Logos concept had its origin in Greek thought. It ~~would~~ {was} only natural that the early Christians, after coming in contact with the Greeks would be influenced by their thought.

But by no means can we designate this as the only clue to the rise of this doctrine. Saint Paul and the early church followers could have never come to the conclusion that Jesus was divine if there had not been some uniqueness in the personality of the historical Jesus. What Jesus brought into life was a new personality and those who came under {its} spell were more and more convinced that he with whom they had walked and talked in Galilee could be nothing less than a divine person. To the earliest Christians this breath-taking conviction was not the conclusion of an argument, but the inescapable solution of a problem. Who was this Jesus? They saw that Jesus could not merely be explained in terms of the psychological mood of the age in which he lived, for such explaination failed to answer another inescapable question: Why did Jesus differ from many others in the same setting? And so the early Christians answered this question by saying that he was the divine son of God. As Hedley laconically states, "the church had found God in Jesus, and so it called Jesus the Christ; and later under the influence of Greek thought-forms, the only begotten Son of God."* The Church called Jesus divine because they had found God in him. They could only identify him with the highest and best in the universe. It was this great experience with

* Hedley, op. cit., p. 37.

2. George Hedley, *The Symbol of the Faith: A Study of the Apostles' Creed* (New York: Macmillan, 1948), p. 34: "The first three Gospels portray [Jesus] as growing, learning, contending, suffering, being defeated: all of which are universal human experiences."

the historical Jesus that led the early Christians to see him as the divine son of God.

The second doctrine in our discussion posits the virgin birth. This doctrine gives the modern scientific mind much more trouble than the first, for it seems downright improbable and even impossible for anyone to be born without a human father.[3]

First we must admit that the evidence for the tenability of this doctrine is to shallow to convince any objective thinker. To begin with, the earliest written documents in the New Testament make no mention of the virgin birth. Moreover, the Gospel of Mark, the most primitive and authentic of the four, gives not the slightest suggestion of the virgin birth. The effort to justify this doctrine on the grounds that it was predicted by the prophet Isaiah is immediately eliminated, for all New Testament scholars agree that the word virgin is not found in the Hebrew original, but only in the Greek text which is a mistranslation of the Hebrew word for "young woman." How then did this doctrine arise?

A clue to this inquiry may be found in a sentence from St. Justin's First Apology. Here Justin states that the birth of Jesus is quite similar to the birth of the sons of Zeus. It was believed in Greek thought that an extraordinary person could only be explained by saying that he had a father who was more than human. It is probable that this Greek idea influenced Christian thought.[4]

A more adequate explanation for the rise of this doctrine is found in the experience which the early christians had with Jesus. The people saw within Jesus such a uniqueness of quality and spirit that to explain him in terms of ordinary background was to them quite inadequate. For his early followers this spiritual uniqueness could only by accounted for in terms of biological uniqueness.[5] They were not unscientific in

---

3. Hedley raises the same objection in *Symbol of the Faith*, p. 39: "To our minds it seems improbable in itself that anyone should be born without a human father."

4. Davis underlined "probable," wrote a question mark above it, and asked, "Is there any doubt about it?"

5. Hedley, *Symbol of the Faith*, pp. 45–46: "[Jesus] was so extraordinary a person that ordinary backgrounds seemed for him quite inadequate. The character of Jesus stands out, quite separately from this ancient attempt at explaining it, and surviving that attempt without loss of any kind. We shall not try to account for Jesus' moral uniqueness by a theory of biological uniqueness; but the moral uniqueness of Jesus stands, and still defies our own attempts at its explaining."

their approach because they had no knowledge of the scientific. They could only express themselves in terms of the pre-scientific thought patterns of their day. No laws were broken because they had no knowledge of the existence of law. They only knew that they had been with the Jesus of history and that his spiritual life was so far beyond theirs that to explain his biological origin as identical with theirs was quite inadequate. We of this scientific age will not explain the birth of Jesus in such unscientific terms, but we will have to admit with the early Christians that the spiritual uniqueness of Jesus stands as a mystery to man.

The last doctrine in our discussion deals with the resurrection story. This doctrine, upon which the Easter Faith rests, symbolizes the ultimate Christian conviction: that Christ conquered death. From a literary, historical, and philosophical point of view this doctrine raises many questions.[6] In fact the external evidence for the authenticity of this doctrine is found wanting. But here again the external evidence is not the most important thing, for it in itself fails to tell us precisely the thing we most want to know: What experiences of early Christians lead to the formulation of the doctrine?

The root of our inquiry is found in the fact that the early Christians had lived with Jesus. They had been captivated by the magnetic power of his personality. This basic experience led to the faith that he could never die. And so in the pre-scientific thought pattern of the first century, this inner faith took outward form.[7] But it must be remembered that before the doctrine was formulated or the event recorded, the early Christians had had a lasting experience with the Christ. They had come to see that the essential note in the Fourth Gospel is the ultimate force in Christianity: The living, deathless person of Christ.

---

6. Hedley, *Symbol of the Faith*, p. 75: "Easter symbolizes the ultimate Christian conviction. The Easter message is that he who was born of a woman, he who died on Calvary, became the conqueror of death: . . . When, however, we enquire into the documentary evidence for the resurrection faith, we are beset at once by intricate literary, historical, and philosophical problems."

7. Hedley, *Symbol of the Faith*, p. 80: "For those who knew him, he could never die. His moral imperatives were immortal, his gentleness triumphed over the brutality of the cross, his love lived on without reference to his body's death. He could not die: that certainty was at the beginning. Out of it came the assurance that still he lived. By the necessities of symbolic expression, and especially in the terms of first-century thinking, the faith took outward form in an increasingly objective way of expression."

They expressed this in terms of the outward, but it was an inner experience that lead to its expression.

BIBLIOGRAPHY

Hedley, George, The Symbol of the Faith, New York: The Macmillan Co., 1948.

Holman, C. T., Psychology and Religion for Everyday Living, New York: The Macmillan Co., 1949.

Micklem, Nathaniel, What is the Faith, Nashville, Tenn: Cokesbury Press, n.d.

THDS. MLKP-MBU: Box 112, folder 14.

"The Place of Reason and Experience in Finding God"

[*13 September–23 November 1949*]
[*Chester, Pa.*]

King wrote this essay for the second assignment in Davis's course Christian Theology for Today. In the paper, King poses the neo-orthodox theology of Karl Barth against the theological liberalism of Baptist Edwin E. Aubrey, Methodist Edgar Sheffield Brightman, and Quaker Rufus Jones.[1] Barth denied the capacity of human reason and experience to attain knowledge of God; the liberal theologians sought to vindicate the human capacity to know the divine. King sides with the liberals against Barth, asserting the primacy of experience and the responsibility of reason to interpret experience and "lead man into the presence of God." The essay includes the earliest indications of King's awareness of Brightman, Reinhold Niebuhr, and Henry Nelson Wieman. Davis marked the paper B + without further comment.

It seems that man is animated by an unquenchable desire to enlarge his vision and to know the ultimate

---

1. Karl Barth (1886–1968) was a Swiss Reformed theologian who taught at the universities of Göttingen, Münster, Bonn, and Basel. Perhaps the foremost of the neo-orthodox theologians, Barth restored a biblical basis to Protestant theology. He challenged Emil Brunner's natural theology and Friedrich Gogarten's doctrine of the state and, as a leader of the German Confessing Church, opposed Adolf Hitler. Edwin Ewart Aubrey (1896–1960) was a Baptist theologian and ethicist. He taught at the University of Chicago from 1929 to 1944 and was president of Crozer Theological Seminary from 1944 to 1949. In 1949 he founded the Department of Religious Thought at the University of Pennsylvania. Edgar Sheffield Brightman (1884–1953) was a Methodist theologian who taught at Brown, Nebraska Wesleyan, and Boston universities. Brightman developed his interests in epistemology and metaphysics into an empirical theological personalism. Rufus Jones (1863–1948) was a Quaker mystic, philosopher, and theologian. The author of more than fifty books, he was the founder and lifetime president of the American Friends Service Committee. He taught for forty years at Haverford College.

meaning of things. Man is a metaphysical animal ever longing for answers to the last questions. This in some way accounts for mans continual search for the object of religious faith known as God. The search has often been a difficult and devious one, yet amid all of its difficulties many have continued to search for the un- failing source of eternal value. In this great religious odyssey many have fallen out on the way, some disil- lusioned and some content.

Those who are content may be divided into two groups, one ostensibly religious and the other irreli- gious. The irreligious group has resolved the prob- lem by eliminating all mystery from the universe. For them the natural cause is an adequate explanation of anything they may perceive.

The religious group on the other hand will admit that there is mystery in the universe, but they claim to know to much about this eternal mystery. They will speak as if they have just had a chat with the divine on the cosmic Boulevard. Dr. Reinhold Niebuhr has said that many people in this group will speak as if they know the geography of heaven and hell and the furniture of the one and the temperature of the other.[2] At least the agnostics and fundamentalist have one thing in common: they have given up the search for the eternal mystery of the universe.

But any genuine Christian faith will not be content with such dogmatic assertions. It sees that there is an element of mystery both in the natural world and the unseen world, and that the search for God is a process not an achievement. We never find all of God.

There is also another group which has given up this great religious search. This group is represented by Karl Barth and the crisis theologians.[3] They argue that it is almost blasphemous to talk about man seek- ing or finding God. Does not God, rather, find us? Are not Rufus Jones and other liberal theologians a little wrong when they speak of a "double search?"[4]

---

2. Reinhold Niebuhr (1892–1971) was one of the most influential figures in American reli- gious and political thought. As a founder of the journal *Christianity and Crisis*, and the political group Americans for Democratic Action, he exercised considerable influence as a proponent of Christian or liberal realism. King refers to *The Nature and Destiny of Man: A Christian Interpretation* (New York: Scribner, 1943), 2:294: "It is unwise for Christians to claim any knowledge of either the furniture of heaven or the temperature of hell."

3. The phrase "crisis theologians" is often used interchangeably with "neo-orthodox theo- logians."

4. The "double search" is God's search for man and man's search for God.

Such are their questions and they occur over and over again in their theology. Their basic argument is that man was once made in the image of God, but this image and likeness of God were totally effaced by the fall, leaving not a trace behind. In this fall man's humanity was so corrupted by sin that even his reason was distorted. And so they conclude that man can never know God through reason or experience, for God is "wholly other." Following the Hegelian dialectics they see God as the synthesis between every thesis and antithesis. We may know the thesis and antithesis, but never the synthesis. "The reason sees the small and the larger but not the large."*

* Karl Barth, The Word of God and The Word of Man, p. 9.

This view of the fall of man held by Dr. Barth and others seems to me quite inadequate. It seems more reasonable to hold that the fall of man is psychological rather than historical. In other words, I would be inclined to accept, along with many others, an individual fall rather than a racial fall. Moreover, I cannot follow the Barthian interpretation of reason. This Barthian attempt to undermind the rational in religion is one of the perils of our time.[5] As Dr. Brightman says, "unless religion allows man to retain some degree of self respect and of intelligence, it is doomed. A God about whom we dare not think is a God a thinking mind cannot worship."†

* E. S. Brightman, The Finding of God, p. 26.

Although there are some who have given up this search for God, we must realize that a vast majority of believers are still seaching and will continue to search for the being who is the "source of human good."[6] Those who seek with clear heads and sincere hearts will in some measure find. Of course the true seeker will realize that there is no one way to find God. To be sure, there are many possible ways of finding God. Hence he will seek to find God in as many ways as possible in order to enrich his own experience. Here we will discuss the place of two methods that men have constantly used in seeking God: reason and experience. Let us first turn to the realm of experience since it is the logical prelude of reason.

First we may say that religious experience is the awareness of the presence of the divine. Religious experience is not an intellectual formulation about God,

---

5. Davis corrected "undermind" to "undermine."

6. This phrase is from Henry Nelson Wieman, *The Source of Human Good* (Chicago: University of Chicago Press, 1946).

it is a lasting acquaintance with God. So it is quite obvious that religious experience ranges from an every day experience with reality to the very height of mystic ecstasy.[7] Although this great range has brought about a variety of religious experiences, as William James reminded us in his Giffort Lectures, there is one common trait running throughout.[8] "Religious experience is always a thou experience."* In every religious experience the creature is standing in relation with that other than self or other than human factor in the universe. It is the "I" seeking the "thou."

* Brightman, op. cit., p. 101.

Before carrying this discussion to its logical conclusion we must at least recognize the fact that there are many individuals who distrust religious experience as evidence for God. The first group has a psychological objection. They argue that religious experience is subjective and emotional. Therefore they would contend that through so called religious experience we find our nerves, our sex nature, our wishes, or our subconscious, but not God.†[9]

† Brightman, op. cit., p. 111.

We must admit that error and illusion result from many religious experiences, but is not this true in every other field of human endeavor, including psychology? It seems that these psychologist dwell on the abnormal cases rather than the perfectly normal cases of religious experience.

On the other hand the Barthians, who were mentioned above, give a negative answer to the value of religious experience because it implies that there is something that man can do to find God. So they have a disdain for the very use of the word experience in a religious context. But I have never been able to see how the Barthians can call the divine confrontation or the crisis situation anything less than experience. It seems at this point that we are lead into another Barthian paradox.

However, religious experience is important and it

---

7. Edgar S. Brightman, *The Finding of God* (New York: Abingdon Press, 1931), p. 95: "The religious experience ranges from an almost commonplace atmosphere of every day to the ineffable heights of mystic ecstasy."

8. Davis corrected "Giffort" to "Gifford."

9. Brightman, *Finding of God*, p. 111: "The distrust of religious experience as evidence for God is, however, so widespread that more should be said about it. Certain psychologists regard religious experience as subjective and emotional. It is true that religion, like every other great value in life, arouses intense emotions. . . . These facts lead some to deny the truth of the claim that we can find God through religious experience. We may find our nerves, our sex nature, our susceptibility to drugs, our wishes, or our subconscious, say these doubters, but we do not find God."

has a place in the finding of God. For an instance, the very idea of God is an outgrowth of experience. The idea of God did not burst forth in the mind of man with no concomitant experience. On the contrary, man noticed the order and beauty of the cosmic universe amid all of its disorder and ugliness; he came to a realization of his own needs and fears; he came to realize his dependence on his fellows; and from these experiences he framed the idea of God.

Then again it is through experience that we come to realize that some things are out of harmony with God's will. No theology is needed to tell us that love is the law of life and to disobey it means to suffer the consequences; we see it every day in human experience. It is religious experience which shows us that much of the misery and weakness of men's lives is due to personal fault of the individual. It is through religious experience that we come to see that social and biological urges often overwelm reason. No profound theology is needed to set forth these facts. We need only turn to the verdict of experience.*

* Brightman, op. cit., p. 114.

Although experience is not the only way to find God,, it is probably the primal way. It is a road that every man can travel. This way is open to all levals of human intelligence. Every man, from the ordinary simplehearted believer to the philosophical intellectual giant, may find God through religious experience.

Now we turn to the realm of reason in finding God. Certainly we are aware of the fact that men throughout the ages have believed in the validity of reason in finding God. We find it in a Plato teaching that God is a rational being to be found by reason. We find it in a Jesus speaking of loving God with our minds. We find it in a Spinoza speaking of "the intellectual love of God." Certainly this list could go on ad infinitum. On the other hand we must recognize the fact that many seekers have a persistent suspicion of reason as a road that leads to God.[10] We have already stated above the Barthian objection to this method. Briefly we might discuss the objections which an earlier theologian gives to the validity of reason in finding God, viz., Kierkegaard. He reverses the Hegelian dialectic

---

10. Brightman, *Finding of God*, p. 54: "Yet long before Tertullian, Plato had taught that God was a rational spirit to be found by reason; and long after Tertullian, Spinoza's religious experience was 'the intellectual love of God.' . . . It would seem to follow that, if there is a reasonable God, reason must be a road to him."

in such a way as to place the unity (synthesis) prior to the diversity (thesis and antithesis); and he goes on to attribute the diversity to the inevitable limitation of human thought.[11] In others words the Divine synthesis manifest itself to reason as a contradiction. Therefore, he argues, reason can never lead to God because it is by nature self-contradictory.*

* E. E. Aubrey, Present
Theological Tendencies,
p. 70.

† Brightman, <u>op. cit.</u>, p.
11.

But as Dr. Brightman has reminded us, "if God exist at all, he must be the Supreme Reason, and hostility to reason is one form of hostility to the divine."† If God is Supreme Reason, then it seems to follow that reason is the road that leads to him, notwithstanding the fact that God is far above man.

The reasoner, then, starts his search with the facts of experience.[12] It must be remembered that it is the duty of reason to examine, interpret, and classify the facts of experience. In other words, experience is the logical subject matter of reason. And so the reasoner takes the clues of experience and carries them through the method of analysis. Of course, this must not be a stopping point, because analysis alone is an incomplete picture of reason. The reasoner must somehow understand the experience as it relates to the wholeness of the universe. When experience is interpreted in the light of the wholeness of the universe, reason will come closer and closer to the eternal value of the universe.

We must grant freely, however, that final intellectual certainty about God is impossible. Our knowledge of the absolute will always remain relitive. We can never gain complete knowledge or proof of the real. This, however, does not destroy the stream of rational religion. On the contrary, it reveals to us that intellectual finality is unattainable in all fields; all human knowledge is relative, and all human ideas are caught in the whirlpool of relativity. But we cannot give up the search because of this limitation. Certainly if God is the real that we are seeking, we can always learn more about him.[13] Thus, reason, when sincerely

---

11. E. E. Aubrey, *Present Theological Tendencies* (New York: Harper & Brothers, 1936), p. 83: "Kierkegaard, as we saw, reversed the Hegelian dialectic in such a way as to place the unity prior to diversity; and attributed the diversity to the inevitable limitations of human thought."

12. Brightman, *Finding of God*, p. 64: "The reasoner, then, starts with the facts of experience as they are present to him whenever he begins a thinking enterprise."

13. Brightman, *Finding of God*, p. 69: "We have granted freely, however, that final intellectual certainty is impossible. . . . we can never attain complete knowledge or proof of the real. . . . Thus, if God is the real that we are seeking, we can always learn more about him."

and honestly used, is one of supreme roads that leads
man into the presence of God.[14]

BIBLIOGRAPHY

E. E. Aubrey, <u>Present Theological Tendencies</u>, New
York: Harper and Brothers Publishers., 1936.

John Baillie, <u>Our Knowledge Of God</u>, New York:
Charles Scribners Son, 1939.

E. S. Brightman, <u>The Finding of God</u>, New York:
The Abingdon Press, 1931.

THDS. MLKP-MBU: Box 112, folder 17.

---

14. Brightman, *Finding of God*, p. 72: "Carried far enough and honestly enough, reason is one
of the ways that leads man into the very presence of God."

"The Sources of
Fundamentalism and Liberalism
Considered Historically and Psychologically"

[*13 September–23 November 1949*]
[*Chester, Pa.*]

*This essay for Davis's Christian Theology for Today focuses primarily on religious
liberalism and its ability to accommodate scientific discoveries. King makes substantial
use of The History of Fundamentalism, by a former Crozer professor, Stewart
G. Cole. King's interpretation of the two movements is for the most part uncritical
of liberalism and scornful of fundamentalism: "Unlike liberalism, fundamentalism
is essentially a reactionary protest, [fighting] to preserve the old faith in a changing
milieu." Davis circled the word "Psychologically" in the title and commented: "You
do not do justice to this. Think of what the psychological factors are which lie back
of these two movements." King received a B + on the paper.*

As we look through the arena of contemporary history we are immediately struck by the salient changes
which have taken place in modern society. Any serious observer can notice, with a deal of facility, the
changes in the social, economic, and scientific realms
of modern life. Whether these changes have been for
the best or for the worse, it is not mine to discuss at
this point, but the fact remains that they have come

about. Notice how different the structure of Western society is today from what it was three generations ago. In the course of its development western civilization has shifted from a colonial naivete of the frontier to the far-reaching machination of nationalism and from an agrarian pattern of occupation to the industrial one.[1] Certainly these momentous transformations have made modern man more material minded. Moreover, these great transformations have brought about a highly urbanized society which has caused amusements and fellowship to pass largely out of the home and the church into the hands of commercial agencies.

Also notice the continual rise of the scientific spirit in modern culture. Ever since the days of the Renaissance men have continually subpoenaed ideas and theories to appear before the judgment seat of the scientific method. As Bacon would say, "they are taught to weigh and consider." Modern man is forever standing before the store-house {of nature} with his inevitable interrogative, what? As the new scientific method began to develope many of its decoveries were found to be contradictory to the old ways of thinking which had been basic for religious belief. Newtonian science reduced Providence to the reign of the natural law; Copernicus eliminated man fron the center of the universe and posited a heliocentric theory of the universe. In his theory of organic evolution Dawin placed supernatural man within the natural order.[2] In philosophy positivism emerged in Comte. This scientific spirit invaded the whole of modern life. It seems that the renaissance deviated man's thinking from a theocentric world-view to an antropocentric cosmology.[3] Modern man turned away from metaphysical speculation and decided to worship at the shrine of empiricism.

The question immediately arises, why these propaedeutic concerns in a paper which deals with the

---

1. Stewart G. Cole, *The History of Fundamentalism* (New York: Richard R. Smith, 1931), p. xi: "How different the structure of American society is today from what it was two generations ago is obvious to every student. In the course of its development western civilization has shifted from a colonial naiveté of the frontier to the far-reaching machinations of nationalism and from an agrarian pattern of occupation to the industrial one, with a consequent revolution in human desire, ideal and behavior."

2. Davis circled "supernatural" and wrote a question mark above the word.

3. Davis suggested "directed" rather than "deviated."

sources of fundamentalism and liberalism? The answer of this question lies in the fact that liberalism and fundamentalism grew out of these changing conditions. Whenever man finds himself amid a changing society, his thinking goes in one of two directions. Either he attempts to adjust his thinking to the changing conditions or he attempts to hold to old dogmatic ideas amid the new. Fundamentalism chose the latter while liberalism chose the former. In other words, the changing cultural conditions described above gave rise to both liberalism and fundamentalism; these conditions caused one group to seek adjustment and the other to revolt. Let us turn first to a discussion of liberalism.

As implied above liberalism is a progressive movement which came into being in an attempt to adjust religion to all new truth. Just as the Scholastics attempted to wed theology to the dominant thought pattern of their day, viz., Aristotelian philosophy, the modern liberal attempts to wed theology to the dominant thought pattern of his day, viz., science. The liberal doesn't mind changing old world views to fit the scientific world view. As Dr. Aubrey succinctly stated, "the Christian liberal attempts to incarnate in history the meaning of God's will, as Christ Himself did, by keeping faith relevant to man's expanding knowledge and his common struggles."*

* {E. E. Aubrey, "Our Liberal Heritage," The Chronicle, October, 1944.}

It is of greatest importance to state at the outset that liberalism is a method not a creed. "Liberals are united not by a set of dogma agreed upon but by a common spirit, a common purpose, and a freedom for all."† To be sure, the beliefs of the liberal are individual and, in any case, they are subject to constant revision. His certainties about religion are not found in a set of dogma but in vital experience.[4] So from this we can see that it is impossible to set forth a definite date for the beginning of liberalism, we can only state its method.

† T. G. Soares, Three Typical Beliefs, p. 111.

The liberal method is first historical. Its historical study is directed at recapturing the human experiences out of which the classic doctrines arose. He re-

---

4. Theodore Gerald Soares, *Three Typical Beliefs* (Chicago: University of Chicago Press, 1937), p. 71: "But the beliefs of the liberal are individual; no congress has ever been commissioned to formulate them; and, in any case, they are subject to constant revision. Yet the liberal believes that he can have real religion without static certainty. His spiritual certainties are not in formulated dogmas but in vital experiences."

alizes that before the doctrine was formulated there was an experience, and that the experience is more lasting than the expression of the experience.* From this it is quite evident that the liberal stresses the primacy of experience. The liberal starts with experience and constantly returns to experience to test his findings. For an instance, the authority of the Golden Rule is not that Jesus proclaimed it. On the contrary, its authority lies in the fact that it has received raison d'être in the experences of life. Of course, that Jesus uttered it, and more because he lived it, enhances our moral estimate of him.[5]

The liberal would insist that he can never speak in terms of the absolute. He is humble enough to see that he is locked up in the prison of relativity. Moreover, he sees that we do not have an infallible science therefore truth must be discovered from age to age.† The liberal does not discard old beliefs neither does he discard the Bible. On the contrary, he seeks the truth that is in them. With supreme reverence he joyously cherishes the religious heritage of the past. Only he feels free to bring it to all critical examination of the modern historical method.[6] Thus he attempts to make the spiritual discoveries of the Christian traditions available for modern use.‡ The liberal does not see the Bible as the only source of truth, but he finds truth in numerous other realms of life. He would insist that truth is not a one-act drama that appeared once and for all on the Biblical stage, but it is a drama of many acts continually appearing as the curtains of history continue to open. He sees the light of God shining through history as the blossom shines through the bud; God is working through history.

The liberal does not agree with the orthodox views of human nature. For him there never was a fall of man.[7] Rather than a fall of man he speaks of an upward (evolutionary) movement of man. The liberal

* H. E. Fosdick, <u>Modern Use of the Bible</u>, p. 55.

† Sores, <u>op. cit.</u>, p. 72.

‡ Cf. the title of H. E. Fosdick's the Modern Use of the Bible.

---

5. Soares, *Three Typical Beliefs*, p. 74: "The authority of the Golden Rule is not that Jesus proclaimed it. It makes its own inherent appeal of social sympathy and demand for social justice. That Jesus uttered it, and more that he lived it, enhances our moral estimate of Jesus."

6. Soares, *Three Typical Beliefs*, p. 72: "We do not have an infallible science but must discover truth from age to age. . . . The liberal does not lightly discard old beliefs. He treats them with reverence. He seeks the truth that is in them. He joyously cherishes the religious heritage of the past. Only he feels free to bring it all to the critical examination of the new day."

7. Soares, *Three Typical Beliefs*, pp. 83–84: "The liberal completely repudiates the orthodox views of human nature. . . . There never was a fall of man."

sees value in human nature. He cannot sing with sincerity the hymn:

> Would he devote the sacred head
> for such a worm as I?[8]

"Each human personality," says Sores, "is the object of divine love and holds in himself the possibility of a son of God."[*] This is essentially the liberal view toward man.

* Sores, op. cit., p. 105.

From this brief discussion it seems quite obvious that Liberal theology resulted from mans attempt to answer new problems of cultural and social change. It was an attempt to bring religion up intellectually. Frieddrick Schleiermacher, the ninteenth century theologian, has been called the precursor of the liberal movement. When Schleiermacher stressed the primacy of experience over any external authority he was sounding a note that would ring aloud in the twentieth century.

Unlike liberalism, fundamentalism is essentially a reactionary protest, frighting to preserve the old faith in a changing milieu.[9] In a sense we may say that fundamentalism is as old as the Reformation, but as an organized movement it is of recent origin.[10] We may date the beginning of the fundamentalist movement in 1909 with the Publication of The Fundamentals.[†] This work was published in twelve volumes with the aim of re-establishing the "treasured faith."[11] This volume could well be called the "fundamentalist manifesto."

† S. G. Coe, History of Fundamentalism, p. 52.

These men argued that there could be no compromise on the unchanging fundamentals of the Christian faith. To gain support for their stand, the fundamentalist claimed that they were reaffirming the faith as Luther, Calvin, Knox, and Wesley held it. Of course, in that claim they were undoubtedly correct. It was the Protestant Reformation which enunciated the doctrines which are now called "fundamentalist."[12]

---

8. Soares, *Three Typical Beliefs*, p. 105: "The liberal finds value in man. He dissents from the old creeds that belittled man. He cannot sing the hymn: 'Would he devote that sacred head / For such a worm as I?'"

9. Davis deleted the *r* in "frighting."

10. Soares, *Three Typical Beliefs*, p. 37: "Fundamentalism is as old as the Reformation, though the name is of recent origin."

11. Cole, *History of Fundamentalism*, p. 52.

12. Soares, *Three Typical Beliefs*, pp. 37–38: "Asserting that there could be no compromise on the unchanging fundamentals of the Christian faith, they adopted as a rallying cry the name

The use of the critical method in approaching the Bible is to the fundamentalist downright heresy. He sees the Bible as the infallible word of God, from the dotting of an "i" to the crossing of a "T". He finds it to be a unity and a coherence of parts; "the New Testament is in the old contained, and the Old Testament is in the new explained."[13] Upon this first proposition (the infallibility of the Bible) all other fundamentalist views depend. They argue that if the Bible is true— that is, so divinely inspired as to be free from error—then all other truths follow inevitably, because they are based upon what the Bible actually says in language clear and unmistakable.

When the fundamentalist comes to the nature of man he finds all of his answers in the Bible. The story of man in the garden of Eden gives a conclusive answer. Man was created by a direct act of God.[14] Moreover, he was created in the image of God, but through the workings of the devil man {was} lead into disobedience. Then began all human ills: hardship and labor, the agony of childbirth, hatred, sorrow, suffering, and death.[15] The fundamentalist is quite aware of the fact that scholars regard the garden of Eden and the serpent Satan and the hell of fire as myths analogous to those found in other oriental religions. He knows also that his beliefs are the center of redicule by many. But this does not shake his faith— rather it convinces him more of the existence of the devil.[16] The critics, says the fundamentalist, would never indulge in such skeptical thinking if the devil hadn't influenced them. The fundamentalist is con-

'fundamentalist.' They claimed that they were reaffirming the faith as Luther held it, and Calvin, and Knox, and Robinson, and Bunyan, and Wesley, and the great missionaries and evangelists, and most of the theologians until very recent times. And in that claim they were undoubtedly correct. The great Protestant creeds enunciated the doctrines which are now called 'fundamentalist.' "

13. Soares, *Three Typical Beliefs*, p. 41: "When the fundamentalist studies the Bible, he sees in it a unity, a coherence of its parts, the complementary nature of the two Testaments, 'the New is in the Old contained, the Old is by the New explained.' "

14. Soares, *Three Typical Beliefs*, p. 51: "Man was so created by a direct act of God."

15. Soares, *Three Typical Beliefs*, p. 54: "Then began all human ills: hardship and labor, the agony of childbirth, the subjection of woman, anger, hatred, malice and all uncharitableness, sorrow, suffering, and death."

16. Soares, *Three Typical Beliefs*, pp. 53–54: "The fundamentalist knows that scholars regard the Garden of Eden and the serpent Satan and the hell of fire as myths analogous to those in other oriental religions. He knows also that the belief in these ideas has waned markedly in recent years and that they are made the subject of humor. But this does not shake his confidence— rather he feels that these very facts attest the existence of the devil, whose supreme success in leading men astray is that they have been brought to doubt his existence."

vinced that this skepticism of scholars and cheap humor of the laity can by no means prevent the revelation of God.* [17]

Others doctrines such as a supernatural plan of salvation, the Trinity, the substitutionary theory of the atonement, and the second coming of Christ are all quite prominent in fundamentalist thinking. Such are the views of the fundamentalist and they reveal that he is oppose to theological adaptation to social and cultural change. He sees a progressive scientific age as a retrogressive spiritual age. Amid change all around he was {is} willing to preserve certain ancient ideas even though they are contrary to science.

BIBLIOGRAPHY

Coe, S. G., The History of Fundamentalism, New York: Richard R. Smith, Inc. 1931.

Roberts, D. E., and Van Dusen H. P., Liberal Theology, New York: Charles Scribner's Sons, 1942.

Soares, T. G., Three Typical Beliefs, Chicago: The University of Chicago Press, n.d.

Vanderlaan, E. C., Fundamentalism versus Modernism, New York: H. W. Wilson Co., 1925.

THDS. MLKP-MBU: Box 115, folder 32.

---

17. Soares, *Three Typical Beliefs*, p. 54: "The skepticism of scholars and the cheap humor of the laity cannot annul the revelation of God, who has warned us that this evil being is our enemy, from whom we can be saved only by divine power."

"Six Talks in Outline"

[*13 September–23 November 1949*]
[*Chester, Pa.*]

For the course Christian Theology for Today, Davis required his students to submit outlines for six talks based on William Newton Clarke's An Outline of Christian Theology.[1] *King reproduces Clarke's outline in condensed form in most of these talks, but in the third and fourth, "Who Was Jesus of Nazareth?" and "What Did Jesus Achieve Through His Life and Death?" he deviates from Clarke's*

---

1. William Newton Clarke (1841–1912) was a liberal Baptist theologian. From 1883 to 1887, he was professor of New Testament interpretation at Toronto Baptist College; from 1890 to 1908, he was professor of Christian theology at Colgate University. From 1908 until his death in 1912, he was professor of Christian ethics at Colgate. Clarke's *An Outline of Christian Theology* (1898) was an essential text of liberal American Protestant thought.

*interpretations of the life of Jesus. In emphasizing Jesus' firm roots in the Judaic
tradition and expanding on his method of teaching, King presents a portrait of
a man working for change within the Judaic tradition rather than radically
departing from it. Davis gave the paper a B + and commented: "Your outlines
are clear and progressive. I think you will find them useful. Aim at illustrations
from life."*

"The Character of the Christian God"

The Character of God

I. The Christian Conception of God.

In order to get at the character of God we will discuss the overall Christian conception of God.

A. The Definition of God.—

God is the personal spirit, perfectly good, who in love creates, sustains, and orders all.

The essential matters covered by this statement;—

(1) The nature of God: He is a personal spirit.

(2) The character of God: He is perfectly good.

(3) The relation of God to all other existence: He creates, sustains, and orders all.

(4) The motive of God in his relation to all other existence: His motive is holy love.

B. The Nature of God.—"God is the personal spirit."

(1) Spirit—

a. Greek view—By spirit the Greeks meant that which was invisible, incorporeal ect. In other words their view was philosophical.

b. Christian view—The early Christians conceived of spirit as meaning that man could have spiritual followship with God. It meant that spirit could meet spirit. This was a practical view.

(2) Personal—The word "Personal" in this definition asserts self-consciousness and self-direction in God.

C. The Character of God.—"God is the personal spirit, perfectly good."

(1) The definition "perfectly good" attributes to God all possible excellence. The use of the word good in this context goes beyond its use in popular venucular-kind or gracious. Here it reaches its acme, and stands for the highest that the human mind can conceive.

(2) The goodness of God must not be confused with the goodness of man—the former is absolute and the latter is relative. Indeed the word "good" means the same in both cases, except for God it reaches its highest expression. When the highest conception of good that man can conceive has been set in his mind, it will be found that God corresponds to that conception, and yet he transcends it.

D. The Relation of God to other existence.—God is the personal spirit, perfectly good, who . . . creates, sustains, and orders all.

    (1) Who creates all—The assertion is that the good personal spirit lies back of the universe as the ground of its being.

    (2) Who sustains all—Here it is asserted that he who is the original cause is also the perpetual cause, the upholder of all things, who preserves them in existence.

    (3) Who orders all—Here it is asserted that he who creates and sustains the universe is also governing it, and directing it to an end.

E. The motive of God in his relation to other existence.—"God . . . in Holy love creates sustains, and orders all."

    (1) In Holy Love—Through Christ there has come to us a knowledge of the motive of God. The definition asserts that the motive of God in the universe is holy love. From Christ we learn that "God is Love."

    (2) Holy love is a combination of perfect goodness and immeasurable self-giving. Such holy love, our definition asserts, being the substance of his character, is the motive of God's activity in relation to other existence.

"The Nature of Man———"

I. Man is an animal.

Man is properly a part of animated nature, and cannot disown his kinship with the earth and the creatures that live upon it. No one can doubt the fact that the organization of man's body resembles the bodies of animals in general.

A. The career of the body.—

    (1) Man's body is clearly part of the natural world.

    (2) The body is immediately dependent on innumerable phases of its environment.

    (3) Upon the breakdown of the body, which is called death, the body eventually loses its complex structure and returns to the dust.

B. Our knowledge of the body.—

    (1) There is much about the body which is not yet known. The operation of the ~~bra~~ brain, the nervous system, the subtle changes that take place within the body, contain a story whose details are still to be unfolded.

    (2) We do know something about the history of the body. Biologist have long since developed and increasingly confirmed a theory of organic evolution which traces the development of animal forms from lowly unicellular beginnings to the higher and more complex structures.

II. Man is a being of spirit.

The human spirit cannot be analysed as the body can, and we have no means of defending its essential nature. It is manifested only in action.

Observation upon the action of man reveals three modes of activity which cannot merely be explained in terms of zoology.

A.   Intellect.—
   (1)   In man self-consciousness has a strength, a definiteness, and an intelligence that it does not possess elsewhere.
   (2)   In man the power of abstract throught not only exist, but is capable of vast extension.
B.   Sensibility.—
   (1)   Man feels.—
      (a)   He experiences mental pain or pleasure
      (b)   He lives an affectional life.
      (c)   He loves and hates.
C.   The Will.—
   (1)   Man has within himself the power of choosing his supreme end. Animals follow their nature; man has the power of acting upon his own nature almost as if from without, of guiding it within cer- limits, of modifying it by the choice and prosecution of ends in life.
   (2)   Man entertains ideals, and ideals become his inspiration. Man can be true or false to his nature. He can be a hero or a fool. Both possibilities, the noble and the base alike, indicate man's greatness.

"Who Was Jesus of Nazareth?"

I.   Jesus was a Jew.
It is impossible to understand Jesus outside of the race in which he was born. The Christian Church has tended to overlook its Judaic origins, but the fact is that Jesus of Nazareth was a Jew of Palestine. He shared the experiences of his fellow-countryman. So as we study Jesus we are wholly in a Jewish atmosphere.

A.   His attitude toward the Jewish religion—There is no justification of the view that Jesus was attempting to find a church distinct from the Synagogue. The gospels themselves bear little trace of such a view. Throughout the gospels we find Jesus accepting both the Temple and the Synagogue. He was brought up in the Synagogue and he participated in it during the height of his earthly mission. Though he condemned some of those who took part, speaking scathingly of elders and rabbis when they deserved it, he referred to the instition itself with complete respect.
B.   His attitude toward the Jewish law.—It is quite evident that Jesus had profound respect for the law as did every true Jew. He never opposed it or hinted that it would ever pass away. But it is significant to note that he always sought to get at the spirit of the law. He sought to get back to the ultimate purpose of the law rather than the exact latter. For an instance, when dealing with the sabbath, a common sense interpretation of the purpose of the law lead him to a lenient position.

II. Jesus was a popular teacher of religion.

It is quite evident that Jesus was a religious teacher in the hills of Galilee. Because of the freshness and force to his teaching and above all his practical common sense and unflinching bravery, he was able to get a hearing. He was a representative of the popular religious movement that emphasized liberalism in religion. He was a modernist of his day.

A. His method of teaching.—

(1) His method of teaching was that of a layman. His teaching was given when the occasion and situation arose. We find no exhaustive treatment of any topic.

(2) His teaching was concrete, personal, illustrative, and direct. This means that our approach to the teaching of Jesus must be an informal and common sense approach. Any attempt to classify or analyze his teaching in accordance with a rationalized system or principle is quite misleading. The unifying force in his teaching was his religious experience. His experience determined what topics he discussed.

B. Guiding principles in a modern approach to Jesus teaching.—

(1) The spirit of Jesus teaching is more significant than its detailed form or content. Someone will probably say, "we only know its spirit by its content." This is quite true. However, the spirit of Jesus teaching has not the limitations of its mere content.

(2) Any approach to Jesus teaching should be from the whole to the parts. Its parts must not be detached for independent consideration without reference to the whole.

III Jesus was a momentously influential character—

Jesus remains the most persistent, inescapable, and influential figure that ever entered history. It was such a personality that split history into A.D. and B.C. It was this personality, born under the humblest of conditions in a conquered province of the Roman Empire, that was able in some thirty years only, of which only a few month were spent in public ministry, to change for many the whole complexion of the world. Here we find a man who, through the process of struggle, so submitted his will to God's will that God used him to reveal his divine plan to man.

A. The personality of Jesus.—The chief and abiding significance of Jesus lay in his personality. Many of his sayings faded out of the memory of the disciples, but him they remembered. "Words effect nothing" says Harnack, "it is the power of the personality that stands behind them." (What is Christianity, p. 48)[2]

B. Jesus' influence in personal experience—It is not abstractions but persons who most deeply influence us, e.g., William James was

---

2. Adolf Harnack, *What Is Christianity? Lectures Delivered in the University of Berlin During the Winter-Term, 1899–1900*, trans. Thomas Bailey Saunders (New York: Putnam, 1908).

once asked to give his definition of spirituality. After a moments hesitation he answered that he was not sure he could give the meaning in words, but he could point to a person who was it— Phillips Brooks. Likewise when asked to give a definition of Christianity we may not know an abstract theological definition, but we can point to a personal spirit—Jesus Christ.

"What Did Jesus Achieve Through His Life and Death"

I. Through his life, Jesus achieved unity with God and with the human race.

The appearance of such a person, more divine and more human, than any other, and standing in closest unity at once with God and man, is the most significant and hopeful event in human history. This divine character or this unity with God was nothing thrust upon Jesus from above, but it was a definite achievement. (Contrary to Clark's view)

A. Revelation of God—In the very quality of his life, Christ gave expression to the character of God. In particular, Christ showed men what attitude of mind and heart God held toward them, and consequently, how they should feel toward him. Jesus reveals to us a God who works in the world to bring goodness to pass, and who through human beings is striving to achieve a social order that is moral in its nature and capable of expressing love. So to the early Christians Jesus was more than Jesus. He was the Logos, they said, the Word of God, God's expression, the forthgiving of the Eternal, revealing himself in one life.

B. Revelation of man—As a typical human being, Christ illustrated what man was intended to become. By knowing him man may learn their ideal and their proper destiny. At the same {time} he revealed the actual moral state of men. This he did by contrast. He saw that the best way to throw light upon sin is not by living a life of sinfullness, but by living a sinless life among the sinful. At one and the same time, Christ shows us what we are and what we ought to be. Here is a life that revealed both God and man.

II. Christ brought about the reconciliation between God and man.

Here we approach that special work for the good of a sinful world which the Scriptures attribute to Christ.

A. The condition of the reconciliation—Because of the sinfulness of human beings they need to be brought to God in penitence, to be forgiven by him, and to receive new disposition and power to live in goodness. This is the only way of exchanging the life of sin for the life which man was made. In the experience of such reconciliation there will be three elements:

(1) On the part of man, penitent turning from sin to God. (illus. The prodigal son in the parable)

(2) On the part of God, pardon and fatherly acceptance of man. (illus. the father in the parable of the prodigal son)

(3) In the mutual relation that follows, the imparting by God and the receiving by man of the spiritual quality and power by which they can live in fellowship with him.

B. The Work of Christ in effecting this reconciliation.—

(1) The action of God in the work of Christ was self expression with reference to sin, as hating sin, as Savior, and as sin-bearer. In the attitude of Christ with reference to sin, in these two respects, God was expressing his own:

(a) God's attitude toward sin is that of one who hates it and condemns it: and this truth he expressed in Christ.

(b) God's attitude toward sinners is that of one who desires to save them: and this truth he expressed in Christ.

(2) The twofold object in making this self expression of God in Christ was to win men, and to satisfy God.

(a) The work of God in Christ was intended to win men out of sin to God.

(b) The work of self-expression in Christ was further intended to satisfy God.

III. Conclusion.

The outcome of Christ's mission and achievement may be made plain by the Christian answer to three questions: how God thinks of the world, how God thinks of men, and how men think of God. In all these relations Christ stands as the point of reconciliation and of unity.

"How God Works Today Through His Spirit"

I. How God works through his spirit in the world. It is a common tendency today to be sceptical concerning the presence of the Holy Spirit in the world. Even Christians have fallen victim to this notion. Many suppose it irreverent to believe that the Holy Spirit is as great in the world now as it was in the days of the ap apostles. But by such thoughts we do injustice to God and render our faith ineffective. We must believe that the living Spirit—that is, the present living God—is working through history.

A. Man's growing understanding of the world.—More and more man is coming to understand the complexities of nature both physical and human. Through increased scientific learning he has been able to free himself from the bondage of drudgery and has stamped out many dreaded plagues and diseases, alleviated his pain, prolonged his life and given greater security and physical well-being. All of these advances have come about because of the constant work of God's spirit in the life of man and in the world. Even the scientists who do not recognize God are guided by his spirit. (Illustration: quotation from a verse of Isaiah where the prophet pictures God saying to Cyrus the Persian, "I girded thee, though thou hast not known me." How familiar an experience it is to be ministered to by forces we do not recognize.)

B. His work in bringing about moral progress in the race.—Not only is the spirit of God working that we might differentiate between right and wrong, but he is also working that we will chose the right. He is forever seeking us only hoping that we will seek him. The search is a double one, and the good life is the work of both the spirit of God and the effort of man. All good that appears in men grows up under the fostering care of the Holy Spirit.

II. How God works through his spirit in the church.

In speaking of "the Church" as it has historically appeared, we shall define it in a very catholic and comprehensive manner, as including the sum of those organizations which have been formed to serve as organs of Christ, for the expression and promotion of his religion.

A. His work in bringing about a more Catholic Church.—

B. His work through the Church in revealing eternal truths.—

  (1) In all ages the spirit brings the words of Christ to remembrance, by reviving forgotten or neglected Christian truths in forms suited to the new times, thus never suffering what he taught to pass out of life.

  (2) The Church is not assured of unfailing correctness in thinking neither is it assured of absolute truth. The Chur Church, just as individuals, is in history, therefore it must deal with the relative. However, toward the perfect truth in this highest and most practical realm, the Holy Spirit is steadily leading his people.

III. How God works through his spirit in the individual.—

AS the circle is narrowed from the world to the Church and from the Church to the individual, the work of the Holy Spirit becomes more specific and intense. In the individual human beings is done the fundamental work.

A. A brief discussion of individuals who greatly reveal the working of the Spirit of God.—

  (1) David Livingstone.—

  (2) Mahatma Gandi.—

  (3) Albert Schweitzer.—

  (4) Jesus of Nazareth.—

B. The working of the spirit of God in bringing about moral transformation within the individual.—

  (1) God, the conductor of this moral transformation, is pledged in truth and love to complete it.

  (2) This moral transformation cannot take place, except by the co-operation of man with God in promoting it.

"What Christians Believe About History and the Future"

I. What Christians believe about History.

Most Christians have been very firm on the view that God is working in the historical process, where he has willed that men should learn to be efficient instruments of the divine energy.

A. The direction of history.—Christians over the years have seen the direction of history in the hands of God. God is the ultimate ground of the historical process. A clearer understanding of this view may come from an illustration contrasting the Greek and the Christian conceptions of history.
   (1) Greek—Here the movement of history is cyclical. It has no ultimate goal. Like an ever moving merry-go-round, history is continually moving never getting anywhere.
   (2) Christian view—Here we find history {moving} foward to a meaningful goal. It has an ultimate purpose.

B. The Kingdom of God.—It is a common Christian view that history is moving toward the kingdom of God. This Christian Ideal has often been interpreted in many ways.
   (1) The view that Christ will come again, and established the kingdom.
   (2) The view that the kingdom will come to realization by means of the increasing influence of the Church which is destined to dominate the world.
   (3) However varied the interpretations are, it is probably commonly agreed by all Christians that God's final purpose is the building of a regenerated human society which will include all mankind in a common fellowship of well-ordered living.

II. What Christian believe about the future.

A. Death, and the continuance of the spirit.—
   (1) Death—death is the cessation of the physical life,—the stopping of the unexplained vital process by which the physical organism is maintained in action. It closes life in earthly environment.
   (2) Continuance of the Spirit.—The spirit leaves the material body, but lives on, and enters new scenes of action. In this statement it is assumed that all men continue to exist after death. It is true that there is no demonstrative proof of universal immorality, for the region of the unseen life is one concerning which strict demonstration is impossible. But because it is unseen doesn't mean that it has no reality. (Illustration: Our bodies can be seen but not our personalities. But who can argue that the personality does not exist. No one ever saw an idea or an ideal, or a love or a truth. But who can deny that these are not the deepest forces in our lives). This is the Christian faith of immortality.

B. Judgment.—Most Christians have believed that there will be a judgment of God concerning the life that a man has lived.
   (1) Popular view.—It is commonly held by many Christians that there will be a judgment at the end of this earthly career; that all who have ever lived will there be assembled, and that each will then receive the final sentence.
   (2) Personal view.—The highest court of justice is in the heart of man when he has been inspired by the teaching of Chirs

Christ. Rather than being the Judge, Chirst is the light in which we pass judgment on ourselves. The truth is that everyday our deeds and words, our silence and speech, are building character. Any day that reveals this fact is a day of judgment.

23 Nov 1949

THDS. MLKP-MBU: Box 113, folder 19.

"How to Use the Bible in Modern Theological Construction"

[13 September–23 November 1949]
[Chester, Pa.]

In this paper written for Christian Theology for Today, King directly confronts a question many of his earlier papers had skirted: how does one reconcile the Bible with science? King finds a solution by following the example of biblical critics such as Millar Burrows and Harry Emerson Fosdick.[1] He defines their approach: "It sees the Bible not as a textbook written with divine hands, but as a portrayal of the experiences of men written in particular historical situations," so "that God reveals himself progressively through human history, and that the final significance of the Scripture lies in the outcome of the process." Davis gave the paper an A − and wrote: "I think you could be more pointed in just how you apply progressive revelation to theological construction. Nonetheless, you do a good piece of work and show that you have grasped the theological significance of biblical criticism."

The question as to the use of the Bible in modern culture stands as a perplexing enigma troubling multitudes of minds. As modern man walks through the pages of this sacred book he is constantly hindered by numerous obstacles standing in his path. He comes to see that the science of the Bible is quite contrary to the science that he has learned in school. He is unable to find the sun standing still in his modern astronomy. His knowledge of biology will not permit him to conceive of saints long deceased arising from their graves. His knowledge of modern medicine causes him to look with disdain on the belief that epilepsy, deafness, blindness and insanity result from the visi-

---

1. Millar Burrows (1889–1980) received a B.A. from Cornell in 1912, a B.D. from Union Theological Seminary in 1915, and a Ph.D. from Yale in 1925. An ordained Presbyterian minister, Burrows taught at Brown and Yale and authored a number of books, including *Outline of Biblical Theology* (1946), *Palestine Is Our Business* (1949), *The Dead Sea Scrolls* (1955), and *More Light on the Dead Sea Scrolls* (1958).

tation of demons. Yet he finds each of these unscientific views in the Bible.

Here is the practical difficulty that has confused the minds of many educated people in using the sacred Book. Some have tried to solve this problem by seeing the old Book, "as an inferior record produced by an inferior race."* Others have attempted to solve this problem by avoiding many areas of the Scripture altogether. Still others have tried to solve the problem by discarding the entire Book. But these solutions are far to evanescent for the person who wishes to think wisely about religion. He comes to see that the influence of the Bible is so embedded in the fibre of Western Culture that to remove it would mean a removal of much of our intellectual heritage.

* Danby, H., "The Old Testament," Study of Theology, edited by Kenneth Kirk, p 189

Before considering a more adequate solution of our problem, we may well state that our generation is not the first to have been distressed and puzzled over some of the modes of thought found in the sacred Book. This attempt to accommodate the sacred Book to changing conditions has appeared over and over again in every age (and in every religion for that matter). Whenever this situation arose early man had one supreme resource: allegory.[2] It was though this method of interpretation that Philo found Greek philosophy anticipated by Moses. This method was also used by the Apostle Paul on many occasions.† Probably the greatest developement of this method is found in the works of Origen. This great Christian scholar and apologist frankly admitted that many sections of the Old Testament, taken literally, were to him quite bizarre. When he turned to the New Testament, Origen concluded that the Gospels taken literally were also filled with discrepancies, contradictions, and even impossibilities.[3] Faced with this problem, Origen attempted to find a way out. And allegory was the solution.

† Cor. 10:4; Gal. 4:21–31.

---

2. Harry Emerson Fosdick, *The Modern Use of the Bible* (New York: Harpers, 1942), p. 65: "Ours is not the first generation that has found itself surrounded by new circumstances and using new modes of thought. Therefore, ours is not the first occasion in history when folk who venerated and believed in a sacred book have been distressed and puzzled because so many things in it seemed unfitted to their modern world. In this recurrent situation there has been one supreme resource: allegory."

3. Fosdick, *Modern Use of the Bible*, p. 75: "And turning his attention to the New Testament, Origen said that the Gospels taken literally contained discrepancies, contradictions, and impossibilities."

23 Nov
1949

Faced with the same problem that early Christians was faced with, modern man cannot use the same method of solution, for he is aware of the fact that allegory is empty speculation. As Dr. Fosdick says, "We face the old problem but we cannot use the old solution."* How then are we to use the Bible?

* Fosdick, H. E., Modern Use of The Bible, p. 88.

A solution of the modern Biblical predicament lies in an intelligible way of handling the Bible. The interpretation of any portion of the Bible must be both objective and disinterested. All attempts to read one's own opinions and desires into the Bible and then claiming authorith for them must be avoided.[4] This, in short, is the method used in modern theological construction. For the want of better name this method has been called "higher criticism." It is called "higher criticism," not to suggest superciliousness and fancied superiority as has often been imagined, but in contrast to lower or textual criticism. Instead of dealing with texts the higher critic deals with the sources and methods used by the particular author in question. This process supported by modern instruments of literary, historical, and archeological research has brought about amazing results. The conclusions which are offered from time to time are not always correct, but they are always efforts to increase our understanding of the Scripture. The purpose of "higher criticism" is solely to prepare the ground for constructive building. It sees the Bible not as a textbook written with divine hands, but as a portrayal of the experiences of men written in particular historical situations. As Burrows succiently states, "Correct interpretation requires recognition of the fact that the knowledge of truth and right revealed in the Bible is not stated in abstract universal propositions, but in specific, concrete applications to particular situations, and in literary, not scientific or philosophical, language."†

† Burrows, Millar, An Outline of Biblical Theology, p. 53.

The results of this modern study of the Scripture have brought about two great advances. First we have come to see that the old proof text method of citing Scripture to establish points of doctrine is both un-

4. Millar Burrows, *An Outline of Biblical Theology* (Philadelphia: Westminster Press, 1946), p. 53: "A sound interpretation of any part of the Bible must be, first of all, objective and disinterested. Wishful thinking, reading one's own opinions and desires into the Bible and then claiming its authority for them, has been responsible not only for false exegesis but for division and unchristian attitudes throughout the history of the church, and not least in Protestantism."

sound and inconclusive.[5] Secondly, we are now able to arrange the writings of the Bible in their approximately chronological order.[6] This means that we can trace the great ideas of the Scripture from their elementary form to their point of maturity. This advance has revealed to us that God reveals himself progressively through human history, and that the final significance of the Scripture lies in the outcome of the process.

For the sake of clarity and content we may give brief illustrations of this new and rewarding approach to the Bible. Obviously the length of this paper will not permit me to trace in detail all of the great Biblical ideas, but at least we may discuss in some detail three of these developing ideas.

First let us turn to the idea of God. At the beginning of the Old Testament we are immediately struck by the anthropomorphical interpretation of God. He walks in the garden of Eden in the cool of the day,* shows to Moses his back,† and is so localized that he lives on Mount Sinai and can be thought of as being with his chosen people only when they carry with them a box called the ark. Moreover, the early Old Testament God was a tribal God. Yahweh's love for Israel was so great that it often caused vehement hatred of Israel's enemies. Even more significantly, he was a god of war, battling for the triumph and victory of his people.‡ And so the early Hebrews could say with ease, "Yahweh is a man of war: Yahweh is his name."§[7]

But compare the picture of a god who walks in a garden in the cool of the day with the view that, "God is a Spirit: and they that worship him must worship in spirit and truth."‖ In the early Old Testament God loved his chosen people, but hated his enemies. Think of the difference in atmosphere when you read, "God

* Gen. 3:8.

† Exod. 33:23.

‡ Fosdick, A Guild To Understanding The Bible, p. 5.

§ Exod. 15:3.

‖ John 4:24.

---

5. Burrows, *Outline*, p. 52: "The proof-text method of citing Scripture to establish points of doctrine is unsound and inconclusive."

6. Fosdick, *Modern Use of the Bible*, p. 6: "For the first time in the history of the church, we of this generation are able to arrange the writings of the Bible in approximately chronological order."

7. Fosdick, *A Guide to Understanding the Bible: The Development of Ideas Within the Old and New Testaments* (New York: Harper & Brothers, 1938), p. 5, quoting Exodus 15:3: "Even more significantly, he was a god of war, battling for his people and leading them to victory. The ascription in the so-called Song of Moses, 'Yahweh is a man of war: / Yahweh is his name,' is typical of the earliest traditions."

so loved the world."* Compare the early Hebrew's statement, "Let not God speak with us, lest we die,"† with the words of Jesus, "When ye pray, say, Our Father."‡ As one realizes this immense developement of thought, he immediately finds a growing understanding of the meaning and the relevance of the amazing things that Jesus revealed about God.

Secondly, let us turn to the idea of man. In early Old Testament days the tribe was the basic unit of society. In this leval of thought the individual man was hardly recognized apart from the tribe. "The social fabric was everything and in it the separate threads were barely distinguishable items."§ There was no sense of injustice when the leaders of Israel saw the sin of Achan not as his alone but all his family's. He stole, and the whole family was put to death. Yahweh was "a jealous God" and thrented to visit, "the iniquity of the father upon the children, upon the third and upon the fourth generation of them that hate me."‖ This is not an early reference to the laws of heredity, but it is reference to the solidity of the tribe or to use [*strikeout illegible*] Fosdick's term, "coporate personality."# [8]

With the new chronological arrangement of the Bible one can pass through the pages of the Old Testament and watch the old idea of the "coporate mass" deminish like melting snow. He can hear Jeremiah saying, "O Yahweh, my strength, and my stronghold, and my refuge in the day of affliction"**—that is personal religion.[9] He can watch Ezekiel as he revolteth wholeheartedly against tribal solidarity. Each individual is penalized exclusively for his own iniquity. "The soul that sinneth, it shall die."†† [10] He can finally come to the consummation of the whole idea in Jesus who found the center of all spiritual values on earth in personal lives and their possibilities.

* John 3:16.

† Exod 20:19.

‡ Luke 11:2.

§ Fosdick, op. cit., p. 55.

‖ Exod 20:5.

Fosdick, op. cit., p. 55.

** Jeremiah 15:17.

†† Ezekiel 18:2.

---

8. Fosdick, *Modern Use of the Bible,* p. 17: "Even in earthly justice the individual was treated only as part of the group. When Achan secreted booty from Jericho his whole family was put to death; . . . When Jehovah visits 'the iniquity of the fathers upon the children, upon the third and upon the fourth generation of them that hate' him, we are dealing not with a premonition of modern ideas of heredity, but with a very ancient idea of corporate responsibility in which the separate rights of the individual had no place."

9. The quotation is from Jeremiah 16:19. See Fosdick, *Guide,* p. 65: "'O Yahweh, my strength, and my stronghold, and my refuge in the day of affliction'—that is personal religion."

10. The quotation is from Ezekiel 18:20. See Fosdick, *Guide,* pp. 67–68: "each [individual] is penalized exclusively for his own iniquity. 'The soul that sinneth, it shall die.'"

Consider a third and last illustration of this new approach to the Bible. The hope of immortality seems to be a missing aspect in early Hebrew religion. While the early Hebrews did believe that the physical body survived after death, they did not believe that the soul as an immaterial reality survived. The body's future state in sheol was vague and ghostly. There was a shadowy simi-existence which the Psalmist called "the land of forgetfullness."* But if one knows the new approach he can notice how the old idea of sheol gradually loses its meaning. He hears the Psalmist as he cries, "God will redeem my soul from sheol."†[11] In passing from pre-Christian Judaism into the New Testament one sees the belief in immortality reach its greatest expression in the words of Paul: "For this corruptible must put on incorruption, and this mortal must put on immortality."‡ What a great journey, from a shadowy simi-existence to a profound belief in the immortality of the soul.

* Psalm 88 : 12.

† Psalm 49 : 15.

‡ 1 Corinthians 15 : 53.

This is the new approach to the Bible. Here the phrase "progressive revelation" becomes a reality. We can start with the major ideas of the scripture and follow them as they develope from the acorns of immaturity to the oaks of maturity, and see them as they reach their culmination in Christ and his Gospel.

BIBLIOGRAPHY

Burrows, Millar, <u>An Outline Of Biblical Theology</u>, Philadelphia: The Westminister Press, n.d.

Danby, H., "The Old Testament," <u>Study of Theology</u>, edited by Kenneth Kirk, New York: Harpers, 1939.

Fosdick, H. E., <u>A Guild To Understanding The Bible</u>, New York: Harpers, 1938.

Fosdick, H. E., <u>The Modern Use Of The Bible</u>, New York: Harpers 1942.

THDS. MLKP-MBU: Box 112, folder 14.

---

11. Fosdick, *Guide*, p. 264: "'God,' cried the psalmist, 'will redeem my soul from sheol.'"

"The Humanity and Divinity of Jesus"

[*29 November 1949–15 February 1950*]
[*Chester, Pa.*]

*This paper, written at the beginning of the second term of Davis's course Christian
Theology for Today, indicates King's estrangement from the conservative Baptist
theology he learned as a child. As he had done in his earlier outline of William
Newton Clarke's* An Outline of Christian Theology, *King dismisses the
conception of an inherent divinity in Jesus and concludes: "The true significance
of the divinity of Christ lies in the fact that his achievement is prophetic and
promissory for every other true son of man who is willing to submit his will to the
will and spirit [of] God." By establishing Jesus as human, King allows for the
possibility of progressive improvement in earthly society through individual action.
Commenting on the essay, Davis warned: "You need to proofread your papers before
turning them in. Note corrections on p. 4." Nevertheless, he marked the work a
B + and praised the paper as "a solution which would appeal to the liberal mind."*

Many years ago a young Jewish leader asked his followers a question which was all but astounding. He
had been working with them quite assiduously. During their work together he was constantly asking them
what his contemporaries were saying about him. But
one day he pressed the question closer home. It is all
very well to say what other people think of me, but
what do you think? Who do you say that I am?

This question has gone echoing down the centuries ever since the young Jewish prophet sounded
its first note.[1] Many have attempted to answer this
question by attributing total divinity to Jesus with
little concern for his humanity. Others have attempted
to answer this question by saying that Jesus was a
"mere" good man with no divine dimensions. Still
others have attempted to get at the question by seeing
Jesus as fully human and fully divine. This question,
which was so prominent in the thinking of the early
Christian centuries, was not answered once and for

---

1. William Adams Brown, *How to Think of Christ* (New York: Scribner, 1948), p. 3: "Many years
ago a young Jew put to a little group of his companions what in its setting seems a strange
question. He had been asking them what his contemporaries were saying about him and they had
repeated a variety of answers. Now he presses the questions closer home. It is all very well to tell
me what other people are thinking about me. What do you *think* I am? . . . It has been so ever
since. The question of the young Jewish Rabbi has gone echoing down the centuries."

all at the council of Chalcedon, rather it lurks forth in modern theological thinking with an amazing degree of freshness. In grappling with the question of the person of Christ, modern Christian thinking is unanimous in setting forth the full humanity of Jesus, yet Christians have not been willing to stop there. Despite all the human limitations of Jesus, most Christian thinkers have been convinced that "God was in Christ."[2] To be sure, Christian thinkers are often in conflict over the question of how and when Jesus became divine, but as to the presence of the divine dimension within him we find little disagreement in Christian circles. At this point we may turn to a detailed discussion of the humanity and divinity of Jesus.

The Humanity of Jesus

If there is any one thing of which modern Christians have been certain it is that Jesus was a true man, bone of our bone, flesh of our flesh, in all points tempted as we are.[3] All docetist, Eutychean, Monophysite errors which explained away the humanity of our Lord have now been jettisoned be all serious theological thought.[4] Theologians of all shades of opinions have declared that in respect to His human nature Christ is consubstantial with ourselves.

We need only read the Gospels to attest to the fact of Jesus' genuine humanity. There is not a limitation that humanity shares that Jesus did not fall heir. Like the rest of us, he got hungry. When at the well of Sameria he asked the women who was drawing water for a drink. When he grew tired, he needed rest and sleep. He leared obedience, we are told, in the way we must learn it. When his disciples were unfaithful it was very cutting to his heart. The blindness of the city he longed to save moved him to tears. In the garden he experienced the normal agony of any individual in

---

2. See Donald Macpherson Baillie, *God Was in Christ* (New York: Scribner, 1948), cited in King's bibliography.

3. Brown, *How to Think of Christ*, pp. 6–7: "If there is any one thing of which Christians have been certain it is that Jesus is true man, bone of our bone, flesh of our flesh, in all points tempted as we are."

4. Baillie, *God Was in Christ*, p. 20: "all serious theological thought has finished with the docetist, Eutychean, Monophysite errors which explained away the humanity of our Lord and thus the reality of the Incarnation."

the same situation. On the Cross, he added to all physical tortures the final agony of feeling God-forsaken.[5]

Notice how the unknown writer of the Epistle to the Hebrews speaks of the humanity of Jesus. Nowhere in the New Testament is the humanity of Jesus set forth more vividly. We see him agonising in prayer (5:7) embracing the Cross with joy and faith (12:2). Springing from the tribe of Judah, He passed through the normal development of human life, learning obedience, even though a Son, by the things which he suffered (5:8). Like all other men he was tempted. Yet no corrupt strain existed in His nature to which temptation could appeal. Here we find a frank emphasis of the humanity of Jesus, paralleled nowhere in the New Testament.[*][6]

Again we may notice that Jesus was by no means omnicient. His knowledge was essentially limited by human conditions. This fact was set forth as for back as 1912 by the notable theologian, H. R. Mackintosh. In dealing with this question of Jesus' omnicience He states: "The question can be decided solely by loyalty to facts; and these, it is not too much to say, are peremptory. Not only is it related that Jesus asked question to elicit information—regarding the site of Lazarus tomb, for example, or the number of the loaves, or the name of the demented Gadarene—but at one point there is a clear acknowledgment of ignorance. 'Of that day or that hour,' He said, respecting the

* H. R. Mackintosh, The Doctrine of The Person of Jesus Christ, p. 78.

---

5. Brown, *How to Think of Christ*, p. 7: "If further evidence of Jesus' genuine humanity were needed, one has only to read the Gospels. There is not a limitation to which our human kind is heir but Jesus shares it with us. Like the rest of us, he was hungry. At the well at Samaria he asked the woman who was drawing water for a drink. When he grew tired, he needed rest and sleep. He asked questions, and expected answers. He was a learner, and not from books alone. He learned obedience, we are told, in the way in which we must all learn it, by the things which he suffered. He was cut to the heart by the faithlessness of disciples. He knew what it was to be betrayed by a friend. The blindness of the city he longed to save moved him to tears. In the garden he was in agony and sweated blood. On the Cross, he added to all physical tortures the final agony of feeling God-forsaken."

6. H. R. Mackintosh, *The Doctrine of the Person of Jesus Christ* (Edinburgh: T. & T. Clark, 1913), p. 79: "Nowhere in the New Testament is the humanity of Christ set forth so movingly . . . We see Him proclaiming salvation (2:3), agonizing in prayer (5:7), embracing the Cross with joy and faith (12:2), suffering the last penalty without the city gate (13:12) . . . Sprung from the tribe of Judah, He passed through the normal development of human life, learning obedience, even though a Son, by the things which He suffered (5:8). . . . Yet no corrupt strain existed in His nature to which temptation could appeal. . . . A frank emphasis, without parallel in the New Testament, is laid on His human virtues."

Parousia, 'knoweth no man, not even the angels in heaven, neither the Son, but the Father.' If he could thus be ignorant of a detail connected in some measure with his redemptive work, the conclusion is unavoidable that in secular affairs His knowledge was but the knowledge of His time."[*]

Again we may notice the human character of our Lord's moral and religious life. His religious experience was in the human realm. Certainly he had a human faith in God. As Dr. Baille has so cogently stated, "Our Lord's life on earth was a life of faith, and His victory was the victory of faith. His temptations were real temptations, which it was difficult and painful for Him to resist."[†] Jesus overcame his temptations not by relience on some inherent divine dimension, but by the constancy of his will.[7] So we are moved to the conclusion, on the basis of peremptory evidence, that Jesus shared fully our human life.

[*] Ibid, p. 397.

[†] D. M. Baille, God was In Christ, p. 14.

The Divinity of Jesus

After establishing the full humanity of Jesus we still find an element in his life which transcends the human. To see Jesus as a "mere" good man like all other prophets is by no means sufficient to explain him. Moreover, the historical setting in which he grew up, the psychological mood and temper of the age and of the house of Israel, the economic and social predicament of Jesus family—all these are important. But these in themselves fail to answer one significant question: Why does he differ from all others in the same setting. Any explanation of Jesus in terms of psychology, economics, religion, and the like must inevitably explain his contemporaries as well. These may tell us why Jesus was a particular kind of Jew, but not why some other Jews were not Jesus. Jesus was brought up in the same conditions as other Jews, inherited the same traits that they inherited; and yet he was Jesus and the others were not. This uniqueness in the spiritual life of Jesus has lead Christians to see him not only as a human being, but as a human

---

7. Baillie, *God Was in Christ,* p. 15, quoting William Temple's *Christus Veritas,* p. 147: "He overcame them exactly as everyman who does so has overcome temptation—by the consistency of his will."

being surrounded with divinity.[8] Prior to all other facts about Jesus stands the spiritual assurance that He is divine. As Dr. Brown succinctly states in a recent book, "That God was in Christ is the very heart of the Christian faith. In this divine human person the ever recurring antinomy of the universe is presented in a living symbol—the antinomy of the eternal in the temporal, of the infinite in the finite, of the divine in the human."*

* W. A. Brown, How To Think of Christ, p. 9.

As stated above, the conflict that Christians often have over the question of Jesus divinity is not over the validity of the fact of his divinity, but over the question of how and when he became divine. The more orthodox Christians have seen his divinity as an inherent quality metaphysically bestowed. Jesus, they have told us, is the Pre existent Logos. He is the word made flesh. He is the second person of the trinity. He is very God of very God, of one substance with the Father, who for our salvation came down from Heaven and was incarnate be the Holy Ghost of the Virgin Mary.

Certainly this view of the divinity of Christ presents many modern minds with insuperable difficulties. Most of us are not willing to see the union of the human and divine in a metaphysical incarnation. Yet amid all of our difficulty with the pre existent idea and the view of supernatural generation, we must come to some view of the divinity of Jesus. In order to remain in the orbid of the Christian religion we must have a Christology. As Dr. Baille has reminded us, we cannot have a good theology without a Christology.[9] Where then can we in the liberal tradition find the divine dimension in Jesus? We may find the divinity of Christ not in his substantial unity with God, but in his filial consciousness and in his unique dependence upon God. It was his felling of absolute dependence on God, as Schleiermaker would say, that made him divine. Yes it was the warmnest of his devotion to God and the intimatcy of his trust in God that accounts for his being the supreme revelation of God. All of this reveals to us that one man has at last realized his true divine calling: That of becoming a true son of man by becoming a true son of God. It is

---

8. Davis underlined "surrounded with divinity," and asked, "Was not divinity 'in' him?"
9. Baillie, *God Was in Christ*, pp. 42–43.

the achievement of a man who has, as nearly as we can tell, completely opened his life to the influence of the divine spirit.

The orthodox attempt to explain the divinity of Jesus in terms of an inherent metaphysical substance within him seems to me quite inadaquate. To say that the Christ, whose example of living we are bid to follow, is divine in an ontological sense is actually harmful and detrimental. To invest this Christ with such supernatural qualities makes the rejoinder: "Oh, well, he had a better chance for that kind of life than we can possible have." In other words, one could easily use this as a means to hide behind behind his failures. So that the orthodox view of the divinity of Christ is in my mind quite readily denied. The true significance of the divinity of Christ lies in the fact that his achievement is prophetic and promissory for every other true son of man who is willing to submit his will to the will and spirit og God. Christ was to be only the prototype of one among many brothers.

The appearance of such a person, more divine and more human than any other, ~~andstanding~~ and standing in closest unity at once with God and man, is the most significant and hopeful event in human history. This divine quality or this unity with God was not something thrust upon Jesus from above, but it was a definite achievement through the process of moral struggle and self-abnegation.[10]

Bibliography

1. Baille D. M., God was in Christ, Scribner's, 1948.
2. Brown, William A., How To Think of Christ, Scribner, 1945.
3. Hedley, George, The Symbol of the Faith, Macmillan, 1948.
4. Mackintosh, H. R., The Doctrine of the Person of Jesus Christ, Scribner, 1912.

THDS. MLKP-MBU: Box 112, folder 17.

---

10. A version of this paragraph appears in a previous paper for Davis during the first term of Christian Theology for Today: "The appearance of such a person, more divine and more human, than any other, and standing in closest unity at once with God and man, is the most significant and hopeful event in human history. This divine character or this unity with God was nothing thrust upon Jesus from above, but it was a definite achievement" ("Six Talks in Outline," 13 September–23 November 1949, p. 247 in this volume).

[*29 November 1949–15 February 1950*]
[*Chester, Pa.*]

In this paper written for Davis's course Christian Theology for Today, King's
theological liberalism is apparent in his historical analysis of the development of the
doctrine of atonement and in his conclusion that humanity, not God, is at the
center of the process of redemption. This essay includes King's first reference to
Anders Nygren's influential work Agape and Eros. *Davis gave King an A and*
commented, "Well done."

The cross has stood out as the supreme symbol of he Christian religion for almost two thousand years. Theologians of all shades of opinions and from all ages of the Christian era have attempted to come to some view of the cross with a definite spiritual and Biblical justification in the forefront. This attempt to come to some adequate theory of atonement has not lead to a unity of thought on the matter, rather it has resulted in diverse interpretations. Before turning to our main objective, that of giving a specific view of the cross possessing spiritual and Biblical justification, we might give a brief historical introduction representing the various views of the atonement.

In the history of the doctrine of the atonement it is customary to distinguish three different periods or three different types of thought. The first period, that of the early church, covered nearly a thousand years and is usually referred to as the Greek or patristic period.[1] Here it is held that Christ delivered men from sin by offering a ransom in their behalf to Satan, who was their rightful or actual Lord. This doctrine took various forms and exerted a profound influence on the theology of the early church.

Another creative period in the history of the doctrine of the atonement was that inaugurated by Anselm in the eleventh century. It assumed three main forms: the Anselmic theory of satisfaction. the penal

---

1. Albert C. Knudson, "A View of Atonement for the Modern World," *Crozer Quarterly* 23 (January 1946): 52: "In the history of the doctrine of the atonement it is customary to distinguish three different periods or three different types of thought. . . . The first period, that of the early church, covered a thousand years and is usually referred to as the Greek or patristic period."

theory of the Reformers, and the governmental theory of Grotius. These three theories are by no means identical, but they represent the same general point of view insofar as they found the primary obstacle to man's redemption, not in Satan and other evil spirits, but in the nature of God or in his function as ruler.[2] Each of these theories represents the idea that the satisfaction was paid by Christ not to Satan but to God.

From the middle ages on until now, there has appeared by way of reaction from other systems of doctrine, the Moral Influence Theory of the work of Christ. Here the emphasis is not on the Godward but on the manward side of the atonement. According to this theory, the atoning work of Christ was a revelation of the heart of God, not intended to remove obstacles to forgiveness on God's side, of which there was no need, but designed to bring sinful men to repentance and win their love to himself. First formulated as an independent theory by Abelard in the twelfth century, it was rejected by the Church. But in modern times it was revived, and under the influence of Schleiermacher, Ritschl, and others gained wide currency, becoming the dominant theory in progressive theological circles, so that it is often referred to as the modern theory. of atonement.[3]

Turning now to our main objective, I begin with a process of elimination. First we may say that any doctrine which finds the meaning of atonement in the truimph of Christ over such cosmic powers as sin, death, and Satan is inadequate.[4] This dualistic view is

---

2. Knudson, "View of Atonement," pp. 52–53: "The great creative period in the history of the doctrine of the atonement was that inaugurated by Anselm in the eleventh century. . . . It assumed three main forms: the Anselmic theory of satisfaction, the penal theory of the Reformers, and the governmental theory of Grotus. These three theories differed from each other in some important respects, but they represented the same general point of view insofar as they were forensic in character and found the primary obstacle to man's redemption, not in Satan and other evil spirits, but in the nature of God or in his function as Ruler."

3. Knudson, "View of Atonement," p. 53: "Opposed to this Latin or forensic type of theory is the moral or personal type with its emphasis not on the Godward but on the manward side of the atonement. First formulated as an independent theory by Abelard in the twelfth century, it was rejected by the church. But in modern times it was revived, and under the influence of Schleiermacher, Ritschl, and others gained wide currency, becoming the dominant theory in progressive theological circles, so that it is frequently referred to as the modern theory of the atonement."

4. Knudson, "View of Atonement," p. 53: "Turning now to our main objective, that of defining a doctrine of atonement for the modern world, I begin with a process of elimination. And first no doctrine in my opinion can meet contemporary needs, which finds the meaning of the

15 Feb
1950

* A. C. Knudson, "A Doctrine of Atonement for The Modern World," The Crozer Quarterly, January, 1946.

imcompatible with a thoroughgoing Christian theism.* Such a view impresses "the modern mind ad mythological rather than theological."

The objection to the Latin type of theory—the Anselmic theory of satisfaction, the penal theory of the reformers, and the governmental theory of Grotius—is found in the abstract and impersonal way in which it deals with such ideas as merit, guilt and punishment; {the guilt of others and the punishment} due them are transferred to Christ and borne by him. Such views taken literally become bizarre. Merit and guilt are not concrete realities that can be detached from one person and transferred to another. Moreover, no person can morally be punished in place of another. Such ideas as ethical and penal substitution become immoral.†

† {Knudson, op. cit.}

In the next place, if Christ by his life and death paid the full penalty of sin, there is no valid ground for repentance or moral obedience as a condition of forgiveness. The debt is paid; the penalty is exacted, and there is, consequently, nothing to forgive.

Again, it may be noted that the Latin theory falls short of the fully personal and Christian conception of God as Father. It presents God as a kind of feudal Overlord, or as a stern Judge, or as a Governor of a state.[5] Each of these minimizes the true Christian conception of God as a free personality.

Now we turn to a theory which seems to me best adapted to meet the needs of the modern world, viz., the moral or personal type. Here we move into a different realm of thought, a change from the abstract

---

atonement in the triumph of Christ over cosmic powers of evil such as Satan, sin, and death, to which man is subject."

5. Knudson, "View of Atonement," pp. 55–56: "One [objection] is the abstract, mechanical, and impersonal way in which it deals with the ideas of merit, guilt, and punishment. Merit is acquired by Christ and transferred to others; and the guilt of others and the punishment due them are transferred to Christ and borne by him. All this, taken literally, is fictitious. Merit and guilt are inalienable from personality. They cannot be detached from one person and transferred to another. Nor can one person morally be punished in place of another. The whole idea of ethical substitution is immoral, and so also is the idea of a penal example.

"In the next place, it is obvious that in its strictly objective and substitutionary form the forensic theory leads logically to antinomianism. If Christ by his life and death paid the full penalty of sin, there is no valid ground for requiring anything further in the way of repentance or moral obedience as a condition of forgiveness. Indeed, there is no longer any need of forgiveness at all. The debt is paid; the penalty is exacted, and there is, consequently, nothing to forgive. . . .

"Again, it may be noted that the forensic theory assumes a sub-Christian conception of Deity. It represents God as a kind of feudal Overlord, or as a stern Judge, or as a Governor of a state."

to the empirical. The other theories of atonement have dealt in meaningless abstractions with no basis in concrete reality. Penalty has been treated in such an abstract manner that it may be transferred to an innocent person. Mechanical relations have taken the place of personal relations. But the atonement will not be understood in such abstract and speculative terms; it is from the standpoint of humanity as the growing family of God that the atonement is to be understood. As Dr. Knudson has stated, "We should approach it (the death of Christ) from the standpoint of moral and spiritual dynamics; and if we do so, we shall find in it two great sources of regenerative power: the perfect revelation of the divine love and righteousness and a profoundly moving example of absolute faithfulness to duty. It is here that we find the key to the cross. Not its Godward or Satanward but its manward side is the all-important thing."* The cross represents the eternal love of God seeking to attract men into fellowship with the divine. The chief source of the inspiring and redeeming power of the cross is the revelation of the divine love and righteousness. This theory, often spoken of as the modern theory of atonement, is actually as old as Paul. It is at this point that it receives Biblical justification. "God commendeth his love toward us, in that, while we were yet sinners, Christ died for us" (Rom. 5:8). "The love of Christ contraineth us; for we thus judge that . . . he died for all, that they who live should no longer live unto themselves but unto him who for their sakes died and rose again" (II Cor. 5:14ff.).

It is this aspect of the death of Christ that alone gives it profound moral significance. Any theory of atonement which does not recognize this fact is quite inadequate. The true meaning of the atonement must be interpreted in the light of the incarnation, whose purpose and cause was, in the words of Abelard, "that he might illuminate the world by his wisdom and excite it to the love of himself . . . Our redemption, therefore, is that supreme love of Christ shown to us by his passion, which not only frees us from slavery to sin, but acquires for us true liberty of the sons of God . . . so that kindled by so great a benefit of divine grace, charity should not be afraid to endure anything for his sake."†

The spiritual justification of this view is found in the emphasis that it places on the sacrificial love of

* A. C. KNudson, The Doctrine of Redemption, p. 370.

† Quoted by H. Rashdall, The Idea of the Atonement in Christian Theology, pp. 358f.

God. As stated above, the death of Christ is a revelation or symbol of the eternal sacrificial love of God. This is the agapa that Nygren speaks of in his Agapa and Eros. The love of God is spontaneous in contrast to all activity with a eudaemonistic motive. The divine love is purely spontaneous and unceasing in character. God does not allow his love to be determined or limited by man's worth or worthlessness. "For he maketh His sun to rise on the evil and the good and sendeth rain on the just and unjust" (Mt. 5:45). The divine love, in short, is sacrificial in its nature. This truth was symbolized, as stated above, by the death of Christ, who, because of his unique relation to God and his moral perfection, made this truth more efficacious than any other martyr. Here is the doctrine of the atonement presented in a moral, spiritual, and personal form. This seems to me the only theory of atonement adequate to meet the needs of modern culture.

Some of life is an earned reward, a commercial transaction, quid pro quo, so much for so much, but that is not the major element. The major element arrives when we feel some beauty, goodness, love, truth poured out on us by the sacrifices of others beyond our merit and deserving. It is at this point that we find the unique meaning of the cross. It is a symbol of one of the most towering facts in life, the realm of grace, the sacrificial gifts bought and paid for by one who did what we had no right to ask.

> Were the whole realm of nature mine,
> That were a present far to small;
> Love so amazing so divine,
> Demands my soul, my life, my all.

Bibliography

1. Clark, Henry W. The Cross and the Eternal Order, New York: The Manmillan Co., 1944.
2. Jones, E. S., Christ and Human Suffering, New York: Abingdon Press, 1933.
3. Aulen, G., Christus Victor, N.Y., Manmillan, 1931
4. Cave, S., Doctrine of the Work of Christ, Cokesbury, 1937.
5. Bushnell, H., The Vicarious Sacrifice, Scribner & Co. 1865.

THDS. MLKP-MBU: Box 112, folder 14.

"The Christian Pertinence
of Eschatological Hope"

[*29 November 1949–15 February 1950*]
[*Chester, Pa.*]

*In this essay for Christian Theology for Today, King attempts to find the "spiritual
meaning" of four Christian concepts: the second coming of Christ, the day of
judgment, immortality, and the Kingdom of God. He asserts that in a "Copernican
universe" a literal interpretation of these concepts is "quite absurd." Following
Davis's instructions, King drew from George Hedley's* Symbol of the Faith,
*which examines the Apostles' Creed. In the final paragraph, King links the coming
of the Kingdom of God to the rise of "a society governed by the law of love." Davis
gave the paper an A — without further comment.*

In the early years of the Christian era primitive
Christians set forth certain religious beliefs which
have come to be looked upon by the modern mind as
quite erroneous. To be sure, some modern minds of
the orthodox temperament are willing to hold on to
these traditional beliefs quite tenaciously. But the
more objective modern minds are confronted with insuperable difficulties when such issues arise. They argue that such beliefs are unscientific, impossible, and
even bizarre. Among the beliefs which many modern
Christians find difficult to accept are those dealing
with eschatological hopes, particularly the second
coming of Christ, the day of judgment, and the resurrection of the body. In an attempt to solve this difficult problem many modern Christians have jettisoned these beliefs altogether, failing to see that there
is a profundity of spiritual meaning in these beliefs
which goes beyond the shackles of literalism. We must
realize that these beliefs were formulated by an unscientific people who knew nothing about a Copernican universe or any of the laws of modern science.
They were attempting to solve basic problems which
were quite real to them, problems which to them dealt
with ultimate destiny. So it was only natural for them
to speak in the pre-scientific thought pattern of their
day. They could do no other. Inspiration did not
magically remove the limitations of the writers. It
heightened their power, but did not remove their dis-
tortions. Therefore it is our job as Christians to seek
the spiritual pertinence of these beliefs, which taken
literally are quite absurd. We would probably all agree

with the spiritual meaning of what these early Chris- 15 Feb
tians were trying to say, although we would disagree 1950
with how they said it. At this point we may turn to a
discussion of the more significant eschatological hopes
and attempt to find the Christian pertinence embedded therein.

The Second Coming of Christ

It is obvious that most twentieth century Christians
must frankly and flatly reject any view of a physical
return of Christ. To hold such a view would mean
denying a Copernican universe, for there can be no
physical return unless there is a physical place from
which to return. In its literal form this belief belongs
to a pre-scientific world view which we cannot accept.[1]
Where then do we find the Christian pertenence of
this belief? We may find it in the words of one of the
greatest Christians the world has ever known—St.
Paul. "Nevertheless I live: yet not I, but Christ liveth
in me."*[2] Also we may turn to the words of the
Fourth Gospel, "I will not leave you comfortless; I
come to you. Because I live, ye shall live also." The
most precious thought in Christianity is that Jesus is
our daily friend, that he never did leave us comfortless or alone, and that we may know his transforming
communion every day of our lives. As Dr. Hedley succinctly states, "The second coming of the Christ is not
an event in space-time, but an experience which transcends all physical categories. It belongs not to the
sky, but to the human heart; not to the future, but to
whatever present we are willing to assign to it."†

Actually we are celebrating the Second Advent every time we open our hearts to Jesus, every time we
turn our backs to the low road and accept the high
road, every time we say no to self that we may say yes
to Jesus Christ, every time a man or women turns
from ugliness to beauty and is able to forgive even
their enemies. Jesus stands at the door of our hearts
if we are willing to admit him. He is far away if with

* Galatians 2:20.

† George Hedley, The
Symbol of the Faith, p. 97.

---

1. George Hedley, *Symbol of the Faith* (New York: Macmillan, 1948), p. 2: "It is obvious that we
must reject, frankly and flatly, any thought of a physical return of Jesus of Nazareth. To try to
hold to it is to repudiate a Copernican universe, for there can be no physical return from heaven
unless there is a physical heaven from which to come. In its literal form the whole doctrine
belongs to that pre-scientific world view which we cannot for a moment accept."

2. This biblical passage is cited in Hedley, *Symbol*, p. 97.

ugliness and evil we crowd him out. The final doctrine of the second coming is that whenever we turn
our lives to the highest and best there for us is the
Christ.[3] This is what the early Christians were trying
to say. To be sure they got in unscientific realm because they began by saying that Jesus was the promised Messiah. But the question arises, what led them
to say that in the first place? It was the magnetic personality of this historic Jesus that caused men to explain his life in a category beyond the human. Here
we are one with the unscientific early Christians, for
all of our thoughts and teachings about the second
coming, whether it be physical or spiritual, stem from
the personality of that Jesus whom the Christians
chose to call the Christ.

The Day of Judgment

Orthodox Christianity has held that when a man
dies he sleeps until the general resurrection on the
last day at which time Christ, the judge, will appear to
summonn all to a bar of justice. He will separate tham
"as a shepherd divideth his sheep from the goats,"
sending the former to eternal bliss and the latter to
endless hell. Needless to say the average modern
Christian finds it quite difficult to accept such a view
of judgment.

However, we must agree with the spiritual value of
this view held by the early Christians, for the personality of Jesus does serve as a judgment upon us all.[4]
When we set aside the spectacular paraphernalia of
the judgment scene and the literal throne we come to
the real meaning of the doctrine.[5] The highest court
of justice is in the heart of man after the light of
Christ has illumined his motive and all his inner life.
Any day when {we} waken to the fact that we are making a great moral decision, any day of experienced
nearness to Christ, any day when in the light of
Christ, we see ourselves, is a day of judgment. In
speaking of Jesus as judge of all human life Hedley
remarks, "We have found no better pattern, nor do

---

3. Hedley, *Symbol,* p. 99: "He is in us, if we are willing to admit him. He is far away, and never
shall return, if in us ugliness, and lies, and evil, crowd him out. The final doctrine of the second
coming is that we determine its reality, each of us for himself."

4. Hedley, *Symbol,* p. 105: "The personality of Jesus . . . is in itself a judgement upon us all."

5. Hedley, *Symbol,* p. 106: "Set aside the spectacular paraphernalia of the judgement scene."

we think to seek another. When we are dishonest, we remember in embarrassment the absolute honesty of his mind. When we are disloyal, we are challenged by the find loyalty of his behavior. When we allow ourselves to become cheap, we are reminded of how much his way of living cost him."*[6] In this sense Christ has already come to judge the world. Already and here he is judging every one of us. This is the ultimate meaning of the Christian doctrine. Dare we judge ourselves by the Christ?[7]

* Hedley, op. cit., p. 105.

Immortality

Immortality to our fore fathers in the Christian tradition meant eternal rest and peace in a physical place called Heaven and everlasting communion with God. Those who failed to achieve this immortal life were subjected to a physical place called Hell in which they would suffer eternal misery by burning in a blazing fire. In modern times we have come to see that such eschatological thinking is by far incompatible with the modern scientific world view. A physical Heaven and a physical Hell are inconceivable in a Copernican universe. This changing world view has caused many modern minds to lose faith altogether in the immortal hope. But the question immediately arises, does a changing worly-view necessarily make the immortal hope impossible? What is the Christian pertinence of this doctrine?

Belief in immortality means primarily belief in God. It would be very difficult to conceive of God as blotting out the choicest fruit of the evolutionary process. The Christian sees reality in immortality because he sees reality in God. God is a God that will conserve all values of the universe.

Again the worthfulness of the personal life of Jesus makes immortality meaningful. Through his spirit Jesus brought the immortal hope to light. He had a quality of spirit that death couldn't hold (cf. Acts 2:24). His love was too powerful for death. His truth was too eternal for death. His goodness was too influential for death. Dr. Brown has put this idea in words that are quite apt at this point. He says: "Many arguments may be given for believing in a life after death

6. King omitted one sentence from the original (Hedley, *Symbol*, p. 107).
7. Hedley, *Symbol*, p. 109: "Dare we judge ourselves by the Christ?"

but the greatest of them all is the creative experience; the new life which Jesus makes possible for us here and now—a life which reveals to us capacities in ourselves which require another life for their fulfilment."*

* W. A. Brown, Beliefs
that Matter, p. 280.

It is here that we find the Christian pertinence of this immortal hope. This is what the early Christian Fathers were attempting to say. Because of the world view of their day they could with ease posit a physical immortality. But with all of their unscientific thinking they were saying essentially what we may say—God is a conserver of values. For us immortality will mean a spiritual existence. All of the details of what this existence will be like are somewhat beyond our intelligence. But with faith in God we may rest assure that death will not be a period that will end this great sentence of life, but it will be a comma punctuating it to more loftier significance.

The Kingdom of God

The eschatological thinking of the Christian religion is not without its social emphasis. Throughout nineteen hundred years Christian thinking has centered on the kingdom of God. Some have seen this kingdom in political terms in which there would be established a theocratic kingdom on earth which would triumph over all rival and satanically inspired regimes. Others have seen the kingdom of God coming to realization by means of the increasing influence of the church ultimately destined to dominate the world. Others have seen it as the day when Jesus shall return on the clouds bringing about a cataclysmic end of history and establishing God's eternal purpose. Certainly we in the modern world find it very difficult to accept many of the older interpretations of the kingdom of God. But however varied our interpretations may be, there is at bottom a profound spiritual {meaning} in the concept. "The phrase meant literally the reign of God, the condition of things in which God's will is everywhere supreme."[8] Here we are left in no doubt as to the true meaning of the concept. Whether it come soon or late, by sudden crisis of through slow development, the kingdom of God will be a society in which all men and women will be con-

---

8. This quotation is from William Adams Brown, *Beliefs That Matter: A Theology for Laymen* (New York: Scribner, 1928), p. 56.

trolled by the eternal love of God. When we see social relationships controlled everywhere by the priciples which Jesus illustrated in his life—trust, love, mercy, and altruism—then we shall know that the kingdom of God is here. To say what this society will be like in exact detail is quite hard for us to picture, for it runs so counter to the practices of our present social life.[9] But we can rest assure that it will be a society governed by the law of love.

BIBLIOGRAPHY

1. Brown, W. A., Beliefs that Matter, Scribner, 1928.

2. Clarke, W. N., An Outline of Christian Theology, Scribner, 1898.

3. Hedley, George, The Symbol of the Faith, Macmillan, 1948.

THDS. MLKP-MBU: Box 112, folder 17.

---

9. Brown, *Beliefs That Matter*, p. 59: "Here we are left in no doubt as to Jesus' meaning. Whether it come soon or late, by sudden crisis or through slow development, the Kingdom of God will be a society in which men and women live as children of God should live. When we see social relationships everywhere controlled by the principles which Jesus illustrated in his own life—the principles of trust, of love, of generous and unselfish service—we shall know that the Kingdom is here.

"What this society will be like in detail, it is hard for us to picture, for it runs so counter to the ideals and practices which still dominate much of our social life."

"How Modern Christians Should Think of Man"

[*29 November 1949–15 February 1950*]
[*Chester, Pa.*]

In this paper, written late during the second term of Davis's Christian Theology for Today, King begins to depart from theological liberalism, balancing neo-orthodoxy and liberalism to express his understanding of humanity and religion. For example, he acknowledges elements of determinism in human experience in one section of the paper but stresses the roles of sin and choice in an individual's life in another. He cites personal experiences of racism to show the "vicious" potential of human beings, but, following liberal theologians, King also praises the "noble possibilities in human nature" when people choose to fight this evil. The reference to racism marks this paper as more personal than others King wrote for this course

273

and reveals his belief in the connection between personal experience and theology.
Davis gave King an A and commented, "Very well done. You preserve balance
throughout."

In writing a paper on how modern Christians should think about man I find myself confronted with a difficulty. This difficulty is found in the fact that my thinking about man is going through a state of transition. At one time I find myself leaning toward a mild neo-orthodox view of man, and at other times I find myself leaning toward a liberal view of man. The former leaning may root back to certain experiences that I had in the south with a vicious race problem. Some of the experiences that I encounted there made it very difficult for me to believe in the essential goodness of man. On the other hand part of my liberal leaning has its source in another branch of the same root. IN noticing the gradual improvements of this same race problem I came to see some noble possibilities in human nature. Also my liberal leaning may root back to the great imprit that many liberal theologians have left upon me and to my ever present desire to be optimistic about human nature.

In this transitional stage I must admit that I have become a victim of eclecticism. I have attempted to synthesize the best in liberal theology with the best in neo-othodox theology and come to some understanding of man. Of course I must again admit that the insights which I have gained from neo-orthodox theology about man are quite limited. Its one-sided generalizations are by no means appealing to me. However I do see value in its emphasis on sin and the necessity of {for} perpetual repentance in the life of man. I think liberal theology has to easily cast aside the term sin, failing to realize that many of our present ills result from the sins of men. With these propaedeutic concerns in mind we may turn to a more detailed discussion in which I shall list what seems to me the most important things that modern Christians should believe about man.

1. Man is neither good nor bad by nature, but has potentualities for either

It is a mistake to look upon man as naturally good or naturally bad. Any one-sided generalization about man, whether it be a doctrine of original sin or a romantic idealization of man, should be rejected. Unfortunately, we too often find in the modern world this tendency to overemphasize the goodness or the badness of man. On the one hand we find it in neo-orthodox thought, particularly Barthianism. Here the view is posited that man was once completely good, made in the image of God. This complete goodness, however, was lost in the fall when man misused his freedom. Not only was his goodness lost, but the once present image of God was also totally effaced, leaving him totally helpless in his desire for salvation. Any such generalization about man is preposterous unless it be merely an inaccurate way of stating the fact that man sins on every leval of moral and spiritual achievement.[1]

On the other hand this tendency to generalize about man is found in extreme liberal and so called religious humanistic circles. Here there is the strong tendency toward sentimentality about man. Man who has come so far in wisdom and decenncy may be expected to go much further as his methods of attaining and applying knowledge are improved. This conviction was put into a phrase by an outstanding Humanist: "The supreme value and self perfectibility of man."*[2] Although such ethical religion is humane and its vision a lofty one, it has obvious shortcomings. This particular sort of optimism has been discredited by the brutal logic of events. Instead of assured progress in wisdom and decency man faces the ever present possibility of swift relapse not merely to animalism but into such calculated cruelty as no other animal can practice.

It seems that we shall be closest to the authentic Christian interpretation of man if we avoid both of these extremes. As seen in the life and teaching of Jesus, humanity remains conscious of its humble dependence upon God, as the source of all being and all goodness. "There is none good save one, even God." Yet in his dealing with even the worst of men, Christ

* C. F. Potter, Humanism A New Religion, p. 14.

---

1. John C. Bennett, "The Christian Conception of Man," in *Liberal Theology, an Appraisal: Essays in Honor of Eugene William Lyman,* ed. David E. Roberts and Henry Pitney Van Dusen (New York: Scribner, 1942), p. 192: "Any such generalization about man is preposterous unless it is merely an inaccurate way of stating the fact that man does sin on every level of moral and spiritual achievement."

2. The quotation should end with "self-perfectibility of human personality."

constantly made appealed to a hidden goodness in their nature. The modern Christian must believe that lives are changed when the potential good in man is believed in patiently, and when the potential bad in man is sought to be overwelmed.[3]

2. Man as a Finite Child of Nature

Every modern {Christian} should see man not only as a being made in the image of God, but also as a finite child of nature. He is subject to the laws of nature both in his growth and in many of his actions. So that when we speak of the freedom of man, it is quite obvious that it has a limit. On every hand "human freedom is mixed with natural necessity." This idea affirms that in many instances the laws of nature interfere with the higher life of man. Man is not only a victim of his own sins, but he is a victim of nature. Moreover, he is a victim of the blindness and cruelty of his neighbors. This is a liberal emphasis which must not be lost in the modern world, for it takes into account those non-moral sources of evil which often interfere with man and his salvation.*[4]

3. Man as a Rational Being

The modern Christian should never lose faith in rationality as one of the supreme resources of man. It is the mind of man that distinguishes him from his animal ancestry. Through memory man is able to in-

* John C. Bennett, "The Christian Conception of Man," In: Roberts and Van Dusen, <u>Liberal Theology</u>, p. 195.

---

3. Walter Marshall Horton, "The Christian Understanding of Man," in *The Christian Understanding of Man,* ed. T. E. Jessop et al. (London: Allen & Unwin, 1938), p. 240: "We shall be closest to the authentic Christian interpretation of man's higher nature if we avoid both of these extremes. As seen in the life and teachings of the Christ Himself, divine humanity remains conscious of its clear distinction from God, and its humble dependence upon Him, as the source of all being and all goodness. 'There is none good save one, even God.' Yet in His dealing with even the worst of men, Christ constantly made appeal to a hidden goodness in their nature, . . . Lives are changed, when the potential good in man is believed in, patiently, in the face of repeated rebuffs."

4. Bennett, "Christian Conception," p. 195: *"Man Is a Finite Child of Nature:* It is a mistake to look upon man only as a being made in God's image and as sinner. Man is also as a finite child of nature, subject to the laws of nature which often interfere with his higher life just as they are also the means of his growth . . . a victim of his own sin . . . and a victim of nature. One of the most important elements in liberal thinking about man and his salvation is that emphasis has been placed upon these many non-moral sources of evil. . . . Man is . . . a victim of nature and of the blindness and cruelty of his neighbors."

terpret the present and forcast the future in the light of the past. Moreover, man is able to think abstractly. He can delve into the eternal aspects of reality. By emperical science he can grasp many facts and and aspects of the concrete world. It is the rational element in human nature which serves as a check on false thinking, and without it we would have no way to be protected against false revelation.

It must be admitted, however, that this higher aspect of man's nature is a peril as well as a supreme gift. It often serves to create pride and self-sufficiency within man.[5] It is at this point that many neo-orthodox theologians speak of "the pride of reason."* But here it is well to emphasize the fact that reason rightly used remains the prize gift of man.

* Reinhold Niebuhr, The Nature and Destiny of Man, Vol. I, p. 195.

4. Man as a Free and Responsible Being

Any form of mechanical determinism is outside the orbit of the Christian tradition. Man is a free and responsible being. The Kantian "I ought therefore I can" should stand out as a prelude in the modern Christian's thinking about man. There have been attempts in theological thinking, specifically Calvinistic and contemporary Barthian thought, that {to} maintain that man is a responsible being yet lacking freedom. But such thinking leads us into needless paradoxes. How can there be responsibility with no freedom? The tendency in liberal theology has been to affirm that man is free and then to deny that his conscious purposes are predestined by God.[6] This seems to me a more logical mode of thought. We must believe that man has the power of choosing his supreme end. He can choose the low road or the high road. He can be true or false to his nature.

---

5. Bennett, "Christian Conception," p. 196: "*Man Is a Rational Being:* . . . His memory enables him to interpret the present and forecast the future in the light of the past. He can understand many of the eternal aspects of reality through his grasp of abstract thought and he can by empirical science understand large areas of the concrete world. . . . these higher aspects of man's nature are the source of his greatest temptations as well as his greatest gifts. . . . reason tempts man to be proud and self-sufficient. . . . without [reason] we have no protection against false 'revelations.'"

6. Bennett, "Christian Conception," pp. 196–197: "The tendency in liberal theology has been to affirm this kind of freedom and then to deny that our conscious purposes are predestined by God."

5. <u>Man as a Sinner</u>

The view that man is a sinner is basically a neo-orthodox view, and one that the modern Christian should not so easily overlook. I realize that the sinfullness of man is often over-emphasized by some neo-orthodox theologians, but at least we must admit that many of the ills in the world are due to plain sin. The tendency on the part of some liberal theologians to see sin as a mere "lag of nature" which will be progressively eliminated as man climbs the evolutionary ladder seems to me quite perilous. I will readily agree, as stated above, that many of man's shortcomings are due {to} natural necessities, but ignorance and finiteness and hampering circumstances, and the pressure of animal impulse, are all insufficient to account for many of our shortcomings.[7] As Dr. Horton has cogently stated, "we have to recognize that we have misused man's kingly prerogative as a rational animal by envisaging and pursuing ends that are unworthy of pursuit; and we have misused man's prerogative as a social animal by making others bear the burden of our selfishness."*

We must come to see that every human good has its own form of corruption. Dr. Reinhold Niebuhr has pointed out with great illumination how men sin through intellectual and spiritual pride.† The world is full of examples of such sin.[8] So that the modern Christian must see man as a guilty sinner who must ask forgiveness and be converted.[9]

* W. M. Horton, "The Christian Understanding of Man," (an Oxford Conference Book), {The Christian Understanding of Man, p. 235.}

† Niebuhr, <u>op. cit.</u> Chapter IX.

6. <u>Man as a Being</u>
<u>in need of Continuous Repentance</u>

Repentance is an essential part of the Christian life. Through repentance man is converted and brought into fellowship with God. Repentance as seen in the New Testament—the turning away from a life of sin because of a change of mind in which a new and bet-

---

7. Horton, "Christian Understanding," p. 236: " . . . that ignorance, and finiteness, and hampering circumstance, and the pressure of animal impulse, are all insufficient to account for it."

8. Bennett, "Christian Conception," pp. 199–200: "Every human good has its own form of corruption. Reinhold Niebuhr has written with extraordinary illumination concerning the ways in which men sin through intellectual and spiritual pride. . . . The world is full of examples of the corruption."

9. Horton, "Christian Understanding," p. 236: "We are guilty sinners who must ask forgiveness and be converted."

ter standard of life has been accepted—is something that may occur again and again in a man's experience.[10] The habit of perpetual repentance enables us to grow; it helps us to keep our conscience awake; it preserves us from the sin of self righteousness; it helps us to concentrate on our sins, rather than the sins of others.[11] Repentance is in fact to any man an inestimable privilege.[12] As Dr. Clarke laconically states: "Perpetual repentance is simply perpetual fellowship with Christ. Performed once or a thousand times, it is a most precious act of moral unity with Christ the Savior."*

* W. N. Clarke, An Outline of Christian Theology, p. 403.

In this discussion I have tried to put down six elements that should enter into the modern Christian's doctrine of man. I have tried to show that there are some insights about man to be gained from both liberal and neo-orthodox thinking. However, it is clear that all one-sided generalizations about man must be rejected, whether found in liberal or neo-orthodox thinking. Such doctrines are misleading and they detach man from the understanding of his origin, place, and destiny.[13]

BIBLIOGRAPHY

1. Calhoun, R. L., What Is Man, Association Press, 1940.
2. Clarke, W. N., An Outline of Christian Theology, Scribner, 1898.
3. Niebuhr, R., The Nature and Destiny of Man, vol. I, Scribner, 1941.
4. Symposium, The Christian Understanding of Man, Willett, Clark and Co.

THDS. MLKP-MBU: Box 112, folder 14.

---

10. William Newton Clarke, *An Outline of Christian Theology* (New York: Scribner, 1927), pp. 401–402: "Through repentance and faith a man is converted, or turned, to God, and brought into fellowship with him. . . . Repentance, in the New Testament . . . is the turning away from a life of sin, the breaking off from evil, because of a change of mind in which a new and better standard of life has been accepted. . . . Repentance, thus defined, is something that may occur again and again in a man's experience."

11. Bennett, "Christian Conception," p. 203: "The habit of continuing repentance enables us to grow; it keeps the conscience awake; it helps to preserve us from self-righteousness. It may keep us from the . . . tendency to concentrate upon the sins of others."

12. Clarke, *Outline of Christian Theology*, p. 403: "Repentance is in fact to any man an inestimable privilege."

13. Horton, "Christian Understanding," p. 241: "When will modern man return to this understanding of his origin, place, and destiny?"

Six Talks Based on
Beliefs That Matter by William Adams Brown

[*29 November 1949–15 February 1950*]
[*Chester, Pa.*]

For the final assignment in Christian Theology for Today, Davis required six outlines based on William Adams Brown's book Beliefs That Matter.[1] *The first talk, "What a Christian Should Believe About Himself," is the most notable. In discussing slave religion, King makes one of his few references in his student papers to the African-American experience: "as they gathered in these meetings they gained a renewed faith as the old unlettered minister would come to his triumphant climax saying: 'you—you are not niggers. You—you are not slaves. You are God's children.'" King refers to Leslie Weatherhead's metaphor of the global breakfast in this paper and returned to the metaphor throughout his life. King's second outline, "A Christian View of the World," argues for the achievement of social justice and thus the possibility for realizing the kingdom of God on earth. "How a Christian Overcomes Evil" presents a theme King would often articulate: evil is not driven out by force but crowded out by love. Davis judged the outlines "well done. A."*

"What a Christian
Should Believe About Himself"

I. Each Christian should believe that he is made in the image of God.
   A. The meaning of the image of God.
      1. The ultimate meaning of the view that man is made in the image of God is that man is somewhat like God. He is more than flesh and blood.
      2. God creates every individual for a purpose, to have fellowship with him, to trust him. This is a second meaning of the image of God. It is not that man as he is in himself bears God's likeness, but rather that man is designated for and called to a particular relation with God. (Brunner) It is not that there is such a thing as a divine substance of which man is made. Rather, it is that man partakes of the divine image in a functional way.
   B. The value of the concept.
      1. The concept of the image of God assures man that he is capable of having fellowship with the divine. Unlike his animal ancestry and the many inanimate objects of the universe, man is privileged with a dynamic relationship with God.

---

1. William Adams Brown (1865–1943) studied at Yale University, Union Theological Seminary, and the University of Berlin. He joined the Union faculty in 1892 and served as its Roosevelt Professor of Systematic Theology from 1898 to 1930. Brown's *The Essence of Christianity* (1902), *Christian Theology in Outline* (1906), *Beliefs That Matter* (1930), and *How to Think of Christ* (1945) were essential texts of liberal American Protestant thought in their era.

2. Such a concept also keeps man aware of the fact that he is made for that which is lofty and noble. Man, with such a concept, is able to realize that when his actions, thoughts, and feelings are determined by anything less than God, he fails to partake of the divine image.

II. Each Christian should believe that he is a member of a larger family of which God is Father. Jesus expresses the view throughout the Gospels that we are members of one family, meant to live as brothers and to express our brotherhood in helpfulness. A failure to realize this truth is a failure to realize one of the main tenets of the Christian religion. The Fatherhood of God and the Brotherhood of man is the starting point of the Christian ethic.

A. The Fatherhood of God.

1. First we might say that our view of God as Father should be in definite agreement with Jesus' view of God as Father. Such a view assures us that God is not a mere stern judge that sits upon the divine bench forever ready to punish his children, but he is an all loving Father forever willing to meet the needs of his children. He is not the Aristotelian God who merely contemplates upon himself; not only is God a self knowing Father, but he is an ever {other} loving Father.

2. Secondly, the Christian view of God as Father immediately gives the Christian a sense of belonging. When the Christian comes to believe that he is a child of an all loving Father he feels that he counts, that he belongs. He senses the confirmation of his roots, and even death becomes a little thing. Let me give an illustration. During the years of slavery in America it is said that after a hard days work the slaves would often hold secret religious meetings. All during the working day they were addressed with unnecessary vituperations and insulting epithets. But as they gathered in these meetings they gained a renewed faith as the old unlettered minister would come to his triumphant climax saying: "you—you are not niggers. You—you are not slaves. You are God's children."[2] This established for them a true ground of personal dignity. The awareness of being a child of God tends to stablilize the ego and bring new courage.

B. The Brotherhood of Man.

---

2. This story was known to many southern black preachers. Howard Thurman's grandmother told him the story of a slave preacher who was allowed to visit the plantation and preach to the slaves. "When the slave preacher told the Calvary narrative to my grandmother and the other slaves, it had the same effect on them as it would later have on their descendants. But this preacher, when he had finished, would pause, his eyes scrutinizing every face in the congregation, and then he would tell them, 'You are not niggers! You are not slaves! You are God's children!'" (Howard Thurman, *With Head and Heart: The Autobiography of Howard Thurman* [New York: Harcourt Brace Jovanovich, 1979], p. 21).

1. Man's relationship to God is dependent upon man's relationship to man. It is impossible to simultaneously love God and hate your brother.
2. The brotherhood of man is an established fact by the findings of modern science. There are four types of blood, called O, A, B, and AB. These four types of blood are found in all races.
3. The destiny of each individual wherever he resides on the earth is tied up with the destiny of all men that inhabit the globe. We literally cannot live entirely to ourselves. Let us illustrate how we all share in the assets of the human family. When we rise and go to the bath, a cake of soap is handed us by a Frenchman, a sponge is handed us by a Pacific Islander, a towel by a Turk, our underclothes by an American or Englishman. We go down to breakfast, our tea is poured out by a Chinese. Our toast we accept at the hads of an English speaking farmer, not to mention the baker. We are indebted to half of the world before we finish breakfast. The secret of all our happiness is that we are one amid many brothers. This, every Christian should believe.[3]

"A Christian View of the World"

I. The world as a revelation of God.
   Christians of all ages have testified that the good in nature is a revelation of the eternal God. This means that true Christians have no sympathy with those who think of matter as evil and the body as a thing to be depreciated. God is in the world and he is constantly using parts of it to reveal his nature to man. This has not led most Christians to say that nature is God; this would be pantheism. Rather they have said that nature is one of the avenues through which God reveals himself to man.
   A. The reality of the world.—Unlike Buddha, Christians have always insisted the physical universe has real existence. It is not a mere creation of our imagination, as some philosophers have tried to persuade us; A picture world which we have made for ourselves out of our dreams, an illusion from which we need to wake to reality. The Christian would not flee from the world as Gautama bids him, but he uses it, because God has made it for his sustenance, his discipline, and his happiness.

---

3. Leslie Weatherhead, *Why Do Men Suffer?* (New York: Abingdon-Cokesbury, 1936), pp. 69–70: "When I rise and go to my bath, a cake of soap is handed me by a Frenchman, a sponge is handed me by a Pacific Islander, a towel by a Turk, my underclothes by one American or Englishman, my outer garments by another. I come down to breakfast. My tea is poured out by an Indian or a Chinese. My porridge is served by a Scottish farmer. My toast I accept at the hands of an English-speaking farmer, not to mention the baker. My marmalade is passed to me by a Spaniard, my banana by a West Indian. I am indebted to half the world before I have finished breakfast. The secret of half my happiness is that I belong to a family."

B. God in nature.—Throughout the ages Christians have stood in the midst of the beauties of nature with an assurance that God is revealed therein. Man observes the splendor of the skies, the radiancy of the beaming sun, the fragrant {rose} ose, the melodies of the morning bird, and from such beauty he gains a feeling that causes him to rise above the hurly burly of everyday life and dwell in lofty atmosphere which blows the wind of God's eternal nature. Such beauty has always caught the mind of the affirmation mystic. Such beauty causes the poet to reach up and pull the abstract into the concrete. Such beauty serves as a source of reference for the musician. Whenever man is confronted with such experiences he is aware of the fact that he stands in the presence of the Eternal God who is forever revealed in the beauties of nature.

II. The world as a training school for the Kingdom of God.

Christians have joined in one accord in seeing the world as a place in which God is preparing his children for membership in a society in which all the relationship os life will be controlled by love.

A. The meaning of the Kingdom of God.

1. Political view.—Many have seen the Kingdom in political terms in which there would be established a theocratic kingdom on earth which would triumph over all satanically inspired regimes.

2. Cataclysmic view.—Others have seen the Kingdom as the day when Jesus shall return on the clouds bringing about a cataclysmic end of history and establishing God's eternal purpose.

3. Triumphant church view.—Here it is held that the Kingdom will come to realization by means of the increasing influence of the church ultimately destined to dominate the world.

4. Jesus' view.—Jesus took over the phrase "the Kingdom of God," but he changed its meaning. He refused entirely to be the kind of a Messiah that his contemporaries expected. Jesus made love the mark of sovereignty.[4] Here we are left with no doubt as to Jesus' meaning. The Kingdom of God will be a society in which men and women live as children of God should live. It will be a kingdom controlled by the law of love.

B. The coming of the Kingdom in the world. Many have attempted to say that the ideal of a better world will be worked out in the next world. But Jesus taught men to say, "thy will be done in earth, as it is in heaven." Although the world seems to be in {a} bad shape today we must never lose faith in the power of God to achieve his purpose. Let us illustrate this. Imagine a building in course of construction. The place is littered with all kinds of debris. Over there

---

4. William Adams Brown, *Beliefs That Matter: A Theology for Laymen* (New York: Scribner, 1928), p. 57: "Jesus took over the phrase 'the Kingdom of God,' but he changed its meaning. He refused entirely to be the kind of Messiah that his contemporaries expected. . . . Jesus made love the mark of sovereignty."

is a heap of sand. Near by is a cement mixer, and stones of various sizes are piled up everywhere. Let us imagine ~~tat~~ {that} we know nothing of the art of building, but that we know the architect. How impossible it would be to believe that before the building was funished the architect, who chose the site and chose his his workmen, decided that he was already defeated, that the builders were too stupid, and that therefore he had decided to build elsewhere with other builders. If we believe in the architect, we will believe that at last he will use everything in this muddled building site to work out his plan.

God, the great architect, chose this world as a site on which to build a wonderful structure; a global union of real brothers sharing in his good gifts, and offering all achievement as a form of worship to him. It would seem odd if the architect, who chose the site and intrusted the building to beings ~~elled~~ {called} men, suddenly threw up his hands, left the muddle and chose another site in another world and other workmen. The Great Architect may be saying, "Don't be impatient. Wait and see what I can do with this material which contains so many splendid qualities." It is very early to give up building. One geologist has said that if a movie film of the history of the earth were to be produced lasting twenty-four hours, then man would not appear until the last five seconds of the film. Let us have faith and cooperate with God and in the next few seconds we will be able to see the Kingdom in the world. Every Christian should believe this.

"How a Christian Overcomes Evil"[5]

I. The first step in overcoming evil is to discover what is worst in us.
   A. Discovering the evil. This is done by an examination of that sin to which we are most frequently tempted. It is very wrong to think that simply because we are tempted, that therefore we are wicked. The blessedness of temptation is that it only reveals the weak spot in our character, thereby providing the raw material for victory.
   B. Admitting the evil. One of the peculiar things about the human mind is that it can convince itself that the wrong is right. But if we are to overcome an evil we must first admit that it is an evil. The hidden fault must be called by its right name, otherwise we miss seeing our pride under fear of an inferiority complex.
II. The second stip in overcoming evil is to combat the interior defect in cooperation with God's grace.
   There are generally three ways in which this is done.
   A. We must ask God's grace to overcome the evil.

---

5. Brown's prescription for overcoming evil differs from King's. Brown emphasizes the mystic aspects of the cross, whereas King focuses on individual efforts to overcome evil through self-examination, self-control, and love, which "crowds out" evil.

B. By daily examination of conscience. As a person counts the money in his pocket daily to determine whether the current expense of the day can be met, so we balance our consciences to see if they are going in debt morally and spiritually.

C. By turning the predominant fault into its opposite virtue. Goodnss is not to be confused with passivity, but with activity in an opposite direction.

III. The third step in overcoming evil is: Concentrate not on the eradication of evil, but on the cultivation of virtue.

A. The difference in the two techniques of fighting evil and loving goodness is illustrated in an ancient Greek story. Ulysses returning from the siege of Troy, knew the danger of listening to the sirens tempting many a salor to doom. So Ulysses put wax in the ears of his sailors, strapped himself to the mast of the ship, so that even though he wished to follow the appeal of the sirens, he would not be able to do so. Some years later, Orpheus, the divine musician passed by the same sea, but refused to plug up his sailor's ears or bind himself to a mast. Rather he played his harp so beautifully that the song of the sirens had no appeal. It is not a hatred of evil but a love of God which crowds out evil, for hate is useless unless we love something else more.

B. Evil is never to be attacked directly, but indirectly. Evil is not driven out, but crowded out. Sensuality is not mastered by saying: "I will not sin," but through the expulsive power of something good.

"What Shall We Think About the Church"

I. The church as a religious institution for the perpetuation of a religious tradition.

A. Religion is not a private matter.—It is intensely personal, to be sure, but not therefore private. It is completely social as we human beings are. The church is the institution which has gathered together the various insights of spiritual giants through the ages and welded them into a body of belief and conviction which has passed from one generation to another with cumulative conviction. Without the institution working through the centuries, these insights would have perished long ago.

B. This does not mean that the church perfectly perpetuates the ideal for which it stands. It is an obvious fact that the church, while flowing through the stream of history has picked up the ~~ends~~ {evils} of little tributaries, and the evils of these tributaries, have been so powerful that they have been able to overwhelm the main stream. But amid all of its weaknesses, we must admit that the church enlarges our sympathy and reinforces our power by uniting us with those who have followed Jesus before us, or who will follow him after us.

II. The church as a nucleus of fellowship.
  A. It is the place of the church to make people feel at home, not in a superficial sense but in the deep and abiding sense of finding peace in the fellowship which we have one with another. The church must stress fellowship as being more important than creed, and experience as being more important than doctrinal uniformity.
  B. The memory of what Christian fellowship can mean can become a strong factor in a man's life. Let us illustrate. Dr. Leslie Weatherhead, in one of his books, speaks of a man who had been a victim of sex temptation and successfully resisted it over a long number of years. Only his best friends knew what a battle this particular problem was for him. One evening he found himself on business in Berlin with time on his hands. As he strolled down the Friedrichstrasse, his attention was caught by a large framed photograph of nude women. You can guess the kind of place that was ~~this~~ {then} adverised. He was greatly tempted to go in. No one would have known. His character would not have been damaged in the eyes of his friends. His respectability would have been unsoiled at home. Then suddenly, with great resolution, he walked away. A hundred yards from the place he had an immense sense of relief and spiritual power. When asked how he had found strength to make that great decision, he answered without hesitation, "My church at home." Even the memory of the fellowship, even the thought that he belonged to a company who loved him and who, with him, were seeking together the high and the lovely and the true and the beautiful thngs, strengthened him in the hour of temptation.
III. The church as a religious communion.
  A. To say that the church is a communion distinguishes it at once from any other kind of social institution. The church is the disciples listening to the sermon on the mount, or following Jesus along the roadways of Palestine. It is Peter and his comrades eyeing the leaders of Judaism and saying, "We must obey God rather than men!" It is Kagawa keeping the spirit of the Christian group in Japan alive during the desperate days of war.
  B. The church must confront men with the fact of the living God. The church must make this fact real in terms not alone of vision but also of judgment and light shed on the road ahead. We are supposed to be, to borrow Alfred Noyes' famous phrase, "the light bearers of mankind."

"What Should the Christian Do About the Bible"

I. Accept the Bible as a Spiritual Guide in finding God.
  A. The Bible is a sacred book of the Christian church.—It is the record of God's progressive self-revelation, first to the people of Is-

rael, afterward to the world in Jesus Christ.[6] It tells us not only what men have thought of God and what they have done for God but what they have experienced of God. Thus by bringing us in touch with the men and women who have found God before us, it encourages us to believe that we can find God for ourselves and it shows us how to do so.

    B. The Bible makes us acquainted with Jesus Christ, in whose person the divine revelation culminates.—The Christian religion has always insisted that through Jesus the character of God is revealed to man. God is like Christ. This is the basic affirmation of the Christian faith.

II. Christians should know the meaning of the Bible.

    A. The Bible as a book of progressive revelation.—Every book in the Bible is not equally valuable. This has been made plain to us by the modern critical method. It has proved to us that the Bible is a book of progressive revelation. Notice the development of the great ideas in the Bible such as God, man, sin, and immortality. To understand how these great ideas progresssed to their final culmination is to know the meaning of the Bible.

    B. The Bible as literature.—The Bible is not stated in abstract, universal propositions, but in concrete applications to specific situations, it was written in literary, not scientific or philosophical, language.

    C. The Bible as the ~~gook~~ {[bo]ok} of life.—The Bible is great literature because it is a great book of life. The Bible does not merely tell about life. It grows out of life in an extraordinarily direct and vivid way.

III. Christians should realize what the Bible can do for them.

    A. The Bible helps us to realize afresh the perennial vitality of the central convictions of the Christian life, such truths as the love of God, the Lordship of Christ, the fact of sin, the need of redemption, the vitalizing influence of the Spirit of God, and the hope of immortality.

    B. The Bible clarifies our thinking by making us acquainted with what the great men of the past have thought before us. It helps us to make right decisions by introducing us to those who have lived nobly and dared greatly for their faith.[7]

    C. The Bible can deepen and purify our emotional life. We live by our appreciations, our hopes and our fears, our aspirations and our loyalties, our sympathies and our affections. If we are to make our lives what they ought to be, we must bring order into this often discordant realm.[8]

---

6. Brown, *Beliefs*, p. 221: "[The books of the Bible] tell the story of God's progressive revelation, first to the people of Israel and afterward to the world through Jesus Christ."

7. Brown, *Beliefs*, p. 231: "As the Bible clarifies our thinking by making us acquainted with what the great men of the past have thought before us, so it helps us to make right decisions by introducing us to those who have lived nobly and dared greatly for their faith."

8. Brown, *Beliefs*, p. 231: "[The Bible] can deepen and purify our emotional life. We live by our appreciations, our hopes and our fears, our aspirations and our loyalties, our sympathies and

"The Christian Faith
in the Immortal Life"

I. The Wide-spread doubt of immortality.
   A. The extent of the doubting.—For our forefathers the soul's death-lessness was as a premise to be assumed, not as a conclusion to be established. Today we can no longer take belief in immortality for granted. Multitudes of people, even religious people, have lost the old, unquestioning faith in a life after death. Even where the fact is {not} denied, it is no longer confidently affirmed.
   B. Reasons for this wide-spread loss of faith in immortality in our day.
      1. The Darwinian discovery concerning the evolutionary origin of man.
      2. Men have gathered new hopes of racial progress in our day, and at their best are increasingly inclined to sink their individual prospects in their expectations for humanity.
      3. The minds of men have been so preoccupied with the fascinating advances of this modern age that interest has been totally lost in anything beyond the grave.
II. How to recover lost faith in immortality.
   A. The contribution of this life to faith in immortality. If we are to make belief in immortality again a living issue to those who for the moment have it, we must begin by making them feel that life here is so significant that it deserves to go on. Men will recover faith in immortality when they have recovered faith in life.
   B. The creative experience as a means of recovering lost faith in immortality. We shall recover, faith in immortality as we rediscover in ourselves and in others the possibilities of growth and progress which Jesus, our Lord, attributed to human beings. There are some people who make it easy to believe in immortality.
      1. Lincoln
      2. Dante
      3. Shakespeare.
      4. David Livingstone.
      5. Jesus Christ.[9]
III. The Christian's reason for believing in immortality.
   A. The resurrection of Jesus a proof of immortality. Christian belief in immortality seems to have began with the resurrection of Jesus. Of course there are two ways to interpret the resurrection.
      1. Physical resurrection.
      2. Spiritual resurrection.

---

our affections. If we are to make our lives what they ought to be, we must bring order into this often discordant realm."

9. King replaced Brown's example of Michelangelo with Jesus Christ; otherwise, the list and the two sentences preceding it are also found in Brown, *Beliefs*, p. 301.

B.   The reasonableness of the universe as evidence of immortality.
     Statement by Charles Darwin: "It is intolerable thought that man
     and all other sentient beings are doomed to complete annihilation,
     after such long continued slow progress."[10] The late professor
     Palmer of Harvard expressed faith in the reasonableness of the
     universe when he said the following words after the death of his
     wife. "Though no regrets are proper for the manner of her death,
     who can contemplate the fact of it and not call the world irrational,
     if out of deference to a few particles of disordered matter it ex-
     cludes so fair a spirit."[11]
C.   The beneficence of God evidence of immortality. Man cannot con-
     ceive of God as blotting out the choicest fruit of the evolutionary
     process. Faith in immortality boils down to a faith in God. Chris-
     tians believe that God will conserve all values of the universe.
D.   In the final analysis we believe in immortality because Jesus Christ
     has revealed to us within ourselves, and in others, capacities which
     require another life for their full expression. When a man of in-
     sight demands a life to come, it is not because he seeks outward
     recompense for a good life here; it is because his goodness here,
     if it is to be passionate and earnest, must have the eternal chance
     of being better. His value lies in what he may become, not in what
     he [*remainder missing*].

THDS. MLKP-MBU: Box 115, folder 32.

---

10. The quotation is from *The Life and Letters of Charles Darwin*, ed. Francis Darwin (1887):
"Believing as I do that man in the distant future will be a far more perfect creature than he is
now, it is an intolerable thought that he and all other sentient beings are doomed to complete
annihilation after such long-continued progress. To those who fully admit the immortality of the
human soul, the destruction of our world will not appear so dreadful" (quoted in *Bartlett's Familiar
Quotations*, 11th edition [Boston: Little, Brown and Co., 1946], p. 515).
11. George Herbert Palmer, *The Life of Alice Freeman Palmer* (New York: Houghton Mifflin,
1909), p. 327.

Examination Answers,
Christian Theology for Today

[*13 September 1949–15 February 1950*]
[*Chester, Pa.*]

These essays were written for Davis's course Christian Theology for Today,
probably as part of the final examination. The questions have been lost, but these
essays stand on their own as illustrations of King's evolving conception of God. This
topic continued to evoke King's interest, and he later devoted his dissertation to an
examination of two theologians' conceptions of God. In these answers King is

*straightforward in his description of his own views: "I feel that the most valid
conception of God is that of theism. God, for me along with other theist[s,] is a
personal spirit immanent in nature and in the value structure of the universe."
King's first essay examines the ways in which the theories of evolution can be
incorporated into theological concepts of the origin of the world. The final two
essays discuss the theory of "emergent evolution" and the importance of miracles
to a religious view of the world. Although a grade is not indicated on these
fragments, Davis gave King an A for the course.*

I With the rise of the scientific interpretation of the origin of the world and
the emergence of the theory of evolution many thought that the basic Christian view of creation was totally destroyed. This belief might be right in seeing
the invalidity of the older view of a first creation, but it is wrong in thinking
that all views of creations were destroyed with the rise of scientific interpretation. It seems quite possible to get an adequate religious view of the world
in the light of emergent evolution and cosmic theism. Is it not possible for
God to be working through the evolutionary process? May it not be the God
is creating from eternity? Emergent evolution says essentially that in the evolutionary process there is a continuous incoming of the new. The question
arises, from whence comes this emergence of new elements in the evolutionary process. The religious man answers, with a degree of assurance, that God
is the source of the new emergents. In other words, God is working through
the evolutionary process. As cosmic theism would say, there is an intelligent
conscious mind working out its purpose through the evolutionary proces. So
that in the light of emergent evolution and cosmic theism we can come to an
adaquate religious view of the world, viz., creative evolution. Here we find
creation and evolution existing together. Here we may still hold to a creator
God. Maybe we will conclude with Origin that God is creating from eternity,
but this does not destroy the basic Christian concept of a God who is creator
and sustainer of the universe[1]

II I feel that the most valid conception of God is that of theism. God, for me
along with other theist is a personal spirit immanent in nature and in the value
structure of the universe.

This theistic view carries with it many additional assumptions. First it means
that God is conscious mind and spiritual personality. It is not conceivable that
an unconscious impersonal God could have given rise to consciousness in
man. So that any view of God which emphasizes "his" impersonality fails to
explain adequately how consciousness arose. Moreover any view of an impersonal God fails to explain adequately religious experience. It is only a personal
God who can confront man in a religious experience. So we conclude that
God is conscious mind and personal spirit. This does not mean that his personality is ~~identif~~ identical to man's. God is the supreme personality.

This theistic view also means that God is immanent in the world. This seem
the only adequate way to explain religious experience. A God who is totally

---

1. Davis gave this answer fourteen points out of an unknown number of possible points.

transcendent and out of touch with the world cannot come to man in religious experience. Moreover, this view of the immanence of God is more in as accord with the theory of evolution.

The theistic view also means that God is more than nature and in a real sense not dependent on it. Here the transcendence of God is emphasized. This does not mean that God is spacially transcendent but it means that he is not dependent on the world for his existence. God has <u>aseity</u>. He exist in his own rights. Frankly I feel that unless God were transcendent he would not be God at all.

For the above reasons I feel that theism is the most valid conception of God. With pantheism it stresses the immanence of God. With deism it stresses the transcendence. So that it synthesizes the two and come to a working philosophy[2]

I   In the light of modern scientific knowledge religion proposes as its view of the world a theory of creative evolution. Here we find creation and evolution existing together. The religious man sees God working through the evolutionary process. Closely related to this point is the view of emergent evolution which was posited by the philosopher Morgan. Here it is held that in the evolutionary process there is a continuous incoming of new elements For an instance life seems to be the emergent of matter and mind seems to be the emergent of life. Now the question arises, from whence comes these new elements? Do they result from the working of unconscious forces or do they result from the working of a purposeful, intelligent conscious mind? The religious man answers with a deal of assurance that it is God who is bringing the continuous flow of the new into being. In other words it is the work of a personal spirit who is immanent in the world of nature and its value structure. This theory does in some measure break with the old religious view of the world, but it does not at all destroy a creator God. May it not be that God is creating from eternity? This certainly seems to me a valid conclusion.

Such a view of the world is far from unscientific. It still insist on a creative God and at the same time remains in the orbits of recent scientific findings. The religious will not be content to see the world as a result of chance combination (the interaction of atoms of molecules); neither is he content to see it as the result of unconscious quasi purposeful forces. Rather he is convinced that the world is the results of the workings of a creative mind who {is} still working through the evolutionary process. So that for the religious man emergent evolution serves as a scientific explanation of the continual workings of God.[3]

II   I would say that miracle holds a very important place in a religious view of the world. This does not mean that the older views of miracle are indispensable; but it does mean that the ideas which they attempted to convey are all well-nigh indispensable for any religious view of the world. At this point

---

2. Davis gave this answer sixteen points.
3. Davis gave this answer fifteen points.

seem the only adequate way to explain religious experience. A God who is totally transcendent and out of touch with the world cannot come to man in religious experience. Moreover, this view of the immanence of God is more in accord with the theory of evolution

The theistic view also means that God is more than nature and in a real sense not dependent on it. Here the transcendence of God is emphasized. This does not mean that God is specially transcendent but it means that he is not dependent on the world for his existence. God has aseity. He exist in his own right. Frankly I feel that unless God were transcendent he would not be God at all.

For the above reasons I feel that theism is the most valid conception of God. With pantheism it stresses the immanence of God. With deism it stresses the transcendence. So that it synthesizes the two and come to a working philosophy

Manuscript page 4 from Martin Luther King, Jr.'s examination answers; the transcription begins on page 290 and ends near the beginning of page 291.

II I would say that miracle holds a very important place in a religious view of the world. This does not mean that the older views of miracle are indispensable, but it does mean that the ideas which they attempted to convey are ~~the~~ well-nigh indispensable for any religious view of the world. At this point we might list the reasons why we give such an important position to miracle in a religious view of the world.

(1) First it is important because it insists on a living God. For the Christian God is a God who is living and active. He is not the Aristotelian God who merely contemplates upon himself. He is an ither loving God who is continually working with his children. Such a view is emphasized by the concept of miracle.

(2) Miracle is also important because it insists on a God who can do new and unpredictable things.

(3). Miracle is important, moreover, because

Manuscript page 3 from Martin Luther King, Jr.'s examination answers; the transcription begins near the bottom of page 291 and continues on page 294.

we might list the reasons why we give such an important position to miracle in a religious view of the world.

(1)   First it is important because it insists on a living God. For the Christian God is a God who is living and active. He is not the Aristotelian God who merely contemplates upon himself. He is an other loving God who is continually working with his children. Such a view is emphasized by the concept of miracle.

(2)   Miracle is also important because it insists on a God who can do new and unpredictable things.

(3)   Miracle is important, moreover, because it hold to a God who answers prayer. Christian insist that when man prays he is not talking to his subjective self, but he is talking to an objective God who answers prayer. Such a view is emphasized by the concept of miracle.

(4)   Miracle is important, finally, because it hold to an immanent God. God is not a deity who stands outside of the world and does nothing, but he is a deity immanent in the process of history.

For these reasons I feel that miracle is all important for any religion view of the world. If we accept Dr. Fosdicks definition of miracle the point is made clearer. Says he: "A miracle is God's use of his own law abiding powers to work ~~surprises his will~~ in ways surprising to ~~men~~ us his will in our lives and in the world." If we are to remain truely religious we must believe in miracles. We must believe in the light of emergent evolution that God is continually doing new and unpredictable ~~thig~~ things in the sequence of natural law. God is not a static dead God. He is a God who is alive today and will be forever more.[4]

AHDf. MLKP-MBU: Box 113, folder 23.

---

4. Davis gave this answer sixteen points.

"The Influence of the Mystery Religions on Christianity"

[29 November 1949–15 February 1950]
[Chester, Pa.]

King wrote this paper for the course Development of Christian Ideas, taught by Davis. The essay examines how Christianity developed as a distinct religion with a set of central tenets and how it was influenced by those pagan religions it assimilated. King repeats material from an earlier paper, "A Study of Mithraism," but he extends the discussion here to the influence of other mystery religions.[1] Davis

---

1. See "A Study of Mithraism," 13 September–23 November 1949, pp. 211–225 in this volume.

gave the essay an A, stating: "This is very good and I am glad to have your conclusion. It is not so much that Christianity was influenced by the Mystery Cults, or borrowed from them, but that in the long process of history this religion developed. It, Christianity, is the expression of the longing of people for light, truth, salvation, security.

"That is, with this study you have made, we see the philosophy both of Religion and History. Underneath all expression, whether words, creeds, cults, ceremonies is the spiritual order—the ever living search of men for higher life—a fuller life, more abundant, satisfying life.

"That is essential. Never stop with the external, which may seem like borrowing, but recognize there is the perennial struggle for truth, fuller life itself. So through experience, knowledge, as through other forms, the outer manifestations of religion change. The inner spiritual, continues ever."

The Greco-Roman world in which the early church developed was one of diverse religions. The conditions of that era made it possible for these religions to sweep like a tidal wave over the ancient world. The people of that age were eager and zealous in their search for religious experience. The existence of this atmosphere was vitally important in the development and eventual triumph of Christianity.

These many religions, known as Mystery-Religions, were not alike in every respect: to draw this conclusion would lead to a gratuitous and erroneous supposition. They covered an enormous range, and manifested a great diversity in character and outlook, "from Orphism to Gnosticism, from the orgies of the Cabira to the fervours of the Hermetic contempla-

* Angus, The Mystery Religions and Christianity, p. vii.

tive."*2 However it is to be noticed that these Mysteries possessed many fundamental likenesses; (1) All held that the initiate shared in symbolic (sacramental) fashion the experiences of the god. (2) All had secret rites for the initiated. (3) All offered mystical cleansing from sin. (4) All promised a happy future life for

† Enslin, Christian Beginnings, pp. 187, 188.

the faithful.†

It is not at all surprising in view of the wide and growing influence of these religions that when the disciples in Antioch and elsewhere preached a crucified and risen Jesus they should be regarded as the heralds of another mystery religion, and that Jesus

---

2. S. Angus, *The Mystery-Religions and Christianity* (London: John Murray, 1925), p. vii: "These Mysteries covered an enormous range, and manifested a great diversity in character and outlook, from Orphism to Gnosticism, from the orgies of the Cabiri to the fervours of the Hermetic contemplative."

himself should be taken for the divine Lord of the cult through whose death and resurrection salvation was to be had.[3] That there were striking similarities between the developing church and these religions cannot be denied. Even Christian apologist had to admit that fact.

Christianity triumphed over these mystery religions after long conflict. This triumph may be attributed in part to the fact that Christianity took from its opponents their own weapons, and used them: the better elements of the mystery religions were transferred to the new religion. "As the religious history of the empire is studied more closely," writes Cumont, "the triumph of the church will, in our opinion, appear more and more as the culmination of a long evolution of beliefs. We can understand the Christianity of the fifth century with its greatness and weakness, its spiritual exaltation and its puerile superstitions, if we know the moral antecedents of the world in which it developed."[*4] The victory of Christianity in the Roman empire is another example of that universal historical law, viz., that that culture which conquers is in turn conquered. This universal law is expecially true of religion. It is inevitable when a new religion comes to exist side by side with a group of religions, from which it is continually detaching members, introducing them into its own midst with the practices of their original religions impressed upon their minds, that this new religion should tend to assimilate with the assimilation of their members, some of the elements of these existing religions. "The more crusading a religion is, the more it absorbs." Certainly Christianity has been a crusading religion from the beginning. It is because of this crusading spirit and its superb power of adaptability that Christianity ahs {has} been able to survive.

* Cumont, Oriental Religions in Roman Paganism, p. xxiv.

---

3. The preceding three paragraphs are similar to a passage in King's earlier paper, "A Study of Mithraism," p. 211 in this volume.

4. Grant Showerman, introduction to Franz Cumont, *Oriental Religions in Roman Paganism* (Chicago: Open House Publishing Company, 1911), pp. xi–xii: "Christianity triumphed after long conflict . . . It took from its opponents their own weapons, and used them; the better elements of paganism were transferred to the new religion. 'As the religious history of the empire is studied more closely,' writes M. Cumont, 'the triumph of the church will, in our opinion, appear more and more as the culmination of a long evolution of beliefs. We can understand the Christianity of the fifth century with its greatness and weaknesses, its spiritual exaltation and its puerile superstitions, if we know the moral antecedents of the world in which it developed.'"

It is at this point that we are able to see why knowledge of the Mystery religions is important for any serious study of the history of Christianity. It is well-nigh impossible to grasp Christianity through and through without knowledge of these cults.[5] It must be remembered, as implied above, that Christianity was not a sudden and miraculous transformation, springing, forth full grown as Athene sprang from the head of Zeus, but it is a composite of slow and laborious growth. Therefore it is necessary to study the historical and social factors that contributed to the growth of Christianity. In speaking of the indispensability of knowledge of these cults as requisite for any serious study of Christianity, Dr. Angus says: "As an important background to early Christianity and as the chief medium of sacramentarianism to the West they cannot be neglected; for to fail to recognize the moral and spiritual values of Hellenistic-Oriental paganism is to misunderstand the early Christian centuries and to do injustice to the victory of Christianity. Moreover, much from the Mysteries has persisted in various modern phases of thought and practice."*

* Angus, The Mystery Religions and Christianity, p. viii.

This is not to say that the early Christians sat down and copied these views verbatim. But after being in contact with these surrounding religions and hearing certain doctrines expressed, it was only natural for some of these views to become a part of their subconscious minds. When they sat down to write they were expressing consciously that which had dwelled in their subconscious minds. It is also significant to know that Roman tolerance had favoured this great syncretism of religious ideas. Borrowing was not only natural but inevitable.[6]

The present study represents an attempt to provide a survey of the influence of the mystery religions on Christianity. In order to give a comprehensive picture of this subject, I will discuss ~~Four~~ {Five} of the most popular of these religions separately, rather than to view them en masse as a single great religious system. The latter method is apt to neglect the distinctive contribution of each cult to the religious life of the age

---

5. The preceding two sentences are similar to a passage in "A Study of Mithraism," p. 211 in this volume.

6. The preceding paragraph is similar to passages in two of King's earlier papers: "Light on the Old Testament from the Ancient Near East," 14 September–24 November 1948, p. 163 in this volume; "A Study of Mithraism," p. 212 in this volume.

and, at the same time, to attribute to a given cult phases of some other system. However, in the conclusion I will attempt to give those fundamental aspects, characteristic of all the cults, that greatly influenced Christianity.

The Influence Of
The Cult Of Cybele and Attis

The first Oriental religion to invade the west was the cult of the Great Mother of the Gods. The divine personage in whom this cult centered was the <u>Magna Mater Deum</u> who was conceived as the source of all life as well as the personification of all the powers of nature.*[7] She was the "Great Mother" not only "of all the gods," but of all men" as well.[8] "The winds, the sea, the earth, and the snowy seat of Olympus are hers, and when from her mountains she ascends into the great heavens, the son of Cronus himself gives way before her, and in like manner do also the other immortal blest honor the dread goddess."†

At an early date there was associated with Cybele, the Great Mother, a hero-divinity called Attic who personified the life of the vegetable world particularly. Around these two divinities there grew up a "confused tangle of myths" in explanation of their cult rites. Various writers gave different Versions of the Cybele-Attis myth. However these specific differences need not concern us, for the most significant aspects are common in all the various versions.[10] We are concerned at this point with showing how this religion influenced the thought of early Christians.

Attis was the Good Shepard, the son of Cybele, the Great Mother, who gave birth to him without union

* Willoughby, <u>Pagan Regeneration</u>, p. 114.

† Quoted in Willoughby's, <u>Pagan Regeneration</u>, p. 115.[9]

---

7. Harold R. Willoughby, *Pagan Regeneration* (Chicago: University of Chicago Press, 1929), p. 114: "Of these Oriental mystery religions the first to invade the west was the cult of the Great Mother of the Gods, . . . The divine personage in whom this cult centered was the *Magna Mater Deum* who was conceived as the source of all life as well as the personification of all the powers of nature."

8. Willoughby, *Pagan Regeneration*, p. 114: "She was the 'Great Mother' not only 'of all the gods,' but 'of all men' as well."

9. Willoughby quoted from Apollonius *Argonautica* 1.1098 ff. (*Pagan Regeneration*, p. 115).

10. Willoughby, *Pagan Regeneration*, pp. 116–117: "With [the Great Mother] was associated a hero-divinity called Attis who personified the life of the vegetable world particularly. . . . Around these two divinities, the Great Mother and the god of vegetation, there grew up a confused tangle of myths in explanation of their cult rites. Various writers, pagan and Christian, gave different versions of the Cybele-Attis myth. . . . The specific variations in all these diverse statements do not concern us, for certain significant elements were common to all the various versions."

with mortal man, as in the story of the virgin Mary.[11] According to the myth, Attis died, either slain by another or by his own hand. At the death of Attis, Cybele mourned vehemently until he arose to life again in the springtime. The central theme of the myth was the triumph of Attis over death, and the participant in the rites of the cult undoubtedly believed that his attachment to the victorious deity would insure a similar triumph in his life.

It is evident that in Rome there was a festival celebrating the death and resurrection of Attis. This celebration was held annually from March 22nd to 25th.* The influence of this religion on Christianity is shown by the fact that in Phrygia, Gaul, Italy, and other countries where Attis-worship was powerful, the Christians adapted the actual date, March 25th, as the anniversary of our Lord's passion.†[12]

Again we may notice that at this same Attis festival on March 22nd, an effigy of the god was fastened to the trunk of a pine tree, Attis thus being "slain and hanged on a tree." This effigy was later buried in a tomb. On March 24th, known as the Day of Blood, the High Priest, impersonating Attic, drew blood from him arm and offered it up in place of the blood of a human sacrifice, thus, as it were, sacrificing himself. It is this fact that immediately brings to mind the words in the Epistle to the Hebrews: "But Christ being come an High Priest . . . neither by the blood of goats and calves, but by his own blood . . . obtained eternal redemption for us."‡ Now to get back to the festival. That night the priests went back to the tomb and found it empty, the god having risen on the third day from the dead; and on the 25th the resurrection was celebrated with great rejoicing. During this great celebration a sacramental meal of some kind was taken, and initiates were baptised with blood, whereby their sins were washed away and they were said to be "born again."§[13]

* Frazer, Adonis, Attis, Osiris, p. 166.

† Ibid, p. 199

‡ Heb. 9:11, 12.

§ Weigall, The Paganism In Our Christianity, pp. 116, 117.

---

11. Arthur E. Weigall, *Paganism in Our Christianity* (n.p.: Putnam, 1928), p. 121: "Attis was the Good Shepherd, the son of Cybele, the Great Mother, or, alternatively, of the Virgin Nana, who conceived him without union with mortal man, as in the story of the Virgin Mary."

12. Weigall, *Paganism in Our Christianity*, pp. 121–122: "In Rome the festival of his death and resurrection was annually held from March 22nd to 25th; and the connection of this religion with Christianity is shown by the fact that in Phrygia, Gaul, Italy, and other countries where Attis-worship was powerful, the Christians adopted the actual date, March 25th, as the anniversary of our Lord's passion."

13. Weigall, *Paganism in Our Christianity*, pp. 122–123: "At this Attis festival a pine-tree was felled on March 22nd, and to its trunk an effigy of the god was fastened, Attis thus being 'slain

There can hardly be any doubt of the fact that these ceremonies and beliefs strongly coloured the interpretation placed by the first Christians upon the life and death of the historic Jesus.[14] Moreover, "the merging of the worship of Attis into that of Jesus was effected without interruption, for these pagan ceremonies were enacted in a sanctuary on the Vatican Hill, which was afterwards taken over by the Christians, and the mother church of St. Peter now stands upon the very spot."[*]

* Ibid, p. 117.

The Influence of Adonis

Another popular religion which influenced the thought of early Christians was the worship of Adonis. As is commonly known Antioch was one of the earliest seats of Christianity. It was in this city that there was celebrated each year the death and resurrection of the god Adonis. This faith had always exerted its influence on Jewish thought, so much so that the prophet Ezekiel[†] found it necessary to scold the women of Jerusalem for weeping for the dead Tammuz (Adonis) at the very gate of the temple. When we come to Christian thought the influence seems even greater, for even the place at Bethleham selected by the early Christians as the scene of the birth of Jesus was none other than an early shrine of this pagan god—a fact that led many to confuse Adonis with Jesus Christ.[‡][15]

† Ezekiel 8:14.

‡ Weigall, op. cit., p. 110

---

and hanged on a tree,' in the Biblical phrase. This effigy was later buried in a tomb. March 24th was the Day of Blood, whereon the High Priest, who himself impersonated Attis, drew blood from his arm and offered it up in place of the blood of a human sacrifice, thus, as it were, sacrificing himself, a fact which recalls to mind the words in the Epistle to the Hebrews: 'Christ being come an High Priest . . . neither by the blood of goats and calves, but by his own blood . . . obtained eternal redemption for us.' That night the priests went to the tomb and found it illuminated from within, and it was then discovered to be empty, the god having risen on the third day from the dead; and on the 25th the resurrection was celebrated with great rejoicings, a sacramental meal of some kind being taken, and initiates being baptised with blood, whereby their sins were washed away and they were said to be 'born again.'"

14. Weigall, *Paganism in Our Christianity*, p. 123: "There can be no doubt that these ceremonies and beliefs deeply coloured the interpretation placed by the first Christians upon the historic facts of the Crucifixion, burial, and coming again to life of Jesus."

15. Weigall, *Paganism in Our Christianity*, pp. 115–116: "Now one of the earliest seats of Christianity was Antioch; but in that city there was celebrated each year the death and resurrection of the god Tammuz or Adonis, . . . This faith had always exerted its influence on Jewish thought, and, indeed, the prophet Ezekiel had found it necessary to scold the women of Jerusalem for weeping for the dead Tammuz at the very gate of the Temple; while, in the end, the place at

It was believed that this god suffered a cruel death, after which he descended into hell, rose again, and then ascended into Heaven. Each following {year} there was a great festival in commemoration of his resurrection, and the very words, "The Lord is risen," were probable used. The festival ended with the celebration of his ascension in the sight of his worshippers.[16] Needless to say that this story of the death and resurrection of Adonis is quite similar to the Christian story of the death and resurrection of Christ. This coincidence had led many critics to suppose that the story of the burial and resurrection of Jesus is simply a myth borrowed from this pagan religion.[17] Whether these critics are right in their interpretation or not still remains a moot question.

However when we come to the idea of Jesus' decent into hell it seems that we have a direct borrow from the Adonis religion, and in fact from other religions also. Both the Apostles Creed and the Athanasian {Creed} say that between the Friday night and Sunday morning Jesus was in Hades. Now this idea has no scriptural foundation except in those difficult passages in the First Epistle of Peter* which many scholars have designated as the most ambiguous passages of the New Testament. In fact the idea did not appear in the church as a tenet of Christianity until late in the Fourth Century.†[18] Such facts led almost inevitably to the view that this idea had a pagan origin,

* I Peter 3:19–4:6.

† Weigall, op. cit., p. 113.

Bethlehem selected by the early Christians as the scene of the birth of Jesus (for want to [*sic*] any knowledge as to where the event had really occurred) was none other than an early shrine of this pagan god, as St. Jerome was horrified to discover—a fact which shows that Tammuz or Adonis ultimately became confused in men's minds with Jesus Christ."

16. Weigall, *Paganism in Our Christianity*, p. 116: "This god was believed to have suffered a cruel death, to have descended into Hell or Hades, to have risen again, and to have ascended into Heaven; and at his festival, as held in various lands, his death was bewailed, an effigy of his dead body was prepared for burial by being washed with water and anointed, and, on the next day, his resurrection was commemorated with great rejoicing, the very words 'The Lord is risen' probably being used. The celebration of his ascension in the sight of his worshippers was the final act of the festival."

17. Weigall, *Paganism in Our Christianity*, p. 117: "This coincidence has, of course, led many critics to suppose that the story of the burial and resurrection of Jesus is simply a myth borrowed from this pagan religion."

18. Weigall, *Paganism in Our Christianity*, pp. 118–119: "But there is one feature of the Gospel story which seems really to have been borrowed from the Adonis religion, and, in fact, from other pagan religions also, namely, the descent into Hell. The Apostles Creed and Athanasian Creed say that between the Friday night and the Sunday morning Jesus was in Hell or Hades; . . . It has no scriptural foundation except in the ambiguous words of the First Epistle of Peter; it did not appear in the Church as a tenet of Christianity until late in the Fourth Century."

since it appears not only in the legend of Adonis, but also in those of Herakles, Dionyses, Orpheus, Osiris, Hermes, Balder, and other deities.*

* Ibid, p. 114.

The Influence
of Osiris and Isis

The Egyptian mysteries of Isis and Osiris exerted considerable influence upon early Christianity. These two great Egyptian deities, whose worship passed into Europe, were revered not only in Rome but in many other centers where Christian communities were growing up. Osiris and Isis, so the legend runs, were at one and the same time, brother and sister, husband and wife; but Osiris was murdered, his coffined body being thrown into the Nile, and shortly afterwards the widowed and exiled Isis gave birth to a son, Horus. Meanwhile the coffin was washed up on the Syrian coast, and became miraculously lodged in the trunk of a tree. This tree afterwards chanced to be cut down and made into a pillar in the palace at Byblos, and there Isis at length found it. After recovering Osiris' dismembered body, Isis restored him to life and installed him as King in the nether world; meanwhile Horus, having grown to manhood, reigned on earth, later becoming the third person of this great Egyptian trinity.† [19]

† Weigall, op. cit., p. 119.

In the records of both Herodotus and Plutarch we find that there was a festival held each year in Egypt celebrating the resurrection of Osiris. While Herodotus fails to give a date for this festival, Plutarch says that it lasted four days, giving the date as the seventeenth day of the Egyptian month Hathor, which, according to the Alexandrian claendar used by him, corresponded to November 13th.‡ Other Egyptian

‡ Frazer, op. cit., p. 257.

---

19. Weigall, *Paganism in Our Christianity*, pp. 124–125: "The popular and widespread religion of Osiris and Isis exercised considerable influence upon early Christianity, for these two great Egyptian deities, whose worship had passed into Europe, were revered in Rome and in several other centres where Christian communities were growing up. Osiris and Isis, so runs the legend, were brother and sister and also husband and wife; but Osiris was murdered, his coffined body being thrown into the Nile, and shortly afterwards the widowed and exiled Isis gave birth to a son, Horus. The coffin, meanwhile, was washed up on the Syrian coast, and became miraculously lodged in the trunk of a tree, . . . This tree afterwards chanced to be cut down and made into a pillar in the palace at Byblos, and there Isis at length found it. . . . Afterwards, however, he returned to the other world to reign for ever as King of the Dead; and meanwhile Horus, having grown to manhood, reigned on Earth, later becoming the third person of this great Egyptian trinity."

records speak of another feast in honour of all the dead, when such lamps were lit, which was held about November 8th.*[20]

* Ibid, p. 258.

It is interesting to note that the Christian feast of all Souls, in honor of the dead, likewise falls at the beginning of November; and in many countries lamps and candles are burned all night on that occassion. There seems little doubt that this custom was identical with the Egyptian festival. The festival of all Saints, which is held one day before that of all Souls is also probably identical with it in origin.† This still stands as a festival in the Christian calendar; and thus Christians unconsciously perpetuate the worship of Osiris in modern times.[21]

† Weigall, op. cit., p. 121.

However this is not the only point at which the Religion of Osiris and Isis exerted influence on Christianity. There can hardly be any doubt that the myths of Isis had a direct bearing on the elevation of Mary, the Mother of Jesus, to the lofty position that she holds in Roman Catholic theology. As is commonly known Isis had two capacities which her worshippers warmly commended her for. Firstly, she was pictured as the lady of sorrows, weeping for the dead Osiris, and secondly she was commended as the divine mother, nursing her infant son, Horus. In the former capacity she was identified with the great mother-goddess, Demeter, whose mourning for Persephone was the main feature in the Eleusinian mysteries. In the latter capacity Isis was represented in tens of thousands of statuettes and paintings, holding the divine child in her arms. Now when Christianity triumphed we find that these same paintings and fig-

---

20. Weigall, *Paganism in Our Christianity*, pp. 125–126: "Herodotus states that the festival of the death and resurrection of Osiris was held in Egypt each year, though he does not give the date; . . . Plutarch also records the annual Osirian festival, and says that it lasted four days, giving the date as the seventeenth day of the Egyptian month Hathor, which, according to the Alexandrian calendar used by him, corresponded to November 13th. Now we know from old Egyptian records that a feast in honour of all the dead, when such lamps were lit, was held . . . about November 8th."

21. Weigall, *Paganism in Our Christianity*, pp. 126–127: "But the Christian feast of All Souls, in honour of the dead, likewise falls at the beginning of November; and in many countries lamps and candles are burnt all night on that occasion. . . . there seems little doubt that this custom was identical with the Egyptian festival. . . . the festival of All Saints, which is held one day before that of All Souls and which was first recognised by the Church in A.D. 835, is undoubtedly identical with it in origin. This still stands as a festival in the ecclesiastical calendar; and thus Christians unconsciously perpetuate the worship of Osiris and the commemoration of all his subjects in the Kingdom of the Dead."

ures became those of the Madonna and child with little or no difference.* In fact archaeologists are often left in confusion in attempting to distinguish the one from the other.[22]

* Ibid, p. 123

It is also interesting to note that in the second century a story began to spread stating that Mary had been miraculously carried to Heaven by Jesus and His angels.† In the sixth century a festival came to be celebrated around this event known as the festival of Assumption, and it is now one of the greatest feasts of Roman Catholicism. It is celebrated annually on August 13th. But it was this very date that the festival of Dianna or Artemis was celebrated, with whom Isis was identified. Here we see how Mary gradually came to take the place of the goddess.‡[23]

† The spreading of this story has been attributed to Melito, Bishop of Sardis.

‡ Weigall, op. cit., p. 125.

The Influence Of
The Greater Mysteries
At Eleusis

In the first century of the Christian era the Eleusinian mystery cult was more favorable known than any of the cults of Greece.[24] Its fame and popularity was largely due to the connexion of Eleusis with Athens. The origin of this cult is obscure and uncertain. Some writers traced its origin to Egypt while others upheld Eleusis in Greece as the place of its birth.

In order to understand the type of religious experience represented by this important cult, we must turn to the myth of the rape of Demeter's daughter

---

22. Weigall, *Paganism in Our Christianity*, pp. 129–130: "There were two aspects of Isis which commended themselves particularly to her worshippers: firstly, that of the lady of sorrows, weeping for the dead Osiris, and, secondly, that of the divine mother, nursing her infant son, Horus. In the former capacity she was identified with the great mother-goddess, Demeter, whose mourning for Persephone was the main feature in the Eleusinian mysteries; ... In her aspect as the mother of Horus, Isis was represented in tens of thousands of statuettes and paintings, holding the divine child in her arms; and when Christianity triumphed these paintings and figures became those of the Madonna and Child without any break in continuity: no archaeologist, in fact, can now tell whether some of these objects represent the one or the other."

23. Weigall, *Paganism in Our Christianity*, pp. 131–132: "At about this time a story, attributed to Melito, Bishop of Sardis in the Second Century, but probably of much later origin, began to spread that Mary had been miraculously carried to Heaven by Jesus and His angels; and in the Sixth Century the festival of the Assumption, which celebrates this event, was acknowledged by the Church, and is now one of the great feasts of Roman Catholicism, ... It is celebrated on August 13th; but that was the date of the great festival of Diana or Artemis, with whom Isis was identified, and one can see, thus, how Mary had gradually taken the place of the goddess."

24. Willoughby, *Pagan Regeneration*, p. 36: "Among the cults of Greece none was more favorably known in the first century of the Christian era than the Eleusinian mysteries."

by Pluto. It is stated with sufficient elaboration in the Homeric Hymn to Demeter. In this myth, Persephone is depicted playing in the meadows of Mysia in Asia with the daughters of Oceanus and Tithys. While playing she was stolen by Pluto and carried off to the underworld to be his bride. The mother, frenzied with grief, rushed about the earth for nine days in search for her lost daughter,[25] As a result of her wandering, she came to Eleusis where she was seen, although not recognized, by the four daughters of Kekeas sitting near a public well called the Fountain of Maidenhood. After telling a fictitious tale of her escape from pirates, she won the sympathy of the girls who took her home and at her own request was given a job to nurse their infant brother, Demophon. After making herself known, she commanded the people of Eleusis to build her a temple. In connection with the temple, she established certain ceremonies and rites for her worship.

During her short stay at the temple of Eleusis, the whole earth grew barren. Men began to die for the lack of food while the sacrifices to the gods decreased in number because the animals were dying out. The other gods pleaded with her to relent but she refused to do so until Persephone was restored to her. Pluto, (also called Hades) therefore, at the request of Zeus released her but not before he had caused her to eat a pomegranate seed which magically required her return after a period of time. Demeter, in her joy at the restoration of her lost daughter, allowed the crops to grow once more and institute in honor of the event the Eleusinian mysteries which gave to mortals the assurance of a happy future life.[26]

The significance of this story is immediately clear. It was a nature myth portraying a vivid and realistic picture of the action of life in the vegetable world in regards to the changing seasons. Every year nature

---

25. Willoughby, *Pagan Regeneration*, p. 41: "In order to understand the type of religious experience represented by this important cult, it is necessary clearly to keep in mind the main points of the Eleusinian myth which was developed to explain and justify the cult rites. These are stated with sufficient elaboration in the Homeric Hymn to Demeter, . . . According to the story, Persephone, . . . was stolen by Pluto and carried off to the underworld to be his bride. . . . The mother, frenzied with grief, rushed about the earth for nine days."

26. Willoughby, *Pagan Regeneration*, p. 42: "Demeter, in her joy at the restoration of her lost daughter, allowed the crops to grow once more and instituted in honor of the event the Eleusinian mysteries which gave to mortals the assurance of a happy future life."

passes through a cycle of apparent death and resurrection. In winter, all plants die, this represents the period of Demeter's grief over her daughter. Spring, the time when all plants come back to life, indicates the return of plenty when the goddess maintains all life until autumn when her daughter returns to Hades and the earth becomes once more desolated.*[27]

The myth is also an example of poignant human experience, reflecting the joys, sorrows, and hopes of mankind in the face of death. The mysteries of human life and death are vividly enacted by Demeter, Persephone, and Hades. Hades, the god of death, stole the beloved daughter, Persephone, from Demeter, the life giver, who refused to admit defeat until she secured her daughter's resurrection. In this legend, human beings, who are always loved and lost, are depicted as never or seldom loosing hope for reunion with their God. These fundamental human experiences and the life of nature are the main substances of the Eleusinian Mysteries.[28] To the searchers of salvation, the Eleusinian cult offered not only the promise of a happy future, but also a definite assurance of it.†

† Nilsson, Greek Popular Religion, p. 54.

Now when we observe the modern Greek Easter festival it seems certain that it preserves the spirit if not the form of the old Eleusinian worship. In the spring, those who had shared Demeter's grief for the loss of her daugher welcomed the return of Persephone with all the joy that the returning life of vegetation might kindle. And today similar experiences are represented by Greek Christians. After

---

27. Willoughby, *Pagan Regeneration,* p. 42: "The experiential basis for this story is quite clear. It was a nature myth, a vivid depiction of the action of life in the vegetable world with the changing of the seasons. Each year nature passed through the cycle of apparent death and resurrection. In winter vegetable life was dead while Demeter, the giver of life, grieved for the loss of her daughter. But with the coming of spring the life of nature revived again, for the sorrowing mother had received her daughter back with rejoicing. Through the summer the mother abundantly maintained the life of nature until autumn, when again her daughter returned to the underworld and earth became desolate once more."

28. Willoughby, *Pagan Regeneration,* pp. 42–43: "It was also a reflection of poignant human experiences, mirroring the joys, sorrows, and hopes of mankind in face of inevitable death. The three actors of the Eleusinian tragedy, . . . enacted the mystery of human life and death. The god of death himself stole the beloved daughter away from the life-giver; but the divine mother would not give up her loved one, and in the end she accomplished her daughter's resurrection. Here was human experience made heroic and divine; for man has ever loved and lost, but rarely has he ceased to hope for reunion with the loved one. The Eleusinian myth told of these fundamental human experiences as well as of the life of nature."

mourning over the dead Christ, represented most conspicuously by a wax image carried through the streets, there comes an announcement by the priest, on the midnight before Easter Sunday, that Christ is risen. At this moment the light from the candle of the priest is passed on to light the candles of his companions; guns and firecrackers are discharged as they prepare to break the Lenten fast.* [29] As in the Eleusinian mysteries the modern Greek Christian finds this a moment of supreme joy. So we might say that Eleusinianism was not blotted out by Christianity. On the contrary many of its forms and some of its old content has been perpetuated in Christianity.[30]

* Fairbanks, Greek Religion, p. 288.

The Influence of Mithraism

Mithraism is perhaps the greatest example of paganism's last effort to reconcile itself to the great spiritual movement which was gaining such sturdy influence with its purer conception of God.† Ernest Renan, the French philosopher and Orientalist, expressed the opinion that Mithraism would have been the religion of the modern world if anything had occured to halt or destroy the growth of Christianity in the early centuries of its existence. All this goes to show how important Mithraism was in ancient times. It was suppressed by the Christians sometime in the latter part of the fourth century A.D.; but its collapse seems to have been due to the fact that by that time many of its doctrines and practices had been adopted by the church, so that it was practically absorbed by its rival.[31]

† Dill, Roman Society From Nero to Marcus Aurelius, p. 585.

---

29. Arthur Fairbanks, *A Handbook of Greek Religion* (New York: American Book Company, 1910), p. 288: "Certainly the Greek Easter festival seems to preserve the spirit if not the forms of the old Eleusinian worship. In the spring, those who had shared Demeter's grief for the loss of her daughter welcomed the return of Persephone with all the joy that the returning life of vegetation might kindle. And today the Greeks mourn over the dead Christ, represented most realistically by a wax image borne through the streets on a bier; then at midnight before Easter Sunday the Metropolitan at Athens, the priest in smaller towns, comes out of the church announcing that Christ is risen; the light from his candle is passed to the candles of his companions and on to candles throughout the crowd, guns and firecrackers are discharged, and as they prepare to break their Lenten fast the multitude drop all restraint in the expression of wild joy."

30. Fairbanks, *Greek Religion*, p. 293: "This religion was not blotted out by Christianity. On the contrary, whatever real life it had was perpetuated in Christianity, since the conquering religion had adopted many of its forms and some of the old content in these forms."

31. Weigall, *Paganism in Our Christianity*, p. 135: "It was suppressed by the Christians in A.D. 376 and 377; but its collapse seems to have been due rather to the fact that by that time many of

Originally Mithra was one of the lesser gods of the ancient Persian pantheon, but at the time of Christ he had come to be co-equal with Ahura Mazda, the Supreme Being.[32] He possessed many attributes, the most important being his office of defender of truth and all good things. In the Avesta,* Mithra is represented as the genius of celestial light. He emerges from the rocky summits of eastern mountains at dawn, and goes through heaven with a team of four white horses; when the night falls he still illumines the surface of the earth, "ever walking, ever watchful." He is not sun or moon or any star, but a spirit of light, ever wakeful, watching with a hundred eyes. He hears all and sees all: none can deceive him.†[33] Tarsus, the home of Saint Paul, was one of the great centres of his worship; and there is a decided tinge of Mithraism in the Epistles and Gospels. Such designations of our Lord as the Dayspring from on High, The Light, the Sun of Righteousness, and similar expressions seem to come directly from Mithraic influence.‡[34]

Again tradition has it that Mithra was born from a rock, "the god out of the rock." It must also be noticed that his worship was always conducted in a cave. Now it seems that the general belief of the early church that Jesus was born in a cave grows directly out of Mithraic ideas. The words of St. Paul, "They drank of that spiritual rock . . . and that rock was

* This is the sacred book of the religion of Iran.

† Cumont, Mysteries of Mithra, pp. 2, 3.

‡ Weigall, op. cit., p. 129.

---

its doctrines and ceremonies had been adopted by the Church, so that it was practically absorbed by its rival."

32. Weigall, *Paganism in Our Christianity*, pp. 135–136: "Originally Mithra was one of the lesser gods of the ancient Persian pantheon, but . . . already in the time of Christ he had risen to be co-equal with, though created by, Ormuzd (Ahura-Mazda), the Supreme Being."

33. The previous five sentences are similar to a passage in King's earlier paper, "A Study of Mithraism," pp. 213–214 in this volume. Franz Cumont, *The Mysteries of Mithra* (Chicago: Open Court, 1910), pp. 2–3: "In the Avesta, Mithra is the genius of the celestial light. He appears before sunrise on the rocky summits of the mountains; during the day he traverses the wide firmament in his chariot drawn by four white horses, and when night falls he still illumines with flickering glow the surface of the earth, 'ever waking, ever watchful.' He is neither sun, nor moon, nor stars, but with 'his hundred ears and his hundred eyes' watches constantly the world. Mithra hears all, sees all, knows all: none can deceive him."

34. Weigall, *Paganism in Our Christianity*, pp. 136–137: "Tarsus, the home of St. Paul, was one of the great centres of his worship, being the chief city of the Cilicians; and, as will presently appear, there is a decided tinge of Mithraism in the Epistles and Gospels. Thus the designations of our Lord as the Dayspring from on High, the Light, the Sun of Righteousness, and similar expressions, are borrowed from or related to Mithraic phraseology."

Christ" also seem to be {a} direct borrow from the Mithraic scriptures.[35]

The Hebrew Sabbath having been abolished by Christians, the Church made a sacred day of Sunday, partly because it was the day of resurrection. But when we observe a little further we find that as a solar festival, Sunday was the sacred day of Mithra; it is also interesting to notice that since Mithra was addressed as Lord, Sunday must have been "the Lord's Day" long before Christian use.* It is also to be noticed that our Christmas, December 25th, was the birthday of Mithra, and was only taken over in the Fourth Century as the date, actually unknown, of the birth of Jesus.[36]

To make the picture a little more clear, we may list a few of the similarities between these two religions: (1) Both regard Sunday as a holy day. (2) December 25 came to be considered as the anniversary of the birth of Mithra and Christ also. (3) Baptism and a communion meal were important parts of the ritual of both groups. (4) The rebirth of converts was a fundamental idea in the two cults. (5) The struggle with evil and the eventual triumph of good were essential ideas in both religions.[37] (6) In summary we may say that the belief in immortality, a mediator between god and man, the observance of certain sacramental rites, the rebirth of converts, and (in most cases) the support of high ethical ideas were common to Mithraism as well as Christianity. In fact, the comparison became so evident that many believed the Christian movement itself became a mystery cult. "Jesus was the di-

* Ibid., p. 137.

---

35. Weigall, *Paganism in Our Christianity*, p. 137: "Mithra was born from a rock, as shown in Mithraic sculptures, being sometimes termed 'the god out of the rock,' and his worship was always conducted in a cave; and the general belief in the early Church that Jesus was born in a cave is a direct instance of the taking over of Mithraic ideas. The words of St. Paul, 'They drank of that spiritual rock . . . and that rock was Christ' are borrowed from the Mithraic scriptures."

36. Weigall, *Paganism in Our Christianity*, p. 145: "The Hebrew Sabbath having been abolished by Christians, the Church made a sacred day of Sunday, partly because it was the day of the resurrection, but largely because it was the weekly festival of the sun; for it was a definite Christian policy to take over the pagan festivals endeared to the people by tradition, and to give them a Christian significance. But, as a solar festival, Sunday was the sacred day of Mithra; and it is interesting to notice that since Mithra was addressed as *Dominus*, 'Lord,' Sunday must have been 'the Lord's Day' long before Christian times. . . . December 25th was the birthday of the sun-god, and particularly of Mithra, and was only taken over in the Fourth Century as the date, actually unknown, of the birth of Jesus."

37. The preceding five sentences are similar to a passage in "A Study of Mithraism," pp. 222–223 in this volume.

vine Lord. He too had found the road to heaven by his suffering and resurrection. He too had God for his father. He had left behind the secret whereby men could achieve the goal with him."*

Although the above paragraph makes it obvious that there are many similarities between these two religions, we must guard against the fallacy of seeing all similarity as direct borrowing. For an instance, the sacraments of baptism and the eucharist have been mentioned as rites, which were ~~preactice~~ {practiced} by both Christians and pagans. It is improbable, however, that either of these were introduced into Christian practices by association with the mystery cults. The baptismal ceremony in both cases (Christian and Pagan) was supposed to have the effect of identifying the initiate with his savior. But although baptism did not originate with the Christians, still it was not copied from the pagans. It seems instead to have been carried over from Jewish background and modified by the new ideas and beliefs of the Christians. The eucharist, likewise through similar in some respects to the communion meal of Mithraism, was not a rite borrowed from it. There are several explanations regarding the beginning of the observance of the Lord's Supper. Some held that the sacrament was instituted by Jesus himself. Others saw it as an out-growth from Jewish precedents. Still others felt that, after the death of Jesus, the disciples saw in their common meal an opportunity to hold a kind of memorial service for him.

On the whole, early Christians were not greatly concerned about the likenesses between the Mithraic cult and their own. They felt at first that these competitors were not worthy of consideration, and few references to them are found in Christian literature. When Mithraism became widespread and powerful, it attracted so much attention that certain Christian apologists felt the need to present an explanation for the similarities in their respective characteristics. The only one they could offer was quite naive, but it was in keeping with the trends of thought in that age. They maintained that it was the work of the devil who helped to confuse men by creating a pagan imitation of the true religion.[38]

---

38. The preceding two paragraphs are similar to a passage in "A Study of Mithraism," pp. 223–224 in this volume.

There can hardly be any gainsaying of the fact that Christianity was greatly influenced by the Mystery religions, both from a ritual and a doctrinal angle. This does not mean that there was a deliberate copying on the part of Christianity. On the contrary it was generally a natural and unconscious process rather than a deliberate plan of action. Christianity was subject to the same influences from the environment as were the other cults, and it sometimes produced the same reaction. The people were conditioned by the contact with the older religions and the background and general trend of the time.[39] Dr. Shirley Jackson Case has written some words that are quite apt at this point. He says: "Following the lead of the apostle Paul, the Christian missionaries on gentile soil finally made of Christianity a more appealing religion than any of the other mystery cults. This was accomplished, not by any slavish process of imitation, but by {a} serious attempt to meet better the specific religious needs that the mysteries had awakened and nourished, and by phrasing religious assurances more convincingly in similar terminology."*

* Case, "The Mystery Religions," The Encyclopedia of Religion, Edited by Vergilius Ferm, pp. 511–513

The greatest influence of the mystery religions on Christianity lies in a different direction from that of doctrine and ritual. It lies in the fact that the mystery religions paved the way for the presentation of Christianity to the world of that time. They prepared the people mentally and emotionally to understand the type of religion which Christianity represented. They were themselves, in verying degrees, imperfect examples of the Galilean cult which was to replace them. They encouraged the movement away from the state religions and the philosophical systems and toward the desire for personal salvation and promise of immortality. Christianity was truly indebted to the mystery religions for this contribution, for they had done this part of the groundwork and thus opened the way for Christian missionary work. Many views, while passing out of paganism into Christianity were given a more profound and spiritual meaning by Christians, yet we must be indebted to the source. To discuss Christianity without mentioning other religions

---

39. The preceding four sentences are similar to a passage in "A Study of Mithraism," p. 224 in this volume.

would be like discussing the greatness of the Atlantic Ocean without the slightest mention of the many tributaries that keep it flowing.[40]

Christianity, however, [*strikeout illegible*] survived because it appeared to be the result of a trend in the social order or in the historical cycle of the human race. Forces have been known to delay trends but very few have stopped them. The staggering question that now arises is, what will be the next stage of man's religious progress? Is Christianity the crowning achievement in the development of religious thought or will there be another religion more advanced?

BIBLIOGRAPHY

1. Angus, S., The Mystery Religions and Christianity, (Charles Scribner's Sons, New York: 1925),

2. Cumont, Franz, The Mysteries of Mithra, (The Open Court Publishing Co., Chicago: 1910).

3. Cumont, Franz, The Oriental Religions in Roman Paganism, (The Open-House Publishing Co., Chicago: 1911).

4. Dill, Samuel, Roman Society From Nero To Marcus Aurelius, (Macmillan and Co., New York: 1905), pp. 585–626.

5. Enslin Morton S., Christian Beginnings, (Harper and Brothers Publishers, New York: 1938), pp. 186–200.

6. Frazer, J. E., Adonis, Attis, Osiris, (London, 1922), Vol. I.

7. Fairbanks, Arthur, Greek Religion, (American Book Co, New York: 1910).

8. Halliday, W. R., The Pagan Background of Early Christianity, (The University Press of Liverpool, London: N.D.), pp. 281–311.

9. Hyde, Walter, W, Paganism To Christianity in the Roman Empire, (University of Pennsylvania Press, Philadelphia: 1946).

10. Moore, George F., History of Religions, (Charles Scribner's Sons, New York: 1913), Vol. I, pp. 375–405.

11. Nilsson, Martin P., Greek Popular Religion, (Co-

---

40. The preceding two sentences are similar to a passage in "A Study of Mithraism," p. 224 in this volume.

lumbia University Press, New York: 1940), pp. 42–64.

12. Weigall Arthur, <u>The Paganism in Our Christianity</u>, (Hutchinson and Co. London: N.D.).

13. Willoughby, Harold R., <u>Pagan Regeneration</u>, (University of Chicago Press, Chicago: 1929).

THDS. MLKP-MBU: Box 112, folder 17.

"The Chief Characteristics
and Doctrines of Mahayana Buddhism"

[*28 April 1950*]
[*Chester, Pa.*]

In this paper for Davis's course History of Living Religions, King explores the tenets of Mahayana Buddhism and implicitly associates that religion's morality and popular appeal with the ideals of Christianity. King drew chiefly on S. Radhakrishnan's Indian Philosophy *and J. B. Pratt's* The Pilgrimage of Buddhism. (*King later met Radhakrishnan during his 1959 trip to India.*) *Davis gave King an A for the paper, calling it "a clear statement," and a B + for the course.*

Immediately after the death of Buddha schismatic tendencies began to develop within the religion which he had founded. Even in Buddha's lifetime there were tendencies to schism among his followers, but his magnetic personality was able to prevent their development.[1] The first great doctrinal controversy in Buddhism was about the nature of Buddha. The school of the great council (<u>Mahasanghikas</u>) maintained that Buddha's nature was transcendent, and free from all earthly limitations. The conservatives, while exalting Buddha, above common humanity, would not admit that he was exempt from all the limitations of mankind.

These were but the first steps in a path which led to a radical transformation of Buddhism. The progressive group gave itself the name Mahayana, "the great vehicle," that is, the comprehensive scheme of

---

1. S. Radhakrishnan, *Indian Philosophy*, vol. 1, (New York, Macmillan, 1923), p. 581: "Even in the lifetime of Buddha there were tendencies to schism among his followers, though they did not develop on account of the magnetic personality of the founder."

salvation; with a deragatory comparison they called the old fashioned religion Hinayana, "the little vehicle," a scheme of individual salvation.

Hinayana Buddhism was called Southern Buddhism, since it prevailed in southern countries like Burma and Ceylon. On the other hand Mahayana Buddhism was called Northern Buddhism, since it flourished in northern countries like China and Japan. However this dividion seems to be an artificial one. Says Rhys Davids: "There is not now, and never has been, any unity either of opinion or of language in what is called Northern or in what is called Southern Buddhism."*[2] Although the division is artificail from a geographical point of view it is all important on higher grounds: the "southern" school insists that it has preserved the original teachings of Buddha with no accresions; the "northern" school is manifestly a broader interpretation. The northern school has never been essentially dependent upon the historical Buddha. Dates and documents have never mattered much to this Idealism.

As time passed on Hinayana Buddhism became the "incarnation of dead thought and the imprisonment of spirit." It could give neither a warm faith for which to ~~work~~ {live, nor a real ideal for which to work.} It set forth a sort of world hatred as its inspiring motive. It preferred negative philosophical speculation, rather than a warm and positive religious expression. But this negative philosophy of the Hinayana could never become a popular religion.[3] Its cold, passionless metaphysics could never inspire a real emotional uplifting.[4] "The Hinayana ignored the groping of the spirit of man after something higher and wronged the spiritual side of man. The philosophical atheism of the Hinayana is the skeleton in the box, the diseased worm in the beautiful box."†[5] Thus the Hina-

* R. Davids, Buddhist India, p. 173.

† S. Radhakrishnan, Indian Philosophy, p. 589

2. Radhakrishnan, *Indian Philosophy*, p. 584: "Hīnayāna Buddhism was called Southern Buddhism, since it prevailed in southern countries like Ceylon, while Mahāyāna is called the Northern, since it flourished in the North, Tibet, Mongolia, China, Korea and Japan. But this division seems to be an artificial one. Rhys Davids observes: 'There is not now, and never has been, any unity either of opinion or of language in what is called Northern or in what is called Southern Buddhism.'"

3. Radhakrishnan, *Indian Philosophy*, p. 590: "The negative philosophy of the Hīnayāna could not become a popular religion."

4. Radhakrishnan, *Indian Philosophy*, p. 589: "A cold, passionless metaphysics devoid of religious teaching could not long inspire enthusiasm and joy."

5. The end of the quotation should read "the diseased worm in the beautiful flower" rather than "in the beautiful box" (Radhakrishnan, *Indian Philosophy*, p. 589).

yana Buddhism had to give way to a more positive and religious mode of expression. As Buddhism became more catholic, the Hinayana became less useful. As Buddhism spread throughout India and even beyond it, it had to adjust itself to new modes of thought. It had to present its message in language understandable to the masses. This challenge was met by Mahayana Buddhism. Mahayanism was able to capture the minds of the masses by giving up the icy coldness of some forms of early Buddhism and framing a relgion that could appeal to the inner emotions.*[6]

* Ibid, p. 591.

The Mahayana Buddhism gives us positive ideas of the ultimate issues of life. The Mahayana, or Great Vessel, offers to all beings salvation, by faith and love as well as by knowledge, while the Hinayana only seeks those few strong souls who require no external aid nor the consolation of worship. The Hinayana is exceedingly hard; whereas the burden of the Mahayana is light, and does not require one to totally renounce the world and his affections for humanity. "The Hinayana emphasises the necessity of saving knowledge, and aims at the salvation of the individual, and refuses to develop the mystery of <u>nibbana</u> in a positive sense; the Mahayana lays as much or greater stress on love, and aims at the salvation of every sentient being, and finds in nirvana the One Reality, which is void only in the sense that it is free from the limitations of every phase of the limited or contingent experience of which we have emperical knowledge."†[7] The Hinayanist would protest that the Mahayanist too easily capitulated the pure teachings of Buddha to the necessities of human nature. But such

† A. Coomaraswamy,
Buddha and the Gospel of
Buddhism, p. 227.

---

6. Radhakrishnan, *Indian Philosophy,* p. 591: "The Mahāyāna found that it could capture the peoples' minds only if it gave up the icy coldness of some forms of Buddhism and framed a religion which could appeal to the human heart."

7. Radhakrishnan, *Indian Philosophy,* pp. 591–592, quoting A. Coomaraswamy, *Buddha and the Gospel of Buddhism,* pp. 226–227: "The Mahāyāna Buddhism gives us positive ideas of God, soul and human destiny. 'The Mahāyāna, or Great Vessel, is so called by its adherents in contradistinction to the Hīnayāna, or little vessel, of primitive Buddhism; the former offers to all beings in all worlds salvation by faith and love as well as by knowledge, while the latter only avails to convey over the rough sea of becoming to the farther shore of nibbāna, those few strong souls who require no external spiritual aid nor the consolation of worship. The Hīnayāna, . . . is exceeding hard; whereas the burden of the Mahāyāna is light, and does not require that a man should immediately renounce the world and all the affections of humanity. . . . The Hīnayāna emphasizes the necessity of saving knowledge, and aims at the salvation of the individual, and refuses to develop the mystery of nibbāna in a positive sense; the Mahāyāna lays as much or greater stress on love, and aims at the salvation of every sentient being, and finds in nirvāṇa the One Reality, which is "void" only in the sense that it is free from the limitations of every phase of the limited or contingent experience of which we have empirical knowledge.'"

capitulation was inevitable if Buddhism was to win converts. The Hinayana Buddhism was a religion for the thinking and the strong in spirit. Its lack of any supernatural power, its morbid way of solving the central problems of life, its reduction of nirvana to ultimate extinction, and its relegation of the ethical life to a streneous asceticism, could never satisfy the masses. A new development had to arise for the emotional and the worshipful.[8] Such was found in Mahayana Buddhism. At this point we may turn to a more detailed study of the chief characteristics and doctrines of Mahayana Buddhism.

The Mahayana
Methaphysics

The metaphysics of Mahayana is monistic in character. All that exist in the world is of one reality. The nature of this reality is beyond description.[9] "Things in their fundamental nature cannot be named or explained. They cannot be adequately expressed in any form or language. They are beyond the range of perception, and have no distinctive features. They possess absolute sameness, and are subject neither to transformation nor to destruction. They are nothing else but one soul, for which _tathata_ is another designation."[*][10] No relativity whatsoever can be attributed to the absolute. However it is the self-existent and the source of all. It is "the effulgence of great wisdom; the universal illumination of the _dharmadhatu_ (universe), the true and adequate knowledge, the mind pure and clean in its nature; the eternal, the blessed,

* Suzuki's translation of, The Awakening of Faith, p. 56.

---

8. Radhakrishnan, _Indian Philosophy_, p. 592: "The Hīnayāna protests against the Mahāyāna as an accommodation of the pure teaching to the necessities of human nature. . . . The absence of the supernatural and the consequent lack of any scope for imagination, the morbid way of solving the central problems of life, the reduction of nirvāṇa to extinction and ethical life to a monastic asceticism, made the Hīnayāna a religion for the thinking and the strong in spirit, while a new development had to arise for the emotional and the worshipful."

9. Radhakrishnan, _Indian Philosophy_, p. 593: "Mahāyāna metaphysics is monistic in character. All objects in the world are of one reality. The nature of this reality is beyond language and description."

10. Radhakrishnan, _Indian Philosophy_, p. 593, quoting Suzuki's translation of _The Awakening of Faith_, p. 56: "'Things in their fundamental nature cannot be named or explained. They cannot be adequately expressed in any form of language. They are beyond the range of perception, and have no distinctive features. They possess absolute sameness, and are subject neither to transformation nor to destruction. They are nothing else but one soul, for which tathatā is another designation.'"

* Ibid, p. 96.

† Radhakrishnan, op.
cit., p. 593.

‡ Suzuki, op. cit., p. 59.

the self-regulating and the pure, the immutable and the free."*[11]

The Mahayana Buddhists see the world of experience as phenomenal and not real. They liken it to a maya, mirage, flash of lightning or froth.† All existent things have three aspects: (1) quintessence, (2) attributes, and (3) activities. This may be illustrated by a simple jar. Its quintessence is the earth, its attribute is the form of the jar, and its activity is to keep water. The attribute and activity are by nature mutable, subject to the law of birth and death. On the other hand the quintessence is indestructible.[12] The whole universe has its unchanged aspect as well as its changeable one. The term most frequently used to name the ultimate cosmic principle or the unchangable aspect of the universe is Bhutatathata. This universal absolute is above all predicates. It can best be expressed in terms of the mystic, i.e., by negatives: "Bhutatathata is neither that which is existence nor that which is plurality, nor that which is at once unity and plurality."‡[13] It is quite significant to note the similarity of this conception with the Brahman of the Upanishads. However it seemed that the Mahayanists were quite aware of the similarity of their position with the Upanishadic view.[14] In fact there was a steady influence of the spiritualistic monism of the Upanishads upon the thought of Mahayana Buddhism. The acceptance of the cosmic and monistic Bhutatathata on the part of the Mahayanists was quite significant for later Buddhism, for it meant the transformation of

---

11. Radhakrishnan, *Indian Philosophy*, p. 593, quoting Suzuki's translation of *The Awakening of Faith*, p. 96: "It is 'the effulgence of great wisdom; the universal illumination of the dharmadhātu (universe), the true and adequate knowledge, the mind pure and clean in its nature; the eternal, the blessed, the self-regulating and the pure, the immutable and the free.'"

12. Radhakrishnan, *Indian Philosophy*, p. 593: "The world of experience is phenomenal and not real. . . . The Mahāyāna Buddhists liken the universe to a māyā, mirage, flash of lightning or froth. All things of the world have the three aspects of (1) quintessence, (2) attributes, and (3) activities. If we take a jar, its quintessence is the earth, its attribute is the form of the jar, and its activity is to keep water. The attribute and activity are subject to law of birth and death, while the quintessence is indestructible."

13. J. B. Pratt, *The Pilgrimage of Buddhism* (New York: Macmillan, 1928), pp. 249–250, quoting Suzuki's translation of *The Awakening of Faith*, p. 59: "Pure being, if so I may for the moment render Bhutatathata, is above all predicates. It can best be expressed as the mystics have always expressed it, by negatives: 'Bhutatathata is neither that which is existence nor that which is nonexistence; it is neither that which is unity nor that which is plurality, nor that which is at once unity and plurality, nor that which is not at once unity and plurality.'"

14. Radhakrishnan, *Indian Philosophy*, p. 594n: "The Mahāyānists seemed to have been aware of the similarity of their position to the Upaniṣad view."

Buddhism from an individualistic and either pluralistic or nihilistic philosophy into a monistic and spiritualistic view, strikingly similar to neo-Hegelian absolute idealism.* [15]

The rise of the world of multiplicity is accounted
for by a metaphysics of metaphors. Ignorance or <u>avi-
dya</u> is said to be the cause of the world. [16] As stated
previously <u>Bhutatathata</u> is pure spirit or pure awareness without multiplicity or character; but it is infected with multiplicity through the action of ignorance, a process which the author of the <u>Awakening</u>
seeks to make plainer by the simile of "perfuming."
Just as clothes when new have no odor but are
scented by the perfumes which one puts upon them,
so the pure, undifferentiated mind is "perfumed" by
ignorance. From this perfuming there results the
mind of man, and from the mind of man results the
dream or vision of an external world. [17] However this
illusion of an external world is a defect of true vision;
it is "a cataract on the spiritual eye." This world of
multiplicity is indeed ultimately attributable to, it flows
from, the One Reality. At this point, as Pratt reminds
us,† we find the Mahayana asserting the same general
thesis as Spinoza. Like Spinoza again, the Mahayana
does not pretend to be able to follow out the details
of derivation. They are quite aware of the impos-
sibility of ascertaining where the many appear and
where they disappear; for that we must look to the
Supreme Nature. However we can know that the
many are illusory, like the "flower-shaped apparition"
which a man would get, "who with perfect sight, beheld the pure void of space, but fixed his eyes on one
particular spot, beyond which he did not look or
move his eyes, staring until his sight was fatigued." [18]

* J. B. Pratt, The Pil-
grimage of Buddhism,
p. 248.

† Ibid, p. 253.

---

15. Pratt, *Pilgrimage of Buddhism*, p. 248: "It meant the transformation of Buddhism from an
individualistic and either pluralistic or nihilistic philosophy into a monistic and spiritualistic view,
an absolute idealism in many ways strikingly similar to neo-Hegelianism."

16. Radhakrishnan, *Indian Philosophy*, p. 594: "The rise of the world is accounted for as usual
by a metaphysics of metaphors. Ignorance or avidyā is said to be the cause of the world."

17. Pratt, *Pilgrimage of Buddhism*, p. 250: "*Bhutatathata* and *Alaya-vijnana* are pure spirit or pure
awareness without multiplicity or character; but they are infected with multiplicity through the
action of ignorance, a process which the author seeks to make plainer by the simile of 'perfuming.' Just as our clothes when new have no odor but are scented by the perfumes which we put
upon them, so the pure, undifferentiated mind is 'perfumed' by ignorance. From this perfuming
there results the mind of man, and from it the dream or vision of an external world—a world of
things which are nothing but the percepts of the various observers."

18. Pratt, *Pilgrimage of Buddhism*, p. 253: "The illusion of a real material world is a defect of
true vision; it is, as it were, the effect of a cataract on the spiritual eye. This world of multiplicity

We are immediately led to ask the question, whence arises in our finite minds the illusion of the many? This question is never completely and satisfactorily answered. The Mahayana struggles with it, but its attempts at explanation seldom satisfy the western reader. It seems that their explanation boils down to this point: since an illusion is really a negation of reality, consisting of non-being, no explanation is required. In other words, since it is a form of nothing, it is not necessary to attribute a cause to it.

This then is the explanation of the phenomenal world; this expresses the way in which the many evolve from the one through the intervention of ignorance. Obviously this is not wholly clear. But it need not perplex us to much, for even the author of the <u>Awakening</u> does not claim to have full understanding of the matter himself. In fact, he tells us that "the mind which starts from the perfuming influence of ignorance which has no beginning cannot be comprehended by common people nor even by Sravakas and Pratyekalriddhas. It is partly comprehended by some Bodhisattvas; but even those who bave reached the highest stage of Bodhisattvahood cannot thoroughly comprehend it. The only one who can have a clear and consummate knowledge of it is the Tathagata."*[19]

* Suzuki, <u>op. cit.</u>, p. 78.

The Mahayana Religion

From a doctrinal point there is no unity in the Mahayana religion. It is characterized by a great degree

is indeed ultimately attributable to, it flows from, the One Reality—here we find the Mahayana philosophy asserting the same general thesis as Spinoza. Like Spinoza again, the Mahayana does not pretend to be able to follow out the details of the derivation. To ascertain the precise point where the many appear and where they disappear is not possible; for that we must look to the Supreme Nature, and beyond that we can ascertain nothing. But we know that the many are illusory, like the 'flower-shaped apparition' which a man would get 'who with perfect sight, beheld the pure void of space, but fixed his eyes on one particular spot, beyond which he did not look or move his eyes, staring until his sight was fatigued.'"

19. Pratt, *Pilgrimage of Buddhism*, p. 254: "This, then, in general, is the explanation of the world of multiplicity; this expresses the way in which the many evolve from the One through the intervention of ignorance. If it is not wholly clear to the reader, let him blame neither himself nor me. . . . Thus the author of the *Awakening* does not claim to have the matter clear nor fully to understand it himself. In fact, he tells us that 'the mind which starts from the perfuming influence of ignorance which has no beginning cannot be comprehended by common people nor even by Sravakas and Pratyekabuddhas. It is partly comprehended by some Bodhisattvas; but even those who have reached the highest stage of Bodhisattvahood can not thoroughly comprehend it. The only one who can have a clear and consummate knowledge of it is the Tathagata.'"

of diversity. This lack of doctrinal unity in Mahayana Buddhism may be attributed to its amazing amount of tolerance, something quite conspicuously missing in Hinayana Buddhism. Wherever Mahayana Buddhism prevailed the indigeneous religions were tolerated, while it took care to teach them a new respect for life, kindness to animals and resignation. So long as they followed certain ethical rules, the new converts were not forced to give up their numerous superstitions. Any god could be believed in so long as one was ethical. This protean character of Mahayana Buddhism is another example of that universal historical law, viz., that that culture which conquers is in turn conquered.[20] This universal law is especially true of religion. It was true when Christianity proved victorious in the Roman empire and it was true when Mahayana Buddhism won converts from the regions of China, Korea, Siam, Burma and Japan. "The more crusading a religion is, the more it absorbs."

The amazing amount of tolerence of Mahayana Buddhism is in consonance with its metaphysical views. It is asserted that all religions are revelation of the same Dharmakaya and bring out some aspects of truth.* Dharma is the all-pervading spiritual force, the ultimate and the supreme principle of life. It is interesting to note that there is an attempt to personify dharma in the conception of Buddha. He is considered the first cause, the eternal God, superior to all things the supreme and first of all Buddhas.[21] He is the devatideva, the paramount God of gods. He is the creator of all bodhisattvas. All beings are his children. "The tathagata, having left the conflagration of the three worlds, is dwelllng in peace in the tranquillity of his forest abode, saying to himself all three worlds are my possession, all living beings are

* Radhakrishnan, op. cit., p. 597.

---

20. Radhakrishnan, *Indian Philosophy,* pp. 596–597: "There is no unity in the Mahāyāna religion. It suffered religious superstitions gladly. Wherever it prevailed, India, China, Korea, Siam, Burma and Japan, the indigenous religions were tolerated, while it took care to teach them a new respect for life, kindness to animals and resignation. So long as men conformed to certain ethical rules and respected the order of monks, the Buddhist teachers did not feel called upon to condemn the superstitious usages. It does not matter what gods you worship, so long as you are good. The protean character of Mahāyāna Buddhism is due to this tendency."

21. Radhakrishnan, *Indian Philosophy,* p. 597: "The freedom of opinion in religious matters is in consonance with the metaphysical views of the Mahāyāna. All religions are revelations of the same Dharmakāya and bring out some aspects of truth. Dharma is the all-pervading spiritual force, the ultimate and the supreme principle of life. The first attempt at personifying dharma is in the conception Ādi Buddha, the first cause, the eternal God, superior to all things, the supreme, the first of all the Buddhas, without equal or comparison."

* Quoted in Radakrish-
nan, op. cit., p. 600.

† Indra becomes Sata-
manyu and Vajrapani,
with his own kingdom of
heaven. Brahma had his
chief characters trans-
ferred to Manjusri, the
lamp of wisdom. Vishnu
passes his attributes to
Avalokitesvara or Padma-
pani. Virupaksa is one of
the names of Shiva,
though in Buddhistic leg-
end he is one of the four
kings. Ganesa is taken
over both as Vinayaka and
demon Vinatakn. Ajita
formed with Sakyamuni
and Avolokitesvara a
triad.[24]

‡ Radhakrishnon, op.
cit., p. 598.

my children, the world is full of intense tribulation, but I myself will work out their salvation." "To all who believe me I do good, while friends are they to me who seek refuge in me."*[22] However there is more than one Buddha. There are a number of Buddhas endowed with the highest intelligence and love. They too are working constantly to save the world. There have been an infinite number of these Buddhas in the past, and there will be an infinite number in the future. All of these Buddhas are transitory manifestations of the one eternal being.[23]

Many of the Vedic gods are brought over into Mahayanism, and thus become aspects of the One Supreme Reality. Nagarjuna who, with Asvaghosha is commonly considered the founder of Mahayana Buddhism, by his precept and practice taught that the Hindu gods of Brahma, Vishnu, Shiva and Kali had the attributes assigned to them in Brahmanical scriptures, and were proper objects of worship. The traditional Hindu gods were easily adjusted to this new system, and their function and assignments were readily given.† A close analysis of Mahayanism will reveal that a vast number of its bodhisattvas, archangels and saints are only Vedic Aryans "thinly disguised by Buddhistic symbolism."‡

On the surface Mahayana religion seems to be polytheistic, in contrast to its monistic metaphysics. But a more scrutinizing study would reveal that the several gods are subordinate to a single head.[25] It is the <u>Dharmakaya</u> which is the ultimate foundation of existence.

22. Radhakrishnan, *Indian Philosophy*, p. 600: "All beings are his children. 'The Tathāgata, having left the conflagration of the three worlds, is dwelling in peace in the tranquillity of his forest abode, saying to himself all three worlds are my possession, all living beings are my children, the world is full of intense tribulation, but I myself will work out their salvation.' 'To all who believe me I do good, while friends are they to me who seek refuge in me.'"

23. Radhakrishnan, *Indian Philosophy*, p. 597: "The work of saving the world is done by the Buddhas, or the beings endowed with the highest intelligence and love. There have been an infinite number of these Buddhas in the past, and there will be an infinite number in future. . . . They are all transitory manifestations of the One Eternal Being."

24. Radhakrishnan, *Indian Philosophy*, p. 598n: "Indra becomes Śatamanyu and Vajrapāṇi, with his own kingdom of heavens (svarga), called Trayastṛmśaloka. Brahmā had his chief characters transferred to Mañjuśrī, the lamp of wisdom. Sarasvatī continued to be one of his wives, the other being Lakṣmī. Avalokiteśvara or Padmapāṇi has the attributes of Viṣṇu or Padmanābha. Virūpāksa is one of the names of Śiva, though in Buddhistic legend he is one of the four kings. Gaṇeśa is taken over both as Vināyaka and demon Vinataka. The Sapta tathāgatas are the seven ṛsis. Ajita formed with Śākyamuni and Avalokiteśvara a triad."

25. Radhakrishnan, *Indian Philosophy*, p. 598: "The monistic metaphysics of the Mahāyāna has given rise to an apparently polytheistic religion, but we should note that the several gods are subordinate to a single head."

This metaphysical conception of <u>Dharmakaya</u> as the ground of all existence makes Mahayana religion essentially compatible with its metaphysics.

The Ethics of Mahayana

The ethical ideal of the Mahayana is the Bodhisattva. Etymologically the term Bodhisattva means simply one whose being consists of insight. But historically it means "one who is on the way to the attainment of perfect knowledge, a future Buddha."[26] The term was first applied to Gotoma during his previous births and throughout the earlier years of his historical life up to the time of his enlightenment. It therefore came to mean a man destined to become a Buddha in this or in some future life.*[27] To understand this ideal it is necessary to go back to the teaching and life of the founder. His own example was quite free from selfishness and narrowness. He taught that each man should avoid giving pledges to Fortune and should seek the desireless and sorrow-free life. But beyond this his own heart was so full of love for every form of suffering creature that he long postponed <u>Parinivana</u> for their sake. It was this point of the Buddha's teaching and example that the Mahayanist seized upon and it was upon this that they based their moral ideal. The <u>Arat</u>[28] of the Hinayana, busy about his own salvation, was considered too narrow and selfish by the Mahayana, and they erected in his stead the ideal of the earnest seeker after the welfare of others, who in unselfish devotion to his fellow creatures accumulates great stores of merit and dedicates it not to his own salvation but to that of all suffering beings. Merit is thought by the Mahayana as being transferable. There is also the element of vicarious suffering in Mahayana religion. The Bodhisattva is able to present his merit to a needy world, and for its sake he is willing to be a meritless sinner.†[29] It is interesting at

* Pratt, <u>op. cit.</u>, pl 217.

† Ibid, 218.

---

26. Radhakrishnan, *Indian Philosophy*, p. 600: "But historically it means 'one who is on the way to the attainment of perfect knowledge, a future Buddha.'"

27. Radhakrishnan, *Indian Philosophy*, p. 600: "It therefore came to mean 'a Buddha designate,' or a man destined to become a Buddha in this or some future life."

28. Davis corrected "Arat" to "Arhat."

29. Pratt, *Pilgrimage of Buddhism*, pp. 217–218: "To understand this ideal it is necessary to go back to what I have referred to as the heart element in the teaching and life of the Founder. His own example, as I have so often pointed out, was quite free from that implication of selfishness

this point to note the similarities of this conception of vicarious suffering and the transference of merit to many of the theories of atonement that have appeared in the history of Christian thought.

The Mahavastu, a late Hinayana work, gives a list of ten stages in the progress of the Bodhisattva, and the same number is retained, with modifications in detail, by the Mahayana authorities.[30] The first stage is the joyful (pramudita) one characterised by the rise of the thought of bodhi. It is here that the Bodhisattva makes sincere resolutions which determine the future course. One such vow is the resolution of Avalokitesvara not to accept salvation until the last particle of dust shall have attained to Buddhahood. The recognition of the impermanence of things brings the stage of Vimala or purity into being. In it came the practice of morality and the exercise of wisdom (adhicitta). In the next stage the Bodhisattva goes through the process of blotting out anger, hatred, and error, and promoting faith, compassion, charity, and disinterestedness. This is the third stage (prabhakari), where the seeker shines with patience and forbearance. In the fourth stage the Bodhisattva surrenders all traces of egoism by training himself in good work and applying himself specially to the cultivation of virtues connected with bodhi. In the fifth

---

or narrowness . . . Whatever might be the natural deduction from his teaching that each of us should avoid giving pledges to Fortune and should seek the desireless and sorrow-free life, his own heart was so full of love for every form of suffering creature that he long postponed Parinirvana for their sake, and fired the imaginations of many of his disciples with the longing to be of service to others at any cost. It was this aspect of the Buddha's teaching and example that the Mahayana thinkers seized upon and it was on this that they based their moral ideal. The typical Arhat (= Arahant), busy about his own salvation, wandering alone as a rhinoceros, they felt to be narrow and unworthy, and they erected in his stead the ideal of the earnest seeker after the welfare of others, who in unselfish devotion to his fellow creatures accumulates great stores of merit and dedicates it not to his own salvation but to that of all suffering beings. For in the faith of the Mahayana, there are many such ardent saviors of others. All the Buddhas had dedicated themselves, for ages before their complete enlightenment, to this unselfish task: and as there will be an endless line of Buddhas in the infinite future, as there has been in the infinite past, so there must now be an incalculable multitude of future Buddhas, i.e., Bodhisattvas, who have dedicated themselves to the same endless task as that for which Gotama went through so many births and deaths. This faith involves not only a new ideal but a new conception of the acquisition of merit and of salvation. Merit is thought of by the Mahayana as being transferable. Suffering and goodness are vicarious. The Bodhisattva is able to present his merit to a needy world, and for its sake he is willing to be himself a meritless sinner."

30. Pratt, *Pilgrimage of Buddhism*, p. 221: "The Mahavastu, a late Hinayana work, gives a list of ten stages in the progress of the Bodhisattva, and the same number is retained, with modifications in detail, by the Mahayana authorities."

stage the seeker begins a course of study and meditation to understand the four noble truths in their true light. In the next stage the seeker turns to the basic principles of "dependent origination and non-substantiality." This stage is called the abhimukhi, or "turned towards." The seeker now devotes himself to the attainment of that knowledge which would enable him to effect his aim of universal salvation. He is now in the seventh stage, called duramjama. Next the seeker comes to the eithth stage in which the supreme virtue of (anutpattiladharmacaksuh) seeing all things such as they are dominates. In the ninth stage the seeker reaches the point when all his acts are unselfish, done without desire. Finally the Bodhisattva reaches the tenth stage in which he becomes a tathagata, a cloud of dharma.*[31]

* Radhakrishnan, op. cit., pp. 601, 602.

In this upward pathway from the phenomenal world to the Real world we see something of the Mahayana view of salvation. Just before his death, Buddha had said to his followers, "Work out your own salvation with diligence." The Mahayana accepts this

---

31. Radhakrishnan, *Indian Philosophy,* pp. 601–602: "The first stage is the joyful (pramuditā) one characterised by the rise of the thought of bodhi. It is here that the bodhisattva makes those pregnant resolutions (praṇidhāna) which determine the future course. The resolution of Avalokiteśvara not to accept salvation until the last particle of dust shall have attained to Buddhahood before him is such a vow. The insight is developed gradually so as to render the heart pure and the mind free from the illusion of self. The recognition of the impermanence of things enlarges the aspirant's compassionate nature, and we get next the stage of vimalā, or purity. In it we have the practice of morality and the exercise of wisdom (adhicitta). In the next stage the bodhisattva engages himself in the various bhāvanās which enable him to annihilate anger, hatred and error, and promote faith, compassion, charity, and disinterestedness. This is the third stage (prabhākarī), where the seeker shines with patience and forbearance. The bodhisattva, to surrender all traces of egoism, trains himself in good work and applies himself specially to the cultivation of virtues connected with bodhi (bodhipaksa dharma). It is the fourth radiant stage (arciṣmatī). Then does the seeker begin a course of study and meditation to understand the four noble truths in their true light. It is the fifth invincible (sudurjayā) stage where dhyāna and samādhi predominate. As a result of moral practice and meditation, the seeker turns to the basic principles of dependent origination and non-substantiality. This stage is called abhimukhī, or 'turned towards.' Here prajñā reigns. Yet he is not completely free from passion, and still has the desires of becoming a Buddha and the intention of saving mankind. He devotes himself to the attainment of that knowledge which would enable him to effect his aim of universal salvation. He is now in the seventh stage, called dūraṁgamā. When he is free from the eager desire for the particular, his thoughts are not bound to any special objects, and he becomes immovable (acala). This is the eighth stage where the supreme virtue of (anutpattikadharmacakṣuḥ) seeing all things such as they are, i.e. rooted in tathatā, dominates. The activity of the bodhisattva is tainted by no duality or selfishness. He is not content with tranquil repose, but is actually engaged in the teaching of dharma to others. It is the ninth stage, that of the good ones (sādhumatī) when all his acts are unselfish, done without desire. . . . The bodhisattva becomes a tathāgata in the tenth stage, a cloud of dharma (dharmamegha)."

command and urges the necessity of individual effort in the salvation process. But they do not stop here. The help of a saviour is necessary. The Mahayana would reword the Buddha's sentence and cry with St. Paul: "Work out your own salvation with fear and trembling, for it is God who worketh in you, both to will and to do of his good pleasure."* It is the Buddha nature within us that unites itself with our wills in the struggle for salvation. Without this more than human aid, salvation from ignorance and desire would be impossible.

* Philippians 2 : 12.

The principles of the moral life for the Mahayana are five in number, viz., dana (charity), virya (fortitude) sila (morality), ksanti (patience), and dhyana (meditation). The severity of monasticism is relaxed. It is possible for one to reach the goal and remain married. Asceticism and poverty are not emphasized as they are in Hinayana ethics. The doctrine of karma is tempered with mercy. Emphasis is placed on faith as a way of salvation.[32] The Mahayana insists on the turning over of ethical merit to the advantage of others. They insist that no man lives to himself alone. The good or evil of one affects the whole. Whether the metaphysical truth that nothing on earth is real, can be reconciled with the ethical law that we should work and suffer for our neighbor, is apparently a problem which the Mahayanist never solved.[33] He would still insist that he must save the world. When the question of nirvana is brought forth the Mahayanists are anxious to make out that it is not annihilation.[34] It is real freedom where ignorance is overcome.[35] It is the union with the great soul of the

---

32. Radhakrishnan, *Indian Philosophy*, pp. 602–603: "The principles of moral life are dāna (charity), vīrya (fortitude), śīla (morality), kṣānti (patience), and dhyāna (meditation), and crowning all, prajñā, the home of peace and blessing. The severity of monasticism is relaxed. . . . It is possible to reach the goal though married. Asceticism and poverty, so common in Hīnayāna ethics, are almost exceptional. . . . The doctrines of karma, or the continuous working of our deeds good or bad, is tempered by mercy, which finds expression in the easier way of salvation by faith."

33. Radhakrishnan, *Indian Philosophy*, p. 603: "No man lives to himself alone. The good or evil of one affects the whole. Whether the metaphysical truth that nothing on earth is real, and the ethical law that we should work and suffer for our neighbour, can be reconciled or not, is a problem for the Mādhyamika system."

34. Radhakrishnan, *Indian Philosophy*, p. 605: "The Mahāyānists are anxious to make out that nirvāṇa is not annihilation."

35. Radhakrishnan, *Indian Philosophy*, p. 604: "It is not non-existence pure and simple, but real freedom, where ignorance is overcome."

universe.[36] To become a Buddha is to become one in essence with the infinite.[37]

Conclusion

Now we may see why Mahayana Buddhism gradually won out over Hinayana Buddhism. The Hinayana was for the Buddhist elect chiefly: the Mahayana is for everybody. It has its obstruse philosophical appeal for the thinker, as was noticed in its metaphysical system; and at the same time it provides something for the most naive mind, as was noticed in the amazing degree of tolerance in its religion.[38] "Its thinkers were well aware of Hegel's distinction between religion and philosophy at least sixteen hundred years before Hegel was born. The truths of philosophy need not be studied in their obstruse form by the beginner; for him the simpler and symbolic figures that speak to the imagination may well suffice."*

Thus Buddhism became a religion for the laymen as well as for the monk. The emphasis on fleeing from the world was replaced by a desire to live in the world, while yet being not of the world. In the words of Coomaraswamy, "the development of the Mahayana is the overflowing of Buddhism over the limits of Order into the life of the world."†[39]

* Pratt, op. cit. p. 231.

† op. cit. p. 228

BIBLIOGRAPHY

1. Ashvaghosha, <u>Awakening of Faith</u>, trans. by D. T. Suzuki, Chicago, 1900.
2. Coomaraswamy, A. <u>Buddha and the Gospel of Buddhism</u>, New York, 1916.
3. Davids, R., <u>Buddhist India</u>, New York, 1903.

---

36. Radhakrishnan, *Indian Philosophy*, p. 605: "According to Asaṅga, nirvāṇa is the union with the Great Soul of the universe, or Mahātman."

37. Radhakrishnan, *Indian Philosophy*, p. 604: "To become a Buddha is to become one in essence with the infinite."

38. Pratt, *Pilgrimage of Buddhism*, p. 231: "The Hinayana was for monks chiefly; the Mahayana is for everyone. As we shall see in the next chapter, it has its abstruse philosophy for the thinker, but it has something also for the simplest and even for the most superstitious."

39. Pratt, *Pilgrimage of Buddhism*, p. 232: "In the words of Coomaraswamy, 'the development of the Mahayana is the overflowing of Buddhism over the limits of the Order into the life of the world.' Thus Buddhism became a religion for the layman quite as much as for the monk.... [T]he old fear of the world, the fleeing from the world was replaced by the desire to live *in* the world, while yet being not *of* the world."

4. Pratt, J. B., <u>The Pilgrimage of Buddhism</u>, New York, 1928.
5. Radhakrishnan, S., <u>Indian Philosophy</u>, New York, 1923.

20 July
1950

THDS. MLKP-MBU: Box 115, folder 31.

Statement on Behalf of
Ernest Nichols, *State of New Jersey vs. Ernest Nichols*, by W. Thomas McGann

20 July 1950
Moorestown, N.J.

On 12 June 1950, King, Walter R. McCall, Pearl E. Smith, and Doris Wilson had a confrontation with a New Jersey tavern owner, Ernest Nichols, who refused to serve them.[1] King and his friends charged Nichols with violation of a state civil rights law. Nichols's statement, prepared by his lawyer, defends his refusal to serve the group and his brandishing of a gun. McGann implies wrongdoing on the part of one of the complainants, who was described as "quite insistent that Mr. Nichols sell him package goods or a bottle and this caused Nichols to become upset and excited because he knew that he was being asked to do something which constitutes a violation." McGann argues that Nichols did not generally refuse to serve blacks: "it is well known and can be proven without doubt, that for years Mr. Nichols has served colored patrons." Nichols promises to obey the civil rights statute in the future: "Mr. Nichols steadfastly maintains that he is willing to serve colored folks and knows that under the law he must serve colored patrons." The case was dropped when three witnesses refused to testify on behalf of the complainants.

State of New Jersey Vs. Ernest Nichols, Defendant.

Around 12:45 A.M., Monday morning June 12th, 1950 four colored persons came into the tavern of Ernest Nichols, which is located at Route S-41 and Camden Pike, in the Township of Maple Shade, and County of Burlington. At the time in question, one of the four walked up to the proprietor, Ernest Nichols, and asked him for "package goods." This Mr. Nichols refused to sell and stated that it was Sunday and that he could not sell "package goods" on Sunday or after 10:00 P.M. on any day. Then the applicant asked for a bottle of beer and it is alleged that Mr. Nichols answered "no beer, Mr! Today is Sunday." The

---

1. Walter Raleigh McCall (1923–1978), a Morehouse classmate of King's, graduated from Crozer in 1951. He later pursued postgraduate work at Temple University in 1952–1953 and at Atlanta University in 1958. McCall served as dean and chaplain at Fort Valley State College from 1951 until 1957, when he became pastor of Providence Baptist Church in Atlanta. He was the director of Morehouse's School of Religion from 1965 until 1969.

applicant was quite insistent that Mr. Nichols sell him package goods or a bottle and this caused Nichols to become upset and excited because he knew that he was being asked to do something which constitutes a violation and which might get him into trouble, were he to submit to the request of the colored man.

It is alleged that Mr. Nichols, while the colored folks were still in his tavern, obtained a gun and walked out of the door of his tavern and while outside fired the gun in the air. Mr. Nichols claims that this act was not intended as a threat to his colored patrons. The colored patrons, on the other hand, while they admit that the gun was not pointed at them or any of them, seemed to think that it was a threat. Mr. Nichols on the other hand states that he has been held up before and he wanted to alert his watchdog who was somewhere outside on the tavern grounds.

Admittedly my client was excited and upset and perhaps gave the impression that he was and is antagonistic to negroes and did not want to serve them because of their color. On the other hand, it is well known and can be proven without doubt, that for years Mr. Nichols has served colored patrons. I might point out that at the arraignment before Judge Charlton, the Judge, and the prosecuting attorney, George Barbour, Esquire, readily admitted that they know that Mr. Nichols has served colored folks in the past.

Mr. Nichols became so excited and upset because he was under the impression that the visit by the four colored patrons was an obvious attempt to get him to violate the law so that they could report his misconduct and violation to the authorities. He felt that the colored gentleman, who asked for "package goods," who appeared to be an intelligent man, was well acquainted with the regulation prohibiting taverns from selling bottle goods or "package goods" on Sunday and after 10:00 in the evening. This circumstance, in itself, made my client very suspicious of the actions and requests of the complainants. He thought at the time that surely the colored gentleman knew that his request constituted a violation. I might point out here that at the hearing in Maple Shade one of the colored witnesses admitted that he was asking for something that might constitute a "violation."

The colored patrons left the tavern and within a few minutes returned again to chat with certain patrons at the bar. This tended to confirm my client's conviction that the complainants were endeavoring to in some way ensnare him in some violation of the law.

Mr. Nichols steadfastly maintains that he is willing to serve colored folks and knows that under the law he must serve colored patrons so long as their requests are lawful and the patrons in question are not under the influence of intoxicants. Mr. Nichols further says that in the past he has served colored patrons and is presently continuing to do so.

This statement is submitted in the spirit of assisting the Prosecutor of the Pleas, of Burlington County in the investigation of the case in question. The statement is submitted without prejudice to the rights of the defendant.

[*signed as below*]
W. Thomas McGann,
Attorney for Ernest Nichols.

TDS. WTMc.

Municipal Court

Township ___ of ___ Maple Shade ___ County of ___ Burlington ___

State of New Jersey

State of New Jersey

vs.

Ernest Nichols
....
Defendant.

Complaint for

.... Refusal to serve stimulating beverage in
a public place, etc

State of New Jersey,
County of.......... Burlington .... } ss.

Pearl B. Smith, 735 N. 40th St. Phila. Pa., W. L. King, 755 Walnut St. Camden,
and Harris Wilson Doris Wilson, 735 N. 40th St. Phila., and W. R. McCall of
residing 755 Walnut St., Camden, N.J. ...., New Jersey,

their
upon his oath says that..... Ernest Nichols ....,

residing at...... E. Main St., Maple Shade ...., ..., New Jersey,

on. 12th of June (12.45 A.M.) 50, in the. Township.........of. Maple Shade ....,

County of.... Burlington ...., and State of New Jersey, did. wilfully refuse to serve

beverages of any kind, used profane and obscene language, and intimidation by weapon

to the complainants named above.......

"Annex as follows — Such refusal being by reason
of complainants color, in violation of R.S. 10:-1-3
and supplements thereto

(State essential facts constituting the offense charged. If a statute or ordinance has been violated, insert
brief title and section violated.)

these
WHEREFORE the complainants prays that the said. Ernest Nichols, may be apprehended

may be apprehended* and dealt with according to law.

Pearl E. Smith
Complainant.

Subscribed and sworn to before me this

..12th.........day of.... June......

19..50..

W. L. King Jr.
W. R. McCall

Percy D. Charton

(Name and official title of person administering the oath)

Municipal Magistrate

*In the case of a violation of an ordinance, use the following: "may be summoned to appear and that this court may
award judgment pursuant to the terms of the ordinance above mentioned."

Crozer Theological Seminary
Field Work Questionnaire

13 September 1950
[*Chester, Pa.*]

*On his placement form for Crozer's ministerial field work program, King states
that his strongest talents lie in preaching and pastoral work and that he wishes to
be assigned as a pastor's assistant. King was assigned in the fall of 1950 to a
bimonthly student pastorate at the First Baptist Church of East Elmhurst in
Queens, New York, under the guidance of Rev. William E. Gardner.*

NAME (LAST FIRST MIDDLE)   **King Martin Luther**
ADDRESS   (HOME)   (STREET CITY STATE)   **193 Boulevard N.E. Atlanta, Ga**
      (CROZER)   ~~Dom~~ **Dormitory Box 27**
BIRTHPLACE   **Atlanta Ga**   DATE OF BIRTH   **Jan. 15 1929**

EDUCATION:

INSTITUTION	DATES	DEGREE
Morehouse College	**1944–1948**	**A.B.**

ORDAINED?   **yes**

EXPERIENCE:

(IF A CHURCH)

CHURCH OR ORGANIZATION	TITLE	DATES	MEMBERSHIP	BUDGET	SALARY

**Ebenezer Baptist Church—Assistant Pastor—For the last three summers—
4000—$40,000—$200.00 a month**

CHECK WHAT YOU CONSIDER YOUR OWN STRONGEST POINTS IN YOUR MINISTRY:
PREACHING AND WORSHIP **X**   PASTORAL WORK **X**   RELIGIOUS EDUCATION
ORGANIZATION   AGE GROUP WITH WHICH YOU WORK BEST (CHILDREN, TEEN-
AGE, ETC.)   ANY SPECIAL ABILITIES, (MUSIC, ATHLETICS, ETC.)

MEMBERSHIP IN RELIGIOUS, CIVIC, SERVICE ORGANIZATIONS, COMMITTEE
SERVICE INCLUDING DENOMINATIONAL WORK: **Y.M.C.A.—N.A.A.C.P.—Ministers
conference—**

HONORS: (CITATIONS, MILITARY HONORS, INCLUDING DATES)

DO YOU WISH TO HAVE YOUR NAME LISTED FOR POSSIBLE FIELD WORK?   **yes**
IF SO, INDICATE PREFERENCE: PASTOR   PASTOR'S ASST.   **X**   DIRECTOR OF
EDUCATION   YOUTH ACTIVITIES, CHRISTIAN CENTER, ETC.   OTHER

NAMES, ADDRESSES, AND POSITIONS OF PERSONS WHO MAY BE CONSULTED RE-
GARDING YOUR WORK:
**Rev. M. L. King Sr. 193 Boulevard N.E. Atlanta Ga.
Pastor of the Ebenezer Baptist Church in Atlanta**

330   **Rev. J. P. Barbour Calvery Baptist Church Chester, Pa.
Pastor of Calvery Baptist Church in Chester**

MARRIED TO **Not married** DATE   13 Sept
   EDUCATION: 1950
   ANY SPECIAL ABILITIES:
   CHILDREN: (GIVE NAMES AND BIRTH DATES)

PLEASE ATTACH A PHOTOGRAPH OF YOURSELF, IF POSSIBLE.

BUDGET FOR THE ACADEMIC YEAR (9 MONTHS): (PLEASE ESTIMATE)
   RESOURCES: **Supported by[1] parents and also remuneration from preaching.**
   TOTAL
EXPENSES: **$1,000 Tuition $150.00**
                 Board 288.00
                 Rent 51.00
                 Traveling exp to N. York 200.00
                 Laundry 75.00
                 Books 75.00
                 Extra Spending 150.00
                 $989.00

TOTAL **$1,000**
MY PRESENT INDEBTEDNESS IS **$196.00**

ADDITIONAL REMARKS:

ASSIGNED TO:
NAME OF CHURCH   SUPERVISOR
OR ORGANIZATION   DATE   REMUNERATION   NAME   ADDRESS[2]

AHFmS. CRO-NRCR.

---

1. Someone wrote: "(Bd. & R., Tuition)."
2. Someone wrote and typed the name of a church: "First Bapt. Ch. Corona, L.I., New York
9/50–12/1/50 Rev. M. Gardner."

From Charles E. Batten

11 October 1950
Chester, Pa.

*Batten, dean of Crozer, asks King to write a recommendation for applicant Worth
Littlejohn Barbour, the son of J. Pius Barbour. Worth Barbour was accepted by
Crozer and graduated in 1954.*

Martin Luther King
Crozer Theological Seminary
Chester, Pennsylvania

Dear Martin:

Your name has been given as a personal reference by Worth L. Barbour,
Shaw University, Raleigh, N.C., who has applied for admission to Crozer
Theological Seminary to prepare for the ministry.

Realizing the importance of the contemplated step both for the candidate
and for the seminary, we would highly appreciate a frank and confidential
letter from you conveying your knowledge of the candidate's native ability
and particular aptitudes as well as his spiritual qualifications for the pastorate
or other form of Christian services. Please include comment on character,
personality, academic ability, and any other observations that you would care
to add indicating why you believe he would be useful in this calling.

Your letter may be of value to us not only in deciding the question of
Worth L. Barbour's admission to the seminary, but also in guiding him during
his period of study with us.

Thank you for your help. We are looking forward to a reply at your first
opportunity.

Sincerely,
[*signed as below*]
Charles E. Batten, Dean

CEB/bt

TLS. MLKP-MBU: Box 117, folder 50.

To Charles E. Batten

30 October 1950
Chester, Pa.

Dean Charles E. Batten
Crozer Theological Seminary
Chester, Pennsylvania

I have known Worth L. Barbour for a number of years, but for the last three years our relationship has been much more intimate than in previous years. In my dealings with him I have been greatly impressed with his sincerity of purpose, his conscientiousness, and his enthusiasm for the Christian ministry. I feel that he knows what he wants to do and he is settled enough to attempt to do it. He has a very [*mark illegible*] approach to life, and one which I think beneficial to any young man entering the ministry.

I am not in a position to give quite an objective statement of Littlejohn's academic because of my limited contact with him in that area, however I might say that in ordinary conversational dealings I have found him to be mentally alert and quite open-minded. He confronts issues on quite a mature leval. While I have not received the impression that Littlejohn is of superior intelligence, I feel that he can do the work at Crozer on the leval of an average student.

TLc. MLKP-MBU: Box 116, folder 49.

To Hugh Watt

5 November 1950
Chester, Pa.

This letter to professor Hugh Watt at the University of Edinburgh is the earliest extant document indicating King's interest in graduate study. Six weeks after he wrote this letter King was accepted by Edinburgh. He chose to attend Boston University.

Professor Hugh Watt
The Post Graduate School of Theology
7 Mayfield Terrace
Edinburgh, Scotland

I am interested in taking work toward the Ph.D degree in Theology. At present I am a senior student of the Crozer Theological Seminary (U.S.A.), and plan to finish in May of 1951. I would like very much to start my work toward the Ph.D degree in the fall term of that same year.

For sometime now I have had a great deal of interest in Edinburgh, and would like very much to study there. I would appreciate it very much if you would send me an application form, a catalogue of the Divinity school, and any information that would be valuable to me at this point. Please let me know of the possibilities of my entering in the fall term of 1951.

Thank you for your help. An immediate reply would be appreciated.

TLc. MLKP-MBU: Box 116, folder 49.

Crozer Theological Seminary Placement Committee: Confidential Evaluation of Martin Luther King, Jr., by George W. Davis

15 November 1950
Chester, Pa.

The Placement Committee, headed by Sankey L. Blanton, asked for Davis's "estimate of [King's] general and special abilities and character, together with any added remarks you deem helpful to the Placement Committee." [1]

1. Exceptional intellectual ability—discriminating mind.
2. Very personable.
3. Makes good impression in public in speaking and discussion. Good speaking voice.
4. A man of high character.
5. Should make an excellent minister or teacher. He has the mind for the latter.

AFmS. CRO-NRCR.

---

1. Morton Scott Enslin, Raymond J. Bean, and Charles E. Batten also prepared evaluations for the placement committee; see pp. 354, 392, and 406–407 in this volume, respectively.

"An Appraisal of the Great Awakening"

[*17 November 1950*]
[*Chester, Pa.*]

King wrote this essay for American Christianity (Colonial Period) taught by Raymond J. Bean at Crozer Theological Seminary.[1] Bean lectured on the development of Christianity in the United States from the arrival of the Spanish

---

1. Raymond Joseph Bean (1917–1982) received a B.A. from the University of New Hampshire in 1941, a B.D. from Andover-Newton Theological School in 1944, and a Th.D. from Boston in 1949. He replaced Reuben Elmore Ernest Harkness as Crozer's professor of church history during King's last year at the seminary. Bean remained at Crozer until 1959, when he became minister of the First Baptist Church in East Orange, New Jersey. In 1966, he became pastor of the First Baptist Church in Manchester, New Hampshire.

missionaries in the mid-sixteenth century through the origins of religious liberalism in the early nineteenth century. King was given three options for his term paper topic: the relationship between Catholics and Protestants in the colonies, the relationship between Baptists and the rise of democracy in America, and the Great Awakening in colonial America. His paper on the Great Awakening contains a detailed description of the lives of the ministers who led the movement and the various revivals that occurred between 1720 and 1775. King provides little analysis of either the social and political origins or the consequences of the Great Awakening and no discussion of its role in the development of African-American Christianity. He places great emphasis on the deep religious emotion involved in the revivals and the power of their evangelical preaching. Bean gave King an A for both the paper and the course.

The great spiritual revival of religion in the eighteenth century is usually termed the Great Awakening of 1740, because its chief intensity, in this country, culminated about that time. However it would be a mistake to confine this momentous movement to that year. It commenced more than a decade before that date and continued with power more than a decade after it. It would be well nigh impossible to set forth every single cause of this great religious revival, since social phenomena are usually tied up with a complexity of causes. But some of the causes are quite apparent. Probably the first factor that lead to colonial revivalism was the failure of organized religion to reach the masses. For years organized religion in the American colonies had been a matter of the few. During the early colonial period there were undoubtedly more unchurched people in America, in proportion to the population, than was to be found in any other country in Christendom.* Even in State Churches, as in New England and the Southern colonies, only a comparatively small proportion of the total population were members of the church. It was this situation which necessitated the development of new techniques to win people to the church, and this new method was revivalism. The Great Awakening was the first serious attempt to bring religion to the masses in the American Colonies.

* See Sweet, The Story of Religion in America, p. 5.

The gradual decline of emotional fervor was also a factor which led to the Great Awakening. Religion had become unemotional, with a type of preaching unconducive to revivals and conversion. It was this situation which led to the necessity for the Half-Way Covenant.[2]

---

2. Half-Way Covenant: adopted at the Synod of 1662 in Massachusetts, the covenant stated that children whose parents had been baptised into the Congregational church but not yet had

More and more individuals came to feel that there were certain "means" which might be used in putting the soul in a position to receive the regenerating influence of the Spirit of God. Reliance on these "means" rather than the miraculous power of God led to a cold and unemotional religion.*[3] No wonder Jonathan Edwards came on the scene emphasizing justification by faith and the sovereignty of God. From the moment of his landing in America Theodore Frelinghuysen had noticed this lack of emotional fervor in religion, and he spent most of his time ~~preah~~-{preach}ing against the formality and dead orthodozy that had permeated the Dutch churches in America. Such was the general religious situation when the new and highly emotional reaction set in which we know as the Great Awakening.

    A third factor which led to colonial revivalism was the awareness on the part of religious leaders of a breakdown in moral standards. During the latter years of the seventeenth century and the early years of the eighteenth century New England ministers on every hand were raising their voices against the immoral tendencies then existing. In 1688 Willian Stoughton stood before the Massachusetts legislature and said, "O what a sad metamorphasis hath of later years passed upon us in these churches and plantations! Alas! How is New England in danger to be buried in its own ruins." Increase Mather observed ten years later that "clear, sound conversions are not frequent. Many of the rising generation are profane Drunkards, Swearers, Licentious and Scoffers at the power of Godliness."[4]

* Ibid, p. 65

---

the conversional experience necessary to become full members—that is, "visible saints"—could be baptised by virtue of their parents' "half-way" status. The covenant engendered great theological debate. While adoption of the covenant undermined the "purity" of the community of visible saints, it also increased the size of congregations. The covenant also allowed church fathers to continue to exert ecclesiastical control over the majority of the Puritan community.

    3. William Warren Sweet, *The Story of Religion in America* (New York: Harper & Row, 1950), p. 65: "Thus there came to be more and more reliance upon the use of 'means' and less and less upon the miraculous power of God, which led to a cold and unemotional religion."

    4. Sweet, *Religion in Colonial America* (New York: Scribner, 1942), pp. 272–273: "A third factor which helped set the stage for colonial revivalism was the growing awareness on the part of the religious leaders of the decline of religion throughout the colonies. The sermons of the New England ministers during the latter years of the seventeenth and the early years of the eighteenth centuries are full of gloomy forebodings as to the future because of the low state of religion and public morals. 'O what a sad metamorphosis hath of later years passed upon us in these churches and plantations! Alas! How is New England in danger to be buried in its own ruins,' is the plaint of William Stoughton before the Massachusetts Legislature in 1668. Ten years later Increase

A survey of the subjects of sermons preached at this period also reveals the low state of religious life at that time. In 1700 Samuel Willard preached on "The Perils of the Times Displayed." In 1711 Stephen Buchingham preached from the theme, "The Unreasonableness and Danger of a People's Renouncing Their Subjection to God." In 1730 William Russell's theme was, "The Decay of Love to God in Churches, Offensive and Dangerous."*[5] These and many other subjects could be cited as examples of the uniform denunciation on the part of ministers of the religious conditions of their times. The times were ripe for a new emphasis in religion.[6]

*   I am indebted to Sweet for this list of sermons. See his, Religion In Colonial America, p. 273.

The Revival
in the Middle Colonies

Colonial Revivalism began in the Middle Colonies under the dynamic preaching of Theodore J. Frelinghuysen. He may properly be called the first outstanding revivalist. Frelinghuysen came to America in 1720 at the call of three congregations which had been formed among the Dutch settlers in central New Jersey. Religiously he found the people cold and unemotional with little desire beyond outward formalism. Being educated under pietistic influences, he naturally revolted against this prevelant trend. His first sermon was a call to an inner religion in contrast to conformity to outward religious duties. This passionate preaching soon brought a cleavage among Frelinghuysen's parishioners. On the one hand there were the well-to do whose only desire was to preserve the Dutch Church as a symbol of their Dutch nationality. On the other hand there were the poorer people and the younger generation who were quite in accord with the pietistic teachings of Frelinghuysen.

The conflict between these two parties became so

Mather observed that 'Clear, sound conversions are not frequent. Many of the rising generation are profane Drunkards, Swearers, Licentious and scoffers at the power of Godliness.' "

5. Sweet, *Religion in Colonial America*, p. 273: "A random survey of the subjects of the election sermons preached at this period show that almost all are of a piece in this respect—they were uniformly denunciatory of the religious conditions of their times. In 1700 Samuel Willard preached on 'The Perils of the Times Displayed'; in 1711 Stephen Buckingham's theme was 'The Unreasonableness and Danger of a People's Renouncing Their Subjection to God'; William Russell's subject in 1730 was 'The Decay of Love to God in Churches, Offensive and Dangerous.'"

6. Sweet, *Religion in Colonial America*, p. 273: "Times were ripe for some new emphasis in religion as well as a new type of religious leadership to meet the peculiar situation which the American colonies represented."

intensified that there were even reverberations in Holland. The group opposing Frelinghuysen soon took their complaints to Domine Boel, one of the Dutch collegiate ministers of New York, who labeled Frelinghuysen a heretic. But this did not at all silence the young domine. He continued to preach and even publish sermons defending his views. Converts continued to streem in, and finally Frelinghuysen was able to reach many of his former opposers. The height of this revival came in 1726 when the ingathering of new converts was particularly large. Frelinghuysen eventually came to the point of gaingin{ing} the support of the majority of Dutch ministers, although the division thus created in the Dutch Church was not healed until toward the end of the colonial period.

The Frelinghuysen revival among the Dutch in central New Jersey was highly significant in preparing the way for the next phase of the Middle Colony revival, that among the Scotch-Irish. The most influential figures in this phase of the revival were the graduates of William Tennent's "Log College" at ~~Nosaming~~ {Neshaminy} in Pennsylvania.

The Tennent family consisted of the father, William, and four sons, Gilbert, John, William, and Charles, all five able ministers of the gospel. The senior Tennent, although a powerful preacher, received his chief fame as an educator of young men for the Presbyterian ministry. His school was established primarily for the education of his own sons, but later other young men were admitted. It was not long before this school was derisively called "Log College" by Tennent's opponents, and as such it has passed into history. The classical training obtained at this institution was by no means of light quality. This fact is validated by the scholarly attainments of many of these men; but the chief distinction of these men was their evangelical zeal. Gradually Log College graduates were spreading over central Jersey, and they were preaching a militant revivalism which was sweeping the whole region.[7]

Giblert Tennent, who was educated for the ministry by his father, was destined to be the heart and

---

7. Sweet, *Religion in Colonial America*, p. 276: "Gradually a group of Log College men came to be settled over churches in central New Jersey, and under their preaching developed a militant revivalism which swept the whole region."

center of the revival movement among the Presbyterians. He was the most distinguished member of the noted Tennent family, and by all standards of measurement an able preacher. When he was called to the Presbyterian church at New Brunswick Domine Frelinghuysen was at the height of his revival, and the Dutch minister gave him a hearty welcome and encouraged his members to do the same.

The Scotch-Irish revival mounted high throughout the seventeen-thirites with new converts coming in on every hand. In 1738 the New Brunswick Presbytery was formed, made up of five evangelical ministers, three of whom were Log College men. The reason why these revivalists desired to be formed in a separate presbytery is not far to seek. It is to be noted that opposition to the revival began to manifest itself among the more conservative Presbyterian ministers who had received their training in Scottish universities. These men set out to block the progress of the revivalists by passing certain laws in the Synod requiring all candidates for ordination to present diplomas either from New England or European colleges. This law was obviously aimed at the revivalists, most of whom were Log College graduates. So it can now be seen that a separate presbytery was formed by the Log College men ~~of their own kind.~~ {in order that they might license and ordain men of their own kind.} John Rowland, a recent Log College graduate, was immediately licensed by the New Brunswick Presbytery, a challenge aimed at the conservatives.[8] Thus the Presbyterian ministers in New Jersey were soon divided into two parties, viz., "Old Side" and "New Side."

Such was the general situation among the Presbyterians in the middle colonies when George White-

---

8. Sweet, *Religion in Colonial America*, p. 276: "Throughout the seventeen-thirties the Scotch-Irish revival mounted higher and higher, and new congregations were formed as converts increased and new communities were reached. In 1738 the New Brunswick Presbytery was erected, made up of five evangelical ministers, three of whom were Log College men. The principal reason why the revivalists desired to be formed into a separate presbytery was that they might license and ordain men of their own kind. Meanwhile opposition to the revival began to manifest itself among the older ministers who had received their training in the Scottish universities. These men now sought to control the situation by the enactment of laws in the Synod requiring all candidates for ordination to present diplomas either from New England or European colleges. This enactment was obviously aimed at the revivalists. But at the very time this was happening, John Rowland, a recent Log College graduate, was licensed by the New Brunswick Presbytery, a challenge aimed at the conservatives."

field appeared on the American scene.[9] Landing at Lewes, Delaware, in August 1739, Whitefield immediately began his first American evangelistic tour.[10] One characteristic which he had on his arrival and which he retained throughout his life was a great catholic spirit. On his voyage to America he even lent his cabin to a Quaker preacher, who held meetings there.*[11] Also Whitefield was quite tolerant toward the Baptists, though he himself held the Episcopal theory of ordination and of the real presence of Christ in the elements of the Lord's Supper.† In England he freely collected money for the Lutherans of Georgia‡ and enjoyed fellowship with the Moravians, though they were not in full accord with his Calvinism.§[12] On one occasion, preaching from the balcony of the courthouse in Philadelphia, it is said that Whitefield cried out:[13] "Father Abraham, whom have you in Heaven? Any Episcopalians?' 'No.' 'Any Presbyterians?' 'No.' 'Have you any Independents or Seceders?' 'No.' 'Have you any Methodists?' 'No!' 'no!' no!!' 'Whom have you there?' 'We don't know these names here. All who are here are Christians—believers in Christ—men who have overcome by the blood of the Lamb and the word of his testimony.' 'Oh, is this the case? Thus{en} God help us, God help us all, to forget party names, and to become Christians in deed, and in truth."‖

The preaching ability of this moving spirit of the Great Awakening cannot be exaggerated. His reputation in this area had been established even before his appearance on the American shores. One of the colonial newspapers tells of the great concourse of people that filled the church of St. Mary Magdalene, London, long before the time of service and of sev-

* Whitefield, Journal, No. 5, p. 16.

† Ibid., No. 4, pp. 7, 12, 24.

‡ Ibid., No. 3, p. 7.

§ Ibid., No. 3, p. 97.

‖ Quoted from Sweet, The Story of Religion in America, p. 142.

---

9. Sweet, *Religion in Colonial America*, p. 276: "Such was the situation in central New Jersey when George Whitefield appeared on the American religious scene."

10. Sweet, *Religion in Colonial America*, p. 277: "Landing at Lewes, Delaware, in August 1739, Whitefield immediately began his first American evangelistic tour."

11. Charles Hartshorn Maxson, *The Great Awakening in the Middle Colonies* (Chicago: University of Chicago Press, 1920), p. 45: "On his voyage to America in 1739 he even lent his cabin to a Quaker preacher, who held meetings there."

12. Maxson, *Great Awakening*, p. 45: " . . . with Baptists, though he himself held the Episcopal theory of ordination and of the real presence of Christ in the elements of the Lord's Supper. In England he had collected money for the Lutherans of Georgia and enjoyed fellowship with the Moravians, but his Calvinism was a barrier to the fullest intercourse with them."

13. Sweet, *Story of Religion*, p. 141: "On one occasion, preaching from the balcony of the courthouse in Philadelphia, Whitefield cried out: . . . "

eral hundred persons in the street who in vain endeavored to force themselves into the church and past the constables stationed at the door to preserve the peace. Such was the mad desire to see and hear the eloquent youth who had volunteered to go to Georgia as a missionary.*[14] In speaking of the powerful delivery of Whitefield Tracy says, "Probably, in simply delivery, no man since Demosthenes, has ever surpassed Whitefield as a public orator."†

Whitefield arrived in Pennsylvania in the winter months of 1739. This was his first visit to the Northern Colonies. Great multitudes flocked to hear him. No building being sufficiently large to accomodate the people, he frequently preached from the gallery of the court house on Market Street. It was said that "his voice was distinctly heard on the Jersey shore, and so distinct was his speech that every word was understood on board of a shallop at Market Steet wharf, a distance of upwards of four hundred feet from the court house. All the intermediate space was crowded with his hearers."‡ During his visit at Philadelphia he had intercourse with members of the Society of Friends, and was treated very kindly by many of them. He speaks of them as honest, open-hearted, and true.§ The Presbyterian and Baptist ministers came to his lodgings to tell of their pleasure in hearing "Christ preached in the Church."

The most cherished intercourse that young Whitefield had on his visit to Philadelphia was that with the old gray-headed William Tennent, of Neshaming. Whitefield says in his journal that Tennent was a great friend of the Erskines, and just as they were hated by the judicatories of the Church of Scotland, and as his Methodist associates were dispised by their brethren of the Church of England, so too were Tennent and his sons treated by the majority of the synod. But just as surely as Elijah overcame the prophets of Baal, so would the few evangelicals overcome their opposers, thought Whitefield.|| The aged founder of the Log College had made the journey of twenty miles from Neshaming to hear this great spiritual leader, and the

* See Maxon, The Great Awakening in the Middle Colonies, p. 42.

† Joseph Tracy, "The Great Awakening," The Christian Review. September, 1844.

‡ Quoted from F. G. Beardsley, A History of American Revivals, p. 36.

§ Whitefield, Journal, No. 5, p. 47.

|| Ibid, p. 31.

14. Maxson, *Great Awakening*, pp. 41–42: "The *Virginia Gazette* tells of the great concourse of people that filled the church of St. Mary Magdalene, London, long before the time of service, and of several hundred persons in the street who in vain endeavored to force themselves into the church and past the constables stationed at the door to preserve the peace. Such was the mad desire to see and hear the eloquent youth who had volunteered to go to Georgia as a missionary."

result was an alliance between Whitefield and the New Brunswick Presbyterians.

After nine days at Philadelphia, Whitefield journeyed toward New York, preaching at Burlington, and at New Brunswick, the home of Gilbert Tennent. In New York Whitefield preached in the Presbyterian church, as well as in the fields where great throngs assembled. While in New York Whitefield had the opportunity of listening to a sermon preached by Gilbert Tennent in the Presbyterian church. Whitefield left convinced that he had never before heard such a searching discourse.* So deeply was he moved by the truth presented by his new friend that his own method of preaching was sensibly changed by his intercourse with the Tennents.

* Ibid, p. 35.

Journeying back to Philadelphia Whitefield accepted the previously given invitation of Jonathan Dickinson, Presbyterian pastor at Elizabethtown. In his sermon Whitefield preached against both ministers and people who contented themselves with a bare, speculative knowledge of the doctrines of grace, "never experiencing the power of them in their hearts."†

† Op. cit. {Ibid.,} p. 40)/

Coming again to New Brunswick the evangelist met several of the leaders of the evangelical movement in the Middle colonies. Among them was Domine Frelinghuysen, whom Whitefield called, the "beginner of the great work in these parts."‡ Another was John Cross, Presbyterian pastor of Basking Ridge. Still another was James Campbell, of Newtown, Pennsylvania. These men were greatly moved by the evangelical zeal of Whitefield.

‡ Ibid., p. 41.

Finally Whitefield reached Philadelphia after triumphs in three provinces. The enthusiasm of the people mounted higher and higher. It is estimated that his farewell congregation at Philadelphia numbered ten thousand.§[15] "After five stirring days he left Philadelphia, accompanied by one hundred and fifty horsemen, stopping and preaching at various points until he reached White Clay Creek, the home of Charles Tennent."‖

§ Maxon, The Great Awakening in the Middle Colonies, p. 52.

‖ Ibid., p. 52.

---

15. Maxson, *Great Awakening*, p. 52: "After these triumphs in three provinces Whitefield returned to Philadelphia. The enthusiasm of the people mounted higher and higher. It was estimated that his congregation at Germantown numbered five thousand people, and that his farewell sermon at Philadelphia had ten thousand hearers."

The year 1740 marks the high tide of the revival in the middle colonies. It was in this year that Gilbert Tennent preached his famous sermon on "Danger of an Unconverted Ministry." It was a terrible arraignment of men who enter the ministry as a trade, with no dynamic religious experience. Unconverted themselves, they were unconcerned, though many years passed without a conversion in their congregations.* Whitefield's preaching had touched all classes of people, including the deistic Franklin who became a life long admirer of the evangelist. The revival became exceedingly popular with the common people. But from the beginning the revival had aroused criticism, and unfortunately the revivalists were partly responsible for it because of their tendency to be censorious of those who did not agree with them.

Opposition to the revival among the Presbyterians came to a head at the meeting of the synod in 1740, when the evangelicals were excluded from membership in the synod by the conservatives. The evangelicals attempted to undo the action taken in 1741, but when this failed they formed, in 1745, the New York Synod at Elizabethtown, New Jersey. From this year until 1758 the Presbyterians in the colonies were divided into two distinct bodies. The evangelical or New Side party grew with rapid proportions, while the conservative or Old Side party made very little progress. At the time of the separation the Old Side numbered twenty-five ministers, while the New Side numbered twenty-two. In 1758 when the schism was healed the Old Side had decreased to but twenty-two, while the New Side had grown by leaps and bounds numbering seventy-two.†[16] "These years of separation mark the unmistakable triumph of the revival party within the Presbyterian Church."‡

The great revival in the middle colonies was quite influential in the rise of many educational institutions. Many graduates of William Tennent's Log College went out and established log colleges, or private schools, modeled after that of their Alma Mater. One such school founded on the model of the Log College was that established by Samuel Blair at Fogg's Manor

* Gilbert Tennent, The Danger of an Unconverted Ministry.

† Sweet, The Story of Religion in America, p. 143.

‡ Ibid., p. 143.

16. Sweet, *Story of Religion*, p. 143: "In 1758 at the time of the reunion the Old Side had decreased and numbered but twenty-two, while the New Side had grown by leaps and bounds and numbered seventy-two."

in Chester County, Pennsylvania. Another such school was that established at Nottingham, Pennsylvania, by Samuel Finley. Of greater importance than both of these was the establishment by the New York Synod of the College of New Jersey. This college was established in 1746 with Jonathan Dickinson as its first president. As the years passed by this institution became stronger and stronger. As Sweet succinctly states, "The College of New Jersey, as Princeton was called in its early years, admirably served the purpose of its founding and poured a stream of zealous young men into the ministry of the Presbyterian Church."* * ~~Op. cit.,~~ {Ibid.,} p. 145.

The founding of the University of Pennyslvania came indirectly out of the Great Awakening. When Whitefield first came to Philadelphia he was permitted to preach in the Established Church of the city, but on his later visits this was denied him, and it became necessary for him to preach on the courthouse steps. Finally Whitefield's friends conceived the idea of erecting a building to accommodate the great crowds who wished to hear him.[17] Benjamin Franklin, a great admirer of Whitefield, discribes the erection of the building thus: "Sufficient sums were soon received to procure the ground and erect the building, which was a hundred feet long, and seventy broad. Both house and ground were vested in trustees," of whom Franklin was one, "expressly for the use of any preacher of any religious persuasion, who might desire to say something to the people of Philadelphia."† † Ibid., p. 146.

It was here that Whitefield preached when he visited the city, and it was here that the Second Presbyterian Church of Philadelphia, of which Gilbert Tennent was pastor, worshiped for nine years. In 1753, largely through the efforts of Franklin, the building was chartered as the "College Academy and Charitable School of Philadelphis," which finally (1791) became the University of Pennsylvania.[18] Today there stands

---

17. Sweet, *Story of Religion*, p. 145: "The founding of the University of Pennsylvania came indirectly out of the Great Awakening. . . . At first [Whitefield] was permitted to preach in the Established Church in that city, but on his later visits this was denied him, and it became necessary for him to preach in the fields or from the courthouse steps. Finally Whitefield's Philadelphia friends conceived the idea of erecting a building to accommodate the great crowds who wished to hear him."

18. Sweet, *Story of Religion*, p. 146: "In 1751, largely through the efforts of Franklin, the building was used for an academy, and two years later it was chartered as the 'College, Academy and Charitable School of Philadelphia,' which finally (1791) grew into the University of Pennsylvania."

in one of the quadrangles of that great university a life-size statue of George Whitefield.

The Great Awakening In New England

At the center of the Great New England Awaken~ign~{ng} stands Jonathan Edwards, the minister of the church at Northampton. Edwards was called to the church at Northampton as a young man, fresh from graduate study and a tutorship at Yale, there he became the colleague and ultimately the successor of his grandfather, Solomon Stoddard. Northampton was a prosperous, intelligent and growing community of some two hundred families. The church was famed in New England for its long history of spiritual vigor. The church and the community at this time, however, was going through a state of religious and spiritual decline. Because of this it became Edward's purpose to foster a warmer and deeper piety, and to redeem the community from its moral laxity. With a tremendous earnestness combined with "an almost oriental fertility of imagination, and intellectual acumen," Edwards set out to do this job, and at the end of the winter of 1734–1735 "there was scarcely a single person in the town, old or young, left unconcerned about the great things of the eternal world."* Beginning with a single young woman prominent ~amont~ {among} the "social company keepers" of the town, it overspread the community, until, when spring-time came, this little village of two hundred families sheltered "three hundred souls savingly brought home to Christ."† From Northampton this movement spread like wild fire in all directions, to South Hadley, Suffield, Sunderland, Deerfield, Hatfield, West Springfield, Long-meadow, Enfield, Springfield and Hadley.‡

From the beginning Edwards preached sermons on justification by faith, the justice of God in the damnation of sinners, and the excellency of Christ. In these sermons the doctrine of the sovereignity of God was strongly emphasized. Through Adam's fall man had lost the divine image and was therefore unable to make any move toward God; only God could make the move. Man has the rational power to turn to God, but he lacks the moral power. God is under no obligation to save anyone. However special grace is communicated to such as he has chosen to salvation; all others are left to die in their sins. Satisfaction must be

* Edwards "Works," Vol. IV, p. 23.

† ~Op. cit.,~ {Ibid.,} pp. 18, 28.

‡ Edwards, "Thoughts on Revivals," p. 148.

made for the sins of those who are foreordained to salvation. Such satisfaction was made in the vicarious sacrifice on the cross by Jesus Christ. Such in brief were the elements of Edward's theology. The influence of such doctrines upon the minds of those who had contented themselves with a barren morality can better be imagined than described.

Edwards' method of arousing the sinner was quite different from that of most revivalists. He was never an extemporaneous preacher. He always took his entire manuscript into the pulpit, and his eye never seemed to rest upon his audience, but flashed continually from his manuscript to the opposite wall. However with these strange personal characteristics there was an extraordinary power of fascination in him. In speaking of the amazing power of Edwards Davenport says, "By dint of prodigious intellectual strength, by the wonderfully vivid imaging forth of premises which seem absurd to us but were as fundamental to his auditors as their own being, by the masterly marshalling of terrible argument, he wrought out an appeal to the fears of his hearers which stirred them to the very depths of their souls. They wept, they turned pale, they cried aloud. Some fainted, some fell into convulsions, some suffered thereafter from impaired health and some lost their reason."* Chapell has this to say of Edwards' sermons: "Under the spell of those powerful sermons time and place were all swallowed up in the terrible realities of the eternal world. Once when he preached on the judgment some of his auditors really expected to see the Lord coming in the clouds as soon as the sermon closed. And when he preached at Enfield his famous sermon entitled, "Sinners in the Hands of an Angry God," from the graphic text, "Their feet shall slide in due time," such was the influence upon the congregation, which had assembled in a careless mood, that some of them actually caught hold of the benches to save themselves from slipping into hell."† It was this powerful preaching which was responsible for more than three hundred professed conversions in the first year of the revival in Northampton. About May 1735 the excitement began to die down, probably because the "physical power to endure excitement was exhausted." But in 1740 the revival reappeared, not only in the Northampton vicinity, but in almost every church throughout New England.

346 Whitefield arrived on the shores of New England in this heated year, 1740. He was accepted with a deal

* Davenport, Primitive Traits in Religious Revivals, p. 108.

† Chapell, The Great Awakening, p. 56.

of enthusiasm. Newport and Boston gave him an immense hearing. The students at Harvard heard him gladly "and under the spell of his matchless oratory men wept, women fainted and hundreds professed conversion."* [19] Leaving Boston in October, Whitefield journeyed toward Northampton, and there he met Jonathon Edwards. Edwards was delighted to have him visit Northampton, and himself sat in his own pulpit weeping like a child, as that matchless preacher swayed with his burning pathos the numerous auditors.

Gilbert Tennent also came up from New Jersey and preached with great emotional fervor throughout southern Massachusetts and Connecticut. Later came James Davenport of Long Island, who "more than any other man . . . embodied in himself and promoted in others, all the unsafe extravagances into which the revival was running," and who declared "that most of the ministers of the town of Boston and of the country are unconverted, and are leading their people blindfold to hell." [20]

The New England revival ended with great success in numerical terms. During the years from 1740 to 1742 there were between 25,000 to 50,000 out of a total population of 300,000 added to the church.† Testimonies of moral changes were heard throughout the colonies and there is no doubt but that the whole moral and religious life of New England was raised to a higher plane. [21]

† Ibid, p. 133.

The Revival In
The Southern Colonies

In the south the revival did not commence until 1743, and in Virginia the work was carried on prin-

---

19. Sweet, *Story of Religion*, p. 132: "Everywhere he was received with enthusiasm. Newport and Boston gave him an immense hearing. The students at Harvard heard him and under the spell of his matchless oratory men wept, women fainted and hundreds professed conversion."

20. Sweet, *Story of Religion*, p. 133: "Such a minister was James Davenport of Long Island, who 'more than any other man . . . embodied in himself and promoted in others, all the unsafe extravagances into which the revival was running,' and who declared 'that most of the ministers of the town of Boston and of the country are unconverted, and are leading their people blindfold to hell'" (ellipses in original).

21. Sweet, *Story of Religion*, p. 133: "During the years from 1740 to 1742 there was a wonderful ingathering of members into the New England churches. Out of a population of 300,000, from 25,000 to 50,000 were added. . . . Similar testimonies of moral changes in other communities are numerous and there is no doubt but that the whole moral and religious life of New England was raised to a higher plane."

cipally by laymen in the face of more or less opposition from the Established Church. Here and there throughout the province were to be found men and women hungering for the bread of life, who had become dissatisfied with the abuses of the church.

At Hanover there were a group of such who had been moved greatly by the preaching of Whitefield at Williamsburg in 1740. During the year 1743, Mr. Samuel Morris, one of their number came into possession of a small volume of Whitefield's sermons and a few of Luther's books. Morris invited his neighbors to his home and read them in their hearing. Week after week they met together in one another's houses where these books were read. Finally, the group grew so large that no ordinary house could accommodate them, and special houses were built, the first such building being called Morris's Reading House.* Thus the revival was propagated with spiritual quickening throughout the region. At length there were visits made by Rev. William Robinson, a graduate of the "Log College," who devoted his labors to the neglected districts among the new settlements of Pennsylvania, Virginia and North Carolina. Under his ministrations many were converted and the revival was given a fresh impetus.

This in brief is the rise of Presbyterianism in Virginia. From time to time brief visits were made to this region by other outstanding ministers, among whom were Revs. Gilbert Tennent, Samuel Finley, William Tennent, Samuel Blair, and finally the noted evangelist George Whitefield.† These men were highly accepted and their coming was followed by many converts. But persecutions and seasons awaited them. They were brought into conflict with civil authority and harassed in many ways. In the face of all this embarrassment, the feeble companies of believers grew and churches multiplied, until at length Samuel Davies came to them to minister permanently. Within a short time, through his influence, the churches grew by leaps and bounds. The people were very happy to see Mr. Davies come to their colony, and with tones of joy they exclaimed: "How joyfully were we surprised before the next Sabbath, when we unexpectedly heard that Mr. Davis was come to preach so long among us; and especially, that he had qualified himself according to law, and obtained the licensure of four meetinghous{es} among us, which had never been done before! Thus, when our hopes were expiring, and our liberties more precarious than ever, we

* Ibid, p. 148.

† F. G. Beardsley, A History of American Revivals, p. 46.

were suddenly advanced to a more secure situation. Man's extremity is the Lord's opportunity. For this seasonable instance of this interposition of divine providence, we desire to offer our grateful praises; and we importune the friends of Zion generously to concur in the delightful employ."*

* Quoted in Tracy, The
Great Awakening, p. 384.

Such was the rise of Presbyterianism in Virginia. Notwithstanding many troubles from the partisans of the Church of England, who had the government of the colony in their hands, Presbyterianism continued to gain strength, and the work went forward with uninterrupted success until the commencement of the Revolutionary struggle.

Just five years previous to Samuel Davies' departure from Virginia two separate Baptist preachers, Shubal Stearns and Daniel Marshall, had come down from Connecticut with their families and had settled in Berkeley county (in what is now West Virginia). Both had been converted by Whitefield's preaching and they brought with them the spiritual fervor of the master revivalist. Both had been congregationalists, but soon became convinced of the validity of the Baptist view. Although neither of these revivalist had had a formal education, they were men of great natural ability and good common sense. There were already several congregations of Regular Baptists in Virginia, but they were by no means sympathetic with the revivalistic tendencies of Stearns and Marshall. However the coming of these two separate Baptists into the Southern Colonies marks the beginning of a new phase in the development of the Great Awakening.[22]

Sandy Creek became the living center of the Separate Baptist as Hanover had become the center of Presbytarianism in the Southern Colonies. From a church of sixteen members formed by Stearns and Marshell families at Sandy Creek, the congregation

---

22. Sweet, *Religion in Colonial America*, pp. 301–302: "Just five years previous to Samuel Davies' departure from Virginia two Separate Baptist preachers from Connecticut, Shubal Stearns and Daniel Marshall, settled with their families on Opeguoin Creek in Berkeley county, in what is now West Virginia. Both had been converted under Whitefield's preaching and they brought with them the fervor and spirit of that master revivalist. Both had originally had been Congregationalists, but having become convinced of the futility of infant baptism they withdrew and joined the Baptists. Neither had had the advantage of a formal education, but they were men of superior natural ability and sound judgment. There were already several congregations of *Regular* Baptists in Virginia, but Stearns and Marshall soon found that they were out of sympathy with their revivalistic preaching. . . . The coming of these representatives of the revivalistic Baptists into the Southern Colonies marks the beginning of a new phase in the development of the Great Awakening."

grew within a relative short time to more than six hundred.*[23] One of the things that made the Separate Baptist so popular with the masses was their novel type of preaching, appealing primarily to the emotions. The Presbyterians with their educated ministry had failed to reach the great mass of people, but the Separate Baptist with their uneducated and unsalaried ministry were well suited to the needs of the lower social and economic classes. Extreme emotional revivalism has always been more successful among people of little education than among people of higher educational attainments. The presence of even a few people of high educational attainments will tend to restrain emotionalism to a great degree.[24] This is why Presbyterians were always less overtly emotional than Baptists.†[25]

From the beginning the revivalistic Baptists were a despised people. "The strange mannerisms of their preachers, their odd whoops and whinning tones together with their emotional extravagances aroused digust and contempt."‡ One man is reported to have said that, "he had rather go to hell than be obliged to hear a Baptist in order to go to heaven." But all of this did not stop the growth of the Baptist. After 1770 the growth of Separate Baptist was astounding. In 1771 at the first Baptist Association in Virginia there were fourteen churches and 1335 members. Two years later the number of churches had increased and the total membership had increased to more than four thousand.§

Another phase of southern revivalism was the Methodist phase. This phase gained impetue mainly through Devereux Jarratt and lay preachers sent to America by Wesley. Because of Jarratt's cooperation

* Sweet, Religion In Colonial America, p. 303.

† This is the thesis of F. M. Davenport. See his, Primitive Traits in Religious Revivals, Chapter I

‡ Sweet, Religion In Colonial America, p. 304.

§ Ibid, p. 304.

---

23. Sweet, *Religion in Colonial America*, p. 303: "As Hanover county was the center of an expanding Presbyterianism in the Southern Colonies, so Sandy Creek became the living center of the Separate Baptists. From a church of sixteen members formed by the Stearns and Marshall families at Sandy Creek, the congregation grew within a relatively short time to more than six hundred."

24. Sweet, *Religion in Colonial America*, p. 302: "The Presbyterians with their educated ministry and elaborate creedal demands had failed to reach the great mass of the plain people. The *Separate* Baptists, however, with their uneducated and unsalaried ministry, their novel type of preaching, appealing primarily to the emotions, were well suited to the needs and mental capacities of the lower social and economic classes. Extreme emotional revivalism always has succeeded best among people of little education. But the presence of even a few people of higher educational attainments will tend to restrain the emotionalism of a large concourse of the less educated."

25. Sweet cited the source of this argument to "F. M. Davenport, *Primitive Traits in Religious Revivals, A Study in Mental and Social Evolution*, New York: 1905, Chapter I."

with the Methodist lay preachers Methodism grew more rapidly in Virginia than anywhere else in America. In 1775 Jarratt accompanied Thomas Rankin, Wesley's assistant in America, on a preaching tour of the southern colonies and into North Carolina. They preached to great crowds of people under trees and in "preaching houses. So great was the demand for preaching that Rankin speaks of preaching almost to the point of exhaustion. Jesse Lee, who was an eye witness to many of the revival scenes states: "In almost every assembly might be seen signal instances of divine power; more especially in the meetings of the classes . . . Many who had long neglected the means of grece now flocked to hear . . . This outpouring of the spirit extended itself more or less, through most of the circuits, which takes in a circumference of between four and five hundred miles."*

* Jesse Lee, A Short History of the Methodists, pp. 55, 56.

The results of the revival are reflected in the statistics of the Virginia and North Carolina circuits. In 1774 there were only two circuits in the region, with a combined membership of 291; in 1776 the number of circuits had increased tremendously, with one circuit alone reporting 1,611 members. The following year there were six circuits with a combined membership of 4,379. In this same year the number of Methodists throughout all America was 6,968, which meant that two-thirds of all the Methodists in the colonies were found in Devereux Jarratt's parish.†[26] Such was the rise of Methodism in Virginia.

† Sweet, The Story of Religion in America, p. 154.

The Results of
The Great Awakening

Having given a brief outling of the facts of the Great Awakening it now remains for me to sum up the results of this great movement. The chief value of a revival of religion is seen in its permanent results, that which lives on long after the first excitement has passed away. Bearing this in mind, let us see what were the results of the Great Awakening.

---

26. Sweet, *Story of Religion*, p. 154: "The results of the revival are reflected in the statistics of the Virginia and North Carolina circuits. In 1774 there were but two circuits in the region, with a combined membership of 291; the following year there were 3 circuits with a membership of 935; in 1776 the number of circuits had increased, the Brunswich circuit alone reporting 1,611 members. The following year there were 6 circuits with a combined membership of 4,379. In this year the number of Methodists in America totaled 6,968, which meant two-thirds of all the Methodists in the colonies were found in the vicinity of Devereux Jarratt's parish, a fact which would seem to indicate that this region was the cradle of American Methodism."

First it must be admitted that Church membership was greatly increased with the coming of the Great Awakening. Moreover, the practical influence of Christianity upon colonial society was greatly strengthened. To give an exact figure of the number of individuals converted during the revival would be quite impossible. However various estimates have been made. Careful historians have estimated that from 25,000 to 50,000 were added to the churches of New England in consequence of the Awakening.* Now the population of the New England colonies in 1750 was 340,000. Assuming the smaller number of additions, which is a conservative estimate, to be correct, more than seven per cent of the entire population of these colonies would have been gathered into the churches as a direct result of the revival. A national awakening of similar power at the present time would result in the ingathering of more than nine million souls.

* Tracy, op. cit., p. 388

The increase in the Presbyterian and Baptist churches was proportionately larger. From 1740 to 1760 the number of Presbyterian ministers in American Colonies had increased from 45 to over 100. During this same period the Baptist churches in New England alone increased from 21 to 79.† These and many other figures could be cited to show the numerical results of the Great Awakening. This movement, like a tidal wave swept over the colonies, and gathered multitudes into the church of God.

† Beardsley, op. cit., p. 64.

A second result of the Great Awakening was a Quickening along Missionary and Educational Lines. At this time there came a great concern for Indians and Negroes and underprivileged people in general. Out of this movement was forged the framework of the first anti-slavery impulse in America.‡

‡ Sweet, Religion in Colonial America, p. 317.

The Great Awakening was conducted chiefly by men of education, "and it has left its decided record and invaluable monuments in the way of institutions of learning and religious literature." We have shown above how the College of New Jersey and the Theological Seminary at Princeton grew out of Tennent's Log College at Neshaming. Harvard and Yale received a great impulse from the revival, though they at first set themselves against it. Dartmouth College, in New Hampshire, was a direct outgrowth of the Great Awakening. Brown University, at Providence, the parent of Baptist colleges, was founded during the Great Awakening. Rev. Chapell was quite right when he stated, "many of the colleges and seminaries of the present day largely owe their existence, or their influence as healthful fountains of truth, directly to the Great Awakening."*

* Chapell, op. cit., p. 135.

A third Result of the Great Awakening was its influence upon Religious and Political Liberty. In New England, excepting the colony of Rhode Island, Congregationalism was established by law. In New York, Virginia and the South, Episcopalianism was the established religion. With the coming of the Awakening and the expansion of newer denominations the way was paved for the tolerance of conflicting opinions and a broader conception of liberty of conscience.

Only indirectly did the Great Awakening affect the political liberties of the colonies. But this indirect influence cannot be overlooked. As Dr. Beardsley has laconically stated: "The religious convictions of the American people, which so largely were called into being through the revival, served as a balance to the political revolution which resulted in independence and prevented it from being hurled into the vortex of anarchy and ruin, in which the French Revolution was swallowed up."†

† Beardsley, op. cit., p. 69.

BIBLIOGRAPHY

F. G. Beardsley, A History of American Revivals, (New York, 1904).

Warren A Candler, Great Revivals and the Great Republic, (Nashville, 1904).

F. L. Chapell, The Great Awakening of 1740, American Baptist Publication Society, 1903.

F. M. Davenport, Primitive Traits in Religious Revival (New York, 1906).

Serens E. Dwight, The Life of President Edwards, (New York, 1830).

Jesse Lee, A Short History of the Methodists, in the United States of America, etc. (Baltimore, 1810).

Charles H. Maxson, The Great Awakening in the Middle Colonies (Chicago, 1920).

W. W. Sweet, Religion In Colonial America (New York, 1949).

W. W. Sweet, The Story of Religion in America (New York, 1930).

Joseph Tracy, A History of the Revival of Religion in the Time of Edwards and Whitefield (Boston, 1842).

George Whitefield, Journals

THDS. MLKP-MBU: Box 112, folder 14.

Crozer Theological Seminary
Placement Committee:
Confidential Evaluation of
Martin Luther King, Jr.,
by Morton Scott Enslin

21 November 1950
Chester, Pa.

A very able man. All is grist that comes to his mill. Hard working, fertile minded, rarely misses anything which he can subsequently use. He will probably become a big strong man among his people. Inclined at times to "put on the [*rousers?*]," but I pray that that will not hinder him any in the field he is likely to serve.

AFmS. CRO-NRCR.

Book Review of *A Functional Approach
to Religious Education* by Ernest J. Chave

[*12 September–22 November 1950*]
[*Chester, Pa.*]

King took Davis's course the Religious Development of Personality during the first term of his final year at Crozer. Davis required his students to review five books and offer their "critical reaction to them"; he advised the students: "Do not give back the content of the books."[1] *King chose books on the early stages of personality development, reflecting the course's concentration on the development of religious experience in children. In this first review, he agrees with the author, Ernest Chave, on the importance of a religion informed by scientific insight and discipline, echoing previous comments King had made in other Crozer and Morehouse papers. He finds fault, however, with Chave's implicit humanism, realizing that "I guess I am a little more conservative theologically than I thought I was. Somehow I cannot stop with nature, [for] Christianity to me is a revelation of the nature of nature." Although Davis did not grade the book reviews, he remarked: "This is a good review and the type I believe helpful to the reviewer as well as the reader." He suggested that "for your future use, you should give complete bibliographical details in listing date, author, etc."*

Baron Friedrich Von Hugel. the Roman Catholic interpreter of religion, always said everything he could in praise of a book he was reviewing be-

---

1. King, Class notes, Religious Development of Personality, 12 September–22 November 1950, MLKP-MBU: Box 106, folder 22.

fore he went on to indicate the errors or inadequacies in the volume.[2] We may well follow his example in our consideration of a most interesting book by Dr. Ernest J. Chave entitled, <u>A Functional Approach to Religious Education</u>.

First I think Dr. Chave is quite right in insisting that if religious education is to be meaningful to the modern world it must keep pace with the deepening insights of world thought and keep abreast with the problems of a changing culture. It is at this point that much of our religious education has failed miserably. We to often attempt to indoctrinate young people with outmoulded and unscientific ideas. The young person who goes to school today is taught to be analytical, objective, and scientific; he is taught not to swallow the apple whole, but to chew and digest. In the words of Bacon, he is taught "to weigh and consider." Such modern minds will find it quite difficult to reconcile the unscientific tenets of general education. If religion is to be meaningful to modern man it must be scientifically tenable and intellectually respectable.

Again Dr. Chave strikes a significant note when he speaks of religious education as "the total comprehensive plan by which leaders in all realms of life co-operate to farther the growth of personal-social values and attainments."[3] No one can hardly disagree with the fact that religious education is more than a Sunday affair.[4] It is foolosh to think that an hour of teaching, or preaching, once a week can release the latent spiritual capacities in ones being.[5] Chave is quite emphatic at this point and any well thinking will agree with him.

I was also quite interested in the ten experiences which Chave listed as basic in religious growth.[6] As I read them I could not help from applying them to my own religious development. Certainly educators of all shades of opinion will be in debt to Chave for this analysis of religious development and growth.

Up to this point I have {found} myself in perfect agreement with our author, but this is not the whole story. I find myself parting company with Chave in many instances. I cannot quite accept his extreme naturalistic point of view.[7] I guess I am a little more conservative theologically than I thought I was. Somehow I cannot stop with nature, far Christianity to me is a revelation of the nature of nature. However I am quite sure that Chave found it quite easy to set forth his naturalistic point of view after being in the company of Henry Nelson Wieman for a number of years.

---

2. Davis wrote in the margin, "Good idea! Not only in book reviewing!"

3. Chave's text uses "further," not "farther" (Ernest J. Chave, *A Functional Approach to Religious Education* [Chicago: University of Chicago Press, 1947], p. 6).

4. Davis wrote in the margin, "True."

5. Chave, *Functional Approach*, p. 6: "It is foolish to think that an hour of teaching, or preaching, once a week can transform human nature or release divine powers."

6. Chave's ten experiences are sense of worth, social sensitivity, appreciation of the universe, discrimination in values, responsibility and accountability, cooperative fellowship, quest for truth and realization of values, integration of experiences into a working philosophy of life, appreciation of historical continuity, and participation in group celebrations (Chave, *Functional Approach*, p. 22).

7. Davis commented in the margin, "As far as I am concerned, I agree!"

Does not the functional approach in this book almost border on the lines of humanism.? I think it does.[8] It is not an explicit humanism, but certainly it is implicit.[9] And here again I must part company with Chave. Children must be taught that when they pray they are not merely talking to themselves to bring about a psychological change within, but that they are praying to a being that has objective validity.[10] If religious education is to really be <u>functional</u> it must teach the child that he is dependent on a power greater than himself, which in religious terms is God.

Again it se[e]ms that Chave is so absorbed in the general phase of his functional approach that he forgets the particulars on which religious education is grounded. Theologically speaking he fails to see the necessity of delving into the depths of the Christian tradition.[11] This, he would argue, leads to indoctrination. (Of course he fails to see that the functional approach can also lead to indoctrination)[12] Chave talks so much of an approach to religious education that will transcend dogmas, creeds and religions that he forgets the distinctive elements of the Christian religion, viz., a Book and a Man.

Nevertheless, I must confess that Chave has taken a great venture in setting forth this functional approach to religious education. He writes with enthusiasm and zeal. Even though I parted company with him on many points, I was kept spellbound throughout the book.[13]

THD. MLKP-MBU: Box 113, folder 30.

---

8. Davis wrote in the margin, "You are correct."

9. Chave anticipated this criticism: "[I indict] any attempt to classify this functional approach as either humanistic or theistic; for these terms are too vague to make a meaningful dilemma" (Chave, *Functional Approach,* p. v).

10. Davis wrote in the margin, "Good!"

11. Davis wrote in the margin and on the reverse, "He would disagree. He'd point out historical continuity. Chave prides himself on being able to preach his message with unvarnish, as it were, to people of all theological complexions. Chave would chafe (terrible pun, isn't it?) under your criticism."

12. Davis wrote in the margin, "True."

13. Davis circled "spellbound" and noted, "Isn't this a bit strong?"

Book Review of *Personality, Its Study and Hygiene* by Winifred V. Richmond

[*12 September–22 November 1950*]
[*Chester, Pa.*]

In this ungraded review for Davis's Religious Development of Personality course, King discusses his positive reactions to the theories of Sigmund Freud and John Watson.[1] *He notes that "this is the first time that I was able to read the psychologies of Freud and John Watson with a degree of objectivity" and admits that "I have been somewhat converted to many of their theories." Davis remarked: "This is an excellent review. It is exactly the type I desire. It shows a basic understanding of the volume and your reactions to it. The questions you raise concerning personality development can be asked about any area of psychological inquiry. Have you ever explored the field of 'learning'?"*

Personality, Its Study and Hygiene, by Winifred V. Richmond, New York, Farrar & Rinehart, 1937

After reading about two hundred pages of Gardner Murphy's definitive work on personality, I turned to this work by Winifred Richmond with the sole purpose of clarifying some of the complex ideas and terminology found in the former work.[2] After reading a few pages of Richmond's work I became so enamored of it that I read the whole book. I guess I had certain predilections for Richmond's book because of the simplified manner in which it was presented. Richmond has the rare ability of taking the basic theories of psychological research and presented them in a manner readable to the laymen.[3] The work by Gardner Murphy, although elaborate and probably the most authoritative work in the field of personality, is written for the expert not the laymen. I was somewhat attracted by his chapter on "Heredity and Individual Growth," but other than that I was often lost behind the dim fog of psychological obscurities. (Am I just dumb)[4]

One of the greatest influences that Richmond's book made on me was the deeper insight it gave me into psychological theories that I heretofore scorned. Richmond does a marvelous job in presenting the variour theories of personality development, and although he never sets forth his personal theory, he is quite convincing. For an instance, this is the first time that I was able to read the psychologies of Freud and John Watson with a degree of objectivity. I had read Joshua Liebman's Peace of Mind,[5] and even he was

---

1. John Broadus Watson (1878–1958) began a new school of psychology, behaviorism, with his 1913 article entitled "Psychology as a Behaviorist Views It."
2. Gardner Murphy, *Personality: A Biosocial Approach to Origins and Structure* (New York: Harper & Brothers, 1947).
3. Davis wrote in the margin, "Very interesting comment."
4. Davis answered, "I think not."
5. Joshua Loth Liebman, *Peace of Mind* (New York: Simon & Schuster, 1946).

unable to convince me that there was any truth in Freud.[6] But now I am convinced. It is probably true to say that the basic facts of Freud and Watson are correct, notwithstanding the fact that their bais had conditioned what they observed. I am now willing to admit that they discovered new continents and new areas that had for centuries been overlooked. No one can observe human personality objectively without admitting the truth of many Freudian and Watsonian theories. (Most of us read them with a religious bias as I did in years gone by). I could point out many examples, too numerous to cite in this brief review, of personality traits which are quite in accord with Freudian and Watsonian analysis. This is not to imply that my reading of this book has caused me to accept all of Freud and all of Watson. (I am to much of a religionist for that) I think that much in Freud and Watson which seems to be facts will turn out on examination to be interpretations. Moreover, I am perfectly willing to admit that Freud and Watson didn't go far enough. For an instance, Watson comes to some amazing facts in describing the patterns of behavior of a human organism, but to say that this is describing the person himself is to me a one sided generalization.[7] Man transcends his behavior, if for no other reason than the [strikeout illegible] fact that he knows what he is doing. No matter how completely men succeed in describing all of the patterns of change in the human nervous system, there will remain completely untouched another process which may be called mind or consciousness or the self, and which can be observed only by introspection. This Watson would not accept and similar generalizations can be found in Freud.

From the above discussion one is likely to get the impression that Richmond only adduced the theories of Freud and Watson in personality development. This is by no means the case, but it so happens that my previous disdain for Freud and Watson causes me to spend more time on them. (especially since I have been somewhat converted to many of their theories) Jung and Adler were given quite a bit of attention in Richmond's book, but it so happens that I have always has certain predilections for their theories over against those of Freud and Watson, for this reason I have not said much about them.

As I came to the end of Richmond's book many questions pertaining to the validity of psychological analysis arose in my mind. What theory of personality development is correct? Can psychology be an objective science? These questions inevitably arise because of the diverse theories of personality development. There are at least four different schools of modern psychology with totally different approaches to the problem of personality development, and even some psychologists within the same school differ among themselves. For an instance, Adler, Jung and Freud have totally different approaches to psychoanalysis, albeit they are within the same school. May we not conclude that we have a long way to go in this whole area of the psychological analysis of personality development.

THD. MLKP-MBU: Box 115, folder 30.

---

6. Davis remarked, "That's something."
7. Davis wrote, "I agree."

"An Autobiography of Religious Development"

[*12 September–22 November 1950*]
[*Chester, Pa.*]

*In this revealing essay written for Davis's course the Religious Development of
Personality, King reviews the influences of his family and church on his religious
beliefs. King's essay reflects Davis's emphasis on the experiences of childhood and
adolescence. King recalls a nurturing family life—closely interwoven with
activities in his father's church—which conditioned him to be optimistic about
human nature. "It is quite easy for me to think of a God of love," King writes,
"mainly because I grew up in a family where love was central and where lovely
relationships were ever present." King relates seminal events in his religious
development, including his baptism into the church and his call to the ministry
while in college. He attributes the decision to become a minister to his father's
"noble example"; despite their theological differences, King retains his "admiration
for a real father." He also recounts two formative experiences: the shock of a
childhood confrontation with racism and the death of his grandmother. Davis
marked the paper "Excellent."*

My birthplace was Atlanta Georgia, the capital of the state and the so-called
"gate-way to the south." I was born in the late twenties on the verge of the
great depression, which was to spread its disastrous arms into every corner of
this nation for over a decade. I was much too young to remember the beginning of this depression, but I do recall how I questioned my parent about the
numerous people standing in bread lines when I was about five years of age.
I can see the effects of this early childhood experience on my present anti
capitalistic feelings.

I was the second child of a family of three children, having one brother and
one sister. Because of {our} relative closeness of ages we all grew up together,
and to this day there still exist that intimate relationship which existed between
us in childhood. Our parents themselves were very intimate, and they always
maintained an intimate relationship with us. In our immediate family there
was also a saintly grandmother (my mother's mother) whose husband had
died when I was one years old. She was {very} dear to each of us, but especially
to me. I sometimes think that I was his favorite grandchild. I can remember
very vividly how she spent many evenings telling us interesting stories.

From the very beginning I was an extraordinarily healthy child. It is said that
at my birth the doctors pronounced me a one hundred percent perfect child,
from a physical point of view. Even today this physical harmony still abides,
in that I hardly know how an ill moment feels. I guess the same thing would
apply to my mental life. I have always been ~~somewh~~ somewhat precocious,
both physically and mentally. My I.Q. stands somewhat above the average. So
it seems that from a hereditary point of view nature was very kind to me.[1]

---

1. Davis wrote in the margin, "Good! I like a man who has an intelligent evaluation of his
abilities."

The same applies to my environment. I was born in a very congenial home situation. My parents have always lived together very intimately, and I can hardly remember a time that they ever argued (My father happens to be the kind who just wont argue), or had any great fall out. I have never experienced the feeling of not having the basic necessities of life. These things were always provided by a father who always put his family first. My father has alway been a real father. This is not to say that I was born with a silver spoon in my mouth; far from it. My father has never made more than an ordinary salary, but the secret is that he knows the art of saving and budgeting. He never wastes his money at the expense of his family. He has always had sense enough not to live beyond his means. So for this reason He has been able to provide us with the basic necessities of life with little strain. For the past three years he has had the tremendous responsibility of keeping all of us in school, (my brother in college, my sister in graduate school, and me in the Seminary) and although it has been somewhat a burden from a financial angle, he has done it with a smile. Our mother has also been behind the scene setting forth those motherly cares, the lack of which leaves a missing link in life.

The community in which I was born was quite ordinary in terms of social status. No one in our community had attained any great wealth. Most of the Negroes in my home town who had attained wealth lived in a section of town known as "Hunter Hills." The community in which I was born was characterized with a sought of unsophisticated simplicity. No one in our community was in the extremely poor class. This community was not the slum district. It is probably fair to class the people of this community as those of average income. Yet I insist that this was a wholesome community, notwithstanding the fact that none of us were ever considered member of the "upper upper class." Crime was at a minimum in our community, and most of our neighbors were deeply religious. I can well remember that all of my childhood playmates were regular Sunday School goers, not that I chose them on that basis, but because it was very difficult to find playmates in my community who did not attend Sunday School.

I was exposed to the best educational conditions in my childhood. At three I entered nursery school. This great childhood contact had a tremendous effect on the development of my personality. At five I entered kindergarten and there I remained for one year until I entered the first grade.

One may ask at this point, why discuss such factors as the above in a paper dealing with ones religious development? The answer to this question lies in the fact that the above factors were highly significant in determining my religious attitudes.[2] It is quite easy for me to think of a God of love mainly because I grew up in a family where love was central and where lovely relationships were ever present. It is quite easy for me to think of the universe as basically friendly mainly because of my uplifting hereditary and environmental circumstances. It is quite easy for me to lean more toward optimism than pessimism about human nature mainly because of my childhood experiences. It is impossible to get at the roots of ones religious attitudes without taking in

2. Davis agreed: "Correct!"

account the psychological and historical factors that play upon the individual.[3]
So that the above biographical factors are absolutely necessary in understanding my religious development.

Now for a more specific phase of my religious development. It was at the age of five that I joined the church. I well remember how this event occurred. Our church was in the midst of the spring revival, and a guest evangelist had come down from Virginia.[4] On Sunday morning the guest evangelist came into our Sunday School to talk to us about salvation, and after a short talk on this point he extended an invitation to any of us who wanted to join the church. My sister was the first one to join the church that morning, and after seeing her join I decided that I would not let her get ahead of me, so I was the next. I had never given this matter a thought, and even at the time of {my} baptism I was unaware of what was taking place. From this it seems quite clear that I joined the church not out of any dynamic conviction, but out of a childhood desire to keep up with my sister.

Conversion for me was never an abrupt something. I have never experienced the so called "crisis moment." Religion has just been something that I grew up in. Conversion for me has been the gradual intaking of the noble {ideals} set forth in my family and my environment, and I must admit that this intaking has been largely unconscious.[5]

The church has always been a second home for me. As far back as I can remember I was in church every Sunday. I guess this was inevitable since my father was the pastor of my church, but I never regretted going to church until I passed through a state of scepticism in my second year of college. My best friends were in Sunday School, and it was the Sunday School that helped me to build the capacity for getting along with people.[6]

The lessons which I was taught in Sunday School were quite in the fundamentalist line. None of my teachers ever doubted the infallibility of the Scriptures. Most of them were unlettered and had never heard of Biblical criticism. Naturally I accepted the teachings as they were being given to me. I never felt any need to doubt them, at least at that time I didn't. I guess I accepted Biblical studies uncritically until I was about twelve years old.[7] But this uncritical attitude could not last long, for it was contrary to the very nature of my being. I had always been the questioning and precocious type. At the age of 13 I shocked my Sunday School class by denying the bodily resurrection of Jesus. From the age of thirteen on doubts began to spring forth unrelentingly. At the age of fifteen I entered college and more and more could I see a gap between what I had learned in Sunday School and what I was learning in

---

3. Davis remarked in the margin, "Right!"

4. This event probably occurred at the age of seven. In his Crozer application, King mentions that he joined Ebenezer on 1 May 1936. He was baptized two days later. Reverend H. H. Coleman, the guest evangelist who led a revival at Ebenezer in April 1936, was the former pastor of Atlanta's Beulah Baptist Church and pastor of the Macedonia Baptist Church in Detroit in 1936. See "Revival Drawing Fine Crowds at Ebenezer," *Atlanta Daily World*, 21 April 1936, p. 1.

5. Davis suggested that King "see Mr. [*word illegible*]."

6. Davis commented, "This is interesting, for I do not think it characterizes most people."

7. Davis wrote in the margin, "This is early."

college. This conflict continued until I studied a course in Bible in which I came to see that behind the legends and myths of the Book were many profound truths which one could not escape.[8]

One or two incidents happened in my late childhood and early adolescence that had tremendous effect on my religious development. The First was the death of my grandmother when I was about nine years old.[9] I was particularly hurt by this incident mainly because of the extreme love I had for her. As stated above, she assisted greatly in raising all of us. It was after this incident for the first time that I talked at any length on the doctrine of immortality. My parents attempted to explain it to me and I was assured that somehow my grandmother still lived. I guess this is why today I am such a strong believer in personal immortality

The second incident happened when I was about six years of age. From about the age of three up until this time I had had a white playmate who was about my age. We always felt free to play our childhood games together. He did not live in our community, but he was usually around every day until about 6:00; his father owned a store just across the streets from our home. At the age of six we both entered school—separate schools of course. I remember how our friendship began to break as soon as we entered school, of course this was not my desire but his. The climax came when he told me one day that his father had demanded that he would play with me no more.[10] I never will forget what a great shock this was to me. I immediately asked my parents about the motive behind such a statement. We were at the diner table when the situation was discussed, and here for the first time I was made aware of the existence of a race problem. I had never been conscious of it before. As my parents discussed some of the tragedies that had resulted from this problem and some of the insults they themselves had confronted on account of it[11] I was greatly shocked, and from that moment on I was determined to hate every white person. As I grew older and older this feeling continued to grow. My parents would always tell me that I should not hate the white {man}, but that it was my duty as a Christian to love him. At this point the religious element came in. The question arose in my mind, how could I love a race of people {who} hated me and who had been responsible for breaking me up

---

8. King took George D. Kelsey's two-semester course on the Bible at Morehouse during his junior year.

9. Jennie Celeste Williams died on 18 May 1941, when King was twelve.

10. Davis remarked in the margin, "How tragic!"

11. See King, *Stride Toward Freedom* (San Francisco: Harper & Row, 1958), pp. 18–19: "While I was still too young for school I had already learned something about discrimination. For three or four years my inseparable playmates had been two white boys whose parents ran a store across the street from our home in Atlanta. Then something began to happen. When I went across the street to get them, their parents would say that they couldn't play. They weren't hostile, they just made excuses. Finally I asked my mother about it. . . . My mother took me on her lap and began by telling me about slavery and how it had ended with the Civil War. She tried to explain the divided system of the South—the segregated schools, restaurants, theaters, housing; the white and colored signs on drinking fountains, waiting rooms, lavatories—as a social condition rather than a natural order. Then she said the words that almost every Negro hears before he can yet understand the injustice that makes them necessary: 'You are as good as anyone.'"

with one of my best childhood friends? This was a great question in my mind for a number of years. I did not conquer this anti White feeling until I entered college and came in contact with white students through working in interracial organizations.

My days in college were very exciting ones. As stated above, my college training, especially the first two years, brought many doubts into my mind. It was at this period that the shackles of fundamentalism were removed from my body. This is why, when I came to Crozer, I could accept the liberal interpretation with relative ease.

It was in my senior year of college that I entered the ministry. I had felt the urge to enter the the ministry from my latter high school days, but accumulated doubts had somewhat blocked the urge. Now it appeared again with an inescapable drive. My call to the ministry was not a miraculous or supernatural something, on the contrary it was an inner urge calling me to serve humanity. I guess the influence of my father also had a great deal to do with my going in the ministry. This is not to say that he ever spoke to me in terms of being a minister, but that my admiration for him was the great moving factor; He set forth a noble example that I didn't mine following. Today I differ a great deal with my father theologically, but that admiration for a real father still remains.

At the age of 19 I finished college and was ready to enter the seminary. On coming to the seminary I found it quite easy to fall in line with the liberal tradition there found, mainly because I had been prepared for it before coming.

At present I still feel the affects of the noble moral and ethical ideals that I grew up under. They have been real and precious to me, and even in moments of theological doubt I could never turn away from them. Even though I have never had an abrupt conversion experience, religion has been real to me and closely knitted to life. In fact the two cannot be separated; religion for me is life.

AHDS. MLKP-MBU: Box 106, folder 22.

An Autobiography Of Religious
Development

By :
M. L. King jr.

"My birthplace was Atlanta Georgia, the capital of the state and the so called "gate-way to the south." I was born in the late twenties on the verge of the great depression, which was to spread its disastrous arms into every corner of this nation for over a decade. I was much to young to remember the beginning of this depression, but I do recall how I questioned my parent about the numerous people standing in bread lines when I was about five years of age. I can see the effects of this early childhood experience on my present anti capitalistic feelings.

I was the second child of a family of three children, having one brother and one sister. Because of our relative closeness of age we all grew up together, and to this day there still exist that intimate relationship which existed between us in childhood. Our parents themselves were very intimate, and they always maintained

an intimate relationship with us. In our
immediate family there was also a saintly
grandmother (my mother's mother) whose husband
had died when I was one years old.
She was very dear to each of us, but
especially to me. I sometimes think that
I was his favorite grandchild. I can
remember very vividly how she spent many
evenings telling us interesting stories.

From the very beginning I was an
extraordinarily healthy child. It is said
that at my birth the doctors pronounced
me a one hundred percent perfect child,
from a physical point of view. Even today
this physical harmony still abides, in that
I hardly know how an ill moment feels.
I guess the same thing would apply to
my mental life. I have always been
~~somewhat~~ somewhat precocious, both physically
and mentally. My I. Q. stands somewhat
above the average. So it seems that
from a hereditary point of view
nature was very kind to me.

The same applies to my environment.
I was born in a very congenial home
situation. My parents have always lived
together very intimately, and I can hardly remember a time that they ever argued
(My father happens to be the kind who just wont
argue), or had any great fall out. I
have never experienced the feeling of not
having the basic necessities of life. These
things were always provided by a
father who always put his family
first. My father has always been
a real father. This is not to
say that I was born with a silver
spoon in my mouth; far from it.
My father has never made more than
an ordinary salary, but the secret is
that he knows the art of saving
and budgeting. He never wastes his
money at the expense of his family. He
has always had sense enough not to
live beyond his means. So for this
reason He has been able to provide

us with the basic necessities of life
with little strain. For the past three
years he has had the tremendous
responsibility of keeping all of us in school,
(my brother in college, my sister in graduate
school, and me in the seminary) and although
it has been somewhat a burden from a
financial angle, he has done it with a
smile. Our mother has also been behind
the scene setting forth those motherly cares,
the lack of which leaves a missing
link in life.

The community in which I was
born was quite ordinary in terms of
social status. No one in our community
had attained any great wealth. Most
of the Negroes in my home town who
had attained wealth lived in a section
of town known as "Hunter Hills." The
community in which I was born was
characterized with a sought of unsophisticated simplicity. No one in our
community was in the extremely poor

class. This community was not the slum district. It is probably fair to class the people of this community as those of average income. Yet I insist that this was a wholesome community, notwithstanding the fact that none of us were ever considered members of the "upper upper class." Crime was at a minimum in our community, and most of our neighbors were deeply religious. I can well remember that all of my childhood playmates were regular Sunday School goers, not that I chose them on that basis, but because it was very difficult to find playmates in my community who did not attend Sunday School.

I was exposed to the best educational conditions in my childhood. At three I entered nursery school. This great childhood contact had a tremendous effect on the development of my personality. At five I entered kindergarten and there I remained for one year until I entered the first grade.

One may ask at this point, why discuss such factors as the above in a paper dealing with one religious development? The answer to this question lies in the fact that the above factors were highly significant in determining my religious attitudes. It is quite easy for me to think of a God of love mainly because I grew up in a family where love was central and where lovely relationships were ever present. It is quite easy for me to think of the universe as basically friendly mainly because of my uplifting hereditary and environmental circumstances. It is quite easy for me to lean more toward optimism than pessimism about human nature mainly because of my childhood experiences. It is impossible to get at the root of one religious attitudes without taking in account the psychological and historical factors that play upon the individual. So that

The above biographical factors are absolutely necessary in understanding my religious development.

Now for a more specific phase of my religious development. It was at the age of five that I joined the church. I well remember how this event occurred. Our church was in the midst of the spring revival, and a guest evangelist had come down from Virginia. On Sunday morning the guest evangelist came into our Sunday School to talk to us about salvation, and after a short talk on this point he extended an invitation to any of us who wanted to join the church. My sister was the first one to join the church that morning, and after seeing her join I decided that I would not let her get ahead of me, so I was the next. I had never given this matter a thought, and even at the time of my baptism I was unaware of what was taking place. From this it seems quite clear that I joined the church not out of any dynamic conviction, but out of a childhood desire to keep up with my sister.

Conversion for me was never an abrupt something. I have never experienced the so called "crisis moment." Religion has just been something that I grew up in. Conversion for me has been the gradual intaking of the noble ideals set forth in my family and my environment, and I must admit that this intaking has been largely unconscious.

The church has always been a second home for me. As far back as I can remember I was in church every Sunday. I guess this was inevitable since my father was the pastor of my church, but I never regretted going to church until I passed through a state of scepticism in my second year of college. My best friends were in Sunday School, and it was the Sunday School that helped me to

This is interesting
for I do not
think it
seeming
must appear

Herder 9-

build the capacity for getting along with people.

The lessons which I was taught in Sunday School were quite in the fundamentalist line. None of my teachers ever doubted the infallibility of the Scriptures. Most of them were un-lettered and had never heard of Biblical criticism. Naturally I accepted the teachings as they were being given to me. I never felt any need to doubt them, at least at that time I didn't. I guess I accepted Biblical studies uncritically until I was about twelve years old. But this uncritical attitude could not last long, for it was contrary to the very nature of my being. I had always been the questioning and precocious type. At the age of 13 I shocked my Sunday School class by denying the bodily resurrection of Jesus. From the age of thirteen on doubts began to spring forth

unrelentingly. At the age of fifteen I
entered college and more and more could
I see a gap between what I had
learned in Sunday School and what
I was learning in college. This conflict
continued until I studied a course
in Bible in which I came to see that
behind the legends and myths of the Book
were many profound truths which one
could not escape.

One or two incidents happened
in my late childhood and early
adolescence that had tremendous effect
on my religious development. The first
was the death of my grandmother
when I was about nine years old. I
was particularly hurt by this incident
mainly because of the extreme love I had
for her. As stated above, she assisted
greatly in raising all of us. It was
after this incident for the first time
that I talked at any length on the
doctrine of immortality. My parents

attempted to explain it to me   and I
was assured that somehow my grandmother still lived. I guess this is
why today I am such a strong
believer in personal immortality.

The second incident happened when
I was about six years of age. From
about the age of three up until this
time I had had a white playmate who was about my age. We always felt free to play our childhood
games together. He did not live in our
community, but he was usually around
every day until about 6:00; his father
owned a store just across the streets
from our home. At the age of six we
both entered school - separate schools of
course. I remember how our friendship
began to break as soon as we entered
school, of course this was not my desire but his. The climax came when
he told me one day that his father
had demanded that he would play

with me one more. I never will
forget what a great shock this was
to me. I immediately asked my parents
about the motive behind such a statement. We were at the diner table
when the situation was discussed; and
here for the first time I was made
aware of the existence of a race
problem. I had never been conscious
of it before. As my parents discussed
some of the tragedies that had resulted from this problem and some of the
insults they themselves had confronted
on account of it I was greatly
shocked; and from that moment on I
was determined to hate every white person. As
I grew older and older this feeling
continued to grow. My parents would
always tell me that I should not hate
the white man; but that it was my duty
as a Christian to love him. At this
point the religious element came in.
The question arose in my mind, how

could I love a race of people who hated me
and who had been responsible for
breaking me up with one of my chest
childhood friends? This was a great
question in my mind for a number
of years. I did not conquer this
anti White feeling until I entered
college and came in contact with
white students through working in
interracial organizations.

My days in college were very
exciting ones. As stated above, my
college training, especially the first
two years, brought many doubts into
my mind. It was at this period
that the shackles of fundamentalism
were removed from my body. This
is why, when I came to Crozer,
I could accept the liberal interpretation
with relative ease.

It was in my senior year of
college that I entered the ministry.
I had felt the urge to enter the

the ministry from my latter high school
days, but accumulated doubts had
somewhat blocked the urge. Now it
appeared again with an inescapable
drive. My call to the ministry was
not a miraculous or supernatural
something; on the contrary it was an
inner urge calling me to serve humanity.
I guess the influence of my father also
had a great deal to do with my
going in the ministry. This is not to
say that he ever spoke to me in terms
of being a minister, but that my admiration
for him was the great moving factor;
He set forth a noble example that I
didn't mine following. Today I differ
a great deal with my father theologically,
but that admiration for a real father
still remains.

At the age of 19 I finished college
and was ready to enter the seminary. On
coming to the seminary I found it quite
easy to fall in line with the liberal

tradition there found, mainly because I had been prepared for it before coming.

At present I still feel the affects of the noble moral and ethical ideals that I grew up under. They have been real and precious to me; and even in moments of theological doubt I could never turn away from them. Even though I have never had an abrupt conversion experience, religion has been real to me and closely knitted to life. In fact the two cannot be separated; religion for me is life.

Excellent

Crozer Theological Seminary
Field Work Department: Rating Sheet for
Martin Luther King, Jr., by William E. Gardner

[September–1 December 1950]

William E. Gardner, the probable author of this evaluation, was a friend of the King family and pastor of First Baptist Church in East Elmhurst, Queens, New York. Although Gardner rated King "above average" in pulpit ability, he noted major weaknesses: "An attitude of aloofness, disdain & possible snobbishness which prevent his coming to close grips with the rank and file of ordinary people."

IT IS THE PURPOSE OF OUR FIELD WORK PROGRAM TO AID THE STUDENT IN HIS DEVELOPMENT AS A RELIGIOUS LEADER. WE SHALL APPRECIATE IT IF YOU WILL MARK THE FOLLOWING AS OBJECTIVELY AS POSSIBLE. FOR OUR CONVENIENCE, PLEASE USE THE FOLLOWING SYMBOLS:

A–Superior; B–Above average; C–Average; D–Below average; E–Inferior

Name of Student   **Martin King**[1]

		A	B	C	D	E
I.	PERSONAL QUALITIES					
	DEPENDABILITY		X			
	PROMPTNESS		X			
	INITIATIVE		X			
	JUDGMENT	X				
	DECISIVENESS	X				
	NEATNESS	X				
	COURTESY			X		
	POISE	X				
	SELF-CONFIDENCE	X				
	WILLINGNESS TO LEARN			X		
II.	SOCIAL QUALITIES	A	B	C	D	E
	FRIENDLINESS		X			
	SENSE OF HUMOR		X			
	COOPERATION			X		
	SYMPATHETIC UNDERSTANDING		X			

---

1. An unknown reviewer, perhaps a member of Crozer's field work department, wrote in the margin: "Doing preaching about 2 times each week. Grad. work at U.P. No field work. Middle—Single.—Junior."

III.	PULPIT ABILITY	A	B	C	D	E
	GENERAL IMPRESSION		x			
	ENUNCIATION		x			
	SENTENCE STRUCTURE		x			
	CONTENT		x			
	ORGANIZATION		x			
	USE OF VOICE		x			
	EFFECTIVE OF DELIVERY		x			
	EFFECTIVENESS OF PUBLIC READING		x			
	ABILITY TO LEAD WORSHIP		x			

IV.	GROUP WORK	A	B	C	D	E
	LEADERSHIP		x			
	ABILITY TO PLAN PROGRAMS		x			
	ABILITY TO CARRY THROUGH PROGRAMS		x			
	ABILITY TO ORGANIZE GROUP ACTIVITIES		x			
	ABILITY TO SECURE GROUP PARTICIPATION			x		
	PREPARATION FOR APPOINTMENTS			x		
	UNDERSTANDING OF GROUP WORK TECHNIQUES			x		
	CONCERN FOR INDIVIDUALS IN GROUP			x		
	WILLINGNESS TO ACCEPT SUGGESTIONS AND CRITICISM			x		
	ABILITY TO EVALUATE PROGRAMS		x			

V.	TEACHING ABILITY	A	B	C	D	E
	THOROUGHNESS OF PREPARATION			x		
	UNDERSTANDING OF PUPILS			x		
	ABILITY TO MAINTAIN ORDER		x			
	ORIGINALITY AND VARIETY OF METHODS			x		
	EFFECTIVENESS IN ACHIEVING GOALS			x		
	PERSISTENCE IN FOLLOW-UP			x		

I FEEL THAT THIS STUDENT'S STRONGEST POINTS ARE **superior mental ability, clarity of expression, impressive personality, thoroughness in preparation for academic tasks.**

I FEEL THAT THE CHIEF WEAKNESSES WHICH THE SEMINARY MIGHT HELP HIM OVERCOME ARE **An attitude of aloofness, disdain & possible snobbishness which prevent his coming to close grips with the rank and file of ordinary people.**

Also, a smugness that refuses to adapt itself to the demands of ministering effectively to the average Negro congregation.

AFm. CRO-NRCR.

Morton Scott Enslin
to Chester M. Alter

14 December 1950

Enslin wrote this letter of recommendation in support of King's application to the School of Theology at Boston University.

Dean Chester M. Alter[1]
Boston University Graduate School
725 Commonwealth Avenue
Boston 15, Massachusetts

Dear Dean Alter:

One of our seniors, Martin L. King, Jr., tells me that he has made application for admission to Boston University for graduate work upon completion of his work and the reception of his B.D. from Crozer. He also intimated that a letter from me to your office would be appreciated. I am very glad to be able to recommend Mr. King without qualification for admission to graduate work with an eye to an eventual doctorate. He has proved himself to be a very competent student, conscientious, industrious, and with more than usual insight. He has had several courses with me and in each of them has done able work. He is president of the Student Government and has conducted himself well in this position. The fact that with our student body largely Southern in constitution a colored man should be elected to and be popular {in} such a position is in itself no mean recommendation. Unless I am greatly in error, he will go far in his profession. The comparatively small number of forward-looking and thoroughly trained negro leaders is, as I am sure you will agree, still so small that it is more than an even chance that one as adequately trained as King will find ample opportunity for useful service. He is entirely free from those somewhat annoying qualities which some men of his race acquire when they find themselves in the distinctly higher percent of their group. So far as his moral character is concerned there is no need of any qualification, at least so far as I know, and I think that very few details of that sort escape me. Accordingly I recommend him

---

1. Chester M. Alter (1906–) taught in Indiana public school systems from 1923 to 1925. He studied at Harvard University from 1929 until 1933, earning his Ph.D. in chemistry in 1936. Alter was a professor at Boston University from 1934 to 1953, acting dean of the graduate school from 1944 to 1945, and dean from 1945 to 1953. He became chancellor of the University of Denver in 1953 and remained there until 1967.

with distinct pleasure to you for serious consideration for admission to Boston University.

Very sincerely,
Morton S. Enslin

MSE:eah

TLc. CRO-NRCR.

From Oliver Shaw Rankin

15 December 1950
Edinburgh, Scotland

This letter informs King that the University of Edinburgh has accepted him for graduate work.

Martin Luther King, Junr., Esq.,
Crozer Theological Seminary,
Chester,
PENNSYLVANIA, U.S.A.

Dear Mr. King,

Your transcripts have now arrived and are of sufficiently high quality for us to accept you as a student in the Post-Graduate School for 1951. The session should, I imagine, begin on 4th October. Looking forward to seeing you then.

Yours sincerely,
[*signed*] O. S. Rankin[1]

TLS. MLKP-MBU: Box 117, folder 50.

---

1. Oliver Shaw Rankin (1885–1954) was professor of Old Testament Language, Literature, and Theology in the Faculty of Divinity at the University of Edinburgh from 1937 to 1954.

"A Conception and Impression of
Religion from Dr. W. K. Wright's Book
Entitled *A Student's Philosophy of Religion*"

[*19 December 1950*]
[*Chester, Pa.*]

King wrote this paper during the first term of Davis's course Philosophy of Religion. Davis asked his students to consider several questions: "'If I had never known anything about religion or had never had a religious experience, what pictures of religion would this book impart to me?' . . . What message and impressions of a religious character does the book write upon your mind?"[1] Commenting on Wright's definition of religion as "the conservation of socially recognized values," King says: "Now I want to be religious, but I have some values that I would like to see conserved which are not socially recognized. Would I be excluded? What shall we call the experience in which a prophet, dissenting from socially recognized values, makes appeal to what he regards as a higher standard?"[2] Davis gave the paper an A and commented, "Well done."

After reading this interesting work by Dr. William K. Wright entitled, <u>A Students Philosophy of Religion</u>, I find that religion is something broad and universal covering the whole of life. It seems that the universality and perpetuity of religion result from the fact that it "endeavors to secure the conservation of socially recognized values."[3] What then is religion? In order to answer this question we must deal with both the genus and differentia of our author's definition. In the genus of his definition of religion he attempts to be broad enough to include within its bounds every conceivable form of religion, and in the differentia he seeks to be sufficiently narrow and specific to exclude from the species of religion everything included within the genus that is not properly religious. If, then, we proceed to seek the genus of the definition of religion we come to some such words as those quoted above: the endeavor to secure the conservation of socially recognized values. Let us carefully scrutinize each of the separate expressions in this definition of religion.

By "values" Mr. Wright seems to mean any of a number of things depending on the degree of advancement of the religion and of the civilization in

---

1. George W. Davis, Bibliography and term assignments, Philosophy of Religion and Advanced Philosophy of Religion, 28 November 1950–4 May 1951, MLKP-MBU: Box 113, folder 18.

2. William Kelley Wright (1877–1956) received his B.A. and Ph.D. from the University of Chicago in 1899 and 1906, respectively, and taught at Dartmouth. He wrote several books, including *Ethical Significance of Feeling, Pleasure, and Happiness* (1907), *A Student's Philosophy of Religion* (1922), *General Introduction to Ethics* (1929), and *A History of Modern Philosophy* (1941).

3. William Kelley Wright, *A Student's Philosophy of Religion*, rev. ed. (New York: Macmillan, 1935), p. 41.

which it appears. In lower religions, which Mr. Wright calls "natural religions," the values are all concrete, tangible, practical wants. If food is something scarce, and means of cultivation of the soil is inefficient, there are likely to be religious ceremonials to obtain food. If water is scarce, as in the Arabian desert, every spring of water may be thought of as sacred. If men find themselves in need of protection from perils of thunder, lightning, earthquake, flood and cataract, then these become matters of religious attention. Protection from disease, especially pestilence, and the desire for long life, riches and posterity are values with which natural religions often have been concerned.

In contrast to natural religions our author speaks of "ethical religions". In these man is more self-conscious, and reflective and possesses deeper moral insight. Moral conduct has become the chief value to conserve. The greatest evil that man has to overcome is his own sinful nature, which curses him now and threatens to continue to bring harm upon him in a future life. So ethical religions are usually "religions of redemption," and afford man some way of escape from his sinfulness.

One characteristic applies to all the values of both natural and ehtical religions. The values are all "socially recognized." That is, they are either values that are recognized by many persons, if not by all, to concern the welfare of a whole of the social group, or else they are values recognized to be morally right and proper for individuals to seek for their own benefit. Victory in war, deliverance from pestilence or famine, and counsel regarding important decisions that must be made by the group obviously are matters of general public concern, and endeavor may be made to conserve them through religion. The same is true of the efforts of a family to maintain solidarity with its deceased members, leading it to share delicacies of food with them, to seek the repose of their souls, to ask their counsel, and to endeavor to avert their wrath.[4]

From this it seems that religion only emerges through the social community. I get the impression that social judgments are more important than religious judgments since the latter are derived from the former. Religion, then is something that comes from within the social whole, rather than from a revelation from without. The logical conclusion of this point seems to be that no one can make a religion for himself any more than he can devise a language of his own; religion is a slow development of group life and common experiences.

---

4. Wright, *A Student's Philosophy of Religion*, p. 42: "One characteristic applies to all the values of both natural and ethical religions. The values are all 'socially recognized.' That is, they are either values that are recognized by many persons, if not by all, to concern the welfare as a whole of the social group (family, totem, tribe, nation), or else they are values recognized to be morally right and proper for individuals to seek for their own benefit. Victory in war, deliverance from pestilence or famine, and counsel regarding important decisions that must be made by the group are obviously matters of general public concern, and endeavor may be made to conserve them through religion. The same is true of the efforts of a family to maintain solidarity with its deceased members, leading it to share delicacies of food with them, to seek the repose of their souls, to ask their counsel, and to endeavor to avert their wrath."

Religion is an "endeavor to secure the <u>conservation</u> of socially recognized values." "Conservation" seems to carry with it a very wide connotation, at least for our author it does. It includes quantitative increase of that object that is of value, in the case of food, rain, and other material goods. It also includes enhancement or intensification of the values, especially in the case of more spiritual goods—such as bravery, loyalty, purity of heart, social solidarity, sense of divine presence and support, and the like.[5]

Religion is an "<u>endeavor</u> to secure the conservation of socially recognized values." The "endeavor" need not be successful. Often, indeed, especially in savage religions, we perceive it to be wholly futile, as in the case of the Australian ceremonies to secure rain and to increase the food supply. The practise of religion always involves a minimum of faith, or confidence in the efficacy of the religious act, enough to make it seem worth while to try to secure the result in that way.[6]

As stated above the description of religion just set forth—"the endeavor to secure the conservation of socially recognized values"—is really the genus of the definition of religion and is sufficiently broad to cover all varieties of religion. However any definition to be complete must have a differentia. At first I was about to think that Mr. Wright's definition of religion did not have a differentia, and I was on the verge of accepting the genus as his whole definition. This was about to lead me to the conclusion that many phases of magic, science, art, morality, and law came under the pale of religion, since each of these seeks to secure the conservation of socially recognized values. Reading further, however, I found that Mr. Wright completed his definition by a differentia, which delimited the field of religion from the other forms of endeavor to secure the conservation of socially recognized values that are not religious.

I find that in the case of religious endeavor the conservation of values is always sought through "a specific and peculiar kind of agency and the attitude toward this agency is of a definite sort."[7] In other words, the conservation of values is sought through specific actions that are believed to evoke some agency different from the ordinary ego of the individual, or from other

---

5. Wright, *A Student's Philosophy of Religion*, p. 43: "Religion is an 'endeavor to secure the *conservation* of socially recognized values.' '*Conservation*' is intended in a wide sense of the word. It includes *quantitative increase* of the object that is of value, in the case of food, rain, and other material goods. It also includes *enhancement or intensification* of the value, especially in the case of more spiritual goods—such as bravery, loyalty, purity of heart, social solidarity, sense of divine presence and support, and the like."

6. Wright, *A Student's Philosophy of Religion*, p. 43: "'Religion is an *endeavor* to secure the conservation of socially recognized values.' The '*endeavor*' need not be successful. Often, indeed, especially in savage religions, we perceive it to be wholly futile, as in the case of the Australian ceremonies to secure rain and to increase the food supply. The practise of religion always involves a minimum of faith, or confidence in the efficacy of the religious act, enough to make it seem worth while to try to secure the result in that way."

7. Wright, *A Student's Philosophy of Religion*, p. 44: "In the case of religious endeavor the conservation of values is always sought through *a specific and peculiar kind of agency, and the attitude toward this agency is of a definite sort*."

merely human beings, and that imply a feeling of dependence upon this agency.

"Specific action" seems to have {been} employed in order to make it clear that it includes any kind of act whatsoever that has been employed to serve the purpose—whether a dance about an arrow, a magic spell or incantation, or purely mental acts like concentrating one's thought upon the eightfold path of the Buddha, throughtful meditation upon the meaning of life or the sublimity of nature, or the silent prayer a Christian might momentarily make when confronted by a sudden emergency. Such an action, whatever it may be, is always, in the mind of him who makes it, definite and specific.

The differentia proceeds to describe the agency employed. It is "some agency different from the ordinary ego of the individual, or from other merely human beings."[8] The agency greatly varies in different religions, and is variously regarded by different individuals of the same religious faith. It may be some mysterious impersonal power in things known as mana, it may be a totem pole or fetich or a charm or an amulet, a dead or living animal; it may be the Blessed Virgin or one of the saints; it may be nature as conceived by a romantic poet like Shelley or a philosopher life Marcus Aurelius; it may be the deceased spirit of one's father, or it may be some other spirit or god or God. The agency may even be a human being like an Egyptian King or a Roman emperor provided he is {not} believed to be merely human, but in some respects divine.

The last clase[9] of the differentia is intended to differentiate between religion and science, a dichotomy which I didn't make until I had read beyond the mere genus of the definition. As stated above, I was about to include science along with many other things under the pale of religion, since it to, in a manner, seeks to conserve socially recognized values. However this dichotomy was clearly set forth in the differentia of the definition. The scientific attitude toward nature always reveals a mechanical exploitation of nature. Nature is inert, passive, and man may bend and manipulate it according to his needs if it discovers the "laws" of nature, which are of course only descriptive formulae of the succession of phenomena. On the other hand, the religious attitude always implies a "feeling of dependence" toward power greater than our ordinary selves, and not an attempt to exploit this power.

Interestingly enough, the various religious phenomena which the psychologist interprets are explained under our author's conception of religion. Prayer, for instance, whenever it is clearly distinguishable from the spell, is seen as the endeavor to secure the conservation of socially recognized values through "an imaginative social process" or conversation between the ordinary ego of the individual and the agency invoked. Sacrifice is the offering of gifts to

---

8. Wright, *A Student's Philosophy of Religion*, p. 47: "*Religion is the endeavor to secure the conservation of socially recognized values through specific actions that are believed to evoke some agency different from the ordinary ego of the individual, or from other merely human beings, and that imply a feeling of dependence upon this agency.*"

9. Davis crossed out "clase" and wrote "clause."

propitiate the agency. All religious ceremonials are explained as consisting chiefly in elaborations of prayer and sacrifice. Sacraments are interpreted as rites which {are} believed either spiritually or magically to effect some desired change in the believer by means of the agency invoked. The evangelical revival is seen as a different device to secure a similar purpose; and conversion and sanctification are changes in the personality of the individual attributed to a divine agency. Myths, whenever they have religious significance at all, are interpreted as naive attempts to account for the origin and validity of practices employed in religion, while doctrines and creeds are more elaborate rational and philosophical explanations and justifications. Institutions, like the church or the synagogue, are pictured as organizations for the purpose of preserving and propagating methods of religious endeavor for the conservation of socially recognized values. From all of this I get the impression that all religion can be explained in terms of this endeavor; and the various details of sacrifice, prayer, and other ritual, and the rise of myths, dogmas, and institutions are incidents that appear in the carrying out of this endeavor.

At this point we may consider whether our authors definition has succeeded in differentiating religion from the terms which it is most capable of being confused: animism and magic, in the case of primitive religions, and morals, ethics, and esthetics, in the case of higher religions.

According to the conception of religion set forth here, animism and magic may or may not be religious. They become religious when employed in the endeavor to secure the conservation of socially recognized values. Otherwise they {are} non-religious and on occasion they may become anti-religious. For instance, the simple belief in spirits about one is animism, and may be entirely non-religious. The endeavor to induce these spirits by means of offerings to adopt a desired attitude so as to conserve socially recognized values, is a religious use of animism.

The distinction between religion and morals is not to be made in terms of the content of judgments of good and evil. There is no moral content that is always religious, and none that is always non-religious. The values of religion are all in some sense moral values, though they are occasionally outworn moral values that have survived from a bygone age. What funishes the differentia of religion from merely moral value is the peculiar nature of the agency through which the religious value is conserved.[10]

The distinction between religion and ethics is similar. Ethics is the attempt to put morals upon a systematic basis by philosophically defending its principles. Religion is one of the agencies available for conserving some of the values recognized by ethics.

The differentiation of religion from esthetics is also provided for in our author's definition by the emphasis upon the agency employed. The religious endeavor is never an end in itself. Religious interest is always mediated. Esthetic contemplation is interesting on its own account; it is an end in itself. Religious meditation and prayer are always for the sake of conserving socially

---

10. Davis questioned "funishes."

recognized values important to the believer at other times even more than at the moment of worship.

The genus and differentia of religion have now been explained. It has been shown how religion differs from other attempts to secure the conservation of socially recognized values. The total conception of religion set forth in this book, therefore, may be summed up in the following definition:—Religion is the endeavor to secure the conservation of socially recognized values through specific actions that are believed to evoke some agency differnt from the ordinary ego of the individual, or from other merely human beings, and that imply a feeling of dependence upon this agency.[11]

After being introduced to this all pervasive phenomenon called religion I am left with many impressions. First I get the impression from Mr. Wright's definition that almost anything, even man's dealings with physical forces, can be religious. To be religious, actions must, according to him, be believed "to evoke some agency different from the ordinary ego of the individual, or from other merely human beings, and that imply a feeling of dependence upon this agency." This admits, it seems, within the pale of religion man's dealings with merely physical forces when he uses them for the conservation or the production of values, and when he feels dependent upon them. For the ordinary physical forces—heat, and electricity, for instance—are agencies different from "the ordinary ego of the individual, and from other merely human beings," and upon them we are dependent. Does Mr. Wright intend to include in religion the many specific actions by which we use these forces? Of course who am I to ask such a question or even to discuss the adequacy or inadequacy of Mr. Wright's definition? After all I am just being introduced to the meaning and nature of this great force called religion.

In the genus of his definition Mr. Wright limits the values involved in religious consciousness to those already socially recognized. Now I want to be religious, but I have some values that I would like to see conserved which are not socially recognized. Would I be excluded? What shall we call the experience in which a prophet, dissenting from socially recognized values, makes appeal to what he regards as a higher standard? O well these observations are not too important. The important thing is that the author has convinced me that religion more than anything else effects a certain amount of social and moral solidarity and conservatism within the group of worshipers. Society needs a strong conservative, centripetal agency to solidify its forces and keep it from losing the values it has learned to recognize and appreciate. The author has convinced me that this agency is found in religion. Moreover, he has convinced me that by becoming properly adjusted to the divine power of religion I can become adjusted to myself and to my fellow man. I will now go out and seek that religious experience which Mr. Wright so cogently discusses in this book.

THDS. MLKP-MBU: Box 112, folder 14.

---

11. This definition is taken from Wright, *A Student's Philosophy of Religion*, p. 47; see note 8 above.

[*September–December 1950*]

This statement explains King's interest in pursuing graduate work in systematic theology. Crozer professor Raymond J. Bean, a graduate of Boston University, recommended that King study with Edgar S. Brightman at Boston. King had used Brightman's book A Philosophy of Religion *in a number of classes with George W. Davis. In this fragment, which was copied by S. Paul Schilling, a professor of systematic theology at Boston University, King reveals that he plans a teaching career. He was admitted to Boston University on 11 January 1951.*

For a number of years I have been desirous of teaching in a college or a school of religion. Realizing the necessity for scholastic attainment in the teaching profession, I feel that graduate work would give me a better grasp of my field. At present I have a general knowledge of my field, but I have not done the adequate research to met the scholarly issues with which I will be confronted in thie area. It is my candid opinion that the teaching of theology should be as scientific, as thorough, and as realistic as any other discipline. In a word, scholarship is my goal. For this reason I am desirous of doing graduate work. I feel that a few years of intensified study in a graduate school will give me a thorough grasp of knowledge in my field.

My particular interest in Boston University can be summed up in two statements. First my thinking in philosophical areas has been greatly influenced by some of the faculty members there, particularly Dr. Brightman. For this reason I have longed for the possibility of studying under him. Secondly, one of my present professors is a graduate of Boston University, and his great influence over me has turned my eyes toward his former school. From him I have gotten some valuable information about Boston University, and I have been convinced that there are definite advantages there for me.

TDc. SPS.

"Martin L. King," by Charles E. Batten

[*1951*]
Atlanta, Ga.

Charles E. Batten, dean of Crozer, wrote this sketch of King that appeared in the pamphlet The Achievements of Morehouse Men in the Great Universities. *Benjamin E. Mays, president of Morehouse College, had written to universities attended by Morehouse alumni to gather material for the publication.*

King is one of our most outstanding students, from my point of view. Academically he is doing superior work. We have just had a period of comprehensive examinations and only one man was granted honors in them; it was

King. In the life of the school he is playing an important part and is president Jan
of our student body this year. In an organization such as we have at Crozer, 1951
the president of the student body is a position that carries much reponsibility.
He is held universally in high regard by faculty, staff, and students and is
undoubtedly one of the best men in our entire student body. He reflects fine
preparation, an excellent mind, and a thorough grasp of material. King seems
to know where he wants to go and how to get there. Furthermore, he is making remarkable progress in arriving.

PD. *The Achievements of Morehouse Men in the Great Universities* (Atlanta: Morehouse College, n.d.):
5; copy in CKFC.

To Sankey L. Blanton

[January 1951]
[Chester, Pa.]

*This letter to Blanton applying for a postgraduate fellowship from Crozer is not in
King's handwriting, but was probably written on his behalf during his last year at
Crozer.[1] King received a $600 fellowship for his first year (1951–1952) at
Boston University.*

President

Dear Dr. Blanton:

I anticipate graduating from Crozer——in May 1951. In the forthcoming
academic year I plan to continue my study toward the Doctor of Philosophy
in the field of Systematic Theology.

In accordance with my plans, I have made application at the following
schools: Edinburgh University, Edinburgh, Scotland; Boston University, Boston, Mass, and Yale University, New Haven, Conn. I have {already} been accepted at the former two named schools, however, I have not been accepted
at Yale University because I have not yet taken the graduate examination
which is a prerequisite for acceptance. (It so happens that Yale University is
my preference)

Therefore, in view of the foregoing, and ~~wish to hereby make application
for the J. Lewis Crozer Fellowship Grant~~ my inability to pursue work in this
field without financial aid, I hereby make application for the J. Lewis Crozer
Fellowship Grant.

Your favorable consideration of this matter will be highly appreciate. I
remain

Sincerely,
M. L. King

HLd. MLKP-MBU: Box 116, folder 49.

---

1. Sankey Lee Blanton (1898–1974) earned an A.B. at Wake Forest College (1925), a Th.M. 391
at Southern Baptist Theological Seminary (1929), and an S.T.M. degree at Andover Newton

Crozer Theological Seminary
Placement Committee:
Confidential Evaluation of
Martin Luther King, Jr., by Raymond J. Bean

4 February 1951
Chester, Pa.

Bean taught King in two courses, Outline History of Christianity *and* American
Christianity.

Mr. King is the outstanding student in his class and one who would be
outstanding in any institution. His work is always of the highest grade. The
few questions he has asked in class have revealed a real interest in the subject
under discussion.

I think Mr. King will always be a credit to Crozer. It is gratifying to know
that he plans to continue for his doctorate.

THFmS. CRO-NRCR.

"The Origin of Religion in the Race"

[*9 February 1951*]
[*Chester, Pa.*]

King wrote this paper for Davis's Philosophy of Religion course. In the essay,
which is largely drawn from D. Miall Edwards's The Philosophy of Religion,
King examines various philosophical and anthropological arguments for the origin
of religion. The word "race" in the title refers to the human race, not a particular
group. Davis gave King an A and praised his "thoughtful, critical analysis."

The question of the origin of religion in the human
race still remains one of the insoluble mysteries con-
fronting the mind of man. Men have attempted to
solve this problem through scientific research, only to
find that the results lead to inevitable antinomies.

Theological Seminary (1931). He served at Baptist churches in New Haven, Connecticut, and in
Wilmington, North Carolina. Blanton was dean of the school of religion at Wake Forest from
1946 to 1950, when he became president of Crozer. He remained there until 1962 when he
became director of public relations at Meredith College in Raleigh, North Carolina.

Like all other questions of "origins," the origin of religion is more a matter of speculation than of investigation; or to make it less extreme, it will at all events be admitted that speculation is involved in a problem for which an entirely satisfactory solution cannot be found through historical investigation alone. We may trace a particular religion to its faint beginnings, we may even be able to determine the features which the most primitive form of religion presents, but we shall still be far from furnishing an answer to the question—How did religion arise? What is its source?

It is significant that the question of the origin of religion was not scientifically studied until modern times. Before we come to consider some modern theories it may be well to refer briefly to two views which were once widely prevalent, but which are now obsolete or at least absolescent.[1]

The View of
Divine Revelation

Jewish, Christian, and Mohammedan theologians, for a long time, assumed Divine Revelation as a necessary factor in the rise of religion, either in the form of a primitive Revelation vouchsafed to all mankind, or of a special Revelation to certain peoples singled out for the purpose. This view has usually taken the form of a belief in a primeval monotheism of divine origin, from which polytheism in its many forms is a later relapse. It is now usually held that the doctrine of revelation has explained the origin of religion in far too intellectual and mechanical a fashion, "as if religion began with the impartation to man of a set of ideas, ready-made and finished ideas poured into a mind conceived as a kind of empty vessel."* This is a crudely unpsychological view.[2] Moreover, the theory

* D. Maill Edwards, The Philosophy of Religion, p. 32.

---

1. D. Miall Edwards, *The Philosophy of Religion* (New York: Richard R. Smith, 1930), p. 30: "The question of the origin of religion was not scientifically studied until modern times. Before we come to consider some modern theories it may be well to refer briefly to two views which were once widely prevalent, but which are now obsolete or obsolescent."

2. Edwards, *Philosophy of Religion*, pp. 30–31: "It has usually taken the form of a belief in a primeval monotheism of divine origin, from which polytheism in its many forms is a later relapse. In its usual forms the doctrine of revelation has explained the origin of religion in far too intellectual and mechanical a fashion, as if religion began with the impartation to man of a set of ideas, ready-made and finished ideas poured into a mind conceived as a kind of empty vessel. This is a crudely unpsychological view."

of evolution has led us to conceive of primitive man as utterly incapable of receiving and retaining the highly developed ideas which primitive revelation was supposed to communicate to him.[3]

The View of
the English Deist

The English deist of the eighteenth century came on the scene rejecting the idea of revelation and found the origin of religion in human reason. Through the intellect, they claimed, such fundamental doctrines as the belief in a god and the immortality of the soul could be established with a certainty that could not be shaken. The religion of reason is natural to man and therefore known to him from the beginning. But through the cunning devices of the priests, whose one object was to exploit the fears and credulity of the masses in order to get them under their control, elaborate superstitious beliefs and ritual practices came everywhere to take the place of the simple religion of reason. Thus religion has a twofold origin—viz., reason as the source of pure natural religion, and willful deceit on the part of priest as the source of all the actual historical religions.[4] This theory of the English Deists is now quite obsolete. It has several very serious and obvious defects. (a) It exaggerates the place of reason as the originating source of religion, and underestimates the place of that emotional and intuitional illumination which is such a fruitful source of religious ideas and experience. (b) It attributes to primitive man mature ideas which it took centuries for man to be able to grasp and appreciate.* (c) Most absurd of all is the idea that all the actual religions of history are simply calculating hypocrisies invented by priests in a spirit of selfish

* Ibid, p. 33

---

3. Edwards, *Philosophy of Religion*, pp. 31–32: "The theory of evolution has led us to conceive of primitive man as utterly incapable of receiving and retaining the highly developed ideas which primitive revelation was supposed to communicate to him."

4. Edwards, *Philosophy of Religion*, p. 32: "The religion of reason is natural to man and therefore known to him from the beginning. But through the cunning devices of the priests, whose one object was to exploit the fears and credulity of the masses in order to get them under their control, elaborate superstitious beliefs and ritual practices came everywhere to take the place of the simple religion of reason. Thus religion has a twofold origin—viz., reason as the source of pure natural religion, and willful deceit on the part of priests as the source of all the actual historical religions."

greed and power. Doubtless priests have frequently exploited the religious impulses of men to serve their own ends, but they could only exploit what already existed independently of them.[5] As Sabatier says, "When I hear it said, 'Priest made religion,' I simply ask, 'And who, pray, made the priest?' In order to invent a priesthood, and in order that that invention should find general acceptance with the people that were to be subject to it, must there not have been already in the hearts of men a religious sentiment that would clothe the institution with a sacred character? The terms must be reversed. It is not priesthood that explains religion, but religion that explains priesthood."* After seeing the complete untinability of this theory Dr. Edwards concludes that "this shallow and cynical theory makes religion a matter of deliberate invention rather than a matter of spontaneous growth with its roots in the deep foundation of man's nature."† At present this theory has been discredited by most scholars and probably has no supporters.

9 Feb
1951

* Sabatier, Outlines of a Philosophy of Religion, p. 6.

† Edwards, op. cit., p. 34.

These older and pre-scientific views we may now put on one side and proceed to discuss some of the more important modern theories of the origin of religion. There are two ways in which the question may be approached—the way of the anthropologist and the way of the psychologist. The former is concerned with the historic, or rather prehistoric, origin of religion. The problem of the latter is, What is its source in man's spiritual nature, not at the beginning only, but everywhere and always?[6] In other words, the former deals with the origin of religion in the human race while the latter deals with the origin of religion

5. Edwards, *Philosophy of Religion*, pp. 32–33: "This theory of the English Deists . . . is now quite obsolete. It has several very serious and obvious defects. (a) It exaggerates the place of reason as the originating source of religion, and ignores that emotional and intuitional illumination which is such a fruitful source of religious ideas and experience. (b) . . . It attributes to primitive man mature ideas which it took untold ages for man to be able to grasp and appreciate. . . . (c) Most absurd of all is the idea that all the actual religions of history are simply calculating hypocrisies invented by priests in a spirit of selfish greed for power. Doubtless priests have frequently exploited the religious impulses of men to serve their own ends, but they could only exploit what already existed independently of them."

6. Edwards, *Philosophy of Religion*, p. 34: "These older and pre-scientific views we may now put on one side and proceed to discuss some of the more important modern theories of the origin of religion. There are two ways in which the question may be approached—the way of the anthropologist and the way of the psychologist. The former is concerned with the historic, or rather prehistoric, origin of religion. . . . But the problem of the latter is, What is its source in man's spiritual nature, not at the beginning only, but everywhere and always?"

in the individual. Since this paper only deals with the
origin of religion in the Race we may be content to set
forth the various anthropological theories with little
reference to the psychological views.

The Animistic
Theory of E. B. Taylor[7]

This may be said to be the first theory of the origin
of religion that was backed up by a thoroughly scientific study of the mind and habits of the primitive.
In this momentous work* Tylor shows that at a certain stage of culture men everywhere attribute a kind
of soul to the phenomena of Nature—e.g., to trees,
brooks, mountains, clouds, stones, stars. Primitive man
regarded all he saw as possessing a life like unto his
own.[8] The movement of things around him he accounted for on the analogy of his own movements,
which he knew by immediate experience were due to
the activity of his spirit or will. To early man, as to the
savage today, all Nature was alive, filled with innumerable spirits. Thus religion, Tylor believed, arose
in an effort to propitiate these spirits by offerings and
to win their favor by prayers.[9]

Tylor's conclusions in anthropological researches
have deeply influenced the direction taken by the
study of religion. Yet as an account of the origin of
religion it cannot be regarded as satisfactory.[10]

The chief objections to this theory are, first that the
argument does not account in a satisfactory manner

* E. B. Taylor, Primitive
Culture.

---

7. Except in three cases (this subhead, a footnote, and the bibliography), King typed "Tylor"
throughout the document, then inserted an a to form "Taylor." Davis changed "Taylor" back to
"Tylor" throughout. We have retained the original version.

8. Edwards, *Philosophy of Religion*, p. 36: "*The Animistic Theory of E. B. Tylor*—This may be said
to be the first theory of the origin of religion that was backed up by a thoroughly scientific study
of the mind and habits of the savage. It first appeared in Tylor's monumental volumes, *Primitive
Culture* (first edition 1871, third edition 1891), where it is shown that at a certain stage of culture
men everywhere attribute a kind of soul to the phenomena of Nature—e.g., to trees, brooks,
mountains, clouds, stones, stars. Primitive man regarded all he saw as possessing a life like unto
his own."

9. Edwards, *Philosophy of Religion*, pp. 36–37: "The movements of things around him he accounted for on the analogy of his own movements, which he knew by immediate experience were
due to the activity of his spirit or will. To early man, as to the savage to-day, all Nature was alive,
filled with innumerable spirits. According to Tylor, it was on the basis of this animistic view of
the world that religion arose. . . . and this would lead him to seek to propitiate the powerful spirits
and to exorcise the evil ones."

10. Edwards, *Philosophy of Religion*, p. 37: "Tylor's anthropological researches and theory have
deeply influenced the direction taken by the study of religion. . . . Yet as an account of the origin
of religion it cannot be regarded as satisfactory."

for undoubted cases of direct worship of natural phenomena; second that the most primitive savage does
not possess so clear an idea of spirit in distinction
from body as is here implied.[11] The notion of a soul
as a definite thing is a fairly advanced concept which
must have been beyond the mental reach of primitive
man. And so authorities have come to recognize what
is called a pre-animistic stage of religion which I will
discuss subsequently.[12]

The Ghost-Theory
of Herbert Spencer

Brief reference may be made to Spencer's well-
known theroy which finds the origin of religion in
the worship of ancestors appearing in the form of
ghosts.* The awe inspired by dead {death}, and the
fear created by the dead who had passed beyond the
control of the living, constitute the two factors which
arouse a new sense in man; and as far back as we can
go men are seen offering sacrifices to the spirits of
their ancestors. This Herbert Spencer believed to be
the most primitive form of religion. Animism is not
original but derivative, being a generalized form of
the belief in the spirits of dead ancestors reappearing
as ghosts and choosing certain objects in Nature as
their dwelling-place.[13]

The weakness of Spencer's theory is at the point of
oversimplicity. The deification of ancestors is far too
narrow a basis on which to rear the structure of religion. "Religion is too complex a phenomenon to be accounted for by the growth and spread of a single cus-

* See Spencer's <u>Princi-
ples of Sociology</u>, Chapters viii to xvii.

---

11. E. Washburn Hopkins, *Origin and Evolution of Religion* (New Haven: Yale University Press,
1923), p. 3: "The chief objections to this theory are, first, that the most primitive savage does not
possess so clear an idea of spirit in distinction from body as is here implied; second, that the
argument does not account in a satisfactory manner for undoubted cases of direct worship of
natural phenomena."

12. Edwards, *Philosophy of Religion*, pp. 38–39: "The notion of a soul as a definite thing is a
fairly advanced concept which must have been beyond the mental reach of primitive man. . . .
And so authorities have come to recognize what is called a pre-animistic stage of religion."

13. Edwards, *Philosophy of Religion*, p. 39: "*The Ghost-Theory of Herbert Spencer*—Brief reference
may be made to Spencer's well-known theory which finds the origin of religion in the worship of
ancestors appearing in the form of ghosts. . . . and as far back as we can go men are seen offering
sacrifices to the spirits of their ancestors. This Herbert Spencer believed to be the most primitive
form of religion . . . The fear of the dead who had passed beyond the control of the living was
the motive which led to the observance of religious rites. Animism is not original but derivative,
being a generalized form of the belief in the spirits of dead ancestors reappearing as ghosts and
choosing certain objects in Nature as their dwelling-place."

tom. Worship, of however primitive a character, is not the expression of a single thought or a single emotion, but the product of thoughts so complex, so powerful, as to force an expression in the same way in which a river, swollen by streams coming down the mountains from various directions, overflows its banks."*[14] Dr. Jevons expresses his view in unqualified terms thus: "It never happens that the spirits of the dead are conceived to be gods. Man is dependent on the gods, but the spirits of his dead ancestors are dependent on him . . . The worshipper's pride is that his ancestor was a god and not mere mortal . . . The fact is that ancestors known to be human were not worshipped as gods, and that ancestors worshipped as gods were not believed to be human."†[15] This might be a slight exaggeration, but it does come somewhat within the facts (e.g., the natives of Central Australia, a most primitive type of people, believe in the reappearance of the spirits of ancestors, but do not worship them).‡ The worship of ghost has not been found to be nearly as prevalent among the lower peoples as Spencer imagined, and it certainly cannot be maintained that ancestor-worship is more primitive in character than the worship of the spirits of natural objects.[16]

* M. Jastrow, The Study of Religion, p. 185.

† F. B. Jevons, An Introduction to the History of Religion, pp. 196f.

‡ Edwards, op. cit., p. 40.

The Totemistic Theory

Some authorities have found the origin of religion in totemistic practices. So complex and intricate is

---

14. Edwards, *Philosophy of Religion*, pp. 39–40, quoting M. Jastrow, *The Study of Religion* (1901), p. 185: "Spencer's theory errs on the side of over-simplicity. The deification of ancestors is far too narrow a basis on which to rear the structure of religion. 'Religion is too complex a phenomenon to be accounted for by growth and spread of a single custom. Worship, of however primitive a character, is not the expression of a single thought or a single emotion, but the product of thoughts so complex, so powerful, as to force an expression in the same way in which a river, swollen by streams coming down the mountains from various directions, overflows its banks.'"

15. Edwards, *Philosophy of Religion*, p. 40, quoting F. B. Jevons, *An Introduction to the History of Religion* (1896), pp. 196f.: "Dr. Jevons expresses his view in unqualified terms thus: 'It never happens that the spirits of the dead are conceived to be gods. Man is dependent on the gods, but the spirits of his dead ancestors are dependent on him. . . . The worshipper's pride is that his ancestor was a god and not mere mortal. . . . The fact is that ancestors known to be human were not worshipped as gods, and that ancestors worshipped as gods were not believed to be human.'"

16. Edwards, *Philosophy of Religion*, p. 40: "This may be overstating the case, but this at least may safely be said, that not all savages who are familiar with the idea of ancestral spirits make these spirits objects of worship (e.g., the natives of Central Australia, a most primitive type of people, believe in the reappearance of the spirits of ancestors, but do not worship them). We do not find the worship of ghosts to be nearly as prevalent among the lower peoples as Spencer imagined, and it certainly cannot be maintained that ancestor-worship is more primitive in character than the worship of the spirits of natural objects."

the phenomenon surrounding Totemism that an adaquate description of it cannot be given in so brief a
compass. However we may briefly present its essential
features. A totem is a species of animal or plant, or
more rarely a class of inanimate objects, to which a
social group (a clan) stands in an intimate and very
special relation of friendship or kinship—frequently
it is thought of as the ancestor of the clan—and which
provides that social group with its name. The totem
is not exactly a god, but a cognate being and one to
be respected. It must not be used for common purposes, nor must it be slain or eaten except in some
solemn and sacramental way. It is ~~alsays~~ {all ways} the
species and never an individual animal or plant that
is regarded as a totem. This theory of the totemistic
origin of religion has been highly advocated by W.
Robertson Smith in his <u>Religion of the Semites</u> (1885)
and F. B. Jevons in his <u>Introduction to the History of
Religion</u> (1896). Although Smith's ingenious theory
has greatly influenced the scientific study of religion,
it is far from being adequate to the facts. Jevons maintains that totemism is "the most primitive form of society,"[*] that it "is or has been worldwide,"[†] that polytheism is a relapse from it.[‡] [17]

In criticism of this theory it has been revealed
through recent research that not every religion has
passed through the totemistic stage. It is admitted
that totemism is very ancient, but its universality is
very far from being proved. There are many peoples
of very low culture among whom it is unknown, or at
least unrecognizable. It is not discerned, for instance,
among the Veddas of Ceylon, or among the Andaman Islanders, or among the low Brazilian tribes.[§]

[*] Jevons, op. cit., p. 99.

[†] Ibid, p. 117.

[‡] Ibid, p. 395.

[§] Edwards, op. cit., p. 42.

---

17. Edwards, *Philosophy of Religion*, pp. 40–41: "Some authorities have fastened on totemism
as the most ancient and primitive form of religion. Totemism is such an extraordinarily intricate
phenomenon that we cannot here describe it in its baffling complexity. A totem is a species of
animal or plant, or more rarely a class of inanimate objects, to which a social group (a clan) stands
in an intimate and very special relation of friendship or kinship—frequently it is thought of as
the ancestor of the clan—and which provides that social group with its name. The totem is not
exactly a god, but a cognate being and one to be respected. It must not be used for common
purposes, nor must it be slain or eaten except in some solemn and sacramental way. It is always
the species and never an individual animal or plant that is regarded as a totem. The totemistic
theory of origin of worship had once much vogue, owing to its brilliant and suggestive advocacy
by W. Robertson Smith in his *Religion of the Semites* (1885) whose position was further developed
by F. B. Jevons in his *Introduction to the History of Religion* (1896). Smith's ingenious theory . . . has
greatly influenced the scientific study of religion, but it cannot now be regarded as adequate to
the facts. Jevons maintains that totemism is 'the most primitive form of society' (p. 99), that it 'is
or has been worldwide' (p. 117), that polytheism is a relapse from it (p. 395)."

Other tribes have totems which yet are not worshipped and which are in no sense deities.[18]

A new form has been given to this theory by the French sociological school, of which Emile Durkheim is the most distinguished representative.*[19] Durkheim's theory assumes totemism {as the earlier form of religion although he insist that the importance of totemism} is absolutely independent of whether it was ever universal or not, yet it is practically assumed as the earliest form of society and of religion everywhere. The essence of all religious belief lies in the idea of a mysterious impersonal force controlling life, and this sense of force is derived from the authority of society over the individual. It is this sense of the power of the social group over his life that becomes to man the consciousness of a mysterious power in the world. The totem is the visible emblem of this power; but the reality behind the totem, which the totem symbolized, is the might of tribal custom, emotion, and thought, which seems like an actually existing force weighing upon each individual and dominating his life. His real god is society; the power he really worships is the power of society. It seems quite clear at this point that Durkheim's interest in totenism is determined by his sociological theory of religion as essentially and wholly a social phenomenon. The further discussion of it cannot be undertaken here. We can only repeat that there are large parts of the world in which no traces of totemism have been found, and that strictly speaking, totemism is not a religion at all. "Although regarded with reverence and looked to for help, the totem is never, where totemism is not decadent, prayed to as a god or a person with powers which we call supernatural."†[20]

* See Durkheim's, Elemental Forms of the Religious Life.

† E. S. Hartland, Totemism in Hastings' Encl of Religion and Ethics, vol. xii (1921), pp. 406F.

---

18. Edwards, *Philosophy of Religion*, p. 42: "In criticism of this theory it must be said that the most recent researches have not sustained the view that every religion has passed through the totemistic stage. It cannot be denied that totemism is very ancient, but its universality is very far from being proved. There are many peoples of very low culture among whom it is unknown, or at least unrecognizable. We fail to discern it, for instance, among the Veddas of Ceylon, . . . or among the Andaman Islanders, or among the low Brazilian tribes. Other tribes . . . have totems which yet are not worshipped and which are in no sense deities."

19. Edwards, *Philosophy of Religion*, pp. 42–43: "A new form has recently been given to this theory by the French sociological school, of which Emile Durkheim is the most distinguished representative." Edwards wrote in a footnote to this sentence: "See esp. Durkheim's *Les Formes Elementaires de la Vie Religieuse* (Paris, 1912; Eng. Trans. 1915)."

20. Edwards, *Philosophy of Religion*, pp. 42–43: "Durkheim regards totemism as the most simple and primitive religion which it is possible to find. Though he insists that the importance of totemism is absolutely independent of whether it was ever universal or not, yet it is practically

A more weighty criticism of this theory is set forth by Dr. Hopkins. He states: "The fundamental objection which will eventually overthrow this theory is that it ignores or minimizes beyond reason the individual in favor of the group. . . . While it must be admitted that religious ideas in general reflect a man's habitat and group, it is a serious error to imagine that the habitat or group in which he is born produces his religious state of mind. The French theory does not hesitate to insist that man does not think at all as an individual; there is no such thing as an individual mentality and consequently all religious thought is social. But it is pure assumption that the mind of the group is so overwhelmingly coercive that the individual mind is entirely subservient to it. All that can be affirmed is that the social atmosphere affects the religious consciousness."* On the basis of fact Durkheim's theory cannot be accepted as totally valid. But Durkheim is probably right in seeking to trace religion back to something more primitive than the animistic belief in nature-spirits conceived as personal or in the ghosts of ancestors.[21]

* F. W. Hopkins, <u>Origin and Evolution of Religion</u>, pp; 6, 7.

Pre-Animistic Religion:
The Conception of Mana.

Any satisfactory theory of the origin of religion must be able to account, not only for the prominence of magic and mysticism in religion, but also for the connection of these, from the beginning, with a vital moral element. Recent anthropology tends more and

---

assumed as the earliest form of society and of religion everywhere. The substratum of all religious belief lies in the idea of a mysterious impersonal force controlling life, and this sense of force is derived from the authority of society over the individual. It is this sense of the power of the social group over his life that becomes to man the consciousness of a mysterious power in the world. The totem is the visible emblem of this power; but the reality behind the totem, which the totem symbolized, is the might of tribal custom, emotion, and thought, which seems like an actually existing force weighing upon each individual and dominating his life. His real god is society; the power he really worships is the power of society. Durkheim's interest in totemism is determined by his sociological theory of religion as essentially and wholly a social phenomenon. The further discussion of it cannot be undertaken here. We can only repeat that there are large parts of the world in which no traces of totemism have been found, and that, strictly speaking, totemism is not a religion at all. 'Although regarded with reverence and looked to for help, the totem is never, where totemism is not decadent, prayed to as a god or a person with powers which we call supernatural.'" Edwards attributed this quote to "E. S. Hartland, art. on 'Totemism' in Hasting's *Enc. of Religion and Ethics*, vol. xii. (1921), pp. 406f."

21. Edwards, *Philosophy of Religion*, pp. 43–44: "But Durkheim is probably right in seeking to trace back religion to something more primitive than the animistic belief in nature-spirits conceived as personal or in the ghosts of ancestors."

more to find this satisfactory theory in the conception of <u>mana</u>. Here the origin of religion is found in a pre-animistic period or stage characterised by a sense of awe in the presence of a diffused, indefinable, mysterious power or powers not regarded as personal.[22] This potency has been given many names, but for the sake of uniformity we may call it <u>mana</u>, as the Polynesians do, amongst whom this potency as such was first discovered by modern investigators.

It is believed that <u>mana</u> is everywhere, intangible and all-pervasive. All things have it: of course this does mean that <u>mana</u> is something universal or of abstract reality—the primitive has not risen high enough to generalize a universal reality—but it means that there is potency in every object to which man's attention is given. <u>Mana</u> by no means has any moral quality. It may be good or bad, favorable or dangerous, according to time or place.

Here, then, we seem to have the common root of magic and religion. Here is an attitude of mind which supplies religion with its raw material. It is obviously more primitive in character than animism, and may be assumed to be chronologically prior to it. It "may provide the basis on which an animistic doctrine is subsequently constructed . . . Of such powers (towards which awe is felt) spirits constitute but a single class among many; though, being powers in their own right, they finish a type to which the rest may become assimilated in the long run."*[23] Religion in its origin is thus seen to be a sense of awe and mystery in the presence of the indefinable and incalculable power manifested in things, p persons, and events, together with the attendant effort on man's part to adjust himself negatively and positively to that power, with a view to satisfying certain felt needs of his life.[24]

* R. R. Marett, <u>The Threshold of Religion</u>, pp. 1–2.

---

22. Edwards, *Philosophy of Religion*, p. 44: *"Pre-Animistic Religion: The Conception of Mana.—* Recent anthropology tends more and more to find the origin of religion . . . in a pre-animistic period or stage characterized by a sense of awe in the presence of a diffused, indefinable, mysterious power or powers not regarded as personal."

23. Edwards, *Philosophy of Religion*, p. 46, quoting Marett, *Threshold of Religion* (1914), pp. 1–2: "Here, then, we seem to have the common root of magic and religion. . . . Here is an attitude of mind which supplies religion with its raw material. It is obviously more primitive in character than animism, and may be assumed to be chronologically prior to it. It 'may provide the basis on which an animistic doctrine is subsequently constructed. . . . Of such powers [toward which awe is felt] spirits constitute but a single class among many; though, being powers in their own right, they finish a type to which the rest may become assimilated in the long run.'"

24. Edwards, *Philosophy of Religion*, p. 47: "Religion in its origin is thus seen to be a sense of awe and mystery in the presence of the indefinable and incalculable power . . . manifested in

It has been implied above that religion and magic have a common root. At this point we may state this position more fully. The question of the relation between these two attitudes or types of behaviour has often been discussed by anthropologists, and has an important bearing on the problem of the origin and nature of religion. In dealing with this relationship many questions inevitably arise. Have we sufficient grounds for assigning logical or chronological priority to the one rather than to the other? If so, to which of the two does priority belong? Can we place a genetic relation between them? Did the one spring from the other, by way of development or else by way of relapse? Or did they have independent origins? In an attempt to answer these questions at least three positions have emerged.[25]

* Jevons, op. cit., p. 25.

† Cf., however, Andrew Lang's theory. He is an exception at this point. He set forth the theory that spiritual intuition rather than magic accounted for the rise of religion. He sees primitive monotheism as the root of religion out of which animism and myth grew. See his Making of Religion (1898; 2nd ed., 1900).

The first position holds that religion was prior to magic, or, in the words of Dr. Jevons, "that belief in the supernatural (religion) was prior to the belief in magic, and that the latter whenever it sprang up was a degradation or a relapse in the evolution of religion."* [26] This doctrine of relapse implying that man started with a relatively pure form of religion, recurs in other contexts in Jevon's book, for an instance he holds that polytheism is a relapse from a kind of monatheism. This view, however, has few, if any, supporters among modern anthropologists,† nor is it antecedently probable.[27]

---

things, persons, and events, together with the attendant effort on man's part to adjust himself negatively and positively to that power, with a view to satisfying certain felt needs of his life."

25. Edwards, *Philosophy of Religion*, pp. 47–48: "*Magic and Religion.*—We have said that religion and magic have a common root. This position has now to be more fully stated. The question of the relation between these two attitudes or types of behaviour has often been discussed by anthropologists, and has an important bearing on the problem of the origin and nature of religion. Have we sufficient grounds for assigning logical or chronological priority to the one rather than to the other? If so, to which of the two does priority belong? Can we place a genetic relation between them? Did the one spring from the other, either by way of development or else by way of degradation or relapse? Or did they have independent origins? At least three positions may be held in reference to these questions."

26. Edwards, *Philosophy of Religion*, p. 48: "It may be maintained that religion was prior to magic, or, in the words of Dr. Jevons, 'that belief in the supernatural was prior to the belief in magic, and that the latter whenever it sprang up was a degradation or a relapse in the evolution of religion.'"

27. Edwards, *Philosophy of Religion*, p. 48: "This doctrine of relapse, implying that man started with a relatively pure form of religion, recurs in other contexts in Jevon's book (cf. our reference above to his view of polytheism as a relapse from a kind of monotheism). It has, however, so far as we are aware, few, if any, supporters among modern anthropologists, nor is it antecedently

A second position holds that magic was prior to religion, and that the latter evolved in some way out of the former.[28] Sir James Frazer is the outstanding exponent of this view.* His famous theory may be thus briefly summarized. "In the evolution of thought, magic as representing a lower intellectual stratum, has probably everywhere preceded religion." At first man sought adjustment through magic, but "a tardy recognition of the inherent falsehood and barrenness of magic set the more thoughtful part of mankind to cast about for a truer theory of Nature and a more fruitful method of turning her resources to account." Thus man's bitter experience of the failure of magic drove him to a different and better method of dealing with the unseen.[29] "The age of magic" gradually gave way to the "age of religion." In a word, man's despair of magic is the genesis of religion.[30]

* Frazer's Golden Bough, "The Magic Art," vol. 1., esp. pp. 220–243.

Frazer's theory has proved quite suggestive and thought provoking. But, though doubtless it contains elements of truth, it cannot be accepted in the sharp antithetical way in which he presented it.[31] As Edwards laconically states, "It is far too intellectualistic a view of the origin of religion. It seems to represent early man (of the more 'sagacious' type) as almost a full-blown arm chair philosopher in search of a working theory of life and the world, and ignores the spontaneous emotional response to environment which played a much greater part in the life of primitive man than reflective thought did."† Further, the theory only offers a negative explanation of the genesis of

† Edwards, op. cit., p. 50/

---

probable." In a footnote placed after "modern anthropologists," Edwards wrote: "Cf., however Andrew Lang's theory of degeneracy from a kind of primitive theism. See his *Making of Religion* (1898; 2nd ed., 1900)."

28. Edwards, *Philosophy of Religion*, p. 49: "It may be held that magic was prior to religion, and that the latter evolved in some way out of the former."

29. Edwards, *Philosophy of Religion*, p. 49: "Sir James Frazer's famous theory may be thus briefly summarized. 'In the evolution of thought, magic, as representing a lower intellectual stratum, has probably everywhere preceded religion.' . . . But 'a tardy recognition of the inherent falsehood and barrenness of magic set the more thoughtful part of mankind to cast about for a truer theory of Nature and a more fruitful method of turning her resources to account.' Thus man's bitter experience of the failure of magic drove him to a different and better method of trafficking with the unseen." In a footnote to the first sentence Edwards cited "Frazer's *Golden Bough*, 'The Magic Art,' vol. i., esp. pp. 220–243."

30. Edwards, *Philosophy of Religion*, p. 50: "Thus 'the age of magic' gradually gave place to 'the age of religion' . . . In a word, man's despair of magic is the genesis of religion."

31. Edwards, *Philosophy of Religion*, p. 50: "Frazer's theory has proved most suggestive and provocative . . . But though doubtless it contains elements of truth, it cannot be accepted in the sharp antithetical way in which he has presented it."

religion—the failure of magic. A positive motive for religion still needs to be found.[32]

A third position maintains that magic and religion had a common root in man's experience of the mysterious forces of the world, but that in the course of human evolution they revealed their mutual incompatibility even to the extent of active hostility.[33] In this theory, then, religion and magic are thought of as issuing out of common conditions, being the results of man's more or less conscious experiments with the unseen powers in his keen struggle for existence, and of his endeavour to utilize the mysterious potency around him which is generally called <u>mana</u> to help him in the battle of life.[34] This, as indicated above, is the view accepted by most modern anthropologists, and from my way of thinking it is quite valid.

Conclusion

The above brief study of the origin of religion in the light of anthropological research seems to culminate in the view that the most primitive religious idea is that of mana, that this arises in the actual ceremonial performances of the primitive groups, and that subsequently, as Marett says, "Gods start, in fact, as no more than portions of the ritual apparatus." However we must not reject the other theories as totally untenable. There seems to be some truth in each of these theories; none of them can be accepted as absolute. Maybe after all we will never get all of the facts as to the origin of religion in the race. Like Troeltsch we will probable have to be content to deal with religion in terms of what it has become, rather than from whence it came. After all this is the true essence of religion.

If, however, it can be proved that the origin of religion in the race was very crude we need not despair.

---

32. Edwards, *Philosophy of Religion*, pp. 51–52: "Finally, the theory only offers a negative explanation of the genesis of religion—the failure of magic. A positive motive for religion still needs to be found."

33. Edwards, *Philosophy of Religion*, p. 52: "It may be maintained that magic and religion had a common root in man's experience of the mysterious forces of the world, but that in the course of human evolution they revealed their mutual incompatibility even to the extent of active hostility."

34. Edwards, *Philosophy of Religion*, p. 53: "We may then think of religion and magic as issuing out of common conditions, being the results of man's more or less conscious experiments with the unseen powers in his keen struggle for existence, and of his endeavour to utilize the mysterious potency around him which the Melanesian calls *mana* to help him in the battle of life."

The question of origins is relatively independant of the question of values. If religion can be traced back to lowly origins, that should not in itself be regarded as prejudicial to its real value in the higher stages of its development, or to its relative value even at the l lower stages, any more than the fact that science and art have s sprung from most crude and unpromising beginnings should discredit the value of the final results or of the painful and often bungling efforts which have contributed to those results. It seems more rational to maintain that the final achievement enhances the worth of the crude beginnings than to say that the crudeness of the beginnings depreciates the value of the results.

Bibliography

1. Emile Durkheim: Elemental Forms of the Religious Life. Geo. Allen and Unwin, 1915.
2. D. Miall Edwards: The Philosophy of Religion. Richard R. Smith, 1930
3. James G. Frazer: The Golden Bough. Macmillan, 3rd ed. 1911.
4. F. W. Hopkins: Origin and Evolution of Religion, Yale Uni. Press, 1923.
5. Morris Jastrow: The Study of Religion, Charles Scribner's Sons, 1902.
6. F. B. Jevons: An Introduction To the History of Religion, Methuen, 1896.
7. R. R. Marett: The Threshold of Religion, Methuen, 1914.
8. Auguste Sabatier: Outlines of a Philosophy of Religion, James Pott and Co., 1897.
9. E. B. Taylor: Primitive Culture, Brentans, 1924.

THDS. MLKP-MBU: Box 115, folder 33.

Crozer Theological Seminary Placement Committee: Confidential Evaluation of Martin Luther King, Jr., by Charles E. Batten

[23 February 1951]
Chester, Pa.

406   King is one of the most brilliant students we have had at Crozer. He has a keen mind which is both analytical and constructively creative. While inter-

ested in social action, he has a fine theological and philosophical basis on which to promulgate his ideas and activities. He is particularly interested in philosophy and has done fine work in it both at Crozer and at Penn. He is a real leader as evidenced by the confidence his fellow students have in him by electing him president of the student body.

THFmS. CRO-NRCR.

6 Mar 1951

Graduate Record Examination
Scores for Martin Luther King, Jr.

6 March 1951
Princeton, N.J.

King took the examination on 3 February. A table enclosed with the test report indicated that his verbal aptitude score was in the second lowest quartile and his quantitative score was in the lowest ten percent of those taking the test. In the advanced test in philosophy, King's score (on a scale of 100) placed him in the lowest third, while his other scores (on a scale of 800) were in the lowest quartile in all the subject areas except literature, where he placed in the top quartile.

	EXAMINATION DATE		EXAM. NO.	COLLEGE
King Martin L Jr	**Feb 51**		**45982**	**1 567**
Aptitude	**V 350**	**Q 270**		
Philosophy	**58**			

PROFILE	**310**	**280**	**360**	**320**	**470**	**340**
	PHYSICS	CHEMISTRY	BIOLOGY	SOC. STUDIES	LITERATURE	FINE ARTS

TFm. CSKC.

"A Conception and Impression of Religion
Drawn from Dr. Brightman's Book
Entitled *A Philosophy of Religion*"

[*28 March 1951*]
[*Chester, Pa.*]

King wrote this essay as the first paper for the second term of Davis's Philosophy of Religion course. Although the essay derives largely from Brightman's Philosophy of Religion, *King grapples with various conceptions of God, a topic he would later discuss in greater depth in his dissertation. In contrast to his firm adherence*

407

to theism in early 1950, King, after reading Brightman's book, admits to being
"quite confused as to which definition [of God] was the most adequate." [1] *King's*
conclusion to this essay vividly illustrates Brightman's impact: "How I long now
for that religious experience which Dr. Brightman so cogently speaks of throughout
his book. It seems to be an experience, the lack of which life becomes dull and
meaningless. As I reflect on the matter, however, I do remember moments that I
have been awe awakened; there have been times that I have been carried out of
myself by something greater than myself and to that something I gave myself."
Davis gave King an A and commented, "Well done."

After reading Dr. Brightman's most scholarly work entitled, <u>A Philoso-</u>
<u>phy Of Religion</u>, I find that religion is a universal phenomenon involving
a set of beliefs about reality in addition to attitudes and practices of various
sorts. More specifically, religion seems to be "concern about experiences
which are regarded as of supreme value; devotion toward a power or powers
believed to originate, increase, and conserve these values; and some suitable
expression of this concern and devotion, whether through symbolic rites
or through other individual and social conduct."[2] Religion, then, seems to
be a total experience which includes this concern, this devotion, and this
expression.[3]

Dr. Brightman makes it very clear that religion is not to be confused with
magic, science, morals and art. Religion differs from magic in being devoted
to the power that is the source of values, whereas magic is a kind of mechanical compulsion of that power. Religion differs from science in being concerned about values, while science ignores the value of its facts and confines
itself to objective description. Religion resembles morals and art in being concerned with values, but differs from them in its primary devotion to the power
or powers that originate the supreme value of life, as well as in the use of
ritual for its expression.[4]

Interestingly enough I find that religion is a characteristically human experience From all known facts, the lower animals have no religion. Religion is
man's concern about his own value and destiny. From this I get the impression
that if there were no men, and if there existed only pure intelligences with no

---

1. In a final examination for Davis, King wrote: "I feel that the most valid conception of God
is that of theism. God, for me along with other theist is a personal spirit immanent in nature and
in the value structure of the universe" (see Examination answers, Christian Theology for Today,
13 September 1949–15 February 1950, p. 290 in this volume).

2. Edgar S. Brightman, *A Philosophy of Religion* (New York: Prentice-Hall, 1940), p. 17.

3. Brightman, *Philosophy of Religion*, p. 17: "Religion, then, is a total experience which includes
this concern, this devotion, and this expression."

4. Brightman, *Philosophy of Religion*, p. 17: "Religion differs from magic in being devotion
to the power that is the source of values, whereas magic is a kind of mechanical compulsion
of that power. Religion differs from science in being concerned about values, while science
ignores the value of its facts and confines itself to objective description. Religion resembles
morals and art in being concerned with values, but differs from them in its primary devotion to
the power or powers that originate the supreme value of life, as well as in the use of ritual for its
expression."

ideal save that of scientific knowledge, physics and mathematics would be as true for them as for men, but they would have no religion.[5]

From my reading of this interesting work by Dr. Brightman, I find that there are certain essential religious beliefs which underlie the whole phenomenon of religion. These essential religious beliefs, according to our author, have been found to pervade every religion. What then are these essential beliefs?

The first essential religious belief is that there are experiences of great and permanent value.[6] In the above definition of religion it was revealed that every religious experience is an experience of value. Science is objective, disinterested description. Religion, according to our author, is never merely disinterested, however objective it may be. It is "interested," that is, it takes sides for value as against disvalue. Religion is definitely for the good and against the evil, whereas science is interested only in knowing the facts of good and evil, their causes and their effects.[7]

Our Author makes it quite clear that religion is an experience of value in two senses. In the first place, as has been said, it is a choice of value, an appreciation or adoration of value, or the source of value. But in the second place, it is also a faith in the friendliness of the universe to value. The first point means that value experience can be created by human enjoyment, choice, or appreciation; the second means that value experience will somehow be preserved in the universe, because there is in the very nature of things an unfailing source of value.[8]

The belief in gods or God is the second essential religious belief. According to our author most religions from the start rest on belief in divine beings, or a divine being, viewed as a source of value, if not the source of all value. Even those religions, like Jainism, Buddhism, and Communism, which begin with atheism tend to develop a belief in some objective source of value, that is to say, a god.[9]

---

5. Brightman, *Philosophy of Religion*, p. 342: "Religion is a characteristically human experience. As far as we know, the lower animals have no religion. If there were no men, and if there existed only pure intelligences with no ideal save that of scientific knowledge, physics and mathematics would be as true for them as for men, but they would have no religion. . . . Religion is man's concern about his own value and destiny."

6. Brightman, *Philosophy of Religion*, p. 81: "*The belief that there are experiences of great and permanent value.*"

7. Brightman, *Philosophy of Religion*, p. 85: "The survey of the facts of religion (its phenomenology, as such a survey is called) has revealed the fundamental fact that every religious experience is an experience of value. . . . Science is objective, disinterested description. Religion is never merely disinterested description, however objective it may be. It is 'interested,' that is, it takes sides for value as against disvalue. Religion is definitely for the good and against the evil, whereas science is interested only in knowing the facts of good and evil, their causes and their effects."

8. Brightman, *Philosophy of Religion*, p. 86: "In two senses, religion is an experience of value. In the first place, as has been said, it is a choice of value, an appreciation or adoration of value, or the source of value. But in the second place, it is also a faith in the friendliness of the universe to value. The first point means that value experience can be created by human enjoyment, choice, or appreciation; the second means that value experience will somehow be preserved in the universe, because there is in the very nature of things an unfailing source of value."

9. Brightman, *Philosophy of Religion*, p. 81: "*The belief in gods or God.* Most religions from the start rest on belief in divine beings, or a divine being, viewed as a source of value, if not the source

I was amazed to find that the conception of God is so complex and one about which opinions differ so widely. There have been at least nine conceptions of God in the history of religious thinking which have been quite prominent. The first conception of God that we might refer to is that of Polytheism. Here there is a belief in many gods, each god regarded as a vaguely personal (or impersonal-mana) spirit which is the source of some energy which brings value to man. There are gods of rivers, springs, trees, rains; of fertility, of motherhood, of fatherhood, and of love. It is believed that even when man sees disaster, some one of these gods is at work or may be called on. According to our author polytheism is religiously important as a phenomenon which has continued for centuries and still persists in some sections of Asia and Africa.[10]

A second conception of God that has arisen is referred to as Henotheism. This term is used to describe belief in and worship of one god as supreme, accompanied by recognition that others exist.[11]

A third conception of God sees him as "Supreme Personal Creator." This is the view of monotheism. Here it is held that there is only one God, and that this supreme personal spirit is the source of all value and the creator of all that exist other than himself.[12]

A fourth conception of God sees him as the "Whole of Reality." This is known as the pantheistic view. In this view God is not a spirit separate from nature and man, who creates them and imparts value to them. Rather God is conceived as the whole of which nature and man are parts.[13]

A fifth conception of God sees him as the Unknowable source of all being. Our author refers to this view as agnostic realism. Here it is held that God exists, but he is essentially unknowable. Those who hold such a view point out that religion does not pretend to be a matter of human knowledge, scientific or philosophical. It is rather an aspiration toward the infinite but unknown source of our experience of values, and of nature. Religion is humble, and religion moves in the atmosphere of mystery.[14]

---

of all value. We have found that even those religions, like Jainism, Buddhism, and Communism, which begin with atheism tend to develop a belief in some objective source of value, that is to say, a god."

10. Brightman, *Philosophy of Religion*, pp. 137–138: "What we are sure of is that we find man for a long time in his history believing in many gods, each god regarded as a vaguely personal (or impersonal-mana) spirit which is the source of some energy which brings value to man. There are gods of rivers, springs, trees, rains; of fertility, of motherhood, of fatherhood, of love; . . . It is believed that even when man sees disaster, some one of these gods is at work or may be called on. . . . Polytheism is, however, religiously important as a phenomenon which has continued for centuries and still persists in some sections of Asia and Africa."

11. Brightman, *Philosophy of Religion*, p. 139: "The term henotheism is often used to describe belief in and worship of one god as supreme, accompanied by recognition that others exist."

12. Brightman, *Philosophy of Religion*, p. 140: "More or less independently, there grew up the idea of one supreme personal spirit, the source of all value and the creator of all that exists other than himself."

13. Brightman, *Philosophy of Religion*, p. 141: "God is not a spirit separate from nature and man, who creates them and imparts value to them. Rather, these thinkers hold, God is the whole of which nature and man are parts."

14. Brightman, *Philosophy of Religion*, p. 142: "Those who hold such a view point out that religion does not pretend to be a matter of human knowledge, scientific or philosophical. It is

A sixth view of God sees "Him" as human aspiration for Ideal Values. This view is often referred to as Humanism. The essence of this view is that God is to be found in man's highest social experiences, not in any reality beyond man.[15]

A seventh conception of God sees him as the superhuman and supernatural revealer of values. Our authors refers to this view as deistic supernaturalism. According to this view, God is not found in human experience at all except in so far as he chooses to reveal himself; when he reveals himself it is not as the highest man can think, but rather as something "totally other" than everything human, of a radically different quality from human hopes and strivings—as different from our best as eternity is from time.[16]

An eighth conception of God sees "Him" as the system of ideal values. This view is referred to by Brightman as impersonal Idealism. The members of this group go back to Plato, and think of God as the eternal Forms (or Ideas) of Justice, Truth, and Love. Since the Forms are thought of as eternally valid ideals or principles, God is not a person or conscious mind for members of this group, and their view may well be called impersonal idealism.[17]

A ninth view of God see "Him" as the tendency of Nature to support or produce value. This view is known as religious naturalism. Here God is seen as the tendency of nature to support or produce movement toward perfection. God is the name for "the growth of meaning and value in the world."[18]

After reading so many different definitions of God, I found myself quite confused as to which definition was the most adequate, only to find as I continued to read that the question of whether God is finite or infinite raises a whole new problem. The former view is referred to as theistic absolutism. The latter is referred to as theistic finitism. Our author seems to deal with this problem of the finite or infinite God mainly when he comes to a discussion of the problem of evil. For this reason we may reserve our discussion of this

---

rather an aspiration toward the infinite but unknown source of our experience of values, and of nature. Religion is humble, and religion moves in the atmosphere of mystery."

15. Brightman, *Philosophy of Religion*, p. 144: "In America, . . . there has arisen a movement known as religious humanism, the essence of which is the view that God is to be found in man's highest social experiences, not in any reality beyond man."

16. Brightman, *Philosophy of Religion*, p. 145: "According to this view, God is not found in human experience at all except in so far as he chooses to reveal himself; when he reveals himself it is not as the highest man can think, but rather as something 'totally other' than everything human, of a radically different quality from human hopes and strivings—as different from our best as eternity is from time."

17. Brightman, *Philosophy of Religion*, p. 147: "Hence this group defines God as the system of ideal values. Its members go back to Plato, and think of God as the eternal Forms (or Ideas) of Justice, Truth, and Love, although Plato himself never identified God with the Forms. Since the Forms are thought of as eternally valid ideals or principles, God is not a person or a conscious mind for members of this group, and their view may well be called impersonal idealism."

18. Brightman, *Philosophy of Religion*, pp. 151, 152: "Thinkers of this sort would agree in defining God as the tendency of nature to support or produce values. . . . the same general formula applies equally well to Wieman's God and to Alexander's: God is the tendency of nature to support or produce movement toward perfection. . . . For Wieman, likewise, God is the name for 'the growth of meaning and value in the world.'"

problem until we come to a discussion of the existence of evil as an essential religious belief.

In bringing this section on belief in God to a close, I cannot avoid being impressed by the variety of opinion about God. Yet what the author said at the start is now seen more clearly to be true; that in all variety of opinion there is one common insight about experience coming to expression, namely, that the object to which all religions have directed their worship and service is a divine source and conserver of values.[19]

The third essential religious belief is that <u>man is a soul or spiritual being, and not merely a physical organism</u>. All religions, according to our author, have found the chief meaning of existence in man's spiritual nature and attitude, rather than in any purely material condition or possession. The most crude idolatry is always regarded as a relation of the human spirit to a divine spirit.[20]

The belief in man as a spiritual being leads us inevitably to the problem of personality. Dr. Brightman goes to great pains to deal with this question. He concludes that a <u>person</u> is a self that is potentially self-conscious, rational, and ideal. That is to say, when a self is able at times to reflect on itself as a self, to reason, and to acknowledge ideal goals by which it can judge its actual achievements, then we call it a person. The question immediately arises at this point as to the personality of lower animals. Dr. Brightman answers this question by saying that there is no reason on the basis of known evidence to draw the line sharply and say that only human beings are persons; pigs, dogs, apes, and horses seem to be at least elementary persons. But this consideration, he continues, is of no vital importance to a philosophy of religion, for the very good reason that, as far as is known, human persons are the only ones who have religious experience.[21] Such a fact reveals the spiritual nature of man.

A Fourth essential religious belief is that <u>there is purpose in human existence</u>. This purpose is thought of as being for the group, and in higher religions, also for the individual; it is not merely man's purpose, but also God's. Thus religion is always a relation of man to the whole of existence or at least to the whole which he believes to be supremely important and worthy of his

---

19. Brightman, *Philosophy of Religion*, p. 161: "In bringing this chapter to a close, we cannot avoid being impressed by the variety of opinion about God. Yet what was said at the start is now seen more clearly to be true; that in all the variety of opinion there is one common insight about experience coming to expression, namely, that the object to which all religions have directed their worship and service is a divine source and conserver of values."

20. Brightman, *Philosophy of Religion*, pp. 81–82: "*The belief that man is a soul or spiritual being, not merely a physical organism.* All religions have found the chief meaning of existence in man's spiritual nature and attitude, rather than in any purely material condition or possession. The most crude idolatry is always regarded as a relation of the human spirit to a divine spirit."

21. Brightman, *Philosophy of Religion*, p. 350: "A *person* is a self that is potentially self-conscious, rational, and ideal. That is to say, when a self is able at times to reflect on itself as a self, to reason, and to acknowledge ideal goals by which it can judge its actual achievements, then we call it a person. There is no reason on the basis of known evidence to draw the line sharply and say that only human beings are persons; pigs, dogs, apes, and horses seem to be at least elementary persons. But this consideration is of no vital importance to a philosophy of religion, for the very good reason that, as far as we know, human persons are the only ones who have religious experience."

purposive devotion. Says our author, even when belief in purpose is faint or absent, its effects abide in the form of belief in man's membership in a larger whole on which he depends.[22]

A Fifth essential religious belief is that <u>there is valid religious experience</u>. This is the conviction that there are experiences, such as sacraments, conversion, worship, mystical moments, and prayer, when the religious person comes into actual and immediate relation with the divine being.[23] More specifically our author speaks of religious experience as any experience of any person taken in its relation to his God. Religious experience is not a unique kind or quality of experience; it is rather a unique way of apprehending experience. There are therefore many degrees of religious experience according to Dr. Brightman. The experience of believing nature to be a deed (or creation) of God is a religious experience; so is the experience of prayer. But the latter, being less apparently impersonal than the system of nature and being more directly concerned with spiritual values and hence with the essential nature of God, is more intensely religious.[24]

A sixth essential religious belief is that <u>the human soul is immortal</u>. This belief has been so widespread that some have called it universal. Traces of it may be found in almost every primitive tribe, as well as in almost every developed religion. Dr. Brightman makes it quite clear that there are some religions (such as Old Testament Judaism) in which belief in conscious, personal immortality is inconspicuous, and others from which it is entirely absent (such as Hinayana Buddhism). But, like belief in the personality of God, he argues, it tends to develop in the later stages of a religion, even if it was lacking from the earlier.[25]

I was interested to find our author speaking of the great religious value of

---

22. Brightman, *Philosophy of Religion*, p. 82: "*The belief that there is purpose in human existence.* This purpose is thought of as being for the group, and in higher religions, also for the individual; it is not merely man's purpose, but also God's. Thus religion is always a relation of man to the whole of existence or at least to the whole which he believes to be supremely important and worthy of his purposive devotion. Even when belief in purpose is faint or absent, its effects abide in the form of belief in man's membership in a larger whole on which he depends."

23. Brightman, *Philosophy of Religion*, p. 82: "*The belief in valid religious experience.* This is the conviction that there are experiences, such as sacraments, conversion, worship, mystical moments, and prayer, when the religious person comes into actual and immediate relation with the divine being."

24. Brightman, *Philosophy of Religion*, pp. 415–416: "Religious experience is *any experience of any person taken in its relation to his God.* Religious experience is not a unique kind or quality of experience; it is rather a unique way of apprehending experience. There are therefore many degrees of religious experience. The experience of believing nature to be a deed (or creation) of God is a religious experience; so is the experience of prayer. But the latter, being less apparently impersonal than the system of nature and being more directly concerned with spiritual values and hence with the essential nature of God, is more intensely religious."

25. Brightman, *Philosophy of Religion*, p. 387: "Belief in the survival of bodily death is so widespread that some have called it universal. Traces of it may be found in almost every primitive tribe, as well as in almost every developed religion. There are, it is true, some religions (such as Old Testament Judaism) in which belief in conscious, personal immortality is inconspicuous, and others from which it is entirely absent (such as Hinayana Buddhism). But, like belief in the personality of God, it tends to develop in the later stages of a religion, even if it was lacking from the earlier."

this belief in immortality. His argument may be summarized thus. The good life is a life of goal-seeking; it is a life of forward-looking purpose. Immortality symbolizes the faith that good purpose never fails to all eternity. The taproot of all human endeavor is in the hope that purpose can acheive values. Those who deny immortality continue to strive largely because they beleive that they are laying foundations for the next generation. If courage and meaning are imparted to life by a short {look} into the future, how much more dignity, hope, and perspective arise from the faith that every life capable of purposive development is eternal. Immortality symbolizes the intrinsic value of the individual person, the intrinsic value of shared, cooperative living, and the goodness of God.[26]

A seventh essential religious belief is that there is evil as well as value. All religions, according to Brightman, have recognized that there is something in the universe to be opposed and feared. In primitive religion, it is hard to distinguish good from evil in the taboo; but the belief in demons, Satan, Ahriman, sin, the need of redemption, longing for individual conversion and social reform all imply recognition of something evil. Even a religion like Christian Science, which denies the reality of evil, recognizes it in the fact of "error of mortal mind" and in "malicious animal magnetism."[27]

It seems fair to say from an interpretation of our authors conclusions that good is a principle of totality, of coherence, of meaning; evil is a principle of fragmentariness, of incoherence, of mockery. Hence there is no immanent logic in evil; "evil is the Satan that laughs at logic. Yet many religionist believe that there is logic in thought about evil, and from my reading I find that many more or less logical solutions of the problem have been proposed. Those most often discussed in the modern world, according to Brightman, are as follows: (1) Moral evils may be explained as a result of human freedom. (2) Nonmoral evils are sometimes viewed as a punishment for moral evils. (3) Nonmoral evils, if not penal, may be regarded as disciplinary. (4) Evil, it is said is incomplete good. (5) Some adherents to the foregoing theory, as well as some who do not hold it, advance the idea that evil is needed as a contrast to good. (6) It is sometimes argued that nonmoral evils, as well as moral ones, are a result of

---

26. Brightman, *Philosophy of Religion*, pp. 409–410: "The good life is a life of goal-seeking; it is a life of forward-looking purpose. Immortality symbolizes the faith that good purpose never fails to all eternity. The taproot of all human endeavor is in the hope that purpose can achieve values. Those who deny immortality continue to strive largely because they believe that they are laying foundations for the next generation. If courage and meaning are imparted to life by a short look into the future, how much more dignity, hope, and perspective arise from the faith that every life capable of purposive development is eternal. Immortality symbolizes the intrinsic value of the individual person, the intrinsic value of shared, coöperative living, and the goodness of God."

27. Brightman, *Philosophy of Religion*, p. 81: "*The belief that there is evil as well as value.* All religions recognize that there is something in the universe to be opposed and feared. In primitive religion, it is hard to distinguish good from evil in the taboo; but the belief in demons, Satan, Ahriman, sin, the need of redemption, longing for individual conversion and social reform all imply recognition of something evil. Even a religion like Christian Science, which denies the reality of evil, recognizes it in the fact of 'error of mortal mind' and in 'malicious animal magnetism.'"

freedom. (7) It is often argued that even though certain evils may be intrinsic surds so far as man is concerned, it may be that those very evils are needed in the universe as instruments to beings rather than men. (8) The theory just stated often takes a more general form in the proposition that all evils intrinsic or instrumental—serve an unknown good. (9) In sharp contrast with the view which justifies all evil as good is the view, held by some Hindus and by Christian Scientists, that evil is unreal. (10) There remains as a solution of the problem of evil the one which is most popular among nontheistic and nonidealistic thinkers, namely, the view that good and evil are the outcome of processes or entities which are axiologically neutral.[28]

As Dr. Brightman continues his discussion on good-and-evil he makes it very clear that his solution to the problem ~~resols~~ resolves around a {the} positing of a finite God. Here God is described as a self struggling with recalcitrant factors within himself. He is a personal finite God whose finiteness consists in his own internal structure: an eternal unitary personal consciousness whose creative will is limited both by external necessities of reason and by eternal experiences of brute fact. These limits Brightman calls The Given. In short he concludes that God's Power is Finite, while his Will for Good is infinite.

After being introduced to this all pervasive phenomenon called religion I am now convinced that it is one of the most fruitful adventures that man [strikeout illegible] can take. With H. G. Wells I might now say that "if a man is not religious he begins at nowhere and ends at nothing." It is religion that gives meaning to life. It is religion that gives meaning to the Universe. It is religion that is the greatest incentive for the good life. It is religion which gives us the assurance that all that is high noble and valuable will be conserved. Such fruits of religion I find to be its greatest virtues, and certainly they cannot be ignored by any sane man. I must now conclude that any atheistic view is both philosophically unsound and practically disadvantageous. How I long now for that religious experience which Dr. Brightman so cogently speaks of

---

28. Brightman, *Philosophy of Religion*, pp. 259–260: "Good is a principle of totality, of coherence, of meaning. Evil is a principle of fragmentariness, of incoherence, of mockery. Hence there is no immanent logic in evil; evil is the Satan that laughs at logic. Yet there is logic in thought about evil, and many more or less logical solutions of the problem of evil have been proposed. Those most often discussed in the modern world will now be briefly stated and criticized."

Brightman then presents a detailed list on pp. 260–271; King used the first sentence of each point in the list: "(1) *Moral evils* may be explained as *a result of human freedom.* . . . (2) *Nonmoral evils* are sometimes viewed as *a punishment for moral evils.* . . . (3) *Nonmoral evils*, if not penal, *may be regarded as disciplinary.* . . . (4) *Evil*, it is said, *is incomplete good.* . . . (5) Some adherents to the foregoing theory, as well as some who do not hold it, advance the idea that *evil is needed as a contrast to good.* . . . (6) It is sometimes argued that *nonmoral evils*, as well as moral ones, *are a result of freedom.* . . . (7) Even though certain evils may be intrinsic surds so far as man is concerned, *it may be that those* very *evils are needed in the universe as instruments to beings other than men.* . . . (8) The theory just discussed often takes a more general form in the proposition that *all evils*—intrinsic or instrumental—*serve an unknown good.* . . . (9) In sharp contrast with the view which justifies all evil as good is the view, held by some Hindus and by Christian Scientists, that *evil is unreal.* . . . (10) There remains as a solution of the problem of evil the one which is most popular among nontheistic and nonidealistic thinkers, namely, the view that *good and evil are the outcome of processes or entities which are axiologically neutral.*"

throughout his book. It seems to be an experience, the lack of which life be-comes dull and meaningless. As I reflect on the matter, however, I do remember moments that I have been awe awakened; there have been times that I have been carried out of myself by something greater than myself and to that something I gave myself. Has this great something been God? Maybe after all I have been religious for a number of years, and am now only becoming aware of it.

AHDS. MLKP-MBU: Box 112, folder 14.

"Religion's Answer to the Problem of Evil"

[*27 April 1951*]
[*Chester, Pa.*]

In this paper for the second term of Davis's Philosophy of Religion course, King examines the explanations of ancient and modern philosophers for the existence of evil in the world. He follows Harris Franklin Rall's analysis of the problem of evil in Christianity: An Inquiry into Its Nature and Truth, *concluding that "the ultimate solution is not intellectual but spiritual. After we have climbed to the top of the speculative ladder we must leap out into the darkness of faith." Davis gave King an A − and commented, "Well done."*

The problem of evil has always been the most baffling problem facing the theist. Indeed, it is belief in a personal God which constitutes the problem in all its known acuteness. At the heart of all high religion there is the conviction that there is behind the universe an ultimate power which is perfectly good. In other words the theist says: the power that is behind all things is good. But on every hand the facts of life seem to contradict such a faith. Nature is often cruel. "Nearly all the things which men are hanged or imprisoned for doing to one another", says John Stuart Mill, "are nature's every day performances. Nature kills, burns, starves, freezes, poisons."*[1] Not only that, but the world seems positively immoral. If we look through the pages of history what do we find?

* Three Essays on Religion, p. 28.

---

1. Harris Franklin Rall, *Christianity: An Inquiry into Its Nature and Truth* (New York: Scribner, 1940), p. 313: "That is what faith in God means: the power that is back of all things is good; goodness has ultimate power. But on every hand the facts of life seem to contradict that faith. . . . Nature is cruel. 'Nearly all the things which men are hanged or imprisoned for doing to one another,' says John Stuart Mill, 'are nature's every day performances. Nature kills, burns, starves, freezes, poisons.'"

Jesus on a cross and Caesar in a places; truth on the
scaffold and wrong on the throne;[2] the just suffering
while the unjust prosper. How explain all this in the
face of a good and powerful God? If the universe is
rational, why is evil rampant within it? If God is all
powerful and perfectly good why does he permit such
devastating conditions to befall the lives of men? Why
do the innocent suffer? How account for the endless
chain of moral and physical evils?

These are questions which no serious minded religionist can overlook. Evil is a reality. No one can make
light of disease, slavery, war, or famine. It might be
true that God is in his heaven, but all is not right with
the world, and only the superficial optimist who refuses to face the realities of life fails to see this patent
fact. Evil is not rational, on the contrary it is non-
rational. It is a "principle of fragmentariness, of incoherence, of mockery." It is not logical; evil is the
Satan that laughs at logic.[3] It is in this great inescapable conundrum that we find the "theistic dilemma."
I must hasten to say, however, that the theists have
not been content to pass over this problem as just another problem with no serious import; theists of all
shades of opinion have been willing to face the problem with all the intellectual equipment that the human mind has afforded. At this point we may turn to
a critical discussion of those solutions most often set
forth in the modern world. In conclusion I will present what I feel to be the most adequate solution to
this pressing problem.

Modern Answers

(1) First there is the position that moral evils result
from the human misuse of freedom. Certainly this
position has much weight, and cannot be easily cast

---

2. Davis corrected "places" to "palace." King often quoted this James Russell Lowell poem in
sermons and speeches throughout his life, including "Facing the Challenge of a New Age" (1956)
and "Remaining Awake Through a Great Revolution" (1968) (see James Washington, ed., *A Testament of Hope* [San Francisco: Harper & Row, 1986], pp. 52, 141, 207, 243–244, 277, 507). The
section of the poem favored by King is:

> Truth forever on the scaffold, Wrong forever on the throne,—
> Yet that scaffold sways the future, and, behind the dim unknown
> Standeth God within the shadow, keeping watch above his own.
>   (*The Present Crisis* [1844, stanza 8]).

3. The quotation and the phrase "evil is the Satan that laughs at logic" are from Edgar S.
Brightman, *A Philosophy of Religion* (New York: Prentice-Hall, 1940), p. 259.

aside. Nevertheless, human freedom leaves many aspects of evil, even of moral evil, unexplained. With Dr. Brightman we would ahave to raise the following questions. Why are there in the nature of things, independent of human choice, so many temptations and allurements of evil choices? And why are the consequences of some evil choices so utterly debasing and disastrous? Is it just to ascribe all of the sins and vices of poverty-stricken refugees or unemployed families to their own freedom, or even to all human freedom put together?* This seems to be putting too much weight on the back of human freedom. Freedom may explain much of moral evil, but it fails to explain physical evil. Moreover, it does not explain the force of temptation or the debasing consequences of moral evil.[4]

* Brightman, A Philosophy of Religion, p. 260.

(2) A second view explains physical evils as a punishment for moral evils.[5] Such a view rests in the principle of retribution. This view goes back to the old Deuteronomic idea that prosperity follows piety and righteous, while suffering follows sin. Even in the days of Jesus we find traces of this theory. Hence the question is put to Jesus: "Who sinned, this man, or his parents, that he should be born blind."† The most rigorous expression of this viewpoint is found in India's ancient doctrine of Karma. Karma means literally deed. Suffering is explained as the consequence of a man's deeds, whether committed in this present life or in some prevoius existence. Views of this variety continue to exist in the modern world. But such views are repugnant to the ethical sense of modern idealist.[6] Does a good God harbor resentment? Does perfect love achieve its purpose in such cruel ways? This crude theory was rejected long ago by the writer of the book of Job and by Jesus (according to John

† John 9:2

---

4. Brightman, *Philosophy of Religion*, pp. 260–261: "*Moral evils* may be explained as *a result of human freedom*. Much weight may be granted to this argument. . . . Nevertheless, human freedom leaves many aspects of evil, even of moral evil, unexplained. Why are there in the nature of things, independent of human choice, so many temptations and allurements to evil choices? And why are the consequences of some evil choices so utterly debasing and disastrous? . . . Is it just to ascribe all of the sins and vices of poverty-stricken refugees or unemployed families to their own freedom, or even to all human freedom put together? . . . Freedom, we repeat, explains much of moral evil, but it does not explain either the force of temptation or the debasing consequences of moral evil."

5. Brightman, *Philosophy of Religion*, p. 261: "*Nonmoral evils* are sometimes viewed as *a punishment for moral evils*."

6. Davis corrected "idealist" to "idealism." Brightman, *Philosophy of Religion*, p. 261: "Yet it is repugnant to the ethical sense of modern idealists."

9:3). The whole theory of punishment as a solution of the problem of evil collapses with a series of ethical objections.[7]

(3) A third view explains nonmoral evils as disciplinary rather than penal. Here the purpose of evil is to reform or to test rather than to punish. It is quite obvious that this view cannot be totally rejected. Who can deny that many apparent evils turn out in the end to be goods in disguise. Character often develops out of hardship. Unfortunate hereditary and environmental conditions often make for great and noble souls. Suffering teaches sympathy.[8] But is this the whole story? We must answer with an emphatic no. Character is not always developed through hardship. Unfortunate hereditary and environmental conditions do not always make for noble spirits, they more frequently make for resentful, depressed ahd hopeless living.

A more serious criticism of this view is pointed out very cogently by Dr. Brightman. He argues that if discipline is the purpose of all evil, and God is both omnipotent and just, then disciplinary evils should meet at least two conditions, viz, (1) they should appear wherever they are needed and only where they are needed and (2) they should be perfectly adapted to their ideal end. It is perfectly clear that neither of these conditions is met.[9] Says Brightman: "Diciplinary evil fail to appear for the moral ecucation of the world's worst characters; and the innocent and already overdiciplined victims of these very characters receive repeated superfluous and unjust diciplines. Even if all evils were wisely and justly disciplinary and none were wasted unjustly, the second condition would remain unsatisfied. When one contemplates the actual evils of a wind storm at sea, the experiences of freezing and starving, or the symptoms of syphilis or arteriosclerosis, it would be most extravagant to as-

---

7. Brightman, *Philosophy of Religion*, pp. 261–262: "This crude theory of punishment was rejected by the writer of the book of Job and by Jesus (according to Jn. 9:3). . . . The whole theory of punishment as a solution of the problem of evil collapses of its own weight."

8. Brightman, *Philosophy of Religion*, p. 262: "*Nonmoral evils*, if not penal, *may be regarded as disciplinary*. Their purpose is then to reform or to test, . . . It cannot well be denied that many apparent evils (disvalue-claims) turn out to be goods in disguise (true values). Hardship often develops character. . . . Suffering teaches sympathy."

9. Brightman, *Philosophy of Religion*, p. 263: "If discipline is the purpose of all evil, and God is both omnipotent and just, then disciplinary evils should meet at least two conditions. First, they should appear wherever they are needed and only where they are needed. Secondly, they should be perfectly adapted to their ideal end. It is clear that neither of these conditions is met."

sert not only that these experiences may be disciplinary, but also that they are the most perfect means to the ideal ends of personal and social development that an infinitely good and powerful imagination could devise. As a philosophical explanation of evil, the appeal to discipline entails incoherences so far-reaching that it cannot serve its purpose."*

In the final analysis we must reject the disciplinary theory because it fails to give a true picture of the whole. It only faces the problem piecemeal. Any explanation of the problem of evil must (at least any adequate explanation) present evidence that fits all the facts and is contradicted by none.

(4) There is a fourth position which explains evil as incomplete good. Absolute idealist like Hegel and his followers have been strong proponents of this view. They have insisted that the true is the whole, and that a partial view of anything is inadequate and irrational. Many patches of color within a painting are ugly; but the entire painting is beautiful. This argument on the surface seems quite cogent, yet if we probe deeper we find that its cogency depends on whether or not every whole is necessarily good. From incompleteness alone, the goodness of the complete cannot be derived. In fact such a view boils down to inane speculation. It is as logical at some points to argue that good is incomplete evil as it is to argue that evil is invomplete good.† The question of whether the whole is good or evil must therefore be settled on other grounds than the incompleteness of our experience.[10] Moreover, even if the whole could be proved to be good, the question would still remain as to whether destructive means justify constructive ends. As Dr. Rall laconically states, "the Christian faith which follows Jesus in his belief in the sacredness of a moral personality cannot let even God (God, indeed, least of all) use human beings as mere means to some supposedly higher ends."‡[11]

* Brightman, op. cit., p. 263.

† Brightman, op. cit., p. 264.

‡ Rall, Christianity, p. 316.

---

10. Brightman, *Philosophy of Religion*, p. 264: "*Evil*, it is said, *is incomplete good*. Absolute idealists like Hegel have dwelt on the principle that the true is the whole, that a partial view of anything is inadequate and irrational, and that the whole alone is truly good. . . . Many patches of color within a painting are ugly; but the entire painting is beautiful. . . . Yet [this argument from synoptic logic] is cogent only if we know in advance that every whole is necessarily good, or that this is true of the universe as a whole. From incompleteness alone, the goodness of the complete cannot be derived. In fact, it is as true in some cases to say that good is incomplete evil as to say that evil is incomplete good. . . . The question of whether the whole is good or evil must therefore be settled on other grounds than the incompleteness of our experience."

11. Rall's final word is "end," not "ends" (Rall, *Christianity*, p. 316).

(5) Another view, quite similar to the foregoing, advances the idea that evil is needed as a contrast to good. Proponents of this view argue that no one would appreciate the goodness if all were good; indeed goodness could not even be defined if there were nothing by way of contrast.[12] So from this point of view evil is not an unfortunate blot which the finished can't help having; the blot is essential to its beauty; the artist deliberately put it there; it is an element contributing to the perfection of the whole, like those momentary discords in a symphony which enhance the total harmony. Presumably, then, in the eternal order of things pain and sin are nothing to worry about; they are as necessary to its perfection as are beauty and joy and virtue, Like the dark places in Rembrandt's pictures, they make the high lights possible.

There are many objections to this view, in fact they are too numerous to mention at this point, but at least we may allude to two. First, this theory implies that God not only permits evil (which is obviously true), but that he deliberately creates it; He purposely does evil that good may come. Now we may ask as we did in our criticism of the theory of the absolute idealists, does the means justify the end? We must conclude that the argument that the end j justifies the means is as morally unjustified for God as for men.

Again, if the existence of evil is necessary to the good of the whole, will it not be a mistake to try to get rid of evil? To lessen evil would surely be to lessen the good of the whole; presumably the universe would be less perfect if its evil were removed; and therefore suffering men need not strive to change anything; all their high moral aspirations all their dreams of betterment, are vain; which is absurd. This theory defeats its own ends.

(6) In sharp contrast with the view which justifies all evil as good is the view that evil is unreal. It is "maya" or illusion; it is "error of mortal mind." This view has its strongest proponents in Christian Scientists and Hindus.

Objections to this are obvious, but two must suffice

---

12. Brightman, *Philosophy of Religion*, p. 265: "Some adherents to the foregoing theory, as well as some who do not hold it, advance the idea that *evil is needed as a contrast to good*. A monotonous world, it is held, would be wearisome; and if all were good, no one would appreciate the goodness; perhaps no one could even define it if there were nothing by way of contrast."

here.[13] First: if the natural order in so far as it seems evil is nonexistent, the next step is to deny the existence of the natural order as good. If all nature is illusion there is no good reason for believing anything to be objective. Second: even if evil is error it is just as harmful as it would be if it were objective; the problem is not solved, it is merely pushed one stage further back.[14] "Errors of mortal mind" would still be a problem clamoring for solution. As Dr. Whole so congently states in a criticism of this theory, "To say that all suffering is a delusion of man's mind would be to make the existence of the mind the worst of evils; there is not much to choose between pain that is objectively real and mind which necessarily imagines the pain that tortures it."*

* J. S. Whole, The Christian Answer to The Problem of Evil, p. 21 [15]

The Doctrine
Of A Finite God

We may consider in a special group those who have found a solution to the problem of evil by setting forth a limitation of the power of God. They believe that in the face of evil God must either be lacking in power or goodness; they choose the former.[16]

The historical root of theistic finitism is to be found in plato. For him God's will is confronted by limits set by the uncreated discordant and disorderly aspects of being. "God is not the cause of all things, but only of the good things."† This is explained more fully in the Timaeus, where divinity is represented, not as omnipotent creator of all, but simply as a good God who desires "that, so far as possible, all things should be good and nothing evil." What is the meaning of "so far as possible?" It simply means that God's will did not create the conditions under which it worked, but "took over all that was visible, seeing that it was not in a state of rest, but in a state of discordant and disor-

† Rep. II, 380 c.

---

13. J. S. Whale, *The Christian Answer to the Problem of Evil* (New York: Abingdon Press, 1936), p. 20: "Objections to this are obvious, but two must suffice here."

14. Whale, *Christian Answer*, p. 21: "The other objection is that if one of the fundamental elements of human experience is an illusion, this fact is itself an evil; the problem is not solved, it is merely pushed one stage further back."

15. Davis corrected "Whole" to "Whale," both in this footnote and in the text above.

16. Rall, *Christianity*, p. 317: "We may consider in a special group those who in one way or another have set forth a limitation of the power of God as the answer to this problem. It is their reply to the old alternative: in the face of the fact of evil, God must be lacking in either goodness or power."

derly motion," and "he brought it into order out of disorder."[17]

Plato's view of God is then clear. God is a will for good, not infinite but finite, limited on the one hand by rational principles of order and control (Philebus) and on the other by "discordant and disorderly motion" (Timaeus) which he finds in existence.[18]

We find something of this view in Nicholas Berdyaev, who was the great modern exponent of the theology of the Orthodox Chruch. His system seems to be through and through dualistic. He sees a duality in man, in the world and even in God Himself. This duality has a non-rational basis, an element of the inexplicable. Speaking in mystical language, he declared that God himself is born out of the divine Nothing, the Ungrund. The duality in God is not that of good and evil, but rather a conflict between equally good values; yet there enters in an uncreated, nonrational element which is basic or or elemental in the universe. In the resultant conflict is found the source of evil in the world.[19]

Berdyaev's views of freedom are quite important in his overall explanation of evil. In his The Meaning of History Berdyaev argues that history is a product of three factors: human freedom, n natural necessity and divine Grace. Now the usual teaching of "positive" theology is that the first and second factors are derived from the latter; i.e., God made nature and man, giving to man the power to use nature's re-

---

17. Brightman, *Philosophy of Religion*, p. 288: "Plato . . . puts into the mouth of Socrates the principle that 'God is not the cause of all things, but only of the good things.' This is explained more fully in the *Timaeus*, where divinity is represented, not as omnipotent creator of all, but simply as a good God who desires 'that, so far as possible, all things should be good and nothing evil' (30A). So far as possible! His will, then, did not create the conditions under which it worked, but 'took over all that was visible, seeing that it was not in a state of rest, but in a state of discordant and disorderly motion,' and 'he brought it into order out of disorder.'"

18. Brightman, *Philosophy of Religion*, p. 288: "Plato's picture of God is now before us. God is a will for good, not infinite but finite, limited on the one hand by rational principles of order and control (*Philebus*) and on the other by 'discordant and disorderly motion' (*Timaeus*) which he finds in existence."

19. Rall, *Christianity*, p. 318: "Nicholas Berdyaev, modern exponent of the theology of the Orthodox Church, shows the influence of Plato and of the mystics, Eckhart and Boehme. His system has a strong emphasis on duality, which appears not only in man and the world but in God himself. This duality has a non-rational basis, an element of the mysterious, the inexplicable. In terms gained from the mystics, he declares that God himself is born out of the divine Nothing, the *Gottheit* or *Ungrund*. The duality in God is not that of good and evil, but rather a conflict between equally good values; yet here there enters in an uncreated, nonrational element which is basic or elemental in the universe. In the resultant conflict is found the source of evil in the world."

sources and his own faculties well or ill, as he chose. Thsi theology, thinks Berdyaev, is a prolific source of atheism, for freedom is admitted to lead to sin and, for at least a great proportion of mankind, to eternal punishment; and yet God, foreseeing these terrible consequences, bestowed this fatal gift upon his ignorant and unsuspecting creatures! In contrast to this teaching of "positive" theology, according to which God the Creator himself is eternally born out of a dark abyss of deity or divine Nothingness; and man and universe are then created by God out of the same ultimate, indeterminate metaphysical stuff from which he himself proceeds. Since non-being is of the very essence of the primal stuff, freedom is uncreated, co-eternal with God, and man may be described as the child of two parents: God, the formative agent in the process, and "meonic freedom," the passive stuff which simply "consented" to God's creative act. The element of uncreated freedom in man's nature is the source of his instinctive urges and creative powers; it is also the source of his ability to rebel against God and resolve himself back into the chaos of non-being. So that freedom is here with its noble possibilities as well as its tragic elements. But so also is "fate or destiny, i.e., nature, the solidified, hardened outcome of the dark meonic freedom." Thus we have a God who is limited by a nonrational ultimate which is the source of tragedy and suffering.[20]

We also find the idea of a finite God in the thinking of John Stuart Mill. Says he, "If the maker of the world can do all that he will, he wills misery, and there is no escape from the conclusion . . . Not even on the most distorted and contracted theory of good which was ever framed by religious or philosophical fanaticism, can the government of Nature be made to resemble the work of a being at once good and omnipotent. The only admissible theory of Creation is that the Principle of Good cannot at once and altoghther subdue the powers of evil, either physical or moral; an incessant struggle with the maleficent powers, or make them always victorious in that struggle, but could and did make them capable of carrying on that

---

20. Rall, *Christianity*, pp. 318–319: "Freedom is here, rich in noble possibilities, as well as in tragic elements. But so also is 'fate or destiny, *i.e.*, nature, the solidified, hardened outcome of the dark meonic freedom.' Thus we have a God who is limited and a world that is conditioned by a non-rational ultimate, not unconquerable, it is true, but the source of tragedy and suffering."

fight with vigor and with progressively increasing success."*[21]

* Three Essays On Religion, pp. 37–39.

In recent times this idea of a finite God has been set forth by E. S. Brightman and W. P. Montague. For both God is the creative power throught the evolutionary process. But for both it is equally clear that this power is limited or hindered. For Montague God is not an omnipotent monarch, but "an ascending force, a nisus, a thrust toward concentration, organization, and life." But there is a world of finite existences "that in God which is not God," in God yet each with "its measure of a self-affirming spontaneity or primary causality, and also its inertia or passivity." God's will is pure and good, but it is finite. As a mind God is infinite, extending through the whole universe. As will he is finite, "a self struggling to inform and assimilate the recalcitrant members of his own organism or the recalcitrant thought of his own intellect."†[22]

† Befief Unbound, pp. 74, 83, 84, 91.

For Brightman the problem of evil is especially acute. Holding that the only existent reality is personal (finite persons and the infinite), he can account for moral evil by the freedom given to men, but not for evil in the physical universe. From this point Brightman comes to the conclusion that the will of God is pure and good, but there is something within God that hinders the expression of his will. God finds

21. Rall, *Christianity*, p. 319: "John Stuart Mill was first among the moderns to suggest the idea of a finite God. 'If the maker of the world can [do] all that he will, he wills misery, and there is no escape from the conclusion. . . . Not even on the most distorted and contracted theory of good which was ever framed by religious or philosophical fanaticism, can the government of Nature be made to resemble the work of a being at once good and omnipotent. The only admissible theory of Creation is that the Principle of Good *cannot* at once and altogether subdue the powers of evil, either physical or moral; could not place mankind in a world free from the necessity of an incessant struggle with the maleficent powers, or make them always victorious in that struggle, but could and did make them capable of carrying on that fight with vigor and with progressively increasing success.'" Rall cited Mill's *Three Essays on Religion*, pp. 37–39; brackets, italics, and ellipses are in Rall's original.

22. Rall, *Christianity*, pp. 319–320: "Two interesting and more recent discussions develop this suggestion of Mill: *The Problem of God*, by E. S. Brightman, and *Belief Unbound*, by W. P. Montague. For both the idea of evolution is important and both find in this developing world a creative and directing Power. But for both it is equally clear that this Power is limited or hindered. For Montague God is not an omnipotent monarch, but 'an ascending force, a nisus, a thrust toward concentration, organization, and life.' But there is a world of finite existences, 'that in God which is not God,' in God and yet each with 'its measure of a self-affirming spontaneity or primary causality, and also its inertia or passivity.' God's will is pure and good, but it is finite; . . . As mind God is infinite, extending through the whole universe. As will he is finite, 'a self struggling to inform and assimilate the recalcitrant members of his own organism or the recalcitrant thoughts of his own intellect.'" Rall cited Montague's *Belief Unbound*, pp. 74, 83, 84, 91.

within hinself, as a part of his nature, a "Given," an element that is irrational, passive, and resistant.[23] To clarify this point we may refer to Brightman's own words. Says he: "God's will, then, is in a definite sense finite. But we have called him 'finite-infinite.' Although the power of his will is limited by the Given, arguments for the objectivity of ideals give ground for the postulate that his will for goodness and love is unlimited; likewise he is infinite in time and space, by his unbegun and unending duration and by his inclusion of all nature within his experience; such a God must also be unlimited in his knowledge of all that is, although human freedom and the nature of The Given probalby limit his knowledge of the precise details of the future."*

* Brightman, op. cit., 337.

There are numerous criticisms that have been raised against these theories of a finite God, but three will suffice at this point (1) Its anthropomorphism. Here it is argued that belief in a finite God humanizes him too much. (2) Its failure to absolve God of responsibility for creation. This is probable the strongest objection to the theory of theistic finitism. Here it is argued that if God is regarded as a creator, however finite his power, he must still be held responsible for having created man, knowing that man would necessarily suffer from surd evils. (3) Its dualism. Each of these theories break down into dualism. Brightman and Montague might escape a cosmis dualism, but they fall right back into the dualistic trap by setting forth a dualism in the nature of God.[24] But dualism affords no real answer to the problem of evil. With such a view faith in a supreme God is endangered and the triumph of good left uncertain.

Toward a More
Adequate Solution

After a brief resume of the most frequently discussed views on the problem of evil in the modern world, we now turn to a discussion of the view which

---

23. Rall, *Christianity*, p. 320: "For the personal idealism which Professor Brightman represents, the problem of evil is especially acute. Holding that the only existent reality is personal (finite persons and the Infinite), he can account for moral evil by the freedom given to men, but not for evil in the physical universe. . . . the will of God is pure and good, but there is something within God that hinders the expression of his will. . . . So he holds that God finds within himself, as a part of his nature, a 'Given,' an element that is irrational, passive, and resistant."

24. Rall, *Christianity*, p. 321: "Both he and Brightman escape a cosmic dualism by introducing a dualism into the nature of God."

I feel to be a more adequate solution to this difficult problem. In this view I have attempted to look at the problem in all of its complexity, avoiding as far as possible any piecemeal solutions. I have attempted to deal with both moral and physical evil, feeling that any discussion of one without the other is inadequate and fails to meet the philosophical demand for coherence.

Our first task in any adequate solution of the problem of evil is to give a new consideration to the ideas of goodness and power as they refer to God. It seems that at this point philosphers have often been as shallow as popular writers; and that often the high insights of the Christian faith have been lacking in the discussions of theologians.

(1). What do we mean by the goodness of God? The word "good" is not limited here, as it often is in the popular speech, to mean kind, or gracious. It affirms that God possesses every excellence that can belong to a personal spirit, unmixed with evil, unweakened by defect, unsurpassable in degree. The goodness of God is, indeed, as tender as that of a mother, as patient as a father's love. But this love is ethical, redemptive, creative. Dr. Rall has written something at this point that is quite significant. Says he; "His goodness is good will, that is, it is a high and fixed purpose aiming at the supreme good of man. It is redemptive and therefore set against all evil. It is creative: It is goodness at work, active, unswerving, sparing no toil or pain in itself or in its object, seeking to give its own life to this creature man, not intent or granting pleasure and sparing sorrow, but rather on the creation in men, and the sharing with men, of its own life, the life of truth and wisdom, of holiness and love."* If we are to deal adequately with the problem of evil we must come to some such view of the goodness of God.

(2). What, we must ask next, is our conception of the power of God? Probably in all our thinking about God our thoughts at this point have been most shallow. So careful a philosopher as C. E. M. Joad settles the question in such an offhand manner as this: "Pain and evil are either real or unreal. If they are real then God, who, being omnipotent, was bound by, no limitations and constrained by no necessities, wilfully created them. But the being who wilfully creates pain and evil cannot be benevolent." If evil is due to man, he argues further, remember man is a creature of God. If man was not evil to begin with but wilfully generated evil, then how can man coming from God

* Rall, op. cit., p. 323.

have a will of his own which is not also a part of God's will?*[25] Such a view of God's power certainly needs clarification. It seems to imply that power is abstract, irresistible, and externalistic.

* Joad, <u>Mind and Matter</u>, p. 119.

How then are we to think of God's power? We are never to think of God's power in terms of what he could conceivably do by the exercise of what we may call sheer omnipotence which crushes all obtacles in its path. We are always to think of God's power in terms of his purpose. If what he did by sheer omnipotence defeated his purpose, then, however startling and impressive, it would be an expression of weakness, not of power. Indeed, a good definition of power is "ability to achieve purpose. This applies to the power of a gun, or a drug, or an argument, or even a sermon! Does it achieve its end? Does it fulfill its purpose?

We must realize that God's power is not put forward to get certain things done, but to get them done in a certain way, and with certain results in the lives of those who do them. We can see this clearly in human illustrations. My purpose in doing a crossword puzzle is not to fill in certain words. I could fill them in easily by waiting for tomorrow morning's paper. Filling them in without the answers is harder but much more satisfying, for it calls out resourcefulness, ingenuity, and discipline which by the easier way would find no self expression.

Similarly, to borrow an illustration from William James, eleven men battle desperately on a field, risking falling and injury, using up a prodigious amount of energy, and when we ask why, we learn that it is to get an inflated, leather covered sphere called a football across a goal. But if that is all, why doesn't someone get up in the night and put it there? Football games are not played to get a ball across a goal, but to get it there under certain conditions, in a certain way, with certain results in the lives of those concerned. Power to get the ball across the goal is to be interpreted in terms of purposes and only makes sense in the light of those purposes. Action, then, which defeats purpose is weakness. Power is the ability to fulfill purpose. No one knows what it cost God to refrain from intervention when wicked men put his beloved Son to death. But the restraint was not

25. This quotation appears in Rall, *Christianity*, p. 324.

weakness. The Cross became the power of God unto salvation.

And now the outline of our problem begins to grow clear. We cast aside as inadequate all naive puerile conceptions of God's goodness and power. Our problem now is to discover the purpose of God and see if that purpose is being carried out in the world of our everyday existence. Now its seems that any theist would accept the fact that God's purpose is to achieve the good in the world and in the lives of men. If the good can never be handed over as a finished product to a passive recipient, if it can only be an achievement, then a good world will be one which is adpated for such attainment. Then our great question is: What kind of world is fitted for the attainment of God's purpose?

(1). In a world where good is to be achieved, there must be freedom. This is most obvious in the case of man. In reality the whole idea of morality and religion presupposes the existence of freedom. Thomas Huxley once said that "if some great power would agree to make me think always what is true and do what is right on condition of being turned into a sort of clock, I should instantly close with the bargain. The only freedom I care about is the freedom to do right; the freedom to do wrong I am ready to part with."*[26] But freedom to do only what is right is not freedom; it is mechanical coercion. A being incapable of worng is also incapable of of right; he is not a human being at all but an antomatic machine. Huxley's hypothesis nullifies his conclusion, because its sells the birthright of human personality. A much more profound remark is that of Lessing: "If God held in His right hand all truth, and his left only the ever-active impulse to search for truth, even with the condition that I must always make mistakes, and said to me 'Choose!' I should humble bow before His left hand and say, 'Father, give me this. Pure truth belongs to Thee alone."[27] Freedom is necessary for human personality.

* {Collected Essays I, 192.}

---

26. This quotation appears in Rall, *Christianity*, p. 329.

27. Whale also cited Huxley but did not quote him. Whale, *Christian Answer*, p. 49: "Huxley's hypothesis nullifies his conclusion, because it sells the birthright of human personality; a being incapable of wrong is also incapable of right; he is not a human being at all but an automatic machine. . . . This, surely, is the meaning of Lessing's profound remark: 'If God held in His right hand all truth, and in His left only the ever-active impulse to search for truth, even with the condition that I must always make mistakes, and said to me, "Choose!" I should humbly bow before His left hand and say, "Father, give me this. Pure truth belongs to Thee alone."'"

It is from the misuse of this freedin that the dark shadow of moral evil appears. The necessity of freedom brings the possibility and practical inevitability of sin. Most of the ills in the world today could be eliminated if knowledge was the only factor needed. We could conquer poverty, for there is "enough and to spare" for all. We know enough, if we would only work together, to wipe out all plagues. We could have decent living conditions for all if we used only the means that went into one item, the preparation of war. The difficulty, however, does not lie here. It is selfishness, pride, greed, lust for power and love of pleasure—in a word it is the sin of man that is the source of our ills and much of our unhappiness.[28] Yet if God's purpose is to be achieved freedom must be maintained. Just as a child cannot learn to walk without the possibility of falling, man cannot learn the ways of God without the possibility of going wrong. Dr. Whale has put this whole idea in words well worth our quoting. He says, "freedom—though it involves grievous error and pain—is the very condition of our being human. There can be no other way for men and women called of God to vindicate the moral order. We cannot have it both ways. It is only in a world where the horror of war, slavery, and prostitution can happen, that the learning of self-sacrifice, fellowship, and chivalry will happen. Indeed if God were to suppress the possibility of moral evil, He would be doing evil, for He would be preferring the worse to the better."*

(2) A world fitted for the achievement of life must be one of order, and an order that is universal and dependable.[29] By order we mean that all things have their own specific nature and behave accordingly, and that they will always and everywhere behave the same way. H_2O, for example will always be water. Water will always be water. Water will always become vaporous with heat; it will always condense as it becomes

* Whale, op. cit,
p. 49–50.

---

28. Rall, *Christianity*, p. 330: "We could conquer poverty, for there are resources enough for all peoples. We could furnish decent living conditions for all if we used only the means that went into one item, the preparation for war and the prosecution of war. We know enough, if we could all work together, to wipe out all the great plagues. The difficulty does not lie here. It is the indifference, the selfishness, the greed, the lust for power and love of pleasure—in a word, it is the sin of man that is the great source of our ills and that prevents our working together for their abolition."

29. Rall, *Christianity*, p. 332: "A world fitted for the achievement of life must be one of order, and an order that is universal and dependable."

colder; becoming still colder and solidifying, it will
expand as ice. Upon that order depends fertile fields,
pleasant streams, equable climate, power for man's
use, and indeed the very existence of life. At the same
time its inevitability may mean tornados and flood
and destruction in which the good suffer with the
evil.[30]

But such a universal order is the <u>sine quo non</u> of a
moral world, it is the only basis on which moral
achievement can be built.[31] If our environment were
a chaos rather than cosmos, and if we never knew
within reasonable limits what was going to happen
next our lives would be a nightmare, not merely because it would be unpleasant but because it could have
no moral meaning. Moreover if t there were no order
in the world reason could not develop in man, for
man's reason develops in response to the reason, or
order, that is in the universe. Again without this order science could not be possible, for science is simply
the discovery of order and its setting forth in terms
of what we call natural laws.[32] And finally it is the
presence of such order that, while it brings certain
evil, at the same time makes possible their overcoming. So that distructive floods may be part of the order of nature, but the knowledge of this same order
of nature makes it possible to halt forest destruction,
impound waters, and change the process from destruction to service.[33] Now we can see that the gains
of an orderly universe far outweigh the losses. The
possibility of physical evil is necessary for the existence of order, while the existence of order is neces-

---

30. Rall, *Christianity*, pp. 333–334: "[Order] means that all things have their own specific nature and behave accordingly, and that they will always and everywhere behave the same way.
Water, for example, will always follow a given course: become vaporous with heat; as vapor will
expand and rise; will condense as it becomes colder, as when struck by a cold-air current; will
then be heavier, fall to earth, and seek its lowest level; becoming still colder and solidifying,
will expand as ice. Upon that order depend fertile fields, pleasant streams, equable climate, power
for man's use, beauty of rainbows and clouds, and indeed the very existence of life. At the same
time its inevitability may mean tornado and flood and destruction in which the good suffer per-
force with the evil."

31. Davis replaced "quo" with "qua."

32. Rall, *Christianity*, p. 334: "But such a universal order, which makes our world cosmos instead of chaos, is not only necessary for physical existence; it it [*sic*] the indispensable condition
of the achievement of all higher life. (1) Only in such a world could reason develop in man, for
man's reason develops in response to the reason, or order, that is in the universe. (2) Only in such
a world is science possible, for science is simply the discovery of this order and its setting forth in
terms of what we call natural laws."

33. Rall, *Christianity*, p. 334: "The floods may destroy, but we can halt forest destruction, impound waters, and change the process from destruction to service."

sary for the achievement of all higher life. So it seems that while freedom is responsible for moral evils, order is r responsible for physical evils; the possibility of moral evil is necessary for the existence of freedom while the possibility for physical evil is necessary for the ecistence of order. This is not to say that evil is really good, or that the existence of evil is necessary to God.

Conclusion

The existence of evil in the world still stands as the great enigma wrapped in mystery, yet it has not caused Christians to live in total despair. The Christian religion has offered men a way for the overcoming of evil through insight and faith and a life in right relations with God and man.[34]

It is right and inevitable to attempt to come to an intellectual solution of this problem. Men of all ages and all religions have set out on this difficult venture. Yet some of the proposed solutions are no solutions at all. To deny the reality of evil is all but absurd. To posit the existence of another cosmic power opposed to God is taking a speculative flight which can have no true philosophical grounding. To suggest a finite God as a solution to the problem is to fall in the pit of humanizing God.

The discussion which we have offered above on this dark problem seems to me to shed more light on the problem than most of the familiar theories; It maintains the triangle of the sovereignty of God, the goodness of God, and the reality of evil, attemptint to shed new light on each of these old corners of the triangle.

Yet with all of the new light that has been shed on the old problem we still come to a point beyond which we cannot go. Any intellectual solution to the problem of evil will come to inevitable impasses. The ultimate solution is not intellectual but spiritual. After we have climbed to the top of the speculative ladder we must leap out into the darkness of faith. But this leap is not a leap of dispair, for it eventually cries with St. Paul, "For now we see through a glass darkly; . . . but then shall I know even as I am known."[35] The Chris-

---

34. Rall, *Christianity*, p. 343: "And it offers to men a way for the overcoming of evil through insight and faith and a life in right relations with God and man."

35. 1 Corinthians 13:12.

tian answer to the proboem of evil is ultimately contained in what he does with evil, itself the result of
what Christ did with evil on the cross.

BIBLIOGRAPHY

1. E. S. Brightman, A Philosophy Of Religion, N.Y.
   Prentice-Hall, 1940
2. H. F. Rall, Christianity: an Inquiry into its Nature and Truth, N.Y. Scribner's, 1940
3. L. D. Weatherhead, Why Do Men Suffer, N.Y.
   The Abingdon Press, 1935
4. J. S. Whale, The Christian Answer To The Problem of Evil, N.Y. The Abingdon Press, 1936

THDS. MLKP-MBU: Box 112, folder 14.

"War and Pacifism"

[20 February–4 May 1951]
[Chester, Pa.]

*In Kenneth L. Smith's course Christianity and Society, each student chose to speak
on one topic from the course syllabus, distributing a short summary of his
argument to other class members.[1] King kept eleven of these summaries, only two of
which are of known authorship. Although this essay has often been attributed to
him, internal evidence raises questions about King's status as its author. Several
lines at the top of the page identifying the course, presumably written by the author
of "War and Pacifism," are not in King's handwriting. His handwriting does
appear elsewhere on the document—he conjugated three French verbs on the
reverse of the second page and wrote at the bottom of that page, "See Crozer
Quarterly, Jan. 1949 an artical on Pascifism"—but he also wrote comments on
other outlines for this class. A plausible explanation for these marginal comments is
that King received the outline during a classmate's presentation, wrote a note to
himself to check the article referenced in the talk, and practiced French during a
break in the presentation.*

*Whether or not King was the author of this essay, the views presented herein are
consistent with those he expressed in* Stride Toward Freedom. *The author of
"War and Pacifism" criticizes "absolute pacifism" on the grounds that it ignores
the essentially sinful side of human nature and the need for coercion to avoid anarchy.
The author questions the applicability of Gandhi's example to the world: "That
Gandhi was successful against the British is no reason that the Russians would
react the same way." This argument reflects both King's class notes on Smith's
lectures and the assigned readings of Reinhold Niebuhr's works. In a later article,
Smith recalled that as a student in 1951 King had argued that "Niebuhr's
emphasis upon 'original sin,' the ambiguous nature of historical*

---

1. Kenneth L. Smith, Syllabus for Christianity and Society, 20 February–4 May 1951, MLKP-
MBU: Box 112, folder 16.

*existence, and the ethic of love as 'an impossible possibility' were inadequate as the
bases for a dynamic theory of social change." But, Smith speculated, King's later
commitment to nonviolent direct action reflected "the realism of Niebuhr."* [2]

{Christianity and Society
Dr. Kenneth L. Smith
Crozer Theological Seminary
Sem II, 1951}

Though I cannot accept an absolute pacifist position, I am as anxious as any to see wars end and have no desire to take part in one. Man being what he is it seems to me that struggle wll be a necessary part of human existance for a long time to come. I could not present my view as one to which there is no exception. No one can work out a theological or philosophical system which is perfect.

I found the position of Nels Ferré interesting especially since he was for a time a pacifist.[3] He presents conflict as a part of the evolutionary process. Man struggles with his fellow man because he has not yet overcome the animal nature which is his. He sees war as a creative part of this process, but it is creative only as long as it is used to work toward peace. The true aim of war is peace. War has been creative in the past and might possibly be so in the future. A third world war might give us a united world. The development of larger units of government from smaller ones has often come about as a result of war. However he is not sure that war can be creative any more. War has been necessary under the concept of natural law and national sovereignty. The time has come for the nation to give way to world government. Under world government man could learn to control war with proper world police. He find the cause of war in the sinful nature of man and the proper attitude one of the practice of Christian justice.

John H. Hallowell of Duke University in an article in the Crozer Quarterly writes largely in criticism of a book by A. J. Muste.[4] I think that his criticisms are valid. He first points out the strong emphasis of the pacifists on the im-

---

2. Kenneth L. Smith, "Martin Luther King, Jr.—Reflections of a Former Teacher," *Bulletin of Crozer Theological Seminary* 57, no. 2 (April 1965): 2–3.

3. Nels Fredrik Solomon Ferré (1908–1971) was a Congregational minister and professor of philosophical theology. Ferré taught at Andover Newton Theological School (1937–1965) and the Divinity School at Vanderbilt University (1950–1957). He was the author of many books and articles, including *The Christian Faith* (1948); *Faith and Reason* (1946); *Evil and the Christian Faith* (1947); *The Christian Understanding of God* (1951); and his most popular work, *Strengthening the Spiritual Life* (1951).

4. John H. Hallowell, "Pacifism—The Way to Peace," *Crozer Quarterly* 26, no. 1 (January 1949): 30–40. Hallowell (1913–) was an Episcopal layman educated at Princeton (Ph.D., 1939) and professor of political science at Duke from 1942 to 1981. He wrote *The Decline of Liberalism as an Ideology* (1943); *Main Currents of Political Thought* (1950), which he considered his most important work; and *The Moral Foundation of Democracy* (1954). A. J. Muste (1885–1967) was a militant pacifist who opposed both World Wars, served the Fellowship of Reconciliation, helped establish the Congress of Racial Equality (CORE), and chaired the Committee for Non-Violent Action. Under Muste's leadership, American pacifists adopted Gandhi's tactics for nonviolent social change.

portance of the pacifist position since the atomic bomb has been developed. I
think he rightly sees that the ethical and moral problems are exactly the same as they were. It matters little how one kills; the victim is just as dead. It may shock the sensitivity of men to kill many but if it is wrong to kill many with an atomic bomb it would be just as wrong to kill one with a stone axe. In fact the position of non-participation advocated by Muste might cause a more horrible death by starvation. His so called non-violence may become more violent than war. That Gandhi was successful against the British is no reason that the Russians would react the same way.

A position of absolute pacifism allows no grounds for maintaining even a police force, since there is no real difference in kind between war and police action. Their position logically results in anarchy. Perhaps the most serious criticism is that they fail to recognize the sinfulness of man. The believe that if we just assume that the enemy will react favorably he will. They isolate war from other ethical problems and ignore the fact that war is actually a symptom of deeper trouble. By their total absorption in the question of war they neglect the deeper underlying causes of war.

It seems to me that we must recognize the presence of sin in man and that it can be done without seeing that there is also good. Since man is so often sinful there must be some coercion to keep one man from injuring his fellows. This is just as true between nations as it is between individuals. If one nation oppresses another a Christian nation must, in order to express love of neighbor, help protect the oppressed. This does not relieve us of our obligation to the enemy nation. We are obligated to treat them in such a way as to reclaim them to a useful place in the world community after they have been prevented from oppressing another. We must not seek revenge.

THD. MLKP-MBU: Box 112, folder 14A.

Notes on American Capitalism

[20 February–4 May 1951?]
[Chester, Pa.?]

*King wrote these two paragraphs, probably as notes to himself, during the
Christianity and Society course. He criticizes aspects of Marxist thought but asserts
that "capitalism has seen its best days."*

Will

Karl Marx, the German philosophy and economists, statted that capitalism carries the seed of its own destruction. There is an obvious fallacy in that statement. The fallacy is that it to is limited to capitalism leaving the impression that other social movements do not carry the seed of their own destruction. The actual fact is that [*strikeout illegible*] every social institution carries the seed of its own destruction; its survival depends on the way way the seed is norished. Now after admitting that there is a fallacy in Marx' statement, do we find any truth therein? It is my opinion that there is. I am conviced that capitalism has seen its best days in American, and not only in America, but in the entire world. It is a well known fact that no social institut can survive when it has outlived its usefullness. This, capitalism has done. It has failed to meet the needs of the masses.

We need only to look at the underlying developements of our society. There is a definite revolt by, what Marx calls, "the preletarian", against the bourgeoise. Every where we turn we turn we are faced with stricks and a demand for socialized medicine. In fact, what is more socialistic than the income tax, the T.V.A., or the N.R.B. "What will eventually happen is this, labor will become so power (this was certainly evidenced in the recent election) that she will be able to place a president in the White House. This will inevitably bring about a nationalization of industry. That will be the end of capitalism. I am not saying that there is a conscious move toward socialism, not even by labor, the move is certainly unconscious. But there is a definite move away from capitalism, whether we conceive of it as conscious or unconscious Capitalism finds herself like a losing football team in the last quarter trying all types of tactics to survive.

AD. MLKP-MBU: Box 113, folder 21.

"Jacques Maritain"

[20 February–4 May 1951]
[Chester, Pa.]

King delivered this presentation for Smith's course Christian Social Philosophy,[1] *which surveyed the ethical and social thought of Christianity from the era of the New Testament to the 1950s. King explains that Jacques Maritain, a Catholic theologian, was critical of modern philosophy's move away from theology toward agnosticism and atheism.*[2] *"Maritain feels that atheism was one of the causes for the rise of communism rather than a mere consequence," King writes. He insists that although Maritain did not equate Christianity with democracy, "the only valid assumption that one can draw from Maritain's conclusions on democracy is that he sees it as the nearest political approximation of Christian principles." Smith made no comments on the paper and gave King an A for the course.*

---

1. "Each student will prepare a paper, which will be presented orally in class. These reports should be 45 minutes long. On the day of the report, the student will submit a two-page, typed summary of his report to each member of the class." Maritain was listed as one of the "representative proponents" under the section heading "Contemporary Responses to the Social Crisis" (Kenneth L. Smith, Syllabus for Christian Social Philosophy II, 10 February–4 May 1951, CSKC).

2. Jacques Maritain (1882–1973) was a French Catholic theologian. King also examined Maritain's theology in an essay at Boston University. See "Contemporary Continental Theology," 13 September 1951–15 January 1952, MLKP-MBU: Box 112, folder 14; to be published in volume II.

I. Analysis of The Present Situation

Jaques Maritain stands out as one of the foremost Catholic philosophers of the contemporary scene. From his chair in the Institut Catholique in Paris, Maritain views the whole modern age with a critical eye, diagnoses its diseases, and prescribes "Integral Thomism" as the infallible antidote for all its ills.[3] He diagnoses the ills of modern culture in intellectual terms. The disease of modernity began, according to Maritain, when modern philosophy abandoned its dependence on theology. This separation started a process of dissociation which could not be checked short of the very verge of dissolution.[4] The three great symptoms of this state of dissociation, in the last stages, are (1) agnosticism, or the complete separation of the knowing mind from the object of knowledge; (2) naturalism, or the complete separation of the world from its divine Source or Ground, and (3) individualism, or the complete separation of the rebellious human will from any object of trust and obedience. Maritain now goes on to show that Thomism is the specific antidote for these alarming symptoms, and the disease that underlies them.[5] In applying Thomism as the general solution to the various problems of the modern era, Maritain gives special attention to two closely related questions: the question of freedom, and the question of the destiny of man.[6]

II. Views on Communism.

In a sense Maritain sees Communism as the final great symptom of the disease of modernity. Here he finds atheism exalted to the position of a religion for which dialectic materialism supplies the dogma, and of which communism as a rule of life is the social and ethical expression. This atheism, according to Maritain, is not a necessary consequence of the social system, but on the contrary is presupposed as the very principle of the latter. In other words, Maritain feels that atheism was one of the causes for the rise of communism rather a mere consequence. He attempts to prove historically that Marx was an atheist before he was a communist. The origin

---

3. Walter Marshall Horton, *Contemporary Continental Theology: An Interpretation for Anglo-Saxons* (New York: Harper & Brothers, 1938), pp. 48–49: "From his chair in the *Institut Catholique* in Paris [Maritain] views the whole modern age with a critical eye, diagnoses its diseases, and prescribes 'Integral Thomism' as the infallible antidote for all its ills."

4. Horton, *Contemporary Continental Theology*, p. 55: "The disease of modernity began, according to Maritain, in the realm of the mind. When modern philosophy abandoned its dependence on theology, it started a process of dissociation which could not be checked short of the very verge of dissolution."

5. Horton, *Contemporary Continental Theology*, p. 55: "The three great symptoms of this state of dissociation, in its last stages, are (1) *agnosticism*, or the complete separation of the knowing mind from the object of knowledge; (2) *naturalism*, or the complete separation of the world from its divine Source and Ground, and (3) *individualism*, or the complete separation of the rebellious human will from any object of trust and obedience. Thomism is the specific antidote for these three alarming symptoms, and for the disease that underlies them."

6. Horton, *Contemporary Continental Theology*, p. 56: "In applying this general solution to the various problems of the modern era, Maritain gives special attention to two closely related questions . . . the question of *freedom*, and the question of the *destiny of man*."

of Marx's communism was not economic, as it was in the case of Engels, but philosophical and metaphysical. Maritain is very insistent at this point and he takes great pains to establish his thesis. But he does not stop here. He sees another cause for the rise of communism which immediately reveals his objectivity. Communism arose as a revolt against Christianity itself. It originated chiefly through the fault of a Christian world unfaithful to its own principles.

III.   Views on Democracy.

When Maritain comes to a discussion of democracy he quite readily speaks of it as the most ideal political system created by the mind of man. Its virtue lies in the fact that it grew out of Christian inspiration. Says Maritain, "the democratic implulse burst forth in history as a temporal manifestation of the inspiration of the gospel." (Christianity and Democracy, p. 36) But if democracy has its virtues it also has its concomitant vices, and its vices are found in the fact that it has failed to remain true to its virtues. To often has the democratic principle attempted to subsist without the Christian principle. In this attempted dichotomy Maritain finds the "tragedy of the democracies." He feels that the survival of the democracies will rest on condition that the Christian inspiration and the democratic inspiration recognize each other and become reconciled.

From this brief resume of Maritain's views on democracy we must not draw the conclusion that he identifies democracy with Christianity. Such a conclusion would be unwarranted and gratuitous in the light of Maritain's overall thought. For him, Christianity transcends all political systems, and it can never be made subservient to democracy as a philosophy of human and political life nor to any political form whatsoever. So that the only valid assumption that one can draw from Maritain's conclusions on democracy is that he sees it as the nearest political approximation of Christian principles.

IV.   Views on Politics and The Relation of Church and State

As we have no doubt noticed in the foregoing discussion, Maritain is far from Catholic in many of his views. This fact is probably nowhere better revealed than in his political views. He has no desire to see the mediaeval supremacy of Church over state restored; he only hopes for a day when "an entirely moral and spiritual activity of the Church shall preside over the temporal order of a multitude of politically and heterogeneous nations, whose religious differences are still not likely to disappear." He deplores the social inertia and reaction which beset so many Catholics.[7] Some years back he in-

---

7. Horton, *Contemporary Continental Theology,* p. 49: "He has no desire to see the medieval supremacy of Church over State restored; he only hopes for a day when 'an entirely moral and spiritual activity of the church shall preside over the temporal order of a multitude of politically and culturally heterogeneous nations, whose religious differences are still not likely soon to disappear.' He deplores the social inertia and reaction which beset the Catholics."

curred considerable criticism by many of his fellow Catholics because he refused to see in General Franco the perfect Christian knight-errant that the
Vatican saw him to be.[8]

If it be asked how a loyal Catholic can thus take sides against the interest of
his own Church, the answer is very clear. Maritain refuses to identify the
interests of Catholics with the interest of the church, or the kingdom of God.
The Invincible Armada was sent out by his Most Catholic Majesty, Philip II of
Spain, with holy intent and with prayers upon the lips of the faithful; but in
Maritain's candid opinion, God was against it.[9] For him, Catholics are not Catholicism, and the errors, apathies, shortcomings and slumbers of Catholics
do not involve Catholicism.

BIBLIOGRAPHY:

Maritain, J. Christianity and Democracy
    Charles Scribner's Sons, 1944
————. Freedom in the Modern World
    Charles Scribner's Sons, 1936
————. Scholasticism and Politics
    MacMillan Co. n.d.
————. The Angelic Doctor: The Life and Thought of St. Thomas Aquinas
    Snodd and Ward Publishers, n.d.
————. True Humanism
    The Contcrary Press, 1938

TDS. CSKC.

---

8. Horton, *Contemporary Continental Theology*, p. 50: "He has lately incurred considerable op-
probrium among his fellow Catholics by refusing to see in General Franco the perfect Christian knight-errant that Spanish landed proprietors—yes, and the Vatican itself—seem to take
him to be."

9. Horton, *Contemporary Continental Theology*, p. 50: "If it be asked how a loyal Catholic can
thus take sides against the interests of his own church, the answer is very clear. Maritain refuses
to identify the interests of Catholics with the interests of the Church, or the Kingdom of God.
The Invincible Armada was sent out by his Most Catholic Majesty, Philip II of Spain, with holy
intent and with prayers upon the lips of the faithful; but in Maritain's candid opinion, God was
against it."

Alberta Williams King to Charles E. Batten

10 May 1951
Atlanta, Ga.

*In response to this letter, Batten wrote the article "Son of Noted Atlanta Family
Wins High Graduation Honors," which appeared in the* Atlanta Daily World *on
20 May 1951.*

Dean Charles E. Batten
Crozer Theological Seminary
Chester, Pennsylvania

My Dear Mr. Batten,

I am writing to ask a favor of you, something I forgot to mention ere I left there Tuesday.

I would like to send an account of Martin Luther's graduation to our paper here, mentioning the honor and awards here received. Realizing that you can do a much better job of this than I (having all facts at hand) I am asking if you will word such article for {me} and send at your earliest convenience. Your ~~cons~~ kindness in this matter will be highly appreciated.

M. L. wishes me to say to you that his address for the summer will be, 193 Boulevard N.E. and to have any mail he might receive, forwarded here. He also wishes you to send him Jessie Brown's address.

Thanking you in advance, I am,

Yours truly,
[*signed*] (Mrs) M. L. King

ALS. CRO-NRCR.

To Charles E. Batten

1 June 1951
Atlanta, Ga.

Dean Charles E. Batten
Crozer Theological Seminary
Chester, Pa.

Dear Dean Batten,

After checking my communications from Boston University I find that it will be necessary for me to file a certificate of my B.D. degree. The letter states that this certificate is necessary for the completion of their record. I will appreciate it very much if you will send this certificate to Boston University. It will be addressed to Dean Chester M. Alter, Boston University Graduate School, 725 Commonwealth Avenue, Boston 15, Mass.

I trust that all goes well with you and the Seminary. Please give my regards to all my friends on the campus.

Thanks for the fine write-up that you sent my Mother about me. It appeared in our local newspaper and was highly appreciated. I remain

Sincerely yours,
[*signed as below*]
Martin Luther King, Jr.

MLK/w

TLS. CRO-NRCR.

4 June 1951

Reverend Martin Luther King, Jr.
193 Boulevard N.E.
Atlanta, Georgia

Dear Martin:

Thank you very much for your letter of June 1. I shall send the certificate to Boston University today. I trust it is warmer in Atlanta than it is in Chester. We are really in the middle of a big heat wave.

I am glad the newspaper write-up was satisfactory. If you have an extra copy, send one along for our files. I hope you will stop off and see us when you are on your way to Boston. Here's wishing you the very best of everything. Please remember me to your mother and dad. With all good wishes, I am,

Sincerely,
Charles E. Batten, Dean

CEB/bt

TLc. CRO-NRCR.

Charles E. Batten to Chester M. Alter

4 June 1951

Dean Chester M. Alter
Boston University Graduate School
725 Commonwealth Avenue
Boston 15, Massachusetts

Dear Dean Alter:

This is to certify that Martin Luther King, Jr., 193 Boulevard, N.E., Atlanta, Georgia received the degree of Bachelor of Divinity at the Crozer Theological Seminary, Chester, Pennsylvania on Tuesday, May 8. Mr. King was graduated as the number one man in the class and was granted the Pearl Ruth Plafker award as being the outstanding member of the graduating class. If you wish any other information, I shall be very happy to supply it.

Sincerely yours,
Charles E. Batten, Dean

CEB/bt

TLc. CRO-NRCR.

Each volume of the *Papers of Martin Luther King, Jr.,* includes a "Calendar of Documents" that provides an extensive list of significant King-related material for the period. In addition to specifying those documents selected for publication, the calendar includes other research material relevant to the study of King's life and work. It is generated from an online database maintained at the King Project's Stanford University office.

In the case of this volume, archival research by the King Papers Project has resulted in the identification and dating of hundreds of documents pertaining to King's maternal and paternal ancestors and his years in college and seminary. Space limitations prevent the publication of all such documents, but researchers can utilize the information in the calendar to identify documents of interest among the many available in archives. This inventory includes not only all significant documents in the King collection at Boston University, but also documents obtained from King's relatives and acquaintances as well as material in archives such as the Moorland-Spingarn Research Center at Howard University. Listed, for example, are citations to all King-authored material, all correspondence sent to King, and programs of events in which King participated. Because of the unique nature of the first volume, the calendar also includes many documents that are not strictly related to Martin Luther King, Jr., but to the lives of his ancestors. Slave records, census forms, church minutes, legal documents, and family photographs are listed as well as early sermons and speeches by King's grandfather and father. The calendar in volume I includes a large proportion of the extant material; due to the vast amount of documentary material, calendars in later volumes will necessarily be more selective.

School essays and notes constitute the bulk of the documentary material. Such items include class syllabi, lecture notes, papers written by his classmates, and other materials relating to King's intellectual development and his interaction with academic mentors. Although many papers lack identifying information, we determined their provenance by examining class notes and syllabi, course catalogues and other documentary material. In this way, many documents from King's schooling could be assigned to a time span corresponding to one of the courses King completed during his nine years of postsecondary education. Documents that could not be identified with a specific course were assigned generally to the years King spent at Morehouse College, Crozer Theological Seminary, or Boston University. The calendar does not include published material about King unless the document appeared in a relatively obscure publication such as the Morehouse college newspaper, the *Maroon Tiger.*

Each calendar entry provides essential information about the document. Italics and brackets indicate information assigned by the editors based on evidence contained in the document. Question marks are used when the evidence is not conclusive. The entry adheres to the following format:

Date | Author (Affiliation). "Document Title." Date. Place of origin. (Physical description codes) Number of pages. (Notes.) Archival location. King Papers Project identification number.

11/22/1950 | King, Martin Luther, Jr. (Crozer Theological Seminary). "An Autobiography of Religious Development." [*9/12–11/22/1950*]. [*Chester, Pa.*] (AHDS) 16 pp. (Marginal comments by George W. Davis.) MLKP-MBU: Box 106, folder 22. 501122–000.

Date. In those cases where the original bears no date, the editors have assigned one. Range dates that correspond to the dates of a school term are given to some undated papers such as school essays. Those documents bearing range dates are arranged after precisely dated documents, unless logic dictates another order. The date of photographs is presented without brackets if the donor provided a date. The date of published or printed papers is the date of publication or public release rather than the date of composition. The date in the left margin is intended to aid the reader in looking up specific documents. Complete date information is provided in the entry.

Author. A standardized form of an individual's name (based on Anglo-American Cataloging Rules, Second Edition) is provided in both the author and title fields. Forms of address are omitted unless necessary for identification, such as a woman who used her husband's name. The calendar provides only one author for documents with multiple authors. For photographs, the photographer is considered the author. King's authorship has been conjectured only when he is the *probable* author. Since King's script is distinctive, his unsigned handwritten documents are identified as of certain authorship. Institutional authorship is provided when appropriate.

Affiliation. Affiliation information is provided if the author wrote in his or her capacity as an official of an organization. No brackets or italics have been used in the affiliation field. King's affiliation as a student at Morehouse, Crozer, or Boston is indicated in entries for documents produced during his formal education.

Title. In general, the title as it appears on the document is used, with minor emendations of punctuation, capitalization, and spelling for clarity. Phrases such as "Letter to," "Photo of," "Examination answers" are used to create titles for otherwise untitled documents; in such titles, words are generally lower-case letters and names are standardized. For academic essays written by King's classmates, the name of the course is provided in the title.

Place of Origin. This field identifies where the document was completed or, in the case of a published document, the place of publication. If the document does not contain the place of origin and the information can be obtained, it is provided in brackets; such information is offered only for documents written by King.

Physical Description. This field describes the format of the document, type of document, version of document, and character of the signature (see "List of Abbreviations"). Documents that consist of several formats are listed with the predominant one first.

Notes. In this optional field, miscellaneous information pertaining to the document is provided, such as the enclosures to a letter; routing information ("Copy to Martin Luther King, Jr."), since King often received copies of correspondence addressed to others; and remarks concerning the legibility of the document or the authorship of marginalia.

Archival Location. The location of the original document is identified using standard abbreviations based on the Library of Congress's codes for libraries and archives (see "List of Abbreviations"). When available, box and folder numbers are provided.

Identification Number. The nine-digit identification number is based on the date and uniquely identifies the document.

Documents that are published in the volume are set in boldface type.

11/1846   Porter, James (Shiloh Baptist Church). "Shiloh Baptist Church minutes."
           11/1/1846. [*Greene County, Ga.*] (ADS) 1 p. SBCM-G-Ar: Drawer 34, box
           36. 994611–000.

7/1848   Edmonds, R. B. (Shiloh Baptist Church). "Shiloh Baptist Church minutes."
           7/16/1848. [*Greene County, Ga.*] (ADS) 1 p. SBCM-G-Ar: Drawer 34, box
           36. 994807–000.

8/1848   Edmonds, R. B. (Shiloh Baptist Church). "Shiloh Baptist Church minutes."
           8/20/1848. [*Greene County, Ga.*] (ADS) 1 p. SBCM-G-Ar: Drawer 34, box
           36. 994808–000.

10/1848   Edmonds, R. B. (Shiloh Baptist Church). "Shiloh Baptist Church minutes."
           10/15/1848. [*Greene County, Ga.*] (ADS) 1 p. SBCM-G-Ar: Drawer 34, box
           36. 994810–000.

1850   U.S. Department of Commerce, Bureau of the Census. "Census entry for
           William Williams." 1850. [*Greene County, Ga.*] (AFm) 1 p. DNA.
           995000–000.

1850   Greene County (Ga.) "Slave Digest Record for William Williams." 1850.
           Greene County, Ga. (AFm) 2 pp. G-Ar. 995000–001.

1854   Greene County (Ga.) "Tax Digest Record for William Williams." 1854.
           Greene County, Ga. (AFm) 4 pp. G-Ar. 995400–000.

4/1855   Sanders, William (Shiloh Baptist Church). "Shiloh Baptist Church minutes."
           4/15/1855. [*Greene County, Ga.*] (ADS) 1 p. SBCM-G-Ar: Drawer 34, box
           36. 995504–000.

1859   Greene County (Ga.) "Tax Digest Record for William Williams." 1859.
           Greene County, Ga. (AFm) 2 pp. G-Ar. 995900–000.

6/1860   U.S. Department of Commerce, Bureau of the Census. "Census entry for
           William Williams." 6/8/1860. Scull Shoals, Ga. (AFm) 1 p. DNA.
           996006–000.

8/1867   Henry County (Ga.) "Voter Qualification Form for James Long." [*8/1867*].
           Henry County, Ga. (AFmS) 1 p. G-Ar. 996708–000.

6/1870   U.S. Department of Commerce, Bureau of the Census. "Census entry for
           Willis Williams and family." 6/22/1870. Greene County, Ga. (AFm) 1 p.
           DNA. 997006–000.

1870   U.S. Department of Commerce, Bureau of the Census. "Census entry for
           James Long and family." 1870. Henry County, Ga. (AFm) 1 p. DNA.
           997000–000.

1870   U.S. Department of Commerce, Bureau of the Census. "Census entry for
           Jane Linsey and family." 1870. Henry County, Ga. (AFm) 1 p. DNA.
           997000–001.

6/1880   U.S. Department of Commerce, Bureau of the Census. "Census entry for
           Jane Linsey and family." 6/28/1880. Henry County, Ga. (AFm) 1 p. DNA.
           998006–000.

6/1880   U.S. Department of Commerce, Bureau of the Census. "Census entry for
           James Long and family." 6/29/1880. Henry County, Ga. (AFm) 1 p. DNA.
           998006–001.

6/1880   U.S. Department of Commerce, Bureau of the Census. "Census entry for
           Adam Daniel (A. D.) Williams and family." 6/15/1880. Greene County, Ga.
           (AFm) 1 p. DNA. 998006–002.

1880   U.S. Department of Commerce, Bureau of the Census. "Census entry for
           Robert Burgess and family." 1880. [*Oconee County, Ga.*] (AFm) 1 p. DNA.
           998000–002.

9/1885   Jeruel Baptist Association. "Minutes." 9/25–9/28/1885. Augusta, Ga. From:
           Minutes of Jeruel Baptist Association, Convened with Springfield Baptist Church,
           Crawford, Georgia, September 25th, 26th, 27th, and 28th, 1885 (Augusta:
           Georgia Baptist Book Print, 1885). (PDf) 3 pp. GMM. 998509–000.

9/1891   Jeruel Baptist Association. "Minutes." 9/24–9/27/1891. Augusta, Ga. From:
           Minutes of Jeruel Baptist Association, Convened with Thankful Baptist Church,
           Days Station, Oglethorpe County, Georgia, September 24th, 25th, 26th, and 27th,
           1891 (Augusta: Georgia Baptist Book Print, 1891). (PDf) 1 p. GMM.
           999109–000.

9/1892   Jeruel Baptist Association. "Minutes." 9/21–9/24/1892. Augusta, Ga. From:

Minutes of Jeruel Baptist Association, Convened with Spring Creek Baptist Church, The Fork, Greene County, Georgia, September 21st, 22nd, 23rd, and 24th, 1892 (Augusta: Georgia Baptist Book Print, 1892). (PDf) 1 p. GMM. 999209–000.

8/1895   Henry County (Ga.) "Marriage license for James Albert·King and Delia Linsey." 8/20/1895. Henry County, Ga. (AFmS) 1 p. (Filed 8/24/1895.) HCPC. 999508–000.

5/1899   Fulton County (Ga.) "Indenture between Oscar Davis and the Trustees of Ebenezer Baptist Church." 5/26/1899. Fulton County, Ga. (ADS) 3 pp. (Filed 7/6/1900.) EBCR. 999905–000.

10/1899   Fulton County (Ga.) "Marriage license for A. D. Williams and Jennie Celeste Parks." 10/29/1899. Fulton County, Ga. (AFmS) 1 p. (Filed 1/29/1900.) FCPCR-GAFC. 999910–001.

6/18/1900   U.S. Department of Commerce, Bureau of the Census. "Census entry for A. D. Williams and Jennie Celeste Parks Williams." 6/18/1900. Fulton County, Ga. (AFm) 1 p. DNA. 000618–000.

6/20/1900   Fulton County (Ga.) "Indenture between Mrs. D. C. Shaw and the Trustees of Ebenezer Baptist Church." 6/20/1900. Fulton County, Ga. (AFmS) 1 p. (Filed 7/7/1900.) EBCR. 000620–000.

6/23/1900   U.S. Department of Commerce, Bureau of the Census. "Census entry for James Albert King and family." 6/23/1900. Clayton County, Ga. (AFmS) 1 p. DNA. 000623–000.

12/12/1900   Fulton County (Ga.) "Indenture between Fifth Street Baptist Church and the Trustees of Ebenezer Baptist Church." 12/12/1900. Fulton County, Ga. (AFmS) 3 pp. (Filed 12/18/1900.) EBCR. 001212–000.

2/14/1906   Metropolitan Mercantile and Realty Company. "Stock certificate for A. D. Williams." 2/14/1906. East Orange, N.J. (AFm) 1 p. CKFC. 060214–000.

1906   "Photo of Jennie Celeste Parks Williams and Alberta Williams." 1906. Atlanta, Ga. (Ph) 1 p. CKFC. 060000–001.

1907   Henry County (Ga.) "Tax Digest Records for James Albert King." 1901–1907. Stockbridge, Ga. (AFm) 8 pp. G-Ar. 070000–001.

1/28/1908   Silver Queen Mining Company. "Stock certificate for A. D. Williams." 1/28/1908. Parral, Mexico. (AFm) 2 pp. CKFC. 080128–000.

1908   "Photo of Jennie Celeste Parks Williams and Alberta Williams." 1908. Atlanta, Ga. (Ph) 1 p. CKFC. 080000–000.

1908   "Photo of Jennie Celeste Parks Williams, Alberta Williams, and a group of Ebenezer members." 1907–1908. Atlanta, Ga. (Ph) 1 p. CKFC. 080000–001.

4/28/1910   U.S. Department of Commerce, Bureau of the Census. "Census entry for A. D. Williams and family." 4/28/1910. Fulton County, Ga. (AFm) 1 p. DNA. 100428–000.

5/11/1910   U.S. Department of Commerce, Bureau of the Census. "Census entry for James Albert King and family." 5/11/1910. Henry County, Ga. (AFm) 1 p. DNA. 100511–000.

9/24/1912   Fulton County (Ga.) "Deed Book Entry for A. D. Williams." 9/24/1912. Fulton County, Ga. (AFmS) 1 p. EBCR. 120924–000.

1/10/1913   Fulton County (Ga.) "Bond for Title between A. J. Delbridge and A. D. Williams." 1/10/1913. Fulton County, Ga. (AFmS) 2 pp. EBCR. 130110–000.

3/11/1913   Williams, A. D. "Bill of Sale and Transfer from A. D. Williams to the Trustees of Ebenezer Baptist Church." 3/11/1913. Fulton County, Ga. (TD) 1 p. EBCR. 130311–000.

11/10/1913   Fulton County (Ga.) "Indenture between the Trustees of Ebenezer Baptist Church and L. C. Butler, et al." 11/10/1913. Fulton County, Ga. (AFmS) 6 pp. EBCR. 131110–001.

1913   Henry County (Ga.) "Tax Digest Records for James Albert King." 1910–1913. Stockbridge, Ga. (AFm) 4 pp. G-Ar. 130000–000.

1/8/1917   National Association for the Advancement of Colored People (NAACP). "Minutes of Meeting of Board of Directors." 1/8/1917. (TDf) 1 p. NAACPP-DLC: Part I, reel 1. 170108–000.

2/13/1917   National Association for the Advancement of Colored People. "Minutes of Meeting of Board of Directors." 2/13/1917. (TDf) 1 p. NAACPP-DLC: Part I, reel 1. 170213–000.

3/12/1917   National Association for the Advancement of Colored People. "Minutes of

Meeting of Board of Directors." 3/12/1917. (TDf) 1 p. NAACPP-DLC: Part I, reel 1. 170312–000.

4/9/1917   National Association for the Advancement of Colored People. "Minutes of Meeting of Board of Directors." 4/9/1917. (TDf) 2 pp. NAACPP-DLC: Part I, reel 1. 170409–000.

1917   Caldwell, A. B. "Adam Daniel Williams." 1917. Atlanta, Ga. From: *History of the American Negro and His Institutions: Georgia Edition* (Atlanta: A. B. Caldwell Publishing Co., 1917), pp. 210–214. (PD) 5 pp. TAP. 170000–000.

5/18/1918   Calcasieu Drilling Company. "Stock certificate for A. D. Williams." 5/18/1918. New Orleans, La. (AFm) 2 pp. CKFC. 180518–000.

6/25/1919   Finley, Cora (National Association for the Advancement of Colored People). "Speech at the Tenth Annual Conference of the National Association for the Advancement of Colored People." 6/25/1919. (TAD) 5 pp. NAACPP-DLC: Part I, reel 8. 190625–000.

6/26/1919   Williams, A. D. "Speech at the Tenth Annual Conference of the National Association for the Advancement of Colored People." [6/26/1919]. Atlanta, Ga. (TD) 3 pp. NAACPP-DLC: Part I, reel 8. 190626–000.

1/14/1920   U.S. Department of Commerce, Bureau of the Census. "Census entry for James Albert King and family." 1/14/1920. Henry County, Ga. (TFm) 3 pp. DNA. 200114–000.

1920   Henry County (Ga.) "Tax Digest Records for James Albert King." 1916–1920. Stockbridge, Ga. (AFm) 6 pp. G-Ar. 200000–003.

1923   "Photo of Alberta Williams and three other women, Hampton Institute." 1922–1923. Hampton, Va. (Ph) 1 p. CKFC. 230000–000.

1923   "Photo of Alberta Williams, Hampton Institute." 1922–1923. Hampton, Va. (Ph) 1 p. CKFC. 230000–001.

3/16/1924   Ellington, G. S. (Ebenezer Baptist Church). "Short Sketch of the Life and Work of Rev. A. D. Williams." 3/16/1924. Atlanta, Ga. From: Programme of the Thirtieth Anniversary of the Pastorate of Rev. A. D. Williams. (PHD) 15 pp. CKFC. 240316–000.

5/27/1924   Georgia State Board of Health, Bureau of Vital Statistics. "Certificate of Death for Delia Linsey King." 5/27/1924. Henry County, Ga. (AFmS) 1 p. (Filed 5/29/1924.) GAHR. 240527–000.

1924   "Photo of Martin Luther King." 1924. Atlanta, Ga. (Ph) 1 p. CKFC. 240000–000.

1924   "Photo of James Albert King." 1920–1924. Atlanta, Ga. (Ph) 1 p. CKFC. 240000–001.

1925   "Photo of Ebenezer Baptist Church with insert of A. D. Williams." 1925. Atlanta, Ga. (Ph) 1 p. EBCR. 250000–000.

1/31/1926   Ebenezer Baptist Church. "Program of the Thirty-second Anniversary of Rev. A. D. Williams." 1/25–1/31/1926. Atlanta, Ga. (PD) 1 p. EBCR. 260131–000.

11/25/1926   Williams, A. D. "Wedding Invitation for Marriage of Alberta Christine Williams and Michael Luther King." 11/25/1926. Atlanta, Ga. (PD) 1 p. EBCR. 261125–000.

1928   "Photo of Christine King." [1928]. Atlanta, Ga. (Ph) 1 p. CKFC. 280000–001.

1928   "Photo of Alberta Williams King and Christine King." [1928]. Atlanta, Ga. (Ph) 1 p. CKFC. 280000–002.

1/15/1929   **Georgia Department of Public Health, Bureau of Vital Statistics. "Certificate of Birth for Martin Luther King, Jr." 1/15/1929. Atlanta, Ga. (TAFmS) 1 p. (Filed 4/12/1934 and revised 7/23/1957; name changed from "Michael.") GAHR. 290115–000.**

6/3/1929   Williams, A. D. "Last Will and Testament." 6/3/1929. Fulton County, Ga. (TFmS) 3 pp. (Filed 4/23/1931.) EBCR. 290603–000.

1929   "Photo of A. D. Williams." 1920–1929. Atlanta, Ga. (Ph) 1 p. CKFC. 290000–005.

6/1930   "Photo of Martin Luther King, Morehouse College graduation." 6/1930. Atlanta, Ga. (Ph) 1 p. CKFC. 300600–000.

1930   "Photo of Martin Luther King, Jr., and Christine King." 1930. Atlanta, Ga. (Ph) 1 p. CKFC. 300000–002.

1930   "Photo of Martin Luther King, Martin Luther King, Jr., and Christine King." 1930. Atlanta, Ga. (Ph) 1 p. CKFC. 300000–000.

1930   "Photo of Martin Luther King, Jr., and Christine King." 1930. Atlanta, Ga. (Ph) 1 p. CKFC. 300000–001.

1930	"Photo of Jennie Celeste Parks Williams." 1925–1930. Atlanta, Ga. (Ph) 1 p. CKFC. 300000–004.
3/21/1931	Georgia State Board of Health, Bureau of Vital Statistics. "Certificate of Death for A. D. Williams." 3/21/1931. Atlanta, Ga. (AFmS) 1 p. (Filed 3/24/1931.) GAHR. 310321–000.
3/24/1931	Ebenezer Baptist Church. "Program, A. D. Williams funeral service." 3/24/1931. Atlanta, Ga. (PD) 4 pp. CKFC. 310324–000.
3/1931	Ellington, G. S. (Ebenezer Baptist Church). "Short Sketch of the Life and Work of Rev. A. D. Williams." [*3/1931*]. (THD) 6 pp. EBCR. 310300–000.
1931	"Photo of Martin Luther King, Jr., and Christine King." 1931. Atlanta, Ga. (Ph) 1 p. CKFC. 310000–000.
1931	"Photo of Martin Luther King, Jr." 1931. Atlanta, Ga. (Ph) 1 p. RKC-WHi. 310000–001.
11/17/1933	Georgia Department of Public Health, Bureau of Vital Statistics. "Certificate of Death for James Albert King." 11/17/1933. College Park, Ga. (AFmS) 1 p. (Filed 11/23/1933.) GAHR. 331117–000.
6/26/1935	"Photo of Martin Luther King, Jr., at a birthday party." 6/26/1935. Atlanta, Ga. (Ph) 1 p. SCRBC-NN-Sc. 350626–000.
1935	"Photo of Martin Luther King, Jr." 1935. Atlanta, Ga. (Ph) 1 p. CKFC. 350000–000.
6/13/1937	**King, Martin Luther, Jr. "Father's Day telegram to Martin Luther King." [*6/13/1937*]. Atlanta, Ga. (PWSr) 1 p. CKFC. 370613–000.**
1938	"Photo of Alberta Williams King, Morris Brown College graduation." 1938. Atlanta, Ga. (Ph) 1 p. CKFC. 380000–000.
1938	"Photo of Martin Luther King and Christine King." 1938. Atlanta, Ga. (Ph) 1 p. CKFC. 380000–001.
1/1939	"Photo of Martin Luther King, Alberta Williams King, Jennie Celeste Parks Williams, Christine King, Alfred Daniel King, and Martin Luther King, Jr." 1/1939. Atlanta, Ga. (Ph) 1 p. CKFC. 390100–000.
4/1/1939	**Williams, Jennie Celeste Parks. "Poem in honor of A. D. Williams." 4/1/1939. Atlanta, Ga. From: *Georgia Baptist*, 4/1/1939. (PD) 1 p. (Co-authored by Martin Luther King, Jr.) 390401–000.**
12/14/1939	Karger, George (*Life*). "Photo of Ebenezer Baptist Church choir, 'Gone With the Wind' premiere." 12/14/1939. Atlanta, Ga. From: *Life*, 12/25/1939, p. 11. (PPh) 1 p. 391214–001.
1939	"Photo of Martin Luther King, Jr., and Alfred Daniel King." [*1938–1939?*]. Atlanta, Ga. (Ph) 1 p. CKFC. 390000–004.
1939	"Photo of Martin Luther King, Jr., and Alfred Daniel King." [*1938–1939?*]. Atlanta, Ga. (Ph) 1 p. RKC-WHi. 390000–005.
1/18/1940	**King, Martin Luther, Jr. "Letter to Martin Luther King." 1/18/1940. Atlanta, Ga. (TL) 1 p. CKFC. 400118–000.**
1/24/1940	**King, Martin Luther, Jr. "Letter to Martin Luther King." 1/24/1940. Atlanta, Ga. (TLS) 1 p. CKFC. 400124–000.**
4/4/1940	Sutton, Willis A. (Board of Education of the City of Atlanta). "Letter to Martin Luther King." 4/4/1940. Atlanta, Ga. (TLS) 1 p. CKFC. 400404–000.
6/20/1940	**King, Martin Luther, Jr. "Letter to Alberta Williams King." 6/20/1940. Atlanta, Ga. (ALS) 2 pp. CKFC. 400620–000.**
6/23/1940	**King, Martin Luther, Jr. "Letter to Martin Luther King." 6/23/1940. Atlanta, Ga. (ALS) 3 pp. CKFC. 400623–000.**
10/17/1940	King, Martin Luther (Atlanta Missionary Baptist Association, Inc.). "Moderator's Annual Address." 10/15–10/17/1940. Cartersville, Ga. From: Minutes of the Thirty-sixth Annual Session of the Atlanta Missionary Baptist Association, Inc., held with the Mt. Zion Baptist Church. (PD) 3 pp. CKFC. 401017–000.
1940	Atlanta Public Schools. "Report cards and records for Martin Luther King, Jr." 1934–1940. Atlanta, Ga. (AFm) 4 pp. (Nearly illegible.) APS-GAP. 400000–012.
1940	"Photo of Martin Luther King, Jennie Celeste Parks Williams, and three others." 1939–1940. Atlanta, Ga. (Ph) 1 p. CKFC. 400000–014.
1940	"Photo of Christine King." [*1939–1940*]. Atlanta, Ga. (Ph) 1 p. CKFC. 400000–015.
5/11/1941	"Photo of Jennie Celeste Parks Williams and Alberta Williams King, Mother's Day." 5/11/1941. Atlanta, Ga. (Ph) 1 p. CKFC. 410511–000.
5/18/1941	Georgia Department of Public Health, Bureau of Vital Statistics. "Certificate

of Death for Jennie Celeste Parks Williams." 5/18/1941. Atlanta, Ga. (TAFmS) 1 p. (Filed 5/21/1941.) GAHR. 410518–002.

5/18/1941 "Photo of Martin Luther King, I. P. Reynolds, Arthur Henderson, Edward Boykin, Martin Luther King, Jr., and Alfred Daniel King." 5/18/1941. Atlanta, Ga. (Ph) 1 p. CKFC. 410518–001.

5/18/1941 "Photo of Alfred Daniel King, Christine King, and Martin Luther King, Jr." 5/18/1941. Atlanta, Ga. (Ph) 1 p. CKFC. 410518–003.

5/21/1941 Ebenezer Baptist Church. "Program, Jennie Celeste Parks Williams funeral service." 5/21/1941. (PD) 2 pp. CKFC. 410521–000.

6/1941 "Photo of Alberta Williams King." 6/1941. Atlanta, Ga. (Ph) 1 p. CKFC. 410600–001.

10/16/1941 Atlanta Missionary Baptist Association, Inc. "Program." 10/14–10/16/1941. Atlanta, Ga. (TD) 2 pp. EBCR. 411016–000.

1941 "Photo of Martin Luther King, Martin Luther King, Jr., and Alfred Daniel King." 1941. Atlanta, Ga. (Ph) 1 p. CKFC. 410000–005.

1941 "Photo of Alberta Williams King, Martin Luther King, Jr., Alfred Daniel King, and Aretha English." [*1941*]. Atlanta, Ga. (Ph) 1 p. CKFC. 410000–009.

1/1942 Bolen, Beulah (Atlanta University Laboratory High School). "Report Card in Science for Martin Luther King, Jr." 1/1942. [*Atlanta, Ga.*] (TFmS) 1 p. CKFC. 420100–000.

1/23/1942 Jones, B. A. (Atlanta University Laboratory High School). "Report Card in 8th Grade Social Studies for Martin Luther King, Jr." 1/23/1942. Atlanta, Ga. (TFm) 1 p. CKFC. 420123–000.

1/23/1942 Thomas, E. R. (Atlanta University Laboratory High School). "Report Card in 8th Grade Shop for Martin Luther King, Jr." 1/23/1942. [*Atlanta, Ga.*] (TFmS) 2 pp. CKFC. 420123–001.

1/23/1942 Thomas, E. R. (Atlanta University Laboratory High School). "Report Card in Physical Education for Martin Luther King, Jr." 1/23/1942. [*Atlanta, Ga.*] (AFmS) 1 p. CKFC. 420123–002.

1/26/1942 Henderson, Roland G. (Atlanta University Laboratory High School). "Report Card in 8th Grade Math for Martin Luther King, Jr." 1/26/1942. [*Atlanta, Ga.*] (TFmS) 1 p. CKFC. 420126–000.

1/26/1942 Dean, Mary J. (Atlanta University Laboratory High School). "Report Card in 8th Grade Art for Martin Luther King, Jr." 1/26/1942. [*Atlanta, Ga.*] (TFmS) 1 p. CKFC. 420126–001.

6/1942 Atlanta University Laboratory High School. "Report Card in 8th Grade English for Martin Luther King, Jr." [*9/1941–6/1942*]. Atlanta, Ga. (ATFm) 1 p. CKFC. 420600–000.

1942 "Photo of Alberta Williams King." [*1938–1942*]. (Ph) 1 p. CKFC. 420000–003.

10/14/1943 King, Martin Luther. "Moderator's Annual Address." [*10/13/1943*]. Atlanta, Ga. From: Minutes of the Thirty-ninth Annual Session of the Atlanta Baptist Missionary Association, Inc., held with the Zion Hill Baptist Church. (PD) 3 pp. CKFC. 431014–001.

1943 King, Martin Luther (Ebenezer Baptist Church). "Ebenezer Baptist Church Annual Conference Message and Recommendations." 1943. [*Atlanta, Ga.*] (THD) 4 pp. EBCR. 430000–006.

1943 "Photo of Alberta Williams King." [*1943*]. Atlanta, Ga. (Ph) 1 p. CKFC. 430000–001.

1943 "Photo of Martin Luther King, Alberta Williams King, Martin Luther King, Jr., Christine King, and Alfred Daniel King." [*1942–1943*]. Atlanta, Ga. (Ph) 1 p. CKFC. 430000–010.

1943 "Photo of Martin Luther King, Jr., Christine King, and Alberta Williams King." [*1942–1943*]. Atlanta, Ga. (Ph) 1 p. CKFC. 430000–009.

1943 "Photo of Martin Luther King, Jr., Christine King, and Alfred Daniel King." [*1942–1943?*]. [*Atlanta, Ga.*] (Ph) 1 p. RKC-WHi. 430000–008.

1943 "Photo of Alfred Daniel King." [*1940–1943*]. Atlanta, Ga. (Ph) 1 p. CKFC. 430000–007.

1/28/1944 Booker T. Washington High School. "Report Card for Martin Luther King, Jr." 1/28/1944. [*Atlanta, Ga.*] (AFmS) 1 p. CKFC. 440128–000.

4/16/1944 "Contest Winner, M. L. King, Jr." 4/16/1944. Atlanta, Ga. From *Atlanta Daily World*, 4/16/1944, p. 2. (PD) 1 p. 440416–000.

5/1944   King, Martin Luther, Jr. "The Negro and the Constitution." [*5/1944*]. Atlanta, Ga. From: *The Cornellian*, Booker T. Washington High School, 1944, p. 54. (PD) 1 p. EPH. 440500–000.

6/11/1944   King, Martin Luther, Jr. "Letter to Alberta Williams King." 6/11/1944. Simsbury, Conn. (ALS) 2 pp. (Envelope included.) CKFC. 440611–000.

6/15/1944   King, Martin Luther, Jr. "Letter to Martin Luther King." 6/15/1944. Simsbury, Conn. (ALS) 2 pp. (Envelope included.) CKFC. 440615–000.

6/18/1944   King, Martin Luther, Jr. "Letter to Alberta Williams King." 6/18/1944. Simsbury, Conn. (ALS) 3 pp. (Envelope included.) CKFC. 440618–000.

8/5/1944   King, Martin Luther, Jr. "Letter to Alberta Williams King." 8/5/1944. Simsbury, Conn. (ALS) 3 pp. (Envelope included.) CKFC. 440805–000.

8/12/1944   King, Alberta Williams. "Letter to Lillian Barbour." 8/12/1944. Atlanta, Ga. (ALS) 3 pp. MLKJrP-GAMK. 440812–000.

8/30/1944   King, Martin Luther, Jr. "Letter to Alberta Williams King." 8/30/1944. Simsbury, Conn. (ALS) 4 pp. (Envelope included.) CKFC. 440830–000.

9/1944   "Photo of Martin Luther King, Jr., and Morehouse Student Body." [*9/1944*]. Atlanta, Ga. (Ph) 1 p. CA–GAM. 440900–000.

1944   "Photo of Martin Luther King, Jr." [*1943–1944?*]. Atlanta, Ga. (Ph) 1 p. RKC-WHi. 440000–004.

2/27/1946   King, Alberta Williams (Ebenezer Baptist Church). "Letter to Benjamin Elijah Mays." 2/27/1946. Atlanta, Ga. (TLS) 1 p. BEMP-DHU: Box 1, folder 10. 460227–000.

3/2/1946   Mays, Benjamin Elijah (Morehouse College). "Letter to Alberta Williams King." 3/2/1946. (TLc) 1 p. BEMP-DHU: Box 1, folder 10. 460302–000.

4/1946   "Photo of Martin Luther King, Jr., Family Life seminar, Morehouse College." [*4/1946*]. Atlanta, Ga. (Ph) 1 p. GD. 460400–000.

8/6/1946   King, Martin Luther, Jr. (Morehouse College). "Kick Up Dust, Letter to the Editor." 8/6/1946. Atlanta, Ga. From: *Atlanta Constitution*, 8/6/1946, p. 6. (PD) 1 p. 460806–000.

1946   "Photo of Martin Luther King, Jr., and Christine King." [*1945–1946?*]. [*Atlanta, Ga.*] (Ph) 1 p. RKC-WHi. 460000–003.

1946   "Photo of Alberta Williams King, Martin Luther King, Christine King, and Martin Luther King, Jr." [*1944–1946?*]. Atlanta, Ga. (Ph) 1 p. CKFC. 460000–001.

1/1947   King, Martin Luther, Jr. (Morehouse College). "Purpose of Education." [*9/1946–1/1947?*]. [*Atlanta, Ga.*] (ADS) 4 pp. MLKP-MBU: Box 118, folder 6. 470100–000.

2/1947   King, Martin Luther, Jr. (Morehouse College). "Purpose of Education." 1/1947–2/1947. Atlanta, Ga. From: *Maroon Tiger*, 1/1947–2/1947, p. 10. (PD) 1 p. GD. 470200–000.

7/1/1947   Morehouse College. "Report Card for Martin Luther King, Jr." 7/1/1947. Atlanta, Ga. (TFm) 1 p. CKFC. 470701–000.

10/27/1947   King, Martin Luther, Jr. "Letter to Crozer Theological Seminary." 10/27/1947. Atlanta, Ga. (TLS) 1 p. CRO-NRCR. 471027–000.

10/29/1947   Batten, Charles E. (Crozer Theological Seminary). "Letter to Martin Luther King, Jr." 10/29/1947. (TLc) 1 p. CRO-NRCR. 471029–000.

1948   Young Men's Christian Association (YMCA). "Certificate of Participation in YMCA Annual Basketball League," 1947–1948. [*Atlanta, Ga.*] (AHFmS) 1 p. (Signed by King.) ATL-AAHM. 480000–015.

1948   Scott, Coretta. "Why I Came to College." 1948. From: *Opportunity* 26 (1948): 42+. (PD) 2 pp. 480000–019.

1948   "Photo of Martin Luther King, Jr., and Martin Luther King." 1948. Atlanta, Ga. (Ph) 1 p. CKFC. 480000–014.

1948   "Photo of Martin Luther King, Jr., and woman." [*1947–1948?*]. (Ph) 1 p. RKC-WHi. 480000–020.

1/31/1948   "Examination questions, Social Institutions." [*9/24/1947–1/31/1948*]. [*Atlanta, Ga.*] (TD) 1 p. MLKP-MBU: Box 113, folder 19. 480131–000.

1/31/1948   King, Martin Luther, Jr. (Morehouse College?). "Ritual." [*9/24/1947–1/31/1948?*]. [*Atlanta, Ga.?*] (THDS) 18 pp. (Marginal comments by professor.) MLKP-MBU: Box 113, folder 19. 480131–001.

2/1948   King, Martin Luther, Jr. "Application for Admission to Crozer Theological Seminary." [*2/1948*]. [*Atlanta, Ga.*] (AFmS) 5 pp. CRO-NRCR. 480200–000.

2/4/1948	**Watkins, Lillian D. (Ebenezer Baptist Church). "Certification of Minister's License for Martin Luther King, Jr." 2/4/1948. Atlanta, Ga. (TLS) 1 p. CRO-NRCR. 480204–000.**
2/18/1948	**Batten, Charles E. (Crozer Theological Seminary). "Letter to Martin Luther King, Jr." 2/18/1948. (TLc) 1 p. CRO-NRCR. 480218–000.**
2/20/1948	Morehouse College. "Program, Memorial Service for John Hope and Samuel Howard Archer." 2/20/1948. Atlanta, Ga. (TD) 2 pp. SWWC-GAU. 480220–000.
2/25/1948	**Tobin, Lucius M. (Providence Baptist Church). "Letter to Charles E. Batten." 2/25/1948. Atlanta, Ga. (TLS) 1 p. CRO-NRCR. 480225–000.**
2/28/1948	**Mays, Benjamin Elijah (Morehouse College). "Letter to Charles E. Batten." 2/28/1948. Atlanta, Ga. (TLS) 1 p. CRO-NRCR. 480228–000.**
3/5/1948	**King, Martin Luther (Ebenezer Baptist Church). "Letter to Charles E. Batten." 3/5/1948. Atlanta, Ga. (THLS) 1 p. CRO-NRCR. 480305–000.**
3/9/1948	**Burney, Phoebe (Clark College). "Letter to Charles E. Batten." 3/9/1948. Atlanta, Ga. (TLS) 1 p. CRO-NRCR. 480309–000.**
3/12/1948	**Kelsey, George D. (Morehouse College). "Letter to Charles E. Batten." 3/12/1948. Atlanta, Ga. (TLS) 1 p. CRO-NRCR. 480312–000.**
3/23/1948	**Brazeal, Brailsford R. (Morehouse College). "Letter to Charles E. Batten." 3/23/1948. Atlanta, Ga. (TLS) 1 p. CRO-NRCR. 480323–000.**
3/23/1948	**Batten, Charles E. (Crozer Theological Seminary). "Notes on Martin Luther King, Jr.'s academic standing at Morehouse College." [3/23/1948]. (AD) 1 p. CRO-NRCR. 480323–001.**
4/26/1948	King, Martin Luther, Jr. "Matriculation Form of Crozer Theological Seminary." 4/26/1948. [Atlanta, Ga.] (AFmS) 1 p. CRO-NRCR. 480426–000.
4/27/1948	Batten, Charles E. (Crozer Theological Seminary). "Letter to Martin Luther King, Jr." 4/27/1948. (TLc) 1 p. CRO-NRCR. 480427–000.
5/31/1948	Williams, Samuel W. (Morehouse College). "Class Record, Philosophy." 9/22/1947–5/31/1948. (AFmS) 22 pp. SWWC-GAU. 480531–000.
6/1948	"Photo of Martin Luther King, Jr., Morehouse Chapel." [9/1944–6/1948]. Atlanta, Ga. (Ph) 1 p. BEMP-DHU: Box 49. 480600–008.
6/1948	"Photo of Martin Luther King, Jr., Morehouse Chapel." [9/1944–6/1948]. Atlanta, Ga. (Ph) 1 p. DCF-GAM. 480600–009.
6/1948	King, Martin Luther, Jr. (Morehouse College?). "Notes on Marriage." [1/1946–6/1948?]. [Atlanta, Ga.?] (AD) 1 p. MLKP-MBU: Box 113, folder 19. 480600–005.
6/6/1948	"Photo of Martin Luther King, Jr., and Christine King, Morehouse and Spelman Joint Baccalaureate." 6/6/1948. Atlanta, Ga. (Ph) 1 p. MLKJrP-GAMK. 480606–000.
6/8/1948	Morehouse College. "Transcript for Martin Luther King, Jr." [6/8/1948]. Atlanta, Ga. (TAFmS) 1 p. CRO-NRCR. 480608–012.
6/8/1948	"Photo of Alberta Williams King, Martin Luther King, and Christine King, Spelman Commencement." 6/8/1948. Atlanta, Ga. (Ph) 1 p. CKFC. 480608–002.
6/8/1948	"Photo of Alfred Daniel King and Joel Lawrence King, Morehouse Commencement." 6/8/1948. Atlanta, Ga. (Ph) 1 p. CKFC. 480608–005.
6/8/1948	"Photo of Alberta Williams King, Martin Luther King, and Christine King, Spelman Commencement." 6/8/1948. Atlanta, Ga. (Ph) 1 p. CKFC. 480608–006.
6/8/1948	"Photo of Martin Luther King, Alberta Williams King, Martin Luther King, Jr., Alfred Daniel King, Christine King, and Joel Lawrence King, Morehouse Commencement." 6/8/1948. Atlanta, Ga. (Ph) 1 p. CKFC. 480608–007.
6/8/1948	"Photo of Martin Luther King, Jr., and Martin Luther King, Morehouse Commencement." 6/8/1948. Atlanta, Ga. (Ph) 1 p. CKFC. 480608–008.
6/8/1948	"Photo of Martin Luther King, Jr., Morehouse Commencement." 6/8/1948. Atlanta, Ga. (Ph) 1 p. RKC-WHi. 480608–013.
6/8/1948	"Photo of Martin Luther King, Jr., and Christine King, Spelman Commencement." 6/8/1948. Atlanta, Ga. (Ph) 1 p. RKC-WHi. 480608–014.
6/8/1948	"Photo of Martin Luther King, Jr., and the Class of 1948, Morehouse Commencement." 6/8/1948. Atlanta, Ga. (Ph) 1 p. CA-GAM. 480608–015.
6/8/1948	"Photo of Martin Luther King, Alberta Williams King, Christine King, Mar-

tin Luther King, Jr., Alfred Daniel King, Rebecca Jackson, and Nannien W. Crawford, graduation reception." 6/8/1948. Atlanta, Ga. (Ph) 1 p. CKFC. 480608–009.

6/8/1948   "Photo of Alfred Daniel King, Christine King, and Martin Luther King, Jr., graduation reception." 6/8/1948. Atlanta, Ga. (Ph) 1 p. CKFC. 480608–010.

6/8/1948   "Photo of Alfred Daniel King, Christine King, Martin Luther King, Jr., Alberta Williams King, and Martin Luther King, graduation reception." 6/8/1948. Atlanta, Ga. (Ph) 1 p. CKFC. 480608–011.

6/8/1948   "Photo of Martin Luther King, Jr., and Alberta Williams King." 6/8/1948. Atlanta, Ga. (Ph) 1 p. CKFC. 480608–016.

7/12/1948   Morehouse College. "Report Card for Martin Luther King, Jr." 7/12/1948. Atlanta, Ga. (TFm) 2 pp. CKFC. 480712–000.

8/22/1948   De Kalb County (Ga.) "Marriage Certificate for Samuel Preston Long, Jr., and Ruth Argenis Bussey, ceremony performed by Martin Luther King, Jr." 8/22/1948. De Kalb County, Ga. (TFmS) 1 p. SLP. 480822–000.

8/22/1948   "Photo of Martin Luther King, Jr., presiding at wedding ceremony of Samuel Preston Long, Jr., and Ruth Argenis Bussey." 8/22/1948. Decatur, Ga. (Ph) 1 p. SLP. 480822–001.

10/1948   **King, Martin Luther, Jr. "Letter to Alberta Williams King." [*10/1948*]. [*Chester, Pa.*] (ALS) 4 pp. CKFC. 481000–000.**

11/24/1948   **King, Martin Luther, Jr. (Crozer Theological Seminary). "Light on the Old Testament from the Ancient Near East." [*9/14–11/24/1948*]. [*Chester, Pa.*] (THDS) 22 pp. (Marginal comments by James B. Pritchard.) MLKP-MBU: Box 113, folder 19. 481124–000.**

11/24/1948   **King, Martin Luther, Jr. (Crozer Theological Seminary). "The Significant Contributions of Jeremiah to Religious Thought." [*9/14–11/24/1948*]. [*Chester, Pa.*] (THDS) 17 pp. (Marginal comments by James B. Pritchard.) MLKP-MBU: Box 115, folder 17. 481124–004.**

11/24/1948   King, Martin Luther, Jr. (Crozer Theological Seminary?). "Meet Amos & Hosea." [*9/14–11/24/1948?*]. [*Chester, Pa.?*] (AD) 14 pp. MLKP-MBU: Box 115, folder 27. 481124–001.

11/24/1948   King, Martin Luther, Jr. (Crozer Theological Seminary). "Class notes, Orientation for Juniors." [*9/14–11/24/1948*]. [*Chester, Pa.*] (AD) 20 pp. MLKP-MBU: Box 115, folder 27. 481124–003.

11/24/1948   Aubrey, Edwin Ewart (Crozer Theological Seminary). "Final examination questions, Orientation for Juniors." [*9/14–11/24/1948*]. [*Chester, Pa.*] (THD) 1 p. (Marginal comments by King.) MLKP-MBU: Box 115, folder 27. 481124–002.

2/16/1949   **King, Martin Luther, Jr. (Crozer Theological Seminary). "The Ethics of Late Judaism as Evidenced in the Testaments of the Twelve Patriarchs." [*11/30/1948–2/16/1949*]. [*Chester, Pa.*] (THDS) 18 pp. (Marginal comments by Morton Scott Enslin.) MLKP-MBU: Box 113, folder 19. 490216–017.**

2/16/1949   King, Martin Luther, Jr. (Crozer Theological Seminary). "Class notes, Great Theologians." [*11/30/1948–2/16/1949*]. [*Chester, Pa.*] (AD) 22 pp. MLKP-MBU: Box 115, folder 29. 490216–011.

2/16/1949   King, Martin Luther, Jr. (Crozer Theological Seminary?). "Class notes, Great Theologians." [*11/30/1948–2/16/1949?*]. [*Chester, Pa.?*] (ADf) 7 pp. MLKP-MBU: Box 115, folder 29. 490216–014.

2/16/1949   King, Martin Luther, Jr. (Crozer Theological Seminary?). "Notes on *On the Trinity* by Augustine." [*11/30/1948–2/16/1949?*]. [*Chester, Pa.?*] (AD) 15 pp. MLKP-MBU: Box 113, folder 21. 490216–002.

2/16/1949   King, Martin Luther, Jr. (Crozer Theological Seminary?). "Thomas Aquinas." [*11/30/1948–2/16/1949?*]. [*Chester, Pa.?*] (AD) 7 pp. MLKP-MBU: Box 115, folder 29. 490216–015.

2/16/1949   King, Martin Luther, Jr. (Crozer Theological Seminary?). "Divine Revelation." [*11/30/1948–2/16/1949?*]. [*Chester, Pa.?*] (AD) 1 p. MLKP-MBU: Box 115, folder 29. 490216–016.

2/16/1949   King, Martin Luther, Jr. (Crozer Theological Seminary?). "Anselm." [*11/30/1948–2/16/1949?*]. [*Chester, Pa.?*] (AD) 3 pp. MLKP-MBU: Box 115, folder 29. 490216–012.

5/6/1949   King, Martin Luther, Jr. (Crozer Theological Seminary?). "Quest for Balance." [2/22–5/6/1949?]. [Chester, Pa.?] (ADd) 1 p. MLKP-MBU: Box 118, folder 6. 490506–018.

5/6/1949   King, Martin Luther, Jr. (Crozer Theological Seminary?). "Notes on the minister, his world and his work." [2/22–5/6/1949?]. [Chester, Pa.?] (ADf) 3 pp. MLKP-MBU: Box 118, folder 6. 490506–020.

9/1949   "Photo of Martin Luther King and Alberta Williams King en route to National Baptist Convention in California, 9/1949." Salt Lake City, Utah. (Ph) 1 p. CKFC. 490900–003.

10/8/1949   **Gray, William H., Jr. "Letter to Martin Luther King." 10/8/1949. Philadelphia, Pa. (TALc) 1 p. (Copy to Martin Luther King, Jr.) MLKP-MBU: Box 117, folder 50. 491008–000.**

10/28/1949   "Junior orientation exam." 10/28/1949. [Chester, Pa.] (THD) 1 p. (Marginal comments by King.) MLKP-MBU: Box 115, folder 33. 491028–001.

11/23/1949   King, Martin Luther, Jr. (Crozer Theological Seminary). "Class notes, Greek Religion." [9/13–11/23/1949]. [Chester, Pa.] (AD) 39 pp. MLKP-MBU: Box 115, folder 28. 491123–001.

11/23/1949   King, Martin Luther, Jr. (Crozer Theological Seminary). "Notecards on Greek Religion." [9/13–11/23/1949]. [Chester, Pa.] (AD) 6 pp. MLKP-MBU: Box 115, folder 28. 491123–002.

11/23/1949   **King, Martin Luther, Jr. (Crozer Theological Seminary). "A Study of Mithraism." [9/13–11/23/1949]. [Chester, Pa.] (THDS) 18 pp. (Marginal comments by Morton Scott Enslin.) MLKP-MBU: Box 113, folder 19. 491123–000.**

11/23/1949   King, Martin Luther, Jr. (Crozer Theological Seminary). "Class notes, Christian Theology for Today." [9/13–11/23/1949]. [Chester, Pa.] (AD) 81 pp. MLKP-MBU: Box 113, folder 20. 491123–006.

11/23/1949   **King, Martin Luther, Jr. (Crozer Theological Seminary). "What Experiences of Christians Living in the Early Christian Century Led to the Christian Doctrines of the Divine Sonship of Jesus, the Virgin Birth, and the Bodily Resurrection." [9/13–11/23/1949]. [Chester, Pa.] (THDS) 7 pp. (Marginal comments by George W. Davis.) MLKP-MBU: Box 112, folder 14. 491123–007.**

11/23/1949   **King, Martin Luther, Jr. (Crozer Theological Seminary). "The Place of Reason and Experience in Finding God." [9/13–11/23/1949]. [Chester, Pa.] (THDS) 8 pp. (Marginal comments by George W. Davis.) MLKP-MBU: Box 112, folder 17. 491123–003.**

11/23/1949   **King, Martin Luther, Jr. (Crozer Theological Seminary). "The Sources of Fundamentalism and Liberalism Considered Historically and Psychologically." [9/13–11/23/1949]. [Chester, Pa.] (THDS) 8 pp. (Marginal comments by George W. Davis.) MLKP-MBU: Box 115, folder 32. 491123–004.**

11/23/1949   **King, Martin Luther, Jr. (Crozer Theological Seminary). "Six Talks in Outline: The Character of the Christian God; The Nature of Man; Who Was Jesus of Nazareth?; What Did Jesus Achieve Through His Life and Death; How God Works Today Through His Spirit; What Christians Believe About History and the Future." [9/13–11/23/1949]. [Chester, Pa.] (THDS) 19 pp. (Marginal comments by George W. Davis.) MLKP-MBU: Box 113, folder 19. 491123–005.**

11/23/1949   **King, Martin Luther, Jr. (Crozer Theological Seminary). "How to Use the Bible in Modern Theological Construction." [9/13–11/23/1949]. [Chester, Pa.] (THDS) 9 pp. (Marginal comments by George W. Davis.) MLKP-MBU: Box 112, folder 14. 491123–008.**

11/23/1949   King, Martin Luther, Jr. (Crozer Theological Seminary). "Examination answers, Christian Theology for Today." [9/13–11/23/1949]. [Chester, Pa.] (AHDS) 13 pp. (Marginal comments by George W. Davis.) MLKP-MBU: Box 113, folder 30. 491123–009.

1949   "Photo of Martin Luther King, Martin Luther King, Jr., and Joel Lawrence King." 1949. Philadelphia, Pa. (Ph) 1 p. CKFC. 490000–001.

1949   "Photo of Martin Luther King." [1940–1949]. (Ph) 1 p. CKFC. 490000–010.

1949   "Photo of Martin Luther King." [1940–1949]. Atlanta, Ga. (Ph) 1 p. CKFC. 490000–009.

2/15/1950   King, Martin Luther, Jr. (Crozer Theological Seminary). "Paper topics and assignments, Christian Theology for Today." [9/13/1949–2/15/1950]. [Chester, Pa.] (AD) 3 pp. MLKP-MBU: Box 106, folder 21. 500215–001.

5/5/1950	Bean, Raymond J. (Crozer Theological Seminary). "Course outline, Outline History of Christianity." [2/21–5/5/1950]. [Chester, Pa.] (TD) 1 p. MLKP-MBU: Box 106, folder 18. 500505–006.
5/5/1950	King, Martin Luther, Jr. (Crozer Theological Seminary). "Examination answers, Outline History of Christianity." [2/21–5/5/1950]. [Chester, Pa.] (AHDS) 9 pp. (Marginal comments by Raymond J. Bean.) MLKP-MBU: Box 113, folder 30. 500505–009.
5/5/1950	King, Martin Luther, Jr. (Crozer Theological Seminary?). "List of five authors on John Calvin and Martin Luther." [2/21–5/5/1950?]. [Chester, Pa.?] (AD) 1 p. MLKP-MBU: Box 106, folder 19. 500505–010.
5/5/1950	King, Martin Luther, Jr. (Crozer Theological Seminary?). "Sample budget for a church or individual." [2/21–5/5/1950?]. [Chester, Pa.?] (AD) 1 p. MLKP-MBU: Box 106, folder 19. 500505–011.
6/10/1950	King, Martin Luther, Jr. (University of Pennsylvania?). "Class notes, Philosophy of History." [9/26/1949–6/10/1950?]. [Philadelphia, Pa.?] (AD) 35 pp. MLKP-MBU: Box 115, folder 29. 500610–000.
6/10/1950	King, Martin Luther, Jr. (University of Pennsylvania?). "Class notes, Philosophy of History." [9/26/1949–6/10/1950?]. [Philadelphia, Pa.?] (ADf) 4 pp. MLKP-MBU: Box 115, folder 29. 500610–001.
6/10/1950	King, Martin Luther, Jr. (University of Pennsylvania?). "Eckhart's Philosophy of History." [9/26/1949–6/10/1950?]. [Philadelphia, Pa.?] (ADd) 2 pp. MLKP-MBU: Box 115, folder 29. 500610–002.
6/10/1950	King, Martin Luther, Jr. (University of Pennsylvania?). "Schlegel's Philosophy of History." [9/26/1949–6/10/1950?]. [Philadelphia, Pa.?] (TDfS) 3 pp. MLKP-MBU: Box 115, folder 29. 500610–003.
6/10/1950	King, Martin Luther, Jr. (University of Pennsylvania?). "Notes on Philosophy of History." [9/26/1949–6/10/1950?]. [Philadelphia, Pa.?] (ADd) 1 p. MLKP-MBU: Box 115, folder 29. 500610–005.
6/12/1950	Township of Maple Shade (N.J.) "Complaint lodged by Walter R. McCall, State of New Jersey vs. Ernest Nichols." 6/12/1950. Maple Shade, N.J. (TAFmS) 1 p. (King's signature struck out.) WTMc. 500612–000.
6/12/1950	Township of Maple Shade (N.J.) "Record of the Case, State of New Jersey vs. Ernest Nichols." 6/12/1950. Maple Shade, N.J. (TFmS) 1 p. WTMc. 500612–001.
6/15/1950	Township of Maple Shade (N.J.) "Complaint lodged by Walter R. McCall, State of New Jersey vs. Ernest Nichols." 6/15/1950. Maple Shade, N.J. (AFmS) 1 p. WTMc. 500615–000.
6/15/1950	Township of Maple Shade (N.J.) "Record of the Case, State of New Jersey vs. Ernest Nichols." [6/15/1950]. Maple Shade, N.J. (TFmS) 1 p. WTMc. 500615–002.
6/17/1950	"Photo of Alfred Daniel King and Naomi Barber King at their wedding, with Martin Luther King, Jr., and Christine King." 6/17/1950. Atlanta, Ga. (Ph) 1 p. CKFC. 500617–001.
6/22/1950	Johnson, Robert Burk. "Letter to Harold T. Parker." 6/22/1950. Camden, N.J. (TLS) 1 p. WTMc. 500622–000.
7/20/1950	**McGann, W. Thomas. "Statement on Behalf of Ernest Nichols, State of New Jersey vs. Ernest Nichols." 7/20/1950. Moorestown, N.J. (TDS) 2 pp. WTMc. 500720–000.**
9/8/1950	"Comprehensive examinations, Crozer Theological Seminary." [9/7/1950–9/8/1950]. [Chester, Pa.] (TD) 12 pp. CSKC. 500908–000.
9/8/1950	Smith, Kenneth L. (Crozer Theological Seminary). "Examination questions, Christian Ethics." [9/7/1950–9/8/1950]. [Chester, Pa.] (THD) 1 p. CSKC. 500908–001.
9/13/1950	**King, Martin Luther, Jr. (Crozer Theological Seminary). "Crozer Theological Seminary Field Work Questionnaire." 9/13/1950. [Chester, Pa.] (AHFmS) 2 pp. CRO-NRCR. 500913–000.**
9/26/1950	King, Martin Luther, Jr. (Crozer Theological Seminary). "Examination answers, American Christianity—Colonial Period." [9/26/1950]. [Chester, Pa.] (AHD) 5 pp. (Marginal comments by Raymond J. Bean.) MLKP-MBU: Box 115, folder 27. 500926–000.
10/11/1950	**Batten, Charles E. (Crozer Theological Seminary). "Letter to Martin Luther King, Jr." 10/11/1950. Chester, Pa. (TLS) 1 p. MLKP-MBU: Box 117, folder 50. 501011–000.**
10/27/1950	King, Martin Luther, Jr. (Crozer Theological Seminary). "Examination an-

swers, American Christianity—Colonial Period." [*10/27/1950*]. [*Chester, Pa.*] (AHD) 4 pp. (Marginal comments by Raymond J. Bean.) MLKP-MBU: Box 115, folder 27. 501027–000.

10/30/1950   **[*King, Martin Luther, Jr.*] "Letter to Charles E. Batten." 10/30/1950. Chester, Pa. (TLc) 1 p. MLKP-MBU: Box 116, folder 49. 501030–000.**

10/31/1950   King, Martin Luther, Jr. "Letter to Ebenezer Baptist Church Members." 10/31/1950. Chester, Pa. (TALd) 2 pp. MLKP-MBU: Box 116, folder 49. 501031–000.

11/5/1950   **King, Martin Luther, Jr. "Letter to Hugh Watt." 11/5/1950. Chester, Pa. (TLc) 1 p. MLKP-MBU: Box 116, folder 49. 501105–000.**

11/15/1950   **Davis, George W. (Crozer Theological Seminary). "Crozer Theological Seminary Placement Committee: Confidential Evaluation of Martin Luther King, Jr." 11/15/1950. Chester, Pa. (AFmS) 1 p. CRO-NRCR. 501115–000.**

11/17/1950   **King, Martin Luther, Jr. (Crozer Theological Seminary). "An Appraisal of the Great Awakening." [*11/17/1950*]. [*Chester, Pa.*] (THDS) 25 pp. (Marginal comments by Raymond J. Bean.) MLKP-MBU: Box 112, folder 14. 501117–000.**

11/21/1950   **Enslin, Morton Scott (Crozer Theological Seminary). "Crozer Theological Seminary Placement Committee: Confidential Evaluation of Martin Luther King, Jr." 11/21/1950. Chester, Pa. (AFmS) 1 p. CRO-NRCR. 501121–000.**

11/21/1950   King, Martin Luther, Jr. (Crozer Theological Seminary). "Final examination answers, Religious Development of Personality." [*11/21/1950*]. [*Chester, Pa.*] (AHDS) 14 pp. (Marginal comments by George W. Davis.) MLKP-MBU: Box 106, folder 22. 501121–001.

11/22/1950   Davis, George W. (Crozer Theological Seminary). "Selected bibliography, Religious Development of Personality." [*9/12–11/22/1950*]. [*Chester, Pa.*] (THD) 2 pp. (Marginal comments by King.) MLKP-MBU: Box 106, folder 22. 501122–008.

11/22/1950   King, Martin Luther, Jr. (Crozer Theological Seminary). "Class notes, Religious Development of Personality." [*9/12–11/22/1950*]. [*Chester, Pa.*] (AD) 22 pp. MLKP-MBU: Box 106, folder 22. 501122–003.

11/22/1950   King, Martin Luther, Jr. (Crozer Theological Seminary). "Class notes, Religious Development of Personality." [*9/12–11/22/1950*]. [*Chester, Pa.*] (ADf) 1 p. MLKP-MBU: Box 106, folder 22. 501122–010.

11/22/1950   **King, Martin Luther, Jr. "Book review of *A Functional Approach to Religious Education* by Ernest J. Chave." [*9/12–11/22/1950*]. [*Chester, Pa.*] (THD) 4 pp. (Marginal comments by George W. Davis.) MLKP-MBU: Box 113, folder 30. 501122–001.**

11/22/1950   King, Martin Luther, Jr. (Crozer Theological Seminary). "Book review of *When Children Ask* by Margueritte Harmon Bro." [*9/12–11/22/1950*]. [*Chester, Pa.*] (THD) 2 pp. (Marginal comments by George W. Davis.) MLKP-MBU: Box 113, folder 30. 501122–002.

11/22/1950   **King, Martin Luther, Jr. (Crozer Theological Seminary). "Book review of *Personality, Its Study and Hygiene* by Winifred V. Richmond." [*9/12–11/22/1950*]. [*Chester, Pa.*] (THD) 3 pp. (Marginal comments by George W. Davis.) MLKP-MBU: Box 115, folder 30. 501122–009.**

11/22/1950   King, Martin Luther, Jr. (Crozer Theological Seminary). "Book review of *Children Need Adults* by Ruth Davis Perry." [*9/12–11/22/1950*]. [*Chester, Pa.*] (THD) 2 pp. (Marginal comments by George W. Davis.) MLKP-MBU: Box 106, folder 22. 501122–011.

11/22/1950   **King, Martin Luther, Jr. (Crozer Theological Seminary). "An Autobiography of Religious Development." [*9/12–11/22/1950*]. [*Chester, Pa.*] (AHDS) 16 pp. (Marginal comments by George W. Davis.) MLKP-MBU: Box 106, folder 22. 501122–000.**

11/22/1950   King, Martin Luther, Jr. (Crozer Theological Seminary). "Class notes, American Christianity—Colonial Period." [*9/12–11/22/1950*]. [*Chester, Pa.*] (AD) 70 pp. MLKP-MBU: Box 115, folder 27. 501122–007.

11/22/1950   Bean, Raymond J. (Crozer Theological Seminary). "Final examination questions, American Christianity—Colonial Period." 11/22/1950. [*Chester, Pa.*] (THD) 1 p. (Marginal comments by King.) MLKP-MBU: Box 115, folder 27. 501122–005.

11/22/1950   King, Martin Luther, Jr. (Crozer Theological Seminary). "Final examination answers, American Christianity—Colonial Period." [*11/22/1950*]. [*Chester, Pa.*] (AHD) 9 pp. (Marginal comments by Raymond J. Bean.) MLKP-MBU: Box 112, folder 17. 501122–006.

12/1/1950   **[*Gardner, William E.*] (First Baptist Church, East Elmhurst, N.Y.). "Crozer Theological Seminary Field Work Department: Rating Sheet for Martin Luther King, Jr." [*9/1950–12/1/1950*]. (AFm) 3 pp. CRO-NRCR. 501201–000.**

12/14/1950   Enslin, Morton Scott (Crozer Theological Seminary). "Letter to Chester M. Alter." 12/14/1950. (TLc) 1 p. CRO-NRCR. 501214–000.

12/15/1950   Rankin, Oliver Shaw (Edinburgh University). "Letter to Martin Luther King, Jr." 12/15/1950. Edinburgh, Scotland. (TLS) 2 pp. MLKP-MBU: Box 117, folder 50. 501215–000.

12/19/1950   King, Martin Luther, Jr. (Crozer Theological Seminary). "A Conception and Impression of Religion from Dr. W. K. Wright's Book Entitled *A Student's Philosophy of Religion*." [*12/19/1950*]. [*Chester, Pa.*] (THDS) 10 pp. MLKP-MBU: Box 112, folder 14. 501219–000.

12/21/1950   Smith, Kenneth L. (Crozer Theological Seminary). "Quiz questions, Christian Ethics." 12/21/1950. [*Chester, Pa.*] (THD) 3 pp. MLKP-MBU: Box 113, folder 21. 501221–000.

12/1950   **King, Martin Luther, Jr. "Fragment of application to Boston University." [*9/1950–12/1950*]. [*Chester, Pa.*] (TDc) 1 p. (S. Paul Schilling's copy of original.) SPS. 501200–005.**

1950   "Photo of Rebecca Jackson, James Dixon, Juanita Sellers, Martin Luther King, Jr., Christine King, Mattiwilda Dobbs, and June Dobbs at the home of Nannien W. Crawford." 1949–1950. Atlanta, Ga. (Ph) 1 p. CKFC. 500000–023.

1950   [*Shaw, C.*] "Rev. John Parker." [*1950?*]. (AD) 2 pp. EBCR. 500000–024.

1950   "Photo of Martin Luther King and Martin Luther King, Jr., Ebenezer Baptist Church." [*1948–1950?*]. Atlanta, Ga. (Ph) 1 p. CKFC. 500000–026.

1951   **Batten, Charles E. (Crozer Theological Seminary). "Martin L. King." [*1951*]. Atlanta, Ga. From: Morehouse College, *The Achievements of Morehouse Men in the Great Universities*, p. 5. (PD) 1 p. CKFC. 510000–012.**

1/24/1951   Schrecker, Paul (University of Pennsylvania). "Midyear examination questions, Kant." 1/24/1951. [*Philadelphia, Pa.*] (THD) 2 pp. (Marginal comments by King.) MLKP-MBU: Box 106, folder 23. 510124–000.

1/24/1951   King, Martin Luther, Jr. (University of Pennsylvania). "Notes for examination, Kant." [*1/24/1951*]. [*Philadelphia, Pa.*] (AD) 1 p. MLKP-MBU: Box 106, folder 23. 510124–001.

1/1951   **King, Martin Luther, Jr. "Letter to Sankey L. Blanton." [*1/1951*]. [*Chester, Pa.*] (HLd) 1 p. MLKP-MBU: Box 116, folder 49. 510100–000.**

2/3/1951   King, Martin Luther, Jr. (University of Pennsylvania?). "Class notes, Kant." [*9/25/1950–2/3/1951?*]. [*Philadelphia, Pa.?*] (ADf) 22 pp. MLKP-MBU: Box 106, folder 23. 510203–001.

2/3/1951   King, Martin Luther, Jr. (University of Pennsylvania?). "Notes on Kant." [*9/25/1950–2/3/1951?*]. [*Philadelphia, Pa.?*] (AD) 1 p. MLKP-MBU: Box 106, folder 23. 510203–002.

2/3/1951   King, Martin Luther, Jr. (University of Pennsylvania?). "Notes on books on Kant." [*9/25/1950–2/3/1951?*]. [*Philadelphia, Pa.?*] (AD) 5 pp. MLKP-MBU: Box 106, folder 23. 510203–003.

2/3/1951   King, Martin Luther, Jr. (University of Pennsylvania?). "Study questions, Kant." [*9/25/1950–2/3/1951?*]. [*Philadelphia, Pa.?*] (AD) 1 p. MLKP-MBU: Box 106, folder 23. 510203–000.

2/3/1951   University of Pennsylvania. "Graduate school transcript for Martin Luther King, Jr." [*2/3/1951*]. Philadelphia, Pa. (TFmS) 1 p. CRO-NRCR. 510203–004.

2/4/1951   **Bean, Raymond J. (Crozer Theological Seminary). "Crozer Theological Seminary Placement Committee: Confidential Evaluation of Martin Luther King, Jr." 2/4/1951. Chester, Pa. (THFmS) 1 p. CRO-NRCR. 510204–000.**

2/9/1951   **King, Martin Luther, Jr. (Crozer Theological Seminary). "The Origin of Religion in the Race." [*2/9/1951*]. [*Chester, Pa.*] (THDS) 15 pp. (Marginal comments by George W. Davis.) MLKP-MBU: Box 115, folder 33. 510209–000.**

2/15/1951   Davis, George W. (Crozer Theological Seminary). "Definition of Religion." [*11/28/1950–2/15/1951*]. [*Chester, Pa.*] (TD) 5 pp. MLKP-MBU: Box 113, folder 18. 510215–002.

2/15/1951   King, Martin Luther, Jr. (Crozer Theological Seminary). "Class notes, Philosophy of Religion." [*11/28/1950–2/15/1951*]. [*Chester, Pa.*] (AD) 76 pp. MLKP-MBU: Box 113, folder 20. 510215–001.

2/15/1951   King, Martin Luther, Jr. (Crozer Theological Seminary). "Examination answers, Philosophy of Religion." [*11/28/1950–2/15/1951*]. [*Chester, Pa.*] (AHDS) 14 pp. (Marginal comments by George W. Davis.) MLKP-MBU: Box 113, folder 30. 510215–000.

2/23/1951   **Batten, Charles E. (Crozer Theological Seminary). "Crozer Theological Seminary Placement Committee: Confidential Evaluation of Martin Luther King, Jr." [*2/23/1951*]. Chester, Pa. (THFmS) 1 p. CRO-NRCR. 510223–000.**

3/6/1951   **Educational Testing Service. "Graduate Record Examination, report of test scores for Martin Luther King, Jr." 3/6/1951. Princeton, N.J. (TFm) 6 pp. CSKC. 510306–000.**

3/28/1951   **King, Martin Luther, Jr. (Crozer Theological Seminary). "A Conception and Impression of Religion Drawn from Dr. Brightman's Book Entitled *A Philosophy of Religion*." [*3/28/1951*]. [*Chester, Pa.*] (AHDS) 21 pp. (Marginal comments by George W. Davis.) MLKP-MBU: Box 112, folder 14. 510328–000.**

4/20/1951   Nates, John (Crozer Theological Seminary). "H. Richard Niebuhr, paper for Christian Social Philosophy." 4/20/1951. [*Chester, Pa.*] (THD) 2 pp. (Marginal comments by King.) CSKC. 510420–000.

4/27/1951   **King, Martin Luther, Jr. (Crozer Theological Seminary). "Religion's Answer to the Problem of Evil." [*4/27/1951*]. [*Chester, Pa.*] (THDS) 20 pp. (Marginal comments by George W. Davis.) MLKP-MBU: Box 112, folder 14. 510427–000.**

5/4/1951   Davis, George W. (Crozer Theological Seminary). "Bibliography and term assignments, Philosophy of Religion and Advanced Philosophy of Religion." [*11/28/1950–5/4/1951*]. [*Chester, Pa.*] (THD) 4 pp. (Marginal comments by King.) MLKP-MBU: Box 113, folder 18. 510504–000.

5/4/1951   King, Martin Luther, Jr. (Crozer Theological Seminary). "Class notes, Advanced Philosophy of Religion." [*2/20–5/4/1951*]. [*Chester, Pa.*] (AD) 71 pp. MLKP-MBU: Box 113, folder 18. 510504–018.

5/4/1951   Smith, Kenneth L. (Crozer Theological Seminary). "Syllabus, Christianity and Society." [*2/20–5/4/1951*]. [*Chester, Pa.*] (THD) 4 pp. (Marginal comments by King.) MLKP-MBU: Box 112, folder 16. 510504–005.

5/4/1951   King, Martin Luther, Jr. (Crozer Theological Seminary). "Class notes, Christianity and Society." [*2/20–5/4/1951*]. [*Chester, Pa.*] (AD) 44 pp. MLKP-MBU: Box 112, folder 16. 510504–007.

5/4/1951   King, Martin Luther, Jr. (Crozer Theological Seminary). "Study questions, Christianity and Society." [*2/20–5/4/1951*]. [*Chester, Pa.*] (AD) 2 pp. MLKP-MBU: Box 112, folder 16. 510504–006.

5/4/1951   **[*King, Martin Luther, Jr.?*] (Crozer Theological Seminary). "War and Pacifism." [*2/20–5/4/1951*]. [*Chester, Pa.*] (THD) 2 pp. (Marginal comments by King.) MLKP-MBU: Box 112, folder 14A. 510504–020.**

5/4/1951   **King, Martin Luther, Jr. (Crozer Theological Seminary?). "Notes on American Capitalism." [*2/20–5/4/1951?*]. [*Chester, Pa.?*] (AD) 2 pp. MLKP-MBU: Box 113, folder 21. 510504–002.**

5/4/1951   "Christianity and Democracy, paper for Christianity and Society." [*2/20–5/4/1951*]. [*Chester, Pa.*] (THD) 2 pp. MLKP-MBU: Box 112, folder 17. 510504–036.

5/4/1951   "Christian Response to the State, paper for Christianity and Society." [*2/20–5/4/1951*]. [*Chester, Pa.*] (THD) 2 pp. MLKP-MBU: Box 112, folder 17. 510504–001.

5/4/1951   "Family Problems in Western Culture, paper for Christianity and Society." [*2/20–5/4/1951*]. [*Chester, Pa.*] (TD) 5 pp. MLKP-MBU: Box 112, folder 16. 510504–008.

5/4/1951   "Church and State Relationship, paper for Christianity and Society." [*2/20–5/4/1951*]. [*Chester, Pa.*] (TD) 3 pp. MLKP-MBU: Box 112, folder 16. 510504–009.

5/4/1951   "Religious Liberty Under Law in the United States, paper for Christianity and Society." [2/20–5/4/1951]. [Chester, Pa.] (THD) 4 pp. (Marginal comments by King.) MLKP-MBU: Box 112, folder 16. 510504–010.

5/4/1951   "A Critical Study of Capitalism in the Light of Christianity, paper for Christianity and Society." [2/20–5/4/1951]. [Chester, Pa.] (THD) 2 pp. MLKP-MBU: Box 112, folder 16. 510504–011.

5/4/1951   Snoad, Dick (Crozer Theological Seminary). "Individual Freedom and Planning, paper for Christianity and Society." [2/20–5/4/1951]. [Chester, Pa.] (TD) 2 pp. MLKP-MBU: Box 112, folder 16. 510504–012.

5/4/1951   "United Nations—Possibilities and Realities of World Government, paper for Christianity and Society." [2/20–5/4/1951]. [Chester, Pa.] (TD) 2 pp. MLKP-MBU: Box 112, folder 16. 510504–013.

5/4/1951   "Church and Labor Movement, paper for Christianity and Society." [2/20–5/4/1951]. [Chester, Pa.] (THD) 3 pp. (Marginal comments by King.) MLKP-MBU: Box 112, folder 16. 510504–014.

5/4/1951   "Ethical Implications of the Atomic Bomb, paper for Christianity and Society." [2/20–5/4/1951]. [Chester, Pa.] (TD) 2 pp. MLKP-MBU: Box 112, folder 16. 510504–015.

5/4/1951   McCall, Walter R. (Crozer Theological Seminary). "Contribution of Religion to Social Work, paper for Christianity and Society." [2/20–5/4/1951]. [Chester, Pa.] (THDS) 2 pp. (Marginal comments by King.) MLKP-MBU: Box 112, folder 16. 510504–016.

5/4/1951   Smith, Kenneth L. (Crozer Theological Seminary). "Syllabus, Christian Social Philosophy." [2/20–5/4/1951]. [Chester, Pa.] (TD) 4 pp. CSKC. 510504–023.

5/4/1951   King, Martin Luther, Jr. (Crozer Theological Seminary). "Class notes, Christian Social Philosophy." 2/20–5/4/1951. [Chester, Pa.] (AD) 52 pp. CSKC. 510504–024.

5/4/1951   King, Martin Luther, Jr. (Crozer Theological Seminary). "Notes, Christian Social Philosophy." [2/20–5/4/1951]. [Chester, Pa.] (AD) 3 pp. CSKC. 510504–022.

5/4/1951   **King, Martin Luther, Jr. (Crozer Theological Seminary). "Jacques Maritain." [2/20–5/4/1951]. [Chester, Pa.] (TDS) 2 pp. CSKC. 510504–028.**

5/4/1951   King, Martin Luther, Jr. (Crozer Theological Seminary?). "Notes on the new movement in America." [2/20–5/4/1951?]. [Chester, Pa.?] (ADf) 1 p. MLKP-MBU: Box 113, folder 21. 510504–003.

5/4/1951   King, Martin Luther, Jr. (Crozer Theological Seminary?). "Draft of paper on nature of human history." [11/28/1950–5/4/1951?]. [Chester, Pa.?] (ADd) 6 pp. MLKP-MBU: Box 113, folder 18. 510504–019.

5/4/1951   Hanson, Stanley A. (Crozer Theological Seminary). "Eugene William Lyman, paper for Christian Social Philosophy." [2/20–5/4/1951]. [Chester, Pa.] (TD) 2 pp. CSKC. 510504–025.

5/4/1951   [Sakurabayashi] (Crozer Theological Seminary). "Critique of the Social Gospel, paper for Christian Social Philosophy." [2/20–5/4/1951]. [Chester, Pa.] (TD) 2 pp. CSKC. 510504–026.

5/4/1951   Marques, Cal (Crozer Theological Seminary). "Walter Rauschenbusch, paper for Christian Social Philosophy." [2/20–5/4/1951]. [Chester, Pa.] (THD) 2 pp. (Marginal comments by King.) CSKC. 510504–027.

5/4/1951   Lawrence, George W. (Crozer Theological Seminary). "Papal Encyclicals, paper for Christian Social Philosophy." [2/20–5/4/1951]. [Chester, Pa.] (THD) 2 pp. (Marginal comments by King.) CSKC. 510504–029.

5/4/1951   Stom, Fred Eugene (Crozer Theological Seminary). "Christopher Dawson, paper for Christian Social Philosophy." [2/20–5/4/1951]. [Chester, Pa.] (THD) 1 p. (Marginal comments by King.) CSKC. 510504–030.

5/4/1951   Reardon, B. Clifton (Crozer Theological Seminary). "William Temple, Archbishop of Canterbury, paper for Christian Social Philosophy." [2/20–5/4/1951]. [Chester, Pa.] (THD) 2 pp. (Marginal comments by King.) CSKC. 510504–031.

5/4/1951   Piper, Royden (Crozer Theological Seminary). "T. S. Eliot, paper for Christian Social Philosophy." [2/20–5/4/1951]. [Chester, Pa.] (THD) 2 pp. (Marginal comments by King.) CSKC. 510504–032.

5/4/1951   Seyler, L. (Crozer Theological Seminary). "Emil Brunner, paper for Christian Social Philosophy." [2/20–5/4/1951]. [Chester, Pa.] (THD) 2 pp. (Marginal comments by King.) CSKC. 510504–033.

5/4/1951   "Karl Barth, paper for Christian Social Philosophy." [2/20–5/4/1951]. [Chester, Pa.] (TD) 2 pp. CSKC. 510504–034.

5/4/1951	Fagons, George E. (Crozer Theological Seminary). "John Coleman Bennett, paper for Christian Social Philosophy." [2/20–5/4/1951]. [Chester, Pa.] (TD) 2 pp. CSKC. 510504–035.
5/10/1951	**King, Alberta Williams. "Letter to Charles E. Batten." 5/10/1951. Atlanta, Ga. (ALS) 2 pp. CRO-NRCR. 510510–000.**
5/1951	King, Martin Luther, Jr. (Crozer Theological Seminary). "Total Significance of the Titles Lord and Messiah." [9/1948–5/1951]. [Chester, Pa.] (THD) 4 pp. (Marginal comments by professor.) MLKP-MBU: Box 113, folder 30. 510500–006.
5/1951	King, Martin Luther, Jr. (Crozer Theological Seminary). "Collected quotations from Shakespeare." [9/1948–5/1951]. [Chester, Pa.] (TD) 6 pp. JOG. 510500–008.
5/1951	King, Martin Luther, Jr. (Crozer Theological Seminary?). "Notes on Marxism." [9/1948–5/1951?]. [Chester, Pa.?] (AD) 1 p. MLKP-MBU: Box 115, folder 27. 510500–002.
5/1951	King, Martin Luther, Jr. (Crozer Theological Seminary?). "What is Man?" [9/1948–5/1951?]. [Chester, Pa.?] (ADf) 1 p. MLKP-MBU: Box 115, folder 27. 510500–007.
5/1951	King, Martin Luther, Jr. (Crozer Theological Seminary?). "Aphorisms and quotations." [9/1948–5/1951?]. [Chester, Pa.?] (AD) 30 pp. CSKC. 510500–009.
5/1951	King, Martin Luther, Jr. (Crozer Theological Seminary?). "Notes on knowledge, religion, race, and other topics." [9/1948–5/1951?]. [Chester, Pa.?] (AHD) 17 pp. CSKC. 510500–010.
5/1951	King, Martin Luther, Jr. (Crozer Theological Seminary?). "Controlled by a Culture-transcending Devotion." [9/1948–5/1951?]. [Chester, Pa.?] (AD) 2 pp. MLKP-MBU: Box 106, folder 27. 510500–012.
5/1951	King, Martin Luther, Jr. (Crozer Theological Seminary?). "Notes on Albert Schweitzer." [9/1948–5/1951?]. [Chester, Pa.?] (AD) 3 pp. MLKP-MBU: Box 106, folder 27. 510500–013.
5/1951	King, Martin Luther, Jr. (Crozer Theological Seminary?). "Notes on Jesus." [9/1948–5/1951?]. [Chester, Pa.?] (AD) 1 p. MLKP-MBU: Box 115, folder 27. 510500–014.
5/1951	King, Martin Luther, Jr. (Crozer Theological Seminary?). "First sentence of a parable." [9/1948–5/1951?]. [Chester, Pa.?] (ADf) 1 p. MLKP-MBU: Box 113, folder 21. 510500–015.
5/1951	King, Martin Luther, Jr. (Crozer Theological Seminary?). "Niebuhr on Democracy." [9/1948–5/1951?]. [Chester, Pa.?] (ADf) 1 p. MLKP-MBU: Box 113, folder 20. 510500–016.
5/1951	King, Martin Luther, Jr. (Crozer Theological Seminary?). "Examination answers, Philosophy." [9/1948–5/1951?]. [Chester, Pa.?] (AHD) 5 pp. (Marginal comments by professor.) MLKP-MBU: Box 115, folder 31. 510500–017.
5/1951	"Filing System for Illustrations." [9/1948–5/1951?]. (TD) 16 pp. CSKC. 510500–011.
5/8/1951	Crozer Theological Seminary. "Transcript for Martin Luther King, Jr." [5/8/1951]. Chester, Pa. (THFm) 1 p. CRO-NRCR. 510508–000.
5/8/1951	Crozer Theological Seminary. "Program, Graduation Exercises." 5/8/1951. Chester, Pa. (PD) 2 pp. JK. 510508–001.
5/8/1951	"Photo of Martin Luther King, Jr., and the Class of 1951, Crozer Commencement." 5/8/1951. Chester, Pa. (PPh) 1 p. JK. 510508–002.
5/8/1951	"Photo of Martin Luther King, Christine King, Martin Luther King, Jr., Alberta Williams King, Alfred Daniel King, and Walter R. McCall, Crozer Commencement." 5/8/1951. Chester, Pa. (Ph) 1 p. CKFC. 510508–004.
5/8/1951	"Photo of Martin Luther King, Jr., and the Class of 1951, Crozer Commencement." 5/8/1951. Chester, Pa. (Ph) 1 p. RKC-WHi. 510508–005.
6/1/1951	**King, Martin Luther, Jr. "Letter to Charles E. Batten." 6/1/1951. Atlanta, Ga. (TLS) 1 p. CRO-NRCR. 510601–000.**
6/4/1951	**Batten, Charles E. (Crozer Theological Seminary). "Letter to Martin Luther King, Jr." 6/4/1951. (TLc) 1 p. CRO-NRCR. 510604–000.**
6/4/1951	**Batten, Charles E. (Crozer Theological Seminary). "Letter to Chester M. Alter." 6/4/1951. (TLc) 1 p. CRO-NRCR. 510604–001.**
7/1951	Morehouse College. "Morehouse Men Receive Advanced Degrees: Martin Luther King, Jr." 7/1951. Atlanta, Ga. From: Morehouse Alumnus, 7/1951,

Calendar

1951   p. 8. (PD) 2 pp. HSl-GAU. 510700–000.

1951   "Photo of Alfred Daniel King, Alberta Williams King, and Christine King." [*1951*]. [*Atlanta, Ga.*] (Ph) 1 p. CKFC. 510000–003.

1951   Reid, Ira (Baptist Inter-Convention Committee). "Negro Baptist Ministry: An Analysis of Its Profession, Preparation, and Practices." 1951. (PDf) 18 pp. BEMP-DHU: Box 77. 510000–013.

1951   "Photo of Martin Luther King, Jr." [*1948–1951*]. (Ph) 1 p. RKC-WHi. 510000–014.

1951   "Photo of Martin Luther King, Jr., and Alberta Williams King." [*1948–1951*]. (Ph) 1 p. RKC-WHi. 510000–015.

1951   "Photo of Martin Luther King, Jr., and Alfred Daniel King." [*1948–1951*]. (Ph) 1 p. CKFC. 510000–016.

Boldfaced page numbers in entries indicate that the material can be found in documents authored by Martin Luther King, Jr.

Italicized page numbers in entries are used to indicate the location of the main biographical entry for an individual.

University of Michigan, 151n
University of Pennsylania, 88, 89, 126, 162n, 230n, **344**, 459, 460
University of Tennessee, 115n

Vanderlaan, E. C., **242**
Van Dusen, H. P., **242**
Virgin birth, doctrine of, **228–29**
Virginia Union University, 151n
Voice of the Negro (newspaper), 10
Voter registration, 15–16, 17, 18, 19, 33, 77, 78, 80, 81, 85

Wallace, Henry A., 45
Walton County, Georgia, 121
"War and Pacifism," 54–5, **433–35**, 461
Washington, Booker T., 9, 10
Booker T. Washington High School (Atlanta), 17, 35, 36, 83, 84, 107, 109, 111, 450
Watkins, Lillian D., **105**, 150, 452
Watson, John, **357–58**, *357n*
Watson, Melvin H., 25, 80
Weatherhead, Leslie, 280, 282n, **286**, **433**
Webb, John W., 84
Weigall, Arthur E.
    Paganism in Our Christianity by, **299**, **300**, **301**, **302**, **303**, **304**, **308**, **309**, **313**; compared to King's text, 299–304nn, 307–9nn
Welch, Adam C., **186**
Wells, H. G., **415**
Wesley, John, **240**, **350**, **351**
Westminster Atlas of the Bible, **163**, 163n; compared to King's text, 179n
Whale, J. S.
    Christian Answer by, **422**, **430**, **433**; compared to King's text, 422n, 429n
Wheat Street Baptist Church (Atlanta), 9, 10, 13, 14n, 18, 25, 78, 85
Whitefield, George, **340–42**, **344**, **345**, **346–47**, **348**, **349**, **353**
White, Walter, 14, 15
White, William Jefferson, 10
Whiting, Joseph L., 39
Wieman, Henry Nelson, 230, **355**, 411n
    Source of Human Good by, compared to King's text, 232n
Willard, Samuel, **337**
Williams, A. D. (King, Jr.'s grandfather)

activism of, 10, 14–17, 18
and Atlanta Baptist Ministers Union, 9
and Atlanta Missionary Baptist Association, 13, 17
and Baptist Young Peoples Union and Sunday School Board, 9
birth of, 4, 4n, 75
childhood of, 4
and civil rights activism, 10, 11, 14–18, 26
death of, 26, 28, 76, 102, 448, 449
education of, 4, 7, 25, 36, 43
and entrepreneurial activity, 11, 13, 447, 448
and family, 7, 446, 447
and General State Baptist Convention, 9
and Georgia State Baptist Convention, 14
King, Sr., as protege of, 25–26
and marriage of, 7, 76, 447
memorial poem to, 102
and move to Atlanta, 6
and ministry at Ebenezer Baptist Church, 1, 6–7, 9, 13, 18, 75
and Morehouse College Alumni Association, 14
NAACP activities of, 14–17, 18, 448
and National Baptist convention, 9, 13, 17
as Odd Fellows member, 11
photos of, 448
and Silver Queen Mining Company, 11, 447
as student at Morehouse, 7, 25, 36
and YMCA (Atlanta), 13
Williams, Alberta Christine. *See* King, Alberta Williams
Williams, Jennie Celeste Parks (King, Jr.'s grandmother), 1, 7, 29–30, 34, 75, 79, 82, 102, **359**, **362**, **449**
    marriage of, 76, 447
    photos of, 447, 449
Williams, Lacey Kirk, 18
Williams, Lucrecia (Creecy) Daniel (King, Jr.'s great–grandmother), 2, 75
Williams, Mamie, 105
Williams, R. S., 10
Williams, Samuel W., 45, 153, 451, 452
Williams, William N., 1, 2n, 446
Williams, Willis (King, Jr.'s great–grandfather), 1–2, 4, 75, 446
Willoughby, Harold R.
    Pagan Regeneration by, **298**, **306**, **313**; compared to King's text, 298n, 304–6nn
Wilson, Doris, 327
Winchester, Massachusetts, 126n
World Baptist Alliance, 30
Worship, artificial **186–89**
Worthem, Ida, 107